YOUR SONS ARE
AT YOUR SERVICE

COLUMBIA STUDIES IN TERRORISM AND IRREGULAR WARFARE

COLUMBIA STUDIES IN TERRORISM AND IRREGULAR WARFARE
Bruce Hoffman, Series Editor

This series seeks to fill a conspicuous gap in the burgeoning literature on terrorism, guerrilla warfare, and insurgency. The series adheres to the highest standards of scholarship and discourse and publishes books that elucidate the strategy, operations, means, motivations, and effects posed by terrorist, guerrilla, and insurgent organizations and movements. It thereby provides a solid and increasingly expanding foundation of knowledge on these subjects for students, established scholars, and informed reading audiences alike.

For a complete list of titles, see page 379

YOUR SONS ARE AT YOUR SERVICE

Tunisia's Missionaries of Jihad

AARON Y. ZELIN

Columbia University Press
New York

Columbia University Press
Publishers Since 1893
New York   Chichester, West Sussex
cup.columbia.edu

Copyright © 2020 Columbia University Press

All rights reserved

Library of Congress Cataloging-in-Publication Data
Names: Zelin, Aaron Y., author.
Title: Your sons are at your service : Tunisia's missionaries of jihad / Aaron Y. Zelin.
Other titles: Columbia studies in terrorism and irregular warfare.
Description: New York : Columbia University Press, 2020. | Series: Columbia studies in terrorism and irregular warfare | Includes bibliographical references and index.
Identifiers: LCCN 2019025150 (print) | LCCN 2019025151 (ebook) | ISBN 9780231193764 (cloth) | ISBN 9780231193771 (paperback) | ISBN 9780231550499 (ebook)
Subjects: LCSH: Jihad. | Terrorist organizations—Tunisia. | Islamic fundamentalism—Tunisia. | Islam and politics—Tunisia. | Terrorism—Religious aspects—Islam.
Classification: LCC BP182 .Z45 2019 (print) | LCC BP182 (ebook) | DDC 297.7209611—dc23
LC record available at https://lccn.loc.gov/2019025150
LC ebook record available at https://lccn.loc.gov/2019025151

Cover design: Milenda Nan Ok Lee
Cover photo: © Zoubeir Souissi / © Reuters

For the people of Tunisia in their quest for dignity, freedom, democracy, and justice, or, as they would say, shughl, huriya, karama wataniya

CONTENTS

Acknowledgments ix
Abbreviations xiii
Note on Transliteration xv

Introduction 1

1. The Generation of Zaytunah 23
2. A Scattered Group with a Less-Than-Perfect Image 41
3. Come Do Jihad 71
4. Sons of Tunisia 96
5. Tunisia Is a Land of *Dawa* 114
6. Hear from Us, Not About Us 135
7. Tunisians Can Be Found Everywhere in the Land of Jihad 159
8. It Was Mostly the Tunisians Who Were Involved in *Takfir* 188
9. Honest Ones Among the *Dawa* People Must Come to al-Sham 204
10. We Are Here to Protect You from This Nonbeliever Government 233
11. The Future of the Tunisian Jihadi Movement 257

Author's Note on Terminology 273
Notes 279
Bibliography 339
Index 365

ACKNOWLEDGMENTS

It is a pleasure to thank those who made this book possible. Without the continued support of the Washington Institute for Near East Policy, this book would not have been possible. The organization and its leadership have granted me the independence to explore a multitude of research questions and issues that were intellectually stimulating since I became a senior fellow in May 2012. Therefore, I want to extend special thanks and appreciation to Robert Satloff, Patrick Clausen, and Matthew Levitt for continuing to support my pursuits and being patient throughout this entire process. Furthermore, I appreciate the unwavering support from Dick Borow, who endows my position at the Washington Institute. Likewise, I would be remiss not to mention Kayvan Chinichian, who helped secure the fellowship as part of the institute's development team in 2012.

I am especially grateful to King's College of London's Peter Neumann, who pushed me over the years to write an analytically and empirically rich product, resulting in this unique contribution to the literature on jihadi studies. I am also very appreciative of David Martin-Jones and Fernando Reinares, who provided useful feedback that helped improve this book. Furthermore, Neumann and the International Centre for the Study of Radicalisation and Political Violence (ICSR) funded the early stages of this research. Without such financial support, it would have been difficult to undertake this research. I would also like to thank others at ICSR who gave advice and support along the way, especially Shiraz Maher.

I would likely not be at this juncture in my professional life without the support from Dr. Jytte Klausen, my professor at Brandeis University, where I completed my master's degree. Since 2010, she gave me to access her Western Jihadism Project database, which includes information on all Westerners involved in jihadism dating back to the early 1990s. This was extremely useful when exploring Tunisians based in Western countries. More importantly, when I worked for her from 2010 to 2012, she allowed me to pursue my own research in my free time. This gave me the opportunity to write in places like *Foreign Policy*, *Atlantic*, *Foreign Affairs*, and *CTC Sentinel* at a young age. This in turn provided a platform that helped me secure my position as the Richard Borow Fellow at the Washington Institute for Near East Policy in May 2012. As such, I am deeply indebted to Dr. Klausen for her ongoing advice and encouragement.

Beyond organizational affiliations, I would also like to express my deep gratitude to those who provided guidance as I was first starting in the field of jihadi studies. When I began writing publicly Brian Fishman, Leah Farrall, Will McCants, and Jarret Brachman gave me crucial direction when I had specific questions. Others in the field were also helpful. Thank you to Jean-Charles Brisard, Pieter Van Ostaeyen, and Lorenzo Vidino, who shared court documents that were useful when exploring different Tunisian networks in Belgium, France, Germany, Italy, and Spain. Moreover, special thanks to Thomas Hegghammer who gave me to access to his archive of jihadi primary sources from the 1980s and 1990s, which helped piece together information about Tunisians involved in jihadism prior to the 2011 revolution.

I would also like to thank friends and colleagues who I have made in the field over the years. Through our private conversations, you have enriched my understanding of various issues related to jihadism. There is one person who deserves specific mention, J. M. Berger. J. M. not only continues to be a close friend but also read the entire manuscript and provided crucial feedback that helped strengthen the final copy of this book.

I would also like to thank the following individuals who assisted me at various points in the process of developing this book (in no particular order): Oula A. Alrifai, Montassar J., Safouene G., Houssem M., Sameh B., Michael Marcusa, Erik Churchill, Cole Bunzel, Timothy Holman, Samar Batrawi, Jonathan Prohov, Alex Schnapp, Joakim Bjornestad, Timothy Rhein, Elspeth Carruthers, Isabel Lopez, Ryan Pereira, Jeffry Halverson, Habib Sayah, Adam Heffez, Patrick Hoover, Nour Chaaban, Yousif Kalian, Jackson Doering, Nicolette San Clemente, Marina Poudret, and Noaman Mousa.

The publication of this book would not have come to fruition without Columbia University Press. First, I would like to thank Stephen Tankel and Marc Lynch for providing useful feedback on my original book proposal. I am especially grateful to Bruce Hoffman, the doyen of terrorism studies, for accepting my proposal and agreeing to publish my first book. More importantly, this book would not have made it to press without the support and assistance of the editorial team at CUP: Caelyn Cobb, Monique Briones, Zachary Friedman, and Leslie Kriesel. I would also like to thank Patti Bower of Diligent Editorial and Book Production Service for copyediting the manuscript, and Robert and Cynthia Swanson and Eric and Doreen Anderson of Arc Indexing, Inc., for indexing the book.

Finally, I want to thank my family for always being there and encouraging me over the years. Special thanks to my sister, Naomi, and especially my mom. Thank you for everything. I could not have done this without you.

Unfortunately, three of my four grandparents are no longer with us. It's a shame they will not be able to see the publication of this book. I'm thinking of you Savta, Grandma Doris, and Grandpa Norman. My only grandparent still alive is my Saba. Thanks for teaching me so much over the years.

Last, but certainly not least, I want to thank my Dad. You have been my mentor in life and helped me grow intellectually. Ever since I can remember, we always had deep conversations about politics, history, and philosophy. Thank you for showing me the pleasures and rewards of the life of the mind.

There are many individuals who have provided guidance, advice, and assistance in the process of completing this book, but all errors and mistakes are mine alone.

ABBREVIATIONS

AIS	Armée islamique du salut
AQ	Al-Qaeda
AQAP	Al-Qaeda in the Arabian Peninsula
AQI	Al-Qaeda in Iraq
AQIM	Al-Qaeda in the Islamic Maghrib
ASL	Ansar al-Sharia in Libya
AST	Ansar al-Sharia in Tunisia
CPR	Congrés pour la république
FIS	Front islamique du salut
FIT	Front islamique tunisien
GIA	Groupe islamique armé
GSPC	Groupe salafiste pour la prédication et le combat
ICI	Islamic Cultural Institute
ISI	Islamic State of Iraq
ISIS	Islamic State of Iraq and al-Sham
IS	Islamic State
JABF	Jund Asad Bin al-Furat
JI	al-Jama'ah al-Islamiyah
JN	Jabhat al-Nusra
JNIM	Jama'at Nusrat al-Islam wa-l-Muslimin
JT	Jama'at al-Tabligh
JTWJ	Jama'at al-Tawhid wa-l-Jihad
KSM	Khalid Shaykh Muhammad

KUBN	Katibat 'Uqbah Bin Nafi
MAK	Maktab al-Khidamat al-Mujahidin
MB	Muslim Brotherhood
MSM	Majlis Shura al-Mujahidin
MTI	Mouvement de la tendance islamique
SDF	Syrian Democratic Forces
SMT	social movement theory
ST	Shabab al-Tawhid
TADA	Tunisian Association for Drama Arts
TCG	Tunisian Combatant Group
UGTT	Union générale tunisienne du travail

NOTE ON TRANSLITERATION

The transliteration of Arabic in this book follows the rules of the American Library Association/Library of Congress (for further details: Randal K. Berry, ed., "Arabic: ALA-LC Romanization Tables: Transliteration Schemes for Non-Roman Scripts," Library of Congress, 1997, 10–19). For ease of reading, though, I did not include the diacritics. Arabic names, places, or terms that are common in English are not transliterated, nor are Arabic words that have been Anglicized, such as words ending with -ic, -ist, or -ism. Finally, any quotations from secondary literature kept the author's original spellings.

**YOUR SONS ARE
AT YOUR SERVICE**

INTRODUCTION

We are trying to save people from the black tunnel the old regime placed them in.... We believe that prosperity comes from the governance of sharia [Islamic law] and that everything bad comes from following civil laws.... Our dawa [outreach/proselytization] is to bring people back to salvation and we will wait for no one to approve of our message.... We are not looking for elections or power, but our goal is to bring people back to faith.[1]

The seeds for this book were planted on May 18, 2011, when I was conducting my daily routine of checking new online forum posts from jihadis. This was before jihadis were using social media. One thread in particular titled "Important News/Glad Tidings: Convening of the Ansar al-Sharia Forum in Tunis on May 21, 2011—God Willing" caught my eye. Within four months of Tunisia's revolution, a jihadi group was establishing itself. The quote above is the words of Sayf Allah Bin Hasin (better known as Abu 'Iyadh al-Tunisi), the founder and leader of Ansar al-Sharia in Tunisia (AST), at the opening of this first forum.

At the time this was curious since many within the scholarly community and media consistently highlighted the highly secular and cosmopolitan nature of Tunisian society. Even Tunisia's main Islamist movement, Harakat al-Nahdah, was being described as very moderate compared with other regional

Muslim Brotherhood–like organizations. This notice for the opening event on the Ansar al-Mujahidin Arabic Forum piqued my interest and started my search to better understand this new and somewhat surprising phenomenon. It was difficult then to know the trajectory of this new group and what would come of the broader Tunisian jihadi movement in the following years. Suspicious that it would become a larger trend, I decided to investigate it more deeply.

This book reflects nine years of in-depth research into the topic of Tunisian jihadism, first as a curious intellectual interest and later as the basis for my PhD dissertation. The dissertation explored this phenomenon through the lens of AST until the organization became illegal in Tunisia in late August 2013. This book, however, delves into this movement through mid-2019, so it includes everything related to the most recent foreign fighting and the Islamic State. Without crucial historical context, the payoff in understanding the most recent aspect of this trend would be facile. Therefore, this book seeks to explain why jihadism became a force in Tunisia and among Tunisians following the January 2011 revolution.

To answer this overarching question on why jihadism became an important mobilizing factor and ideology following the Tunisian revolution, this book investigates subsidiary questions and answers: (1) What conditions (historical and contemporary) led to the rise of AST? (2) Why did AST pursue a *dawa*-first approach in contrast to a jihad-first approach? (3) How did AST implement its strategy? (4) What led to AST's downfall? (5) Why did so many Tunisians following AST's terrorism designation become foreign fighters in Iraq, Libya, and Syria with the Islamic State (IS)? (6) And how did the Tunisian state grapple with the terrorism campaign that IS wrought locally in 2015–2016?

The case of jihadism in Tunisia after its revolution is unique in part because of the particular historical context and conditions within Tunisia. One could potentially compare the cases of AST with the Ansar al-Sharia groups created in Egypt and Libya after 2011, but the scope of the research would be limited to comparisons between conditions in each country and likely overlook the deep historical processes that allowed AST to flourish. It would only scratch the surface. A limited focus on the Tunisian case allows one to go below the surface and better situate Ansar al-Sharia within the Tunisian context. While this book will be relevant for broader discussions and understandings of Sunni jihadism after the Arab uprisings, it also seeks to participate in debates within scholarship on Tunisia and Islamism in Tunisia.

From the beginning of the Arab uprisings, many scholars believed these revolutionary events would prove detrimental to al-Qaeda (AQ) and ideologically aligned groups. However, contrary to some early optimistic predictions, the uprisings did not marginalize al-Qaeda's "narrative" or the new groups that sprang up in their aftermath. Although jihadis did not play a visible role in the protests that led to the downfall of various regimes in the Middle East and North Africa, they took advantage of changing circumstances that had resulted from the opening of society, prisoner amnesties, and greater freedom of expression. This new unprecedented environment allowed groups to operate in ways that were previously impossible and employ lessons learned from previous mistakes over the past four decades.[2] This evolution is best exemplified by AST.

While few took notice of AST until after the September 2012 attack on the U.S. Embassy in Tunis, by then the group had already built a strong base and constituency within Tunisian society, largely through its provision of social welfare and outreach. By using these tactics, AST recruited members and spread its ideas more successfully than any other global jihadi group before within a particular country. The group did this not by wielding a sword but rather through *dawa*.[3]

This emphasis on *dawa* might be taken for granted now, but at the time it signaled a significant divergence from the conventional tactics used by the global jihadi community and highlighted the group's abilities to adapt to new environments. It is true that some jihadis in Europe had been using similar methodologies, but this case was within a Muslim-majority Arab country and not a Western context.[4] AST's methodology would later become a model for Ansar al-Sharia groups in Libya and Egypt as well as for jihadis in Syria. Its efforts were also commended by al-Qaeda in the Islamic Maghrib (AQIM).[5] AST highlighted a new complexity: jihadi groups' transformation from purely terrorist entities or insurgent forces to social movements. A greater understanding of the changes that jihadi groups underwent following the uprisings is important.

The ascendancy of AST as a relevant player within the postrevolution debate came as a surprise to many, especially given the attempts of successive Tunisian regimes postindependence to impose staunchly secular values on Tunisian society. Although AST's *dawa*-first approach was unsustainable in the end, it broadened the pool of recruits for future foreign fighting in Iraq, Libya, and Syria, with IS in particular. This next generation remains relevant to this day.

Surveying the Field

To better situate how this book and research fits into other works related to this topic, it is worth exploring five areas within the academic literature that this book communicates with and builds off. I consider literature on Tunisian Islamism and jihadism, jihadi studies, jihadism post–Arab uprisings, jihadi governance, and the debate on leader-led versus leaderless jihad.

Tunisian Islamism and Jihadism

Tunisian Islamism and jihadism have seen more interest since Tunisia's uprising, yet the subject matter is still very much small in scale compared with other Arab countries. Although studies have been written about the case of the Muslim Brotherhood–associated party al-Nahdah as early as the 1980s, there has been a paucity on the topic of Tunisians involved with jihadism more specifically.

Within the literature on Tunisian Islamism, over the years scholars such as Marion Boulby, Nikki R. Keddie, Bruce Maddy-Weitzman, and Susan Waltz have attempted to trace the rise of the movement more broadly and its biggest organization, al-Nahdah, as it developed and became a perceived threat to the Tunisian state in the 1980s.[6] Since the revolution, newer books from Anne Wolf and Rory McCarthy have been far more comprehensive and gained access to previously unexamined historical data and conducted many interviews with senior and lay members of al-Nahdah.[7]

Others, such as Alaya Allani, explore al-Nahdah's oscillating position between confrontation with and participation in the Tunisian state system. Allani also argues that "with the recent rise of a violent Salafist movement in the Maghreb, there is a possibility of future political participation in Tunisia by moderate Islamists movements such as al-Nahdah, and that the cost of such participation is far better than the cost of their non-participation."[8] This belief is borne out of the notion that engagement and exposure to power moderates the group. Allani's hypothesis, however, is flatly rejected by more recent literature from Francesco Cavatorta and Fabio Merone, who argue that, in fact, "it has been exclusion through repression and social marginalization that has led the Islamist party al-Nahdah to move from its extreme anti-systemic position of the 1970s to become the mainstream conservative party it is today."[9] Anne Wolf, after the revolution, relayed counternarratives explaining that the rise of al-Nahdah as a political force post-uprising was not necessarily unique since Islamists "have always played an important part in Tunisian society."[10] Others, like Khaled Elgindy and Abdullah Saeed, attempted to understand al-Nahdah by studying the ideological works and production of its leader, Rashid Ghannushi.[11]

With the public rise of salafism in Tunisia after the uprising, some researchers began to delve into the topic for the first time, even though salafism has existed in Tunisia since the 1980s, as Rikke Hostrup Haugbølle has explored.[12] Within the Tunisian context, "the degree of AST's popularity, according to unofficial estimates, is far superior to that of all other Tunisian salafi movements and parties."[13] This is why focusing on the jihadi side of the salafi spectrum is worthy of research. Researchers like Merone and Cavatorta explore salafism in Tunisia in a broad sense, showing how it is not a homogenous movement but rather contains many debates related to contours, tactics, and relations with the state.¹⁴ Both later refined their ideas with Stefano M. Torelli and highlighted historical aspects of the movement, showing "that Tunisian salafism is not a foreign import, but represents the political demands of a sector of the population."¹⁵ Cavatorta also argues that "AST was caught in the dilemma of how to stay radical and true to its ideological core while remaining within the framework of the nascent liberal democratic structures without falling foul of them."¹⁶ As is seen in chapters 4 through 7, however, this argument is not valid since AST never had an intent to work within the new system.

Similarly, Monica Marks uses Quintan Wiktorowicz's salafi schema (purist, politico, and jihadi) in the Tunisian context to analyze the differing trends. Based on field research, Marks identifies flaws in Merone's and Cavatorta's argument that economic deprivation motivates people's involvement in salafism. Rather, Marks concludes, many affluent individuals are part of the salafi community. Furthermore, many Tunisians who experience economic misfortune do not become salafis. Marks believes that many wish to "circumvent institutionalized obstacles and upend long-standing hierarchies." Additionally, salafism "offers an inspirational opportunity for Tunisian youths to fight for something larger than themselves and inject a sense of higher purpose into their lives."¹⁷ In short, salafism is a counterculture. While both sides of the argument have truth, there is no monocausal reason behind individuals' involvement with salafism; individuals each have their own set of factors.¹⁸

On the more securitized end, scholars such as Alison Pargeter have uncovered important details related to the North African/Tunisian jihadi immigrant communities in Europe and involvement in terrorism. She argues that "a closer look suggests that these first generation immigrants continue to be preoccupied as much by national politics as any notion of a globalized form of Islam."¹⁹ The issue of Tunisian jihadis who were exiled in Europe is a very important factor in understanding the growth of jihadism in Tunisia after 2011. However, as I explain in chapters 2 and 3, these jihadis were far more connected to the global aspects of the movement than Pargeter acknowledges. She also wrote an important chapter about the so-called Sulayman Group that was involved in a low-level insurgency against the Tunisian government for three to four weeks in late 2006 to early 2007. One of her most important findings is that these individuals had previously been involved in jihadism and had not come out of nowhere.²⁰ To further our understanding of these events and the broader dynamics that led to greater acknowledgment of jihadis in Tunisian society, this book uses access to previously unutilized court documents and primary sources as well as Jytte Klausen's Western Jihadism Project database that catalogs all cases of jihadism in the West since the early 1990s. The latter allows greater opportunities for cross-country analysis of the connections and networks of Tunisians within the West prior to 2011.

While all of the above sources and research on Tunisian Islamism and jihadism helps us better understand the phenomenon, none truly answer the question of why jihadism, especially that espoused by AST and later IS, came to be such a force in the country. Although each provides a part of the story, there are still many missing aspects. Therefore, this book aims to do this by analyzing the history of the movement prior to 2011, which allows individuals to better appreciate the scale and embeddedness of Tunisian involvement in the jihadi milieu following the revolution.

A Note on Jihadi Studies

The field of studying jihadi groups, while almost two decades old, is still maturing. Two downsides of this status are worth pointing out. First, it is a unique field due to the nature in which it straddles both academia and the policy world. As a result, many of the articles related to jihadi groups can be found in both peer-reviewed journals and more mainstream publications. Therefore, one must be careful in assessing the rigor of articles outside academically peer-reviewed systems.

More substantively and structurally, an additional issue within the field that makes it difficult for scholars to contextualize research in the post–Arab uprising environment within the academic literature: the rise of the Islamic State. IS's reemergence resulted in a shift away by most researchers and in a redirection of funding. This shift led to a lack of robustness on other topics within the field, especially those that directly preceded IS or were not related to Syria: namely, the development of jihadism in other post–Arab uprising contexts, including Tunisia, Libya, Egypt, and Yemen. By the time researchers might have made unique contributions about occurrences in these spaces from 2011–2013, much of the energy had shifted toward the IS phenomenon.

That said, some efforts like the Project on Middle East Political Science's "Studies" series did produce research on certain aspects of these topics. For instance, Marc Lynch notes that "while much remains unclear, there appears to be a new al-Qaeda strategy focused on building ties with local jihadist movements, including the various Ansar al-Sharia factions."[21] Yet these studies fall short, not for a lack of quality but because the research focused on broader issues following the Arab uprisings, such as Arab monarchies, sectarianism, the Syrian war, and Muslim Brotherhood–like Islamist groups. In individual capacities, Daveed Gartenstein-Ross and Donald Holbrook wrote journal articles on how al-Qaeda and its allies interpreted the Arab uprisings.[22] Beyond this limited analysis, however, there has been very little academic exploration of the early periods in the post–Arab uprising era on jihadi groups.

This dearth of research leads to one conclusion: there needs to be more in-depth examination of jihadi movements in countries affected by the Arab uprisings from 2011 to 2013. Such research would not only enhance the knowledge base of the field but it could also provide greater insights into the foreign fighter phenomenon, the reemergence of the Islamic State, and its later spread beyond Iraq and Syria. Based on these caveats, the following sections provide a backdrop of key works and debates in the aftermath of the Arab uprisings and their effects on jihadi groups.

Jihadi Metastasization Post–Arab Uprisings

Following the Arab uprisings that began in December 2010 and January 2011, the jihadi studies community debated whether the uprisings benefited or hurt al-Qaeda. As with the leadership question that is addressed below, the scope of the debate appears narrow since so much has changed and evolved within the broader movement. Today a discussion purely based on al-Qaeda seems quaint. The rise of the Islamic State signaled the creation of a competitor network and, with it, the emergence of a bipolar jihadosphere. As a consequence, it is important to highlight that the post–Arab uprising era can be divided into two parts when exploring the jihadi phenomenon. The first part, from 2011 to 2013, saw the growth of new groups in new locales, while the second part, since 2014, saw the rise of IS and the clear split between its leadership and that of AQ. Since this book primarily focuses on the first part, this section focuses on the growth of the new groups.

In the year after the uprisings, a lively debate ensued between William McCants and Daveed Gartenstein-Ross. McCants argued that "Al Qaeda has also struggled to respond to the Arab Spring. In Egypt, Libya, and Tunisia, Islamists have rejected al Qaeda's model of autocratic governance through sharia law in favor of parliamentary politics. Even many of al Qaeda's theological fellow travelers, such as the ultraconservative salafis in Egypt, have embraced the democratic process and formed political parties to compete in elections."[23] On the other hand, Gartenstein-Ross argued that in fact, "al-Qaeda isn't anywhere near defeated—for all our triumphalism, it appears to be winning."[24] Alex S. Wilner was correct to note that there would be both costs and benefits in this new era.[25]

Years later, due to the evolution of events, it appears that both McCants and Gartenstein-Ross's arguments were flawed, while Wilner's was more insightful. For one, except for al-Nahdah in Tunisia, the space for parliamentary politics closed in the years after the uprisings. Unlike in Egypt, however, the Tunisian salafi trend veers more toward the jihadi end of the spectrum than toward the purist or politico side. Additionally, while it is true that AQ was not fully defeated, it is still a bit of an exaggeration to say that it was winning. Rather, the group was able to take advantage of the new environment. Peter Neumann and Shiraz Maher aptly highlighted in the fall of 2012 that while "the problem for al-Qaeda was that its own people had played no actual role in the unfolding revolutions[,] . . . the Arab Spring's violent turn in Libya and Syria has provided al-Qaeda with an opportunity to insert itself back into the public consciousness."[26] Indeed, al-Qaeda's branch in Syria, Jabhat al-Nusra, was able to make a name for itself as a result of the conflict in Syria. Likewise, Libya provided a safe haven for the training and organizing that benefited Ansar al-Sharia in Libya, AST, AQIM, and the foreign fighters preparing for the Syrian jihad.

Instead of purely focusing on al-Qaeda and the Arab uprisings' costs or benefits for it, Clinton Watts argued that the uprisings would lead to more competition within the global jihadi movement: "Arab Spring uprisings in the Middle East and North Africa have introduced a wide range of resistance groups seeking manpower, resources and operational space. New upstart groups enmeshed in the Arab Spring may cooperate with al-Qaeda at times, but in the long run, these groups may be more incentivized to compete with al-Qaeda for influence among young vulnerable male populations."[27] Further to this point, Leah Farrall believed that the opening of societies after the Arab uprisings, coupled with the attrition of al-Qaeda leaders in Afghanistan and Pakistan as a result of drone strikes, would cause the overall milieu to become more extreme. Farrall questioned, "what will happen when authoritative voices who can restrain the actions of those left and, importantly, those newer folks still seeking to join the cause, no longer exist? When indiscriminate becomes the norm."[28]

Both Watts and Farrall identify key ways in which the landscape changed. They both provide relevant discussions about the rise of the Islamic State. Watts' notion of competition, however, falls short in its examination of other groups such as Ansar al-Sharia. Instead of competitors, these new groups were more like fig leaves that were part of AQ's post-uprising strategy to mask its relations with the new groups. This idea is further explored in chapter 5's discussions of AST as an organization. That said, while many of these new groups were on the same "team," they still had different immediate interests that could clash over time. This explanation is drawn out in greater detail in chapter 7, which explores the downfall of AST as AQIM inserted itself more overtly into the Tunisian context.

In many ways the post–Arab uprising scene established a global jihadi international system parallel to the actual international system respected by nation-states. Because they do not believe in nation-states and in the United States' world order, jihadis' main goal is to upend the Westphalian nation-state model and the architecture of the United States' post–World War II international system. Jihadis instead view society through the prism of religion, which encompasses anyone under the umbrella of a particular religion. In the case of Islam, the *umma* (the global Islamic religious community) should be organized under a caliphate (the historic system of Islamic governance).

Broadly speaking, this is where all jihadis agree. Leaving aside the IS and focusing specifically within the AQ ecosystem, there are differing tactical and interest-related views that prompt the movement to articulate different paths even if its members are all technically part of "Team AQ." As such, there is a de facto jihadi international system in which different organizations operate based on their own immediate interests. For example, AST primarily operated on a local and regional basis. Its local interests of attempting to perform *dawa* activities contradict the interests of AQIM, which would prefer to attack the Tunisian government. As a result, if AQIM chooses to conduct insurgent attacks, such activity harms AST since the Tunisian government views both groups as one and the same. This is the scenario that led to the eventual designation of AST as a terrorist organization by the Tunisian government. As such, the policies of the two groups clash even if—broadly speaking—they want the same result.

In contradistinction to their local interests, AST and AQIM's regional interests are more aligned. Whether AST is helping with Tunisian recruitment into AQIM for operations in Mali or assisting with training individuals in Libya to fight jihad in Syria, both organizations agree on the fundamental basics of regional issues or policies. Therefore, when examining this new jihadi international system, one has to identify the core raison d'être of each group as well as where groups' interests overlap in order to understand how they might operate together in certain instances. As such, a more granular understanding of different jihadi groups is necessary since groups will often balance different interests according to particular situations or evolving local climates. For instance, Mukhtar Bilmukhtar left AQIM and created al-Murabitun while still pledging fealty to AQ's leader, Ayman al-Zawahiri. He returned to the AQIM fold a couple of years later. Likewise, Jabhat al-Nusra's announcement that it was leaving AQ did not mean that it had left AQ's orbit completely. Such developments indicate that the global jihadi ecosystem is both complex and intertwined. The old debates about al-Qaeda are obsolete because there is so much happening beneath the surface. This case study on Tunisian jihadism thus helps shed greater light on these post-2011 dynamics.

The Growth in Jihadi Social Services/Governance

One of the most important trends within the global jihadi movement after the Arab uprisings is groups' ability to move beyond the terrorism box to add tools to its repertoire to expand support from its clandestine base. While it is true that organizations such as Harakat al-Shabab al-Mujahidin in Somalia had been involved in *dawa* and protogovernance principles prior to 2011, it became more of a norm with new open spaces or liberated territories, depending on the country-specific context. More freedoms have allowed global jihadi groups from Yemen to Tunisia to Libya to Syria evolve into multipurpose organizations.

As Gartenstein-Ross and Amichai Magen argue, the topic of jihadi social services/governance "is an area ripe for more detailed examination."[29] Thus far, individuals such as Brian Fishman have explored the Islamic State's original governance project from last decade prior to the *sahwa* (awakening) movement and the U.S. troop surge. First, he examines how jihadis legitimized the governance project since it was a controversial decision even within the milieu.[30] Second, he explains the failure of the project by stating its two major flaws: "First, it incited a sectarian backlash from Iraqi Shi'a without the means to defend Iraq's Sunnis from the onslaught it provoked. Second, AQI created a formal political entity, the Islamic State of Iraq (ISI), to dominate Iraq after a U.S. withdrawal without adequate support from Iraq's Sunni population."[31] Lastly, Fishman explains how the organization recovered by transforming itself once again from an insurgent force to an entity that relied on terrorist tactics: "The ISI increasingly resembles other al-Qaeda franchises that are more focused on terrorist attacks as opposed to the ISI of 2006, which was unique in its ambitious concentration on controlling territory and building a governance structure."[32]

This evolution is important since it explains the jihadi life cycle as articulated by Gartenstein-Ross:

> A clear pattern emerges in which the extremist group gains ground, announces the imposition of sharia, and governs territory. This alarms nearby states, and often those that are further away as well. So the extremist group's enemies strike. They topple it from power rather quickly.... The extremist group does its best to melt away rather than face a decisive battlefield defeat. It regroups with the intention of coming back stronger than before. The disturbing thing is the frequency with which militant groups are able to succeed in mounting this comeback.[33]

We have seen this phenomenon with the Islamic State as it retook territory in Iraq and new territory in Syria from 2013 to 2014. In the 2000s it solely relied on terror and judicial punishments to subdue territory. Today, as I explain, it has coupled those tactics with a soft power strategy that uses social services and governance to pacify the population or force residents to become dependent on IS. It has established quite a sophisticated bureaucracy.[34] Many of these developments are a result of a lessons-learned process that has taken place since the group's dark days in Iraq in the mid-2000s. They are also relevant to the study of AST because, according to members and sympathizers of the Islamic State, Tunisian foreign fighters that were previously in AST helped set up the Islamic State's *dawa* program.[35] Moreover, the face of the Islamic States' *dawa* campaign when it first began in the summer and fall of 2013 was the Tunisian Abu al-Waqas. The legacy of AST's *dawa* program is examined in greater detail when describing how former members of AST applied themselves within the jihadi movement following the designation of AST as a terrorist organization.

Other lessons learned and best practices from correspondences between the different al-Qaeda leaders in private provide more background on how the groups have learned from past experiences. Following the French invasion of Mali, investigative reporter Rukmini Callimachi found a trove of documents in AQIM safe houses in Timbuktu. One of the documents included correspondence from al-Qaeda in the Arabian Peninsula's (AQAP) emir at the time, Nasir al-Wihayshi, to AQIM's emir, 'Abd al-Malik Drukdal, in the spring and summer of 2012.[36] In the correspondence, Wihayshi "provides a step-by-step assessment of what worked and what didn't in Yemen."[37] Moreover, one of AQAP's ideologues, Abu Zubayr 'Adil Bin 'Abd Allah al-Abab, who was later killed in a drone strike, wrote an after-action report on AQAP's control of parts of the south in July 2012 titled "Gains and Benefits of Control Over Parts of Abyan and Shabwah."[38] This professionalization highlights the evolution and progression of jihadis' attempts to govern and provide social services in a more efficient and beneficial manner so as not to cause a backlash.

Since the failed "Islamic state" project last decade, the Somali jihadi group Harakat al-Shabab al-Mujahidin has been cultivating its own governance strategy as it has taken, relinquished, retaken, and lost territory on multiple occasions. Christopher Anzalone explains that al-Shabab undertook a protogovernance approach partly because of its competition with the Transitional Federal Government for resources and recruits. Anzalone also highlights how al-Shabab was able to capitalize on the Transitional Federal Government's poor governance record. As a result, al-Shabab "has undertaken and publicized a number of small-scale public works projects and social services in the areas of southern and central Somalia that it controls."[39] Moreover, Robin Simcox has written on a similar trend that can be seen in the context of AQAP when it captured territory in Yemen in 2011 and 2012: "[The] Yemeni state's inability to provide basic provisions and services is a key driver behind AQ's growth."[40]

Similarly, in the aftermath of the Arab uprisings when the Tunisian government was attempting to settle the politics of the capital instead of focusing on the needs of the average citizen, groups like AST began conducting relief caravans to rural parts of the country. This activity aimed to fill the vacuum left by the government's poor governance. The services were not perfect, but they provided a level of trust and soft power. Moreover, as I first noted in early 2012, "assisting in social work gave space to preach one's [AST's] ideology."[41]

Therefore, service provision can benefit the group and movement in multiple ways. AST's use of social services through its *dawa* program adds another layer to the explanation of why the movement grew so quickly after the Tunisian uprising. AST's innovation also provides another case study in the growing literature on jihadi social services and governance tactics to assuage populations and gain new supporters and recruits. These issues are explored in greater depths in chapters 5 and 6. The fifth chapter focuses more on decisions and reasons behind AST's outreach and social services, while the sixth chapter shows how AST implemented these programs on the ground throughout Tunisia.

The Leader-Led Versus Leaderless Debate

As a consequence of changes within the global jihadi movement in response to the post–Arab uprising landscape, some of the old debates within the literature were no longer relevant. In particular, the debate about leader-led versus leaderless jihad became less germane since it related more to threats faced by the West than to the dynamics of jihadism in the Arab world. And yet, as that debate evolved, it became more nuanced and provided a link to new explanations of how organizations such as AST could fit into or rearrange the framework of the debate.

One of the liveliest debates within the field of jihadi studies broke out between two well-respected scholars: Bruce Hoffman and Marc Sageman. In latter half of last decade there were major questions about the state of al-Qaeda and its relevance to the global jihadi scene. Was it still a centralized organization that controlled everything within the broader global jihadi movement, or had it devolved to the point that the grass roots had detached or started operating independently? It is important to remember that before the post–Arab uprising metastasization of jihadi groups, al-Qaeda was the only large player.

Historically, al-Qaeda believed that in order to defeat the so-called apostate Arab regimes, it first had to take down the Western countries that were propping them up. Al-Qaeda's main raison d'être up until 2011 had been to target Western countries with attacks. As such, there are some limitations in Hoffman and Sageman's debate when applying it to more localized/regionalized jihadi groups like AST since the arguments focus solely on al-Qaeda's connections to attacks against Western states. As is discussed below, the debate is relevant in other ways that help elucidate the organizational structures and methodologies of jihadi groups' operations, especially those of groups like AST established after 2011.

In his 2008 book, *Leaderless Jihad: Terror Networks in the Twenty-First Century,* Sageman argues that "al-Qaeda [Central] is of course not dead, but it is still contained operationally. It puts out inspirational guidance on the Internet, but does not have means to exert command and control over the al-Qaeda social movement."[42] Therefore, while al-Qaeda has been "in hiding, the al-Qaeda social movement has flourished." Sageman also argues that because of this dynamic, the "self-generated" networks in the West do not have any connective tissues to al-Qaeda.[43] This in turn would suggest that the more immediate threat facing Western countries is homegrown terrorists more so than al-Qaeda and its training camps in Afghanistan and Pakistan.

In contrast, Hoffman argues in a review of Sageman's book that in fact al-Qaeda still poses a greater threat. Hoffman bases his argument off of "the two most recent authoritative analyses of terrorist threats to the United States: the July 2007 National Intelligence Estimate and the annual threat assessment presented by the director of national intelligence," among other publicly available resources.[44] These two reports claim that al-Qaeda is still the largest threat to the homeland. Hoffman thus concludes from this that "the unmistakable message is that al Qaeda is a remarkably agile and flexible organization that exercises both top-down and bottom-up planning and operational capabilities."[45]

After the U.S. killed Usamah Bin Ladin in Abbottabad, Pakistan, in May 2011, information was declassified about documents recovered during the raid. In many ways the documents confirmed Hoffman's view that al-Qaeda was still intimately involved in plots against the United States. Hoffman argued after the raid that "it is clear that bin Laden was more involved in al Qaeda operations than many officials and experts had previously imagined. Far from having become an operational anachronism, bin Laden remained a driving force behind al Qaeda's undiminished terrorist ambitions."[46]

While the debate still continues for some, there are others who have taken different views on the issue. For example, Eliane Tschaen Barbieri and Jytte Klausen argue, based on a network analysis of all Western jihadis between 1998 and 2011 and British jihadis in particular, that both models have some truth: "A network analysis of the study's data indicates that while neither model accurately describes Western jihadism as a whole, each model fits specific geographically and temporally bound segments of the networks."[47] They conclude that Hoffman's model is accurate when examining the British network from 1998 to 2008, while Sageman's becomes more relevant post-2008 due to the degradation of al-Qaeda and its leadership network in "Londonistan" (and its outlying networks elsewhere in the United Kingdom).[48]

Others, such as Peter Neumann, Ryan Evans, and Raffaello Pantucci, explore the role of middle managers within the global jihadi network: those between the grass roots and the top leadership. "Middle managers, in short, are the only members of the group who are connected to both the *grassroots* and top leadership."[49] Using the Carl von Clausewitz idea of center of gravity to determine organizational pull, Neumann, Evans, and Pantucci argue that "in many instances—al-Qaeda's middle management has been critical in holding the group together and making its terrorist campaign work."[50] As a result, these connective tissues allow for "one (more or less) coherent strategic entity."[51]

In some ways, Neumann, Evans, and Pantucci's arguments are more relevant to the case of AST even if the context surrounding how al-Qaeda operates is different. In contrast to al-Qaeda and its use of middle managers to connect with grass roots in the West, as is shown in chapter 6, AST uses Tunisian locals to serve both as middle managers in its *dawa* campaigns and as faces of the organization at the local level. This tactic allows AST to show a more known or familial face when conducting outreach in areas in which top leadership does not have connections or aims to penetrate. Therefore, when conceptualizing AST as an organization, one must differentiate between the national-level leadership, regional/local-level leadership, and the grassroots activists in different cities and villages. This, in part, helps explain why AST was able to gain support nationally and not just in certain pockets within society. As such, Neumann, Evans, and Pantucci's work provides a base from which to contextualize AST's operations as an organization. It also helps answer one of the overarching questions of this book, which is why AST became relevant so quickly: its leadership structure and strategy for implementing it.

Methodology and Structure

This research is a historical case study informed primarily by qualitative analysis and process tracing a wide variety of primary source material, together with some basic quantitative assessments. Therefore, this research does not aim to provide a new theoretical perspective but rather seeks to produce and contribute a rigorous empirical understanding of the topic. Many within social science fields today scoff at the lack of quantitative or theoretical contribution; however, some, like John Gerring, understand the importance of "mere description," which "aims to answer what questions (e.g., when, whom, out of what, in what manner) about a phenomenon or a set of phenomena."[52] Similarly, Max Besbris and Shamus Khan highlight how "theoretical concepts are emptied of their content fairly quickly to satisfy the requirements of advancing theory. This leads to theoretical concepts that are rarely useful beyond a particular case, and it creates cloudiness instead of clarity." They "stake the position that a theoretically rich landscape, where theories are plentiful, is one wherein ideas are vacuous."[53]

With that being said, this study still attempts to situate the empiricism in social science theory—namely, social movement theory (SMT). This helps extrapolate why AST was so successful in recruitment. Sidney Tarrow defines a social movement as "collective challenges, based on common purposes and social solidarities, in sustained interaction with elites, opponents, and authorities."⁵⁴ Until the past decade or so, much of the SMT literature has dealt with coverage of social movements in the West. As Carrie Rosefsky Wickham observes, many studies on social movements are based in free societies of the West, while her research aims to probe Islamic social movements in Egypt under authoritarian rule.⁵⁵ Other studies, such as Wiktorowicz's edited volume on social movement theory's approach to Islamic activism, helped push the literature forward in terms of analyzing social movements in the Middle East.⁵⁶

Quinn Mecham argues, in his recent comprehensive examination of a spectrum of Islamist-related groups from all over the world in the context of social movement mobilization, that "voting for Islamically oriented political parties, participation in street demonstrations related to religious policy issues, and actions of political violence on behalf of a self-defined Islamist agenda are the core manifestations of mobilization."⁵⁷ This argument helps fit SMT into a Muslim-world context since the variety of activities expounded here, when stripped of the Islamic part, are just like studies on Western social movements: mobilization for elections, issue-specific demonstrations for some policy change, and political violence on behalf of a variety of political ideologies.

I would contend, however, that groups like AST do not fit this mold completely. Yes, AST is in fact a social movement, but the types of activities undertaken are different. Jihadis do not believe in democracy, since they view it as contravening the unicity of God and God's law, the violent parts—whether in relation to *hisba* (vigilante moral policing), terrorism, or insurgency—do apply. But unlike in the Western context, where a lot of the focus is on elections and protest, jihadi social movements have a religious component, which conducts *dawa* activities to bring people to the correct interpretation of Islam according to them, uses educational programs to further indoctrinate a particular worldview, and provides social services in the service of opening space to conduct *dawa* and bring more individuals into the fold of an organization or movement. Therefore, in some ways, one could also say that Muslim Brotherhood–like groups are a hybrid between a purely Western liberal democratic social movement and a jihadi social movement since they do have the *dawa*, education, and social service component but also take part in elections.

Relatedly, unlike traditional Islamist activism, which in the non-Western context has historically taken place under authoritarian regimes, AST developed in a transitioning society, one abandoning authoritarian practices of the past for justice, democracy, and freedom. It should be kept in mind, though, as Charles Tilly notes, that while democratization leads to more social movements, not all movements promote democracy.⁵⁸ This is the case with AST. Moreover, Erica Chenoweth has explained that "relatively poor and transitioning democracies with internally inconsistent institutions were more likely to experience domestic terrorism than advanced democracies and authoritarian regimes." This would also apply to the case of Tunisia.⁵⁹

Within SMT, scholars usually identify three main components: (1) political opportunity structures, (2) resource mobilization, and (3) framing.[60] The first relates to the changing conditions in which a social movement might operate. The second deals with the resources an organization brings when mobilizing itself, supporters, and potential new members. The third examines the narratives put forth by the group to consolidate its support base and use these ideas to recruit new members.

Regarding political opportunity structures, Donatella della Porta and Mario Diani explain that "the characteristics of the political system offer or deny essential opportunities for the development of collective action."[61] Prior to 2011 there was absolutely no space for free political expression, let alone the ability of jihadis to operate openly in Tunisia. This changed after the revolution due to the policies of the successive transitional and al-Nahdah-led governments. While the main focus of this study is to identify key reasons for AST's growth, the state's eventual pushback against AST's rise is—as Tarrow points out—relevant because it changes the environment in which a movement can operate.[62] The change in the status quo would affect how mobilization for jihadism would occur following AST too: more foreign fighting abroad and insurgent/terrorist activity at home. Therefore, this study sheds light on the evolutionary policies of the state during its transition vis-à-vis the activism of AST, which led to not only its meteoric rise but also its demise.

Until the Tunisian government designated AST as a terrorist organization in late August 2013, there was a general opening of freedoms and the public square in society. For example, the 2011 Freedom House report on Tunisia (which evaluates freedoms in the year 2010—the last full year prior to the uprising) rated Tunisia as not free; when broken down further, its rating (1 = best, 7 = worst) on freedom was 6; on civil liberties, 5; and on political rights, 7. Over the following three years when AST was active, Tunisia's overall rating dropped to partly free, and its freedom rating in 2012 and 2013 dropped to 3.5; civil liberties to 4; and political rights to 3. The 2014 report showed slight improvement, with "3" ratings for freedom, civil liberties, and political rights. The 2015 report, published after the designation of AST as a terrorist organization, continued an upward trend. Tunisia's overall rating was considered free, and its freedom rating was 2; civil liberties, 3; and political rights, 1.[63] This illustrates that although Tunisia's record improved, it did not necessarily mean that there would be more jihadism. Rather, after the designation of AST and subsequent crackdown, the conditions changed, as did the political opportunity structures. In other words, societal freedoms do not necessarily lead to jihadi action. Instead, jihadi action is tied to space provided via governmental policies more so than just the general opening of the proverbial public square.

In addition, this study evaluates resource mobilization and framing. Regarding the first concept, Doug McAdam, John D. McCarthy, and Mayer N. Zald define resource mobilization as "those collective vehicles, informal as well as formal, through which people mobilize and engage in collective action."[64] Moreover, Wickham shows that individual/group empowerment and agency are important factors in the development of social movements and that the main conduit through which these actors pursue agency is mobilization.[65] In particular, AST's organization and mobilization of resources are investigated since they are important parts of AST's *dawa* program aimed at growing and recruiting new individuals.

It is crucial to understand the framing narratives that AST uses to recruit and retain commitment among group members. Heather S. Gregg's recent work on the role of religion and how it plays out in social movements is useful in understanding AST since it is not a purely political actor but has a theocratic endgame too. Gregg argues that "religion provides a powerful resource for framing the struggle, a vision for the solution, and moral justification for taking action."[66] Furthermore, narrative ideas and slogans play an important role in AST's messaging arsenal. As Robert D. Benford and David A. Snow note, the purpose of executing a media plan by a social movement is to "negotiate a shared understanding of some problematic condition or situation they define as in need of change, make attributions regarding who or what is to blame, articulate an alternative set of arrangements, and urge others to act in concert to affect change."[67]

Bin Ladin understood these tactics, especially the use of master narratives. He famously remarked in a 2002 letter to the Islamic Emirate of Afghanistan's leader, Mullah Muhammad 'Umar, that: "It is obvious that the media war in this century is one of the strongest methods; in fact, its ratio may reach 90% of the total preparation for the battles."[68] As Jeffry R. Halverson, H. L. Goodall Jr., and Steven R. Corman conclude, "The reason the narratives of al-Qaeda and other Islamist extremists carry such potency is because they posses an internal coherence for their intended audiences that connects them to grand, deeply culturally embedded views of history—to master narratives—that Muslim audiences, in broad terms readily understand, identify with, or feel little need to question."[69]

Similar to Michael Page, Lara Challita, and Alistair Harris's work on understanding the propaganda of al-Qaeda in the Arabian Peninsula, this research examines the collective action frames of AST.[70] By understanding AST's diagnostic, prognostic, and motivational frames and how it hopes to achieve frame alignment, one can gain greater insight into the organization.

By using these three tools (political opportunity structures, resource mobilization, and framing) within social movement theory, we can gain a better understanding and appreciation for AST as an organizational movement. It also helps fill in the gaps for explaining why AST was able to become such a powerful political force in Tunisia after the revolution.

Sources

Before examining the structure of this book, it is worth making a note about the sources used in this study. This book drew upon a number of sources that had not previously been used, particularly old jihadi biographies and magazines from the 1980s and 1990s, which help provide a deeper knowledge of the history of Tunisian involvement in the jihadi movement prior to the revolution. I was also able to cross-reference a variety of court documents from Belgium, the European Union, France, Germany, Italy, Spain, the United Kingdom, and the United States to better explain Tunisian involvement in some of the largest terrorist attacks and plots in the Western world from the mid-to-late 1990s to the Tunisian revolution. Additionally, I exploited Jytte Klausen's Western Jihadism Project database, which has information on jihadism in the West from the early 1990s up until the present, which helped better identify the connections between individuals and organizations with whom Tunisians had been involved. The latter two sources—the court documents and Klausen's database—were crucial since the vast majority of Tunisian jihadis before the revolution used Europe either as a base or as a hub for a number of foreign fighting endeavors.

Additionally, when exploring the postrevolution era, this book used primary source material that was publicly released by AST and archived by this author on his external hard drive because, over the years, a number of AST's accounts online have been taken down. The process of gathering this data included tracking the "official" and the "news" Ansar al-Sharia Facebook pages and its Twitter account for new updates on its activities and ideological narratives. Over the course of its existence, AST used ninety-four Facebook pages and more than ten Twitter accounts as both companies took them down for violating their terms of service. The unprecedented amount of primary data provides a rich overview of many of the activities on the ground in Tunisia that AST has been involved in. Within this data—between the announcement of the organization publicly in May 2011 and its designation in August 2013—I collected more than eighteen thousand files, which include statements, video and audio recordings, essays and papers, magazine issues, pictures, and graphics, among other things.

In addition to primary sources from AST, this book also relies upon hundreds of Islamic State primary sources from Iraq, Libya, Syria, and Tunisia, including its propaganda materials and internal documents. Most notably from the latter is leaked IS border documents, which detail intake information from foreign fighters when they joined the Islamic State. These documents help provide official detail on almost seven hundred Tunisians who joined the Islamic State between 2012 and 2014. On top of this, I have collected more than five thousand documents in multiple languages on foreign fighters. Besides the IS, hundreds of primary sources from AQIM's front group in Tunisia, Katibat 'Uqbah Bin Nafi (KUBN), are used to better understand its transformation between 2012 and 2019. Lastly, I have access to internal governmental documents from both the Libyan attorney general's office (on Tunisian foreign fighters in Libya) and Tunisia's Ministry of Interior (on Tunisian foreign fighter returnees from Iraq, Libya, and Syria).

This is all very useful since Thomas Hegghammer has highlighted the vastness and granularity of primary source data nowadays, which he argues allows for an "ethnography by proxy."[71] However, it is important to highlight that jihadi content is biased toward the information it wants the public to see. That is why it was useful that I had the opportunity to conduct a number of field research trips to Tunisia in 2012, 2013, 2018, and 2019. As Adam Dolnik argues, "field research is useful in helping researchers in navigating with greater certainty through multiple contradictory versions of events available in open sources. It contributes to counterbalancing some of the key research biases that inherently exist. It also enhances the reliability and accuracy of findings, and above all, the process itself can be highly beneficial in educating the researcher by allowing him or her to acquire a tacit knowledge of the context."[72]

While in Tunisia, I had the opportunity to meet with members of AST in a variety of cities and villages as well as with a returned foreign fighter from Syria. To buttress these interviews, meetings with civil society actors, unaffiliated political activists, al-Nahdah and Nida Tunis members and leaders, current governmental officials, and former regime officials from the Bin 'Ali era were undertaken as well. This helped strengthen many of the findings from the primary sources since it is one thing to follow it online and explore where events are occurring via Google Maps; it is another thing to feel it and attend an AST rally, join the prayers at an AST mosque, join AST members attempting to do *dawa* on oneself, or gather physical publications passed out on the streets by AST members that are not posted online, among other activities.

Structure

This study is divided into three parts. The first part explores the historical and postrevolution conditions that provided the opportunity for AST to thrive after 2011. The second part looks at the particular strategic approach AST took when exploiting the post-revolution conditions and investigate how it mobilized its resources, framed its messaging, and cultivated connections with the broader global jihadi movement, leading to its downfall. The third and final part explores the aftermath of AST's designation, the mobilization of Tunisians for foreign fighting abroad, and the renewed terrorism campaign domestically in Tunisia following the rise of IS.

The first chapter covers the history of Islam and Islamism in Tunisia from its independence in 1956 to 2010, when the revolution began. It answers the question of why there was a rise in Islamism and, subsequently, jihadism in Tunisia. It is important to understand the changes that Tunisia's first president, Habib Bourguiba, and later Bin 'Ali made toward the role of Islam in society. Probing this history helps explain the local context of how and why Islamist movements in Tunisia came into being. It also highlights the evolution of Islamism from its beginning in the late 1960s and early 1970s to the present. The chapter is also relevant to the discussion in the fourth chapter since the experience of al-Nahdah after its suppression by the regime in the late 1980s and early 1990s informed the party's decision making and dealings with AST when it came to power in 2011. Lastly, chapter 1 discusses the vacuum created and then filled by salafis after the crackdown on al-Nahdah, which created a space for the beginning of a homegrown jihadi movement that would flower after the revolution.

The second and third chapters look at Tunisians involved in jihadism prior to the 2011 revolution. It seeks to answer the question of how Tunisians gained experience in the jihadi movement. This is one of the most important aspects of understanding the rapid pace with which AST was able to organize following the revolution. Many central figures had a bevy of experience. The main crux of these chapters looks at Tunisians joining foreign fighter mobilizations in Afghanistan, Bosnia, Chechnya, and Iraq; being a part of logistics and facilitation networks based in Europe; plotting terrorist attacks from Afghanistan, Europe, and Turkey; and training regionally with AQIM in Algeria. They demonstrate the rich history of Tunisian involvement in the jihadi movement as well as continuity of some of the key figures that would eventually become leaders in AST. Therefore, with the opening of society after the revolution, there was a base for a new organization to form and take advantage of the opportunity.

The fourth chapter explores the Tunisian government's policies toward jihadis and AST from March 2011 to August 2013. These dates coincide with the prisoner amnesty implemented by the transitional government, which allowed thousands of jihadis imprisoned prior to the revolution to start organizing. The latter date is when the Tunisian government designated AST as a terrorist organization. This chapter aims to answer the question of what postrevolution conditions in Tunisia allowed AST to thrive. It looks at the evolving policies of the transitional- and al-Nahdah-led governments that provided the space for AST to recruit and proselytize its ideas. Furthermore, it explores case studies of incidents in that two-and-a-half-year period to show how the governments approached each episode and how that opened or closed windows for the organization. The latter part on conditions being more restricted is explored in greater detail in the seventh chapter.

The fifth chapter looks at AST's strategic decision making that led to its *dawa*-first approach. To better understand it, the chapter first explores the evolution in jihadi strategic thought post-9/11 to the Arab uprisings. It also analyzes the strategic texts of key jihadi ideologues and leaders, their views of the changing environment after the 2011 uprisings, and their diagnoses on what to do as it related to Tunisia. The new environment wrought by the Arab uprisings, especially in Tunisia, provided an opportunity to implement lessons learned from the Taliban's defeat in Afghanistan, the failed jihad in Saudi Arabia, and the excessively violent experience in Iraq. This helps situate AST's decision on the *dawa*-first approach. The final section examines the particular conditions within Tunisia that solidified the *dawa*-first strategy.

With the previous chapter's background, the sixth chapter examines the implementation of AST's *dawa* program. In order to do this, the chapter looks at the program's organizational structure, missionary activities, social services, outreach, and approach to spreading its ideology and forming its narratives. These actions are an important component in understanding how and why AST gained sympathy within some segments of society so quickly. *Dawa* was the means to spread AST's ideology. Therefore, the chapter also provides a content analysis of key ideas promoted in AST's propaganda and advertisements for its events.

The seventh chapter looks into the more nefarious aspects of AST as an organization that led to its designation as a terrorist organization: most specifically, its *hisba* activities, jihadi terrorist attacks, and foreign fighter recruitment. As such, it explains the downfall of AST and the return of Tunisian foreign fighting. First, I touch upon the vigilantism that has been attributed to its members and how AST as an organization evolved into a more hostile actor as a consequence. Then I survey Tunisian involvement in terrorist attacks within Tunisia with either KUBN or AST. Finally, I discuss Tunisian involvement in training and fighting jihad abroad, specifically in Libya and Syria, prior to the reemergence of IS and its caliphate announcement.

The eighth chapter examines the shifting networks following the designation of AST and how IS was able to take advantage of the changing environment to recruit individuals to join it in Iraq and Syria. It also identifies why so many Tunisian jihadis ended up joining IS even though AST had been an AQ group. It also explains why the crackdown upon AST and some prior international connections that members of the group made during the AST-era led a number of former AST members to become ultra-extremists within the IS.

Chapter 9 provides an in-depth exploration of the Tunisian foreign fighter mobilization to the IS in Iraq and Syria. It explores in detail various statistical data points on the flow, motivations for why Tunisians went and joined, what they actually did while they were with the IS (including women), and how that would affect the future of the movement whether abroad or when they return home to Tunisia.

The final two chapters look at what happened within Tunisia following the designation of AST, particularly how the IS was able to infiltrate KUBN, how the IS's network next door built up in Libya, and how that created a safe haven environment for external operations back into Tunisia that led to mass casualty attacks in 2015 in Tunis and Sousse. It then highlights how the Tunisian government reacted to this challenge; why KUBN was unable to take advantage of the IS's defeats in Iraq, Libya, Syria, and Tunisia; and what that means for the future of the movement.

CHAPTER 1

THE GENERATION OF ZAYTUNAH

In central Tunis, a middle-aged man with slight balding in a dapper suit and with bodyguards behind him approaches a group of women wearing cream-colored *sefsari* (the Tunisian version of the hijab). Holding his "Coke-bottle" glasses in his left hand, he begins to unfurl one of the women's *sefsari* with his right hand. At first, she places her hand up to try and put it back on, but then relents and allows him to fully take off her veil. She has a smile on her face. Another woman next to her then goes up to the man and kisses him on his right cheek before he then takes off her *sefsari*.[1] This man is Habib Bourguiba, Tunisia's founding president who instituted a wide range of secular reforms after coming to power following Tunisia's independence from France in 1956. This scene was part of Bourguiba's drive to take religion out of the public sphere, which over time succeeded in creating a particular perception of Tunisia in comparison with other Arab countries.

Prior to the 2011 revolution, when thinking about Tunisia, many would likely believe that it was a highly educated and secular society. Yet, secularism is a relatively new phenomenon and in many ways is a rupture from Tunisia's past as a religious society. As Kenneth J. Perkins notes, "Islam constituted an inextricable component of Tunisian culture in the view of the secular Young Tunisians as well as in the views of both the conservative and progressive *'ulama* (religious establishment)."[2] Furthermore, as North African scholar Michael Willis explains, "Islam had historically always played a central role in Maghrebi [North African] politics: most notably in legitimising political authority."[3] Therefore, Anne Wolf explains, "the notion of 'secular Tunisia' has always been a myth."⁴ It is no surprise, then, that not everyone in Tunisia was content with relegating Islam to the private sphere.

By understanding this tendency, an appreciation for why there was a rise in Islamism—and, subsequently, jihadism—in Tunisia can better be understood. This chapter aims to set the historical stage for explaining the growth of Tunisian jihadism. To better elucidate this growth, it is necessary to first examine Tunisia's modern history to understand its origins. Bourguiba's Islamic reforms led to the creation of the Tunisian Islamist movement, known as al-Nahdah today. Subsequently, the harsh crackdown against this movement in the 1980s and 1990s by Bourguiba and his successor, Zayn al-'Abidin Bin 'Ali, left a vacuum for new religious contestation.

The latter reason is also relevant to events that transpired after the revolution and is evaluated in greater detail in chapter 4. The crackdown on al-Nahdah in the 1980s and 1990s left a mark on the group's leader, Rashid Ghannushi, insofar as it radicalized some members of the movement to turn toward violence, and an even smaller subset defected and became jihadis. This radicalization because of the government's crackdown would help inform Ghannushi's and al-Nahdah's policies vis-à-vis Ansar al-Sharia in Tunisia (AST) when it came to power in October 2011. Thus, beyond the historical background, it is necessary to understand al-Nahdah's evolution to better appreciate how the government responded to events after the revolution. It will also reveal parallels that will become clearer later in the book between the early growth in what became al-Nahdah and AST. This provides another layer to understanding why al-Nahdah preferred a policy of dialogue with AST over one of conflict.

Bourguiba's Islamic Reforms

Bourguiba's religious reforms were the driving force behind the Islamic activism of men like Rashid Ghannushi in the 1960s and 1970s. Tunisian scholar 'Abd Elbaki Hermassi argues that "the origin of the MTI [Mouvement de la tendance islamique, a prior name al-Nahdah's movement used] one can put forward a reason so obvious that is rarely taken into account or accorded its full weight. It is that out of all the Arab countries, Tunisia is the only one where the modernist elite deliberately attacked the institutions of Islam and dismantled its infrastructure in the name of systematic reform of the social and cultural order."⁵ Sarah J. Feuer describes this process and style as a "non-traditionalist regime ... for which religion, if present at all, remains peripheral to the ruler's rhetoric of self-legitimation."⁶

All founding members of what would eventually become al-Nahdah had been aggrieved by what they felt had been the stripping of their identity. As Ghannushi noted: "I am of the generation of Zaytunah students during the early years of independence. I remember we used to feel like strangers in our own country. We have been educated as Muslims and as Arabs, while we could see the country totally molded in the French cultural identity. For us, the doors for any further education were closed since the university was completely Westernized."[7] Only later in al-Nahdah's development did it feel the need to address economic or political issues. In most Arab countries that have been home to Islamist movements since the abolishment of the Ottoman caliphate in the 1920s, one of the largest grievances was the lack of implementation of true Islam or the correct interpretations of sharia (Islamic law) at executive, legislative, judicial, and military levels. In contrast, the entrepreneurs of Tunisia's Islamist movement simply wanted a place for religion in society. As one of the earliest activists noted, "we started preaching and it was about bring people back to the mosque and back to prayers.... It was about faith and belief as pillars in themselves."[8]

Unlike leaders in other Arab states, Bourguiba eliminated basic aspects of Islam from daily life. He attempted to implement a secular system similar to that of France (laïcité). However, Bourguiba was not always like this. He lost his appreciation of the importance of Islam to some in Tunisian society, which he originally helped drive during the anticolonial struggle against the French. As Marion Boulby explains, "Bourguiba did not present himself as a secularizing reformer in the style of Turkey's Kemal Ataturk. Instead he offered himself to the Tunisians as a modernist reformer of Islam."[9] Moreover, during the fight against the French, Bourguiba framed himself as *al-mujahid al-akbar* (the great holy struggler) and asserted that the Tunisians were fighting a jihad against France. He even urged his supporters to pray the five daily Muslim prayers every day for the martyrs who died at the hands of the French. His party gathered support in mosques and *zawiyyas* (religious schools) in addition to cafés. Therefore, while Bourguiba did not identify as religiously conservative, he understood the pulse of Tunisian society. Even after independence, according to Wolf, "in one speech he denounced France's 'assimilation projects' by defending the *hijab* as well as the traditional veil of Tunisian women, the *sefsari*."[10] As he gained more power, he lost sight of this crucial aspect in a process that Wolf describes as the "trivialization of religious discourse."[11]

Following independence, Bourguiba embarked on widespread reforms of Islam and its role in society. At first he did not receive much pushback—largely a factor of the marginalization of the Tunisian *'ulama* and Sufi brotherhoods during the French colonial period.[12] He also had more luxury to maneuver politically after deposing his rival, Salih Bin Yusuf.[13] From 1956 to 1957, Bourguiba began his sweeping changes with the Code du statut personnel. The Code du statut personnel's biggest legacy—which continues to this day—is the rights granted to women. According to Robert D. Lee, "under the constitution women already enjoyed equality of citizenship. The [Code du statut personnel] created a civil marriage procedure based on mutual consent as well as a legal divorce procedure, abolishing the practice of repudiation; it abolished polygamy, and regulated child adoption."[14] Moreover, the *sefsari* was banned, which led Bourguiba to publicly take them off women, as described earlier.[15]

Part of these reforms derived from what Sana Ben Achour describes as Bourguiba's "new conception of *ijtihad* (independent reasoning)" and from belief that he himself was a mufti (an Islamic scholar who interprets and expounds Islamic law and jurisprudence) with the ability to publish *fatawa* (religious edicts).[16] Bourguiba demonstrated this belief in his most famous public defiance of traditional Islamic practice when he drank orange juice on television during Ramadan in 1964—an act linked to his 1960 ban on fasting during Ramadan.[17] He also discouraged the Muslim practice of hajj to Mecca.[18] Between those two ideas, Bourguiba was undermining two of Islam's five pillars, claiming that these changes were instituted to do "jihad against underdevelopment."[19] Moreover, in 1956 Bourguiba abolished the *habus* (known elsewhere as *waqf*), charitable donations and land given to mosques and religious schools to provide financial independence to the *'ulama*. In addition, Bourguiba suspended the use of sharia courts in favor of a more secular, liberal, and progressive court system governed not by *qadis* (religious judges) but rather by national judges.[20] Lastly, Bourguiba nationalized and centralized religious education by firing and then appointing new teachers at Zaytunah University, the oldest Sunni religious school. In 1960 Bourguiba placed Zaytunah under the authority of the School of Theology at the University of Tunis and created the Directorate of Religious Affairs, which effectively co-opted the *'ulama*.[21] If the *'ulama* had not already been marginalized during the colonial period, these economic, jurisprudential, and educational blows further discredited them. Willis argues that Bourguiba's actions were partly motivated by the *'ulama*'s support for Bourguiba's rival, Bin Yusuf.[22] It is quite possible, too, that the attempted coup plot against Bourguiba by supporters of Yusuf in 1960 may have played a role as well.[23]

Bourguiba truly believed he was establishing a Tunisian and Republican Islam.[24] Part of this project was therefore aimed at educating the populace. Over the next three decades of his rule, Bourguiba rapidly developed the education system on all levels, from primary to tertiary schools. In 1958 he integrated all educational systems into one secular program, making education free to the populace and establishing the University of Tunis.[25] In each level of education, Bourguiba's 1959 program, Nouvelle conception de l'enseignement en Tunisie, emphasized different aspects of republican and Islamic values. One of his key influences had been his time studying and living in France in the 1930s. During this period Tunisians constituted three-quarters of university students coming from French-colonized North African countries.[26] This demographic makeup foreshadowed the birth of a new secular elite.

According to Edward Webb,

Bourguiba adapted a model of state-religion relations originated by the French revolutionary state and pursued by the French Third Republic before 1905, and by the Turkish Republic under Ataturk. In each of these cases a radical state elite sought to adapt the religion of the majority into a new religion of the republic as an instrument in socializing well-disciplined republican citizens. Religion was not eradicated, but subordinated to the state and absorbed into its revolutionary mission.[27]

The main objective of this curriculum was to foster moral citizens that would then adhere to republican values as they progressed through the educational system. The problem with this system was that economic constraints forced certain people to forgo higher levels of education in favor of finding jobs to support their families. Because the educational program was gradualistic, those who left the system earlier gained less knowledge of the duties of the responsible republican citizen, while those who continued with university education shifted focus away from religious morals needed to be upstanding citizens. Therefore, the citizenry became divided in terms of emphasis, norms, and duties, which later came to delineate different classes in Tunisian society. That being said, Webb believes that "republican identity production had some success" considering the continued viability and more recent nostalgia for Bourguiba's ways.[28] Rikke Hostrup Haugbølle also argues that "Islam did not disappear in the decades under President Bourguiba and Bin 'Ali's rule, but shifted from the public to the private realm."[29]

Some members of society were disgusted by Bourguiba's educational reforms. Defiant *'ulama* who had refused to give up their independence to the state (such as Muhammad Salih al-Nayfar, Ahmad Bin Milad, and 'Abd al-Qadir Salamah) and some of the last students who had completed religious primary school before the educational reforms—most notably Ghannushi, but also 'Abd al-Fatah Muru, Hamidah al-Nayfar, and Salah al-Din al-Jurshi—were among those who opposed the revised curriculum.[30] This band of individuals would form the nucleus of what would become the burgeoning Islamist movement in Tunisia.

From *Halaqat* to al-Jama'ah al-Islamiyyah to Harakat al-Ittijah al-Islami to Harakat al-Nahdah

In response to Bourguiba's policies, a number of religious individuals came together to push back against the reforms in the hopes of rebuilding a religious society. Emad Eldin Shahin provides a useful evolutionary framework for understanding the rise of al-Nahdah. He argues that there are four phases that the group has gone through since it first began organizing: the formative phase

(1960s–1973); the expansion phase (1973–1979); the politicization phase (1979–1987); and the post-Bourguiba phase (1987–present [which, in Shahin's book, was 1997; the post-Bourguiba phase here goes up to 2000]).³¹ Since this research extends beyond the date of Shahin's work, this analysis will add a fifth phase, up to the Tunisian Revolution: political normalization (2001–2010). Each phase can be traced to key events or turning points inside and outside Tunisia. The phases also illustrate how the Tunisian government, in the face of the Islamist mobilization, began to slacken its approach related to religion in a way to co-opt the movement, which it was unable to do.

The Formative Phase: 1960s–1973

In the mid-1960s, Ghannushi, Muru, al-Nayfar, and al-Jurshi formed the core of the proto-Islamist movement in Tunisia and created *halaqat* (religious lessons), primarily around Shaykh Milad at Zaytunah mosque in Tunis.³² According to Boulby, *halaqat* were "conceived in social and cultural, rather than in political terms. Discourse was concentrated on issues relating to the individual or the family and much emphasis was placed on the role of women in Islam. Attention was also given to the general decadence of Western institutions."³³

Although Ghannushi had been exposed to the Syrian Muslim Brotherhood when he studied and taught in Syria in the mid-1960s, the first main influence and methodology of organization for Tunisia's Islamist movement stemmed from Jama'at al-Tabligh (JT), an apolitical proselytizing organization focused on education and reintegrating lapsed Muslims into practice through *dawa*. Ghannushi had been exposed to JT during his studies in Paris from 1966 to 1967.³⁴ Others within the Islamist movement inside Tunisia were exposed to JT when its missionaries visited Tunisia in the late 1960s.³⁵ JT's methodology requires *al-khuruj* (to go out)—travel to other cities and villages to do missionary work in streets, cafés, and mosques. It even calls for inviting individuals to members' homes.

Coinciding with the growth in these *halaqat* and *dawa* sessions in the late 1960s and early 1970s, there was a need for Bourguiba to reestablish some religious legitimacy due to the failure of his socialist economic policies over the previous decade. Because his economic policies failed to affect meaningful change, some called into question the legitimacy of his Islamic reforms. In response, Bourguiba created the National Association for the Preservation of the Qur'an in an attempt to placate parts of the populace. To distance himself from the socialist economic policies, Bourguiba began to suppress socialist and leftist activism, especially on college campuses. In addition, while Tunisia's economy sputtered, the foreign policy of Gamal 'Abd al-Nasir—Egypt's president and the bulwark of Arabism in the region—experienced a major setback in the 1967 Six-Day War against Israel. This watershed military loss was the beginning of the end of 'Abd al-Nasir's regional ideological and economic project as well as what many view as the beginning of the Islamist era in the broader Arab world. This confluence of events provided an opening for the Islamist movement in Tunisia.

Through the National Association for the Preservation of the Qur'an, al-Jama'ah al-Islamiyyah (JI), which is what the movement began to call itself in 1972, was able to operate on a more official level and in a legal manner.[36] Although JI did not run the National Association for the Preservation of the Qur'an, it used the organization as a vehicle to further spread its cause. At this point, JI started to grow and formalize its *halaqat* outside the original groupings, specifically targeting baccalaureate students and women.[37] As the baccalaureate students started entering college, this outreach allowed JI to grow on campus, which in turn fueled skepticism among many leftists who questioned the authenticity of the Islamists. Some leftists even felt that JI was part of the regime's conspiracy against them. In reality, JI was just in the right place at the right time to take advantage of these newfound freedoms.

The Expansion Phase: 1973–1979

Until 1973 JI continued its work within the framework of JT's methodology, but this all changed after Ghannushi, Muru, and al-Nayfar were arrested during a *dawa* session in Sousse, ninety miles southeast of Tunis. In 1992 Ghannushi told Muhammad al-Hashimi Hamdi, a former member of al-Nahdah, "we realized that the methods of al-Tabligh may work in Pakistan or India, or even France where democratic traditions exist. But none of this was available in Tunisia."[38] As a result, Ghannushi turned his attention to the Muslim Brotherhood (MB) methodology, which he was first exposed in Syria. The early 1970s also saw the release of many Egyptian MB members from prison as new Egyptian president Anwar al-Sadat aimed to distinguish himself from his predecessor, 'Abd al-Nasir. Al-Nayfar even met with some of the newly released MB members at hajj in Mecca in 1973. In retrospect, al-Nayfar notes that the MB "pushed us to be engaged more directly in political action as well as in setting up an underground organisation."[39] In addition to a greater recruitment focus on universities, JI now also looked to formal mosques.

As JI became more politicized, different topics and narratives were published in its main magazine, *al-Ma'rifa* (Knowledge). In his 1985 book on the Islamist movement in Tunisia, 'Abd al-Latif al-Hermassi tracked these changes, mainly showing how *al-Ma'rifa* shifted its focus from theological to more political issues (see table 1.1). During this same period, *al-Ma'rifa*'s readership grew from 6,000 to 25,000.[40] This growth period and greater focus on politics was

TABLE 1.1 'Abd al-Latif al-Hermassi's Breakdown of *al-Ma'rifa*'s Evolution

Issues Covered	Percent During 1972–1973	Percent During 1979
Cultural and intellectual	43.1	62.6
Theological and moral	44.3	18.3
Social	10.3	6.1
Political	2.3	13

Source: 'Abd al-Latif al-Hermassi, *al-Harakah al-Islamiyyah fi Tunis: al-Yasar al-Ishtiraki, al-Islam, wa al-Harakah al-Islamiyyah* (Tunis: Bayram li al-Nashr, 1985), 101–7.

concurrent with the first Tunisian Book Fair in 1973, which provided JI members access to works from newly released Egyptian MB members.[41] Therefore, in addition to its own magazine, JI began to distribute books by Hasan al-Banna, Sayyid Qutb, Muhammad Qutb, Yusuf al-Qaradawi, and Muhammad al-Ghazali to its membership, which bolstered, according to Ghannushi, "enthusiasm for Islam and disapproval of the current situation."[42]

As JI continued to grow, some members of the movement grew dissatisfied with its direction. The organization experienced its first split in 1976 when founding members al-Nayfar and al-Jurshi left the group and established their own organization, al-Ittijah al-Islami al-Taqadumi (The Progressive Islamic Tendency). Both felt that JI was pursuing political agendas too soon and wanted to have more of a local Tunisian approach instead of importing outside influences like Qutbist ideology.[43] According to al-Nayfar, the MB "did not know anything about what was happening in North Africa. When I asked a simple question [to them at the hajj in 1973], I always just received a quote from Hasan al-Banna as an answer. But al-Banna founded the Muslim Brotherhood in the 1920's and we were living in 1973."[44] This new formation, however, never garnered much popular support.

The three events that drove JI to become fully socially conscious and politicized occurred between late 1977 and early 1979. Throughout the 1970s, as JI grew and the government continued to suppress the leftists, the balance of strength on campuses began to shift in favor of the Islamists—a development that increased the leftists' desperation. On December 26, 1977, knife-wielding leftists attacked a group of Islamists. Such confrontations continued until 1982.[45] This competition led the Islamists on campuses to become more radicalized and tried to outbid the leftists. As al-Nayfar notes, JI's campus members also pushed the leadership of the organization to pursue more political and radical positions: "Since 1977, we can even say that there was a reversal of roles: the university became the locomotive of the movement."[46] According to Wolf, these JI students also "practiced karate on a daily basis, certainly in preparation for future clashes on campus, and possibly even with the regime."[47]

On January 26, 1978, as the fights progressed on campus and a month after the knife attacks, an uprising and riot led by union workers took place, which came to be called Black Thursday. Following the failed socialist economic policies, Bourguiba led an economic liberalization effort, which in its first five years or so showed promise and revitalization of the Tunisian economy. But by the end of the 1970s, the liberalization project's stagnation began to hurt the working class since many of the policies only favored corporations and the wealthy. As a result, the L'Union générale tunisienne du travail (UGTT, Tunisian General Labour Union) called for a strike on January 26, leading to a major confrontation with the regime. Although this "uprising" failed and led to the UGTT's suppression, JI's leadership took several lessons from this experience.

Leaders in JI believed that the workers were a strong political force against the regime and therefore felt the need to address workers' concerns. This realization led JI to adopt economic positions in addition to political ones. Ghannushi noted that "Islamists have no influence over the working class, they leave this strategic sector to the ideologies of the right or the left."[48] As a result, when the Tunisian government restored the UGTT, workers who were members of JI joined UGTT in order to gain influence and proselytize to non-Islamist members.[49]

In addition to events inside Tunisia, the Iranian Revolution in February 1979 was a watershed moment for JI. The movement had been following everything leading up to the revolution and had even started a weekly newspaper called *al-Mujtamah* (The Community) in August 1978 that published pro-revolutionary articles.[50] According to Hamdi, "the Islamists in Iran provided a model of success and political power, which became a source of great motivation for the members of *al-Jama'ah al-Islamiyyah*."[51] Additionally, Ghannushi emphatically stated that "the example of Iran shows us the awakening has come."[52] JI also began to take on more of the rhetoric of Ruhollah Khomeini, replacing the more Marxist sayings of "imperialism," "oppressed classes," and "despotic regimes" with "*al-istikbar al-alami* (the international oppression)," "*al-mustad 'afun al-ard* (the dispossessed on Earth)," and "*al-taghut* (the tyrant)."[53] In response to the internal and external factors leading to JI's politicization, the movement decided to formalize its structures instead of remaining as an ad hoc grouping of *halaqat*.

The Politicization Phase: 1979–1987

Around the time of the Iranian Revolution in early 1979, the Islamist movement applied to become an official association registered by the state called al-Wa'i al-Islami (Islamic Awareness). The state rejected the request.⁵⁴ In August 1979 the Islamist movement officially created an organizational structure for JI when it had its first formal conference in private.⁵⁵ In it, Ghannushi was elected *amir* (leader) of JI after having been its symbolic leader for years. It also named Salah Karkar as Ghannushi's deputy. Karkar, who had previously served as an economics teacher and organizer, would lead the more radical wing of the organization. During the founding conference, the individuals involved formally decided to identify as members of the International Muslim Brotherhood.⁵⁶ As a result, the organization mimicked the classic Egyptian MB pyramid structure, with individuals receiving three years of "educational" training before becoming official members. They were also divided into "informal families" and "formal families."⁵⁷

At that point, this information remained internal and unknown to the government or public until December 5, 1980. This is when two executive bureau members, Karkar and Ben 'Issa Dimini, were arrested, revealing a variety of JI documents in their homes to the police.⁵⁸ Ghannushi decided to dissolve the *majlis al-shura* (consultative council), the central executive bureau, and committees and tell the public about its organization. Six months later the organization reassembled itself, went public with its organization, and tried to become a legal political party, calling itself Harakat al-Ittijah al-Islami (the Islamic Tendency Movement, most known by the French acronym MTI).⁵⁹

As part of its rebranding effort, MTI released a statement highlighting five key points of its program:

1. Reviving the Islamic personality of Tunisia
2. Reformulating Islamic thought
3. Reasserting popular will
4. Establishing a system of social justice
5. Reviving the political and civilizational unity of Islam nationally, regionally, within the Arab world, and internationally⁶⁰

These points were too much for Bourguiba's regime to tolerate. It saw MTI as a direct political threat to the survivability of its government. The regime likely also perceived events such as the February 1981 hostage-taking by Islamist students of the dean of the Faculty of Science at the University of Manouba (a similar incident would occur with AST members at the same university after the revolution) as one of the breaking points.⁶¹ In response, on July 18, 1981, the regime arrested 107 of the movement's activists and leaders, including Ghannushi, Muru, and Karkar. The top leaders were then sentenced to ten years in prison after being appealed down from eleven.⁶² Despite the setback, Ghannushi believed it "was a chance to feed new blood into the movement, thereby preserving its youth, effectiveness, and renewal."⁶³ Notwithstanding this optimism about the future, the organization experienced internal fractures: Muru advocated a more moderate position while Karkar supported a more radical confrontational approach. This rift would become a problem that Ghannushi would have to navigate once the movement's leaders were released from prison early in 1984.[64]

It is important to note that during this time the anti-Soviet jihad in Afghanistan started to pick up steam. Unlike most Arab countries, including those surrounding Tunisia—Algeria and Libya—the mobilization of Tunisians to Afghanistan was quite low. In addition, Tunisia did not experience the returnee problem from Afghanistan that other North African states, as well as Egypt and Yemen, faced in the late 1980s and early 1990s. And although the MTI sympathized with the cause, Alison Pargeter notes that "the Afghan jihad may have seemed like an unwanted distraction by the MTI leadership."[65] Ghannushi and MTI increasingly felt that their opportunities in Tunisia were going to bear fruit soon. Notably, MTI's ability to participate overtly in Tunisian politics—even if not on an official level—delayed the start of any jihadi movement whose members might have been disgruntled with the mainstream Islamist trend, as was the case in other countries. It appeared that MTI would be able to position itself for a potential future takeover of the Tunisian political system. That said, there were some members of the MTI in individual capacities that became foreign fighters and joined the anti-Soviet Afghan jihad, which portended to greater jihadi activism in later years.[66] This lack of organizational interest and broader mobilization for Afghanistan does help explain the delay in jihadism becoming more relevant in Tunisia compared with other regional Arab states in the 1980s and 1990s.

During the three years that MTI's leaders were imprisoned (1981–1984), those who were not arrested elected a new leadership, whose *amir*, Hamadi al-Jabali, an engineer from Sousse (who eventually served as prime minister of Tunisia after the October 2011 elections following the Tunisian Revolution), directed operations from Paris.[67] In addition, MTI created new secret pamphlets called *al-Risalah* (the Message) and *al-Masar* (the Path), and wrote in the opposition press *al-Ra'i* (the Opinion).[68] From this perch abroad, and through these publications, the organization was able to continue its activities, especially on college campuses. MTI was thus able to take advantage of more economic unrest in January 1984 in what became known as the Bread Riots. Unlike in the 1979 uprising pushed by the unions, MTI played a role in agitating this one, illustrating the power it was able to wield even while its top leadership was imprisoned.[69]

Until the fall of Bourguiba in 1987, the movement was still harassed, but it was able to gain more support and sympathy through relationship building across ideological lines, most notably with the Social Democrats, the Communist Party, the Movement of National Unity, and the Socialist Alliance.[70] This outreach allowed it to operate in a way that protected it from reprisal while still posing a threat to the regime. In May 1985 MTI established the Tunisian General Union of Students, marking a major victory for the movement on campus and solidifying its stranglehold over student politics at the University of Tunis. This further emboldened Ghannushi to believe that the time was ripe for his movement to take over Tunisia in the near future, even though the trade unions remained the strongest opposition entity.[71] Over the next few years economic problems continued, and Bourguiba's health deteriorated, leading to internal contestation over who would succeed him. Bourguiba himself became ever more paranoid about the growing power of MTI, remarking once that "the eradication of the Islamist poison will be the last service I'll render Tunisia."[72]

Bourguiba's paranoia was not necessarily unfounded. At its next organizational conference in December 1986, the MTI decided to pursue the more radical policies of Karkar, which Ghannushi endorsed, essentially consolidating gains and advancing the cause instead of returning to a more *dawa*-only organization.[73] According to Hamdi, "the tempting prospect of taking power was so great that no one opted for a change in direction."[74] Moreover, as MTI leadership reactivated the organization, they still maintained a secret aspect to its affairs in addition to the public political party. Karkar's radical wing drafted plans for a potential coup d'état that would be led by Muhammad Shammam, the head of the group's military wing, called al-Majmu'a al-Amniyah (the Security Group).[75]

As this wing planned, the breaking point—which would lead to the third, final, and harshest crackdown against MTI in the Bourguiba era—came when Ghannushi attempted to deliver a speech at a mosque without an official license.[76] This incident would eventually lead to a death sentence, which Bourguiba hoped would end the movement. Many individuals within the political arena—including the powerful interior minister, Bin 'Ali—felt this would make a martyr of Ghannushi and radicalize the movement in the same way that Sayyid Qutb's execution in Egypt had done two decades earlier. Within this environment, a breakaway faction that left the MTI in 1981 and called itself Islamic Jihad, having previously plotted attacks against the government and tourist industry, conducted a series of bomb attacks at four hotels in Monastir and Sousse in August 1987.[77] Only a few months later Bin 'Ali forced Bourguiba out of power through a constitutional decree about the incapacitation of the president on November 7, 1987. Bin 'Ali would later pardon Ghannushi to prevent what many perceived would have led to a civil war if he had been executed.

The next day, following Bin 'Ali's takeover, without the knowledge of Ghannushi, MTI's military wing was planning a coup led by three of its members, Sa'id Firjani, Munsif Bin Salim, and Biljaqim Firshishi.[78] Bin 'Ali, however learned about it three to four days ahead of time. One of the 219-member coup team, which called themselves al-Majmu'a al-Inqadh al-Watani (the National Salvation Front), wrote a will for his wife on November 5.[79] She then mentioned it to her father, who was a master sergeant, and he then relayed this information to his superiors after confronting his daughter's husband about the plan. This led Bin 'Ali to move up plans for his own takeover of the state, thereby thwarting the Islamist coup attempt. According to Wolf, "internal [MTI] estimates placed the expected casualty rate during the planned coup at a minimum of 600 people, including pro-regime security personnel and protesters. In addition, the Security Group managed to secure 5,000 tear-gas bombs, firearms, planes, tanks, and other military vehicles, as well as important communication devices, which were provided by its supporters in the security forces."[80] This illustrates the seriousness of the coup possibly occurring. Even after Bin 'Ali's takeover, Karkar believed that MTI should still follow through with its plans on November 8, but he was overruled by the majority of the organization.[81]

Post-Bourguiba Phase: 1987–2000

The first few years of Bin 'Ali's reign saw a rapprochement between the government and MTI, partially as a result of Bin 'Ali's opening of the political system to differentiate himself from Bourguiba and to signal a new era had begun. Bin 'Ali also took steps to reintroduce Islam into society from 1987 to 1990: the call to prayer was broadcast on radio and television; the moon was once again used to decide when the two main Muslim holidays, Eid al-Fitr and Eid al-Adha, begin; Zaytunah University was reopened; the Islamic High Council was reinstated; the Center for Islamic Studies was formed in al-Qayrawan; the new Ministry of Religious Affairs was established; and two yearly prizes for Qur'an memorization and Islamic sciences were created.[82] Additionally, two weeks following the ascension of Bin 'Ali, "the Interior Ministry announced a 'morality campaign' aimed at cleansing cafes, commercial centers, streets, and public transportation of individuals engaged in immoral acts."[83]

With planned new elections in 1989, MTI decided to change its name to Harakat al-Nahdah in order to de-emphasize its Islamic character. Similarly, its new manifesto, while more or less the same as in 1981, did not discuss Islam quite as much. Despite all of these steps, Bin 'Ali still would not officially recognize al-Nahdah, foreshadowing the showdown that would follow the results of the election—which al-Nahdah members decided to participate in as independent candidates. Officially, al-Nahdah's independent list garnered at least 15 percent of the vote and up to 40 percent in major city centers. Some have even argued that the true overall number was closer to 30 percent, but the regime covered it up.[84] Due to the results, al-Nahdah became the main opposition to the regime in terms of level of support, which made Bin 'Ali nervous, especially if they were allowed to openly recruit in a more liberalized system. Furthermore, as the Algerian Islamist party Front islamique du salut began to gain prominence—a factor that contributed to Algeria's civil war—Bin 'Ali decided to end the period of political opening. This led Ghannushi to exile himself to London in 1989 and not return to Tunisia until after the 2011 revolution. Furthermore, it is believed that eight thousand al-Nahdah members were then arrested between 1989 and 1992.[85]

All these events led al-Nahdah to reactivate its military wing. It was additionally emboldened by the successes of the Front islamique du salut. Ghannushi said that the "splendid Algerian *intifada* (uprising) of 1988" should be viewed as an example for Tunisians.[86] The large anti–Gulf War protests that permeated the broader Islamist movement in the Arab world in the early 1990s also pushed those in Tunisia for greater activism and engagement to alter the situation.[87] This led to al-Nahdah's new strategy of "the enforcement of the liberties," an innuendo for standing up to the regime, confronting it, and making necessary sacrifices for the "promised victory."[88] As a consequence, a series of violent actions culminated with al-Nahdah members burning down an office of Bin 'Ali's political party, the Constitutional Democratic Rally, and killing a guard in Bab Souika in downtown Tunis.[89] This and other plots led the regime to dismantle al-Nahdah's student wing, the Tunisian General Union of Students, which took away an important mobilizing mechanism for the organization. According to Muru, there were even plans at one point to use a stinger missile smuggled from Afghanistan through Algeria to Tunisia to take down Bin 'Ali's presidential plane.[90] There were also other questionable decisions made, such as Ghannushi's attendance at Hassan al-Turabi's "Popular Arab and Islamic Congress" in Khartoum, Sudan, which was attended by various nationalist and Islamist factions from the Palestinian Liberation Organization to Hizballah as well as by jihadis from al-Qaeda and Egyptian Islamic Jihad, including Usamah Bin Ladin and Ayman al-Zawahiri.[91]

Ghannushi became so paranoid during this period by what was happening, he claimed in a 1993 interview that a "new Bosnia [was] taking place in Tunisia without being noticed.... We are now proceeding to prepare an overall plan to liberate our people from dictatorship."[92] This was all talk though. By the mid-1990s, through arrests and al-Nahdah members fleeing to Europe, the movement was no longer able to operate inside Tunisia. Therefore, in 1996, when al-Nahdah had another conference in Belgium, it realized it was not going to be able to change the situation in the country through violence, and it reasserted nonviolence and gave up its confrontation with the regime.[93] For the next five years the movement scaled back its political activities as a result of the exile and imprisonment of its members.

Political Normalization Phase: 2001–2010

Following the end of al-Nahdah-led violence in Tunisia in the early to mid-1990s, the group attempted to repair its image with other opposition forces and rebuild its organizational infrastructure inside Tunisia. According to Esen Kirdiş, al-Nahdah was able undertake these reforms because the organization had "internal pluralism" compared with other MB-like Islamist movements in Egypt, Morocco, and Turkey: "given its emphasis on self-critique, al-Nahdah learned crucial lessons from its past failures."[94]

It is also possible that in the aftermath of 9/11, al-Nahdah (along with other MB-like Islamist movements in the region) wanted to distinguish itself as being different and unaffiliated with al-Qaeda and its excessive violence. Interestingly, these efforts by al-Nahdah began to bear fruit in 2001 when activists and members of Congrés pour la république (CPR) agreed to break the Ramadan fast with al-Nahdah in France a mere two-months after the 9/11 attacks.[95] This led to greater contact in the coming years, which blossomed into a series of agreements about how the broader opposition viewed the future of Tunisia. First, in June 2003, in Aix-en-Provence, France, the Call of Tunis Agreement was signed by al-Nahdah and CPR, among other exiled anti-Bin 'Ali activists, which "called for democracy, the liberation of all political prisoners, and a continuation of the fight against corruption."[96] Two years later, al-Nahdah, along with the Progressive Democratic Party and CPR, among other smaller elements, created the October 18 Collectif, which "attempted to go beyond the pragmatic need for unity against the common enemy and was designed as a vision of a future Tunisia, where shared democratic principles would regulate social and political relations."[97] Some have argued that the early part of Tunisia's transition to democracy succeeded because of this alliance, which began years prior to the outbreak of the revolution and also paved the way for the creation of the original troika government of al-Nahdah, CPR, and Ettakatol after the October 2011 election.

In addition to its political normalization with key opposition elements outside of Tunisia, there had also been other clandestine efforts within Tunisia to reconstitute the movement in general and specifically on university campuses going back to 2003. In Sfax, for example, this effort was led by Munsif Bin Salim (the same individual who helped plan the coup) and his son, Usamah, the latter of whom spearheaded the university initiative and called it the "Independent Students" in an attempt to gradually recreate the same type of dynamic as al-Nahdah's original student wing the Tunisian General Union of Students.[98]

More important, however, was when one of al-Nahdah's key leaders, Hamadi al-Jabali, along with 1,600 other members, were released from prison on February 25, 2006, in an amnesty by the Bin 'Ali regime marking Tunisia's fifty years of independence.[99] Jabali then helped reconstitute the organization inside Tunisia over the next few years.[100] These efforts were guarded and not as assertive as al-Nahdah was in the late 1970s through the early 1990s. This style made it harder to appeal to the younger generation that was coming of age in a more securitized environment for Muslims globally, a generation that was showing greater signs of overt religiosity in Tunisia as a protest against the Bin 'Ali regime as well as the greater involvement of the United States in the Middle East following 9/11.

New Forms of Islamist Contestation

While it is true that al-Nahdah maintained a near monopoly on Islamist activism in Tunisia since the 1970s, by the mid-1990s salafism began to provide alternative avenues after the crackdowns against al-Nahdah in the late 1980s and early 1990s. Although there is certainly a more scholarly and apolitical trend of salafism within Tunisia, most Tunisian salafis subscribe to the more radical jihadi variant. Nevertheless, the depoliticized salafi tendency was seen as nonthreatening to the regime since it focused on studying and proselytizing instead of politics. Therefore, Bin 'Ali looked the other way as it spread its ideas. This policy, however, helped fill an ideological vacuum that had been left by al-Nahdah when its members either went to prison or fled to Europe. Bin 'Ali thereby allowed the younger generation to be exposed to new ideas that, when mobilized, could lead to jihadism, either in the form of foreign fighting or terrorist plotting and attacks.

In line with al-Nahdah's normalization abroad, Wolf argues that "some young activists gradually came to view the ideology of al-Nahdah senior members as too 'weak,' since it had failed to challenge the regime's grip of power, and adapted more radical approaches."[101] Therefore, as Rory McCarthy explains, al-Nahdah "was no longer a defiant young generation newly empowered by their university experiences, but an older more cautious middle class."[102] As a result, the movement's perception among the youth was that it had softened its approach, "which left them out of tune with the satellite preacher-led religious revival of the 2000s."[103]

The mid-1990s also coincided with the return of one of Tunisia's most relevant jihadi-salafi clerics, Shaykh al-Khatib al-Idrisi. He was born in 1953 in Sidi Bouzid and is blind.[104] In 1985 al-Idrisi traveled to Saudi Arabia to learn Islamic scholarship under Wahhabi clerics. He studied with Shaykh Muhammad Sa'id al-Qahtani, Shaykh 'Abd al-'Aziz Bin Baz, Shaykh 'Abd al-Majid al-Zindani, Shaykh Salih al-Luhaydan, and Shaykh Sa'id Shafah, among others. He spent nine years studying and focusing on the sciences of sharia and ethics. According to al-Idrisi, when he returned to Tunisia in 1994, he had wanted to apply the strategy of the Saudi *sahwa* movement to Tunisia. Essentially, this meant calling for more religious action within the political sphere and creating a more conservative society as a defense against Western cultural influences. While al-Idrisi did not openly promote these ideas when he first returned, this more confrontational approach would develop over time and lead him to jihadism.

Al-Idrisi's return to Tunisia has been viewed as a turning point at which salafism began to gain a larger following within Tunisia, especially around universities. The salafi movement was still small though, and because it did not overtly advocate politics, its spread remained within the sphere of one's religiosity. Nevertheless, it provided a more permissive atmosphere for ideas that could turn political or even violent. This was especially pertinent with the rise of access to new information beyond state-controlled television through regional Arab satellite channels in general and salafi-funded ones in particular from the Gulf states and Egypt in the late 1990s and early 2000s. In particular, al-Jazeera in 1996, Iqraa TV in 1998, al-Resalah in 2006, and al-Hiwar in 2006. Alongside the start of the al-Aqsa Intifada in Israel in 2000 and the American invasion of Iraq in 2003, these processes and events played a role in heightening the politicization and mobilization that led some Tunisians to fight jihad in Iraq.[105]

Al-Nahdah's domestic cautiousness after members started leaving prison in 2006, based on its reforms and historical experience, led the movement to counsel young jihadi-salafis to "rein in their ambitions."[106] But this further contributed to a younger generation seeking something greater than moderation and seeking to take on a regime that was seen as unjust, arbitrary, and only enriching those within it. Therefore, as a young salafi from Tunis, Dhia, told Fabio Merone, "jihadi-salafi literature linked to jihadi web-forums (most famously [Shaykh Abu Muhammad al-Maqdisi's] Minbar al-Tawhid wa-l-Jihad) had circulated in Tunisia during the previous decade [before the revolution], and many had developed a sense of belonging, through their own individual paths, to a larger *umma*."[107]

Following the December 2006–January 2007 fight between Tunisian security and the Jund Asad Bin al-Furat jihadi network (popularly called the Sulayman Group by the Tunisian government), the Tunisian state arrested al-Idrisi for allegedly penning a fatwa that sanctioned jihadi activity in Tunisia specifically related to this incident. However, al-Idrisi claims he was only sanctioning jihad abroad in Iraq and Palestine.[108] As a result, al-Idrisi was sentenced to two years in prison and released in January 2009.[109]

Al-Nahdah also used the Jund Asad Bin al-Furat incident as an opportunity to buttress its reformist credentials. At its May 2007 congress in London, the movement advocated itself as a "constructive opposition."[110] Ghannushi went so far as to say that al-Nahdah was willing to dialogue with the regime and that they were "moderate" in comparison to the failed Jund Asad Bin al-Furat–led insurgency.[111] After the fall of the Bin 'Ali regime, al-Idrisi began to gain even more popularity within Tunisia and the broader jihadi-salafi world. Al-Idrisi's sanctioning of jihad abroad also helps explain why domestically a number of Tunisians became foreign fighters in Iraq or joined al-Qaeda in the Islamic Maghrib for training in the latter half of last decade.

* * *

Bourguiba's Islamic reforms in the late 1950s to late 1960s led to a backlash within the conservative Muslim segment of society. This helped spur the creation of Tunisia's indigenous Islamist movement. The Islamist movement's growth and success turned it into a threat not only to Bourguiba but also his successor, Bin 'Ali. This led to the arrest or exile of many members of the movement, which later created a space for salafism and clandestine jihadi activity to grow. As is explained in chapter 4, Ghannushi's and al-Nahdah's experience in the crackdown of the 1980s and 1990s would help inform its decision making regarding dealing with AST when it came into power after the Tunisian Revolution.

Before addressing the policies of al-Nahdah and the Tunisian government following the revolution, this book explores the historical growth of Tunisian jihadism, which provides one of the key explanatory factors for the growth of jihadism inside Tunisia after the 2011 uprising. It will look closely at Tunisians involvement in Afghanistan in the 1980s, Bosnia in the 1990s, and Iraq in the 2000s. In addition, it looks at the Tunisian jihadi networks inside Europe in the 1990s, which eventually also led to the creation of the Tunisian Combatant Group that had a home in both Europe and Taliban-controlled Afghanistan from the late 1990s to 9/11. This history is especially important because some of the key members and leaders within this group in the 1990s then became top leaders and organizers in AST after the Tunisian Revolution. Therefore, this book probes the key individuals and activities associated with Tunisian jihadis during this period and how their experiences influenced their actions after they left prison or returned to Tunisia in 2011.

CHAPTER 2

A SCATTERED GROUP WITH A LESS-THAN-PERFECT IMAGE

Many in Tunisia and the West perceived the rise and growth of Tunisian jihadism following the 2011 revolution as a surprise or new phenomenon. But Tunisians have been involved with the movement since the 1980s anti-Soviet jihad in Afghanistan. Many of the key leaders in Ansar al-Sharia in Tunisia (AST) and among Tunisia's foreign fighter cohort in Iraq, Libya, and Syria were previously involved in jihadi activity (Sayf Allah Bin Hasin, Sami Isid Bin Khamis, Mahdi Kamun, Muʿaz al-Fizani, Hasan Brik, Bubakr al-Hakim, Tariq al-Harzi, Sabri Issid, Muhammad Bakhti, and Wanas al-Faqih). That is why what happened following the revolution was not as new as it seemed. Part of the misperception is rooted in the fact that there was very little jihadi activism within Tunisia prior to the revolution. Tunisian involvement in jihadism occurred outside its borders and fractured across locations and over time. The period of openness that AST was able to exploit after the revolution is an anomaly in the history of Tunisian jihadism. What is discussed in this and the next chapter is more of the norm.

Chapter 2 and 3 seek to answer the question of how Tunisians gained experience in the jihadi movement. This question is crucial in understanding the development of AST postrevolution. Three main explanations are discussed in these two chapters: foreign fighting; running logistics, facilitation, and plot networks; and leading organizations. To tease this out, these two chapters are divided into two time periods that track with two different generations of jihadi activism. This chapter explores those who came of age during the anti-Soviet jihad and its aftermath, while the next chapter looks at those who came of age during the Iraq jihad and its aftermath. In particular, this chapter is divided into sections by time periods and location of activities, which include the anti-Soviet Afghan jihad; the Bosnian jihad; the Algerian jihad; Taliban-run Afghanistan; the Tunisian Combatant Group (TCG); and post-9/11 terrorist plots and attacks. Of course, these categories have some overlap and are not necessarily mutually exclusive. Instead, it is a way to classify content for smoother examination, explanation, and understanding.

While there is much detail in chapters 2 and 3, the purpose is to provide as full of a history of pre-2011 Tunisian involvement in jihadism as possible. Therefore, it relies upon process tracing as a method to paint a full picture of the context pertinent to understanding that Tunisian involvement in jihadism was much more widespread before the revolution than had been previously believed. According to David Collier, "careful description is a foundation of process tracing. Process tracing inherently analyzes trajectories of change and causation, but the analysis fails if the phenomena observed at each step in this trajectory are not adequately described. Hence, what in a sense is 'static' description is a crucial building block in analyzing the processes being studied."[1]

In other words, it is necessary to describe all aspects and angles of the history of the movement. Each section in chapters 2 and 3 lays a foundation that provides an even deeper understanding of the movement's evolution, changes, and consistencies over time. Each helps build the story and history. Without a foundation, it is difficult to paint a complete picture. As Collier continues, "As a tool of causal inference, process tracing focuses on the unfolding of events or situations over time. Yet grasping this unfolding is impossible if one cannot adequately describe an event or situation at one point in time. Hence, the descriptive component of process tracing begins not with observing change or sequence, but rather with taking good snapshots at a series of specific moments. To characterize a process, we must be able to characterize key steps in the process, which in turn permits good analysis of change and sequence."[2]

The account in chapters 2 and 3 provides the richest and most comprehensive history of the Tunisian jihadi movement, which helps fill a gaping lacuna in the academic literature and general knowledge base on this phenomenon.

The Early Adopters

Although there are accounts of Tunisian involvement in the Siege of Mecca in 1979, Tunisian jihadism did not begin in earnest until the infamous Afghan jihad.[3] Like other Arab nationals in the 1980s, Tunisians responded to the call for jihad and went to Afghanistan to fight the Soviets. In contrast to Saudis, Egyptians, and Yemenis, Tunisians joined in smaller numbers and gained a reputation for being unorganized in comparison with other national groups. It is believed that up to four hundred Tunisians went to Afghanistan in the 1980s and early 1990s, with about a quarter losing their lives.[4] The Tunisians were in such disarray that Abu Mus'ab al-Suri, one of the key theorists within the global jihadi movement, lamented the state of the Tunisian contingent in Afghanistan: "Unfortunately, and despite having many faithful and good members among them, the reputation of the Tunisian brothers, among the mujahidin groups in general, became that of a scattered group with a less-than-perfect image."[5] Similarly, Noman Benotman, a former *shura* council member of the Libyan Islamic Fighting Group, explained to Alison Pargeter that Tunisians were so extreme that they could not agree on strategy, ideology, and leadership and therefore never created their own training camp. There was even a joke among other foreign fighters that "if you put two Tunisians together they end up fighting jihad against each other!"[6]

Over time, Tunisians would improve their organizational skills through experience, first with the TCG, formed in 2000, and later, after the revolution, with AST. In the intervening years, however, Tunisians did indeed join a variety of jihads and networks in which individuals gained experience and knowledge that contributed to the creation of AST. Despite early levels of participation that were lower than those of other foreign nationals and groups, Tunisians have maintained intimate involvement in the jihadi movement over the years.

The Afghan Jihad

Five years after the outbreak of the Afghan-Soviet war, 'Abd Allah 'Azzam, viewed by many scholars of jihadism as the godfather of the global jihadi movement, established the Peshawar, Pakistan-based Maktab al-Khidamat al-Mujahidin (MAK; the Services Office of the Holy Strugglers) in 1984.[7] Peshawar would become the key logistics and facilitation hub for the so-called Afghan Arabs in the war. This effort signaled the first overt attempt to systematize and recruit individuals to join the Afghan jihad and assist the local insurgent factions. In addition to 'Azzam and Usamah Bin Ladin, some other individuals, including 'Abd al-Hadi al-Tunisi (the Tunisian), joined the conflict prior to 1984. According to Muhammad al-Qatari, 'Abd al-Hadi was among the first Arabs to come to Afghanistan, joining in 1982.[8] He was famous for never succumbing to torture by the Soviet Union at the Central Intelligence Prison in Kabul, having been tortured and imprisoned for five years. After a year of recovery in Europe, 'Abd al-Hadi returned to Afghanistan and died in a battle in Jalalabad in 1988 along with a Saudi fighter.[9] Another Tunisian—Sadiq al-Tunisi, a former fighter pilot in the Tunisian air force—was captured by Soviet forces and later traded in a prisoner exchange.[10] He went to Afghanistan sometime after the 1985 Israeli Operation Wooden Leg against the Palestinian Liberation Organization in Tunisia, which destroyed the PLO's headquarters in Hammam Chott, fifteen miles southeast of Tunis. The experience radicalized him because his superiors had allegedly told his fellow fighter pilots to disassemble the rockets from their planes and fly in southern Tunisia away from the raid on the day of the Israeli attack.[11] Sadiq would eventually train with AQ in Jaji, Afghanistan, but later found a Pakistani wife, which he claimed ended his jihad.[12] Another early entrant was Ahmad Buʿamra (Ahmad al-Pakistani) who was born on December 30, 1954, in Hadiaf, Tunisia, and went to Peshawar, Pakistan, in 1984. Little is known about his exploits except that he remained in the Afghan arena until 1989, when he returned to Algeria where he had previously been a medical student.[13] Not all Tunisians who joined the Afghan jihad fought with ʿAzzam or Bin Ladin. For instance, Ahmad Nabil al-Tunisi fought with the Afghan mujahidin leader Shaykh Jalal al-Din al-Haqqani.[14]

Other Tunisians assisted the Afghan cause in noncombat roles. For example, although al-Nahdah did not call for individuals to fight in Afghanistan, some of its members were regularly involved in the facilitation and logistics networks that brought Libyans to Afghanistan. In particular, they provided accommodations and facilitated travel arrangements.[15] In recent years, pictures have also surfaced of al-Nahdah leader Rashid Ghannushi with Afghan mujahid leader and warlord Gulbuddin Hekmatyar during the war in the 1980s, which leads to greater questions on whether there was greater al-Nahdah involvement in assisting the fight.[16]

This is important to remember since many al-Nahdah members were exiled to Europe after the crackdown on the organization in the late 1980s and early 1990s. Some left the organization after the crackdown and became more drawn to jihadi and foreign fighter networks. It also did not help that leading al-Nahdah figure Salah Karkar justified support for the Afghan and, later, the Algerian jihad as well as maintained contacts with militants from both countries after he fled to France, even though he claimed that "he would not use violence in Tunisia."[17] These experiences thus provided the backbone to what would become a proficient logistics and facilitation network for which Tunisians gained widespread renown within the jihadi milieu in Europe in the 1990s and 2000s. Another important development in noncombat roles was the Tunisian Abu Jaʿfar helping with the layout of *al-Mujahidun* magazine, funded through MAK, run by Jamiat-e-Islami, and led by Burhanuddin Rabbani, a professor of sharia in Afghanistan.[18] The magazine was first created in 1986, and Abu Jaʿfar joined the team starting with the ninth issue. A Tunisian named Mansur al-Binzurti also wrote a column for the jihadi magazine *al-Bunyan al-Marsus* (The Solid Edifice), starting with issue 18 in February 1988.[19] Other more well-known writers of the magazine included Wadih el-Hage, who is currently serving a life sentence in the United States for involvement in the 1998 embassy bombings in Africa, and Khalid Shaykh Muhammad (KSM), the architect of 9/11.

The first Tunisian martyr of the Afghan jihad died on June 21, 1986. His name was Muhammad Bin Ibrahim (Abu 'Uqbah al-Tunisi). Muhammad was only the sixteenth Arab martyr killed in the Afghan jihad, which happened in Shinari in Kandahar Province in an airstrike.[20] A twenty-five-year-old Tunis-born husband and factory worker living in Bizerte, Muhammad was recruited to fight at al-Madinah Mosque.[21] He arrived in Afghanistan via Turkey, Paris, and Pakistan in August 1985 and gained a reputation for his understanding of hadith transmission. During his time on the front lines, Muhammad served as lieutenant to Hamdi al-Banna and participated in the preparations and fighting around Jaji, prior to the famous battle in April–June 1987 that catapulted Bin Ladin into fame.[22] Prior to the battle, Bin Ladin set up *mu'askar masadat al-ansar* (the lion's den of the supporters military training camp; al-Masadah for short) in Jaji, which included seventy Arabs.[23] This episode illustrates how Tunisians were involved with Bin Ladin's milieu from the start.

Another individual involved with Bin Ladin at Jaji early on was Shafiq al-Tunisi, who had spent time at al-Masadah.[24] He was even involved with the building of that training camp when Bin Ladin first laid the groundwork for it in October 1986, suggesting that he was a trusted confidant.[25] Shafiq first arrived to MAK in Peshawar in late May 1985 and, after ten days, left for training at Jaji with Abu Muhammad al-Sudani and Abu Bara'.[26] Shafiq gained extensive experience in facilitation and training and traveled to Peshawar, Miran Shah, Warsak, Kunar, 'Arin, Nangarhar, and Jalalabad throughout the conflict. He met his demise in the Battle of Jalalabad on May 7, 1989.[27]

The Rise of the *Takfiri* Trend Within the Jihadi Movement

Shafiq's most relevant experience was his time spent training fighters with Usamah Azmara'i.[28] According to Mustafa Hamid, one of the top insiders in the history of Arab involvement in Afghanistan, Azmara'i was one of the early architects (prior to AQ) of the pursuit and execution of terrorist attacks against the West. He was involved (at the very least) with the 1995 Bojinka plot to take down Asian airliners along with Ramzi Yusuf, who helped bomb the New York City World Trade Center in 1993.[29] These ideas first originated from what Hamid describes as the Jalalabad school (also known as the Youth school), what might be described today as the ideology that undergirds the *takfiri* (announcing someone as an apostate and therefore legitimizing the killing of said individual or group) movement or, even more precisely, those who now follow the path of the Islamic State.

The so-called Jalalabad school stemmed from Bin Ladin's failed military campaign in Jalalabad in the summer of 1989—a reversal of the perceived triumphant victory he had at Jaji two years before. Many from North Africa, including Tunisians, did not arrive in Afghanistan until after Bin Ladin's great achievement and therefore were not necessarily loyal to him.[30] Following the defeat, many youths singled out Bin Ladin and 'Azzam.[31] As Hamid explains, one of the characteristics of the Jalalabad school is the youths' refusal to listen to authority; Bin Laden's defeat had a radicalizing and militarizing effect that led to a rise in the *takfiri* trend.[32] Other characteristics of the Jalalabad school are that "[it] operate[s] without leadership, political vision, or strategic planning, and do[es] not care about the consequences of [its] actions."[33] In particular, the *takfiri* trend was strong within the North African milieu—a reality that would further manifest itself in the 1990s with the Algerian al-Jama'ah al-Islamiyyah al-Musallahah (better known by its French acronym, GIA, for Groupe islamique armé). Likewise, as Benotman notes above, many Tunisians were also viewed as extreme.[34] An explanation of this *takfiri* trend is relevant because, as is seen later in this chapter, Tunisians became intimately involved with Algerian support networks in Europe in the 1990s and early 2000s. It is also relevant to the discussion on Tunisian foreign fighters in Iraq in the last decade, which is touched upon in the next chapter, and, more recently, with the Islamic State, which is explored in greater detail in chapters 8 and 9.

Not all Tunisians, however, were part of this *takfiri* trend. One of the individuals loyal to Bin Ladin and most worried about this trend was Abu Zayd al-Tunisi (Abu al-'Atta' al-Sharqi).[35] He was originally recruited in the 1980s to Afghanistan by 'Azzam during one of his tours in the United States, since Abu Zayd was studying at NASA then.[36] Over time, Abu Zayd would rise in the ranks of AQ and become a key reason behind Bin Ladin's ability to restart his jihad in Afghanistan in 1996 following his exile from Sudan. After the fall of the communist regime in Kabul in 1992, the United States and other Arab governments pressured the Pakistani government to expel any foreign fighters left in Peshawar. At the time, according to figures published by the Pakistani government, 2,800 Arabs, including 63 Tunisians, remained in the country.[37] Bin Laden was among those who left. As he prepared to relocate to Sudan, he called for the liquidation of all training camps including Jihadwal, AQ's "mother" camp in Khowst. Abu Zayd served as the *amir* of all AQ training camps in the Khowst region and specifically ran Jihadwal.[38] Sayf al-Adl, AQ's chief military commander, convinced Bin Ladin to maintain a small presence at Jihadwal. Abu Zayd would help train Tajiks and Uzbeks, among others, between 1992 and 1996.[39] He also set up another small camp called Salman al-Farsi, named after a Tunisian who would die with Katibat al-Mujahidin during Operation Miracle on July 21, 1995, in Bosnia.[40] During this time, Abu Zayd traveled to Sudan at least twice, once in 1993 and once in 1995.[41] Hamid recalls that when he returned to Afghanistan with Bin Ladin in 1996, Bin Ladin was pleased that Jihadwal had remained open because he would have otherwise had to restart from scratch.[42] This interaction illustrates the integrality that the Tunisian Abu Zayd played in the continuity of Bin Ladin's network in Afghanistan. Without

Abu Zayd, the history of AQ may have been different, especially considering the competition among the various Arab jihadi factions in Afghanistan in the late 1990s. He also helped provide translations for the journalists that came to AQ's camps in 1997.[43] Abu Zayd would eventually die on July 9, 1998, at the hands of Mullah Taj's men fifteen miles north of Kabul in Murad Beg.[44]

A Tunisian Jihadi Diaspora

Tariq Marufi and Sami Isid Bin Khamis (the latter would become a senior leader in AST) are veterans of the Afghan jihad, though little is known about their time in theater.[45] Both would go on to play a significant role in European jihadi networks in the 1990s following their time in Afghanistan. They would be part of a crop of Tunisian jihadis who would gain new organizational and networking skills relevant to the founding and activities of AST. Many Tunisian jihadis like Marufi and Bin Khamis did not have the option to return to Tunisia following the withdrawal of the Soviet Union and, later, the fall of the Communist regime in Afghanistan.[46] This jihadi activism coincided with the rise of new Tunisian president Bin 'Ali and his crackdown on Islamist and jihadi opposition inside Tunisia. As a consequence of Bin 'Ali's policy, a decentralized Tunisian jihadi diaspora community in Europe would crystallize in the mid-to-late 1990s.

Tunisian Islamic Front

With the internal crackdown against al-Nahdah, many members who were not arrested fled to Europe; in the process, some left al-Nahdah while also becoming radicalized. Those who had already broken with al-Nahdah in 1981 and formed Jabhat al-Islamiyyah al-Tunisiyyah or the Tunisian Islamic Front (better known by its French acronym FIT, for Front islamique tunisien) in 1987 would join up with this milieu, too. Among this group, some would go onto fight in Afghanistan and Bosnia as well as integrate into the maturing European jihadi facilitation and logistics networks.[47] Those who had fought in Afghanistan could not go home. It was not an option, as they would likely go straight to jail due to Bin 'Ali's hardline approach to al-Nahdah.[48] As a result, many sought asylum in Europe instead. Besides those that had prior affiliations, jihadi networks in Europe would recruit Tunisian migrant workers who were not previously connected to jihadi/Islamist networks going forward.

Contrary to many articles that state otherwise, FIT was not a radical wing of al-Nahdah. According to its founder, Muhammad 'Ali Harrath, FIT was established as a breakaway group from al-Nahdah out of displeasure with its way.[49] FIT was created in a similar vein as Algeria's al-Jabhah al-Islamiyah Li-l-Inqadh (better known by the French acronym FIS, for Front islamique du salut). FIT was viewed as a confrontational threat and as a result was quickly suppressed by the Tunisian government. Due to the clandestine and shadowy nature of FIT, there is little information about it, and much of that information subsequently has come from Harrath following the fall of Bin 'Ali. As a result, based on what he is doing now, a lot has changed, and it is possible he is attempting to spin what the true nature of the organization was in the late 1980s and early 1990s. Currently, Harrath is the CEO of Islam Channel, which is a satellite channel he created in 2004 in London that broadcasts shows related to Islam. He returned to Tunisia following the fall of the Bin 'Ali regime.

Looking back on FIT in October 2011, *Time* magazine spoke with Harrath: "We realized engaging with the regime [would be] a waste of time, so the only way forward [would be] to be rid of it. Fighting, coup d'état, whatever you can put your hands on."[50] He is adamant that FIT, unlike many insurrectionist groups, did not itself practice the violence it argued was necessary, at least in its early phase. During his activist years in Tunisia "there were never violent actions, we were clear about that. Action would be one day—if you have a coup d'état you have to do it in a sudden away. . . . We never had any action, not because we didn't believe in action but because action is a strategic move."[51]

This seems to contradict reporting in 1995, which stated FIT took responsibility for murdering four policemen.[52] Additionally, it is believed that Harrath and FIT, after fleeing Tunisia, went to Pakistan, Bosnia, and Algeria.[53] Further, according to the U.S. State Department, FIT was "working in conjunction with the GIA, the successor to the FIS, and . . . its members may be training in GIA camps. Several Tunisians were taken into custody in 1995 for alleged involvement with the GIA network in Europe. FIT claimed responsibility for an attack in February [1995] against a Tunisian border post on the Tunisia-Algeria border in which seven border guards were killed, but some officials blame the GIA possibly in conjunction with the FIT for the attack."[54]

There is further evidence to confirm these reports. In 1994 and 1995 France arrested FIT cells prior to them taking action.[55] There was also alleged collaboration between FIT and GIA cells in France.[56] While much reporting on FIT falls off after 1995, Armando Spataro identifies Bin Khamis, a Tunisian exiled in Italy and the head of the Tunisian Milan network, as being involved with FIT and collaborating with the GIA's successor group, the Groupe salafiste pour la prédication et le combat (GSPC). According to Anne Wolf, "Around seventy people linked to the FIT were imprisoned [by the Bin 'Ali regime] between 1995 and 2006, rendering its activities obsolete."[57]

Since the early 1990s Tunisians have been involved in jihadi networks in Austria, Belgium, Denmark, France, Germany, Ireland, Italy, Luxembourg, the Netherlands, Spain, Sweden, Switzerland, and the United Kingdom.[58] Milan, Italy, was the first important hub for Tunisian involvement in jihadi networks in Europe. It became a base for recruitment, logistics, and facilitation of foreign fighters deploying to Bosnia and assisting the GIA and, later, the GSPC in the Algerian jihad.

The Bosnian Jihad

The activities in Milan were headquartered at the Islamic Cultural Institute (ICI) and led by the Egyptian Shaykh Anwar Shaban, who was a member of the Egyptian jihadi group al-Gama'ah al-Islamiyyah. Norwegian academic Thomas Hegghammer has described Shaban as someone who aspired to play the role that 'Azzam did, but in the Bosnian war.[59] Shaban began to send individuals to Bosnia in the summer of 1992. Shaban's group, al-Gama'ah al-Islamiyyah, is most known for its involvement in the assassination of Egyptian president Anwar al-Sadat in 1981 and the Luxor massacre in 1997, among other insurgent activities in Egypt in the 1990s. Although the Milan-based network was originally an Egyptian network and formed in 1989 with links to Ramzi Yusuf and the 1993 World Trade Center attacks, the center also attracted militants from North Africa, including Tunisians.[60] Shaban's network facilitated Tunisian involvement in Bosnia and the jihadi milieu of Europe more broadly.

Inside Bosnia, Abu 'Abd al-'Aziz (better known as Barbaros), a Saudi veteran of the Afghan jihad, became the leader of Katibat al-Mujahidin, whose members were primarily North African.[61] Because of the extensive involvement of Tunisians and Algerians in Milan and Bosnia, many veterans of the Bosnian conflict participated in the Algerian jihad a few years later. 'Abd al-'Aziz's first headquarters were at the Mehurici training camp, near the central Bosnian town of Travnik.[62] Shaban served as 'Abd al-'Aziz's key recruiter and facilitator in both Europe and the Arab world, shepherding many foreign fighters through Milan to Bosnia. As a result, Milan became the key place for document forgery and other criminal activities with which Tunisians became intimately involved over the next decade or so.[63] In addition, Shaban would travel between Milan and the Bosnian frontlines to gather news and VHS-taped propaganda to support recruitment efforts back in Italy. While in Bosnia, Shaban was seen as the political leader and spokesperson for the foreign fighters.[64]

According to Bosnian government intelligence records on the conflict, Tunisians accounted for 11 percent of known foreign fighters in Bosnia.[65] The French government claimed that more than 1,000 foreign fighters participated in the entire conflict, while Hegghammer put the figure at 1,000–2,000.[66] It is therefore plausible that 110–220 Tunisians fought in the Bosnian conflict. One of the first Tunisians to enter the conflict was Abu Shahid al-Tunisi, who was in his late twenties. He emigrated from Tunisia to Italy for work and settled in Milan, where Shaban encouraged him to travel to Bosnia. He arrived in

Bosnia in late 1992 and joined Katibat al-Mujahidin. He would serve as a trainer in the village of Mahraj and later Auraashist. Like many other foreign fighters in Bosnia, he married a Bosnian woman and received citizenship from the government for his services. While he remained quiet after the war, many other foreigners who received citizenship were later implicated in criminal activities and terrorist attacks. According to documents reviewed by the Bosnian daily, *Glas Srpske*, 741 foreign fighters would receive citizenship, including 49 Tunisians.[67] Although Abu Shahid survived the war, he would later drown in a river.[68]

One such individual who violated Bosnian law was Karray Kamal Bin ʿAli (Abu Hamzah and ʿUmar al-Tunisi). He quit his job at a Fiat car factory in Turin, Italy, and moved to Bosnia in 1992 three days after Shaban gave a guest speech and showed a VHS tape of conditions in Bosnia at Karray's mosque.[69] Like Abu Shahid, Karray survived the war and married a Bosnian woman. Karray murdered a Shiʾa activist in front of the Balkan Islamic Center in Zenica in 1997 at the behest of the Algerian ʿAbd al-Qadir al-Mukhtari (better known as Abu al-Maʿali) at the Zenica mujahidin command center.[70] Al-Mukhtari is believed to have been second in command to Shaban when he went to fight in Bosnia, while the Algerian Fatah Kamal was third in command.[71] Karray would later flee to Germany. In June of 1999 he was involved in a shootout with German police in Frankfurt and arrested on August 11, 1999, in Cologne. He was rendered back to Bosnia to serve time in jail.[72] Like many other Tunisians arrested in Europe from the late 1990s to 2010, Karray would be deported to Tunisia following the uprising in 2011.[73] His current status is unknown.

The Tunisian with the longest staying power within the broader global jihadi movement among those that went to Bosnia is Muʿaz al-Fizani (Abu Nasim al-Tunisi), who, before joining the Bosnian jihad via Shaban's lectures, was selling drugs on the streets of Milan.[74] Following his stint in Bosnia, he would later go onto to fight in Afghanistan and take part in AQ's chemical weapons program at the time. According to Aimen Dean, a former jihadi who defected and became an MI6 operative and who was a part of AQ's chemical weapons unit, describes al-Fizani as a "sociopath" and one who "took great pleasure in torturing the animals on which we experimented and [who] held extreme takfiri views"—that is, a member of the so-called Jalalabad school.[75] It is no surprise, then, that al-Fizani, following the Tunisian Revolution, would eventually become a senior leader within the Islamic State in Libya and would help plan the March 2015 and June 2015 Bardo and Sousse attacks in Tunisia.

In addition to these fighters, a number of lesser-known Tunisian individuals would die fighting in many of the battles between 1992 and 1995, such as Abu Khalid al-Tunisi and those who died in Travnik early in the war.[76] Many also died between May and September 1995 in two of the three key battles (Operation Miracle and Operation Badr) known for foreign fighter involvement.[77]

In addition to those Tunisians who arrived in Bosnia via the Shaban network, there were some with loose ties to AQ. The case of Muhammad Bin Brahim Saydani serves as an example. When Bin Ladin dispatched his envoy from Sudan, Jamal al-Fadl, to Zagreb to glean information about the situation in Bosnia in the fall of 1992, al-Fadl met a number of key figures, including 'Abd al-'Aziz and Saydani.[78] This contact could suggest that Saydani acted as Bin Ladin's associate, albeit on a small scale. After meeting al-Fadl, Saydani went to Abu Zayd al-Tunisi's training camp in Afghanistan in 1993. Upon returning to Italy, Saydani became the cleric of the Massarenti Street mosque in Bologna, where he would then connect with Shaban's network.[79] It is believed that he then recruited thirty young men to Katibat al-Mujahidin in Bosnia. To make it easier for recruits to travel, Saydani created a front business.

Another figure connected to AQ who also spent time in Bologna was Mahriz Bin Sassi al-Amduni (also known as Abu Talhah, Fabio Fusco, and Muhammad Hasan). The case of al-Amduni illustrates the seamlessness between the networks created for the Bosnian jihad and those used during the Algerian jihad in support of the GIA. Like many other figures, al-Amduni fought as a member of Katibat al-Mujahidin in Bosnia (arriving in 1993) and eventually received Bosnian citizenship.[80] Following the war, al-Amduni began gun running weapons to the GIA—a task for which he would be arrested in Spain in 1997. After his release, he returned to Zenica, Bosnia, and attempted to lay low. However, an Italian warrant related to al-Amduni's connections to an alleged plot to kill Western government officials, including Italian foreign minister Lamberto Dini and U.S. assistant secretary of state Marc Grossman, would lead to a second arrest when he was traversing Turkey. Al-Amduni was caught with fake passports and stolen goods. He was allegedly on his way from Bosnia to Chechnya.[81] Unlike in Bosnia, however, there are few known cases of Tunisians fighting in Chechnya.[82] The most significant Tunisian fighter was Mahdi Kamun, a member of the Milan network and later a key associate of Bin Khamis.[83] Moreover, this connection to Bin Khamis would help Kamun rise to become a senior leader in AST. There is also the case of the Tunisian Fathi, who assisted with supply convoys that went through Dagestan to Chechnya to assist the senior foreign fighter leader in the field, Ibn al-Khatab (who is described in greater detail shortly).[84]

The Algerian Jihad

Besides al-Amduni, many Tunisian veterans of the Bosnian war would later join networks supporting the GIA's activities in Algeria. They would also participate in terrorist plots hatched by the GIA and its successor group, the GSPC—founded in 1998. Beyond the Milan network, other Tunisian jihadi hubs in Brussels, London, and Paris that played only small roles in the Bosnian foreign fighter networks became more active during the Algerian jihad.

The Algerian civil war, following the January 1992 coup d'état, at first pitted the mainstream Islamists of FIS against the military; this conflict stemmed from the military's concerns that FIS would win the second round of the Algerian elections after its success in the first round. It was only later that the conflict transformed into a war between the GIA and the military.[85] The GIA was also the first test case of the *takfiri* trend within the global jihadi movement, as many of the combatants were Afghan returnees from the so-called Jalalabad school.[86]

While some Tunisians certainly fought in Algeria alongside the GIA, Tunisians in Europe primarily supported the recruitment, facilitation, and logistics networks as well as attack plots.[87] As noted earlier, many of the Jalalabad school adherents in Afghanistan were the first fighters to be interested in terrorist operations abroad. The GIA was the first organization to have a campaign of attacks and plots abroad.[88] Just as Bin Ladin later criticized the U.S. commitment to propping up "apostate" Arab regimes, the GIA pushed a similar narrative about the French government and Algeria. The GIA thus aimed to exact a price on France for its support of the Algerian military in the war against the GIA. The GIA's first attempted (though unsuccessful) attack was a plot to hijack Air France Flight 8969, flying from Algiers to Paris in December 1994, and crash it into the Eiffel Tower.

One of the key Tunisian cogs in these GIA operations in France from 1994 to 1998 was an Afghan jihad veteran named Tariq Marufi (Abu Isma'il), who was based in Brussels, Belgium.[89] Marufi's connections to the Algerian jihadi scene began in 1991 when he first made contact with an Algerian based in London, Rashid Ramda.[90] Ramda is currently serving a life sentence in France for being the mastermind and financier of the successful 1995 Paris Metro bombings and heading the European GIA cells. While in Brussels, Marufi was the leader of the GIA's Brussels cell. Because of his connections to Ramda, Marufi was arrested with eleven others in 1995 and sentenced to three years in prison for planning a terror attack in Europe. He was released a year later and put on three years' probation.[91] The arrest and probation, though, did not deter his further involvement with the GIA and other jihadi fronts, such as Chechnya.

Around this time another important figure in the history of Tunisian jihadism would become involved in these networks in London. Sayf Allah Bin Hasin (better known now as Abu 'Iyadh al-Tunisi, although he went by Abu Sufyan in London and Abu Muhammad in Afghanistan), would go on to cofound the TCG in 2000 with Marufi and later establish and lead AST after the Tunisian uprising. Abu 'Iyadh has been linked to the European jihadi movement since at least 1994, when he moved to London. According to his Moroccan wife, following a two-year prison sentence for involvement with a student movement in Tunisia in 1987 (most likely the student wing of al-Nahdah), he moved to Morocco to study law.[92] When Abu 'Iyadh moved to the United

Kingdom, he became enmeshed in the so-called Londonistan jihadi counterculture.[93] He quickly became an understudy of the Jordanian-Palestinian 'Umar bin Mahmud 'Uthman (better known as Abu Qatadah al-Filistini), who arrived in London only a few months before Abu 'Iyadh, in September 1993.[94] During this time, one of Abu Qatadah's main projects was supporting the GIA and the Algerian jihad. In particular, he provided religious justifications for the GIA's violence in its official magazine, *al-Ansar*.[95] He also raised money for this cause following his sermons in London.[96]

Unlike other infamous clerics in London at the time, such as Abu Hamzah al-Masri, whose followers were less educated, Abu Qatadah "concentrated his efforts on a handpicked few. His associates were an elite hardcore of activists."[97] This suggests that he viewed Abu 'Iyadh as a good investment that could rise in the ranks of the movement. More recently, on January 20, 2014, Abu Qatadah noted that Abu Iyadh "is among the best of those I have known in intellect and estimation of matters ... [and] is the most knowledgeable of people of my intentions ... for he was the closest of people to me."[98] This is important because, as mentioned earlier, there were already connections between Marufi and Algerians in London, and Abu Qatadah was the most important religious scholar for the GIA. Therefore, because of his respect for Abu 'Iyadh, it is most likely through him that Abu 'Iyadh was exposed to other key Algerian jihadis in London. As a result, Abu 'Iyadh became an important player in the European networks, especially with Marufi and the Algerians in London around 1998. Abu 'Iyadh's relationship with Abu Qatadah also likely connected him to jihadis in Afghanistan when he moved there in 2000.

By 1998, however, a lot had changed for the GIA. At its peak in 1994, the GIA controlled territory and maintained a reputation as the strongest nonstate actor, even more so than the FIS's armed wing, al-Jaysh al-Islami Li-l-Inqadh (better known by its French acronym AIS, for Armée islamique du salut). The GIA's excessive violence and *takfiri* ideology turned the Algerian population—and, later, jihadis inside and outside the country—against it. The event that truly damaged the GIA's reputation was its killing of a number of Libyans from the Libyan Islamic Fighting Group who had assisted in the fighting as well as those who later inquired about their Libyan Islamic Fighting Group brothers who had gone missing. This episode led many—including Abu Qatadah—to rescind their support for the GIA in 1996.[99] As a consequence of both internal and external issues, the GIA began to slowly break up.

In September 1998 the GIAs former commander for Algeria's "second zone," Hasan Hatab, formed the GSPC with other defectors in an attempt to reclaim the banner.[100] In the GSPC's first statement, it noted that it was "a continuation of the [GIA], following its ideology, before it deviated and went astray. Thus, [the GSPC] represents the genuine path that jihad has followed since its inception in Algeria."[101] Similarly, many of the GIA networks inside Europe that grew disgusted with the GIA—including those composed of many Tunisians—simply joined the rebranded GSPC, which began to strengthen even more in 1998. This is likely why the French—along with other European partners (Germany, Italy, Belgium, and Switzerland)—launched a large-scale preventive operation against GIA/GSPC plots and support networks in the run-up to the 1998 World Cup.[102]

The first plot broken up, called "Stade de France," had cells in France and Italy and included six Tunisians. One of those arrested had previously fought in Chechnya and been involved with hostage-taking there.[103] The Italian cell had provided fundraising and falsified documents to the cell in France, which had planned a car bomb attack at France's national stadium, north of Paris, in Saint-Denis.[104] In March, June, and September 1998, European security services broke up fundraising and recruitment cells in Belgium, France (two Tunisians), and Italy (sixteen Tunisians).[105] The French also arrested a Tunisian in the Coupe de Monde plot, which involved guns and grenades.[106]

These raids likely facilitated Abu 'Iyadh and the London-based Algerians' increased coordination with the Brussels cell run by Marufi (who became the head of the GSPC's Belgium network[107]) and the Milan cell run by Sami Isid Bin Khamis (also known as Abu Muhajir). Khamis had been involved at the ICI with Anwar Shaban and the Bosnian support networks in the 1990s. He rose in the ranks and eventually became the head of AST's charity convoys after the 2011 Tunisian Revolution. For the first time, Tunisian jihadis were finally coming together as a more unified network. The coordination served as a precursor to the formation of the TCG two years later and, more importantly, fostered relationships between individuals who would play important roles in the formation of AST.

In London, Abu 'Iyadh became a close confidant of Rashid Bukhalfa (better known as Abu Doha), an Algerian who represented the GSPC in London in 1998.[108] They met one another through Abu Qatadah.[109] Over the next few years, they shared their recruiting and fundraising activities. Moreover, due to Marufi's historical links to the Algerian network in London, Abu 'Iyadh's involvement further solidified arrangements with the Belgian network, which provided recruits with money, accommodation, and forged documents.[110] The third cog in this operation was the Milan network, which also had historical ties to GIA/GSPC networks.[111] It was led at that time by the Tunisian Bin Khamis and best known for its "flawless" fake documents.[112] As a result, both Abu 'Iyadh and Bin Khamis sent Tunisian recruits to Algeria to fight with the GSPC.[113]

As the star of the GIA faded, so too did other jihads in the Arab world. Bin Ladin's interlude in Sudan ended in 1996 as Saudi Arabia and the United States pressured the Sudanese president, 'Umar Bashir, to kick him out of the country. Moreover, both of the insurgencies in Libya and Egypt failed by 1997. Even though there were these setbacks, they happened with auspicious timing for the jihadi movement. This is because the Islamic Emirate of Afghanistan (better known as the Taliban) began to take control of territory in Afghanistan. As a result, Bin Ladin along with competing jihadi organizations and networks (in particular, Abu Zubaydah's Khalden training camp network and Abu Mus'ab al-Suri's network[114]) began to make their way back to Afghanistan. It was where AQ would plan its largest terrorist attacks: the 1998 U.S. Embassy bombings in Dar es Salaam, Tanzania (which a Tunisian named Ahmad 'Abd Allah helped case[115]) and Nairobi, Kenya; the 2000 USS *Cole* bombings; and the 9/11 attacks. It should be noted that while Bin Ladin's, Abu Zubaydah's and Abu Mus'ab al-Suri's networks were in competition, at times they would work together. Algerians and Tunisians connected with the GSPC networks started returning or went for the first time to Afghanistan. Other Tunisians also continued helping rebuild GSPC either from Europe or as fighters inside of Algeria.

Although the focus of the GSPC network was to rebuild itself after the GIA debacle, the group still had ties to networks in Afghanistan, including the ones involved in external operations. In particular, the GSPC maintained links with the Khalden training camp, which was originally established by MAK but after its dissolution became a progenitor of the Jalalabad school in the late 1980s.

The Khalden Network

According to Mustafa Hamid, the two key players at Khalden were Ibn Shaykh al-Libi and Abu Zubaydah. This was a different network from that of Bin Ladin's AQ, which trained more at al-Faruq based in Khowst and, later, Kandahar. Furthermore, when Khalden first formed in the late 1980s, many of those trained were Algerians who helped seed the GIA in the early to mid-1990s.[116] Khalden was also connected to Usamah Azmara'i, Thamir Salih 'Abd Allah (better known as Ibn al-Khatab), Ramzi Yusuf, and KSM, all early adopters of external operations.[117] Omar Nasiri, a pseudonym for a Belgian-Moroccan spy who infiltrated jihadi networks in Europe and Afghanistan in the 1990s and early 2000s, became a key contact point in London between Abu Zubaydah, who provided access to the Khalden training camp when recruits arrived in Pakistan, and Abu Qatadah.[118] It was likely through this connection that Abu 'Iyadh and Abu Doha via Abu Qatadah established contacts and network infrastructure with the scene in Afghanistan. Similarly, the ties built within the Khalden network in the late 1990s and early 2000s are relevant to not only the Iraq jihad network after 2003 but also its recruitment and support networks in Europe that Tunisians would play a significant role in as well.

The 2000 millennium plot by the Khalden network's Abu Zubaydah that sought to bomb Los Angeles International Airport, the USS *The Sullivans*, and four sites in Jordan was one of the earliest and largest plots broken up by the United States, Canada, and Jordan.[119] Tunisians were tied to the plot as well, particularly the Los Angeles airport component of it. The Algerian Ahmad Rissam, who was supposed to bomb the airport, had illegally immigrated to Montreal, Canada, in 1994 and primarily supported himself through crime and welfare benefits. A few years later he was introduced to Ra'uf Hanashi, a Tunisian who acquired Canadian citizenship in 1986. After Hanashi returned from training at Khalden in the summer of 1997, he became the *mu'azin* (the one who performs the call to prayer) at al-Sunnah al-Nabawiyyah Mosque in Montreal.[120] It is believed that through Hanashi's stories of jihad, Rissam decided to go to Afghanistan to train. Hanashi facilitated Rissam's contact with Abu Zubaydah and the Khalden camp, where he allegedly joined a sixty-man group composed mostly of Tunisian veterans of the Bosnian jihad.[121] The latter fact about the veterans would be corroborated by Abu Mus'ab al-Suri.[122] Rissam was in Afghanistan from March 1998 to February 1999 and was eventually arrested on December 14, 1999, as he attempted to cross the Canadian-American border in Vancouver.

Just after Rissam's arrest, the Khalden training camp would close on the Taliban's instruction to Ibn Shaykh al-Libi and Abu Zubaydah. According to Hamid, in the past, Ibn Shaykh had been able to negotiate its continued operations, but when the Taliban called for its closure in 2000, Ibn Shaykh was in Syria looking for a bride, and Abu Zubaydah was unsuccessful in convincing Bin Ladin to vouch to keep it open. This is in part because the Khalden network and AQ were in competition, but also because the Taliban was not fond of the Jalalabad school, due to the school's extreme ideas and Arab members who occasionally used takfir and fought against the Taliban.[123] In turn, when Khalden closed, many went to AQ's al-Faruq training camp.

The Return to Afghanistan

Changing circumstances forced Tunisians previously connected to the Khalden network to start working more closely with Bin Ladin's network (although they would maintain their own guest house in Jalalabad). The leader of the Jalalabad house was Abu 'Iyadh, who arrived in Afghanistan in early 2000 alongside his Londonistan partner, Abu Doha, who would be in control of the Algerian guesthouse in Jalalabad.[124] Once in Afghanistan, Abu 'Iyadh established contact with Abu Qatadah to keep him informed of AQ activities in a correspondence similar to that between Abu Zubaydah and Abu Qatadah, mentioned above.[125] In one message, Abu 'Iyadh discusses Ahmad Fadhil al-Nazal al-Khalaylih (better known as Abu Mus'ab al-Zarqawi). Abu Iyadh calls al-Zarqawi "an honest, generous person who would be happy to sacrifice his soul and property for you."[126] This likely signified that relationships developed between the networks of Abu 'Iyadh and al-Zarqawi. These contacts would become more important after the fall of Tora Bora in 2001. Thus, despite internetwork rivalry, overt hostility like that between AQ and IS currently was less common. A comparison to the current split between AQ and IS thus provides an incomplete understanding of the nuanced relationships in the 1990s and early 2000s.

The Tunisian Combatant Group and Tunisians in AQ

According to the *New York Times*, by 2001 Abu 'Iyadh had become one of Bin Ladin's top ten lieutenants, although there has yet to be any public confirmation.[127] It is certainly possible, given Bin Ladin's instruction to Abu 'Iyadh's TCG (cofounded in June 2000 with Marufi, who remained in Brussels) to assassinate Ahmad Shah Mas'ud, leader of the Northern Alliance and a Western ally in Afghanistan, two days before the September 11, 2001, attacks. This was significant since AQ knew that if the United States invaded Afghanistan following the 9/11 attacks, the United States would have heavily relied upon Mas'ud due to his fighting prowess and command against the Taliban in the previous few years. According to Marufi, he himself met Bin Ladin and al-Zawahiri in Afghanistan 2000 and saw "it [as] the perfect opportunity to gain a foothold in the organization."[128] The fact that Bin Ladin gave this assignment to Abu 'Iyadh and the TCG likely reflects on Abu 'Iyadh's importance.

The Tunisian Ministry of Interior claims that Abu 'Iyadh abdicated his leadership to the Tunisian Muhammad Bin Riyadh Nasri (Abu Dujanah al-Tunisi and Abu Khalid al-Tunisi) in January 2001 after disagreements between the two.[129] Abu 'Iyadh told the Tunisian daily *al-Sabah* that he left Afghanistan in February 2001, suggesting this could have indeed occurred.[130] Although it is possible this trip was more innocuous since French-Algerian jihadi Jamal Beghal, who shared a home with Abu 'Iyadh in Jalalabad and who would later mentor the perpetrators of the January 2015 Charlie Hebdo and kosher supermarket attacks in a French prison, "left Afghanistan with the wife and children of Abu Iyadh, whose youngest son was said to be too sick to go on living in the difficult conditions in Afghanistan" in July 2001.[131] So it is possible Abu 'Iyadh may have left to help his son in some manner. Either way, Abu 'Iyadh fought against the Northern Alliance in November 2001 before escaping to Pakistan and arriving in Turkey.[132] This could explain Abu 'Iyadh's growing importance within AQ and AST's alignment with AQ's post-2011 strategic plans over those of the Jalalabad school, to which Tunisians had historically been closest. (Nevertheless, many Tunisians would return to the so-called Jalalabad school through al-Zarqawi's network and its successor IS networks).

According to Hamid, the TCG had been planning the assassination with AQ for more than a year.[133] Dressed up and pretending to be journalists interested in interviewing Mas'ud, the Tunisians 'Abd al-Satar Dahmani and Burawi al-Awa'ir conducted the operation by planting a bomb in the camera, which they stole from a France 3 network and exploded it while they asked: "Commander, what are you going to do with Usamah Bin Ladin when you have conquered Afghanistan?"[134]

Dahmani's second wife, Malikah al-Arud (Umm 'Ubaydah)—infamous in her own right—encapsulated the nexus between components of the TCG network in Afghanistan, Milan, Brussels, and London in her memoir *Les soldats de lumière*. She explained that prior to Dahmani's travels from Brussels to Afghanistan, he studied *manhaj* (Islamic methodology) with Abu Qatadah in London between May 18, 2000 and August 20, 2000.[135] During this trip Dahmani also got a letter of introduction to interview Mas'ud via al-Gama'ah al-Islamiyyah member Yasir al-Siri.[136] Furthermore, when applying for journalist visas in Pakistan, Dahmani and al-Awa'ir received stolen passports from Marufi, who had procured them from the Milan-based Tunisian Fadhl Sa'adi, who was part of Bin Khamis's network.[137]

The WikiLeaks Guantánamo files database on Tunisians also provides a rich picture on how these networks in Europe facilitated recruitment and travel to Taliban-controlled Afghanistan. Similar to the Bosnian jihad, most of the Tunisian detainees were recruited through the network in Italy. Of the 771 Guantánamo detainees, 12 were Tunisian citizens, and 1 was a French citizen of Tunisian background.[138] Nine of the 13 individuals had connections to or were facilitated through either the network in Milan with Bin Khamis or that in Bologna with Saydani. Six had known connections to the ICI in Milan and 4 had previously fought in Bosnia. Seven of the 13 individuals also had direct ties to the TCG, according to the files from the database.

Little is known about the inner workings of the TCG since it had a small presence compared to other jihadi groups at the time. Between the Guantánamo files and other primary and secondary sources, I have been able to piece together some details on the organization. Since it was a clandestine group, it is likely that there is still missing data. That said, there were at least ten individuals present at the founding of the TCG in June 2000, and at least twenty members total. In addition to the two founders—Abu 'Iyadh, who was in charge of the Tunisian guest house in Jalalabad, and Marufi, who was mainly involved with terrorism plots and the facilitation and logistics network abroad—three other known individuals served on the advisory council of the organization: Lufti Bin 'Ali (Julaybib), 'Adl Bin Ahmad Bin Ibrahim Hakimi (Abu Bilal), and Nasri.[139] The latter two had known leadership positions within the organization. Hakimi served as the deputy to Abu 'Iyadh in Afghanistan and led communications and recruitment efforts. He was also the commander of the "Tunisia Cave" during the battle of Tora Bora in December 2001, while Nasri was the TCG's top military commander for their operations inside

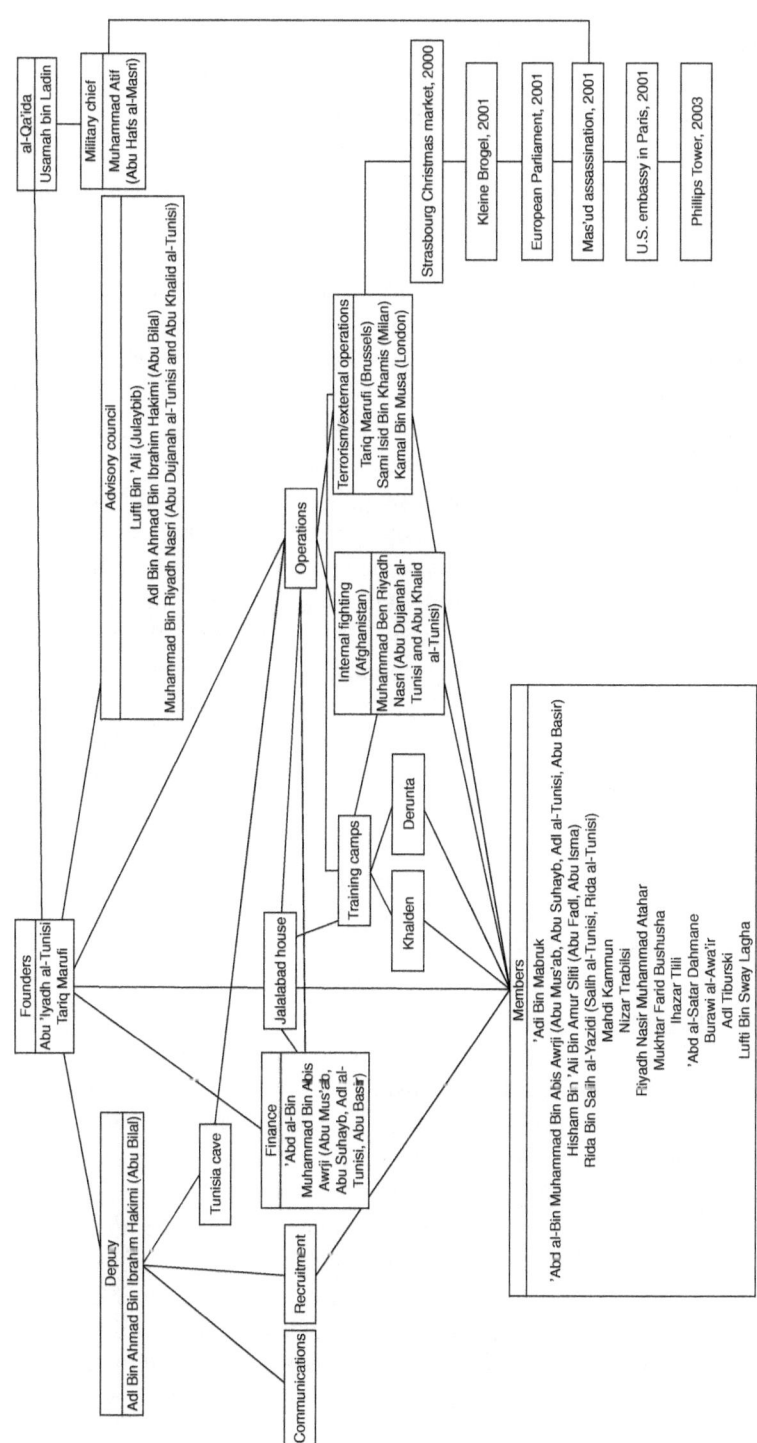

2.1 Tunisian Combatant Group Organizational Chart

Afghanistan.[140] In addition to them, 'Abd al-Bin Muhammad Bin Abis Awrji (also known as Abu Mus'ab, Abu Suhayb, 'Adl al-Tunisi, and Abu Basir) served as head of finance for the group, and Bin Khamis in Milan and Kamal Bin Musa in London acted as members of Marufi's TCG network abroad.[141] This network was involved in several failed terrorist plots in Europe: Strasbourg Christmas Market in December 2000, European Parliament in February 2001, U.S. Embassy in Paris in July 2001, Kleine Brogel in September 2001, and Philipps Tower in February 2003.[142]

Beyond the TCG's successful Mas'ud assassination, which was executed jointly with AQ's military chief, Muhammad Atif (Abu Hafs al-Masri), Tunisians played a role in AQ that was independent of the TCG. Three of the thirteen Tunisian Guantánamo detainees, including Rida Bin Salih al-Yazidi (also known as Salih al-Tunisi and Rida al-Tunisi) were affiliated with AQ. Rida had been arrested in Karachi, Pakistan, in 2002 but had an illustrious career within the jihadi milieu prior to that.[143] According to Fadhl 'Abd Allah Muhammad (better known as Fadhl Harun)—AQ's top operative in East Africa who trained in Afghanistan—Rida was one of Bin Ladin's bodyguards and a founding member of Bin Ladin's al-Masadah training camp in Jaji.[144] After the Afghan jihad, Rida would join the Milan network at the ICI in 1993, fight in Bosnia, become Abu Hafs al-Masri's bodyguard in Khartoum, go to prison for involvement with the GIA cells in 1998, and return to Afghanistan in May 1999.[145] Another relevant Tunisian in AQ and who was not in Guantánamo was a military trainer named Musa, who helped the American AQ senior media operative, Adam Gadahn, when he first joined AQ: "[he] would take us out for morning runs and was very patient with those of us less physically fit."[146]

Furthermore, Tunisians were involved in or had knowledge of the 9/11 attacks, even though none of the hijackers were Tunisian. For one, according to Nasri and Ibn Shaykh al-Libi, the Mas'ud assassination was a signal to the 9/11 hijackers to begin the attack.[147] Days before the assassination and 9/11, on September 6, 2001, 'Adl Bin Sultan, a Tunisian arrested earlier in the year as part of the Bin Khamis Milan network, received an empty wrapper from the popular Italian chewing gum company, Brooklyn, from another jihadi that showed a picture of the Brooklyn Bridge.[148] Investigators believe its purpose was to give Bin Sultan notice of the coming attack on the United States. Furthermore, Spanish courts claim that the Tunisian Hidi Bin Yusuf Budhiba provided logistical, financial, and counterfeit documentation to the 9/11 hijackers in Spain and Hamburg, Germany.[149] Budhiba left Hamburg for Istanbul on September 3, 2001, ahead of the attacks, likely linking up with the AQ network in Turkey, which became an important point of logistics and facilitation for Tunisian jihadis in the following years. Lastly, there is the case of the Tunisian-Canadian 'Abd al-Ra'uf Jiday (Faruq al-Tunisi), who was among twenty-nine candidates for the 9/11 attacks and was later assigned to what KSM dubbed the "second wave" of 9/11-style attacks. He even prepared a martyrdom video tape for the operation.[150] Nasir al-Bahri, Bin Ladin's bodyguard at the time, recalls his stay at the house of KSM, Muhammad Atta, Ramzi bin al-Shibah, and Jiday in Karachi in the summer of 2001. During that time his hosts played a flight simulator game on PlayStation in preparation for the attack.[151] Sometime between the summer and the 9/11 attack, it is believed that Jiday dropped out when he went back to Canada.[152] As of today, Jiday remains on the FBI's Most Wanted List for further questioning, though little is known publicly about what happened to him after he left Afghanistan.[153]

9/11 Aftermath

Following the 9/11 attacks, a number of Tunisians died in the subsequent U.S. invasion. Unlike the many Tunisian jihadis who fled or were captured and then transferred to Guantánamo, individuals like Abu Tariq al-Tunisi, Zakariyya al-Tunisi, and Habib al-Wadhan, remained to fight against American forces in Afghanistan. Abu Tariq was killed sometime in late 2001.[154] Before that he set up Bin Ladin's radio encryption system for when he wanted to talk with leaders, operatives, and trainers at other AQ-run training camps as well as with the Taliban.[155] In addition to that, Abu Tariq was also a trainer at Tarnak Farm, where he along with a couple others provided "specialist instruction" showing recruits "how to make electrical circuits for detonators, ground-to-air missiles SAM-7, Stinger, and anti-tank Milan."[156] He would be killed sometime in late 2001, after the U.S. invasion.[157]

An even more important figure within AQ was Zakariyya al-Tunisi ('Abd Allah al-Tunisi).[158] He was a companion of Fadhl Harun when they first joined the jihadi movement in the early 1990s in Afghanistan, both acting as bodyguards for Sayf al-Adl.[159] Following the departure of most "Afghan Arabs" in 1992, at first Zakariyya remained in Afghanistan with the Tunisian Abu Zayd at Jihadwal, where he would upgrade the training camp from one that was made out of mud to cement.[160] Shortly afterward, at the behest of al-Adl, Zakariyya and Harun made their way to Somalia to assist al-Ittihad al-Islami, a precursor to the Islamic Courts Union and Harakat al-Shabab al-Mujahidin, with training as well as to take part in the Battle of Mogadishu in 1993.[161] During that battle, Zakariyya was the one who launched a rocket-propelled grenade that downed one of the U.S. Black Hawk helicopters in the infamous "Black Hawk Down" incident in early October 1993.[162] A few years later, after the return of Bin Ladin and other jihadis to Afghanistan in 1996, Zakariyya and Harun were dispatched back to the Horn of Africa to help out with training camps and the preparations for the 1998 embassy bombings. Both men helped build up the training camps at Kiamboni, Somalia, in 1996 for al-Ittihad al-Islami.[163] Zakariyya would later travel with Harun to Kiunga, Kenya, while the latter was planning the embassy bombings, although not much is known about Zakariyya's activities afterward and when he traveled back to Afghanistan.[164] His dead body was discovered in the aftermath of a November 15, 2001, airstrike against AQ military chief Abu Hafs al-Masri's house in Afghanistan.[165]

Finally, there is the case of Habib al-Wadhan (Abu Muslim al-Tunisi), who first came into contact with the jihadi milieu in Milan when he attended Shaban's mosque at the ICI sometime in the early to mid-1990s after being inspired by a vision of a wounded Tunisian "brother."[166] He would then study under Shaban until Shaban's assassination in Bosnia in mid-December 1995. With this new fervor, al-Wadhan decided to join AQ's al-Faruq military training camp in Afghanistan after Bin Ladin returned in 1996 and would later be involved in the battles against the Americans in Kabul.[167] Similar to others, he retreated to Pakistan to get reinforcements from the Pashtun tribes and returned to Afghanistan in early 2002 to continue the fight, although he would not last long and was killed from bullet fire.[168]

Following 9/11, Western law enforcement agencies worked hard to prevent another attack. As a result, many of the individuals in the various jihadi networks based in Europe—including many Tunisians—were arrested or sanctioned, largely for their logistical and facilitation support to different organizations and terror plots. One such individual was Shafiq Bin Muhammad al-Ayadi, the head of an Islamic charity, al-Muwafaq Foundation, that provided financial support to AQ and Bin Ladin and was designated as a terrorist entity on October 12, 2002, by the U.S. Treasury Department.[169] Although he remains on the U.S. sanctions list, he has since been removed from the United Nations' and European Union's lists.[170] The British government would arrest the TCG's London leader, Kamal Bin Musa, in December 2001 for his financial and logistical support to the organization.[171] Similarly, the TCG's Milan leader, Bin Khamis, was arrested in April 2001 for involvement in the production of fake passports.[172] Finally, in mid-December 2001, Marufi, the TCG's cofounder, would be arrested by the Belgians for his role in the aforementioned Mas'ud assassination and Kleine Brogel plot.[173] After completing his prison sentence in Belgium in 2012 and being deported back to Tunisia, Marufi would join up as a behind-the-scenes leader within AST (although following the designation of AST as a terrorist organization, he decided to quit the movement and focus on composing poetry as a private citizen).[174]

In addition to these higher profile individuals, a number of non-leadership-level Tunisian operatives were also arrested from 2001 to 2003. Altogether, fifty-five Tunisians were arrested in these various fundraising/logistical networks and broken-up plots.[175]

TABLE 2.1 Tunisians Arrested Post-9/11 for Attack Plots and Associated Networks

2001

Plot name	Country	Description
Operacion Appreciatte	Spain	Fake passport ring
Milan Cell	Italy	Support network for the U.S. Embassy in Rome attack plot

2002

Plot name	Country	Description
Milan Tunisian Terrorism Support Network	Italy	Alleged to have planned an unspecified plot
Ryanair Hijacking	Sweden	Tunisian Karim Saduk Shatti provided material support for the alleged hijackers
Tirana Jihad Recruitment Group	Italy	Recruited people to fight jihad abroad
Chechen Recruitment Ring	France	Recruited people to fight jihad against Russia in Chechnya

2003

Plot name	Country	Description
Operation Alfarroba	Portugal	A forgery network
Cremona Cathedral Bomb Plot	Italy	Planned an attack against the Cremona Cathedral
Cremona Coordination Cell	Italy	Individuals committed fraud, document fabrication, and logistics for the bomb plot
LIFG Turin Fundraising Cell	Italy	Tunisian Muhammad Sassi helped with document production, fundraising, and jihadi propaganda

(continued)

TABLE 2.1 Tunisians Arrested Post-9/11 for Attack Plots and Associated Networks (*continued*)

2003

Plot name	Country	Description
London Ricin Plot	United Kingdom	Tunisian Bin Yamin Ishaq (Bin Yusuf Budhina) arrested in connection and had contact with Mohamed Atta ahead of 9/11 in Germany and Portugal
EU Parliament Bomb Plot	Luxembourg	Planned attack against the EU Parliament
Berlin Demonstration Bomb Plot	Germany	Several simultaneous bomb attacks planned at a demonstration protesting the beginning of the Iraq war
Como Fundraising Support Cell	Italy	Related to the cells in Milan and Turin
American Targets in Rome	Italy	Plan to attack American interests in the Rome area, such as an American army cemetery

Successful Post-9/11 Attacks

Despite many thwarted attacks and dissolved support networks, security services were not able to stop every attack. The first large-scale attack after 9/11 was conducted by a Tunisian in Tunisia, with planning and support from operatives in Afghanistan, France, Germany, Spain, and possibly Canada.

The Djerba Synagogue Bombing

On April 11, 2002, at one of Africa's oldest Jewish synagogues, a Tunisian AQ operative named Nizar Bin Muhammad Nasar Nawar (Sayf al-Din al-Tunisi) drove a truck filled with liquid propane, ignoring security officers' orders to stop, into the wall of al-Gharibah Synagogue in Djerba, Tunisia.[176] Masterminded by KSM, it was AQ's first successful attack after 9/11.[177] The attack killed fourteen Germans, five Tunisians, and two Frenchmen while leaving thirty others injured.

The central figure in the Djerba attack was Nizar Nawar, who was born in 1978.¹⁷⁸ His family was originally from Ben Gardane, a town west of Tunisia's border with Libya that has since become infamous as a recruitment hub for foreign fighters to Iraq, Syria, and Libya. Little is known about Nawar prior to his involvement within AQ, beyond the fact that he was a poor student, which led him to drop out at the age of sixteen and become a small-time salesman. Nawar is known to have traveled to Libya to buy cheap goods and sell them back in the local markets in Ben Gardane.¹⁷⁹ Family members and friends, when interviewed about Nawar following the attack, did not seem to fully know about his activities after he dropped out of school. Many stated they had not observed any outward signs of militancy.¹⁸⁰

According to the autobiography of Fadhl 'Abd Allah Muhammad (better known as Fadhl Harun), then head of AQ in East Africa who spent time in Afghanistan with Bin Ladin in the late 1990s, Nawar had been planning the attack since he first returned to Tunisia from Afghanistan in late 1999.¹⁸¹ Between his original return home in late 1999 and the attack in April 2002, Nawar would travel back and forth between Tunisia and Afghanistan for additional guidance. The Saudi AQ member Hasan Muhammad 'Ali Bin Atash, for example, noted that he saw Nawar at al-Matar airport complex in Kandahar in October 2000.¹⁸²

Fadhl Harun's autobiography also commends Nawar for his training capabilities and independence. Nawar had trained in explosives at the AQ-affiliated Khalden camp (which is different, although the same name, from the one run by Ibn Shaykh al-Libi and Abu Zubaydah) in Paktia Province while in Afghanistan.¹⁸³ According to French court documents on the Djerba attack, this is where Nawar met the Polish-German convert Christian Ganczarski (Abu Muhammad al-Almani).¹⁸⁴ Ganczarski befriended Nawar at Khalden and provided support and guidance to him for the synagogue bombing. In 2009 Ganczarski was convicted in a French court for his role in the Djerba attack.¹⁸⁵

Further evidence from the trial uncovered that Ganczarski and Nawar had many simultaneous travel patterns in the year or two prior to the Djerba attack, suggesting they worked in tandem.¹⁸⁶ Ganczarski allegedly became a mentor to Nawar, possibly due to Ganczarski's high stature and position within AQ.¹⁸⁷ According to testimony by Shadi 'Abd Allah, the leader of a German Jama'at Tawhid wa-l-Jihad cell who was arrested in April 2002 in connection with Abu Mus'ab al-Zarqawi's Turkish network, Ganczarski was very close to top AQ leaders Sayf al-Adl, Abu Hafs al-Masri, and Bin Ladin.¹⁸⁸ According to evidence from the French prosecution, Ganczarski was often seen at al-Adl's logistics base in Afghanistan and was one of the individuals in charge of AQ's information technology, including radio links and AQ's internet activities and passing messages between Bin Ladin and KSM.¹⁸⁹ Ganczarski can also be seen in a January 2000 video sitting near Muhammad Atta, Ramzi Bin al-Shibah, and 'Abd al-Ra'uf Jiday as Bin Ladin gives a sermon at Tarnak Farm.¹⁹⁰

It is certainly possible that Ganczarski was Nawar's handler for the plot. In fact, the French prosecution noted that just prior to the suicide attack in Djerba, Nawar phoned two individuals: Ganczarski and KSM (twice). According to Germany's domestic intelligence agency, the Office for the Protection of the Constitution, which was wiretapping Ganczarski's phone, Nawar asked Ganczarski for his *du'at* (blessings) ahead of the operation, to which Ganczarski replied by wishing him good luck: "Go in peace, God's mercy and blessing be with you."[191] The French were able to determine from wiretapping that Nawar was in constant contact with KSM in the two months leading up to the attack, likely receiving instructions and advice on final plans.[192] For these conversations to take place, Nawar relied on a supportive logistical network in Spain and France; KSM had a hand in the former, specifically connecting individuals from different parts of the broader Djerba attack network.[193] These networks also helped provide the necessary financial resources, which were funneled through Spain, in the planning and execution of the attack, which ended up costing €19,326 (about $17,000 at the time).[194]

Nawar last left Afghanistan on September 4, 2001, and returned to Tunisia via Switzerland on September 5. He may have had a meeting during his layover with one of KSM and Ganczarski's European associates, a Swiss-German named Daniel "Yusuf" Morgenegg, who had originally met Ganczarski in Germany in late 1992.[195] Morgenegg was likely overseeing the logistics of KSM's Djerba attack network in Europe, which, besides himself, included operatives in France and Spain.[196] Once back in Tunisia, Nawar created a front import–export business in Djerba. Final preparations for the attack began in January 2002 when Nawar purchased a used truck and his uncle, Biljakim Nawar, a sheet metal worker, welded a large steel tank inside of it, which Nawar said he planned to use to transport olive oil.[197] In reality, Nawar filled it with liquid propane for his attack.[198] Also in January, Nawar dispatched Tariq Hidiyya (Tahar), one of his associates from his hometown of Ben Gardane, to France with money to purchase a satellite phone through his brother Walid Nawar.[199] Hidiyya and Walid met in Saint-Priest near Lyon where Hidiyya presented Walid with an envelope containing €1,800. The money was used by Walid to buy a phone (as well as a modem) in Paris for his brother Nizar, the Djerba attacker.[200] This allowed Nizar to speak with KSM and others more conveniently since Nizar had previously been using pay phones to remain in contact with the network.[201]

According to Spanish court documents, in early March 2002, in order to acquire additional funds for Nawar's activities, KSM associate Isa Isma'il Muhammad, a Canadian-Pakistani who was based in Karachi, faxed a message to Enrique Cerda Ibanez (Kiké), CEO of the Valencia-based business Hispania de Calcomanias, saying that a man named 'Abd Allah Jafir would be calling him. "Isa Karachi has a gift of €5,720," he stated.[202] The Spanish investigation found that 'Abd Allah Jafir was a pseudonym for Nawar that KSM told Nawar to use when contacting Ibanez.[203] Isa Isma'il Muhammad and Ibanez had business dealings for years, suggesting that transfers between the two men were one way that money was being sent from the Afghanistan-Pakistan region to operatives and cells in Europe.[204]

KSM also gave Nawar the business phone number of Ibanez, which Nawar used to contact Ibanez via his new satellite phone. Apparently, there were issues with Ibanez, however. Morgenegg, the network's Swiss-German logistical coordinator, called KSM saying that the "wedding" (a code term used by AQ for an attack) would happen soon but that those based in Europe and Tunisia were waiting for Ibanez to "arrive" (i.e., provide the money).[205] Morgenegg then ordered Walid Nawar to follow through on KSM's orders to contact Ibanez. Walid called Ibanez on March 16, and Morgenegg then followed up with KSM, Nizar, and Nizar's uncle Biljakim about the status of receiving the payment. On the same day, the Pakistan-based Isa Ismaʿil Muhammad sent another fax to Ibanez, reprimanding him for not yet transferring the funds.[206]

The reprimand appears to have worked because Ibanez finally made the transfers two days later. He deposited €9,500 into a shared Bancaja bank account with Ahmad Rukhsar, the Logroño-based owner of New Lagpal, which was used for *hawala* transfers, among other things.[207] There was also another deposit of €6,000 on April 10, the day before the attack.[208] Given that at least one phone call took place between Nawar and Rukhsar, it is likely that Nawar was the final recipient of these funds.[209] With the money and equipment in place, the attack was imminent. As with other deceptions, on the day of the attack, Nawar told his family he was traveling to Libya.[210] According to French court documents, he also had a specific message for his uncle Biljakim, telling him that after he conducted the attack, Biljakim should contact KSM.[211]

The bomb Nawar prepared for the attack was a smaller version of the one used in the 1998 U.S. Embassy bombing in Tanzania, illustrating how tradecraft was replicated over time.[212] Additionally, similar to the 1998 embassy attacks in Kenya and Tanzania, a statement of responsibility was released by Jaysh al-Islami Li-Tahrir al-Muqadisat (or the Islamic Army for the Liberation of the Holy Sites, a front name for AQ) via fax to the Arabic newspapers *al-Hayat* and *al-Quds al-Arabi* on April 16, 2002.[213] It stated that "Nizar Bin Muhammad Nawar Sayf al-Din al-Tunisi carried out the attack, which was commissioned by Jaysh al-Islami Li-Tahrir al-Muqadisat," that the "martyr" Nawar was a model for the *umma*, and that Nawar carried the attack out in the name of Palestine against the Jews. Attached to the statement was a martyrdom will from Nawar dated July 5, 2000, highlighting the plot's long gestation period. In the will, Nawar reminds the reader to "not be fooled . . . I'm a martyr in the cause of God."[214] Months later, in late June 2002, AQ's spokesperson at the time, Sulayman Abu Ghayth, officially claimed responsibility, stating that the attack was carried out by a "man of the al-Qaʿida organization."[215]

In contrast to the Djerba synagogue bombing, whose perpetrators began planning prior to the 9/11 attacks, other successful post-9/11 attacks were planned after AQ and other jihadi elements had been ejected from their Afghan sanctuary. A number of these individuals, especially those from North Africa, would move to Turkey to plot and plan attacks from Istanbul.

The Turkish Base

Following the fall of Tora Bora in December 2001, Tunisians began to reconstitute their network in Europe and established headquarters in Istanbul, Turkey. This is a relevant development because it not only links the Afghan jihad of the 1980s and 1990s to the Iraqi and Syrian jihads of the 2000s and 2010s; it also helps explain the continuity and evolution of these networks in the post-9/11 world, particularly in the context of Tunisian foreign fighter networks after the Arab uprisings in 2011.

As noted earlier, the Tunisian jihadi networks maintained tight links with the so-called Jalalabad school and the Khalden network inside Afghanistan. Besides Abu Zubaydah, Ibn Shaykh al-Libi, and Abu Mus'ab al-Zarqawi, there was another cog in this broader network: a Syrian Kurd named Luay Sakka. Sakka was based in Turkey and played an important role between two battlefields: facilitating training in Afghanistan at Khalden and dispatching individuals to Chechnya with Ibn al-Khatab. As a result of AQ's interlude in Sudan, Ibn al-Khatab built legitimacy and credibility through his leadership and fighting prowess in Tajikistan and later Chechnya.[216] Because Chechnya was an open front against the Russians in the late 1990s, many wanted to fight there instead of assisting the Taliban in its local political fights against the Northern Alliance. Even al-Zarqawi originally went to Afghanistan to train and then fight in Chechnya.[217] Therefore, Sakka's Turkish base was an important center between two zones of jihad. Moreover, it would provide the building blocks of what later became a key facilitation and logistics hub for individuals traveling to Syria and Iraq for the Iraq jihad following the U.S. invasion in 2003. It is also the point from which the Casablanca, Madrid, and other attacks were planned beginning in February 2002.

In Istanbul in February 2002, top leaders from the Libyan, Moroccan, and Tunisian jihadi networks met to discuss the prospects of bringing jihadi attacks back to the Western countries in which they had previously resided.[218] According to Amir 'Azizi ('Uthman al-Andalusi), a Moroccan with Spanish citizenship who would play an important role in the Madrid attacks, "there have been other meetings there, at which the bombings in Riyadh, Casablanca, Istanbul [which Sakka helped fund and plan], and Madrid were discussed."[219] One of these meetings, during which attendees chose targets for the Casablanca bombings, would take place in Istanbul in January 2003 with the participation of Abu 'Iyadh.[220] Abu 'Iyadh's attendance suggests that, despite his arrest in

Istanbul in March 2003, he was involved in the planning two months prior to the attacks. It would also insinuate that Abu 'Iyadh was likely present at the meeting in February 2002 since he was the leader of the Tunisian jihadi movement. Therefore, Abu 'Iyadh likely had a hand in the early planning of the Madrid train bombings as well, especially due to the overlap in the networks involved in both attacks, which were both conducted in large part by the Moroccan Islamic Combatant Group networks.[221] Beyond Abu 'Iyadh's planning role in Casablanca, there were no other known Tunisians involved in any aspects of the attack.

The Madrid Train Bombings

While Tunisians did not play a large role in the Casablanca bombings, the Tunisian Sarhan Bin 'Abd al-Majid Fakhit organized the Madrid train bombings. Fakhit moved to Spain in 1996 on a scholarship to study economics at Madrid Universidad Autónoma.[222] He seemed to integrate well into Spanish society, but a hajj trip to Mecca in 1998 proved to be a life-altering experience that changed his outlook on religion and non-Muslims.[223] He would abandon his studies to become a real estate agent and join the M30 mosque in Madrid. There, he would query the imam, Munayr Mahmud 'Ali al-Massiri, about whether Arab regimes were apostates and if jihad was a legitimate way to spread Islam.[224] The M30 mosque also facilitated Fakhit's contact with the jihadi network of the Syrian Imad al-Din Barakat Yarkas (Abu Dahdah).[225] Fakhit would become Yarkas's most important and loyal disciple. The aforementioned 'Azizi, who was Yarkas's right-hand man, recruited Fakhit into this network.[226]

Yarkas became the head of the jihadi network in Spain in October 1995 after its original leader, a Palestinian named Shaykh Adnan Muhammad Salih, moved to Peshawar to recruit for Abu Zubaydah.[227] This move illustrates the continued prevalence of the Jalalabad school in many networks that Tunisians would become involved in. This Spanish cell set up by Salih in 1994 was formed from a core of "Afghan Arab" alums and called Jund Allah (Soldiers of God).[228] Yarkas's main contacts in Europe were Abu Qatadah in London and Marufi in Brussels, which would further suggest Abu 'Iyadh's involvement in the early stages of planning for the attack; the former was his mentor and the latter, his main organizational partner.[229] Yarkas was also tied to the Hamburg cell, which was responsible for 9/11. (Muhammad Atta had traveled to Spain twice and met once with al-Shibah ahead of the attack. Yarkas therefore had prior knowledge of 9/11.)[230]

In the aftermath of 9/11, Spanish law enforcement arrested Yarkas—along with most of his network—for his leadership role in Jund Allah and support to the 9/11 conspiracy in what it called Operación Dátil.[231] As the first arrests began,

'Azizi fled Spain and spent his intervening time between Iran and Turkey, ushering individuals from Afghanistan to Europe and Iraq.[232] Fakhit was thus the most respected and senior member left in Spain who had not escaped or been arrested. As a result, he became intimately involved with the planning of the attack and would travel a number of times to Istanbul to meet with 'Azizi and others. Fakhit and 'Azizi met in Istanbul at least four times: shortly after 9/11, the February 2002 joint meeting, at the end of 2002, and in early 2004.[233] It is also believed that Fakhit remained in contact with Yarkas through an intermediary in prison up to five days before the attack.[234]

Following the February 2002 meeting, Fakhit began to recruit individuals into the attack network. All key elements were in order by August 2003.[235] This is when preparation for the attack—which would not occur until March 11, 2004—began.[236] On the morning of March 11, this network of 18 Moroccans, 3 Algerians, 1 Lebanese, and 1 Tunisian would plant 13 IEDs on four trains in Madrid, killing 191 individuals and injuring 2,050 people.[237] In its aftermath, a number of individuals in the network escaped, although the ringleaders remained, possibly to plot further attacks. The investigation by the Spanish police led to an apartment in Leganés, a suburb of Madrid, where Fakhit and others (Jamal Zugham and Jamal Ahmidan al-Sini) were living. Instead of being taken alive, they blew themselves up in the apartment on April 3, 2004.[238] In a video found afterward, Fakhit justified the attacks by harkening back to history: "You know of the Spanish crusade against Muslims and that not much time has passed since the expulsion from al-Andalus and the tribunals of the Inquisition.... Blood for blood! Destruction for destruction!"[239]

As Tunisians and other jihadis were building a base in Turkey to plot terrorist attacks like those in Casablanca and Madrid, al-Zarqawi's network began to take shape in the lead-up to the Iraq war. This is explored in the next chapter, among other developments. The next chapter also introduces new individuals among the second generation that got involved with the jihadi movement and would also become relevant following the Tunisian Revolution.

This first generation of Tunisian jihadis built a foundation that the second generation would be able to build off of, whether in Europe, in foreign fighter zones, or even at home. From a group of random individuals who went to Afghanistan in the 1980s and who were not viewed in the best light to an efficient movement in the 1990s that became infamous for facilitation and document forgery to mature into an actual group with the TCG in 2000, the broader movement became more experienced and institutionalized. The next chapter follows this process, which allowed the movement to then take advantage of the new opportunities after the Tunisian Revolution in 2011, especially as those from both generations would meet and intermingle within Tunisia's prison system.

CHAPTER 3

COME DO JIHAD

The second generation of Tunisia's jihadi movement was in some ways a continuation of the first years of the movement and in other ways something completely new. In this chapter, I explore Tunisian involvement in the Iraq jihad; plots and attacks involving Tunisians in the West from 2005 to 2010; other foreign fighting ventures in Afghanistan, Somalia, and Yemen; and Tunisians getting involved with GSPC/AQIM regional networks. Of course, there are some individuals who play roles from the first generation who continue to act with the second generation since they had yet to be killed or imprisoned. Those among this second generation who are introduced in this chapter and who play important roles with AST or with the Islamic State following the 2011 Tunisian revolution include Hasan al-Brik, Bubakr al-Hakim, Tariq al-Harzi, Sabri Isid, Muhammad Bakhti, and Wanas al-Faqih. Similar to chapter 2, this one relies upon process tracing as a method to better understand the breadth of Tunisian involvement in the global jihadi movement.

The Iraq Jihad

Although many Tunisians partook in jihadism prior to the Iraq war, as described in the previous chapter, the war inspired a new generation and cadre of individuals. For example, Hasan al-Brik, who would become AST's head of *dawa* after the 2011 revolution, traveled to Iraq in 2003. Like many others, he did not actually make it into Iraq but rather took charge of a safe house in Syria where individuals were vetted before traveling to Iraq.[1] For the Tunisians who survived, many, including al-Brik, would be arrested in Syria (and elsewhere) and rendered back to Tunisia to be placed into its prison system.

Tunisia's prisons in the seven to eight years before the revolution would be crucial for bringing together the first generation of Tunisian jihadis associated with Afghanistan and Europe-based networks and the second generation more associated with Iraq and the GSPC/AQIM networks. This prison exchange between the first and second generations of Tunisian jihadis would provide AST's base for activities after the 2011 revolution.

Abu Mus'ab al-Zarqawi's and Mullah Krekar's Network(s)

The rise of al-Zarqawi's network began with the connections he made at the training camp he ran in Herat, Afghanistan, in the year prior to the 9/11 attacks. There he started the organization Jund al-Sham with recruits mainly from Syria, Lebanon, Palestine, and Jordan.[2] It is also where he cultivated ties to Gulf financiers, who would be helpful in the early years of the Iraq war.[3] Most importantly, al-Zarqawi was able to exploit the networks that brought people into Herat via Mashhad, Iran. After the U.S. invasion of Afghanistan, al-Zarqawi redirected this flow in the opposite direction to eventually set up a base of operations in Iraqi Kurdistan with the help of the local jihadi outfit, Ansar al-Islam.[4]

With three hundred fighters, including Tunisians, al-Zarqawi slipped into Mashhad on December 12, 2001.[5] Although his lieutenants and foot soldiers were training and operating out of Iraqi Kurdistan in the first half of 2002, al-Zarqawi was in Syria recruiting individuals and establishing a logistics network to connect with Luay Sakka in Turkey.[6] It was only in August 2002, in a meeting in Tehran, that al-Zarqawi and his associates, along with Ansar al-Islam's leader, Najm al-Din Faraj Ahmad (better known as Mullah Krekar), decided to set up a permanent base in Iraqi Kurdistan. This led to an overwhelming increase in the number of "Afghan Arabs" and new recruits who found safe haven there more than six months before the start of the Iraq war.[7] According to a security source in the Abu Sayda district in the Diyala governorate, al-Zarqawi's first foothold in that governorate in 2002 was in the village of al-Mukhisah and was led by the Tunisian Abu Yahya, who had been living there with his wife and three children. He would eventually be killed in 2007.[8]

After gaining refugee status in Norway in 1991, Krekar took advantage of his new freedoms and began to recruit, fundraise, and establish support networks in Norway, Italy, Germany, the Netherlands, and the United Kingdom. In the 1990s Krekar performed these duties for the Islamic Kurdistan Movement, an organization he participated in prior to its merger with another Kurdish group—Jund al-Islam—and some other Kurdish Islamist factions. This merger created Ansar al-Islam on September 1, 2001.[9] Ansar al-Islam's recruitment network in Europe was vital for al-Zarqawi (in addition to his own cell in Germany). Many of the earliest individuals to join al-Zarqawi's group came from Europe and included a number of Tunisians.

Tunisians Join the Iraq Jihad

The first known foreign fighters to join al-Zarqawi's Kurdistan base were eight Tunisians and three Iraqis from Marseille, France, in the fall of 2002.[10] They first stopped in Damascus, Syria, which would become an important transition point for foreign fighters traveling to Iraq.[11] One of the Tunisians in this group was Fadhl Sa'adi, the same individual involved with the Milan network who provided false documentation for the Mas'ud assassination. Sa'adi would be one of the first suicide bombers after the war started in July 2003.[12] While a second generation of Tunisian jihadis were born as a consequence of the Iraq War, some of the first generation who were not arrested in the post-9/11 sweep played an early role in Iraq as well.

As the war began, many more Tunisians became interested in joining to fight the Americans. Four days before the American intervention, in an intercepted phone call by Italian security, Muhammad Hamid, a Kurdish Ansar al-Islam recruiter in Parma, Italy, noted: "Now that the Americans have decided to go to war against Iraq there are many communities of Moroccans and Tunisians that are getting ready to go and fight against the Americans."[13] Among the individuals Hamid recruited was Lufti Rihani, a Tunisian based in Milan who was previously indicted for working with Bin Khamis. In August 2002 Hamid and Rihani met with two other Kurdish recruiters, Muhammad Amin Mustafa and Mullah Fu'ad, at the infamous Islamic Cultural Institute two months prior to Rihani's travel to Syria and, later, Iraq.[14] Rihani, along with two other Tunisians, would eventually die in a suicide car-bomb attack targeting U.S. forces in September 2003.[15] A month later two other Tunisians, Kamal Murshidi and Habib Waddani (Sa'id), carried out a suicide attack on the al-Rashid Hotel in Baghdad, likely targeting then U.S. deputy defense secretary Paul Wolfowitz.[16] Both men were also part of Bin Khamis's cell in Milan and had previously been implicated in crimes. Murshidi had trained in Afghanistan and allegedly supported the provision of forged documents to prospective foreign fighters going to Iraq. The U.S. designated Waddani for his association with AQ in August 2002, in part because the Italians wanted him in September 2000 for trafficking weapons from Russia to Pakistan to be used at AQ training camps.[17]

In addition to the historical Italian-based Tunisian networks, another network from the 19th arrondissement in Paris began to recruit and send individuals to Iraq. The head of this network was Farid Benyettou, a French-Algerian janitor who first became exposed to jihadism in the mid to late 1990s through Yusuf Zimmuri, his sister's husband. Zimmuri was a leader in the French GSPC network and arrested in 1998 for the World Cup plot mentioned in the previous chapter.[18] Benyettou's exposure to the milieu led him to become a self-styled imam and attract other young radicals around him. An important figure in this network was the Tunisian Bubakr al-Hakim, who served as a leader in AST after the revolution and, later, as part of the Islamic State in Syria until he was killed in a drone strike on November 26, 2016.[19] More importantly, al-Hakim claimed responsibility for the assassination of two leftist politicians in Tunisia in 2013—an event that shook the country and almost derailed the transition after the revolution.[20]

Al-Hakim, who had been studying Arabic at Majma'a al-Fatah al-Islam in Syria since 2000, signed up for Saddam Hussein's foreign legion in order to train to fight the Americans.[21] According to captured documents from Saddam's regime, the foreign legion had been training non-Iraqi Arab fighters as early as the 1980s; some—including eight Tunisians—even fought during the first Gulf War in 1991.[22] While in Iraq, al-Hakim exhorted his friends from the 19th arrondissement to join in an interview with the French radio station RTI: "All of my friends in the 19th, I tell them, come do the jihad. All of my brothers who are over there, come, to defend Islam. They are wimps, wimps and buffoons. The Americans aren't anything. I am ready to fight on the front line. I am even ready to blow myself up. I am ready to blow myself up, to put dynamite and, 'Boom! Boom!' We will kill all of the Americans. We are mujahidin. We want death. We want paradise."[23] These hopes would eventually come to fruition, although under the rubric of al-Zarqawi's network after the disbandment of Saddam's officers.

After returning to Paris in May 2003, al-Hakim joined Benyettou's circle and began to recruit individuals to fight in Iraq with al-Zarqawi's organization, which by then was calling itself Jama'at al-Tawhid wa-l-Jihad (JTWJ). One year later six individuals joined al-Hakim to fight in Iraq or work with the support networks in Syria. The only other Tunisian in this group was al-Hakim's brother, Radwan, who was killed by a U.S. bombing on July 17, 2004.[24] Bubakr fought in the infamous Fallujah battles for five months before getting arrested by the Bashar al-Assad regime for lacking a passport at the border in the fall of 2004. At the time of his deportation back to France in January 2005, other members of the 19th arrondissement clique (Benyettou, a Tunisian named Thamir Bushnak, and Chérif Kouachi; the latter would eventually be involved in the Charlie Hebdo attacks in January 2015) were days away from traveling to Iraq, based on al-Hakim's connections, but were arrested by French police.[25] Al-Hakim described his time in prison with his network as "a great opportunity for preaching to God, to explain this *manhaj* (methodology) to the imprisoned youth."[26]

Statistics on Tunisians Who Fought in Iraq

As the conflict in Iraq simmered, more and more Tunisians signed up to take on roles within al-Zarqawi's JTWJ, which would transform into AQ in the Land of the Two Rivers (more popularly known as AQ in Iraq, or AQI) in October 2004, Majlis Shura al-Mujahidin (MSM) in January 2006, and, finally, after al-Zarqawi's death, the Islamic State of Iraq (ISI) in October 2006.[27] According to AQI internal documents that showed foreign members who entered Iraq in 2004 and 2005, Tunisians made up 9.8 percent and ranked fourth overall among foreign national groups that successfully arrived.[28] Additionally, Tunisians showed up in large numbers in the Sinjar Records, which the U.S. military recovered in October 2007 in a raid on an ISI compound. The records documented foreign fighters that joined MSM/ISI between August 2006 and August 2007. Tunisians were the seventh-highest foreign national group that had passed through Syria to get to Iraq.[29] In per capita terms, Tunisians were the third most represented group, behind only Libyans and Saudis.[30] The most common route that Tunisians traveled to get to Iraq were through Turkey/Syria, Germany/Turkey/Syria, Saudi Arabia/Syria, and Libya/Syria.[31] While the Sinjar Records are better known than the earlier AQI records, when compared, they show that Tunisians came to Iraq in greater numbers in the earlier stages of the war, which tracks with the facilitation networks outlined above.

At the time, some researchers also began to quantify casualties: Evan Kohlmann found that between March 2003 and June 2005, 1.7 percent of the foreign fighters killed in Iraq were Tunisian, while Reuven Paz calculated that 1.3 percent of foreign fighters killed between January 2005 and March 2005 were Tunisian.[32] Furthermore, in June 2005 the U.S. military disclosed that Tunisians were among the top ten foreign nationalities fighting in AQI.[33] In addition, Tunisians were the eighth (or 3.2 percent) most detained foreign national group by coalition forces between April and October of 2005. As of April 7, 2008, Tunisians made up 3.2 percent of foreign fighters held at the infamous Camp Bucca prison.[34]

The jihadi magazine *Majallat Minbar Suriya al-Islami* relayed in its third issue in October 2005 that 1,000 Tunisians had been arrested attempting to travel to Iraq.[35] Moreover, Samir Ben Amor, a Tunisian attorney who defended arrested jihadis, said that from 2005 to 2007, 600 Tunisians were arrested attempting to make it to Iraq.[36] This number does not include Tunisians based outside Tunisia or those who were not arrested prior to 2005. This could suggest that the true pool of individuals would be somewhere between 1,600 and

2,500 for that entire period who were arrested ahead of making it to Iraq and those that made it. These numbers would illustrate the strength of Tunisia's foreign fighter population, especially considering that between 4,000 and 5,000 foreign fighters were involved in the Iraq jihad, according to Thomas Hegghammer. It could also suggest that there were more individuals who went or were arrested attempting to go to Iraq than was originally believed, or that the way individuals now count foreign fighter flows for Syria is different than for Iraq since many now also include those who attempted to go but were stopped ahead of time.[37] Therefore, it is not surprising that so many Tunisians were observed joining the Syrian jihad after 2011 even if they did not all make it during the peak Iraq years.

Roles of Tunisians in the Iraq Jihad

Many of the Tunisians who joined JTWJ/AQI/MSM/ISI were facilitators/recruiters, but a number of others were fighters, suicide bombers, and even leaders.[38] The facilitator/recruiter role provides an important insight into why so many Tunisians have fought in Syria since 2011. In particular, the highly connected nature of their Tunisian brethren allows for easier access to the networks that provide logistics to those wanting to join the fight.

Beyond identifying names of those killed, MSM published martyrdom notices with stories on the backgrounds of individuals and their activities in Iraq prior to their deaths. For example, in April 2006 MSM released a notice about Abu Ibrahim al-Tunisi, a commander who had previously fought in Bosnia and Afghanistan. While in Afghanistan, he allegedly managed guest houses on behalf of Usamah Bin Ladin, fought against the Northern Alliance alongside the Taliban, and defended Kandahar, Jalalabad, and Kabul after the U.S. invasion until he fled to Turkey with al-Hajj Banan al-Turki and later joined the Iraq jihad.[39] Abu Ibrahim first served as head of the security branch in Rawa until he was promoted to head of the security branch of al-Anbar Province and military commander for al-Qa'im, where he oversaw the sniper, intelligence, security, and antiaircraft units.[40] The latter town, located on the border with Syria, was an important passageway for the smuggling of foreign fighters and other illegal activities originating in the town of Albu Kamal on the Syrian side of the border. Albu Kamal likewise served as a stopping point for foreigners traveling from Damascus to Iraq. Abu Ibrahim planned and commanded a number of battles, including the operation of the martyr Shaykh Abu Muhammad al-Lubnani and the first and second operations to conquer Husaybah. He would eventually be killed in a U.S. airstrike during the battles of al-Qa'im, in its subdistrict of al-Karabilah.[41]

A number of other Tunisians, such as Abu Basir al-Tunisi, fought with and were leaders in the MSM/ISI battalion Katibat Umm al-Mu'minin 'A'ishah.⁴² Two of the most prominent Tunisians in this battalion who both went by the name of Abu Usamah al-Tunisi were killed in July 2006 and September 2007, respectively. The first came to Iraq in 2004 and eventually became a commander in Katibat Umm al-Mu'minin 'A'ishah. He led the Battle of Abu Anas al-Shami, commanded the al-Fatah assault, and participated in the Sunni revenge battles and antiterrorism assaults. He was killed by U.S. airstrikes in al-Yusufiyah, a town twenty miles south of Baghdad.⁴³

The other Abu Usamah, whose full *kunya* was Abu Usamah Walid Uld al-Habat al-Tunisi (also known as al-Amir al-Sha'b, the leader of the people), was a senior leader in the ISI. He was the head of Katibat Umm al-Mu'minin 'A'ishah, which was originally founded by Abu Hamzah al-Muhajir (Abu Ayyub al-Masri), the successor to al-Zarqawi. Al-Muhajir eventually became the first minister and the war minister of the ISI under its leader, Abu 'Umar al-Baghdadi.⁴⁴ The second Abu Usamah also came to Iraq in 2004 and fought in the battles of Fallujah, where his close relationship with both al-Zarqawi and al-Muhajir led to his rise in the organization first as the military leader of Baghdad's southern belt and later as the leader of MSM/ISI's entire foreign fighter operation.⁴⁵ This might help explain why Abu Usamah was one of the masked individuals in the video that showed the beheading of the American Nicholas Berg in May 2004.⁴⁶ Therefore, the fact that Tunisians held high-level positions in the organization could help explain why so many Tunisians were connected to these networks that are still relevant to the fighting in Iraq, Libya, and Syria to this day. Like many of the other individuals already mentioned, Abu Usamah would be killed in a U.S. airstrike in the city of Musayyib, in Babil Province, on September 25, 2007, along with a number of other senior ISI leaders.⁴⁷

Another important Tunisian within MSM/ISI was Yusri Bin Fakhr al-Tariqi (Abu Qudamah al-Tunisi and Ziyad al-Saba'). Although he was not a leader like those mentioned above, he would become a symbol for AST of the oppression at the hands of the Shia-led regime in Iraq while he was in an Iraqi prison prior to his execution on November 16, 2011. Al-Tariqi would arrive in Iraq in November 2003 at the age of nineteen, the youngest among the group with which he traveled.⁴⁸ He would operate in Mosul until mid-2004 when he moved to Samarra with other operatives to plan the infamous February 2006 bombing of the Shia Marqad al-Imamayn 'Ali al-Hadi wa-l-Hassan al-Askari Shrine.⁴⁹ This attack was an important catalyst in the overt civil war between Sunnis and Shias inside Iraq. The ensuing sectarianism had been a goal of al-Zarqawi's so that Sunnis would have no choice but to seek security with MSM. Al-Tariqi, following his later arrest, would claim that "the shrines of the al-Askari imams were chosen because of their religious importance and their geographical location, and the choice was meant to cause sectarian division among the people."⁵⁰ Besides that attack, al-Tariqi was alleged to have been involved in the assassination of Iraqi journalist Atwar Bahjat.⁵¹ He would eventually be captured alive in June 2006 during a battle in Ba'qubah, about fifty miles northeast of Baghdad, where all his fellow brethren were killed. He then moved around a number of prisons before being forced into solitary confinement at al-Kazimiyah prison until his death.⁵²

Tunisian Foreign Fighter Facilitation

Beyond Tunisians who took on leadership positions as commanders, fighters, or foot soldiers, Tunisians also played an important role in the logistics and facilitation network for JTWJ/AQI/MSM/ISI. One of these networks was led by the Tunisian Jamal Husni (Jamal al-Maghribi) and his associates, Mahir Buyahiya and 'Ali Bin Sassi ('Ali al-Tunisi). They were involved in the Italian jihadi networks' forging of documents that would be sent to JTWJ's network inside Turkey, which at the time was still led by Sakka.⁵³ The latter two Tunisians—along with another, Farida Bentiwa Bin Bashir—would be arrested in Italy in November 2003, along with one of their associates in Hamburg, Germany, 'Abd al-Razak Mahjub.⁵⁴

Another key individual was Abu 'Umar al-Tunisi. His name continuously appeared in the Sinjar Records as a major facilitator of individuals through Syria into Iraq.⁵⁵ This suggests he was a key middleman between the recruitment and logistics networks in the Arab world and Western Europe and the operatives on the ground inside Iraq. According to the U.S. military, in May 2008 special operations officers arrested Abu 'Umar in western Ninawa Province.⁵⁶ It was later learned that Abu 'Umar's real name was Tariq bin al-Tahar bin al-Falih al-Awni al-Harzi, and that he was still recruiting and facilitating the travel of foreign fighters to the jihadi group in 2013, after its reemergence as the Islamic State of Iraq and al-Sham.⁵⁷ This suggests he was released from prison or was broken out of prison sometime after his arrest by U.S. forces. Two other Tunisians, whose full identities are unknown, were also involved in the facilitation of individuals through Syria into Iraq: Abu Muhammad al-Tunisi, who provided access to foreign fighters from France, and Abu Adam al-Tunisi, who provided access to foreign fighters from Jordan.⁵⁸

Besides Abu 'Umar, another important facilitator was the Tunisian Malik Sharahili, who was the successor to Sakka as the head of AQI/MSM's network in Turkey.⁵⁹ Sharahili took over the network after Sakka was arrested in August 2005 for his planning and financing of the 2003 Istanbul bombings as well as a plot to bomb Israeli cruise ships. Like others, Sharahili left Tunisia in late spring 2003 and arrived in Syria via Libya where he would take religious classes before being arrested in January 2005 by the Assad regime.⁶⁰ While imprisoned, Sharahili would establish many new contacts, which would be helpful after he was released in March 2005. These contacts included the head of the Belgian foreign fighter recruitment network, Bilal Sughir, who was also a Tunisian.⁶¹ Following his release, Sharahili made his way first to Istanbul and then to Hatay Province in southern Turkey near the Syrian border. He operated out of Hatay until he was arrested in August 2006 for involvement with AQI/MSM.⁶² Following his release from prison, Sughir returned to Belgium and began recruiting individuals and shepherding them to Iraq through Sharahili's operation in Turkey. Moreover, Sughir provided Sharahili financing through criminal activities conducted by his network in Belgium and the exploitation of the Belgian social security system.⁶³ Sughir's network even attempted to find a wife for Sharahili.⁶⁴

Besides Sughir's associations with Sharahili, he is also known for recruiting the Western female convert Muriel Degauque to join AQI in 2005. What's noteworthy is that she is considered the first female Western suicide bomber and sixth female suicide bomber overall used for AQI.⁶⁵ Sughir would later be sentenced to five years in prison in 2008 and his Belgian citizenship revoked in December 2017, alongside Malikah al-Arud, mentioned in the previous chapter.⁶⁶

These connections and events all illustrate the crucial role played by many Tunisians in JTWJ/AQI/MSM/ISI's ecosystem of operations, especially as it relates to foreign fighters. Between Abu Usamah, Abu 'Umar, Sharahili, and a number of logistics and facilitation operatives, it is no wonder that Tunisians had so many contacts in Syria when the Syrian Civil War began. Furthermore, after the tribal awakening and surge in Iraq when foreign fighter flows plummeted and ISI transformed to a more Iraqi-centric entity, Tunisians played a role in rebuilding the foreign fighter network in the latter part of the 2000s. In the mid- to late 2000s there were also many other Tunisians arrested attempting to join or help AQI/MSM/ISI. This provided another cadre of individuals who could be involved in recruitment, logistics, and facilitation after the 2011 revolution.

Besides the most-known networks broken up, mentioned above (in January 2005, the 19th arrondissement network with al-Hakim, and in December 2005, the Iraq jihad recruitment network in Belgium with Sughir), there were other known networks involving Tunisians that ultimately led to arrests and extraditions (see table 3.1). Most notable among this group was the French-Tunisian Sabri Isid, who was arrested in December 2006 by Iraqi forces and deported back to Toulouse, France, via Syria.⁶⁷ There are two interesting aspects of Isid's case: first, in 2009, his father married the mother of Muhammad Merah, who committed the Toulouse and Montauban shootings in March 2012; and, second, Isid would return to foreign fighting in May 2013, this time in Syria.⁶⁸

TABLE 3.1 Broken-Up Iraq Jihad Networks That Included Tunisians

Date	Location	Description
May 2004[1]	Florence, Italy	Recruitment to become suicide bombers in Iraq
April 2005[2]	Algeria	Joining GSPC training camps to train for fighting in Iraq
August 2005[3]	Syria	Arrested for clashes with security services in June 2005
September 2005[4]	Paris, France	Recruitment for jihad in Iraq
November 2005[5]	Paris, France	Recruitment for jihad in Iraq
October 2006[6]	Tunisia	Arrested Tunisian GSPC member for attempting to go to Iraq
December 2006[7]	Cairo and Alexandria, Egypt	Recruiting people to fight in Iraq
December 2006[8]	Iraq	French Tunisian extradited back to Toulouse, France
October 2007[9]	Syria	Deported back to Tunisia for trying to cross border with Iraq
November 2007[10]	Perugia, Italy	Recruitment for fighting in Iraq
December 2007[11]	Tunisia	Facilitating individuals across Syrian–Iraqi border
December 2007[12]	Tunisia	Attempting to go fight jihad in Iraq

[1] Mohamed Hafez, *Suicide Bombers in Iraq: The Strategy and Ideology of Martyrdom* (Washington, D.C.: United States Institute of Peace, 2007), 205; and Western Jihadists 1993–2015: Western Jihadists 1993–Present: An Archive and Database Charting the Evolution of Jihadi-inspired Terrorist Networks and Recruitment in Western States. Principal Investigator: Jytte Klausen. Waltham, MA: Brandeis University.
[2] Anneli Botha, "Terrorism in Maghreb: The Transnationalisation of Domestic Terrorism," *Institute for Security Studies*, ISS Monograph Series, no. 144 (June 2008), 121.
[3] Pargeter, "Radicalisation in Tunisia," 93.
[4] Western Jihadists 1993–Present.
[5] Western Jihadists 1993–Present.
[6] Botha, "Terrorism in Maghreb," 120–21.
[7] Botha, "Terrorism in Maghreb," 170; "American Is Among Egypt Terror Suspects," *Washington Post*, December 4, 2006; and Nadia Abou El-Magd, "American Among Group Arrested in Egypt in Alleged Terror Plot," *Associated Press*, December 5, 2006.
[8] Western Jihadists 1993–Present.
[9] Botha, "Terrorism in Maghreb," 168.
[10] Botha, "Terrorism in Maghreb," 154.
[11] "Tunisia Convicts 4 for Insurgency in Iraq," *al-Sumaria TV*, December 15, 2007; and Bill Roggio, "Tunisia," *Long War Journal*, December 26, 2007.
[12] "Tunisia Convicts 4 for Insurgency in Iraq"; and Roggio, "Tunisia."

Regarding Merah, Isid helped radicalize him while he had been imprisoned, leading him to eventually get training in Afghanistan.[69]

Due to these arrests, along with the tribal awakening and surge in Iraq, the flow of foreign fighters was suppressed.

Declining Foreign Fighter Mobilization and Redirection to Lebanon

By December 2007, according to the head of ISI at the time, Abu 'Umar al-Baghdadi, there were only two hundred foreign fighters left in the country.[70] This is a large decrease from the hundreds who had been going there every month.[71] This continued to fall from ninety per month in mid-2007, to fifty per month in early 2008, to ten per month in early 2009.[72] As a result of the decline in foreign fighters beginning in 2006, as well as international pressure on the Assad regime to resolve the flow of foreign fighters, a number of foreign fighters based in Syria turned west to Lebanon—a move in part pushed by the Assad regime to alleviate pressure on the government.[73]

This led to the buildup of the jihadi organization Fatah al-Islam in Lebanon in 2006–7, which eventually took over the Palestinian refugee camp Nahr al-Barid. The takeover, exacerbated by Fatah al-Islam's plots, attacks, and petty crime around Lebanon, led to a confrontation with the Lebanese army from May to September 2007. One thwarted attack involving a Tunisian was planned in Syria and facilitated through Homs, a governorate in the west and central part of the country that hugs the Lebanese border, in February 2006.[74] Moreover, while the majority of Fatah al-Islam's members were either Lebanese, Palestinian, or Syrian, there were a number of other foreign fighters, including Tunisians. For instance, ten of the fifty-nine Fatah al-Islam members arrested in late May 2007 were Tunisian, while eleven more Tunisians were arrested in August and September 2007.[75] It is highly likely that these Tunisians had previously been involved with the logistics and facilitation network inside Syria prior to being redirected to Lebanon.

Rebuilding the Foreign Fighter Networks

This interlude did not last forever. While many stopped paying attention to Iraq due to the tactical successes of the tribal awakening and the surge, ISI began to rebuild its enterprise in early to mid-2009, about twelve to eighteen months after it was at its lowest points. Part of this could have been related to ISI preparations for the U.S. withdrawal at the end of June 2009 as part of President George W. Bush's U.S.–Iraq Status of Forces Agreement with Iraqi prime minister Nouri al-Maliki, signed in mid-December 2008. One of the key indications that the ISI was rebuilding its infrastructure was the rising numbers of foreign fighters on a per month basis. By mid-2009 the number of foreign fighters per month had risen to 20 and continued to increase to 30–40 in late 2009 and possibly as high as 250 by late fall 2010.[76]

Unlike networks that had been based out of Damascus and Aleppo, one of the revamped foreign fighter networks began to operate out of Homs under the leadership of a group of Tunisians and Algerians.[77] Another network facilitated individuals through al-Hasakah, a northeastern Syrian governorate, to go to Mosul, Iraq, which ISI used as a base to rebuild its operations after the tribal awakening and surge. Some of the individuals known to have gone through the second route were Tunisians who would be involved in some of the deadliest attacks in 2009, including the April 10 truck bombing at the gates of U.S. forward operating base Marez in Mosul, which left five soldiers dead.[78] The group of Tunisians had left Tunisia in mid-October 2008 and traveled via Libya with the assistance of the aforementioned network in Syria; they arrived in Iraq in March 2009. The group also received assistance from an Iraqi living in Canada named Faruq Khalil Muhammad 'Isa, as well as ISI's new head of foreign fighter operations, Sa'd Uwayyid 'Ubayd Mu'jil al-Shammari (better known as Abu Khalaf).[79] The members of this Tunisian-Iraqi network would be arrested over the next few months by Iraqi forces.[80] Tunisians would also be arrested in Iraq in August 2010 and, more significantly, in December 2010, after a Tunisian and others plotted terrorist attacks in Europe and the United States for that Christmas under direct orders from AQ in Pakistan.[81]

During this time, ISI began republishing martyrdom stories for its fighters. One of them included an interview in late August 2010 with the alleged mother of Usamah (Abu 'Abd al-Rahman al-Tunisi and Abu Sa'd al-Tunisi), known as the "Sniper of Baghdad" for killing U.S. soldiers.[82] According to Lorenzo Vidino, the interview was likely done by Usamah's sister, who became radicalized following her brother's death and was henceforth active on the jihadi forums under the handle Swissgirl99.[83] Before arriving in Iraq in September 2005, his family moved from Tunisia to Switzerland in 2000, where he had a difficult time adjusting to the different culture since his family was very conservative and religious.[84] According to Swiss security officials, he "spent hours online reading jihadist propaganda."[85] He died sometime in 2006 in an attack on the counterterrorism headquarters in the al-Jihad neighborhood of Baghdad, although an exact date is unknown.[86] In the interview, his "mother" discussed her son's piety, his dislike of their move to Europe when he was a teenager, and his decision to join ISI. She concluded the interview by praising Abu Bakr al-Baghdadi, the successor to Abu 'Umar al-Baghdadi, and exclaiming that she "will meet [him], with God's help, in the shade of the Caliphate, in the land of the Caliphate [i.e. Iraq], God willing."[87] Her words in some ways foreshadowed what was to come in the following years.

Plots in Europe, 2005–2010

While the fighting in Iraq became the biggest priority within the jihadi movement, other types of recruitment as well as plot planning by Tunisians continued to occur in Europe during the mid- to late 2000s. Some plots were less significant than others, such as, in 2006: the Swiss-Italian network, attempting to provide false identification and arms to AQ and Operation Tigris in Barcelona, where one individual was attempting to recruit fighters; and in 2010: Operation Matmata in Rome, with an individual being arrested for membership in the broader network and terrorism incitement in France by the Tunisian Imam Muhammad Hammami, calling for violence against Jews and women.[88]

The largest Tunisian recruitment network in Europe during this period was based out of the Bologna region in Italy and operated from the Faenza Mosque, about thirty miles southeast of the city. Faenza is where the cell's leader, Khalil Jarraya (the Colonel), lived. Jarraya had previously been a member of the GIA (along with his brother Munir, who had been arrested in Bologna in 1998) and fought in the Bosnian war via Saydani's Bologna network in the 1990s.[89] This illustrates again the continuity between past networks and the importance of foreign fighting experience and returnees' ability to recruit easier. The main objective of Jarraya was to provide logistics for potential fighters in Iraq. The cell was successful in getting four Tunisians recruits who wanted to fight abroad. Unfortunately for them, though, they were arrested before they could make it to the battlefield and so was Jarraya, on August 9, 2008.[90]

Beyond this network, the other plots during this period were all attempted attacks in various parts of Europe. For example, a group of Tunisians were arrested on May 18, 2005, in a second attempt at bombing the Cremona Cathedral.[91] This network was a legacy of the original Cremona recruitment and plot network from 2002 to 2003 run by Ansar al-Islam. Similar to other prior networks in Italy, this one was also involved in procuring falsified documents and sending money for potential foreign fighters to Iraq.[92]

Another potential attack, which was closer to actualization than the Cremona Cathedral plot, was the Sauerland plot in Germany, which was led by Fritz Gelowicz, who converted to Islam in his teenage years, and was broken up in early September 2007.[93] The main actors in the plot were German Christian converts to Islam and Turks who went to Waziristan, Pakistan, in March 2006 to train with the Islamic Jihad Union, an AQ-aligned splinter group from the Islamic Movement of Uzbekistan.[94] The leaders of the Islamic Jihad Union convinced the four German and Turkish foreign fighters to whom it provided training to return home and conduct an attack targeting American military installations and American citizens in Germany.[95] The four of them would return between September 2006 and February 2007. To avoid detection in the procurement of military detonators, the network recruited a fifteen-year-old Tunisian German named 'Ala al-Din Ta'ib, allegedly through his jihadi-connected brother-in-law.[96] The individual responsible for this idea as well as the one who provided Ta'ib with twenty-six military detonators that were hidden in the soles of shoes was Mevlüt Kar, who has a long history within the jihadi movement. Kar is a well-connected logistician and facilitator based in Turkey who provided support to the Chechen jihad recruitment networks. He first helped funnel Turkish and German foreign fighters to Chechnya in the 1990s and later to Waziristan in the mid-2000s. In the years between that Kar worked in the same capacity for al-Zarqawi in his Turkish network, even connecting Sakka to the German scene, which led to the German "Tawhid" cell mentioned earlier in this chapter.[97] This showcases again the continuity and evolution in how jihadi networks have worked and changed over time. Ta'ib would return to Germany and give Gelowicz the detonators, although they would all be arrested prior to the attack being actualized.[98]

The final two attack plots were against targets related to the controversial issue of cartoons portraying the Muslim prophet Muhammad in newspapers and magazines that were published in the mid-2000s. In particular, these two attack plots were connected with the Danish newspaper *Jyllands-Posten*'s twelve editorial cartoons it published on September 30, 2005. The most controversial of them was drawn by the Danish cartoonist Kurt Westergaard, who depicted Muhammad wearing a bomb in his turban. The first plot, planned by the Tunisian Slim Shafra, was to assassinate Westergaard; it was to be carried out by the Tunisian Karim Sørensen and a Moroccan. The three of them would be arrested in Aarhus, Denmark, on February 12 for the conspiracy, although they would later be released without charge after eight months.[99] The second plot related to blowback from the cartoons and was led by the Tunisian Swede Munir Bin Dhahri (Shujah). Dhahri, along with another Tunisian Swede, Sahbi Zaluti (aka Sahbi al-Tunisi and Irhabi 9/11), went to Pakistan in November 2008 where they gained training in Miran Shah and came into contact with Ilyas Kashmiri and David Coleman Headley, both senior AQ operatives.[100] Headley began casing the *Jyllands-Posten*'s office in 2008 to attack it directly in a similar manner to the Mumbai attacks, including hostage takings and executions via throat slitting, which he had played a role in as well. Although Headley along with his associate in Chicago, Tahawur Rana, were arrested in October 2009, the two Tunisians continued to work on the plot until they returned to Sweden in early December 2010.[101] In the three weeks leading up to the attack, Dhahri called a number in Pakistan eighty-eight times, which provided local security the ability to intercept the communications, which led to the arrest of both men along with a Lebanese Swede involved in the plots in Herlev and Stockholm on

December 29, 2010, right before they were going to Copenhagen to conduct the operation.[102]

Other Jihads Post-9/11: Afghanistan, Pakistan, Somalia, and Yemen, 2002–2010

Although the Iraq jihad took up much of the bandwidth following the 9/11 attacks, Tunisians also continued to be involved in other theaters of jihad, though on a much smaller scale. One individual who took on importance that became a foreign fighter in Afghanistan was Muʿaz al-Din al-Gharsalawi (Muʿaz al-Qayrawani, Haydar al-Khurasani, and Abu Muʿaz al-Tunisi). Prior to arriving in Afghanistan in late 2007, al-Gharsalawi married Malikah al-Arud (the widow of one of the Tunisians that assassinated Ahmad Shah Masʿud), and they were both involved in administering the French jihadi forums (Minbar-SoS and Ansar al-Haqq) while based in Switzerland.[103] The forums were magnets for potential recruitment of individuals to fight in Afghanistan. As a result, al-Gharsalawi would be arrested in February 2005 but released on bail, and then both of them decided to move to Brussels (where al-Arud previously lived) in 2007 while the court case and then appeal process went through the system.[104] Eventually he would be sentenced but only spent three weeks in prison and then escaped to Afghanistan.[105]

Although al-Arud did not join him in Afghanistan, both of them continued their activities, with her helping recruit individuals in Brussels to go fight in Afghanistan while al-Gharsalawi would connect them to training camps he ran in Miran Shah. Although there is no definitive evidence, it could also suggest his involvement in the second cartoon plot, mentioned above, since they were trained in that area as well. Al-Gharsalawi would also fight American forces in Afghanistan.[106] In December 2007 al-Arud was arrested but later faced no charge for lack of evidence for an alleged plot to break the Tunisian Nizar al-Trabilsi (Abu Qaʿqaʿa) out of prison.[107] Trabilsi had previously been involved in Tariq Marufi's network in Brussels, then joined up with the Tunisian Combatant Group training camps in Afghanistan in the summer of 2000 and would allegedly later be involved in the U.S. Embassy in Paris and Kleine Brogel plots in 2001, which he would be arrested for on September 13, 2001.[108] After al-Arud was let off for the prison break plot, al-Arud and al-Gharsalawi would continue their activities, which would come to a head again a year later when she, along with fourteen other suspects, including three Belgians who had just returned from al-Gharsalawi's training camps in the Afghanistan-Pakistan region, were allegedly planning an attack on the European Union summit meetings that were being held in mid-December 2008 in Brussels.[109] Unlike in the past, there was no escaping, and al-Arud would be convicted in May 2010 to eight years in prison.[110]

This did not end the jihad for al-Gharsalawi, however, who would continue to operate in the Afghanistan-Pakistan region until he was killed in a drone strike in mid-October 2012.[111] He would come to more notoriety for not only his involvement in the kidnapping of two Swiss citizens in Balochistan alongside the Tehrik-i-Taliban Pakistan in 2011 but, more importantly, for helping train and plan the March 2012 shootings by Muhammad Merah (Yusuf al-Faransi) in Toulouse and Montauban.[112] By 2011 al-Gharsalawi had become the leader of the majority-Kazakh jihadi group Jund al-Khilafah, which is the outfit Merah would join up with to train and the group that would claim responsibility for the attacks in France.[113]

In addition to al-Gharsalawi, there were also other smaller cases of Tunisians going to Afghanistan in the latter half of last decade. For example, the Islamic Jihad Union continued to recruit fighters from Germany, including one Tunisian named Atnan J. from a prayer group in Bonn. Atnan, along with five Turks, left Bonn in March 2009 but was arrested when attempting to crossover into Waziristan in May 2009.[114] Unlike Atnan, another Tunisian, named Abu Harith, did make it to an Islamic Movement of Uzbekistan camp and fought with them in Pakistan. There is nothing known about him beyond the fact that he was announced killed in a video celebrating the Islamic Movement of Uzbekistan's martyrs for the Islamic year 1431 Hijri, which coincides with the Gregorian dates of December 2009–December 2010.[115]

Along with Afghanistan, there is also one known case of Tunisians joining up to fight in Somalia in September 2006 with the Islamic Courts Union, which would later be overshadowed by its youth wing, Harakat al-Shabab al-Mujahidin, after the Ethiopian invasion in late December 2006.[116] According to an account by the jihadi Fadhl Harun, a group of Tunisians were involved in a battle in a forest near Kolbio, Kenya, against Ethiopian forces in the first week of January 2007.[117] During the battle Abu Hafs al-Tunisi was killed, whose real name was 'Umar Faruq Shilindi.[118] The rest of the group would eventually be arrested within days of the fighting, including, allegedly, a Tunisian woman who would later give birth in an Ethiopian prison.[119] Interestingly, Shilindi and one of the arrested Tunisians, Ayub Sfaxi, who is from France, were involved in a plot in 2002 that involved a network in Zarzis, Tunisia, called Kata'ib al-Rasul.[120] They were allegedly going to use a rocket launcher to attack a port security official. This plot led to the arrest and charging of six individuals; Sfaxi and a Tunisian in Sweden, Tahar Gu'amayr, were also charged in absentia. The six individuals would be imprisoned from February 2003 to February 2006, when they were provided amnesty during the commemoration of the fiftieth anniversary of Tunisia's independence.[121]

There was also allegedly a small contingent of Tunisians who went to Yemen, although details are scant. Following the American invasion of Afghanistan, the Yemeni AQ operative Imad 'Abd al-Wahid Ahmad Alwan allegedly helped AQ fighters from Algeria, Egypt, Libya, Morocco, and Tunisia settle in Yemen.[122] Further, in Morten Storm's account of joining al-Qaeda in the Arabian Peninsula and then later becoming a double agent for Western intelligence (which led to the droning of the American al-Qaeda in the Arabian Peninsula ideologue and external operator Anwar al-'Awlaqi), Storm notes that he came across Tunisians within the milieu in Yemen.[123]

Regional Jihad: The GSPC and AQIM

Besides these outside theaters, the most important one, which was reinvigorated due to the Iraq jihad, was the regional jihadi milieu next to Tunisia in North Africa and the Sahel. Beginning in 2005 the GSPC developed contacts with AQI to facilitate training in North Africa so that fighters would be prepared by the time they made it to Iraq.[124] This relationship would also provide the contacts necessary for AQ to bring GSPC into the fold by accepting their *baya* (religious pledge of allegiance) to Bin Ladin and becoming AQIM in January 2007.[125]

This is also gave the GSPC/AQIM a new rolodex of recruits who could be part of its network if they did not end up going to Iraq or if they survived Iraq, returned to the region, and still wanted to be involved in jihadism. This provided the backbone for rebuilding GSPC/AQIM's structures following the GIA's failures in the 1990s. Moreover, the failed Algerian jihad spurred the GSPC/AQIM to expand its recruitment base beyond Algerians to many other North Africans as well as those further south in the Sahel and West Africa.[126] Over time this would have larger consequences as Tunisians began to join up.

Although the GIA had previously attempted to integrate Tunisians into its fold in 1995, after Hasan Hatab created the GSPC in 1998, there were small signs that Tunisia was going to play a larger role in its broader strategy.[127] For example, in May 2000 the GSPC attacked a Tunisian border crossing, killing two Tunisian soldiers.[128] Moreover, Algeria deported a member of the Tunisian Islamic Front, Zayd Bashir, who was attempting to join the GSPC in 2001.[129] Likewise, in 2002 Algeria arrested four Tunisian GSPC logistics experts.[130]

This integration became more formalized after Nabil Sahrawi took over the GSPC in September 2003 and brought on a number of Libyan and Tunisian returnees from Afghanistan.[131] A Tunisian named Munir al-Tunisi became a member of the GSPC's *shura* council because he fought in the original Afghan jihad, before being killed in June 2004.[132] Likewise, Abu Ahmad al-Tunisi was the deputy to Yahya Jawadi (Yahya Abu 'Ammar), AQIM's leader of the Sahara-Sahel region based in northern Mali.[133] In addition, after the GSPC became AQIM, it restructured its allocation of resources, which had previously been divided across nine zones only in Algeria. The group decided to break its operations into four areas: central (Algeria), east (Tunisia), south (the Sahel), and west (Mauritania). The new division illustrated the importance that Tunisia and Tunisian members would play after 2007.[134]

The Failed Creation of Jund Asad Bin al-Furat

These changes could explain why a multiweek, low-level insurgency broke out from December 2006 to mid-January 2007 in the mountains of eastern Tunisia.[135] It is possible that AQIM was showing off its new place in the AQ family and attempting to prove its ability to conduct larger-scale operations outside Algeria. The individuals responsible for the attacks were dubbed the Sulayman Group by the Tunisian government since many of the recruits were from the small town of Sulayman, also in the east.[136] At the time Tunisian security services projected confidence; however, the story from the inside was different. According to a former senior-level Tunisian official close to Bin 'Ali, there was a major panic about the cell. There was a fundamental lack of understanding about jihadism, the number of people involved in Tunisia, and the identities of those actually plotting attacks.[137] Part of this panic related to government officials' views that it was a homegrown threat rather than a regional or international issue.

The ringleader of this cell was Shaykh Lassad Sassi (also known as Abu Hashim, Muni 'Ali and Salim Sadiq) who had previously been a member of the Tunisian Islamic Front and the Tunisian Milan network as well as a foreign fighter in Bosnia.[138] Sassi escaped Milan in May 2001 and traveled to Algeria to join the GSPC. Sassi aimed to set up an armed group in Tunisia called Jund Asad Bin al-Furat (JABF), named after the Tunisian scholar and fighter who led a Muslim army against Sicily in 827 CE.[139] In some ways, this was a test run for AQIM's post-Tunisian uprising creation of Katibat 'Uqbah Bin Nafi, which continues to fight a low-level insurgency against the Tunisian state to this day, discussed in chapters 7 and 10. Personal networks, particularly those that targeted individuals who had been interested in fighting in Iraq, were one of the most powerful recruiting tools for JABF.[140]

JABF set up bases in Grombalia, Ain Tebournouk, and, later, Jabal Ressas to begin military training. The recruits' lack of experience as well as Sassi's poor situational awareness and operational security tipped the Tunisian government off to the group's activities and accelerated JABF's plans, which in turn launched the group into a conflict for which it was not prepared. From late December 2006 to mid-January 2007, JABF fought Tunisian security forces. Tunisian officials believed that, in addition to setting up a base inside Tunisia, JABF was also preparing attacks in Tunis against the American, British, and Italian embassies.[141] Eleven of its twenty-four members, including Sassi, were killed.[142] Another thirty individuals associated with the cell were arrested.[143] Two of them were executed while the others were sentenced to either life imprisonment or terms ranging from five to thirty years in prison.[144]

Among them were some figures who would become more prominent after the Tunisian revolution with AST. For example, Muhammad Bakhti became a senior leader in AST, especially regarding its cultural program and *hisba* activities, which are explored in greater detail in chapters 4 and 7. He also took part in the attack on the U.S. Embassy in Tunis in September 2012. Another prominent AST leader who was a part of JABF was Khalifah Qarawi, who worked as a blacksmith before joining JABF. He later became a religious leader within AST, having conducted lectures, events, and training sessions in Gafsa, Naftah, Sidi Bouzid, and Sousse.[145] He was also briefly arrested for a week in early March 2013.[146] Similarly, Wanas al-Faqih also joined JABF and would become a senior ideologue within AST as well as later joining up with AQIM in Niger and being designated as a terrorist by the U.S. government in January 2018.[147]

Tunisian Activity with the GSPC/AQIM

Throughout the decade prior to the 2011 Tunisian uprising, Tunisians continued their involvement with the GSPC/AQIM: some were arrested attempting to join it while others successfully joined and participated in insurgent attacks in the region or fought in Iraq. Those who did not die would be deported or extradited back to Tunisia and end up in the prison system, which facilitated new connections between various cells and networks that operated outside Tunisia. For example, several individuals were arrested or killed trying to join the GSPC/AQIM or participate in associated weapons networks:

- November 2001: Two Tunisians were killed by Algerian security forces in the Zbarbar Mountains near Bouira, 75 miles southeast of Algiers.[148]
- November 2002: Tunisian security forces seized 440 pounds of explosives and ammunition and arrested five Tunisians in the Kasserine region.[149]
- March 2005: Six Tunisians were arrested in Annaba, Algeria, 335 miles east of Algiers, for attempting to join the GSPC. One of them had previously trained in the Meftah Mountains, 20 miles southeast of Algiers. The Tunisian

government believed that they were training to conduct an attack against Western targets in Tunisia.[150]

- April 2005: Seven Tunisians were arrested inside of Algeria and sent back to Tunisia, where they would eventually be convicted and sentenced to ten years in prison in March 2007.[151]
- April 25, 2005: Four Tunisians were arrested attempting to meet up with the GSPC.[152]
- May 2005: A Tunisian, Zayd Ghudhbani, was arrested for trying to join the GSPC.[153]
- August 2005: Five Tunisians were arrested in Ain Barbar, 345 miles east of Algiers, after doing military training with the GSPC. They were on their way to link up with the GSPC network active in the Edough Mountains, 18 miles southeast of Ain Barbar.[154]
- January 24, 2007: Eight Tunisians from Bizerte, 45 miles north of Tunis, were convicted by a Tunisian court for attempting to travel to join up with the GSPC.[155]
- February 11, 2007: Two Tunisians were arrested along with a larger AQIM weapons-smuggling network in Constantine, 250 miles southeast of Algiers. The police raid yielded 165 shotguns, 995 cartridges, and 30 .300 sniper rifles.[156]
- January 9, 2010: A Tunisian was arrested in Zouerate, Mauritania, 475 miles northeast of Nouakchott, for being a member of AQIM.[157]

Tunisians in the GSPC/AQIM's Iraq Jihad Network

Many of the Tunisians who made it to Algeria and succeeded in joining the GSPC/AQIM were most interested in training to fight in Iraq. In part, the GSPC/AQIM role as a conduit for AQI/MSM/ISI proved a shrewd way for the group to remain relevant and gain new recruits, fighters, and adherents, especially if they survived the Iraq experience or stayed in North Africa with the GSPC/AQIM. One of the key conduits and logisticians for this effort was an Algerian named Abu al-Hammam, who had been based in Syria since 2003.[158] He provided support to those who trained with GSPC/AQIM in Algeria and transited through Syria to get to Iraq. He was also tasked with recruiting Tunisians, a number of whom would be caught before making it to Syria and Iraq.

For example, the Tunisian government charged Hisham Issadi for being a member of the GSPC and attempting to fight in Iraq in October 2006. He had been previously imprisoned for three years for the same crime, although he had been released in February 2006 during the amnesty marking the fiftieth anniversary of Tunisia's founding. Moreover, on February 18, 2005, seven Tunisians were charged by the Tunisian government for attempting to train with the GSPC to fight in Iraq.¹⁵⁹ And in April 2007 five Tunisians were convicted on charges of training with AQIM and attempting to fight in Iraq. One of them was Muhammad Munsif Baghdadi, who was involved in not only raising money to send people to Iraq with AQIM but also training to use explosives for the fight in Iraq.¹⁶⁰ Lastly, in May 2007 Algerian security forces discovered an AQIM training camp in El Oued, 390 miles southeast of Algiers and 55 miles west of the Tunisian border. In the three years prior to that, GSPC/AQIM had recruited at least sixty fighters from various nationalities, including Tunisians, to train at that camp for suicide missions in Iraq. They even recorded martyrdom wills.¹⁶¹

Tunisians Involved in GSPC/AQIM Attacks

In addition to training to fight in Iraq, several Tunisians were also involved in attacks or killed while fighting against Algerian or Tunisian security forces. For instance, on October 25 and October 28 in 2001, Tunisian members of the GSPC conducted two attacks against Tunisian border security from the town of Oum Ali, Algeria, just across the Tunisian border.¹⁶² These attacks in particular are an important sign that much of the current militant activity in the Kasserine region on the Tunisian-Algerian border is not necessarily a new trend.

Three Tunisians, along with two Libyans and a Moroccan, were also killed in a security fight with Algerian forces at Bir El-Ater Mountain, 390 miles southeast of Algiers and 16 miles west of the Tunisian border, on August 1, 2007.¹⁶³ In addition, AQIM took responsibility for the kidnapping of two Austrian tourists in southern Tunisia in February 2008. This is the only known time that AQIM has kidnapped Westerners in Tunisian territory; most such kidnappings have occurred in Mali, Mauritania, and Niger.¹⁶⁴

In terms of larger-scale attacks, Tunisians played a role in the two bombings that took place in Algiers on April 11, 2007. Unlike many of the other activities noted earlier, in this case there was more of a support role from abroad. The brothers Zuhayr Riyabi (Amin) and Zayd Riyabi (Tariq), who were part of the Tunisian Milan network, helped finance the attacks, which targeted the prime minister's office and a police station.¹⁶⁵ It left twenty-three people dead.¹⁶⁶ The two brothers came into contact with the Milan network after illegally entering Italy from Tunisia in 1996 through the Islamic Cultural Institute (previously run by Shaban and, later, Sassi—who would later lead the JABF network mentioned above). The brothers, in addition to planning—and later abandoning—two attacks (at a NATO facility in Mondragone, Italy, in 1997 and the Milan train station during Christmas 2000), went to Afghanistan in 1998 to train at AQ's al-Faruq training camp for seven months with another Tunisian, Lahzar Bin Muhammad Tlili ('Abd al-Nasir).¹⁶⁷

Another case that highlights the adaptive nature of individuals within these networks is a failed plot planned by the GSPC and led by the Tunisian Muhammad Bin al-Hadi Masahil. In 2001, Masahil came into contact with radical individuals at a mosque in Segrate, Italy, involved with the Islamic Cultural Institute in Milan.[168] Masahil was introduced to the jihadi circles in the infamous Milan milieu through 'Ali al-Dahawi. He would later join up with AQI in June 2005 and participate in the logistics and facilitation network in Damascus, Syria.[169] Masahil would then return to Italy and travel to Morocco to recruit more individuals to fight in Iraq. Because of his persuasiveness, leaders in the GSPC wanted to redirect his activities to plot an attack inside Italy. Through prior contacts he made in Paris, Masahil was put in touch with the Algerian Abu Hamzah, the GSPC coordinator with AQ.

When Masahil arrived in Algeria from Morocco in January 2006, Abu Hamzah told him that the plot had stemmed from a directive from Bin Ladin.[170] The plan was to attack the Milan Metro and hit the Basilica of San Petronio in Bologna a few days before the Italian elections on April 9–10. The aim was similar to the result in Spain after the Madrid train bombings: the prevention of President Silvio Berlusconi's reelection so that Italy would withdraw its troops from Iraq.[171] Abu Hamzah requested that Masahil recruit someone in Italy with European nationality to travel to Pakistan and receive more concrete instructions from Ayman al-Zawahiri.[172] Before Masahil was able to enact his plans, he and other members of his cell were arrested in Morocco in March 2006.[173] According to the Moroccan prosecution, which sentenced Masahil to fifteen years in prison on March 2, 2007, his cell was also allegedly planning an attack on the U.S. Embassy in Rabat as well as attacks on the Paris Metro, Orly Airport, the French intelligence agency DGSE, and Milan's police headquarters.[174]

While these plots failed, the last known attack involving a Tunisian prior to the fall of Bin 'Ali on January 14, 2011, occurred a week prior in Bamako, Mali. The attack was ominous, considering that it happened during the height of the revolutionary street protests. On January 6, 2011, the Tunisian Bashir Sinun (Abu Dujanah al-Tunisi), originally from Tataouine in southern Tunisia and a member of AQIM, threw an explosive grenade at a French Embassy building in Mali, injuring two people.[175] Prior to the attack, Sinun's journey to Mali illustrates the changing nature of the jihadi movement: one characterized by online radicalization and the more transnational nature of AQIM in general. Five years earlier in 2006, at the age of twenty, Sinun began downloading, tracking, and watching videos of the global jihadi movement online, which led the Tunisian police to check in on him in 2008.[176] This encounter led Sinun to flee the country and to study at four different religious schools in Mauritania, where he would come into contact with an AQIM recruiter at the end of 2009 who said he could connect Sinun to the Malian jihad as an alternative to Sinun's desire to go to Iraq.[177] After showing interest, the AQIM recruiter helped facilitate Sinun's movement to Dakar, Senegal, and then provided details on how to connect with Abu Ishaq al-Shinqiti, a Mauritanian based in Mali with AQIM and who had been exchanged in April 2009 for Canadian UN diplomats Robert Fowler and Louis Guay.[178] In June 2010 Sinun finally took a bus from Dakar to Bamako, Mali, and another one from there to connect with AQIM in Gao. After proving himself and conducting military training, Sinun took part in AQIM's August 2010 attack on a Mauritanian military barracks in Nema in the southeast of the country.[179] By late December 2010, however, leaders in AQIM turned against Sinun due to their paranoia of him being a possible spy after he repeatedly connected their computers to the internet without permission and after the individual who originally recruited him in Mauritania was arrested.[180] Therefore, Sinun fled, but he also sought to redeem himself and possibly prove his legitimacy, deciding to conduct the grenade attack against the French Embassy, for which AQIM never took credit.[181] In the aftermath of the attack, Sinun was arrested by Malian authorities and sentenced to death in early December 2011.[182] With the intercession of Tunisia's president at the time, Munsif Marzuqi, he pleaded for Sinun's extradition instead, to which Mali agreed, although the current whereabouts of Sinun after he returned in January 2012 are unknown.[183]

In some ways this was a harbinger of AQIM's push to the south, especially in Mali, in the coming years. It also highlights the expanding scope of Tunisian involvement within the jihadi movement. Consequently, it should have been a sign of the possible influence that jihadis would garner within Tunisia only months later. Therefore, on the eve of Bin 'Ali's overthrow, Tunisian jihadis were well placed to take advantage of the situation. As noted earlier, many Tunisian jihadis were extradited or deported back to Tunisia after being arrested in Syria or Algeria for involvement in foreign fighting or training with JTWJ/AQI/MSM/ISI and the GSPC/AQIM. Many of the Tunisians who survived Iraq would become the backbone of AST's secret military wing after the uprisings.[184] Likewise, two of Tunisia's Guantánamo detainees, 'Abd Allah Bin 'Umar and Lufti Bin Sway Lagha, were transferred back to Tunisia and placed in prison on June 17, 2007.[185] More significantly, in the decade prior to the Tunisian uprising, Turkey and many European states extradited or deported a number of hardened jihadis back to Tunisia. Some of these figures included Abu 'Iyadh (the co-founder of the Tunisian Combatant Group and eventual leader of AST); members of Ansar al-Islam, GIA, and GSPC cells in Italy (including Sami Isid Bin Khamis and Mahdi Kamun, who would become leaders in AST); and individuals involved in the first and second Cremona Cathedral bomb plot, the EU Parliament plot, and the Westergaard assassination plot.[186]

As a result of these deportations, extraditions, and local arrests, several new connections were made between 2003 and 2010 across generations of jihadis as well as between those who had experiences abroad and those who were homegrown. Moreover, unlike in Egypt, Libya, or Morocco, there were no ideological revisions within the Tunisian jihadi movement in prison during this time. Abu 'Iyadh would describe this as "a merit for the jihadi current in Tunisia," which allowed it to remain true to its ideology.[187] This cocktail of individuals would provide the base for the creation of AST after the uprising. It also highlights how ripe Tunisia was for the rise of a homegrown movement, especially after the February 19, 2011, general amnesty that released 8,700 prisoners, including 3,000 who had been convicted under the controversial 2003 counterterrorism law.[188]

* * *

From the anti-Soviet Afghan jihad to a terrorist attack in Mali, Tunisians had been involved with the jihadi movement for thirty years prior to the Tunisian uprising. They were not mere footnotes either. Tunisians played important roles as foreign fighters in the Afghan, Bosnian, Algerian, and Iraqi jihads. They were also key cogs in a logistics, facilitation, and recruitment network based in Europe, operating mainly out of Milan but also Paris, Brussels, and London. Tunisians also had various leadership and support roles in a variety of large-scale attacks, including the 1998 embassy attacks, the Ahmad Shah Mas'ud assassination, 9/11, the Djerba synagogue bombing, the Casablanca bombings, and the Madrid train bombings, along with many thwarted plots. Some of the individuals involved over this time, such as Abu 'Iyadh, Bin Khamis, Mahdi Kamun, Mu'az al-Fizani, Hasan al-Brik, Bubakr al-Hakim, Tariq al-Harzi, and Muhammad Bakhti, had formative experiences that would prove crucial for the organization and implementation of AST's plans after its founding in May 2011. The number of Tunisian foreign fighters—especially those who went to Iraq and the ones involved with logistics, facilitation, and recruitment—helps explain why there were so many Tunisian foreign fighters that fought in Syria between 2012 and 2019. The growth in the prisoner population over the decade prior to the uprising connected generations of jihadis, including Tunisians who were born or lived abroad, as well as homegrown individuals. Prison networking also provided new opportunities for jihadis to share experiences, lessons learned, and plans for activities after their release.

The opportunity for a golden age of jihadism at home was ripe, but it was not necessarily guaranteed to succeed or proliferate as much as it did. The success of jihadism was in part due to Tunisian governmental decisions between February 2011 and August 2013 that provided the opportunity structures for AST to exploit. This exploitation occurred irrespective of who was in power, from the transitional body to the Constituent Assembly. To better understand Tunisian government actions during this time period, the next chapter explores a variety of decisions and reactions to large-scale public events and shows of force by AST. This exploration allows us to observe the ways in which the government enabled AST to carve out its own space, expand as an organization, and become a national player by the time the government designated it as a terrorist organization in August 2013. Without such space, AST would never have become as relevant or successful in its ability to recruit Tunisians for *dawa* locally or foreign fighting abroad.

CHAPTER 4

SONS OF TUNISIA

In the aftermath of the successful overthrow of Tunisian president Bin 'Ali, a new era began. The public square opened up, civil society flourished, and religious life began to show signs of revival. In addition, a new jihadi group, Ansar al-Sharia in Tunisia (AST), set itself up in an unprecedentedly overt manner. AST played an indirect yet important role in the various discussions and debates that would animate the political process and the writing of Tunisia's constitution. In any other situation, AST would have been considered an illegal organization due to its ideological outlook (openly sympathetic toward al-Qaeda) and medium- to long-term ambitions of establishing an Islamic state. Instead, AST thrived publicly until the Tunisian government designated it as a terrorist organization on August 27, 2013.

Before examining the internal workings of AST in depth, this chapter seeks to unpack the conditions in postrevolutionary Tunisia that allowed AST to thrive. This discussion better contextualizes the strategic calculus that AST took when it was founded. The chapter examines the policies of the transitional government from January to October of 2011 and the al-Nahdah-led government from its election victory in late October 2011 to August 2013, when the government designated AST as a terrorist organization. During these two periods, there are four main reasons for why AST was able to operate freely: (1) the transitional government's lack of scrutiny toward individuals it released from prison in the February 2011 prisoner amnesty; (2) the transitional government's narrow political mandate and lack of public trust; (3) al-Nahdah's view that a "light-touch" approach would hinder radicalization and, over time, incorporate AST into the political system; and (4) al-Nahdah's desire to present itself as the moderate option between what it viewed as an extreme secular left and an extreme salafi right.

To illustrate these conditions, the chapter first explores the outlook and policies of the transitional and al-Nahdah-led governments vis-à-vis jihadis. The second sections examines specific incidents over the two-and-a-half-year period between the postrevolution prisoner amnesty in February 2011 and the designation of AST as a terrorist organization in August 2013. The last section illuminates how these policies played out in practice.

The Original Sin: The Transitional Government's Jihadi Policy

In the aftermath of Bin 'Ali being overthrown, a transitional body was set up to guide Tunisia until it held a Constituent Assembly election, which would elect individuals to draft a new constitution; this ended up taking place in October 2011, ten months later. Although Bin 'Ali was overthrown in mid-January 2011, it was not until February 27 that a final transitional government came to be, with al-Baji Qa'id al-Sibsi's appointment as prime minister.[1] In the intervening time, Muhammad Ghannushi, the prime minister of Tunisia under Bin 'Ali, assumed control. In the five to six weeks between the overthrow of Bin 'Ali and the establishment of the transitional government, street protests continued over a variety of issues. The protests were a check on Ghannushi's power as well as a means to make new political, economic, and social demands. The street—which held true power and inspired fear in government officials—pressured interim authorities to show they were turning the page on the Bin 'Ali regime. As a result, the government yielded to public demands and agreed to the release of all prisoners—a cause célèbre by political organizations, civil society, and human rights activists.

The issue of political prisoners and the 2003 antiterrorism law was important for many civil society activists and political groups that had been affected by Bin 'Ali's authoritarian policies before 2011. As noted in the first chapter, several Tunisian political factions (including al-Nahdah and the Congress for the Republic Party, which would constitute two-thirds of the ruling troika after the Constituent Assembly election) came together to sign the October 18 Collectif in 2005. Some of the complaints included the poor treatment of political prisoners and excessive use of the 2003 antiterrorism law to silence dissent. It demanded the release of those affected by both.[2] Similarly, international and local human rights groups warned against the abusive nature of Bin 'Ali's security architecture and prison system in the years prior to 2011. It is no surprise then that one of the demands after Bin 'Ali's overthrow was the rectification of what many believed was an illegitimate justice and prison system. While there is no question that those arrested for purely political reasons should have been released, the hatred of all aspects of Bin 'Ali's regime blinded activists to the very real threats posed by individuals with histories of jihadi and terrorist activities, as described in the previous two chapters.

This was the original sin of the Tunisian revolution. In the face of these requests, the interim government did not rigorously scrutinize hardened jihadis who had been involved in the foreign fighting and terrorism prior to January 2011. The interim government instead declared a general political amnesty on January 20, 2011, and later decreed a prisoner amnesty on February 18, 2011.[3] Much of this decision making stemmed from the lack of legitimacy and political capital held by the interim government. This would provide jihadis an opportunity to organize, recruit, and plan for the future without harassment. It would lead to the founding of AST, as many jihadis with past histories within the milieu were once again free. Among this group, "1,200 salafis, including 300 who fought in Afghanistan, Iraq, Yemen, and Somalia, left prison."[4]

Some Tunisians have since argued that the release of jihadis from prison was part of a plan by former regime officials to sow discord and essentially communicate the message, "you want freedom, here is your freedom." These arguments are ex post facto based on later events. And while it is true that the Mu'ammar al-Qadhafi and Bashar al-Assad regimes released jihadis from prisons to survive protest movements and, later, civil wars, there is no evidence to suggest that this happened in Tunisia. In fact, the revolutionary fervor, demands of activists, and the interim government's attempts to move beyond the Bin 'Ali era provides a more robust explanation for the interim government's decision.

This capitulation by the interim government provided the space for released jihadis to regroup. In the six months between AST's founding and the Constituent Assembly elections, AST began building its network and pursuing its political agenda. This included occupying and taking over mosques, protesting for imprisoned Tunisian members of the Islamic State of Iraq to be released from Iraqi prisons, and imposing its conservative moral agenda on society.[5] During this time, however, most Tunisians did not even realize that AST existed or simply looked down on them as medieval "beardos."[6] The only policy that came close to dealing with jihadis from the transitional government involved arresting AQIM-connected individuals attempting to traverse Tunisian territory and smuggle weapons from Algeria to Libya.[7]

From the transitional government's perspective, however, it had far more immediate concerns related to the political transition. On March 3 the interim president, Fu'ad Mibaza'a, announced a transition "road map" for the forthcoming Constituent Assembly elections that were originally supposed to take place on July 24, 2011, but were not held until October 23, 2011. Within this road map, the transitional government called for advice on political and legal reforms, an investigation into human rights violations by security forces during the revolutionary protests, and a corruption investigation into the former regime elite.[8] While these initiatives were suggested in good faith, widespread skepticism of the transitional body left little room for meaningful policymaking. As Sabina Henneberg explains, the transitional government "continuously struggled to convince the Tunisian public that it was a legitimate government. Small, local protests, sits-ins and strikes reflected a widespread notion that the decision makers were ignoring the people's demands."[9]

As a result, the transitional government ended up focusing primarily on preparations for the forthcoming elections and neglected other issues.[10] During this time AST maintained a relatively low profile and only began to manifest itself in a larger way in the week prior to the elections when it instigated the violent response to Nessma TV's broadcast of the film *Persepolis*. This incident is described in greater detail later in this chapter. Without any credibility or political mandate, the transitional authorities were not able to react to the instigators who had prior histories within the jihadi milieu. This allowed AST to slowly build its capacities, which would become far more apparent once the al-Nahdah-led government came to power in late October 2011.

Overlearning and Underestimating: al-Nahdah's Jihadi Policy

The case of al-Nahdah provides an informative example of a ruling Islamist party's response to jihadis in a democratic setting. Both directly and indirectly, the al-Nahdah-led government's policies vis-à-vis salafis, in general, and AST, in particular, provided a greater opening in which AST could operate and expand its influence. Al-Nahdah's engagement policy with salafis and AST, as well as its attempt to position itself closer to conservative Islamists in the debate over the constitution, allowed AST to exploit the political and social situation. Although al-Nahdah and AST could argue within the same Islamic and Islamist discourse in a way that a secular Arab government—let alone a liberal Western government—can't, AST and their fellow travelers never had any intention of being co-opted by al-Nahdah's so-called light-touch policy. The outcome of al-Nahdah's policies suggests that a softer approach when dealing with jihadis does just as much to curb their growth as indiscriminate crackdowns—such as those during the Bin 'Ali era.

One of the main reasons for al-Nahdah's decision to take a light-touch approach with AST was based on al-Nahdah's own experiences in the 1980s and 1990s. Because al-Nahdah members suffered torture and repression under Bin 'Ali, its leadership believed that a similar approach to AST would isolate and marginalize the jihadi group and lead to even greater radicalization.[11] This led to what Abu 'Iyadh described as an "undeclared truce" between al-Nahdah and

AST.[12] The truce allowed AST to focus on its *dawa* activities as long as its members were not involved in violence. (Nevertheless, despite AST's failure to adhere to these conditions, the Tunisian government did not fully respond to violations until AST's designation).

According to Rashid Ghannushi, the head of al-Nahdah, Bin 'Ali's actions against al-Nahdah in the late 1980s and early 1990s were not sustainable policies, as al-Nahdah would assume a leading role in politics after the revolution. If al-Nahdah chose the same policies as Bin 'Ali, Ghannushi argued that "in 10 or 15 years [jihadi-salafis] will be in power."[13] According to Monica Marks, "early on, in 2011 and 2012, as young Salafi jihadis began expressing themselves in the public square, [al-Nahdah's] leaders tended to regard them with a kind of puzzled pity."[14] This is because al-Nahdah believed these youth were robbed of true religious nourishment due to Bourguiba and Bin 'Ali's eradicative religious policies. This in turn led curious youth looking for religious meaning to extremist salafi satellite channels and "Shaykh YouTube" that deprived them of contextual knowledge of "Tunisian Islam." Al-Nahdah felt a responsibility to bring these misguided youth back into mainstream society. Hamadi al-Jabali, the Tunisian prime minister at the time, went so far as to say that they "are sons of Tunisia and they are not from Mars."[15]

Therefore, from al-Nahdah's perspective, it was necessary to give these jihadi youth opportunities for advice, dialogue, and reintegration into the political system. Regarding reintegration, al-Nahdah's government legalized a number of salafi political parties—the largest of which was Jabhat al-Islah—to encourage inclusion and show that representation and power could be achieved through non-violent democratic processes.[16] While this approach made sense in theory, most salafis in Tunisia were jihadi-salafis, not purist or political salafis.[17] Furthermore, according to jihadi-salafi ideology, democracy is considered a separate religion from Islam since humans legislate, which contravenes the sovereignty of God.

In the run-up to the October 2011 Constituent Assembly elections, AST posted on its official Facebook page a stern warning to Islamists participating in the election, declaring that they would regret their actions on the Day of Resurrection. In another statement it warned that "these elections are against the sharia because it does not take into account God and the sharia is not the source of the laws therefore participating in these elections is haram."[18] It also posted the fatwa of Abu al-Mundhir al-Shinqiti, an influential Mauritanian jihadi ideologue, against al-Nahdah, which characterized the party's program as a violation of *tawhid* (unicity of god). The fatwa also described Ghannushi and his "ilk" as heretics and declared that al-Nahdah's positions on jihad, *dhimmis* (protected peoples, e.g., Christians and Jews), *kuffar* (infidels), women, and music all "pollute" Islam.[19]

These warning signs ahead of al-Nahdah's rise to power did not impede al-Nahdah's light-touch approach. Despite AST's calls for an alternative governmental model that posed an existential threat to the very system al-Nahdah inherited, al-Nahdah's leaders believed such individuals could be moderated: "most who speak in extreme tones just want a place in the system; if they get it, they will moderate their views."[20] According to Ghannushi, AST "reminded him of his youth and that Tunisians will make them change too just like they had changed al-Nahdah."[21] Publicly, al-Nahdah sought to accommodate AST by promoting the message that they were all the same and wanted the same thing in the end. For example, in late March 2012 Ghannushi announced that he himself was a salafi, insofar as the term referred to a Muslim who believed that one should return to Islam as founded in the Qur'an and the Sunnah.[22] Furthermore, a few months later, in late July 2012, Ghannushi attempted to appeal to the salafi youth by stating how they reminded him of his own youthful activism and zeal in the 1970s.[23] Many within AST would view these actions as patronizing.[24]

Privately, Ghannushi struck an even more conciliatory tone, encouraging their activism but attempting to steer them toward what he perceived to be more fruitful ambitions so they would avoid mistakes like those of other Islamists who had tried to take power. Ghannushi explained that moving too quickly would "spook" opponents in a way similar to what had happened in Tunisia in 1989 and Algeria in 1991.[25] Furthermore, according to one of the founding members of AST, after the revolution he and other members of AST personally attended two meetings at Ghannushi's home in El-Menzah, just north of Tunis.[26] It is possible that the leaked video of Ghannushi advising "salafis" in October 2012 was from one of these encounters. In one part of the video, the al-Nahdah leader warns, "the Army is in their [the secularists] hands. We cannot guarantee the police and the army."[27] Ghannushi's words suggest that while al-Nahdah pushed an Islamist agenda through the political process, AST should attempt to infiltrate the security services. Of course, while these meetings are difficult to completely understand without having the full context of the entire conversation, it illustrates al-Nahdah's perception of AST as a useful asset. This type of atmosphere provided AST with an opportunity to pursue its agenda.

AST was especially useful to al-Nahdah in the various mainstream debates about the nature and drafting of the constitution, especially on issues pertaining to religion. The rocky start to al-Nahdah's transition is exemplified by al-Jabali's statement: "My brothers, you are at a historic moment . . . in a new cycle of civilization, God willing. . . . We are in sixth caliphate, God willing."[28] While this statement was a gaffe, it signified al-Nahdah's naïveté about balancing its former status as a social movement with the responsibilities of a government in power. This balancing act would prove difficult.

There are several reasons why al-Nahdah allowed groups like AST to operate and flourish. According to the International Crisis Group, there was a "discrepancy" between the leadership's more pragmatic approach and its more activist base's yearning for greater religiosity after the era of suppression under Bourguiba and Bin 'Ali.[29] Therefore, it was necessary to allow jihadi-salafis to express themselves to alleviate pressure on the party. It was also a way to convince the secular-left opposition that, without al-Nahdah, religious extremism would flourish. Consequently, the secular left had to meet al-Nahdah halfway on religious issues to cut any potential gains by jihadi-salafis if religious issues were not decided within a democratic framework. This, Erik Churchill argues, allowed al-Nahdah to move the debate further to the right.[30] For instance, Habib al-Luz, an al-Nahdah preacher from Sfax who took part in the salafi dialogue, called for a law against blasphemy to avoid so-called provocations by secular-left intellectuals and artists. This, he argued, would deter extremism: "if you want to see more al-Qaeda supporters in Tunisia, then be flexible on blasphemy."[31]

Ultimately, al-Nahdah would be defeated on this issue and others—including using sharia as a source of law in the constitution, defining the status of women as different from men, and creating a blasphemy provision. In part, these failures occurred because al-Nahdah only maintained a plurality—rather than a majority—of the vote in the Constituent Assembly. More importantly, one of the main reasons for its defeat was AST's low-level public violence and shows of strength, which pushed the secular-left parties to block the passage of such measures due to fears that al-Nahdah was slowly transforming Tunisia into a conservative Islamic state.

These fears were not unfounded, especially since much of the violence that began after al-Nahdah took power was directed at secular-left intellectuals and artists. The International Crisis Group has even noted that "the violence increased and diversified after the new al-Nahdah-dominated government took office in December 2011."[32] Two interrelated issues allowed this violence to fester. The first is that many al-Nahdah leaders believed that the violence was perpetrated by former regime members attempting to destabilize the country.[33] This suspicion would deflect attention from the actual jihadi-salafi violence. The second issue is that certain al-Nahdah officials thought "it [was] useful to encourage salafis who commit minor acts of violence [so as] to deal with institutions legally."[34] Therefore, AST violence would either be brushed under the rug or viewed as an opportunity to initiate dialogue with salafis in AST. This line of thinking illustrates the permissive environment in which AST operated, largely as a result of al-Nahdah members' conciliatory attitudes toward the group. AST aimed to exploit this naïveté over the duration of al-Nahdah's time in power.

Al-Nahdah's views and actions toward AST spurred many on the secular left to criticize the double standard on which the judicial system and security services operated. In particular, officials responded more tolerantly to violent acts committed by jihadi-salafis than to alleged "provocations" by intellectuals and artists. Marks has argued that al-Nahdah's "opponents are right to criticize the government for its hypocrisy in pursuing highly publicized show trials against artists and media activists while hesitating to charge and prosecute those responsible for the recent violence."[35] Part of this also stemmed from al-Nahdah's political posturing for the next election. Arguing that extremism existed on both the secular left and the salafi right, the party presented itself as a moderate guarantor of Tunisian stability. Al-Nahdah was thus "the only political force that can both preserve Tunisia's sacred symbols and traditions, while also bringing law and order to the country."[36] This, in part, could explain why the judiciary and security services under al-Nahdah's control acted more forcefully against secular-left activists than the salafis associated with AST. The party likely felt it could personally deal with the jihadi-salafis while the system itself could deal with the secularists.

In many ways al-Nahdah viewed the secularists as a distraction from the change it hoped to enact. Sa'id Firjani, a high-ranking member of al-Nahdah and one of the individuals involved in the coup attempt in the late 1980s, told the Associated Press: "We are dealing with the business of government, we have floods in the north, a sinking economy and these people are talking about the burqa and the hijab. I don't think they are very grown up."[37] Of course, he also criticized the salafis to show the extremism that needed to be addressed on both sides: "There is a war of lifestyles, someone from one group wants to impose their lifestyle on the other group. They each believe in freedom of speech only for themselves."[38] Al-Nahdah felt that its light-touch approach and dialogue could handle the so-called salafi problem, while it associated the secularists with the past regimes of Bourguiba and Bin 'Ali, who had suppressed Islam and helped create the environment that led to the current so-called "salafi menace."

Regarding the double standard in responses to secular-left activists and jihadi-salafis, the judiciary and security forces seemed to act in tandem. In the case of the judiciary, young activists on Facebook, for example, were sentenced to seven years in prison for promoting atheism, while a member of AST who tore down the Tunisian flag and replaced it with AST's black flag received a six-month suspended sentence. Both involved the issue of free speech; however, the latter can be construed as vandalism. Nonetheless, there is a major discrepancy in sentencing.[39] A number of other instances show similar double standards.[40] Likewise, secular protests against violence were called off by the government while AST-planned protests were allowed.[41] Although the police would attack or crack down upon secular protests, they appeared to play a protector role at protests conducted by AST. In a similar vein, al-Nahdah once ordered the closure of an art gallery in La Marsa, a suburb of Tunis, after jihadi-salafis rioted against the allegedly blasphemous artwork while at the same time allowing an illegal sit-in by conservative Islamists to go on for almost three months at the state television station.[42]

Another related issue was the way in which the police and security dealt with jihadi-salafis caught for violent actions. In many cases, individuals were arrested but released only a few days later.[43] This tactic was used to satisfy al-Nahdah's broader engagement strategy. Furthermore, "judges fear punishment by the justice minister if they take action against the salafis; police officers do not completely enjoy the trust of the new Islamist leaders, who for a long time were their victims."[44] As a result, the police and security services felt they lacked legal protection, which led them to not "take pointless risks by confronting the salafis" since the salafis were viewed as having real power in some districts and villages.[45] Human Rights Watch even wrote a letter to Tunisia's Ministry of Interior and Justice discussing the lack of action by the police after multiple violent incidents.[46] This in many ways accounts for the noticeable difference between how the security services and judiciary dealt with the secular left and how it dealt with the jihadi-salafis associated with AST. Moreover, it shows the greater space granted to AST to continue operating more or less without harassment.

Even al-Nahdah's leaders came under fire. In early August 2012 'Abd al-Fatah Muru, a cofounder and leading ideologue in al-Nahdah, was attacked at a "Tolerance in Islam" conference for allegedly insulting the Prophet Muhammad's wife.[47] This provides yet another example of AST's perception of al-Nahdah as equally illegitimate as secular-left political parties, regardless of how the party framed or pursued its Islamic agenda. Furthermore, many within AST did not even view al-Nahdah as truly Islamic.[48] This raises the question of why it took al-Nahdah so long to realize its inability to "turn" an organization whose ultimate aim was the transformation of the system of governance that al-Nahdah led. Most likely, al-Nahdah's poor judgment was rooted in hubris, willful naïveté about AST's project, and sheer incompetence as well as its perception that it could change others' minds.

The seminal moment at which al-Nahdah's government began to shift its perception of AST was the attack on the U.S. Embassy in Tunis on September 14, 2012. According to Tunisian journalist Hédi Yahmed, "the events of the American Embassy ended the phase of "hidden coexistence" between al-Nahdah and the jihadi-salafis."[49] That said, al-Sadiq Shuru, a senior al-Nahdah ideologue, told the journal *Essarih* that AST was innocent and that it had nothing to do with the attack.[50] As Marks notes, while the attack broke the trust between the two movements, it did not lead to a large-scale crackdown just yet, saying that although "the Embassy attacks tested al-Nahdah's patience with jihadi

Salafism, the party remains unwilling to pursue a comprehensive crackdown on the movement and will likely continue its relatively hands-off policy of integration and conciliation."[51] The lack of seriousness resulted in another three-quarters of a year in which AST operated and proselytized openly to gain more recruits.

Not even the assassination of the secular-left leader of the Democratic Patriots' Unified Party, Shukri Bila'id, on February 6, 2013, led to an outright crackdown. According to Tunisian analyst Habib Sayah, "fear of stoking divisions within [al-Nahdah's] party, in addition to exposing the ambiguous relationship between the party and the jihadi faction, has kept al-Jabali and Larayedh [interior minister at the time] from decisive action."[52] What truly altered al-Nahdah's calculus was the political backlash from the secular left in response to the assassination, which threatened al-Nahdah's ability to maintain power. Its very legitimacy was at stake. Al-Jabali decided to resign as prime minister, and in the following months al-Nahdah put far more pressure on AST, especially when the group began to plan its annual conference for May 2013. Unlike earlier, al-Nahdah began to enforce the requirement that AST obtain licenses for its *dawa* activities and annual conference.[53] These legal actions allowed al-Nahdah to exert control over AST and limit its ability to openly operate. In part, these new policies aimed to send a message about the true holders of power and allow al-Nahdah to exercise the levers of decision making in the country. By then AST was becoming a threat to not only the intellectual and artist class on the secular left but also to al-Nahdah's religious legitimacy.

Around the same time AST held its annual conference, then prime minister Ali Larayedh described AST as "an illegal organization, which defies and provokes state authority."[54] He went so far as to note AST's links to "terrorism" for the first time. This was in part because of the growing evidence that AQIM's Tunisian front group, Katibat 'Uqbah Bin Nafi, and some members of AST had begun working together to overtly conduct attacks on the Algerian-Tunisian border in the Jabal Chambi region in late December 2012.[55] Consequently, in light of the assassination of yet another secular-left politician, Muhammad Brahmi—founder and leader of the People's Movement Party—on July 25, 2013, as well as a Katibat 'Uqbah Bin Nafi attack a few days later that left eight Tunisian soldiers brutally murdered, al-Nahdah decided to finally turn on AST and stop its ability to operate. At the end of August 2013 the al-Nahdah-led government legally designated AST as a terrorist organization, preventing its ability to operate openly and ending the conditions that allowed it to grow.[56] Of course, the two-and-a-half-year period during which AST operated more or less without consequence had provided other possible avenues for jihadi-salafis to continue their movement. Members of AST either quit and returned to their regular life, joined Katibat 'Uqbah Bin Nafi to fight the Tunisian government, became foreign fighters in Libya and Syria, or went to prison.

Case Studies

Four case studies help illuminate why AST could operate openly for so long. These cases include the founding event of AST in May 2011; the Nessma TV incident before the October 2011 Constituent Assembly election; the University of Manouba *niqab* protest; and AST's Avenue Bourguiba clock tower show of strength. Since the U.S. Embassy attack and assassination of two leftist politicians in early to mid-2013 have already been discussed, they are not repeated below. The latter two examples show how the conditions for AST became more restrictive and do not necessarily explain why AST was able to conduct its activities without any scrutiny.

The Founding of AST

AST formally began operating as an organization when it established the blog named after its first media outlet, al-Qayrawan Media Foundation, on April 27, 2011. This was two months after the prisoner amnesty.[57] AST would later announce a call for the founding conference that took place in La Soukra, a suburb of Tunis, on May 21, 2011.[58] At the time, the transitional government was preoccupied with planning the Constituent Assembly election that would occur five months later. Therefore, there was almost no publicity, let alone reporting about this event (with the interesting exception of an al-Hurra TV crew, which is a U.S. government-funded Arabic television station). Based on the videos and pictures that AST posted online, a few hundred individuals attended the opening forum.

What is significant about the forum, though, is not the lack of attention paid to it by the transitional government but rather the presence of two attendees. One was al-Sadiq Shuru of al-Nahdah, who was invited as a guest of honor and spoke about similarities between Tunisia's current situation and the Truce of Hudaybiyyah, a ten-year truce between the followers of the Prophet Muhammad and the tribal pagans of Mecca.[59] Another attendee was 'Abd al-Ra'uf al-'Ayadi, a senior leader in the Congress for the Republic Party, one of the parties that would be in the ruling troika coalition with al-Nahdah after the Constituent Assembly elections. While the Congress for the Republic Party is ostensibly a secular-left party, its presence at the forum illustrates its willingness to follow al-Nahdah's lead both before and after the elections. In an interview with the Tunisian radio station Shems FM after a video leaked of his appearance at the inaugural forum, al-'Ayadi said he was not embarrassed about attending but rather "honored by the salafi youth who honored him." He viewed this reverence "as a sign of gratitude."[60]

From the beginning, AST was able to garner support within the political system to operate in society with almost no interference. These relationships provided AST with the necessary conditions to expand its operations, spread its ideas, and recruit new individuals in the months following the conference. AST's support continued to grow in the run-up to the Constituent Assembly election when the next key event exposed AST's growing strength.

Nessma TV Airing *Persepolis*

In the two weeks prior to the Constituent Assembly election, the role of religion in society came to the forefront. On October 7, 2011, the private television station Nessma TV played the movie *Persepolis*, a film about the Islamic revolution in Iran based off French Iranian author Marjane Satrapi's autobiographical graphic novel of the same title. In it, there is a scene depicting God in human form, which to religious Muslims is blasphemous. This sent shock waves through the burgeoning salafi community in Tunisia. Although many Tunisian salafis are opposed to participating in elections, the controversy provided AST and other conservatives a platform to push their ideas publicly and steal the national debate.

After the screening of *Persepolis*, AST's leader, Abu 'Iyadh, condemned Nessma TV's alleged "heretical" and "malicious" campaign against Islam.[61] The situation escalated on October 9, when Tunisian police entered the AST-affiliated al-Kambis Mosque and arrested approximately two hundred individuals as a preemptive measure.[62] Two days later, on October 11, salafis online began to organize demonstrations for Friday, October 14, which they dubbed "Friday: Overthrow of the Nessma TV Station" and "Friday: Day of Rage."[63]

Online salafi activists also photoshopped Nessma TV's logo, adding a Jewish Star of David and changing the color from red to blue to make it appear like the Israeli flag. Their aim was to discredit the channel by accusing it of supposed links to Israel, even though there is no evidence to support such claims. On Friday, October 14, thousands of salafis, aroused after inciteful sermons during prayers, went into the streets to demonstrate against Nessma TV. At the same time, a smaller group of around one hundred went to the home of Nabil Karoui, the owner of Nessma TV, who had apologized earlier in the week for airing the movie. The salafis chanted through the streets the Muslim testament of faith, "there is no God but God; and Muhammad is the messenger of God," as well as *takbir-allahu akbar* (God is the greatest). Although salafis called for peaceful protests on their online fliers, the demonstration quickly turned violent. Activists came to Karoui's house with batons and knives. His wife and two children escaped minutes before their home was looted and partially burned down. According to female salafi participants in these events, "of course we participated, the whole country did. They don't respect the beliefs of the country so we should do something against it."[64] In response to the violence at Karoui's house and the demonstrations in the streets, Tunisian police used tear gas on the salafis to disperse the crowds.

While the transitional government arrested some salafis, and al-Nahdah condemned the actions of AST's followers, the responses did not raise much concern about AST's growing ability to mobilize and potentially destabilize Tunisia. Al-Nahdah even blamed Nessma TV for the provocation—a move that represented an attitude the party would perpetuate once it came to power. Such an attitude also articulated al-Nahdah's perceptions of dual extremisms, even though one side was not committing violence. There were no large-scale consequences for the organization in this case, or in many other cases. In fact, a week after the incident at Karoui's house AST conducted more protests on October 21, this time in front of the Tunisian telecommunications company Tunisiana.[65] Nessma TV, on the other hand, would be found guilty in early May 2012 of blasphemy and disturbing public order.[66] Roxane Farmanfarmaian also believes that al-Nahdah took this approach as a way of outbidding the challenge from the salafis by "invoking Article 121.3 of the Bin 'Ali–era penal code to accuse Nessma's owners of 'undermining public morality'."[67]

AST's ability to mobilize was not lost on online global jihadi activists. Videos and pictures from the salafi "Day of Rage" spread throughout Arabic, English, German, and Indonesian global jihadi forums. The online global jihadi activists viewed some of the Tunisian salafi protesters carrying AST's black flag as a sign that an Islamic revolution was imminent. In many ways the response portended the role Tunisians would play in the years to come in the broader global jihadi movement.

Manouba College Niqab Protest

Only a month and a half after these events, at the end of November 2011, a group of salafis began protesting at the University of Manouba, west of Tunis. While some, such as Marks, argue that the group of female students were only advocating for rights to wear the *niqab* (full face veil) in the classroom and to have single-gender classes, the issue went much deeper than personal rights.[68] In fact, it was a power play by AST, led by one of its senior members, Muhammad Bakhti, to push its conservative moral code on society.

According to Habib Kazdaghli, the dean of the Letters of Arts, Science, and Humanities at the school, Bakhti enrolled as a student in September 2011.[69] Before the revolution Bakhti was involved in the so-called Sulayman Group from December 2006 to January 2007, which led to a multiweek, low-level insurgency between those militants and Tunisian security services. Bakhti would remain in prison until the prisoner amnesty in February 2011. His later involvement in the attack on the U.S. Embassy in Tunis highlights how the lack of action taken against AST's provocations led to the group's empowerment. Bakhti was believed to be close to Abu 'Iyadh prior to his November 2012 death as a result of a hunger strike after being imprisoned for his involvement in the embassy attack.[70]

Kazdaghli noted that, on campus, Bakhti would discuss imposing the *niqab* on women. Furthermore, beginning in October 2011, Bakhti would challenge the faculty, claiming that only God could run things.[71] No doubt, the five to six female students had legitimate grievances of their own, but it became apparent that AST was also pulling the strings behind the scenes. After Kazdaghli refused to accommodate the students' demands, they decided to barricade and hold him hostage in his office and call for outside backup (a repeat of a similar incident that al-Nahdah student members did in the 1980s, as described in the first chapter).[72] This, in turn, led to violence.[73]

After the incident the *niqab* issue became a way for AST to exert influence. In particular, the group facilitated and promoted the creation of a new religious student movement called *thawrat al-talibah* (revolution of the students), which was established in a variety of Tunisian universities after the start of the sit-in at the University of Manouba. In an interview with *al-Shuruq al-Tunisiyyah*, Abu 'Iyadh argued that the *niqab* ban was unjust because even universities in non-Muslim societies, such as Oxford University and the "finest schools" in New York, gave students the freedom to wear the *niqab*.[74]

Many AST members would stay on campus or just outside its gates to guard against negative action against the *niqabi* women.[75] Their behavior also fulfilled the group's second aim: to gain publicity by showing off their piety by praying in front of anyone driving by or on campus. The members of AST were outfitted with their notorious orange kits that displayed the group's name and were also accompanied by members of the group's "Organizing Committee."[76] In early March 2012 this presence eventually led Yasin al-Briguwi, a member of AST, to climb up to the top of the entrance and replace the Tunisian national flag with AST's black flag.

In response to this disrespect toward the national flag, Khawla Rashidi, a female student, jumped up to tear down the black flag. Even though Yasin pushed her over, Rashidi's actions turned her into an instant hero on the secular left.[77] That symbolic action cooled the *niqabi* protest movement and prompted AST to withdraw so as to not expose itself to scrutiny. Interestingly, following Bakhti's death later in the year, the students associated with the demands left the school, suggesting their loyalty to his cause.[78] A few days after the incident, Rashidi would be honored by Tunisia's president, Munsif Marzuqi, for defending the honor of the national flag.[79]

Beyond that recognition, the government was relatively absent in dealing with the issue that simmered for months. And it is questionable whether the situation would have been resolved at all if not for that flag incident. The multimonth controversy illustrated the al-Nahdah-led government's relatively hands-off approach. As Churchill has argued, "the government has said that it will take steps to control violent movements on many occasions, but oftentimes this has felt like lip-service. . . . A conflict at the Manouba university over niqabs has been left to fester for an entire academic year because the government has decided not to intervene—leaving the university to solve the problem."[80]

Further illustrating this point, al-Nahdah's Firjani stated in the midst of the events at Manouba that "Manouba must find a solution to the niqab dispute without infringing in any shape or form on a woman's fundamental right to choose her own clothing." The *niqab* debate and controversy over women wearing skimpy bikinis on Tunisian beaches, Firjani said, "are two sides of the same issue. We live within the dynamics of a fledgling democracy, and we must respect democratic principles."[81] Firjani's statements reflect al-Nahdah's argument about the presence of two extremisms in Tunisia while neglecting to acknowledge the greater destabilizer: the jihadi-salafi movement. While faculty and students protested in front of the Ministry of Higher Education to resolve the situation, Minister Munsif Bin Salim (another individual involved in the 1980s coup plot) deferred responsibility, stating that it was the college's internal affair and refusing to allow police to enter the school to deescalate the situation.[82] He thus flouted Human Rights Watch's call for the "swift intervention of security forces" to end the "disruption of academic life."[83] Furthermore, al-Briguwi was not even arrested until he turned himself into the police a month after the incident, highlighting the government's lack of concern with the issue.[84]

The deferral of responsibility by the government provided another opportunity for AST to fill a vacuum. It also gave AST another chance to gain notoriety through its actions and recruit more individuals. Only a few weeks after the flag incident, AST once again was flexing its muscles on the main street in downtown Tunis at Avenue Bourguiba in support of Islamic law.

Avenue Bourguiba Clock Tower Sharia Show of Strength

On March 25, 2012, AST held a protest at the famous *tour de l'horloge* (clock tower) on Avenue Bourguiba in downtown Tunis in support of sharia. Thousands of its members from all over the country attended. According to an AST member, the protest was sparked by the recent desecration of the infamous al-Fatah salafi mosque in Tunis with a Jewish star spray-painted on it and of two Qur'ans desecrated (one in a toilet and the other with ripped pages) in Ben Gardane, a border town with Libya.[85] The protest was also an indirect way for AST to exert influence over the constitution drafting process, which involved questions of sharia: "[Secularists] should know that we can mobilize hundreds of thousands on the streets if they refuse the application of sharia."[86]

In and of itself, a protest calling for sharia or support of Islam would not necessarily spark controversy in a state that protects free speech. This protest, however, left many Tunisians, especially those on the secular left, questioning the direction the country was going. At the event, a number of individuals, including Abu 'Iyadh, gave speeches, but the image many Tunisians will have seared into their minds is the cover of this book. AST members were scaling the clock tower and waving AST's black flag atop it. The clock tower was originally built to commemorate Bin 'Ali's ascent to power. Of course, many Tunisians have little sympathy for their former deposed president. Nevertheless, the image of AST members symbolically occupying the clock tower with their black flag left many on the secular left wondering where the country might be heading. AST was attempting to show that a new era had begun and that the past secular state was receding. Many even chanted: "The people want a new caliphate."[87]

In addition, AST contravened the permit given by the Ministry of Interior, which stated that their event was limited to the area around the clock tower due to a concurrent event in celebration of the upcoming World Day of Theater happening down the road on Avenue Bourguiba. Although the Tunisian Association for Drama Arts (TADA)—the group organizing the celebration—received its permit ahead of AST, some AST members, inspired by Abu Iyadh's speech, started an altercation with TADA. Members of AST also damaged the organization's equipment, disrupted outdoor performances, and threw eggs, empty bottles, and sharp objects at those celebrating theater.[88] One member explained that TADA had provoked them simply by showing up and celebrating its cause, suggesting that TADA members were part of the broader attack against Islam.[89]

The spectacle of AST's overly aggressive show of force backfired. While al-Nahdah continued its light-touch approach by not subjecting AST to any consequences for the incident with TADA, a few days after the protest al-Nahdah decided to abandon its push for a provision in the draft constitution about sharia being the sole source of legislation in Tunisia.[90] This decision was partly inspired by the severe backlash against the AST rally and the belief among many on the secular left that al-Nahdah's light-touch approach provided cover for AST. Consequently, there was an outpouring of negativity, which al-Nahdah did not ignore, especially considering its lack of a majority in the Constituent Assembly. AST's response also illustrates the differences in approach between al-Nahdah and AST: while the former is willing to negotiate in the hopes of changing policies over the long-term, AST and its youth constituency are interested in making immediate changes.

It is surprising, then, to see al-Nahdah's continued soft approach toward AST since there was no evidence that AST was interested in being co-opted into the system. As Abu 'Iyadh noted only a week prior to the sharia demonstration, "we are not a puppet in the hands of anyone, and we make our decisions with complete independence without interference of any party."[91] Furthermore, three months prior to the clock tower event Abu 'Iyadh choreographed the movement's uptick in violence: "Don't put obstacles in our way and don't provoke us. Now we are controlling our reactions to provocations but we might reach a stage in which [AST] couldn't control the youth, when there are transgressions against the sacred and God."[92] But because of al-Nahdah's lack of seriousness in responding to AST's leader, AST was able to not only perform its *dawa* activities but also carry out increasingly violent acts.[93] It would still take the U.S. Embassy attack and two political assassinations for al-Nahdah to take any serious action against AST and its members. The rise in violence is further explored in chapter 7, which examines how this violence led to AST's downfall and a return to the type of Tunisian jihadi activism practiced prior to the revolution.

* * *

The two-and-a-half-year period during which AST operated openly is an instructive example of what happens when two governments do not take a jihadi group seriously, especially as that group gains more followers and faces no significant repercussions to its illegal actions. A variety of conditions led to this openness and ability for AST to recruit and proselytize in an unprecedented fashion. During the transitional government, the lack of oversight and pressure from below allowed many hardened jihadis with experiences in terrorism to return to the streets. Moreover, the transitional government had little legitimacy and focused mainly on preparing the country for the forthcoming elections.

Following the elections, the al-Nahdah-led government was more engaged than the transitional government on how to deal with AST, but its gamble on a light-touch policy failed. AST was able to capitalize on al-Nahdah's soft approach to further recruit, embed itself within society, and challenge secular-left intellectuals and artists as well as the Islamic legitimacy of al-Nahdah. As a result, while AST was useful for al-Nahdah to situate itself as a moderating force between what it believed was secular extremism on the left and salafi extremism on the right, mounting AST violence and subsequent critiques from the left prompted al-Nahdah to take the issue more seriously. This eventually led to the designation of AST as a terrorist organization at the end of August 2013. The freedoms granted to AST until August 2013 helped bring tens of thousands of Tunisians into the jihadi-salafi milieu. This new generation would be instrumental in providing a new batch of individuals for foreign fighting in Iraq, Libya, Syria, and elsewhere.

The first four chapters in this book provide background on the conditions that allowed AST to implement its strategy following the Tunisian revolution. The next three chapters of this book explore why and how AST decided to apply its *dawa*-first approach to postrevolution Tunisia. It then shows how AST's inability to control its members' violent impulses and the connections it had abroad—both ideologically and for foreign fighter mobilization—led to its ultimate demise.

CHAPTER 5

TUNISIA IS A LAND OF *DAWA*

In the aftermath of the prisoner amnesty following the revolution, Abu 'Iyadh and his followers began to implement a strategy to create an Islamic state in Tunisia. The planning for it stretches back to 2006, when many future AST leaders began strategizing in prison. Although it would later be revealed that AST maintained a military wing, Abu 'Iyadh publicly preached the idea that Tunisia was a land of *dawa*, not jihad:

> We are at this stage of our project that is based on *dawa*, a reconciliation with our religion against the demolition of all that was built by the rule of Bourguiba and the rule of Bin 'Ali in the minds of the people that religion is backward, and adhering to the *sunnah* [Sunni tradition] is backward. Our project is to restore the confidence that sharia is the guarantor of the good life for the people. And our movement at this stage is a prelude to the establishment of an Islamic state, and it is not subject to the limits of Sykes-Picot, God willing.[1]

This open approach was unprecedented within the jihadi-salafi movement. It was the logical conclusion of a systematic, ideological protection by key leaders and ideologues within the broader jihadi-salafi movement. This evolution dates to the mid-2000s, when excessive use of *takfir* contributed to the failures of the Iraq jihad. The main proponents of this protective school of thought were AQ leaders and disciples of the ideologue Abu Muhammad al-Maqdisi. This line of thinking contrasts with that of Abu Mus'ab al-Zarqawi's school (also described as the Jalalabad school in chapters 2 and 3), an antecedent to what eventually became known as the Islamic State today.

Abu 'Iyadh and AST fell within the AQ and al-Maqdisi ideological trend. When asked about his relationship with AQ, Abu 'Iyadh explained that "our relationship with those who share with us the same *manhaj* [methodology] is an obligatory relationship because God says, 'believers are but brothers.' So our brothers, be it in Afghanistan, Somalia, or any spot in the world, are part of us and we are part of them."[2] Therefore, to better understand why AST was able to take advantage of the conditions described in the previous chapter, this chapter seeks to answer why Abu 'Iyadh and AST decided to take a public *dawa*-first approach, which in turn helps explain the rise in jihadism in Tunisia after the revolution.

There are three main motivations behind this strategy: (1) lessons learned from past jihadi experiences; (2) advice provided by jihadi ideologues and leaders in the aftermath of the Arab uprisings; and (3) the particular conditions within Tunisia. The analysis that follows also allows for a definitive account of how to classify AST as a group—namely, whether AST was a new phenomenon within the jihadi movement, a rebranding of AQ, or some type of hybrid.

The following exploration also adds to the growing literature in what Brynjar Lia and Thomas Hegghammer describe as "jihadi strategic studies."[3] The two authors explain that this genre, unlike the usual videos and texts seen from jihadi ideologues and leaders, "contains very little theological exegesis or exhortative propaganda" and takes an "essentially secular-rational academic" approach to the topics it covers. This type of work within the jihadosphere came to prominence after 9/11. Before then, according to Steven Brooke, most strategic debates had "heavy religious references."[4] That said, as Joas Wagemakers has shown, within the religious scholarly establishment of the jihadi movement, al-Maqdisi was also involved in strategic writings but within the framework of protecting specific religious ideals.[5]

In recent years, a number of studies have examined the influences of leftist strategists (including Mao Tse-Tung, Vo Nguyen Giap, Ernesto "Che" Guevara, and Carlos Marighella, among others) and Western strategists (including Carl von Clausewitz, Robert Taber, and John A. Nagl) on the thinking of jihadi strategic writers such as Abu 'Ubayd al-Qurashi, Abu Bakr Najī, and Abu Mus'ab al-Suri.[6] Furthermore, Dima Adamsky has explained how military pressure on AQ after 9/11 and the failures of the Iraq jihad led to the creation of a jihadi operational art.[7] This art involved a set of strategic guidelines established for all members within the jihadi movement to circumvent the need for command and control and to avoid risky communication. In many ways, Ayman al-Zawahiri's "General Guidelines for the Work of a Jihadi," released in mid-September 2013, was a culmination of such a practice for those within the AQ ecosystem.[8]

The latter point about the development of a jihadi operational art—or something akin to a "cloud-based strategic university" for jihadis—is relevant to AST's choice of strategy in the aftermath of the Tunisian revolution. If there is indeed a jihadi operational art, it would suggest that the strategic guidance of ideologues within the broader jihadi movement would be followed and implemented by Abu 'Iyadh and AST. As is seen later in the chapter, this did in fact occur. Before examining the impact of strategic thought on Tunisia's revolution, it is imperative to first look at the contributing factors to the movement's decision to pursue its strategic thinking. This discussion better contextualizes why the movement's members argued for particular policies and decided on its *dawa*-first approach.

Jihadi Strategy: From the Fall of the Taliban to the Founding of AST

This section explores four interrelated processes that occurred within the intellectual sphere of the jihadi movement between 2001 and 2010. The first subsection looks at the theoretical strategic works of key thinkers, such as al-Qurashi, al-Suri, and Naji; the second examines al-Maqdisi's program of protecting the religious aspects of the jihadi movement; the third explores AQ's practitioner perspective on correcting the mistakes of past jihads; and the fourth discusses the prison experience of Abu 'Iyadh and other Tunisian jihadis.

A Theory for Bringing About "the" Islamic State

Little is known about al-Qurashi, other than that he was an influential writer for the jihadi magazine *al-Ansar* from 2002 to 2003. His writings mainly appropriated the ideas of Mao, especially those concerning the three stages of guerrilla warfare. Al-Qurashi used an Islamicized version of Mao's framework to formulate steps to establish an Islamic state: (1) gain trust and support of the population through *dawa* activities and raise questions about the legitimacy of the regime one is fighting; (2) conduct terrorist attacks and insurgent operations against the regime's military forces and infrastructure; and (3) use conventional warfare to conquer cities, overthrow the regime, and gain control of the country.[9] Al-Qurashi then details how to apply these steps within social, economic, ideological, cultural, psychological, and international "dimensions." Although his writings are not necessarily unique, he helped bring attention to ideas that would be beneficial to AQ. According to Michael W. S. Ryan, AQ would use the work of Saudi AQ leader and military theorist 'Abd al-'Aziz al-Muqrin to further refine and professionalize these ideas.[10] By the time al-Muqrin became leader of AQ in Saudi Arabia in May 2003, the group was already in steep decline and therefore unable to fully implement the ideas. Such thinking would become more relevant when AQ recalibrated itself after what it perceived as the disastrous events in Iraq.

Al-Quarashi's first stage highlights the importance of *dawa*. As Abu 'Iyadh noted, *dawa* was just a stepping-stone to the broader project of establishing an Islamic state. As such, while AST did indeed have a *dawa*-first approach, it was only the first tool to be used in a broader toolkit. Abu 'Iyadh even notes that AST was following a multistage approach and taking advantage of the permissive conditions during al-Nahdah's rule: "We will benefit if we become good at managing the different stages. And I say to you that we will benefit from any other government that grants *da'i* [ones who do *dawa*] the freedom to proselytize in this country."[11] Moreover, as AST grew and began having de facto control over some neighborhoods (through its neighborhood committees, as is discussed in chapter 7), one of AST's most prominent members, Bilal al-Shawashi, reappropriated one of Mao's sayings by noting that their strategy of winning would rely upon them acting "like fish [AST members] swimming in the sea [the people]."[12] Al-Shawashi further explained that AST was "willing to learn from any source."[13]

Another relevant strategic writer is Abu Bakr Naji. The name is believed to be a pseudonym for the Egyptian AQ operative Muhammad Khalil al-Hakaymah, who was close with Sayf al-Adl and Abu Mus'ab al-Zarqawi.[14] Naji's importance continues to resonate. His most prominent work, published in 2005, is *The Management of Savagery: The Most Critical Stage Through Which the Islamic Nation Will Pass*. Naji further develops al-Qurashi's ideas. In addition, both Naji and al-Suri created grand strategies and action plans for how to defeat the United States and implement an Islamic state locally.

Since the jihadi movement does not focus on one particular country, Naji's theory argues that a two-tiered system of priority—with specific actions taken at each level—is necessary to maximize victory. The priority states go through the classic three-stage Maoist process, which Naji describes as "the power of vexation and exhaustion," "the administration of savagery," and "the power of establishing the state." The secondary states experience only two stages: "the power of vexation and exhaustion" and the "establishment," which comes from the outside.[15] Most relevant to this discussion is "the administration of savagery," since it involves service provision, in addition to military aspects, which became a hallmark of AST's *dawa* program. Naji explains that the stage of "managing the people's needs with regard to food and medical treatment may advance to [the stage of] being responsible for offering services like education and so forth. And the preservation of security and securing the borders may advance to working to expand the region of savagery."[16]

The motive behind providing services is not only to build up sympathy but also to contrast the governance ability of jihadis with that of the central government. This is in part why Naji suggests that jihadis should focus on taking territory in more rural areas, à la Guevara, that have historically had less of a connection to the central state. This allows for a higher likelihood of success. Previously, the movement had focused primarily on military training and terrorist actions. It was not until the mid to late 2000s that the movement shifted to one interested in building sympathy and beyond illustrating that its enemies were evil. Jihadis became focused on the provision of services through various *dawa* programs and governance. They were only able to implement these ideas at scale following the opening of public squares and safe havens in the aftermath of Arab uprisings in 2011.

Another key figure in the development of strategic knowledge was Mustafa bin 'Abd al-Qadir Sit Mariam Nasar, better known as Abu Mus'ab al-Suri. Unlike al-Qurashi and Naji, al-Suri had a long career in jihadi activism that precedes both 9/11 and the anti-Soviet jihad of the 1980s. Al-Suri was involved with the insurrection against Hafiz al-Assad in Syria in the late 1970s and early 1980s as a fighter with the Muslim Brotherhood splinter faction al-Tali'ah al-Muqatilah (The Fighting Vanguard). That experience, along with his deep involvement in the Algerian jihad of the 1990s and revulsion to the excessive violence by the GIA, gave al-Suri the reputation as a fierce critic of failed jihads. Similarly, while on the run after the fall of the Taliban, al-Suri drafted his approximately 1,600-page magnum opus *Call to Global Islamic Resistance*, which examined all aspects of the history of the jihadi movement. This book aimed to use historical lessons to inform future jihadi activity in post-Taliban-controlled Afghanistan.

While al-Suri's most widely known innovation within the strategic jihadosphere is his call to implement a decentralized, small, or individual cell model for fighting jihad, his book has other relevant insights. Most pertinent among these is his "theory of resistance," which AQ adopted as an organizational model. Within al-Suri's "theory of resistance," there are three layers of organization for the broader jihadi ecosystem:

1. Central circle: guidance, propaganda, education, funding;
2. Coordination circle: open fronts (safe havens), guerrilla operations in frontline countries, lack of organizational or operational ties to the central circle, setup call circle in targeted countries (United States, Europe, etc.); and
3. Call circle: individuals and small units of ordinary people, provided with curricula for self-preparation, with no law enforcement or intelligence record, not members of coordination circle returned to countries of origin, and no communication with jihadi groups.[17]

While AQ did not follow all aspects of al-Suri's decentralized approach, al-Suri's three "circles" are essentially analogous to what specialists in the field call AQ central, AQ's branches, and individuals inspired by AQ. The creation of such a model allowed AQ central to give ideological and strategic guidance to its branches in the mid to late 2000s through what Christopher Anzalone describes as a "missionary vanguard" of scholar-ideologues, including Abu Yahya al-Libi,

'Atiyat Allah 'Abd al-Rahman al-Libi, Khalid bin 'Abd al-Rahman al-Husaynan, and Anwar al-'Awlaqi.[18] Others would later rise, as all of these individuals were eventually killed in drone strikes. In turn, the branches provided tactical and operational guidance to individual jihadis in publications such as *Inspire* magazine. This development was a result of advice given by Naji and al-Suri on how to connect the broader military strategy to an information strategy, which over time turned into a jihadi operational art.

In their works, Naji and al-Suri explain the importance of expanding their strategies to the media field, which they view as an important avenue by which to influence the masses. This effort was partly informed by Naji's view that the United States was creating a so-called media halo that deceives individuals about its levels of strength. Naji explains that the U.S. "must resort to using a deceptive media halo which portrays these powers as non-coercive and world-encompassing, able to reach into every earth and heaven as if they possess the power of the Creator of creation."[19] The goal of destroying this "halo" is to eventually force the United States into a pitched battle against AQ. This would allow AQ to use the overt suffering and likely civilian casualties for propaganda purposes.

In the context of AST, Naji's idea of the "media halo" would be destroyed by the creation of an alternative messaging system that comes directly from the group. Therefore, instead of the Tunisian government or other anti-AST activists defining the group's ideology and goals, AST could define itself. This is one of the reasons why Abu 'Iyadh constantly repeated the message "hear from us, not about us." The slogan insinuated that once people met members of the movement and became familiar with its ideas, AST would transform from some boogeyman or monster in people's minds into an entity with whom people might actually agree.

Al-Suri explains the failures of AQ's media strategy in the mid-2000s: "In general, the jihadi message is vainglorious, egotistical, and overbearing, it may even be uncompromising, threatening, impassioned, and rigid. It is lacking in sentiment and is non-appealing to the masses and their psychological spirit. Again, it was unilateral and elitist."[20] Furthermore, AQ asserted that the delivery mechanism needed to be filterless, which is one of the reasons why AQ eventually stopped sending its videos to al-Jazeera. Instead, the group further developed its own media apparatus, al-Sahab Media, and created a system of authentication through the jihadi forums.[21] AQ thus began tailoring its messages to supporters and later using its media wing to provide guidance to its branches and other sympathetic organizations rather than solely focusing on targeting its enemies in the West.

These media efforts led to the creation of a library of information whose purpose was to help branches create tactics and operations locally and inspire individuals to conduct attacks on their own in the West. Therefore, by the time the Arab uprisings began, a robust mechanism had already been established to share strategic and ideological guidance that was not contingent upon a command-and-control structure. In other words, this mechanism facilitated a type of jihadi operational art. Daveed Gartenstein-Ross and Tara Vassefi even surveyed jihadi analysis about the first year of the Arab uprisings and noticed relatively coherent interpretations of and advice for the unfolding events.[22]

Protecting the Jihad

According to William McCants's citation analysis of jihadi works, 'Issam Muhammad Tahir al-Barqawi, better known as Abu Muhammad al-Maqdisi, is the most influential jihadi theorist alive.[23] Therefore, the words al-Maqdisi writes have deep influence, especially within the AQ milieu. Al-Maqdisi's career as a jihadi religious scholar began in the 1980s when he used salafi ideas to argue that the Saudi government was failing to live up to the salafi principles of its founding ideology, Wahhabism. In addition to his influential writings and importance to the development of jihadi-salafism as a systematic ideology, al-Maqdisi is also known for his mentorship of al-Zarqawi. Although al-Maqdisi was al-Zarqawi's mentor, the two had different views on implementing jihad and building an Islamic state.

In response to the violent excesses of al-Zarqawi in Iraq, al-Maqdisi wrote a letter in 2004 and, later, a longer book, *Waqafat ma' thamrat al-jihad* (Stances on the fruits of jihad) that criticized al-Zarqawi's practices. According to Wagemakers, al-Maqdisi did this in "an effort to take greater scholarly control of a trend that he feels responsible for but has also witnessed becoming more and more the prerogative of fighters instead of scholars."[24] Al-Maqdisi thus argued that al-Zarqawi and others did not have the necessary religious knowledge or strategic foresight to make the "big decisions" required to implement jihad and build an Islamic state. As a result, al-Maqdisi needed to "protect" the jihad.

One of the main critiques al-Maqdisi presents in his book, and hopes to clarify within the jihadi movement, is his differentiation between the idea of *qital al-nikayya* (fighting to hurt or damage the enemy) and *qital al-tamkin* (fighting to consolidate one's power). Maqdisi argues that the former provides only short-term tactical victories that often do not amount to much in the long term. In contrast, the latter provides a framework for consolidating an Islamic state.[25] In this way, al-Maqdisi highlights the importance of planning, organization, education, and *dawa* activities. One avenue for promoting a more "pure" jihad was al-Maqdisi's website, *Minbar al-tawhid wal-jihad* (The pulpit of the unicity of God and jihad), a library of endorsed jihadi primary source material.

After al-Maqdisi's release from Jordanian prison in 2009, al-Maqdisi established a sharia committee of like-minded scholars for the Minbar website to provide fatwas on a broad range of topics, from matters of daily life to politics to jihad. The purpose of this site was to "protect" the legitimacy of jihad and better pursue a true Islamic state based on the sanctity of the *tawhid* of God. Although al-Maqdisi is not traditionally considered a strategist, in many ways the creation of the website and sharia committee helped cultivate the religious aspects of "jihadi operational art." Anyone could then use this knowledge base to pursue jihad and the development of an Islamic state in a scholarly-approved manner.

In addition to AST's pursuit of ideas from al-Qurashi, Naji, and al-Suri, its *dawa*-first strategy stems from al-Maqdisi's ideas, especially since AST frequently cited him on its official Facebook page and in its propaganda. AST even went so far as to post my *Foreign Policy* article that referred to AST members as "Maqdisi's Disciples" on its Facebook page, translated into Arabic.[26] A *dawa*-first approach, particularly in regard to AST's social services program, was one of the main avenues by which the group advanced its ideas. The goal was to provide an outlet for the consolidation of a future Islamic state that cultivated followers in a broader fashion. This method differs from a more vanguard-oriented organization that had been the norm within the jihadi movement in the thirty years before the Arab uprisings.

This transition from a clandestine organization to one more focused on the masses was a process that AQ took in the mid to late 2000s. It was also a part of the transition to establishing a jihadi operational art and knowledge base for its branches and supporters.

AQ's Corrective Jihad

Following the U.S. invasion of Afghanistan, AQ became what it had always sought to be: the unipolar leader of the jihadi-salafi movement. Because the United States did not differentiate between AQ militants and other jihadis using Afghanistan as a training ground, many groups joined AQ to defend Afghanistan from the American invasion. Prior to 9/11, AQ was one of a few jihadi groups to focus on attacking the so-called far enemy.[27] As al-Suri notes in his *Call to Global Islamic Resistance*, groups "were also not convinced of the attempts bin Ladin and AQ were making, nor of the latter's military unidirectional penchant. Indeed, this was the case with the majority of the organizations and the Arab groups in Afghanistan. Nevertheless, despite all of these facts, when the American attacks occurred, every one of them got involved in that battle."[28] Consequently, Hegghammer argues that an ideological hybridization occurred between the locally-focused jihadi groups and AQ.[29] Each borrowed characteristics of the others, which in effect established a more potent ideology and brought various trends together.

Although fissures remained within the broader movement, this process allowed AQ to take on the role of leader because of the successful 9/11 attacks, the relative weakness of jihadi groups that had failed to wage successful local insurgencies, and the American destruction of many of these groups safe haven networks in Afghanistan. Unlike the period before 9/11 (when various groups focused on their own ventures), the post-9/11 era was defined by a more coordinated jihadi movement. This consensus would not last forever, though, especially with the 2014 split between those who followed AQ's vision for the development of a caliphate and those who pursued the Islamic State's vision. These differences were borne out of what occurred in Iraq in the mid-2000s, but the overt manifestation of this split would not come to fruition until a decade later.

In response to the increasingly draconian rule over Sunni territory in western Iraq and extreme attacks on civilians of all backgrounds, AQ felt the need to rein in al-Zarqawi. Al-Zawahiri thus sent al-Zarqawi a letter on July 9, 2005, because of "fears from the previous experiences," a reference to Algeria and the GIA.[30] Al-Zawahiri famously stated in this letter that "we are in a battle, and that more than half of this battle is taking place in the battlefield of the media. And that we are in a media battle in a race for the hearts and minds of our *umma*." Therefore, "in the absence of this popular support, the Islamic mujahid movement would be crushed in the shadows."[31] According to al-Zawahiri, it was imperative not to "repeat the mistake of the Taliban, who restricted participation in governance to the students and the people of Qandahar alone. They did not have any representation for the Afghan people in their ruling regime, so the result was that the Afghan people disengaged themselves from them."[32]

A half a year later, on December 12, 2005, 'Atiyat Allah 'Abd al-Rahman al-Libi reiterated al-Zawahiri's message and provided more guidance to al-Zarqawi. Al-Libi experienced the horrors of the GIA's excesses up close and therefore wanted to draw upon what he saw and heard in Algeria:

> Ask me whatever you like about Algeria between 1994 and 1995, when [the movement] was at the height of its power and capabilities, and was on the verge of taking over the government. The government was on the verge of a downfall at any moment. I lived through that myself, and I saw firsthand; no one told me about it. However, they destroyed themselves with their own hands, with their lack of reason, delusions, their ignoring of people, their alienation of them through oppression, deviance, and severity, coupled with a lack of kindness, sympathy, and friendliness. Their enemy did not defeat them, but rather they defeated themselves, were consumed and fell.[33]

From this experience, al-Libi realized that "there must be attention paid to raising the mujahidin through continuous modification and not being quiet about our mistakes, especially the exorbitant mistakes. Indeed, it is necessary to try rapidly to treat them and rectify them." Therefore, it is imperative for "the people [to] feel that we value them and appreciate their efforts and that we respect them and want the best for them and that we sympathize with them, this is what will draw their hearts to us."[34]

Al-Zarqawi ignored these pleas. Even after his death, his organization, which later called itself the Islamic State of Iraq (ISI), pursued a similar path. But because the group had been weakened, ISI was in no position to truly challenge AQ. While the situation was allegedly fixed behind the scenes, Adam Gadahn, in a January 2011 letter, wrote that AQ should cut its losses and kick ISI out of its network: "I see that the organization should declare the cut off of its organizational ties with that organization [ISI]. The relations between the AQ organization and 'The State' have been practically cut off for a number of years."[35] His words were a harbinger of what eventually came to pass three years later, when ISI's successor, the Islamic State of Iraq and al-Sham, or ISIS, felt it was strong enough to push back against AQ's leadership. While ISI/ISIS may have learned different lessons from its experience in Iraq, AQ began to build a program that would be a deterrent and corrective against what it viewed as a deviant interpretation of jihadi ideology and methodology.

For instance, al-Libi would begin to more forcefully write about the dangers of the excessive use of *takfir* that leads to unnecessary shedding of Muslim blood.[36] Likewise, AST's Abu 'Iyadh would use language similar to that of al-Libi when discussing the issue of *takfir* and the needless killing of other Muslims. He explained: "We assure our people that Muslim blood is forbidden blood. . . . We will not allow and will not engage in any physical action against the interests of the Muslim people."[37]

More importantly, AQ and its branches began to pursue a digital outreach strategy by releasing religious lectures online since they did not control territory. It was also AQ's approved way of educating supporters and recruits in its understanding of Islam. For example, in 2010 AQ ideologue Khalid bin 'Abd al-Rahman al-Husaynan (Abu Zayd al-Kuwayti), who was killed in a drone strike in December 2012, began releasing a lecture series during Ramadan that discussed basic religious duties and obligations. He would later release a regular "*dawa*" video series from 2011 to 2013.[38] Similarly, AQAP's ideologue Harith bin Ghazi al-Nazari (Muhammad al-Mirshadi), who was killed in a January 2015 drone strike, had a number of *dawa* video series from 2010 to his death: "With the Qur'an," "Thoughts in Testimonial and Behavior," "The Good Reminders," and "The Free Advices," among others.[39] Likewise, AQIM's Shaykh Abu al-Hasan al-Rashid al-Bulaydi had a *dawa* series titled "Sit Down with Us and Have Faith for an Hour," and Dr. Sami al-Uraydi, the senior sharia official of Jabhat al-Nusra, hosted a lecture series called "Milestones in the Methodology of the Pious Predecessors."[40]

These various *dawa* series by AQ's stable of ideologues illustrates its establishment of a "jihadi operational art" for outreach, education, and, most importantly, public support. AST similarly used *dawa* literature and public forums as well as the provision of services to gain new supporters. Once a potential recruit or member was pulled in through more mainstream religious talk and literature, AST could then privately encourage the individual to pursue more extreme ideas. As Abu 'Iyadh would later note, "our image is not tarnished in the eyes of people who take the trouble to know us closely and to avoid prejudice. It is easy to blame people, but the hardest part is getting to know them."[41]

Prison Experience

Although Abu 'Iyadh and other imprisoned Tunisians were unable to view the new AQ videos, they were able to access various writings by top jihadi ideologues and AQ leaders during their prison stints. According to Abu 'Iyadh, it was difficult to get permission for such materials, but receiving them through family members allowed future members of AST to speak with one another in prison about possible post-prison plans and how they sought to implement their vision based on lessons learned and the new internal jihadi debates.[42]

Prison was an opportunity for Tunisians who had been involved in the wars of the 1980s and 1990s to meet many of the youths who had been inspired by the Iraq jihad but were arrested attempting to fight or when trying to return home. The prisons held the largest grouping of Tunisia's jihadis prior to the creation of AST. It was also where Abu 'Iyadh further cemented his role as a leader following the so-called Mar'akat al-azan fi-l-sujun (Battle of the call to prayer in prison) around December 2004.[43] Although he helped cofound the Tunisian Combatant Group, the younger generation was not familiar with him because he had been out of the country since the early 1990s.

When Abu 'Iyadh went to prison in the fall of 2003, he performed the call to prayer in prison even though such an act was illegal. He explains: "I almost lost my life.... I used to call to prayer despite the dictators, and I challenged them on it and I said to them: 'if you just split me piece after piece I would not abandon the call to prayer with God's will.' And despite their blatant offense by which I almost lost my life, the jihadi-salafi movement left victorious.... And thank God, the call to prayer then was allowed in all Tunisian prisons after this incident."[44] It is difficult to confirm that this episode occurred. If taken at face value, however, the moment provided Abu 'Iyadh legitimacy with the youth, which he used to then answer questions and clarify methodological and intellectual points.[45] Furthermore, according to Hasan al-Brik, a facilitator of foreign fighters from Syria to Iraq for al-Qaeda in Iraq and later AST's head of *dawa*, "communal prayer time served as a forum for discussion and refining ideas that would be put into practice on release."[46]

The post–prison release preparation started to come into focus in early 2006. According to a founding member of AST who had been in prison, when Hamadi al-Jebali, a senior member of al-Nahdah who became Tunisia's prime minister (2011–13), was released from jail in February 2006, some jihadis believed they, too, would soon leave prison. They began planning their post-release activities. Although the group did not have a name for itself at the time, twenty individuals, including Abu 'Iyadh, agreed to create a new organization.[47] Through Abu 'Iyadh's guidance, more individuals in prison joined their program in the following years. Moreover, according to al-Brik, this "unit in one jail first developed the idea, which then spread to different prisons to the point when an informal network of people across the country were aware of the project."[48] Abu 'Iyadh even stated: "I consider the period of imprisonment as one of the best periods of my life in the matter of *'ilm* [knowledge-seeking] and jihad."[49] By the time all prisoners were released in February 2011, 90 percent of individuals within the Tunisian jihadi-salafi current allegedly agreed with AQ's corrective ideas.[50]

AQ's refined ideas and the *dawa* push in its media releases aimed to marry AQ's correctives from the Iraq jihad with newer and more popular grassroots support. This new knowledge base would only really be tested after the opening of public squares and new safe havens in the aftermath of the 2011 Arab uprisings. By the time of the Tunisian revolution and formation of AST, there was already a robust mechanism for obtaining advice from AQ and sympathetic ideologues online.

It is no surprise, then, that AST took such recommendations to heart and taught other groups through its own *dawa* experiences. Abu 'Iyadh summed this up in late 2011: "They [our mujahidin brothers] give us advice and we give them our advice and we support them if we are able to support them even by kind words."[51] The advice from outside groups and ideologues would resonate for Abu 'Iyadh until his last public statement before AST's designation as a terrorist organization. In a late May 2013 address to AST members during its third annual conference, Abu 'Iyadh affirmed "a message to the groups, clerics, preachers, and leaders of *tawhid* and jihad in the Islamic world, you are from us, and we are from you, we thank you for your support and advice, so may God give you the best reward for Islam and Muslims."[52] This message highlights the seriousness with which Abu 'Iyadh and AST took the advice of key ideologues within AQ and the broader jihadi movement.

Strategic Advice for Tunisia's Jihadis

Once it was clear that something historic was going to happen in Tunisia, jihadi groups and ideologues began to release audio/video messages and articles about the momentous event and how the movement could take advantage of it. AQIM's leader, 'Abd al-Malik Drukdal (Abu Mus'ab 'Abd al-Wadud), even released an audio message a day before former Tunisian president, Bin 'Ali, fled to Saudi Arabia. In releases following the revolution, five key themes emerged: (1) warnings against complacency in the aftermath of Bin 'Ali's overthrow; (2) the importance of understanding the local conditions and necessity of devising an organizational plan; (3) the need to focus on *dawa* and spread the true message of Islam; (4) the refusal to join the democratic transitional process in general and al-Nahdah in particular; and (5) the aim of outreach to all segments of society without an air of arrogance. These guidelines provided AST with the building blocks to act as an organization after its establishment. They also illustrate how AQ used the *dawa*-first approach as a lens through which to view the situation in Tunisia. These releases also help better inform our understanding of AQ's diagnostic and prognostic framing for AST's venture, which AST follows and therefore in a sense is AST's diagnostic and prognostic framing as well. The former refers to the "identification of a problem and the attribution of blame or causality," while the latter refers to "to not only suggest solutions to the problem, but also to identify strategies, tactics, and targets."[53] The third component of framing, motivation, is discussed in the next chapter as it relates to how AST motivated members to act on its behalf.

Warning Against Complacency

While several key figures and groups acknowledged the immense victory of Bin 'Ali's departure, they also viewed it as a stepping-stone. The success could still be lost to remnants of the regime within the security and military apparatus, secular/leftist activists, and what Tunisian jihadis viewed as the sellout Muslim Brotherhood-style Islamists in al-Nahdah. For instance, on January 19, 2011, Shaykh Abu al-Mundhir al-Shinqiti, a member of al-Maqdisi's Minbar sharia committee, cautioned Tunisia's jihadis to "be wary against political parties and groups from establishing secularism again in the country or participating in laying the groundwork for it."[54] On the same day, Shaykh Abu Basir al-Tartusi, a Syrian jihadi ideologue based in London, reminded Tunisia's jihadis that "you have executed the easiest part of [achieving] victory. The hardest part remains. You have come half way."[55] Two weeks later another ideologue from the Minbar sharia committee, Abu Muslim al-Jaza'iri, continued this theme by stating: "Oh our people in Tunisia, yes, you became victorious in a battle. However, so that I may be frank with you; you have become victorious in a big part of this battle, but not the entire battle. This is because Bin 'Ali's men are still in power. The crucial point in our battle with the rulers in our time is not the fall of a president, a prince or a sultan, but the toppling of the entire system that these tyrants are ruling."[56]

AQIM further emphasized this point and the necessity of eliminating remaining regime elements: "The tyrant has left and the system of tyranny and infidelity remains; you have won a battle but you haven't won the war yet. And here are the Jews, Crusaders, and the apostates plotting against you. Continue your battle to overthrow the tyrannical system, and be cautious, and be ready."⁵⁷ Similarly, by late February 2011, AQAP's Ibrahim Bin Sulayman al-Rubaysh, who was later killed in a drone strike in mid-April 2015, had become disenchanted with the transitional process: "One harm will be removed, yet another will follow, though less in its evil. One tyrant will be removed, yet another will follow. He may reform some aspects of the mundane life for them by providing employment, opportunities, and raising the average income, but the bigger problem still remains. The sharia is still unimplemented, man-made laws are still being obeyed."⁵⁸ This unfinished business, according to al-Rubaysh, necessitated a jihadi movement in Tunisia.

Organizational Plan

As noted earlier, two of the many lessons that al-Maqdisi learned from the Iraq experience were the importance of planning and having a sound organizational objective. These issues would be explored in depth by Hamzah Bin Muhammad al-Bassam, who wrote for the AQ-sympathetic media outlet Nukhbat al-iʻalam al-jihadi (The jihadi media elite) following the uprisings. He explains that "planning war differs from planning [a] *dawa* effort, which in turn differs from developing and building the state. Every [type of] planning has its essential components and principles. It is important for the leadership to determine what the nature of the [particular] stage is, so planning can be done soundly."⁵⁹ This logic in many ways relates to Abu ʻIyadh's message about the importance of managing the stages. Furthermore, al-Bassam recommends that "if it is necessary to operate openly, then it is suitable that operations are done through a hierarchical group where a leader sits on top."⁶⁰ In addition, al-Jazaʻiri advised the Tunisian jihadi movement "to create a cohesive and cooperative organisation, which is linked to your mujahid brothers and with their heroic leader Shaykh Usamah bin Ladin (at least on an intellectual and programmatic level)."⁶¹ AST was willing to do both based on the conditions in Tunisia and their own intellectual backgrounds.

It is worth pointing out, however, that not everyone within the Tunisian jihadi movement agreed that it was necessary to set up an organization. For one, Shaykh al-Khatib al-Idrisi "argued that if the purpose of salafism was to educate people in Islam, an organisation was not necessary."⁶² This is why al-Idrisi, after initially engaging with AST and working with its original propaganda outlet, al-Qayrawan Media, returned to more of a behind-the-scenes role as someone who provided advice to members of AST but was not an official leader within the group itself. Similarly, AST's original spokesperson Abu Ayub al-Tunisi left the organization because he was not happy that it became more formalized: "We are currently in a *dawa* phase, for the most part.... Why should we organize and [thus] alienate ourselves from the [rest of the] people? We live in a Muslim society, [and the existence of] all these movements and [political] parties leads to disunity, rather than unity."[63] Notwithstanding this disagreement, Abu Ayub claimed "there are no differences between us. They [AST] are our brothers ... we are united by our *aqidah* (creed) and *manhaj* (methodology)."[64]

Nevertheless, a week before his death, Bin Ladin wrote a private letter to al-Libi. In it, he asserted that "we must mobilize all the resources that have expressive abilities in speech, poetry, visual, or audio and devote them completely toward directing and guiding the nation's youth."[65] It is unknown whether al-Libi actually received the letter, but this does illustrate how AQ conceptualized planning for the aftermath of the uprisings. While it is impossible and irrelevant to make any direct connections or correlations to Bin Ladin's letter, AST was one of the organizations at the forefront of media activism within the jihadi movement. Because it pioneered in the use of Facebook, it was able to reach much broader audiences than the self-proclaimed jihadis could on password-protected forums. Beyond planning and creating an organization, the consensus among ideologues and jihadi groups was that a *dawa*-first strategy should be implemented to take advantage of the specific conditions in Tunisia.

The *Dawa*-First Approach

In al-Shinqiti's January 19, 2011, fatwa, which answered questions from a Tunisian jihadi-salafi who used the *kunya* Abu Anas Muslim, he described how Tunisia's jihadi movement could take advantage of the unfolding situation. He specifically suggested the creation of a *dawa* program that involved a number of aspects: "Everyone knows his own area best. Not least to proselytize, to spread knowledge and learning, revivify Muslim duties, and to take the initiative to bring back the mosques and to open [propaganda] bookshops, spread books and useful tapes, and to send *dawa* organizations that support *dawa* activities and so on, so that Tunisia can return to its salafi self: the land of al-Qayrawan and al-Zaytuna [the two historical religious locations of learning in Tunisia]."[66] He further explained that it was important to make it appear as if their current was gaining strength so it would be difficult for others involved in the revolution to say they had not been a part of it or a by-product of it: "therefore, there needs to be an initiative to spread religious appearances, like the beard, veil, the *qamis* [traditional garb] and every possible sign of uprightness and religious duty. This will make the size of the Islamic current appear prominent on the national level."[67]

Similarly, in its second message to the people of Tunisia on January 28, AQIM wanted to remind Tunisia's jihadis of the significance of the revolution and how they "have to take advantage of this historical opportunity to spread the *manhaj* of tawhid and jihad between people."[68] Likewise, AQ's al-Libi reemphasized this topic in a late February booklet, explaining that "the reformers, mujahidin, and preachers of the Islamic nation must take this historical opportunity and spring into action and initiate or increase their preaching, education, reformation, and revitalization in light of the freedom and opportunities now available in this post-revolution era."[69] Furthermore, it was an important topic of private interest in Bin Ladin's aforementioned letter: "Our duty at this stage is to pay attention to the *dawa* among Muslims and win over supporters and spread the correct understanding, as the current conditions have brought on unprecedented opportunities and the coming of Islamic governments that follow the salafi doctrine is a benefit to Islam. The more time that passes and the *dawa* increases, the more the supporters will be of the people, and the more widespread will be the correct understanding among the coming generations of Islamic groups."[70]

These releases, especially those from AQ, show the movement's focus on *dawa* and the spread of ideas based on the unprecedented opening of public squares. From the movement's perspective, it validates AQ's correctives and how it hoped it could be implemented in the real world now that a favorable situation had presented itself. This is after years of discussing *dawa* activities on a theoretical and information-operational level. Now the strategy could be put into practice. Since Abu 'Iyadh and AST internalized these correctives in prison and witnessed the conditions in Tunisia, it is no surprise that they considered Tunisia ripe for a *dawa*-first approach. A member of AST even noted that they took Qur'anic verse 16:125 (Surat al-Nahl) as a reference point for their activities: "Invite to the way of your lord with wisdom and good instruction, and argue with them in a way that is best."[71] It is also worth restating that, as quoted earlier, Abu 'Iyadh proclaimed that "we will benefit from any other government that grants preachers the freedom to proselytize in this country."[72]

And for two and half years, AST was afforded this opportunity in part due to the permissive policies of both the transitional and al-Nahdah-led governments. The issues of elections and working with al-Nahdah to gain a more Islamic government were important topics that many ideologues and groups warned against.

Elections and Working with al-Nahdah

The issues of elections and working with al-Nahdah to play the system were first raised in al-Jaza'iri's February 9, 2011, article in which he states that one should "not allow for cooperation with them [al-Nahdah], [as] is related to electoral work, and party-political work like election campaigns. We are dissociating ourselves from this type of work, in preference of God."⁷³ Al-Jaza'iri reiterated this point in a February 25 fatwa, which responded to a series of questions about the situation in Tunisia by a Tunisian with the *kunya*, Abu Hisham. He said, "as for [party] political work, it is all evil. I warn my beloved brothers from this type of grave offense, which leaves its followers in peril. Party activity is a reprehensible innovation, without any legal benefit."⁷⁴

Furthermore, in a March 7 fatwa, al-Shinqiti responded to a question from Abu al-'Iz al-Tunisi about formal affiliation with al-Nahdah. He asserted that "all of the attempts calling for reconciliation between the Brotherhood and the Salafis are deceptive calls meant to obscure the truth with the bad and generalization at a dangerous level that caused the divergence in this group."⁷⁵ It was clear, however, that a number of Tunisians were still not completely convinced, since al-Shinqiti released another fatwa based on questions from Tuwaylib 'Ilm Tunisi on May 10. In it, he explained the corruptions of joining al-Nahdah: "There is no legitimacy in participating or joining these parties that ask the people to submit to Positive Law and to be ruled by it. . . . Joining parties like these means joining *dawa* for polytheism and spreading it to the people. . . . It is incumbent upon whoever desires *tawhid* to isolate them and warn the people of their doctrine. . . . The Muslim Brotherhood has reached a stage of corruption that has seen it leave the Islamic movement and go into the secularist movement."⁷⁶ Moreover, al-Shinqiti released two more scathing fatwas against participating in elections and voting for al-Nahdah in late September and mid-October in the run-up to Tunisia's Constituent Assembly election.⁷⁷

None of this is particularly surprising considering that democracy and Muslim Brotherhood–aligned groups have been considered an anathema to the jihadi-salafi movement since its inception. Al-Zawahiri sums up some of these key ideological points in a mid-June 2012 video message directed at Tunisia's jihadis: "They [al-Nahdah] are inventing an 'Islam' that pleases the American Department of State, the European Union and the Gulf [regime] scholars. . . . Oh honorable, free and protective ones in Tunisia, the masks have fallen and the faces have been unveiled, so rise up to support your sharia. Incite your people on a popular uprising to support the sharia and affirm Islam and rule with the Qur'an."⁷⁸ Consequently, as described in the last chapter, AST was virulently opposed to the election and what its members perceived as al-Nahdah's compromises. Although AST opposed elections and democracy, it still wanted to gain the support of the population so that it could build its grassroots capabilities to begin the process of building an Islamic state in its own image. This was the last important aspect on which AQ and key ideologues provided advice to garner greater chances of success.

Building Communal Relations

One of the fascinating aspects of AST's plan was its effort to build a network throughout the country. This goal differed from those of its sister organization in Libya, which was founded and mostly based in the city of Benghazi. Once freed from prison, the core group began to organize in Abu 'Iyadh's house and implement the plans it had been devising over the previous five years. AST initiated outreach efforts in Tunis, Sousse, Sidi Bouzid, al-Qayrawan, and Bizerte as well as making contact with Tunisia's most famous salafi cleric, the blind Shaykh al-Khatib al-Idrisi.[79]

These types of plans echoed much of the advice given to them. For instance, the day before Bin 'Ali's departure, AQIM's leader, Drukdal, suggested that "in order for your movement to be fruitful, it should not be limited to one city or one front, but the duty is to extend it to the all the sides of the country and its corners and valleys, because the tyrant is able to extinguish any uprising by a limited sect from the nation, but he has no control over the entire nation."[80] Al-Jaza'iri echoed this sentiment by stating that "the most important of your priorities is to establish your group across the Tunisian lands."[81] Over the next few years AST proved its widespread support by conducting various *dawa* sessions and providing services in all corners of the country, which is examined in depth in the next chapter.

Tunisia's Conditions for *Dawa*

Up until the uprising, religion in society was neutered, as described in the first chapter of this book. As a result, in the view of Abu 'Iyadh and other AST leaders, it was necessary to rebuild this knowledge base. It would be far more difficult to advance to the next stage (i.e., violent confrontation) without it since the population would not understand the decision-making behind it.

This reasoning explains why Hasan al-Brik, AST's head of *dawa*, felt the group was obligated to "plant our seeds in the sunlight," which would lead to the bearing of fruit down the road.[82] Such sentiment was repeatedly mentioned by Abu 'Iyadh in the months following the public rise of AST as a relevant player on the national scene in Tunisia. For instance, in December 2011, Abu 'Iyadh said that "in this period we are in the *dawa* phase.... We want to revive the Islamic identity of our people in order to bring them back to their foundations, i.e., to their Islam."[83] A couple of months later, in mid-March, he reiterated that "Tunisia is not a land of jihad and we do not carry weapons."[84] And ten days after this statement he once again emphasized that Tunisia was a land of *dawa*:

"We cannot consider that Tunisia is a land of jihad or take up arms. Since we are out of the prison, we have chosen *dawa* and the correct methodology for the consolidation of Islamic identity and reconciliation with our religion."[85] Abu 'Iyadh further stressed that "all our actions are now summarized in moral preaching and works of charity.... I am convinced that Tunisia is not a land of jihad, but it is a land of religious preaching."[86]

This highlights that, at least on a public level, Abu 'Iyadh attempted to manage the stages according to AST doctrine and preempt any negative narratives about the side activities of AST members. Most importantly, Abu 'Iyadh and AST attempted to legitimize the *dawa*-first strategy through a local lens. Notably, they operated on the assumption that Tunisians lacked proper religious education or background in the nuances of Islam. As a result, AST strategy thought that before individuals could gain the public support needed to conduct jihad against a regime, they needed to understand the justifications for later violent actions. This reasoning is in essence the logical conclusion of the strategic ideas evolving in the mid to late 2000s within the broader jihadi movement sympathetic to AQ. Tunisia was a test case since AST was allowed to operate openly without much state harassment. This of course differed from other areas, including Egypt—where a variety of Islamist trends contested with each other—or other countries such as Libya, Syria, and Yemen that were plagued by new or ongoing wars.

New Phenomenon, Rebranding al-Qaeda, or a Hybrid?

Based on the analysis from this chapter, there is sufficient evidence to suggest that AST's project was indeed part of an AQ rebranding effort. Although the Tunisian government would present an alleged "Allegiance Act" between AST's leader Abu 'Iyadh and AQIM leader Abu Mus'ab 'Abd al-Wadud in the summer of 2013, there has not been publicly available evidence to suggest an outright link insofar as a pledge of allegiance from Abu 'Iyadh to Bin Ladin or al-Zawahiri. That said, based on the various quotes from Abu 'Iyadh in this chapter, one can read between the lines. Also, more recent information has leaked about Abu 'Iyadh's relations with al-Zawahiri, which showed they were writing letters to each other (more on this shortly).

In relation to this from AQ's perspective, according to press reports based on information from the raid that killed Bin Ladin, AQ's central leadership in Pakistan was debating alternative names for the organization ahead of the Arab uprisings.[87] This was spurred in part by the Western habit of referring to the group as just AQ, rather than its official name, Tanzim Qa'idat al-Jihad (The base organization of jihad). AQ's leadership felt that the West's habit of omitting the word "jihad" robbed the group of its religious legitimacy. Although

AQ ended up not changing its name, since the alternatives—Taʿifat at-Tawhid wa-l-Jihad (Sect of the unicity of God and jihad) and Jamaʿat ʾIʿadat al-Khilafah al-Rashidiyyah (Restoration group of the Rashidun caliphate)—were a mouthful, the debate prompted AQ to instruct Harakat al-Shabab al-Mujahidin in Somalia and Jabhat al-Nusra in Syria to refrain from overtly branding themselves as AQ in East Africa or AQ in the Levant.

Furthermore, AQ's strongest branch, AQAP in Yemen, established a front organization in the spring of 2011 called Ansar al-Sharia in Yemen. The name Ansar al-Sharia in Yemen was first mentioned in an unofficial audio release by AQAP's leading sharia official at the time, Shaykh Abu Zubayr ʿAdil Bin ʿAbd Allah al-Abab. Al-Abab conducted a question-and-answer session with online global jihadi activists through the online Paltalk platform in the private chat room Ghorfah Minbar al-Ansar (Pulpit room of the supporters). The first question asked to al-Abab was, "What is the general situation of the mujahidin in Yemen and the status of the youth of ASY [Ansar al-Sharia in Yemen]?" Al-Abab responded that when AQAP pursues recruitment, its members first introduce themselves under the banner of Ansar al-Sharia in Yemen.[88]

Such a response raises the question of whether it was a coincidence that around the same time AQ's strongest branch used this name, other groups espousing pro-AQ viewpoints began to emerge with the Ansar al-Sharia moniker. Moreover, al-Shinqiti wrote an article in mid-June 2012 affirming that the use of Ansar al-Sharia's name was the best way to assert legitimacy in the jihadi movement: "This name is so good, it describes what is considered the goal and the end state that the upholders of *tawhid* unite for . . . a title, a banner and a goal at the same time . . . who can refuse and reject it? Who can be against it?"[89] Al-Shinqiti later in this essay calls for the creation of similar groups that focus on *dawa* in other countries. This would allow for the spread of "useful knowledge" and eventual consolidation of all Ansar al-Sharia entities.

Lastly, in early January 2016, a pro-AQ media outlet, Hidayyah Media Foundation, leaked two letters between Abu ʿIyadh and al-Zawahiri from July and August 2014 to discredit a recently published polemic by a senior IS ideologue named Abu Maysarah al-Shami, better known as the American Ahmad Abousamra, who was killed in an airstrike in Syria in early April 2017.[90] While the content of the letters is not germane to this discussion, it illustrates that Abu ʿIyadh was in contact and on good terms with al-Zawahiri. The letter was also addressed to AQAP leader Nasir al-Wihayshi, al-Shabab leader Mukhtar Abu al-Zubayr, Boko Haram leader Abu Bakr al-Shakaw, and Ansar al-Din (an AQIM-front group) leader Iyad Agh Ghali. Therefore, based on a wide variety of evidence, (1) Abu ʿIyadh's past relations with AQ in Afghanistan (see chapter 2); (2) Abu ʿIyadh's assertion that AST fell within the broader AQ ideological methodology; (3) AST's internalization of lessons learned from the last decade's failed jihads and strategic advice from jihadi ideologues and AQ leaders after the Tunisian revolution; (4) AQ's attempts to test new strategies/tactics in the post-Arab uprising environment; (5) AQ's own use of the Ansar al-Sharia name; and (6) the relationship between Abu 'Iyadh, al-Zawahiri, and other senior jihadi leaders in the AQ network, it would suggest that AST was in fact a front for AQ that simply aimed to distance itself from any negative connotations associated with the AQ brand following the backlash from the Iraq war.

* * *

This chapter sought to answer the question of why Abu 'Iyadh and AST decided on a *dawa*-first strategy after the Tunisian revolution. Based on the available evidence, it can be concluded that it was a result of a number of key factors: (1) lessons learned by the jihadi movement from the failures of the Iraq jihad; (2) strategic advice given by key AQ leaders, its branches, and respected jihadi ideologues on interpreting and taking advantage of opportunities after the overthrow of Bin 'Ali, and (3) Abu 'Iyadh's realization that individuals needed to be educated in the true understanding of Islam before Tunisia would be ripe for jihad. The *dawa*-first approach allowed AST to reach a broader audience than if it had been a clandestine-type of organization similar to AQ historically. Therefore, this decision, along with the conditions (discussed in the previous chapter) helps explain why so many Tunisians became involved with AST and jihadism after the revolution.

In addition, this chapter adds a new layer to the academic literature on jihadi strategic studies. Not only does it expand upon the idea of "jihadi operational art," it also illustrates how it transformed from something aspirational, if not theoretical, into a tangible strategy that could be implemented in the real world. The chapter also highlights how the content of the strategic debates of the mid to late 2000s was implemented following the Arab uprisings, especially in the relatively open setting of Tunisia. Moreover, this chapter definitively identifies the characteristics that defined AST as a group. While the group was new in terms of its approach to capacity building and establishing an Islamic state, it was a rebranding of and front for AQ's efforts. It was a logical conclusion of the strategic ideas from the prior decade that came to fruition in the Tunisian context.

In chapter 7, this book returns to some of the strategic ideas laid out in this chapter, especially as they pertain to AST's failure to manage the so-called stages. Before that explanation, though, it is essential to first examine the implementation of AST's *dawa* program in detail. Chapter 6 also explores how AST's *dawa* work facilitated the spread of the group's ideology. This helps to explain why so many Tunisians joined the jihadi movement following the 2011 revolution and why such a large pool of potential candidates then became foreign fighters in the Libyan and Syrian civil wars.

CHAPTER 6

HEAR FROM US, NOT ABOUT US

Now that AST's motive for pursuing a *dawa*-first strategy has been explained in the previous chapter, this one explores how the group and its leadership implemented it. There are three main reasons behind AST's successful implementation of its approach: (1) its organizational planning; (2) its missionary, outreach, and social service activities; and (3) its framing of ideas to entice individuals to join.

Most of the content in this chapter is based off a primary source archive that I compiled from AST's official Facebook page and website (which was hosted in Germany and registered to an Abu Usamah al-Muslim in Roubaix, France, based on a WHOIS lookup) when the group was active from 2011 to 2013. Although the various Facebook pages and website are no longer available online, I retain the collection on my laptop and two external hard drives. The archive includes more than 18,000 files in Arabic. These files were translated, and from this corpus I created a number of databases. These databases include "AST's Activities—Full," "AST's Leadership Structure," and "AST's Clerical and Religious Establishment." Each is explored in the coming pages.

It should be noted that while the information obtained is substantial, there is still a gap in the understanding of all aspects of AST. For instance, AST neither reported all its activities online nor released information on all mosques in which it was active. Likewise, it did not disclose all key leaders and clerics within the movement. However, based on the plethora of data gathered, the information analyzed provides the greatest window into AST's operations as an organization and a sufficient explanation of the overall phenomenon.

While the main contribution of this chapter is empirical, this chapter also buttresses the empirics with theory to situate it within the broader literature. The two main theories relevant to understanding the processes at play are resource mobilization and framing, which are the second and third pieces of social movement theory. Chapter 4 examines the first aspect—political opportunity structures—which involve the conditions that allowed AST to prosper in the context of the post-revolution governments. This is also explored in the following chapter in the context of changing conditions that led to the downfall of AST and the return of foreign fighting.

According to Diana Kendall, resource mobilization entails the acquisition of adequate resources and the guidance of motivated individuals to perform an action in the service of a group's goals.[1] Therefore, it is necessary to understand AST's goals in order to explain how it conducted its mobilization efforts. The short-term objective of AST was to reeducate Tunisians about Islam since both Bourguiba and Bin 'Ali had pushed religion outside public discourse and practice. Once a sufficient number of individuals were back in the fold, AST's medium- to long-term goal was to establish an Islamic state in Tunisia. This is why it was important for AST to conduct an outreach program based on Tunisia's specific circumstances. As such, individuals and mosques were key resources for this mobilization. To better grasp AST's ability to use human capital and resources, it is essential to examine its organizational and planning structures as well as its conduct of earlier campaigns, which became important models for spreading AST's brand throughout Tunisia.

Organization and Planning

According to AST's website and official Facebook page, the group was organized in a basic structure that included a leader, an official spokesperson, three committees, and three offices (see table 6.1). Not all aspects of the organization could be fully gleaned from primary sources, but the following details are the positions and responsibilities that could be ascertained from the information provided by AST.

Most relevant to this discussion is how AST's leadership connected with its followers and potential new adherents. The work of Peter Neumann, Ryan Evans, and Raffaello Pantucci on "middle managers" is especially relevant in this context.[2] While their research pertained to al-Qaeda and the planning of terrorist attacks in the West, the broader formulation helps explain AST's success. The similarity between the two is related to the existence of "middle managers" or secondary leaders connected to both local supporters and top leadership. In the context of AST, this allows for strategic decision making at the national level, which is then implemented at the local level. This implementation

TABLE 6.1 AST's Leadership Structure

Position	Person/Group
Leader: Responsible for overall maintenance of the organization.	Abu 'Iyadh al-Tunisi (Sayf Allah Bin Hasin)
Deputy Leader: Responsible for press releases, press conferences, radio and television appearances, and relationship building with local Tunisian media.	Wa'il 'Amami
Official spokesperson: Responsible for press releases, press conferences, radio and television appearances, and relationship building with local Tunisian media.	Sayf al-Din al-Rayyis (previously Abu Ayub al-Tunisi)
Sharia Committee: Responsible for religious and political essays and religious rulings.	'Abd al-Hakim al-Mansuri, Abu Ja'afar al-Hatab, Abu Muhammad al-Ansari, Adam Bukadida, and Kamal Zuruq
Organizational Committee: In charge of overseeing all aspects of AST events: the information campaign, local coordination, and necessary logistics. It primarily worked with and provided help to the media, *dawa*, and social offices.	Sami Isid Bin Khamis
Political Committee: In charge of crafting AST's political messaging and outreach to mainstream political entities.	Unknown
Media Office: Involved in all aspects of duties for AST's media outlet, al-Bayyariq Media, including the management of AST's official and "news" Facebook pages, website and forum, and radio station. It also helped produce, edit, and distribute AST's media releases (statements, essays, religious rulings, video and audio messages, *anashid*, and the group's magazine, *al-Wa'ad* [The promise]). Finally, it trained individuals in new types of media-related skills.	al-Bayyariq Media Foundation
Dawa Office: Planned all types of events to spread AST's message and ideas. These included conferences, forums, distribution of AST literature, tours, and street and religious lectures. It was also in charge of compiling the literature that would be passed out.	Hasan Brik
Social Office: Helped coordinate medical and relief convoys as well as cleaning campaigns. It was in charge of the social service aspect of AST.	Ahmad al-Akrami

by local members of communities is especially important to avoid the perception that outsiders are forcing particular beliefs on the population. Essentially, AST decision making is centralized at the top levels of leadership, while implementation is decentralized. The autonomy granted to local actors through this system empowers new supporters who feel as though they have a piece of the organization. Consequently, supporters who think they have good ideas or work hard feel they can make a difference and advance in the organization.

Another aspect of shifting power back to the locals is AST's incubation process. The main avenues through which this process occurs are *dawa* forums and religious lectures. Within AST's clerical establishment, one can categorize different *shayukh* (clerics) and *daʻi* (callers to the correct interpretation of Islam) based on their national, regional, or local presence.

For example, in late March 2013, at the first *dawa* forum in Hammam-Lif, which is about fifteen miles southeast of Tunis, two individuals—Shaykh Abu ʻAbd al-Rahman al-Maliki and Malik ʻAbd al-Rahman—gave lectures at the ʻUmar Bin al-Khattab Mosque.[3] The former had spoken all over Ariana, Tunis, and Nabeul governorates, while the latter only operated in Hammam-Lif. This type of event, in which a cleric of more national or regional scope is paired with a group of local clerics or callers, played out on numerous occasions. The more well-traveled, established, and known religious figures would typically endow legitimacy on the local figures, while the local figures would present the regional or national individuals as harmless and welcome in the community. Following this initial event, AST would conduct similar events with only the local figure, which would further connect the local network to AST's broader organization. This dynamic between national/regional and local leaders also played out in other spheres of AST's organization. However, there are fewer details on specific individuals since AST media primarily promoted religious leaders—as opposed to those who distributed *dawa* literature or provided social services. This organizational dynamic counters the claim by Francesco Cavatorta that "AST was a movement in constant flux with rather unclear hierarchies."[4]

According to a founding member of AST, when the group began to organize in the spring of 2011, those who had been released from prison began organizing in Tunis, Sousse, Sidi Bouzid, al-Qayrawan, and Bizerte.[5] This organization provides a basis for understanding how AST force-multiplied its resources and gained adherents in more rural areas of Tunisia. In its convoy campaigns, AST drove from major urban locales to impoverished and rural areas to provide food and medical services and to fix or rebuild mud-brick structures the residents lived in. It also was able to take advantage of the fact that, compared with other Muslim Brotherhood–like Islamist movements in different parts of the Arab world, al-Nahdah did not have a robust "welfare operation," as Rory McCarthy explains.[6]

AST led its first convoy campaign to Haydrah, in the Kasserine governorate, on February 20, 2012. At the time, the area had been hit hard by subzero temperatures and snow.[7] Because Haydrah and other affected locations were extremely remote, their residents experienced a major shortage of essential goods.[8] AST's convoy began in central Tunis, where Abu 'Iyadh emphasized the *wajib* (obligation) of providing aid to those in need. He further emphasized that such services were an aspect of *jihad fi sabil Allah* (in the cause of God), which he said would hopefully lead to the creation of an Islamic state or Caliphate.[9] The aid provided by AST went to sixty families and included rice, pasta, bread, canned goods, milk, bottled water, winter clothing, and blankets.[10]

This convoy campaign was an important first step for AST in terms of being able to reach out to new individuals. For one, Abu 'Iyadh refocused the meaning of jihad within a jihadi movement. Historically, much of the focus had been on fighting alone. In his Tunis speech, he returned to another aspect: the so-called greater jihad of bettering yourself or community. He justified this *dawa*-first approach by asserting that these types of activities (charity and outreach) were just as relevant for improving the state of the Islamic nation and achieving the greater goal of an Islamic state. It is also a way to empower members of the group, restoring agency to individuals who felt left behind by an extremely old, top-down, and bureaucratic central government. In contrast, AST promoted a form of jihadi civic-mindedness that was young, bottom-up, and dynamic. This approach allows an individual to truly feel valued in the community. In addition, members or recruits feel that because they are partaking with like-minded individuals, they are cultivating a sense of solidarity and brotherhood or sisterhood in the movement. This juxtaposition between the Tunisian government's failure to foster a role for youth in society and the efforts of AST to achieve the same goal provide insight into the appeal of joining AST.

As AST grew, it expanded beyond major cities like Tunis, Sousse, Sidi Bouzid, al-Qayrawan, and Bizerte. At its peak, the organization could be described as having a well-refined organizational apparatus. It included a top leadership structure as described earlier, a clerical establishment (more on this below), local branches in charge of both urban and rural areas, local branches focused entirely on their own cities or towns, and individual members and volunteers.

AST's *Dawa* Program by the Numbers

I have identified twenty-four branches with capabilities beyond their own cities that brought aid to and conducted ideological outreach in rural or remote locations.[11] In total, AST had branches or organized activities in 191 unique locations throughout Tunisia. These numbers illustrate the diversity of locations in which AST operated. They also show that AST did not restrict its organizing and mobilizing efforts to small segments of society. Rather, it organized, mobilized, and recruited individuals from a plethora of places across the country.

From its first activities (helping refugees at the Tunisian-Libyan border March 2–4, 2011) to its last event (a *dawa* forum in al-Qayrawan on December 18, 2013), AST organized 870 specific activities in total. Sometimes these activities occurred simultaneously in more than one location. If considering activities by location in addition to events, there were 895 altogether. While AST may have operated prior to its formal establishment (May 2011) and continued activities after its designation as a terrorist organization (August 2013), the peak of the group's organizing activities was between November 2012 and August 2013 when it conducted 802—or 92 percent—of its 870 activities.

This trend shows that it took AST about a year and a half to become consistently active. It is possible, however, that AST simply did not report its activities consistently on its official Facebook page until November 2012. It is also conceivable that it took some time to build up its operation and capabilities well enough to become a more known entity. Once AST was able to organize multiple activities a day in multiple locations, its growth was exponential, suggesting that a wealth of planning and recruiting preceded the public show of its capabilities.

There is another plausible explanation for why its public operation did not fully emerge until late 2012: before then, the group had little local name recognition and occupied an insignificant segment of the political scene. It is important to remember that most jihadi activism by Tunisians prior to 2011 was conducted outside Tunisia, in Europe or other foreign fighter destinations. As a result, beyond the close-knit network of early AST members, most other Tunisians were unaware of the broader movement or its members.

It was only as AST staged sit-ins and demonstrations, such as the ones covered in chapter 4, that AST gained more national attention, media coverage, and political notoriety. In particular, the sharia demonstration at the clock tower and the subsequent al-Nahdah decision to no longer pursue sharia in the Constitution led some who were disillusioned by al-Nahdah's choice to join up with AST. According to Anne Wolf, "an estimated 10 percent of al-Nahdah's youth branch subsequently left the party, accusing the leadership of betraying the very Islamic principles it claimed to follow. Some of these young activists subsequently joined the salafis, who pledged never to compromise over *sharia*."[12]

Relatedly, the largest of these incidents—the attack on the U.S. Embassy in Tunis—occurred on September 14, 2012. It is quite possible that these episodes increased awareness and curiosity about AST and its mission. As one AST member noted in August 2013, "people were coming up to us to join; many times, we were not actually recruiting."[13] This curiosity—paired with AST's use of the slogan *isma'u mina wa la tasma'u 'anan* (hear from us, not about us)—provided an opportunity for AST members to engage individuals with the message that they were different from the caricatures presented in the media. For many impressionable youths who were educated but jobless or bored with their job, AST presented an exciting and purposeful alternative. This corresponding publicity campaign probably contributed to the greater visibility of AST's infrastructure and capabilities in the fall of 2012.

While it is certainly true that AST was a national organization, the heart of the organization was primarily based in and operating out of Tunis governorate, which encompasses Greater Tunis and parts of its suburbs.[14] An examination of the raw data without adjusting for population size (more on this shortly) shows that the Sidi Bouzid governorate is overrepresented and the Kasserine governorate is underrepresented (see table 6.2) relative to other governorates. It would be reasonable to conclude that the residents of Sidi Bouzid were sympathetic to AST due to the governorate's role as the seat of the revolution and a historical hotbed of discontent with the central government, given its location in the interior of the country, especially since AST is attempting to completely change the order, which some might perceive as being beneficial to them materially. However, according to Michael Marcusa, the individuals in the governorate may have been interested in the group from a social and emotional perspective.[15] As for Kasserine, it is mainly a hub of trafficking and smuggling.[16] Therefore, it is possible that AST would not want to draw negative attention by establishing a base in that region of the country. It is also an area where al-Qaeda in the Islamic Maghrib's Tunisian branch, Katibat 'Uqbah Bin Nafi, is based.[17] AST and AQIM might not have wanted people to confuse their differing strategies, as the former was promoting a *dawa*-first approach and the latter, a jihad-first approach.

A sounder way to assess AST's influence on an area or, at the very least, its commitment to organize in a particular location is to assess its activities on a per capita basis (see table 6.3). This would adjust for any population biases of an area due to the number of residents. An examination of the data from this angle shows that Tunis governorate remains the strongest area of activity and likely the group's biggest support base. Conclusions from table 6.3 about areas overrepresented and underrepresented, however, provide a different picture from what is represented in table 6.2. The Siliana, Kebili, and Tataouine governorates are overrepresented while Sfax, Medenine, and Kasserine are underrepresented. The reasoning behind activity in the Siliana, Kebili, and Tataouine governorates is similar to that of Sidi Bouzid; however, it is difficult to assess the specifics without further interrogation, especially since the Tozeur governorate and others fit a similar profile of grievance or marginalization but experience low levels of AST activity. The Medenine governorate, like the Kasserine governorate, acts as an important hub of smuggling and trafficking, but with Libya instead of Algeria. Lastly, a greater investigation into the reason behind

TABLE 6.2 AST Activities by Governorate

Governorates	Overall Activities	Population Rank
Tunis	261	1
Nabeul	93	3
Bizerte	58	8
Sidi Bouzid	52	12
Ben Arous	50	5
Monastir	48	9
al-Qayrawan	44	6
Ariana	44	7
Sousse	40	4
Sfax	33	2
Siliana	31	20
Kebili	19	22
Gafsa	15	10
Medenine	15	17
Tataouine	15	23
Mahdia	13	13
Manouba	12	15
Béja	11	18
El Kef	6	19
Gabes	5	14

Governorates	Overall Activities	Population Rank
Jendouba	5	16
Zaghouan	3	21
Kasserine	2	11
Tozeur	1	24

low AST activity in Sfax—Tunisia's second-largest governorate—would be worthwhile but is confounding.

It is possible that recent research by Marcusa as well as Christopher Barrie and Neil Ketchley could provide answers for Sfax and other locales like Medenine and Kasserine, beyond the ones already articulated. According to Marcusa, "state-building legacies and collective memory" have played a role in divergences where jihadis have gained ground, while other locales have not. Meaning that those towns in Tunisia with a history of union activism saw little jihadi mobilization.[18] Moreover, within the context of recruitment to the Islamic State, Barrie and Ketchley contend that "where discontent stemming from economic marginalization can be channeled into protest, the Islamic State saw less success at attracting recruits."[19] Therefore, areas that have seen alternative and competitive social movement opportunities arise, Tunisians have chosen the alternative to jihadism.

What Types of Activities Did AST Organize?

AST organized 10 different types of activities within the 870 it performed. Six of them are relatively self-explanatory: annual conferences, press conferences, radio/TV interviews, demonstrations, and funerals. Demonstrations mainly called for the release of Tunisian prisoners in Iraqi prisons who had fought with Abu Musʿab al-Zarqawi's network and its successor organization the Islamic State of Iraq as well as AST members imprisoned by the Tunisian government. The organization also assisted with funerals and processions of the dead through the streets of members' hometowns. The most notable of these was the return of Yusuf al-Tariqi's body from Iraq to Sfax after the government in Baghdad executed him for involvement in the notorious 2006 attack on the Shia shrine and mosque in Samarra.[20] In addition to the above activities, the most significant ones that AST organized were charity/social services, outreach, children's outreach, and religious lectures.

TABLE 6.3 AST Activities Per Capita

Governorates	Activities Per Capita	Activities Rank
Tunis	4,046.9	1
Siliana	7,196.4	11
Kebili	8,261.1	12
Sidi Bouzid	8,267.5	4
Nabeul	8,472.3	2
Bizerte	9,796.9	3
Tataouine	9,963.5	15
Monastir	11,433.9	6
Ben Arous	12,636.8	5
al-Qayrawan	12,968.2	7
Ariana	13,092.9	8
Sousse	16,874.3	9
Gafsa	22,488.7	13
Béja	27,548.4	18
Sfax	28,952.2	10
Mahdia	31,600.9	16
Manouba	31,626.5	17
Medenine	31,968.0	14
El Kef	40,526.0	19
Zaghouan	58,981.7	22

Governorates	Activities Per Capita	Activities Rank
Gabes	74,860.0	20
Jendouba	80,295.4	21
Tozeur	107,912.0	24
Kasserine	219,621.5	23

A variety of actions fall under AST's charity/social services activities. Due to the scale, this chapter just focuses on a few cases, as it does with outreach, children's outreach, and religious lectures sections. These are the range of charitable actions and social services that AST provided to Tunisian residents:

> Helping refugees, organizing convoys (food, medical, religious), selling produce at wholesale price, repairing roads, providing food for the needy during Ramadan, providing sacrificial animal meat during Eid al-Fitr and Eid al-Adha, providing Iftar meals to people in the street and walking by, collecting aid/money for Gaza, collecting donations for the needy/poor, cleaning the streets, landscaping and planting trees, cleaning the weekly market, maintaining buildings, painting walls, visiting hospitals (providing presents and food), fixing homes, organizing blood donations, cleaning cemeteries, providing acupuncture, performing exorcisms, fixing roofs, and visiting the elderly.

The first action that AST organized was helping Libyan refugees who had fled to Tunisia. From March 2–4, 2011, a group of recently amnestied individuals who would form the core of AST went to the Tunisian-Libyan border to help settle newly arrived refugees. AST members helped erect temporary housing, supply tents, and provide aid once the refugees crossed the border.[21] While altruistic, it was also a way for AST to build relationships and an infrastructure of training, facilitation, and logistics within Libya in cooperation with its sister organization, Ansar al-Sharia in Libya, which is discussed in greater detail in chapter 7.

One of the most comprehensive types of charitable actions that AST organized was its medical convoys that provided medical service and medicine to those in need. These convoys also help explain AST's broader network of associations that helped provide a local infrastructure for donations and supplies. Foremost among them was Jama'iah (The Association of) Abu al-Qasim al-Zahrawi.[22] It is named after the tenth-century Arab physician from al-Andalus (today southern Spain) widely considered to be the father of surgery. Originating in AST's Sfax branch, its first publicized convoy went to Ksour Essef, about fifty-five miles north in the Mahdia governorate.[23] Prior to the convoy AST released an online promotion graphic (which it does for many of its activities) that called for monetary or pharmaceutical supplies and medicines, which stated "items needed: antibiotics, analgesics, anti-inflammatories, mucolytics, eye drops: antibiotics and anti-inflammatories, gastric dressings (actrapid insulin), antiseptics (betadine, compresses, cotton, syringes, tensiometer, among other things), stethoscope, glucometers, glucometer strips, urine dipsticks, and ECG." Those interested in donating were told to send them to an AST-controlled mosque called al-Adhar2, across the street from Hédi Chaker Hospital. Based on pictures AST released from the event, it was clear that at least some of the individuals from AST's medical association were also doctors at this hospital.

AST continued organizing similar medical convoys throughout its existence. For instance, on November 11, 2012, in Sidi Bouzid, on AST's behalf, Jama'iah Abu al-Qasim al-Zahrawi provided free medical services, including internal, cardiovascular, and children's medicine as well as general surgery and ophthalmology.[24] Based on AST's public releases, there were at least twenty-six such medical convoys, some that included other medical services as well. It is certainly possible that AST did not publicize all its events online and therefore conducted more of these medical convoys. This was an important part of AST's repertoire because it allowed the group to prove its ability to provide for a population in need. In many ways AST felt that it was competing with the Tunisian state to prove itself more capable of caring for all residents of Tunisia, not just the elite or those in affluent locations. This is why one of the main slogans that AST used when conducting medical convoys and providing other services was *abna'ukum fi khadamatukum* (your sons are at your service), an attempt to illustrate that those in AST were working on Tunisians' behalf and that they are members of the community and not people from a distant faceless entity like the central government. AST promoted the message that, while the central government overpromises and underdelivers, "we" in AST were working hard to improve your health and the broader community. By ingratiating itself to a particular town or community, AST bought goodwill and an opening to perform ideological outreach to facilitate its broader project of building an Islamic state.

In addition to Jama'iah Abu al-Qasim al-Zahrawi, AST maintained a broader network of support and cooperation with a number of charitable and religious associations that provided aid and services to those in need. According to Tunisian academic Alaya Allani, in total there were around two hundred such charities and associations affiliated with AST.[25] These are the ones AST mentioned in its media: the Association of Islamic Cooperation in Ben Gardane, the Abode of Islam Association for Good Works and the Study of Sharia in

Bizerte, the Revival of Islamic Heritage Society in Ennassim, the Sharia Association for Learning of the Qur'an and Sunnah in Hammam Zriba, the Islamic Nation Association in La Cagna, Imam Sahnun Islamic Association in Mahdia, the Mastering Association for the Recitation of the Qur'an in Tunis, the Qur'anic Association of Bini Ghazayil in Medenine, and the Islamic Youth Awakening in Tunis. AST essentially used these associations as auxiliaries to its formal organizing structures to bolster its image as a religiously legitimate group that performs good deeds. These associations expanded AST's mobilizing structures by providing more resources.

In parallel to its network of associations, AST also took control of or, at the very least, affiliated itself with a number of mosques throughout Tunisia (see figure 6.1). By identifying mosques at which AST organized events or to whose members it expressed messages of solidarity, I was able to identify at a minimum the number of mosques AST likely controlled. In total, this research uncovered 135, with the largest number of mosques in the Greater Tunis area. It is possible and even likely that AST controlled even more mosques.

Following the fall of Bin 'Ali, many mosques dropped from state control. State-appointed preachers lost legitimacy and gained a reputation as lackeys of the state. As a result, many were kicked out of their positions and replaced with others. These replacements were often affiliated with al-Nahdah or non-jihadi salafis as well as AST. According to one al-Nahdah member, "we abandoned the mosques, and the salafists came and took the mosques. They spread extremist ideas that we don't adopt. The problem in al-Nahda is that we let ourselves become too preoccupied with political work."[26] Either way, by October 2011 the Tunisian government estimated that up to four hundred mosques had been lost to nonstate actors.[27] By the time the government began to wrest control back in early 2014, up to one thousand were out of state hands.[28] Moreover, according to 'Abd al-Satar Badr, chief of staff for the Ministry of Religious Affairs in 2015, there were also "close to 200 new mosques built without a license" from 2011 to 2013.[29] Since that time, the state attempted to wrest control of the mosques back. According to Muhammad Khalil, Tunisia's minister of religious affairs at the time, the last mosque reclamation by the government happened in early July 2016, five and a half years after the start of the revolution.[30]

These mosques acted as important resources for the mobilization of AST's activities. While the mosques were certainly used for praying and religious lectures, they doubled as locations for preparing service provisions. Namely, they served as hubs to organize the various goods and supplies AST would distribute in packages with a label stating AST's logo, name, and sometimes a slogan or Qur'anic verse. One of the most vital times of year for these activities was Ramadan. The mosques would then be used as headquarters to plan donation drives for needy families during Ramadan as well as during Eid al-Fitr and Eid al-Adha.

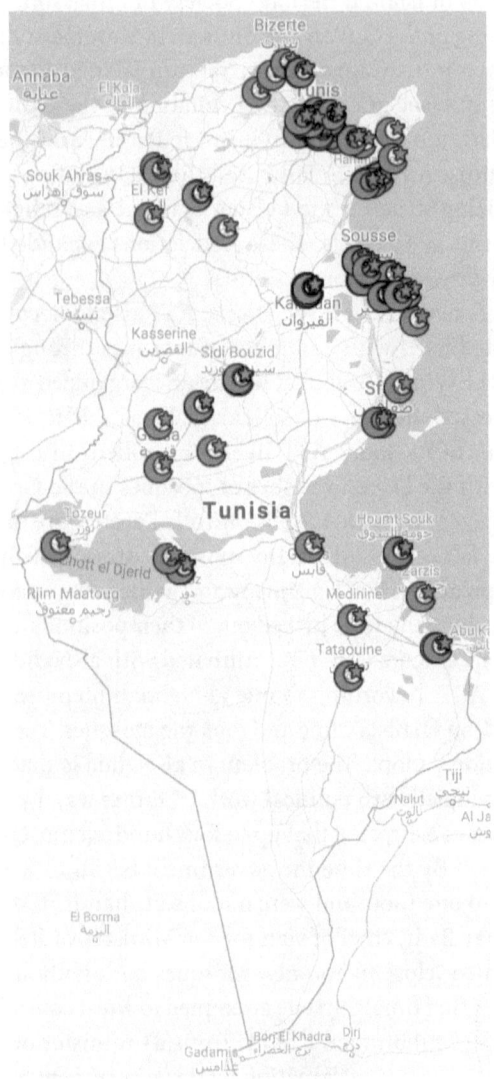

6.1 Ansar al-Sharia in Tunisia's Mosques Network

While AST provided aid during Ramadan in a host of locales, in 2013, it promoted specific donation drives at three mosques in Kebili, five in al-Qayrawan, one in Menzel Bourguiba, four in Le Kram, one in El Mourouj, three in the southern suburbs of Tunis, nine in Douar Hishour, one in Cité El Khadra, and two in Oued Ellil. In Cité El Khadra, it even provided guidelines for the ideal distribution of aid to a family of four so people knew what supplies to bring: Every week for the benefit of four people—1 × chickens is 6,000 millimes,[31]

6 × milk is 6,600 millimes, 30 × eggs is 6,200 millimes, 1 liter of corn oil is 1,500 millimes, 2 × kg semolina is 1,500 millimes, 2 × kg couscous is 1,500 millimes, 1.5 × kg macaroni is 1,300 millimes, 1 × kg sugar is 1,000 millimes, 1/2 × kg soup is 1,000 millimes, 1 × kg tomato is 1,600 millimes, 1 × kg *mesfouf* is 800 millimes, which equals 29 dinars (~US$17.30 at the time).

Another element of AST's broader *dawa* program was its outreach. A large part of this outreach was the education of the local populations in areas in which AST worked. AST therefore organized daily and weekly tents and tables at local markets and schools to pass out its *dawa* literature. Occasionally it would also lead walking tours around the main streets and cafes and visit hospitals to pass out its literature. In addition, AST distributed Qur'ans as well as its own statements, statements from AQIM in Mali, and articles from the jihadi-salafi scholar Abu Muhammad al-Maqdisi, among other things. AST even initiated several mailing campaigns for rural and remote areas.

While AST has released some in-house publications, much of the literature it distributes at its *dawa* events can be traced to at least three book publishing houses in Saudi Arabia: Dar al-Qassem, based in Riyadh; Dar al-Tarafen, based in Taif; and the Cooperative Office for the Call and Guidance and Education Communities, based in Dammam. The nature of the relationship between AST and these publishing houses is unclear, and it is possible that AST did not receive support from any of them since anyone can buy the content online. Nonetheless, the fact that a significant amount of its literature originates in Saudi Arabia—a traditional supporter of salafi organizations—is likely a sign that some of its leaders have liaised with these book shops. Moreover, one of AST's Facebook posts even promoted assisting the group when a package arrived in December in cooperation with two auxiliary charities (Jama'iah al-Jawd al-Khayriyah and Jama'iah al-Khayr al-Islamiyah): "There will be a package sent to Tunisia that has books and promotional information starting from Tuesday. Thus, this is a post to attract helpers to come prepare the packages, who believe in the establishment of an Islamic state within Tunisia."[32]

A significant portion of the literature distributed at markets and schools is not of a militant nature. In fact, a lot of it is orthodox salafi publications on religion that focus on the correct way to pray, ethics in Islam, characteristics of a well-mannered Muslim, religious exegesis, and the hereafter, among other topics. AST uses this literature to present a less extreme ideology than it actually practices. In many ways, AST gradually guides new recruits to become sympathetic to AQ, rather than jarring them with AQ content at the outset. This is why AST reserves special viewings of official AQ videos for its more hardened followers.[33] By ingratiating itself to local residents and students, AST hopes to promote an image of honest and pious Muslims attempting to spread the word of God. While members of AST no doubt view themselves as sincere religious interlocutors, the group does not publicize publicly in local activities its broader ideological affinities and long-term plans with AQ.

Beyond appealing to the broader adult public, AST has also focused on outreach to children and teenagers. The group understood that the future lay with them, especially given that much of the Tunisian population is under the age of twenty-five. If AST could help socialize and mold these young minds, the jihadi-salafi project would be the way of the future. As a result, AST has set up some of its tents in front of primary and secondary schools. It would usually pass out its *dawa* literature alongside sweets and presents for the children to pique the interest of the young children and early teenagers.[34] AST also provided school books and backpacks for children to incentivize parents to allow AST's further engagement with their children or indirectly recruit the parents themselves.[35]

To further encourage children to subscribe to AST ideology, the group organized several social events for kids and young teenagers to expose them to recruiters from the organization. For example, on October 28, 2012, AST provided a soccer lesson and helped referee a game for children no older than ten in Mateur. AST even supplied a quintessential item for anyone who has played youth soccer: juice boxes.[36] An important note here is that, in AST's propaganda, it frames children as "Cubs of Islam." Within jihadi culture, a lion "evokes qualities of bravery, strength, and valor."[37] This is why members of the movement use such symbols to arouse feelings of strength and fortitude. In this same vein, groups such as AST use the word "cub" for children to conjure a similar image of a lion, but one that is still in training with much to learn. At the same time, it provides a sense of pride in a child who believes he is a fierce cub that will eventually become a dominating lion. In the context of jihadism and AST, this would mean spreading the message of Islam and its control over society and the world.

In addition to soccer, other social activities that AST organized for children and teenagers included a sports tournament, hiking in the mountains, and a beach trip.[38] Relatedly, AST also had religious social events to reinforce the importance of religion in its societal project. These included classes with award ceremonies to encourage the continued study of Islam and a number of Qur'anic memorization contests.[39] Moreover, at the end of a religious course or conclusion of a holiday, AST would throw a special party for children and distribute gifts.[40]

Through this soft targeting, AST hoped to gain broader commitment from and role for children and young teenagers interested in the social camaraderie of the organization. As a result, some of the children eventually became involved with AST's services and outreach activities. This led to AST's organization of a road maintenance campaign completed by children in Ariana, painting over graffiti on walls, planting trees and landscaping in Ez Zahra, and leading *dawa* tours to distribute AST literature in al-Mitlawi.[41] From AST's perspective, buy-in with children and young teenagers is vital for the future of its project since these individuals will be the eventual leaders of the movement and hopefully implement AST's ideal theocratic state in the future.

The final aspect of AST's *dawa* campaign was its religious lectures program, which was an opportunity for AST to show that learned individuals with religious bona fides maintained membership in its movement. Based on AST's public releases, there were sixty-five individuals who gave lectures throughout Tunisia when the group was active (see figure 6.2). The most prolific of them were 'Atif al-Matiri, Abu 'Iyadh al-Tunisi, Abu Muhanad al-Tunisi, Kamal

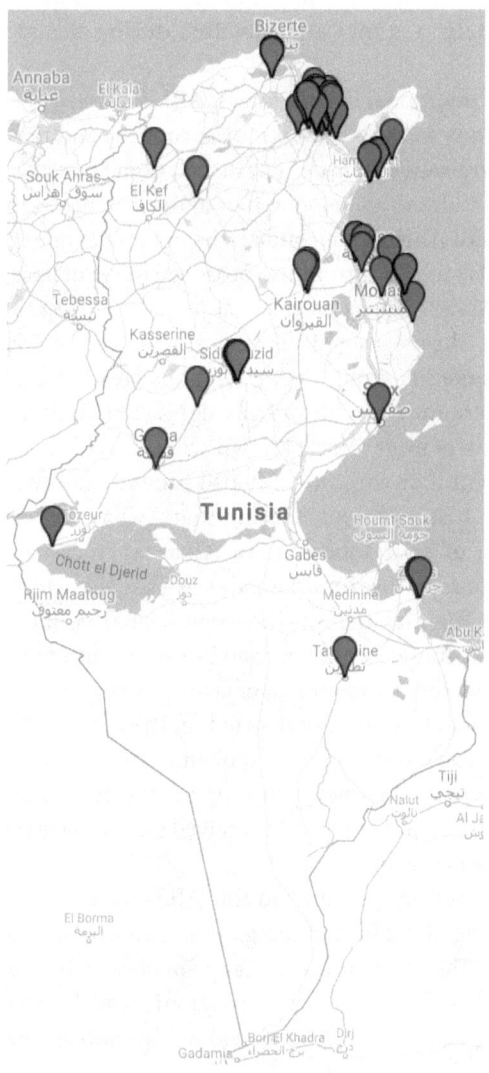

6.2 Locations of Ansar al-Sharia in Tunisia's Religious Lectures

Zuruq, Muhammad al-Fizani, Mujahid Bin Khalid, Sayf al-Din al-Rayyis, Abu 'Abd al-Rahman al-Maliki, and Rida al-Haj Ibrahim.

The lectures given by AST's clerical establishment can be divided into three categories: traditional Islamic topics, Wahhabi theology, and jihadi ideology. The topics most often discussed at these lectures were from Wahhabi theology (more on this shortly). Within the jihadi ideological realm, lectures included topics such as Sayyid Qutb's idea of *jahiliya* (pre-Islamic ignorance) and Shaykh Abu Muhammad al-Maqdisi's works, *al-Dimakratiya din* (Democracy: A religion) and *Millat Ibrahim* (The religion of Abraham). The latter two works are classics within the jihadi-salafi literature. They discuss the incompatibility of Islam and democracy as well as similarities between current Arab "apostate" regimes and idolaters during the age of the Prophet Muhammad.

Regarding the traditional Islamic topics, AST discussed Shaykh Muhammad al-Tahir Ibn Ashur's works on Maliki jurisprudence and praying, Shaykh Ibn Abu Zayd al-Qayrawani's "Epistle" (an instructional book devoted to the education of young children), and biographies of the Prophet Muhammad, his wife 'Aiysha, and Shaykh Ahmad Ibn Hanbal (the founder of one the four main legal schools in Sunni Islam). The group also broached issues of jurisprudence regarding fasting and Maliki fatwas on *zakat al-fitr* (almsgiving to the needy at the end of Ramadan). The most significant aspect of AST's promotion of traditional topics is that despite the group's salafi religious creed, it still draws from Ibn Ashur and al-Qayrawani, two historically significant Tunisian Maliki scholars. This incorporation of more widely known scholars is likely done because local populations are familiar with them. It also provides a way for AST to co-opt Tunisian Islamic history by insinuating that AST is descendant from those scholars. The eras of Bourguiba and Bin 'Ali are then cast as outliers in Tunisia's broader history. The use of Ibn Ashur's work is also a direct message to the members of these regimes and AST's current secular political opponents. This is because, in 1960, Ibn Ashur challenged Bourguiba after being asked to issue a fatwa legitimizing the abandonment of fasting during the Muslim holy month of Ramadan. Ibn Ashur famously retorted on the radio that "God has spoken *haqq* [the truth] and Bourguiba has spoken *batil* [falsehood]."[42] Even if Ibn Ashur or al-Qayrawani were not salafis, AST attempted to carry the banner of Tunisian Islam and continue what it perceived as a positive trajectory of bringing Islam into the hearts of everyone.

As for the lectures on Muhammad Ibn 'Abd al-Wahhab's works and ideas, the speech AST members most often gave was an explanation of his book *al-Usul al-thalatha* (The three fundamental principles), which explores the ideas of "Who is your Lord?," "What is your religion?," and "Who is your Prophet?," AST also gave lectures on Ibn 'Abd al-Wahhab's *Kitab al-tawhid* (The book of monotheism), *Kashf al-shubuhat* (Clarification of the doubts), *al-Qawa'id al-'arba'a* (The four foundations), *al-Usul al-sittah* (The six fundamental principles), *Nawaqid al-islam* (Nullifiers of Islam), and *al-Radd 'ala al-rafidah* (The refutation of the rejectionists). It also discussed specific Wahhabi concepts, including *al-wala' wa-l-bara'* (loyalty [to the Muslims] and disavowal [to the unbelievers]) and *kufr bi-l-taghut* (disbelieving in anything worshipped besides God). These represent key works by Ibn 'Abd al-Wahhab, suggesting that AST attempted to co-opt the Wahhabi scholarly heritage, whose practitioners view themselves as true heirs, unlike members of the Saudi regime who are portrayed as *taghut* (tyrants) by AST and other jihadis. Although AST performed these activities prior to the reemergence of the Islamic State, it professed a similar type of ideational contestation.[43]

Therefore, through its clerical and grassroots charitable/outreach network, AST successfully mobilized human capital, which allowed it to spread its goals and visions throughout Tunisian society. Without such an extensive network that expanded over time, it is unlikely that AST would have been able to succeed in such a manner. But the ability to mobilize, along with the open conditions that allowed AST to thrive, do not fully explain its success. Without a message that resonated with the local population, the ability to operate freely and mobilize would be for naught.

Between Messaging and Narratives

One way to elucidate AST's mechanism for crafting messages is to examine it through the lens of frame analysis. According to Robert D. Benford and David A. Snow, this can be broken down into three parts: diagnostic, prognostic, and motivational framing. The previous chapter identifies the former two frames, while this one focuses on the final aspect of framing: motivational, which "functions as prods to action."[44] Within AST's worldview, its diagnostic framing is related to the lack of Islam in society and the absence of implementation at a governmental level; its prognostic framing is a *dawa*-first strategy; and its motivational framing relates to brotherhood, the defense of Islam, and the creation of an Islamic state.

Prior to discussing AST's motivational framing, it is useful to mention a key factor that social psychologists identify as a reason why individuals join extremist groups. This will help extrapolate the substantive ideas that attract individuals to AST within the context of Tunisian society, especially since framing stems from a top-down process and social psychological aspects come from the bottom (i.e., the individual). Therefore, according to Arie W. Kruglanski and colleagues, the underlying motivation for joining an extremist group is a "quest for significance ... the fundamental desire to matter, to be someone, to have respect."[45]

Within the context of Tunisia, there is a perception that few avenues exist where one can gain some level of significance independently. The original revolution was a youth revolution against an elderly-run state seen as corrupt and unable to provide requisite opportunities or services. Because of the highly educated nature of the populace (as discussed in the first chapter), there was an awareness and political consciousness among the youth and society writ large. At the onset of the revolution, according to Tunisia's National Institute of Statistics, 54 percent of the population was under the age of thirty. Furthermore, 26 percent of university graduates were unemployed, with the percentages even worse outside coastal cities.[46] Despite an entrepreneurial spirit, Tunisia's youth also find it extremely difficult to start their own businesses due the massive governmental bureaucracy that creates unnecessary obstacles and barriers.

Consequently, many Tunisians have decided to move to Europe, both legally and illegally, to improve their prospects and use the skills they acquired in school. The less connected or fortunate, however, remain in Tunisia without many prospects. Therefore, while many Tunisians were happy about the revolution, within a year or two, many had become disillusioned with the lack of substantive changes, even with an Islamist party in power. This provides further backdrop for why individuals in a place like Sidi Bouzid, the birthplace of the revolution, might be inclined to join AST as an alternative to the status quo.

AST aimed to fill the void left by poor governance through providing meaning and understanding in the world. It named the lack of Islam and spiritual vibrancy as the cause for all societal ills. Even al-Nahdah, the so-called Islamist party, was perceived as failing to perpetuate Islamic values. AST's leader, Abu 'Iyadh, questioned, "I ask where is Islam in its meetings in the Constituent Assembly? Where is the Qur'an in those discussions? Where is religion in it? Where is the sanctifying of religion?. . . If Islam has no presence in your meeting, you al-Nahdah people, then what is the point of you being representative of Islam?"[47] AST's *dawa* outreach and alternative vision for society thus aimed to first reeducate Muslims on proper forms of Islam and then provide a base for building an Islamic state. It gave lost youth with very little direction in life a level of significance as well as a means by which to serve their families and society. In many ways AST called on Tunisian youth to do what U.S. president John F. Kennedy once instructed: "ask not what your country can do for you, ask what you can do for your country." However, in this context, AST called for the return of Islam to its rightful place in society. By promoting the message that it was conducting activities on behalf of God, AST sanctified its project and increased its gravitas, respect, and meaning.

With this context in mind, one way to examine AST's promotion and framing of events can be discussed in terms of two categories: slogans and sections from Qur'anic verses. Regarding the former, one of the most widely used motivational themes is the development and assistance of one's brother in religion.

For example, some of the brotherhood-related slogans put forth by AST include The Muslims Are Brothers of Muslims, Worshippers of God Are Our Brothers, and The Believers Are but Brothers. The ideas of brotherhood and solidarity are important selling points to individuals potentially interested in becoming involved with AST. These individuals feel they have an opportunity to join fellow brothers to work together for a better vision in society. This then builds loyalty and willingness to sacrifice for one another in pursuit of AST's goals.

For young individuals struggling to find a place in society, this idea of a family can be seductive. It is even more so the case when AST recruiters approach individuals at markets and in the streets to pass out literature about events that promote familial messages. These recruiters make an individual feel warm, welcomed, and valued. Furthermore, the opportunity to be part of a group that acts on behalf of God provides an added level of significance. These positive emotions, according to Jeff Goodwin and James M. Jasper, give the individual "pride, security, and confidence."[48] They solidify an individual's connection to the organization and his fellow "brothers" since he wants to continue to feel a sense of significance and belonging. An AST member once explained how one of his friends joined the group: "One day he came to see me to understand what was this special feeling that we shared. We are more than friends; we are brothers. We share ethics and between us, there is a special strength and solidarity."[49]

Relatedly, another motivating frame AST used was the necessity of supporting and defending God and Islam. While society had indeed opened up, AST still believed that Islam was under attack and people were unable to properly worship as they saw fit. For instance, a member of AST named Iskander Bughanmi explained that "when we try to spread our message about God's law, we are stopped and we are persecuted."[50] Therefore, AST's pitch was that even under a so-called democratic system, they were still treated as enemies of the state. From AST's perspective, if individuals subscribed to the ideology of the group, they were on the side of God and religion. As such, if they wanted to work on behalf of restoring the place of God and the dignity of Islam in society, they should join the movement. For this reason, AST used the following slogans:

Endowed to Support the Prophet
Be Supporters of God
Safety to Achieve the Law of the Merciful
Be Worshipers of God, Brother
Hasten to God
Worshippers of God Are Our Brothers
They Are Supporters of God
My Religion Is Islam
No Refuge, Except for With God

They Are Supporters of Islamic Law
Best to Repent Wrongdoings
Support for Islamic Law
Return to God

These slogans would signal to individuals that they could join a special movement that provides significance in life. AST's project is a complete break from the status quo and a wholly different idea of how society should function. Therefore, people can join AST to not only support and defend God and religion but also to build something for the benefit of society at large.

Relatedly, the building of an Islamic state is the third motivating frame used by AST to encourage people to join its group. It is so important to the group that, when it published its first advertisement for its second annual conference in May 2012, it framed the event as "a building block in the project to establish the Caliphate State."[51] Furthermore, the title of the third annual conference a year later was "Supporters of Islamic Law, The Islamic State We Are Building," suggesting that it was no longer an objective for the future but rather was a process that AST had already begun. After the third conference, AST began using the slogan We Are Building the Islamic State to further signify the ongoing process and push individuals to join the historic project.[52]

This messaging frame is the ultimate tool in fostering an individual's sense of significance. It asserted that one could be part of a project larger than oneself: the reestablishment of an Islamic state in Tunisia. Therefore, those same youth who have education, skills, and desire to give back to their community can now feel empowered. AST seeks to contrast that feeling of empowerment with the feelings sparked by a corrupt central government that does not want to empower youth. Recognizing these grievances, AST always repeated the slogan Your Sons Are at Your Service. This highlighted the importance of not only giving back to one's neighborhood but also honoring those involved in such work. It also helped that AST provided evidence (by posting all of its activities on its official Facebook page) that it was indeed building this shadow structure of works and services in various communities throughout Tunisia. Consequently, the more charitable and outreach activities AST orchestrated, the more individuals joined up, which in turn allowed AST to organize and conduct more activities more often in more locales.

The final motivational frame used by AST came later in the group's development. It only emerged when the Tunisian government began to crack down on its activities following the assassination of Tunisia's secular politician, Shukri Bila'id, in February 2013 and in the lead-up to AST's third annual conference in May 2013. The government began attempting to completely shut down *dawa* events and prohibit members from legally organizing. Beginning in mid-May 2013 AST began to promote its activities by using the slogan *du'wat Allah baqiya* (the call of God remains).⁵³ Unlike the above frames, which evoked more positive messages to encourage people to join AST, this one used a more negative appeal. It posited that AST needed all the help it could get to defend its vision against an existential threat. It was a rallying cry for support but also a message of defiance in the face of what it perceived to be an oppressive tyrannical regime.

Beyond the slogans, AST also invoked sections of Qur'anic verses to appeal to new supporters and potential recruits.⁵⁴ In many ways AST turned parts of the Qur'an into marketing slogans, including So Do Not Weaken and Do Not Grieve, and You Will Be Superior (3:139); And, [Moreover], This Is My Path, Which Is Straight, So Follow It, (6:153); Remind Them of the Days of God (14:5); They Want to Extinguish the Light of God (9:32); If You Support God, He Will Support You (47:7); Merciful Among Themselves (48:29); and The Believers Are but Brothers (49:10). This reinforces the importance of exploring how these types of groups use religion, and Lorne L. Dawson has challenged those who study jihadi groups to take this more seriously.⁵⁵

Despite the manner in which AST used these verses, none of them are the so-called fighting verses, such as the infamous "sword verse" (9:5). This further confirms results published in 2012 by Jeffry R. Halverson, R. Bennett Furlow, and Steven R. Corman, who analyzed more than two thousand extremist texts from 1998 to 2011.⁵⁶ The results showed that the "verses extremists cite from the Qur'an . . . deal with themes of victimization, dishonor, and retribution."⁵⁷ Regarding AST, the verses cited can be described as relating to enduring hardship, keeping the faith, and surviving in the face of seemingly insurmountable odds. AST's choice of verses does not suggest a message of offensive warfare but the framework of a community under siege (as perceived by its members). This is broadly indicative of a group involved in identity politics (which was partially covered in chapter 4's discussion of AST's promotion of certain social mores. This is further explored in the next chapter's examination of AST's *hisba* activities). AST employed a variety of angles and methods to pull at different individuals who might become curious and later active in the group, depending on the particular motivational frame that spoke to them.

* * *

AST's organizational structure provided space for both national-level strategy and local-level intimacy. Its activities were characterized by a number of opportunities for individuals to become involved, whether through outreach, religious education, or charitable and relief efforts. Moreover, framing provided an individual with a purpose that both benefited himself and encouraged solidarity among group members by helping them to believe that they were fulfilling God's promise and bettering their communities. This incentivized individuals to remain active and encouraged new members to join, even when the group came under threat from the state.

This threat from the Tunisian state will be discussed in the next chapter, which examines the downfall of AST and the return of Tunisian foreign fighting. It will explore the reasons behind the Tunisian government's designation of AST as a terrorist organization in late August 2013. Finally, it will help explain why Tunisians became infamous for foreign fighting and involvement in groups like the Islamic State after 2013.

CHAPTER 7

TUNISIANS CAN BE FOUND EVERYWHERE IN THE LAND OF JIHAD

On Thursday, September 13, 2012, AST posted a flier on its official Facebook page with the caption "They Came to Support Their Prophet." Above this, the organization said it was planning a demonstration in front of the U.S. Embassy the next day after Friday prayers in support of the Prophet Muhammad.[1] This was in response to the controversy surrounding the recently released anti-Islamic film *Innocence of Muslims*. In a similar vein, AST's sister organization Ansar al-Sharia in Libya attacked the U.S. Consulate in Benghazi and killed the American ambassador, J. Christopher Stevens, and Ansar al-Sharia in Egypt conducted a smaller-scale and less violent attack on the U.S. Embassy in Cairo.

Following Friday prayers, hundreds of members of AST began to march from their mosques to the U.S. Embassy. They began chanting: *Obama, Obama, Kulnah Usamah*. Obama, Obama, We Are All Usamah [Bin Ladin].[2] This was anything but a nonviolent protest. Tunisian police attempting to protect the U.S. Embassy became overrun by the sheer number of individuals rushing toward the embassy with AST's black flag (which has the seal of the Prophet Muhammad at the top, the Muslim testament of faith in the middle, and group's name at the bottom). First, they smashed large rocks on the glass windows of the security check entrance. Then a number of individuals who brought ladders with them scaled the ten- to fifteen-foot wall. Others began spray-painting the white exterior walls with the Muslim testament of faith, Muhammad's name inside a heart, X-ing out the acronym USA, and writing *Amirikan yah khamaj* (you rotten/dirty Americans).

After scaling the wall members of AST began to burn rubber tires and set cars in the complex on fire. According to a U.S. Embassy in Tunis official, "they almost killed the motor pool drivers."[3] From there these individuals began to rampage upon the main building and recreation center.[4] Based on pictures released by AST member Abu Turab al-Tunisi, they threw all of the plastic lounge chairs that were surrounding the pool into the pool.[5] Moreover, in a symbolic measure, those involved in this attack took down the American flag from the flagpole and raised AST's black flag.[6] A Tunisian jihadi involved in the attack and interviewed by the French journalist David Thompson explained, "This is a day of glory for God. The Arab people are revived and they understand well who their enemy is. . . . Today we are all Usamah. Today we are all al-Qaeda. Soon there will be no more obstacles standing in the way of the restoration of the caliphate."[7] In many ways those involved in the attack saw this as a legitimate *ghazwah* (raid) and claimed that they also took *ghana'im* (war loot)—in particular, a cargo box full of Apple laptops.[8]

The Tunisian state and security apparatus were very slow to take action. This was likely a consequence of the types of policies related to jihadis, described in chapter 4. Even more callous besides the delayed response was the fact that, during the attack, Tunisian state TV was playing cartoons and not reporting what was going on.[9] No one from the embassy was killed, but it was a close call. According to the same U.S. Embassy in Tunis official, in the safe room in the embassy more than one hundred people were starting to feel the ill effects of the smoke from the burning fires inside and outside the complex. If security had come any later, this official believes that the death toll from the Benghazi attack would have paled in comparison to what could have happened in Tunis because so many could have succumbed to asphyxiation.[10] In the following days senior leaders and members in AST, including Hasan al-Brik, Muhammad Bakhti, and Bilal al-Shawashi, were arrested due to their involvement in the attack. While this was the beginning of the end for AST, it was a confluence of things that led to its eventual downfall.

* * *

At the same time AST was implementing its successful *dawa* outreach, the organization and its members were involved behind the scenes in more covert and nefarious activities. AST's greater popularity and national voice also put a larger spotlight on the organization. In a sense, the seeds of its own destruction were sown in its success. Therefore, this chapter explains the downfall of AST and the return of Tunisian foreign fighting as the dominant form of organization and mobilization for jihadis from Tunisia.

To explain this transformation, this chapter explores a number of interrelated processes inside and outside Tunisia that precipitated the eventual designation of AST as a terrorist organization and incentivized Tunisians to become foreign fighters or commit local acts of terrorism. The dynamics that led to this transformation include the rising level of intimidation and violence through *hisba* (moral policing) activities, transformation of AST to a more overtly hostile actor, and recruitment for training and fighting jihad abroad. Pressure from opposition political parties—combined with al-Nahdah's changing calculus as a result of rising AST-linked violence and instability from al-Qaeda in the Islamic Maghrib's (AQIM) insurgent front group in Tunisia, Katibat 'Uqbah Bin Nafi (KUBN)—spurred the government to push back against AST, even its nonviolent proselytizing.

This pushback changed operating conditions for AST and eventually forced AST to shut down its organization and mobilization efforts for its *dawa* campaign, especially after its designation as a terrorist organization. As Donatella della Porta explains, "encounters between movements and the state, in particular through the policing of protest, are especially influential in radicalization processes"[11] As a result, those who wanted to remain a part of the jihadi movement beyond *dawa* activities began to join groups abroad to train and fight as well as join the small-scale but burgeoning local insurgency led by KUBN.

To untangle the various reasons behind AST's downfall, this chapter again uses primary sources from AST and other jihadi groups. In addition, the chapter relies upon a number of databases that I created to track *hisba* intimidation and violence in Tunisia, jihadi arrests and terrorist attacks in Tunisia, and Tunisian foreign fighters in Algeria, Iraq, Libya, Mali, Niger, Pakistan, Syria, and Yemen. I also have access to the full corpus of early Islamic State foreign fighter border files. They were originally partially leaked by the Syrian news outlet, *Zaman al-Wasl*, in January 2016 and later reported on by Western news outlets in March 2016.

Hisba Intimidation and Violence in Tunisia

Following the revolution, but most notably after al-Nahdah's election victory in October 2011, Tunisia experienced a rise in *hisba*-like violence. Such violence is defined by vigilante-style intimidations and attacks as well as the promotion of conservative social mores. Due to the semiclandestine nature of AST as an organization, it is difficult to prove the extent its leadership planned or organized the *hisba* actions. This is in part because AST continued to push a public message that it viewed Tunisia only as a land of *dawa* not ready for the use of violence. While that may have been the image AST hoped to project, several AST members were nonetheless involved in such incidents at the peak of *hisba* activity from October 2011 to February 2013. Furthermore, certain social media postings and official AST media releases suggest that in some cases it indeed approved of such activity.

It is important to note that some *hisba* activities were conducted at the direction of or by members of other groups, including the League for the Protection of the Revolution, the Committee for the Promotion of Virtue and Prevention of Vice, Hizb ut-Tahrir, and the League for the Fight Against the Spread of Shi'ism. Nevertheless, AST's organizational strength as well as its national brand and level of support caused it to receive much of the blame. It also did not help that AST's leadership and ideology were connected with and inspired by AQ. Therefore, the general trend of such activities negatively affected AST more than any of these other groups.

Based on tracking *hisba* incidents from the start of the Tunisian Revolution to AST's designation in August 2013, I have identified seventy-three cases (see table 7.1). The vast majority, 89 percent, occurred between October 2011 (the election of al-Nahdah) and February 2013 (the assassination of the secular-left leader of the Democratic Patriots' Unified Party, Shukri Bila'id). The greatest number of *hisba* incidents occurred in the Tunis governorate and neighboring Manouba. Both accounted for 47 percent of the disturbances. Given the Tunis governorate's role as the seat of the government and home to 10 percent of Tunisia's population, it is no surprise that vigilante attacks and intimidations became important issues for many members of society.

The types of attacks and intimidations illustrate the type of society AST and others attempted to create as well as the fears they hoped to instill in others who opposed its actions. While there were many types of incidents, the four most common dealt with religion, politics, education, and culture. The most frequent religious *hisba*-type activities were committed against Sufi shrines and tombs as well as Shia Muslims. This targeting stems from the belief among salafis—and AST in particular—that Sufi and Shia Islam are deviations from the true message of the Prophet Muhammad.

In May 2012, Abu 'Iyadh even held a lecture at the Grand Mosque in Ezzahrouni, a neighborhood of Tunis, about the dangers of the *rawafidh* (rejectionists; a derogatory term for Shia) in Tunisia (even though Shia constitute less than 1 percent of the population).[12] These types of ideas were also promoted on AST's official Facebook page with a picture of Muqtada al-Sadr with a bunch of human skulls next to him and behind him with a black background.[13] It also included a caption that says "*rawafidh*" and one that reads "Rejectionist Shia are Evil from Crushed Pebbles," which comes from a poem by Ibn Qayyim al-Jawziya, who is Ibn Taymiyyah's foremost disciple.[14]

Regarding attacks on Sufi religious sites, salafis disturbed the Sayeda Aicha Manoubia Sufi shrine in Manouba, just outside of the capital, on March 6, 2012, and again on October 16, 2012. In March they distributed pamphlets condemning the so-called blasphemous practice of venerating saints, while in

TABLE 7.1 *Hisba* Incidents by Governorate

Governorate	*Hisba* Incidents
Tunis	25
Manouba	9
Bizerte	7
Sidi Bouzid	6
Gabes	4
Jendouba	3
Nabeul	3
Sfax	3
Ariana	2
Kebili	2
Monastir	2
Sousse	2
al-Qayrawan	1
Béja	1
El Kef	1
Kasserine	1
Siliana	1

October individuals set fire to the shrine.[15] Similarly, in January 2013 the Sufi mausoleum in Sidi Bou Said was set on fire.[16] Furthermore, over the course of ten days in mid-September 2012, salafis desecrated both Habib Bourguiba's mausoleum in Monastir (not religious, but political) and the Sufi Sidi Abdelkader Mausoleum in Menzel Bouzelfa.[17] These incidents, however, went against the advice of Abu al-Mundhir al-Shinqiti, who argued that it was only appropriate to do such things "when there is power and control among our brothers. Now, our brothers don't have the needed power; therefore, they should focus on *dawa*."[18] This highlights, as is discussed shortly, AST's inability to manage the stages between *dawa* and jihad.

Likewise, in mid- to late August 2012, three disruptions targeted Iranian and Shia-linked cultural events. In al-Qayrawan, salafis prevented the performance of a Shia concert due to its chants, which they perceived as violating sacred values.[19] On the same day, in Bizerte, salafis armed with swords and other blunt instruments interrupted an Iran-sponsored al-Quds Day celebration and attacked Samir Quntar, an important ally of Iran and Hizb Allah, who has since been killed in an Israeli drone strike in Syria.[20] A day later Abu 'Iyadh denounced the "malignant conquest of Shia" in Tunisia and "urged, at the same time, to stop any kind of 'Shi'itization' of the country and to fight the 'enemies of Islam'" in his Eid al-Fitr sermon.[21] Only a few days after that speech AST members attacked Shia in Gabes while protesting alleged Iranian influence.[22]

On the political front, the highest percentage of incidents occurred against political leaders at party meetings or headquarters. When taken in full, these incidents provide a broader aperture for understanding the eventual assassination of two of Tunisia's leftist politicians in 2013. By that point there had already been a spate of violence and intimidation perpetrated against other political figures with few repercussions. It is not necessarily surprising, then, that Shukri Bila'id and Muhammad Brahmi would eventually be killed. Over the course of two days in April 2012, the leftist party Doustourna was prevented from holding meetings in Douz and Souk El Ahad, in the Kebili governorate. Salafis blocked members from going to the cultural center where meetings were held and threw chairs at party members.[23] Moreover, a few months later, in July, salafis attacked Ahmed Najib Chebbi of the Republican Party in Ghardimaou. They also broke his car's windshield and called him an "atheist" and "infidel."[24] In the days leading up to Bila'id's assassination, three significant incidents occurred: an attack on the headquarters of Nida Tunis in Le Lac, a second attack on Chebbi in Gabes, and damage to the Republican Party's offices in al-Qayrawan.[25]

All these incidents heightened the belief among members of the political opposition that these attacks were a result of one or more of the following: (1) al-Nahdah's desire that these acts occur to instill fear in its political rivals, (2) al-Nahdah's deliberate complacency to maintain good relations with its salafi-right flank, and (3) incompetence. Whatever the case, these attacks emboldened the opposition to push harder against al-Nahdah, which led to a reshuffling in the government and harder stance against AST. This shift would change the conditions in which AST could operate.

Beyond the religious and political incidents, members of AST and others were involved in *hisba*-style activities within the educational sphere. While the standoff at the University of Manouba and AST's approval of the *thawrat al-talibah* movement at universities is better known (as discussed in chapter 4), a number of other cases illustrate salafis' attempts to impose their social mores on institutions of learning. These included

- Students at the local university in Gabes demanding the separation of men and women in classes and the university canteen.[26]
- Salafis confronting Muhammad Naji Matir, the secretary-general of the faculty at the School of Arts and Humanities of Sousse, after the administration prevented a female student wearing a niqab from registering for courses.[27]
- Salafis at the Higher Institute of Theology of Tunis shouting at a secular female professor teaching *aqidah* (Islamic creed): "She is free to decide if she wishes to wear the hijab or not, but if she is going to teach, she must wear it."[28]
- A group of students at the University of Manouba's Business School interrupting a class taught by Rafika Ben Guirat because they objected to her style of dress.[29]
- Students disrupting a class at the Higher Institute of Arts and Crafts in al-Qayrawan by shouting that paintings that personify God are un-Islamic. A professor at the school had been administering an exam that contained a reproduction of the Michelangelo fresco from the Sistine Chapel depicting the creation of Adam. The students followed the professor to the faculty lounge, insulted her, and told her to recite the *shahada* (the Muslim testament of faith).[30]
- A Molotov cocktail being thrown at the Higher Institute of Fine Arts in Sousse.[31]
- Salafis surrounding the Monastir University canteen to demand separate dining rooms for female and male students after salafis observed a female student having lunch with a male peer.[32]
- The storming of a secondary school in Menzel Bouzelfa by salafis because the school's superintendent, 'Abd al-Wahid Sintati, refused entry of a schoolgirl dressed in niqab to the classroom. Sintati was beaten with sticks and stones and suffered several broken bones as antisecular chants were performed.[33]

Similarly, AST and other salafis perpetrated violence and intimidation tactics against those involved in cultural fields, such as comedy, festivals, movies, art, dancing, musicals, and theater. Chapter 4 discusses AST's involvement in the *Persepolis* film controversy and the violence that ensued. There were also the infamous riots at the Palais Abdellia art exhibition in La Marsa in June 2012, where AST members and other salafis demanded the destruction of artwork it deemed offensive to Islam.[34] Additionally, salafis obstructed comedian Lotfi Abdelli's show, "100% Halal," and blocked him from performing in Menzel Bourguiba and Sfax.[35] They claimed that his shows offended Islam. Moreover, there were three cases of salafis preventing college students in Le Kram, Sidi Bouzid, and Manouba from recording their own version of the viral dance video the "Harlem Shake" in late February 2013. One of the salafis wearing military gear and carrying a Molotov cocktail shouted, "Our brothers in Palestine are being killed by Israelis, and you are dancing.... This is a Western dance of the disbelievers."[36]

Lastly, there were a number of violent incidents and intimidations related to the sale of alcohol and opening of restaurants during the Muslim holy month of Ramadan, when individuals are supposed to fast. Beginning in May 2012 salafis repeatedly attempted to burn bars and liquor stores in Sidi Bouzid and Jendouba.[37] There were also attacks on hotels and on individuals selling alcohol. At least one of the perpetrators was a former member of the so-called Sulayman Group, discussed in chapter 3.[38] In another case, salafis even cut four fingers off a man in Manouba.[39] Finally, salafis forced a restaurant to close in the Ennasr neighborhood of Ariana, just north of the capital, after salafis threatened to "break everything" because it was open during Ramadan.[40]

The continuous assaults by AST members, salafis, and others heightened anger and fear among many members of society, including religious individuals with different interpretations of Islam, religious and ethnic minorities, opposition politicians, educators, artists in various fields, and business owners. It is true that not all blame can be pinned on AST and that the perpetrators of many incidents were never discovered. However, AST was the most recognized organization promoting ideologies that encouraged such incidents; therefore, it received the largest spotlight in the aftermath. Relatedly, Munsif Ouerghi, the founder of the Tunisian martial arts practice *zamaqtal*, helped train members of AST—including Bila'id's assassin—in this discipline.[41] AST even showed off the training at its second annual conference in May 2012, which Ouerghi attended.[42] Furthermore, it did not help AST's cause that it set up so-called security committees in October 2012, which it later rebranded "neighborhood committees" in February 2013.

Between the growing *hisba* intimidation and violence, martial arts training, and creation of "security committees," AST illustrated that the organization as a whole was becoming increasingly hostile as a local actor. The group's open proclamation of a peaceful mission began to sound increasingly disingenuous.

Security/Neighborhood Committees

On October 6, 2012, AST set up "security committees" as a preemptive and precautionary measure in the event of a security vacuum in the country. It released an urgent call titled "An Invitation to All Brothers" that said, "We call on all our brothers in the entire territory of the country to set up committees to protect the honor, property, and the blood of our people ... prepare to save the security of our people and provide strength in the event of a chaos."[43] The original intent of these committees was to safeguard individuals if the country spiraled out of control on October 23, 2012, the one-year anniversary of the Constituent Assembly election and end of the assembly's original mandate (although the assembly would extend its mandate to complete the constitution). AST's aim was for these committees to evolve into a de facto non-state-controlled martial law force if needed. No security issue or vacuum developed, and the date passed, but AST still activated these committees on a covert level. This further suggests that some of these *hisba* incidents were caused by individuals emboldened to "safeguard" the community.

AST would officially activate its committees in the aftermath of the Bila'id assassination on February 7, 2013. AST called on its followers to mobilize their "neighborhood committees" to protect individuals' honor, money, and property and to ward off thieves and looters. AST also urged members to remain vigilant and cautious in the face of potential gangs and criminality.[44] Within a few hours, AST mobilized members in Sfax and Hammamet for the night of February 7. The mobilization was even swifter on February 8, when committees, in addition to those in the former two cities, came to the streets in Ez Zahra, El Ouardia, al-Qayrawan, Sousse, Kelibia, Mahdia, Ariana, Sidi Bouzid, the neighborhood of Ettadhamen, Béni Khiar, the Southern Suburbs (Tunis), El Kef, Douar Hishour, Den Den, the neighborhood of al-Nur, Jendouba, the Western Suburbs (Tunis), Mateur, the Braka Coast, the neighborhood of al-Khadra, and Korba.

In the pictures and videos AST posted to its official Facebook page, men were either hanging around in the streets or riding scooters and motorcycles through the center or outskirts of cities. In all cases, they were waving AST's black flag. For added effect in the videos, AST included *anashid* (Islamically sanctioned a capella music) to evoke more visceral emotion meant to elicit pride for their efforts in "protecting" the average citizen in the particular neighborhood, village, or city. The number of AST members who helped on patrols varied by place but ranged from ten to fifty (if not more) individuals. The largest turnout was in al-Qayrawan, where members rode through the center of the city with the black AST flag in a convoy of scooters and cars. AST framed these actions in terms of securing the residents and maintaining stability in the country. Members contrasted their efforts with those of the state by using the slogan Your Sons Are at Your Service. The addition of security patrols to AST's repertoire, along with its missionary and service provision, illustrated AST's continued growth and potential threat to the Tunisian state and society.

It is true that some appreciated such protection and even inspired others to join AST's efforts.[45] However, many Tunisians also began to worry that AST was creating a shadow state, especially in poorer areas of big cities and small villages that were not as policed as major urban centers. Anis Naqash, a jeweler in Ez Zahra, said, "The salafis are pressuring people. I'm a Muslim, and I drink alcohol. Some guys here bother me about that."[46] Karim Razouane in El Ouardia, after seeing members of AST with sticks and swords detaining individuals without probable cause, stated: "When I saw this, I was pessimistic about the future of my country."[47] It is not surprising, then, if those opposed to al-Nahdah might conflate all acts of *hisba* between late 2011 and early 2013 with AST, especially since AST became an increasingly ubiquitous topic of news and conversation.

The Failure to Manage the Stages

As noted in chapter 5, Abu 'Iyadh hoped that he and his organization could properly manage the stages to eventually establish an Islamic state. The problem, though, is that while Abu 'Iyadh promoted a *dawa*-first strategy, the DNA of jihadi-salafism promoted violence. Therefore, while some individuals in the organization adhered to this approach, others were unable to maintain discipline. Abu 'Iyadh even noted in December 2011 that "now we are controlling our reactions to their [al-Nahdah's] provocations, but we might reach a stage in which we can't control the youth."[48] He was referring largely to al-Nahdah's relations with the United States. He even exclaimed that "the American embassy is what really leads the government and unfortunately I say that this embassy is what controls al-Nahdah. Unfortunately, this is a reality."[49] These statements illustrate that ten months prior to the attack on the U.S. Embassy, there was already an intent to strike it. Another crucial factor is Abu 'Iyadh's forthright statement that "in this period we are in the *dawa* phase without abandoning jihad as an obligation. . . . This is not its time, but this doesn't mean that if remnants [Bourguiba's and Bin 'Ali's old guard] set against us that we will surrender to them. If they want to fight us we will not lay down, God willing."[50]

One of the leading voices in what became the vocal opposition to al-Nahdah was the political party Nida Tunis, led by Muhammad al-Baji Qa'id al-Sibsi. Al-Sibsi had previously worked under both the Bourguiba and Bin 'Ali regimes. When al-Sibsi announced the creation of the party in April 2012, he claimed it was in response to "instances of disturbing extremism and violence that threaten public and individual liberties, as well as the security of the citizens."[51] This likely contributed to Abu 'Iyadh's paranoia that AST's open opportunities to proselytize might not last.

Moreover, in the aftermath of the embassy attack, the Tunisian government began to more proactively arrest individuals linked to the attack and AST. One case illustrates AST's organizational transformation, in spite of its efforts to maintain the veneer of a peaceful enterprise. It highlights the intersection of AST's surreptitious *hisba* policy and, at the time of the incident that will be discussed, the security/neighborhood committees that called for jihad and became forces of amateurish yet threatening attacks against the police. A series of incidents that occurred in Douar Hicher, a poor suburb of Tunis, between October 28 and November 2, 2012, changed the tenor of jihadis' public speeches about jihad in Tunisia. It would foreshadow what was already happening to the movement on a small scale: a radicalization in response to the increasing seriousness with which the government was taking its jihadi threat.

On the night of October 28 in Douar Hicher, AST members attacked alcohol vendors, attempting to stab the individuals in the neck. According to Sami Gnaoui, a member of the National Guard, the perpetrators used the nearby al-Nur Mosque "like a military base where salafis are hiding molotov cocktails, knives, and sticks."[52] Al-Nur had been an AST-affiliated mosque and served as a base from which the group had previously conducted lectures and outreach efforts.[53] A couple days later members of AST "patrolling" parts of Douar Hicher yet again attacked local residents, attempting to prevent them from drinking alcohol.[54] This led the National Guard to identify some of the ring leaders the next day, which led to the arrest of AST members.

It is clear that a breaking point had passed, especially since on that same evening, members at the al-Nur Mosque climbed to the top of the minaret and called for jihad and resistance to the *taghut* (tyrants, i.e., the Tunisian government).[55] As a consequence, AST members attacked the local National Guard post to free those arrested.[56] In the ensuing escalation, the National Guard, in an attempt to protect itself, killed two individuals involved in the attack: Khalid Qarawi and Ayman Amduni. The former was the head cleric of the AST-affiliated al-Nur Mosque in Douar Hicher, and the latter performed the call to prayer.[57] In response, Nasr al-Din al-Alawi, a cleric at the same mosque, during a television interview in which he held his burial shroud, told youth to prepare their own shrouds to fight against al-Nahdah. The statements, unsurprisingly, led to his arrest.[58]

In an attempt to calm the situation, Abu 'Iyadh appealed to his supporters in a video message on November 2: "I call on you to heed the words of God and to rely upon patience and prayer."[59] It is clear, however, that Abu 'Iyadh felt pressured to not be completely conciliatory in the face of what AST members viewed as injustice. Therefore, in the same message, he sent a warning to al-Nahdah that it was treading a fine line, which could lead to outright violence: "It is possible that a lot of our youth will not be satisfied by an appeal for calm after the events in Douar Hicher." He also spoke of a potential "explosion of anger": "Our brothers who died as martyrs gave their lives for the worldwide Muslim community . . . and you should be sure that the blood of our brothers will sooner or later bring about the installation of God's law."[60]

It is unlikely that Abu 'Iyadh was interested in or ready for a confrontation with the government. Following the embassy attack, even Hasan al-Brik, the head of AST's *dawa* office, admitted, "Of the violent acts [that] were committed in our name, I do not deny. We have made mistakes."[61] Therefore, it is possible that AST felt forced into a confrontation that it had not planned. Moreover, as is shown later in this chapter, the French intervention in Mali accelerated the closing of opportunities for proselytization and preparation for a fight with the Tunisian government. This is because fleeing AQIM members, including some Tunisian foreign fighters in Mali, returned north and began participating in an insurgency against the Tunisian state.[62] The difficulties that arose from the AQIM influx illustrated the point made in the book's introduction that, despite similar ideologies, AST and AQIM had varying local interests. As a result, Abu 'Iyadh's ability to manage the stages became increasingly difficult, which led to greater violence in Tunisia and more governmental pressure on the organization.

Notwithstanding this, AQIM continued to call for Tunisia's categorization as a land of *dawa* while also building its capabilities to fight the Tunisian state. It is as if AQIM (and, to a lesser extent, Abu 'Iyadh and AST) pursued a dual approach: on the one hand, claiming to focus on *dawa* while, on the other, pursuing overt violence, especially by the end of 2012. This violence took the form of an escalation of hostile AST *hisba* activity and insurgent attacks from fighters in AQIM's KUBN.

In its October 22, 2012, statement, AQIM noted, "We see the necessity of concentrating currently in Tunisia on spreading the *dawa* and raising awareness of the Muslim Tunisian people of its religion and fundamentals."[63] Furthermore, on March 17, 2013, AQIM praised the results of the *dawa*-first strategy following the revolution: "The revolutions had a good impact in changing the reality, and turning the balances, which gave a wide space of *dawa* . . . and more space to practice the rituals of religion and promotion of virtue and prevention of vice."[64] The latter clause is a euphemism for the underground *hisba* activities in which AST members, among others, had been involved. Likewise, on May 18, 2013, AQIM asserted that progress must continue and not be sullied by the provocations of the al-Nahdah-led government: "I say to our loved ones, continue your blessed steps from which its fruit blossomed . . . beware of being provoked by the regime by its brutality to random actions that spoil your blessed popular incubator, so be the people of patience and wisdom."[65] This illustrates AQIM's hopes for the success of AST's *dawa* project in the future.

At the same time, AQIM's KUBN became increasingly involved in recruitment, weapons smuggling, and attacks against security forces. This involvement drew more attention to the insincerity of AQIM's words, especially because AQIM also issued warnings to al-Nahdah. In the October 2012 statement, AQIM explains to al-Nahdah: "We didn't wish . . . to see the return of the oppressive practices of the era of Bin 'Ali after the blessed Tunisian revolution under the government of al-Nahdah. . . . We decided to call to our wise brothers in . . .

al-Nahdah to remedy the situation and correct the compass direction before it is too late."[66]

Additionally, in AQIM's May 2013 statement it made veiled yet specific threats against al-Nahdah for accepting the democratic system and mocked it for misleading religious Tunisians: "They should not be deceived by the people who call to democracy by decorating it under the name of the truth and giving it a religious garment, who have misguided tendencies and the calls that deviate from the straight path."[67] These statements—both conciliatory and hostile at the same time—illustrate AQIM's attempts to pursue a dual strategy it hoped would not affect AST's *dawa* program. Nevertheless, this infringement upon AST's activities eventually escalated, forcing AST to drop any pretenses about its sole focus on *dawa* activities. By Ramadan 2013 a few weeks before the second political assassination, Abu 'Iyadh made it clear that Tunisia was no longer just a land of *dawa* in word and deed: "Those who fight Islam will be signing their own political and existential suicide note."[68] As is discussed below, KUBN's attacks would push Abu 'Iyadh to take a more forceful posture and depart from the original message of the group.

AST's Downfall

While *hisba* incidents and jihadi terrorist attacks occurred during the same period, there were distinct times when one type of activity was happening more often than the other. As noted earlier in this chapter, the *hisba* activities primarily occurred between October 2011 and February 2013, while the jihadi terrorist incidents were most common from September 2012 to December 2013. Overall, between the fall of the Bin 'Ali regime and the end of 2013, seventy-one terrorist incidents (whether attacks, plots, or arrests) occurred at distinct times, with eighty-one incidents overall since members of the same networks were arrested at the same time. With the surge in violence along the Tunisian-Algerian border, the Kasserine governorate accounted for 27.2 percent of incidents, while Tunis, the capital governorate and a symbolic target, incurred 16 percent of the incidents, with the rest of the governorates constituting single-digit percentages.

Prior to the attack on the U.S. Embassy in Tunis in September 2012, most terrorism-related incidents involved AQIM weapons smuggling or small insurgent shootouts. None of the incidents were large-scale, spectacular attacks on major urban centers; rather, the six incidents before the embassy attack occurred in more remote and rural areas of Tunisia, such as Tataouine, Nekrif, Bir Znigra, Rouhia, Bir Ali Ben Khalifa, and El-Stah Hsan.[69]

Due to the nature of AST's attack on the U.S. Embassy in Tunis and U.S. pressure on al-Nahdah, it was the beginning of the end for the group. The

TABLE 7.2 Jihadi Terrorist Incidents by Governorate

Governorate	Jihadi Incidents
Kasserine	22
Tunis	13
Jendouba	6
Sidi Bouzid	5
Kef	5
Tataouine	5
Bizerte	4
Medenine	4
Sousse	3
Manouba	2
Ariana	2
Ben Arous	2
al-Qayrawan	2
Sfax	2
Kebili	2
Béja	1
Monastir	1

embassy attack crossed a line beyond the more localized *hisba*-style attacks and intimidations. From that day forward, al-Nahdah's government gradually took a more forceful approach toward AST. It is true that al-Nahdah squandered its chance to capture Abu 'Iyadh, who gave a fiery speech after the attack demanding the resignation of Tunisian minister of the interior, Ali Larayedh.[70] This failure to capture Abu 'Iyadh suggests a continuation of internal disagreements about how to deal with Abu 'Iyadh and the group.⁷¹ As late as February 2013, members of al-Nahdah, including National Constituent Assembly member Yamina Zoghlami, commended AST for its involvement in the so-called neighborhood committees. She "perceived their deeds as acts of patriotism."⁷² Despite some empathy toward the group within al-Nahdah, for the first time Tunisian security officials were given "written instructions that authorised the police to use lethal force in self-defence if police stations, and therefore their lives, were threatened."⁷³ This instruction provided security officials legal protection that they previously felt did not exist, as discussed in chapter 4.

Another factor that chipped away at al-Nahdah's goodwill toward AST was the emergence of KUBN, which conducted insurgent and terrorist activities in Tunisia. While France's Operation Serval in Mali did not begin until mid-January 2013, the Malian government requested assistance to combat the AQIM-led jihadi insurgency in the northern part of the country in September 2012. This gap between Mali's request and the French intervention allowed AQIM time to plan its resource and personnel reallocation. Tunisian foreign fighters (among others) under the direction of Mukhtar Bilmukhtar in Mali thus felt emboldened to conduct spectacular attacks against the In Amenas gas facility in Algeria in January 2013 and a French military base in Agadez, Niger, in May 2013.⁷⁴ The reallocation of fighters to other theaters and battles also spurred the relocation of AQIM assets to western Tunisia in Jabal Chambi, along the border with Algeria. It is at this juncture that Tunisia fell victim to more sophisticated insurgent-type attacks against its military and security forces. The first of these major attacks, likely conducted by KUBN, targeted a National Guardsman in Bou Chebka, along the Algerian-Tunisian border, on December 10, 2012.⁷⁵

Following this attack, the al-Nahdah-led government announced a series of arrests ten days later in Jabal Chambi and Ain Drahem, in northwest Tunisia, and provided more details on KUBN. This release of information had significant implications for AST.⁷⁶ Larayedh noted that some Tunisians arrested in the sweep had previously been involved with AST's *dawa* activities, though he was "unable to confirm the existence of formal links" between the KUBN cells and AST. This crackdown subjected AST to even greater government scrutiny, especially as KUBN became involved in more insurgent attacks that killed Tunisian soldiers. For a country like Tunisia, with very little history of insurgency or terrorism, even a few deaths in such a manner presented a huge concern and sparked public outrage. It also did not help that AQIM's Abu 'Umar al-Maghribi released a *nashid* (religiously sanctioned a capella) titled "Sons of 'Uqbah Pull Your Courage Swords Out" and incited individuals with lyrics such as "the sword on the necks of the infidels is like a medicine to treat their problem."⁷⁷

It was not until after the second assassination of a politician, Muhammad Brahmi, in July 2013, that the Tunisian government pieced together—or at least publicly disclosed—AST's connections to AQIM and the attacks. In a video confession, Muhammad al-Akari, one of the three leaders of AST's military wing, admitted that he was in charge of "collecting information ... [and that] politicians and journalists are monitored targets."[78] Al-Akari also noted that twenty other public figures, including the speaker of the Constituent Assembly, members of the old regime, and other opposition figures, were planned targets.[79] At the press conference where this information was released, the Ministry of Interior also explained the structure of AST's military wing, which included Abu 'Iyadh at the top, three deputies (al-Akari, Muhammad Awadi, and 'Adl Sa'idi, the last of whom had been killed by then), and three committees under each deputy: a "preparatory operations group," which had six members; the "support and implementation group," which had eight members; and the "mobilisation and armament group," which had two members.[80]

The ministry also showed journalists an alleged handwritten "Allegiance Act" between AST's leader, Abu 'Iyadh, and AQIM's leader, Abu Mus'ab 'Abd al-Wadud, confirming links between the two groups.[81] Furthermore, the ministry's spokesperson explained that their investigation found "strong ties" between the two assassinations, arms smuggling, and the insurgent fight in Jabal Chambi.[82] Moreover, his colleague, Mustafa Bin 'Amur, the head of public security at the ministry, believed that the assassins, Kamal Gafgazi and Bubakr al-Hakim, met with Abu 'Iyadh several times at Jabal Chambi.[83]

Some may have been skeptical of the details given at the time, in part because of a prior lack of government transparency. This skepticism therefore shed doubt on the credibility of the information, which was further questioned because of the alacrity with which the details were provided after the second assassination. That said, Abu 'Iyadh, in a private letter unrelated to this that was written in 2014 to Ayman al-Zawahiri, described himself as the leader of AST and noted in his signature at the bottom of the letter that he was a member of AQIM's sharia committee.[84] Moreover, Bubakr al-Hakim's testimony in an Islamic State video in December 2014 and an interview with the group's English-language magazine *Dabiq* in March 2015, during which he admitted culpability in the assassinations, seems to track with Tunisian government statements. In the video message, al-Hakim triumphantly states: "Yes, tyrants, we are the ones who killed Shukri Bila'id and Muhammad Brahmi."[85] Likewise, in the *Dabiq* interview, al-Hakim explains that Gafgazi shot Bila'id, while he shot Brahmi.[86]

It is unlikely but not impossible that these claims of responsibility suggest Islamic State involvement in the attacks, in part because the organization had just begun operating overtly in Syria by the time of the second assassination. That said, it is important to remember from chapter 3 that al-Hakim (and Gafgazi) were alumni of the Iraq jihad. In addition, in June 2012 Iraqi intelligence reported that letters discovered from the Islamic State of Iraq (ISI) showed that the group was planning to expand operations into Tunisia.[87] Such reports should usually be considered with skepticism, but maybe, in hindsight, ISI was already planning for its return and eventual potential break with AQ. Moreover, U.S. intelligence officials believed that those involved in the Benghazi, Libya attack on the U.S. Consulate in September 2012 maintained connections with ISI operatives (in addition to AQIM ones).[88] Put together:

- Al-Hakim admitted in the *Dabiq* interview that he helped plan and train for the assassinations and other attacks while he was in Libya;[89]
- Ansar al-Sharia in Libya (ASL), AST's sister organization, provided a safe haven for training and was involved in and gave cover to the U.S. Consulate in Benghazi attackers, including the Tunisian 'Ali Bin al-Tahar Bin al-Falih al-'Awni al-Harzi;[90]
- Al-Harzi, another alumnus of the Iraq jihad, member of AST, and suspect in the cell involved in the assassinations and other attacks, trained individuals in Libya to fight in Syria. This was in association with his brother Tariq's network, who was in charge of ISI and later ISIS/IS's efforts to facilitate foreign fighters from North Africa to Syria.[91]

Therefore, it is plausible that elements within ISI/ISIS provided assistance on some level, either directly or peripherally by diverting resources. There is also the possibility that in the aftermath of KUBN's December 2012 attack, ISI's network through al-Hakim may have wanted to outbid KUBN. This would fall in line with Della Porta's idea about "organizational competition within dense milieus of social movements [and] social movement families (made up of social movements that share some general orientations and are often allied). . . . Violent outbidding then develops among different groups that compete for recruits and support from radicalized constituencies."[92]

This is especially the case knowing what we now know about al-Hakim later becoming a senior external operations planner for IS in Syria and having a hand in planning the large-scale attacks in Belgium and France as well as in Tunisia in 2015 at the Bardo National Museum and on a Sousse beach.[93] Additionally, there is also the case of a Tunisian named 'Ali, who in 2013 acted as a courier on behalf of ISI/ISIS between Syria and Tunisia. According to 'Ali, he would relay important news back to ISI/ISIS elements in Tunisia, bring money to cells in Tunisia, and provide propaganda videos so that local Tunisian ISI/ISIS cells could recruit individuals.[94] This illustrates that as early as 2013, even before the announcement of the caliphate, ISI/ISIS was planning for its campaign to recruit Tunisians.

The evidence remains circumstantial, however. Without greater information or details, it is an interesting alternative possibility than the more straightforward explanation. It is important to remember the historical relationship between AQIM's network and ISI's network during the Iraq jihad (as described in chapter 3) as well as the fact that the assassination of Tunisian politicians occurred prior to the formal split between AQ and IS. So it is even conceivable that they were working together due to the overlapping connections. Al-Hakim admitted in the *Dabiq* interview that he would join the fight with ISIS in Syria in 2013 following the Brahmi assassination. Moreover, AQIM has no qualms about assassinating politicians since it claimed responsibility for a failed 2014 plot to kill Lutfi Bin Jiddu, who at that time was the Tunisian interior minister.[95]

Either way, the second political assassination in late July 2013, along with a large-scale mine attack in Jabal Chambi a few days later that killed nine soldiers (at the time the largest attack against Tunisia's soldiers in its modern history), spurred the government to finally end AST's ability to operate openly.[96] Although the al-Nahdah-led government did not designate AST as a terrorist organization until late August 2013, it became evident after the first political assassination in February 2013 that al-Nahdah's top leadership had lost its patience with AST.[97] This initiated a war of words that escalated over time. For instance, in late March 2013 Larayedh told Isabelle Mandraud of *Le Monde* that "Abu 'Iyadh is deeply involved in issues of violence and arms trafficking."[98] Abu 'Iyadh swiftly responded with intimidation: "To your wise men [al-Nahdah] we say: Keep your sick [or diseased] ones from us, or we will direct our war against them until their downfall and their meeting with the dustbin of history."[99]

The event that signaled the end for AST came on May 10 and 11, when the government blocked AST from conducting its *dawa* activities for not having legal permits to set up tents and events. Tunisian security services and police subsequently launched an unprecedented offensive against AST in at least Sidi Hassine, Sijoumi, Tabarka, Tunis, Sousse, Zarzis, Sidi Bouzid, and Mrezga.[100] In response, Abu 'Iyadh threatened that "our youth—who bravely fought for Islam in Afghanistan, Chechnya, Iraq, Somalia, and al-Sham—will not spare any sacrifice to protect their religion in the land of al-Qayrawan."[101]

In response, al-Nahdah cancelled AST's third annual conference, which was expected to take place in al-Qayrawan on May 19, stating that the group did not receive a license to hold the event. Rashid Ghannushi, the head of al-Nahdah, argued that "the authorities must apply the law without distinction; we support a strong government to implement the law for all."[102] The statement signaled a break with al-Nahdah's previous "light touch" policies, as such attention to detail had never been taken with AST previously.[103] This roadblock did not deter AST, which, according to Sami Isid Bin Khamis, expected forty thousand members to attend and argued that it was unnecessary to acquire a license.[104] According to Lilia Weslaty, however, AST actually submitted a request to authorize its rally on May 14, though it is clear that by this time the government was not interested in any type of arrangement or negotiation.[105] On the planned day of the conference—which ended up not taking place due to a police blockade of the streets surrounding the location—Larayedh reiterated that "we will deal with this organization with total seriousness, but in accordance with the law. This organization exists but is not legal. It must either follow the law or end its existence."[106] Abu al-Mundhir al-Shinqiti explained to Tunisia's jihadis that al-Nahdah was taking this action because "this *dawa* in Tunisia is challenging the enemies of Islam because it is exposing them."[107]

This war of words only escalated. On May 23 Abu 'Iyadh released a video message mocking al-Nahdah for allowing AST to proselytize openly in the first place: "Our religion taught us to thank those who is worthy of being thanked . . . and you [al-Nahdah] today are the most worthy of people to be thanked since you committed stupidities that were a reason for the spread of our *dawa*."[108] A few days later, in Ettadhamen, an AST stronghold in Tunis, Ghannushi spoke to al-Nahdah supporters and ended the war of words: "Wherever those jihadis, the kharijites of this age, are, there is destruction and ruin. I challenge them to give me one state where those reckless people have succeeded. Are Somalia, Iraq, or Afghanistan stable countries?"[109] This speech illustrates al-Nahdah's shift in views and public descriptions of AST. It also highlights al-Nahdah's abandonment of the so-called light touch approach.

The Tunisian government formally designated AST as a terrorist organization in late August 2013. For about a year after the designation, AST maintained its propaganda apparatus online even if it was no longer able to organize locally anymore.[110] Much of it related to rejecting the terrorism designation, propaganda against the Tunisian government, the importance of sharia, and continued support for the Syrian jihad (more on this below and the next chapter). This activity came to a halt, however, in early August 2014. It is possible that continued arrests of key figures led to the degradation and inability to continue its online operations. For instance, senior AST leaders such as Slim Kantari (Abu Ayub al-Tunisi), Muhammad Anis Sha'yib, Sami Isid Bin Khamis, Fatimah Zu'aghi, and Hafidh Bin Hasin (Abu 'Iyadh's brother) were arrested in 2014. The case of Fatimah also illustrates how several former AST members began to join KUBN due to greater opportunities to operate. She had originally been the head of AST's online apparatus and would later switch to KUBN's head of online activity until her late October 2014 arrest.[111] Although KUBN continued its momentum of attacks from 2013 (nine attacks) into 2014 (eight attacks), by mid-2014 the Islamic State began to build up its own network within Tunisia and gained more prominence over time. Since the rise of IS locally, KUBN has not been able to get to the level of strength it had in 2013 and 2014. This topic of internal dynamics within Tunisia is covered in greater detail in chapter 10.

Prior to the rise of IS's network within Tunisia, a lot of action occurred outside Tunisia by alumni of AST as well as new Tunisians drawn to foreign fighting abroad. While the designation of AST banned the organization locally, the broader movement of Tunisian jihadism would continue to grow, in part due to the activities conducted by AST members in Libya and Syria as early as 2011 and 2012. This early involvement allowed the movement to morph even if its ability to operate openly and perform *dawa* activities without consequence had been quashed. Some joined the low-level KUBN insurgency in Jabal Chambi, but Tunisian jihadism ultimately reverted to its state prior to the revolution—primarily a movement of foreign fighters, facilitators, and terrorist plotters/attackers.

The Reemergence of Tunisian Foreign Fighting

As described in chapter 3, by early to mid-2009 ISI began rebuilding its organization and networks after the Sunni tribal awakening and U.S. troop surge. As of late fall 2010, just before the Tunisian Revolution, it is believed that ISI was once again receiving up to 250 foreign fighter recruits per month.[112] A foreign fighter network run by a group of Tunisians and Algerians had emerged in Homs, Syria, in 2010.[113] It is no surprise that one of the first Tunisian-related jihadi incidents following the revolution resulted in the arrest on January 25, 2011, of a group of Tunisians and Libyans in Egypt attempting to fight in Iraq with ISI.[114] Similarly, one of the first Tunisians killed abroad as a foreign fighter after the revolution was Yusuf Nur al-Din Mabruk in a raid by Iraqi security forces at the Iraqi-Syrian border on December 14, 2011.[115] As a consequence, a number of Tunisians who joined the fight in Syria had prior jihadi fighting experience. Based on my archive of killed Tunisian foreign fighters in Syria as well as IS's border documents in Syria, Tunisians had previously fought in Libya (eleven), Afghanistan (four), Iraq (three), Mali (three), Gaza Strip (one), and the Sinai Peninsula (one). It is likely that these numbers are low since it is only based on open sources and one corpus of probably more IS border documents that have yet to be discovered or disclosed publicly.

These incidents showed that irrespective of the revolution, it is likely that Tunisians would have continued their involvement in foreign fighting and jihadism. The only difference is that there is instead a wider pool of foreign fighter recruits as a result of the societal opening spurred by the revolution. Consequently, some of the prisoners released following the revolution would eventually return to fighting and join jihadi groups in Syria.[116]

While fighting in Iraq, Libya, and Syria would excite Tunisians the most, Tunisians after the revolution would also join AQIM in Algeria, AQAP in Yemen, and the Islamic Movement of Uzbekistan in the Pakistani tribal areas.[117] Furthermore, groups abroad encouraged training before individuals joined major jihads. On the day Bin 'Ali fled Tunisia, AQIM released a statement advising "our people in Tunisia to be ready and make preparations to send their sons to us to train on weapons and gain military expertise in order to engage in the decisive battle with the Jews and the Christians and their allies who oppress you."[118]

Likewise, Abu 'Iyadh and AST, while sometimes coy about support for fighters abroad, approved of the practice, if not privately encouraged it. For example, in December 2011, when asked in an interview whether he incited youth to join AQIM abroad, Abu 'Iyadh answered slyly: "I would like to hold onto the answer to this question, although me saying 'I would like to hold on to the answer' is in itself an answer to your question."[119] The ambiguity and nondenial suggests that Abu 'Iyadh and AST were likely heeding AQIM's early call for individuals to train with them.

AST Sanctions and Incubates Foreign Fighting

While most researchers recognize that jihadi networks and groups began recruiting individuals to join up with the Syrian jihad in 2012, recruitment to fight in Iraq was ongoing ahead of this, which is an underappreciated dynamic. As a result, efforts to join ISI in Iraq were easily adjusted to instead join up with ISI's front group in Syria at the time, Jabhat al-Nusra (JN). And because most attempting to join up with ISI in Iraq usually traveled via Turkey and Syria, going to Syria took one less step, making it less of a risk, but also allowed the same recruitment, facilitation, and logistics networks to take advantage of the historic opportunity that Syria would bring as a result of the Bashar al-Assad regime's vicious response to the original peaceful uprising.

This is relevant because before the focus of the global jihadi community was on Syria, AST and its leader Abu 'Iyadh was legitimizing joining up with ISI in 2011. In the same interview mentioned above, Abu 'Iyadh provides a clearer response to participation in the Iraq jihad: "Can anyone prevent someone from fighting for the sake of God? So if you come to me and say 'I want to go to Iraq,' I will not prevent you because if I do I will be sinful because you want to realize one of the obligations, which is supporting Muslims and fighting the enemies of our religion."[120] Moreover, a couple of questions later, Abu 'Iyadh drops any pretensions and overtly calls for jihad in Iraq:

> Jihad actually just now began in Iraq because the Americans left behind their bags to the Persians and the *rawafidh* to control Iraq.... You say to me that the American occupation ended? And I say to you that this occupation left the enemies of the *umma* such as the Majus [Iran] and the *rawafidh* selling the umma to the West. My brother, jihad is necessary now, and it is necessary that [then Iraqi Prime Minister Nouri] al-Maliki and his cronies be eradicated from the face of the earth, and the mujahidin in Iraq should escalate their attacks.... We ask God to help our brothers to succeed.[121]

This excitement for jihad and Tunisians' involvement in it did not wane over time. In February 2013 Abu 'Iyadh exclaimed in an interview with Mosaique FM journalist Nasr al-Din Bin Hadid that "Tunisians can be found everywhere in the land of jihad. The ways of going are easy and we don't stop our people from leaving."[122] One of the founding members of AST stated that Abu 'Iyadh worked directly with individuals in Libya and Mali.[123] All of this disproves Fabio Merone's incredulous argument that "Abu 'Iyadh had discouraged Tunisian militants from going to international jihadi battlefields."[124]

Furthermore, in my own experience at an AST mosque, I saw members of the group doing special *du'at* (blessings) after the normal prayers for the "mujahidin in Bilad al-Sham (Greater Syria)," which is the norm in AST's mosques. Such a ritual illustrates that support is encouraged. It is no surprise that AST's official Facebook page posted content in support of groups like JN and, later, ISIS. AST's official media outlet released a video as a gift for the leader of JN, Abu Muhammad al-Jawlani.[125] Likewise, AST posted pictures from children of AST members who had written notes congratulating JN on its battlefield successes.[126] Finally, when former AST members died fighting in the Syrian jihad, AST's official Facebook page would glamorize their martyrdoms.[127]

Just as AST had the space to organize openly, potential foreign fighters had little trouble traveling abroad. The al-Nahdah-led government was occasionally concerned but also apathetic about individuals going to fight abroad. It is possible that some al-Nahdah members sympathized with the cause of overthrowing the Assad regime both because of their own experiences shaking off the yoke of a dictator and because of the overall humanitarian concerns associated with the Assad regime's industrial-scale killing. It is also possible that ideological affinity played a role since some key Syrian opposition members that promoted their cause internationally were associated with the Syrian Muslim Brotherhood. There is also the disturbing response that Ghannushi gave to Amin al-Susi, a retired Tunisian army officer, whose son Muhammad went to Syria, when he was seeking help: "It is better for your son to die in Syria than here. He will be a martyr and he will mediate for you on Judgment Day. Fighting Bashar al-Assad is better than staying here."[128]

Beyond this, the Tunisian presidential spokesperson, Adnan Mancer, argued that "our youth have good intentions, but it is possible they fell into the hands of manipulators."[129] Likewise, Interior Minister 'Ali Larayedh said, "I understand the situation well, and I understand the problems it will cause in the future when the Syrian brothers' ordeal ends."[130] Tunisian president Munsif Marzuqi echoed these latter concerns: "Experience has taught us of the consequences when these fighters give money and arms return to their countries."[131] This highlights the ambiguity of officials' support to the Syrian cause as well as an understanding of potential blowback in the future. That said, some of the government's policies indirectly encouraged some Tunisians to fight abroad. After

Tunis expelled the Syrian ambassador, for example, some Tunisian citizens decided "the situation in Syria was disastrous" and felt they needed to go to Syria to fight against the Assad regime.[132]

Regarding efforts to stop the flow of foreign fighters, the government intervened when parents asked for assistance finding their sons or daughters, but beyond that it did not have much of a stated policy.[133] It is possible, however, that Tunisia's intelligence apparatus entrapped individuals interested in fighting abroad, as AST suggested in a warning on its official Facebook page.[134] Either way, one of the earliest government statements on Tunisian foreign fighting came in February 2012, when Interior Minister Larayedh asserted, "We deplore these young people going on misadventures.... We are watching these things closely."[135] While it is commendable that the government paid attention to those going to fight abroad, Larayedh himself admitted there were few prevention mechanisms: "We cannot legally prevent a citizen from leaving the country if he says he is leaving for work or tourism." Similarly, Habib al-Lawz, a prominent al-Nahdah parliamentarian, stated that "if young Tunisians feel that they are oppressed, they will just go to the training camps of Libya."[136] Therefore, the Tunisian government was not proactive in its attempts to deal with the growing foreign fighter outflow to regional war zones. The government hid behind legal measures unsuited to a problem of unprecedented scale and future ramifications. This inaction provided the space for a record-setting number of individuals to go to places like Libya and Syria between 2011 and 2013, when AST was active.

Libya

Following the outbreak of the Libyan civil war against the Mu'ammar al-Qadhafi regime in 2011, Libya provided a safe haven for a variety of jihadi activities. Tunisians would go to Libya and either fight locally, smuggle weapons back to Tunisia, or train before attempting to conduct an attack in Tunisia or join the fight in Syria. Based on my own collection of primary and secondary sources, between the start of the Libyan war and the end of 2013, more than sixty Tunisians can be identified as foreign fighters who either successfully crossed the border into Libya or were arrested attempting to do so.[137] Furthermore, by the fall of 2013, according to a Tunisian security source, there were up to three hundred Tunisian foreign fighters in Libya.[138]

Many at first believed the Tunisians who fought against the al-Qadhafi regime in Libya yearned to spread the Tunisian Revolution and plant the seeds of democracy in the region. This assessment was incorrect, as Munir, an architectural student from Bizerte, noted after his classmate 'Imad died fighting the al-Qadhafi regime in Benghazi: "At the time, we thought it was just a young death for democracy, whereas it was in fact the first foundations for international jihadi calls to fight wherever their leader asked."[139] Furthermore, individuals like the Tunisian Shukri 'Abd al-Fatah, an alumnus of foreign fighting against the United States in both Afghanistan and Iraq, illustrates that early fighters in Libya had longer-term goals.[140] For one, after the French invasion of Mali to eject AQIM from its safe haven in the northern parts of the country, 'Abd al-Fatah encouraged Tunisians to join the fight against the French: "It is our duty to go to Mali. There is no doubt about that."[141] Moreover, 'Abd al-Fatah believes that Tunisians will eventually subscribe to jihadi ideas on governance via AST's *dawa* efforts: "We are patient. Tunisians will turn to our way. Then they will choose the Caliphate."[142]

AST's efforts to establish the caliphate would be bolstered by the clandestine activities discussed earlier in this chapter through AST's secret military wing. AST would also use its overt *dawa* activities for cover. As mentioned in chapter 6, the first *dawa*-type activity that AST organized was its assistance to refugees on the Tunisian-Libyan border in March 2011.[143] When posting about these activities on its official Facebook page, AST displayed its members erecting temporary housing, supplying tents, and providing aid to refugees once they crossed the border.[144] Unbeknownst to the refugees, and according to the International Crisis Group, AST used this opportunity to buy and sell military equipment in their preaching tents at the refugee camp.[145] These weapons were mainly sold by former al-Qadhafi regime loyalists.[146] Among the individuals involved in this was Miftah Manitah, who would go on to later become a senior leader with the Islamic State in Libya's Tunisia cell in Sabratha, Libya.[147] Manitah helped plan the failed takeover of Ben Gardane in March 2016, during which he was killed; if it had been successful, he would have become the leader of a planned Wilayat Tunis entity within IS's broader caliphate provincial structure.[148] This is discussed in more detail in chapter 10. Prior to the revolution, Manitah was arrested in 2007 for involvement in the Sulayman Group affair.[149]

The so-called democratization of smugglers further exacerbated the growth in weapons smuggling. Jihadis took advantage of this process after the fall of the Bin 'Ali regime. Prior to 2011 the Tunisian government regulated (as well as profited from) the cartels that brought various items across the borders.[150] This arrangement collapsed in 2011 and subsequently caused "an increase in the number of participants in these lucrative activities," including jihadis.[151] Bubakr al-Hakim confirmed this trend, later explaining that after the Tunisian Revolution and start of the Libyan Civil War, there were great opportunities for them to exploit: "Libya was next to us and weapons were widespread there. So we went to Libya and established a training camp. We would train brothers there and at the same time we would work to smuggle weapons into Tunisia."[152] Consequently, Tunisian security forces would find a number of weapons caches or would arrest individuals associated with AQIM and AST. These individuals were smuggling weapons from Libya to Tunisia in locations such as Nekrif, Bir Ali Ben Khélifa, Sfax, Tataouine, El-Stah Hsan, Jabal Chambi, Ain Drahem, Douar Hicher, Medenine, Mnihla, Ben Gardane, and Haffouz.[153]

These smuggling connections facilitated relationships between clandestine AST members or Tunisian foreign fighters in Libya and AST's sister organization, Ansar al-Sharia in Libya. While there are reports of so-called *mujahidin* operating in Libya as early as March 2011, ASL began operating overtly within months of al-Qadhafi's execution in October 2011. It began in Darnah in December 2011 and Benghazi in February 2012.[154] AST members also assisted ASL in the development of its *dawa* program.[155] While the extent of the relationship between AST and ASL was always murky due to its covert nature, one of the key players in the ASL attack on the U.S. Consulate in Benghazi in September 2012 was an AST member, 'Ali Bin al-Tahar Bin al-Falih al-'Awni al-Harzi. Following his interrogation by the FBI in Tunis and subsequent release by Tunisian authorities, AST released a video embracing al-Harzi's freedom (he would later become a foreign fighter with the Islamic State in Syria).[156] Also, ASL's attacks on Tunisia's diplomatic facilities in June 2012—once in Tripoli and twice in Benghazi—are believed to have been in response to the La Marsa art exhibition in a Tunis suburb where jihadi-salafis rioted against what they deemed un-Islamic art.[157] The closeness of this relationship was further clarified when a video leaked online in December 2016 showing the leader of AST, Abu 'Iyadh, praying over the dead body of ASL's founder, Muhammad al-Zahawi, in Benghazi in late 2014.[158] This would also confirm reports about Abu 'Iyadh sneaking out of Tunisia for Libya in October 2013.[159]

Therefore, it is no surprise that evidence of Tunisians training in Libya with ASL appeared. Fighting in Libya provided an avenue for individuals uninterested in AST's *dawa* activities to train for a possible future insurgency against the Tunisian state.[160] Similarly, AQ's 'Atiyat Allah 'Abd al-Rahman al-Libi hoped to exploit these opportunities as well: "Libya now is ready for the jihad, and because of its important location, it will be a jihadi battlefield opening . . . onto Tunisia."[161] Signs of Tunisians training in Libya emerged as early as the spring of 2012, when two Tunisians were detained in the Darnah region after completing military training with ASL in Benghazi.[162] Moreover, a number of Tunisian passports were seized from an ASL base in Benghazi.[163] Beyond Benghazi, ASL also provided training in Darnah, Misrata, Hun, and the Jabal al-Khadra'.[164] These were the same ASL camps that helped prepare the two Tunisian suicide bombers who attempted (and failed) to bomb tourists on the beach in Sousse and the Bourguiba Mausoleum in Monastir in October 2013.[165]

The August 2013 designation of AST, the lack of successful terrorist attacks in Tunisia in the fall of 2013, and the rise of ISIS in the summer and fall of 2013 caused many Tunisians to see greater jihadi opportunities in Syria. These opportunities would be facilitated by legacy AST networks in Tunisia and allies in Libya since many Tunisians went to Libya for training before heading to Syria.[166]

Syria

Tunisians began arriving in Syria to fight the Assad regime as early as March 2012 (if not sooner), but the pace of individuals going to Syria increased throughout 2013. By the end of 2012 it was believed that up to one hundred Tunisians had traveled to fight in Syria—a number that grew to two thousand by the end of 2013.[167] Moreover, according to Tunisian interior minister at the time, Lutfi Bin Jiddu, by the fall of 2013 the Tunisian government had banned the travel of six thousand individuals attempting to fight in Syria.[168] This number illustrates how AST's networks were able to shift from being involved in *dawa* activities to facilitating the travel of individuals to fight in Syria. As Timothy Holman explains, "facilitation enables foreign fighters and travelers to bridge the local and the transnational dimensions of a conflict.... In the absence of facilitation, a foreign fighter departing their country of origin and arriving in a transit location is less likely to cross borders or find and be accepted by an organization operating in a semi-clandestine manner, wary of infiltration by hostile government agents."[169] Therefore, without such organization, it is highly unlikely that so many Tunisians would have been connected so quickly to the necessary networks involved in the facilitation and logistics of foreign fighters. According to an AST member, Abu 'Iyadh would personally provide *tazkiya* (assurance) for potential fighters joining JN.[170] In addition, a number of domestic and foreign preachers helped justify the fighting, while charities associated with AST helped raise funds for individuals to travel abroad.[171]

For example, the Tunisian Shaykh Bilal Sawaysh was arrested in September 2013 for radicalizing and sending Tunisians to fight in Syria.[172] Even non-jihadi clerics in Tunisia promoted and obfuscated the issue of jihad in Syria. The non-AST-aligned salafi cleric Shaykh Bashir Bin Hasan whitewashed the Tunisian foreign fighter issue in his interview with the BBC: "They are on a humanitarian mission. The West insists on associating jihad and salafism to terrorism, which is not true."[173] He even said that he was proud of the "heroic acts of the young jihadists."[174] This sentiment highlights the fact that there were likely others promoting the idea of fighting jihad in Syria, even if they were not jihadis themselves. This promotion of jihad is also a possible consequence of assertions by clerics like the Egyptian Yusuf al-Qaradawi—believed to be one of the most influential Sunni religious leaders in the Middle East and a part of the international Muslim Brotherhood—that fighting in Syria was an individual duty.[175] Furthermore, AST member Bilal Shawashi, not to be confused with the similarly named cleric mentioned above, became a public face for promoting jihad in Syria and encouraging individuals to fight, through his rhetoric on the streets, in interviews with foreign journalists, and on Tunisian television debates.[176] Shawashi would be arrested for involvement in the U.S. Embassy attack in Tunis; after being released from prison, he became a sharia official for IS in Syria.[177] He once told the Associated Press in June 2012 that it was a duty to support jihad in Syria.[178] Shawashi would eventually tell his fellow Tunisians and others to join IS after the announcement of IS's caliphate in late June 2014: "I call all Muslims in the world to give baya to the Amir al-Mu'minin, Caliph al-Qurayshi Abu Bakr al-Baghdadi."[179]

An even more consequential, yet less covered, figure in helping recruit Tunisians is Turki Bin'ali, the leader of IS's Maktab al-Buhuth wa-l-Dirasat (Office of Research and Studies), who came to Tunisia in August 2012 and June 2013.[180] He completed a tour of AST mosques and charities and even had a meeting with AST's leader, Abu 'Iyadh. This is relevant because Bin'ali would become a senior leader in IS and therefore make good use of new contacts he made in Tunisia. While other connective tissues existed between Tunisia's jihadis and IS through Bubakr al-Hakim, it likely did not hurt that individuals also had a personal experience with someone who would become important within IS's leadership. There is no solid proof that Bin'ali was specifically recruiting for Syria at the time. It remains a possibility, though, especially given that his 2013 trip coincided with ISIS operations in Syria and preparations for a caliphate announcement a year later. He was perhaps attempting to gather supporters who would sign onto Abu Bakr al-Baghdadi's plans. Kamal Zuruq, for example—who had conducted a *dawa* event with Bin'ali in Bizerte on August 12, 2012[181]—would be one of the first AST leaders to call for Tunisians to pledge *baya* to al-Baghdadi in early June 2014.[182]

Tunisians also had fellow countrymen as key figures in groups like JN and ISIS that they could emulate from online messages. There were a number of examples of former AST members who had fought in Syria: Ahmad al-Sharni, Baha' al-'Umduni (Baha' al-Tunisi), Mu'az Hizm (Mu'az Harzi), Ziyad, Abu Mariyyah al-Tunisi, Hamzah Bin Jabar (Abu Shahad al-Tunisi), Nidal Mubarak (Abu Suhayb al-Tunisi), Sabir Husni (Sabir Zudum, Abu Khalid), Qays al-Halwami, and Anis al-Hammami, among others.[183] Moreover, Tunisians' experience in *dawa* and administration from their days with AST allowed them to play a key role in developing the *dawa* and outreach programs with Syrian jihadi groups. For example, a Tunisian named Abu Qatadah al-Gharib, who previously served as a foreign fighter in Iraq during the 2000s, was a *dawa* official for JN in Aleppo and helped open religious institutes for the group.[184]

In an even more profound way, Abu Waqas al-Tunisi became the face of ISIS's *dawa* program, appearing in six of its videos by the end of 2013.[185] These activities—which included giving lectures, distributing gifts to children, and reciting the Qur'an in competitions, among other things—allowed ISIS to ingratiate itself with locals and dispel negative views many had of the group as a result of its conduct during the Iraq jihad (even though it would eventually revert to such practices, especially after January 2014 when the Syrian rebel opposition and JN turned against it). The activities were also ways to attract foreigners, including Tunisians, to the group to prove that their previous efforts with AST could continue under ISIS. This idea would resonate with many AST recruits who felt that their mission in Tunisia had only just begun and that they would eventually spread their *dawa* globally according to an AST member I interviewed: "The *dawa* is going on and then after it, it is global work, not just in Tunisia."[186] It is no surprise, then, that ISIS's *Voice of al-Sham* magazine in September 2013 featured a picture of Abu Waqas with the Qur'anic verse 49:10 (Surat al-Hujurat) "the believers are but brothers" next to him.[187] This was one of the same framing devices that AST used to attract followers, as described in the previous chapter.

Tunisians in theater also called on Tunisians at home to conduct jihad and fight in Syria. For example, in July 2013, Abu 'Abd Allah al-Tunisi, a member of the foreign fighter-dominant group Jaysh al-Muhajirin wa-l-Ansar, advised "the Muslim youth in general and the youth of Tunisia in particular to join the fight" and called on Muslim "mothers and sisters" to "incite the youth for jihad and deployment."[188] In addition, an October 2013 ISIS video shows Abu Jihad al-Tunisi inviting and encouraging Tunisians to heed the *nafir* (call to arms) and join the fight.[189] According to Olfa Lamloum, those in theater were also privately Skyping their friends and family members back at home, regaling them with stories "of 'divine assistance' given to these young fighters in the form of 'supernatural apparitions and interventions' on the battlefield."[190] Therefore, the confluence of the AST designation with the strengthening of jihadi groups in Syria had encouraged a robust group of Tunisians to fight jihad in Syria under the banner of ISIS or JN by the end of 2013.

This involvement would continue in the following years as Tunisians became infamous for being one of the largest foreign national groups fighting in Iraq, Libya, and Syria. This in many ways was a direct consequence of the opening of Tunisian society for jihadis to proselytize for two and a half years without much pushback. Compounding this was the Tunisian government's inability to tackle the problem of Tunisians traveling abroad to fight with jihadi groups after finally suppressing AST domestically. As a result, the downfall of AST did not in fact destroy the jihadi movement in Tunisia; rather, the change in operating conditions simply pushed much of its activism outside Tunisia, back to its historic norm. Without a long-term vision for how to deal with these foreign fighters with new military skills or willingness to conduct terrorist/insurgent attacks against the Tunisian state, government, and its people, it is no surprise that such incidents would return home a few years later in 2015 and 2016 (which is discussed in greater detail in chapter 10).

* * *

Abu 'Iyadh's inability to manage the so-called stages led to the downfall of AST as an organization. Not only did members of AST engage in increasing levels of intimidation and personal violence through its *hisba* actions; it also created an atmosphere of impunity through the creation of its security/neighborhood committees. These circumstances, when understood in the context of growing terrorist and insurgent violence, whether against the military in Jabal Chambi or assassinations against politicians, caused the al-Nahdah-led government to finally take seriously the threats that AST posed to society. The designation of AST as a terrorist organization and the subsequent crackdown on its public events led many who wanted to continue pursuing jihadism to fight abroad, particularly in Syria. The justification for doing so had already been laid by Abu 'Iyadh and AST's organization. Therefore, it was not necessarily difficult to get connected to logistics and facilitation networks to go fight there, especially considering Tunisians historical role in these networks in Iraq last decade (as described in chapter 3).

AST was successful in its short time as a group due to the conditions that allowed AST to operate as well as its *dawa*-first approach and how it implemented it and was able to garner support throughout the country. However, this approach was unsustainable because members of AST were involved with the rising level of intimidation and violence through *hisba* activities, the transformation of AST to a more overtly hostile actor as the government began to crack down on it, and the group's recruitment for training and fighting jihad abroad. In a way, this illustrates the aftermath and consequences of this new cohort of individuals that became jihadis through AST from 2011 to 2013, a topic I explore further in the next three chapters.

CHAPTER 8

IT WAS MOSTLY THE TUNISIANS WHO WERE INVOLVED IN *TAKFIR*

Following the fall of AST, the Tunisian jihadi movement changed. No longer was it a cohesive entity that was run by Tunisians and primarily focused on Tunisia. Once again Tunisian jihadism returned to its historical norm of one characterized by foreign fighting as well as individuals involved in facilitating and plotting attacks. While the previous four chapters are connected through their overarching focus on AST and the immediate postrevolution growth in jihadism, the following three chapters explore Tunisian involvement with the Islamic State. Unlike the latter part of the previous chapter, which explains the early mobilization of foreign fighters to Libya and Syria while AST was still an active organization, this one highlights how this network evolved once AST was no longer in existence. Therefore, this chapter examines the shifting networks by answering why so many Tunisians joined up with ISIS when AST was an AQ front group; this in turn helps explain why Tunisians are also considered some of the most extreme among all the jihadis in Syria. As former Saudi ISIS member Sulayman Sa'ud al-Suba'i noted about this extremist trend among Tunisians in ISIS, "it was mostly the Tunisians who were involved in *takfir*, although personally, I doubt they had such extensive religious knowledge."[1]

This chapter relies upon Islamic State primary sources, including its propaganda materials and internal documents. Moreover, primary source data from AST and Shabab al-Tawhid (a network that is explored shortly) help elucidate the reason for and transition of Tunisians affiliating themselves with ISIS over Jabhat al-Nusra (JN) and its successor groups, Jabhat Fatah al-Sham and Hay'at

Tahrir al-Sham. Therefore, this chapter returns to a topic that became less relevant in the latter part of the 2000s and the postrevolution jihadi scene—namely, that Tunisians, while associating with AQ over the decades, have also joined in great numbers with the more extreme trend within jihadism that Mustafa Hamid described as the Jalalabad school, as discussed in chapters 2 and 3. It became less relevant for two reasons: First, Tunisian jihadis were exposed to the leadership and strategy of Abu 'Iyadh within the Tunisian prison system that allowed for a *dawa*-first approach in the postrevolution environment, and, second, the Islamic State of Iraq (ISI) was losing strength as a consequence of the tribal awakening and surge of American troops in Iraq. This changed, however, as ISI gained more strength in 2012 and 2013, leading to the creation of ISIS in April 2013 and eventually the caliphate under the name IS in June 2014.

These dynamics, alongside the waning opportunities and capacity for jihadism in Tunisia, provided space for Tunisian jihadis to become enmeshed once again with ISI/ISIS/IS's network as it did in the prior decade. Therefore, Tunisians joining ISIS following the crackdown upon AST in late 2013 is not necessarily an outlier. There are several contributing factors that allowed ISIS to win the battle with JN over Tunisian foreign fighters since most Tunisians who went to Syria ended up defecting from JN to ISIS or joining ISIS directly.

A Return to the Jalalabad School

Based on data I have collected, most Tunisians who mobilized to join groups in Syria did so between March 2013 and June 2014.[2] This is crucial to remember since much of the mobilization of these individuals was taking place before there had been an overt and final split between AQ's and IS's networks. This was only finalized in February 2014.[3] As such, it was not even seen as a taboo as it would be now for AST, an AQ-related group, to promote ISI/ISIS as described in the last chapter. This is especially so considering Abu 'Iyadh's past relationship with Abu Mus'ab al-Zarqawi in Afghanistan ahead of 9/11, when Abu 'Iyadh described al-Zarqawi as "an honest, generous person who would be happy to sacrifice his soul and property for you."[4]

Alternative Voices Within AST

Even more relevant is the religious legal incentives within AST's sharia committee that helped further push AST members interested in fighting in Syria to join ISIS over JN. In late June 2013, a mere two months after ISI officially went into Syria and became ISIS, Abu Ja'afar al-Hatab, a leading figure on AST's sharia committee, released via AST's al-Bayyariq Media a religious text about the issue of *baya* (a religious pledge of allegiance to a leader) in Islamic history and how it related to the current events in Syria regarding JN's split from ISIS and subsequent *baya* given by its leader, Abu Muhammad al-Jawlani, to Ayman al-Zawahiri instead of Abu Bakr al-Baghdadi. Al-Hatab explained that because ISIS originally created JN, then one's *baya* should remain with the parent leader—in this case, al-Baghdadi. Therefore, according to al-Hatab, "JN['s] action is treason and treachery and is against *sharia*. . . . The JN *baya* [to al-Zawahiri] divided the *mujahidin* into two groups, such divisions have increased recently and that is against *sharia*. . . . JN members must repent and pledge *baya* to ISIS, not only them, but all the other factions and brigades that fight in al-Sham."[5]

As a consequence, it is not surprising that members of AST who then wanted to fight in Syria would heed this ruling considering al-Hatab's position within AST. This was also prior to AST's designation in late August 2013. While al-Hatab claims in this same text that he has not given a *baya* to al-Baghdadi yet, he would later go on to join IS in Syria and become infamous for being part of the so-called Hazimi trend that was viewed as too extreme for IS (which is described in greater detail below). Interestingly, this particular text that al-Hatab wrote was released less than a week after Turki Bin'ali traveled to Tunisia and met with AST members and its leadership, as noted in the previous chapter. Bin'ali himself would write a justification for pledging *baya* to al-Baghdadi two months later.[6] This could further cement the argument that Bin'ali was on a mission to various locales in the Arab world to build support for ISIS over JN and AQ following ISIS's April 2013 entrance into Syria and leading up to its eventual caliphate announcement in late June 2014.

The Shabab al-Tawhid Network

This push to promote IS by some within AST's sharia committee leadership would not end with al-Hatab. In fact, Kamal Zuruq, another senior figure within AST's sharia committee, would play a role as well via a new media and recruitment network called Shabab al-Tawhid (ST). ST was a network of pro-IS Tunisians who had previously been with AST after it was designated as a terrorist organization. ST's online manifestation became public in early March 2014, although it is likely that its on-the-ground network had been operating prior to this. It is possible that the creation of ST is what former AST youth leader Yusuf Mazuz meant in January 2014 when he said a name change from AST was necessary to try to deceive the Tunisian government.[7] Its main media purpose was to serve as a "pulpit of the Sunni people in Tunisia" and express support for ISIS. Much of ST's early content consisted of reposted material from AST and ISIS (including English translations of ISIS releases) as well as information from Tunisian foreign fighters in Syria and ISIS-sympathetic messaging. Most importantly, ST provided guidance on how to travel abroad to Syria through details on personal and operational security.[8] ST also attempted to motivate fighters to come to Syria with poems that had lyrics to inspire, such as "Your knights Tunisia are opening foreign lands and making history with their blood.... It is one life, let it be in the way of God! It is one death, let it be in the way of God!"[9]

At the time, I surmised that ST was a successor network to AST and was attempting to remobilize locally after its designation since it had an on-the-ground network as well.[10] In hindsight, it appears more as a mobilizing structure for foreign fighter recruitment and for turning AST members away from AQ to ISIS. For example, when the central division of al-Qaeda in the Islamic Maghreb (AQIM) expressed support for ISIS, ST highlighted the message.[11] Similar to al-Hatab, ST also released an article justifying pledging *baya* to al-Baghdadi and another article on why it was necessary to do so over AQ/JN.[12] Most important was Zuruq's overt call in early June 2014 via ST's media outlet for Tunisians to support ISIS: "I ask my brothers to support ISIS so that it will protect our Muslim nation as God promised us... jihad in al-Sham is mandatory."[13]

The fact that Zuruq's call was released via the ST network online is relevant because ST's network on the ground inside Tunisia was national in scope just as AST's was prior to the government crackdown (see figure 8.1). It is difficult to ascertain how many individuals were involved in these efforts, but ST had several layers of representation in towns, educational institutions, and mosques:

Towns: Jebel al-Ahmar, Le Kram, Sfax, Sidi Hassine, Guettaya, Megrine, Subaytilah, Bou Salem, Mateur, El Fahs, Hammam Zriba, Hammamet, Jelma, Jemmal, Ksar Hellal, Nefza, Tebourba, Dougga, Foussana, Medenine, Sidi Bouzid, Menzel Hayet, and Kalaa Kebira.

Colleges and mosques: Gafsa University, the March 2nd Institute, Bilal bin Rabah Mosque (in the Suroor neighborhood of Gafsa), the University of Sousse, the University of Sfax, the Higher Institute of Applied Science and Technology in Mateur, the University of Nabeul, the Higher Institute of Nursing Sciences in Sousse, the Vocational Training Center in Mateur, New Neighborhood Mosque in Tunis, the College of Medicine in Sfax, the Higher Institute of Computer and Communication Technologies, and the Higher Institute of Technological Studies in al-Qayrawan.[14]

As a result, this network co-optation of parts of AST's infrastructure by pro-IS Tunisians who had previously been in AST allowed for a smooth transition from one group to the other but also secured many potential recruits who also wanted to fight in Syria and veered them toward ISIS over JN.

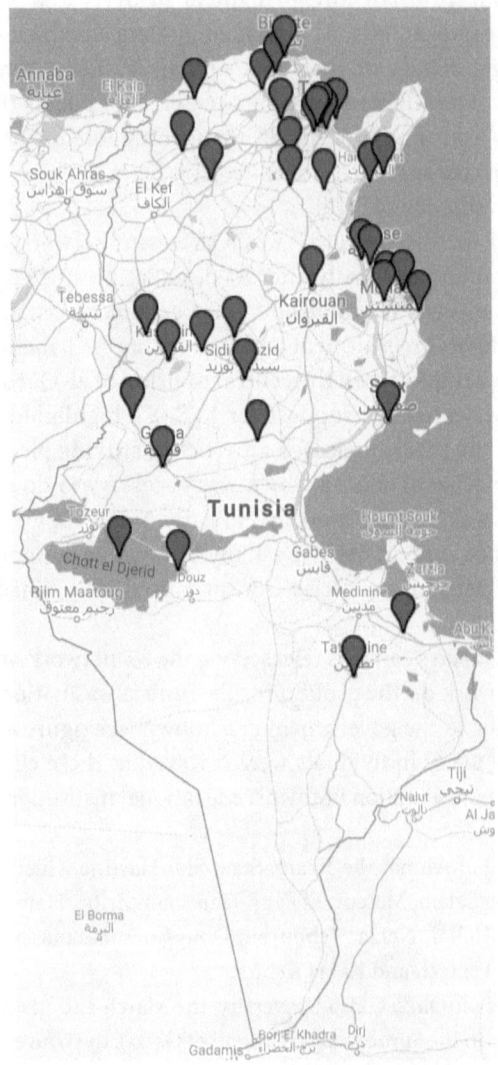

8.1 Shabab al-Tawhid's Network in Tunisia

Abu 'Iyadh Loses the Plot

While this was all unfolding, one might be wondering where Abu 'Iyadh was and what he had to say about all of this since he remained loyal to AQ's broader network. In many ways Abu 'Iyadh and AST's official position as an organization on the growing battle between ISIS and JN provided space for others, like those mentioned above, to fill. At first, in mid-July 2013, AST remained neutral on the issue: "AST announces that it has not declared officially its position regarding the disagreement between ISIS and JN."[15] Furthermore, Abu 'Iyadh was relatively aloof about the various debates, especially as it related to the idea of the caliphate being raised by those sympathetic to ISIS and challenging AQ in the run-up to the actual announcement. In early May 2014, for example, Abu 'Iyadh explained "regarding the conversation about Caliphate based on the prophetic methodology, it is very early and the time for this conversation has not come yet! And I don't think it will happen during our time or even the time of our grandsons! This is not pessimism, but I see that these conversations need a scientific study that will look at the chronological order of events in order for us to understand where we are today!"[16] Only a month and a half later ISIS would announce its caliphate, making Abu 'Iyadh in some ways look out of touch with the third generation of Tunisian jihadis (and anyone who followed ISIS's path among the first two generations).

Following ISIS's takeover of Mosul, Iraq, on June 10, 2014, Abu 'Iyadh released a statement saying he was "inspired by the conquests": "I congratulate our Islamic nation—and the mujahideen in the land of Iraq, [who are] the crown upon our heads—for the victories in the Land of Two Rivers."[17] He also saw it as an opportunity for unity between AQ and ISIS: "I recommend that the two shaykhs, Ayman al-Zawahiri and Abu Muhammad al-Jawlani, rush to congratulate [ISIS on] these victories. This may lead the leaders of the organizations that are fighting each other to put an end to the battle and the struggle between them. Likewise, I call upon Abu Bakr al-Baghdadi to hurry and respond to the calls [for reconciliation issued] by the honorable commanders and clerics who asked him, publicly and in secret." Therefore, at this point Abu 'Iyadh was still unwilling to take a side or condemn ISIS even though AQ itself had already kicked ISIS out of its organization months earlier. As a consequence, there was never any guidance about not joining ISIS, and others who had previously been leaders in AST, like al-Hatab, Zuruq, and Bilal al-Shawashi, who originally joined JN and defected to ISIS in April 2014, were promoting the necessity of joining ISIS.[18] Many young, interested, and impressionable individuals would follow this advice from those three individuals, among others.

In the aftermath of the caliphate announcement, Abu 'Iyadh sent two private letters to Ayman al-Zawahiri. The first one was subsequently leaked online by IS senior leader Abu Maysarah al-Shami (also known as Abu Sulayman al-Shami), who is the Syrian American Ahmad Abousamra. In light of this, to contextualize the matter, the pro-AQ media outlet Hidayyah Media Foundation released both letters.[19] This is because in the first letter, Abu 'Iyadh suggested that al-Zawahiri should pledge *baya* to al-Baghdadi.[20] As a reminder, this is five months after AQ officially kicked ISIS out of its organization. Abu 'Iyadh was proposing that al-Zawahiri would attempt to moderate IS from within by stifling its more extreme tendencies and therefore save them from themselves:

"weaken the extremists of the [Islamic] State who have no project besides murder and *takfir*."[21]

However, in the second letter, which was written in mid-August 2014, just a month and a-half after the caliphate announcement, Abu 'Iyadh told al-Zawahiri to rescind and ignore his original letter: "consider my proposal and advice as if it had never existed."[22] Apparently, in that short amount of time he realized that there was no longer "reasons for giving the benefit of the doubt to the good people among them."[23] Instead, based on consultations with jihadi ideologues Abu Muhammad al-Maqdisi and Abu Qatadah al-Filistini as well as AQ branch leaders Nasir al-Wihayshi (AQAP), Mukhtar Abu al-Zubayr (al-Shabab), Abu Bakr al-Shakaw (Boko Haram), and Iyad Agh Ghali (Ansar al-Din in Mali), a proper strategy was "to turn away from these individuals" and reveal "their extremism."[24] This is not necessarily surprising since Abu Qatadah wrote an article in January 2014 lamenting the trajectory of former AST members that went to Syria and joined ISIS: "My brothers you should know that what hurts this *dawa* is mistakes and fanaticism. . . . But I'm sad to hear that a few of those who went to Syria are radicals."[25] By the time Abu 'Iyadh came to these conclusions, however, around 2,500 of the eventual 2,900 Tunisian foreign fighters had already arrived in Iraq and Syria by that point. Therefore, this epiphany was not all that relevant to those that might have still listened to him by mid-August 2014, especially since those that were in IS by then would have forsworn listening to Abu 'Iyadh anymore since he would have been seen as an enemy within IS circles and a so-called "Jew of Jihad" because he was a leader within AQ's camp.[26] The door was open to ISIS/IS for Tunisian foreign fighters, Abu 'Iyadh dithered, allowing others to take the reins and push former AST members toward ISIS/IS.

Ultra Extremism Among Some Tunisian Jihadis

This might explain why Tunisians ended up with IS over JN in Syria, but it does not necessarily get at why so many within Syria viewed Tunisians as more extreme relative to other foreign fighters.[27] There is a twofold aspect to this. The first relates to the human rights violations that Tunisians have been involved in within Syria, which is not necessarily unique considering all of the human rights violations committed by members of IS, whether local or foreign. And that does not even get into any of the abuses committed by jihadis in other groups, members of the mainstream rebellion, or on a much more industrial scale the Assad regime and its allies from Iran, foreign Shia militias, and Russia. The second relates to some Tunisians involved within an extremist trend within IS called the Hazimis, which is named after the progenitor of the ideas these individuals follow, Ahmad Bin 'Umar al-Hazimi, a Saudi religious scholar.

It should be noted that al-Hazimi is not a member or affiliated with IS; his ideas were co-opted by some members of IS. The next two sections discuss these two interrelated but different reasons why local actors viewed Tunisians as so extreme.

Tunisian Human Rights Violations in Iraq and Syria

Most noteworthy among the abuses Tunisians took part in, two Tunisians were involved in the torture and execution of the captured Jordanian pilot Muʻadh al-Kasasbah. Hamzah Maghrawi (Abu Bilal al-Tunisi), who is originally from the underdeveloped suburb of Tunis called Douar Hicher, was at the scene of Kasasbah's capture and was pictured with his arm around the lieutenant's neck.[28] Maghrawi had previously been a fighter in JN as early as 2012 and later joined IS following the split between the two groups. He would eventually be killed in airstrike in September 2015.[29] Following the capture of al-Kasasbah, Umm Rayan al-Tunisi, the head of IS's infamous, female-led al-Khansa' Brigade, participated in Kasasbah's torture. According to a female IS member who later defected, "It was the most brutal torturing [sic] I have ever seen."[30] This is not necessarily surprising since those who had been imprisoned by IS in other cases also noted that "people from Tunisia were responsible for torturing."[31]

Thereafter, Maghrawi allegedly helped come up with the idea to burn Kasasbah alive in a cage.[32] Similarly, according to Abu Abbud al-Raqqawi, a defected senior commander within IS, Tunisians were involved in other innovative ways to kill people: "some people were boiled alive in oil. Engine oil. They burned wood on a fire for an hour before throwing the victim into boiling oil. It's the Tunisians who were responsible for that."[33] In an event of comparable brutality, at least three Tunisians were involved in the massacre of seven hundred members of the al-Shaitat tribe in Deir al-Zour, an atrocity that took place over a two-week period.[34] In a video that showed executions, you can hear people speaking in Tunisian dialect of Arabic taunting those who had yet to be killed "by swinging severed heads in front of their faces and telling them, 'It's your turn next.'"[35] Even in non-execution punishments, some Tunisian IS leaders were stern. When a Saudi IS member was flogging an individual for breaking an IS law, a Tunisian admonished him for holding back, exclaiming: "Carry out the punishments properly. Whip them firmly!"[36] This is why a local from al-Raqqah once noted when explaining the actions of someone of a different nationality, "He didn't strut around like a Tunisian fighter, high on other people's fear."[37] This illustrates the reputation Tunisians garnered locally.

Tunisian men were also among those that took part in the sexual slavery of Yazidi women. According to a report by the UN Human Rights Council, the women were not given birth control. One woman who was taken from Iraq said in an interview that a Tunisian fighter held her for several months and raped her in the Syrian city of al-Bab.[38] These crimes not only affected the women who were being raped but also the children who were also taken and forced to hear in the next room their mothers being raped. Another women explained in an interview that her son "was one who would scream the loudest when [her Tunisian fighter-owner] locked the children in a room and took her to another room to rape her."[39] According to Ahmet Yayla, who served as the chief of counterterrorism in Sanliurfa, Turkey, on the border with Syria, between 2010 and 2013, IS "gave slaves to Tunisians to try and control them" so those who were among the extreme within this milieu would be preoccupied.[40] There were even reported cases of Tunisian fighters raping children in Buqrus, a small town in the Deir al-Zour governorate, although, due to their seniority in IS, they were never brought to justice.[41] Yet, in Iraq, a Tunisian was stoned to death by locals for raping an Iraqi woman.[42] Similarly, Abu Zayd al-Tunisi, IS's *hisba* official in al-Mayadin, Syria, was strangled to death by locals for his bad treatment of women in the city.[43] Likewise, in Manbij, Syria, there was backlash against a Tunisian IS sharia judge who ordered three members of a local family to be beheaded for allegedly "photographing IS's strongholds." In response, a local resident shot him in the head.[44]

Extreme action even took place within the civil administrative infrastructure of IS. According to Ibrahim, a civilian drilling technician who worked in the oil fields of eastern Syria, "[Fathi bin Awn al-Murad al-Tunisi] (Abu Sayyaf [al-Tunisi]) was a strict and unpopular manager. . . . The areas around the fields became scenes of occasional horror. You go to work and you find someone beheaded."[45] Abu Sayyaf was the head of IS's Diwan al-Rikaz (Administration of Precious Things from the Ground [e.g., oil, gas, antiquities]) in Wilayat al-Khayr (Deir al-Zour governorate) and Wilayat al-Barakah (al-Hasakah governorate) until he was killed in May 2016 during a U.S. Army Delta Force operation.[46] Abu Sayyaf had originally joined IS when Abu Musʿab al-Zarqawi established JTWJ in the aftermath of the 2003 U.S. invasion of Iraq, highlighting the continued relevance of the second generation of Tunisian foreign fighters among the more recent flow.[47]

There were also Tunisian individuals within JN involved in atrocities. For instance, a Tunisian foreign fighter in JN allegedly beat a woman because she violated modesty laws by wearing a coat deemed too short, drawing local demonstrations in Salqin, Syria, against the assailant.[48] Even more egregious was the case of Abu ʿAbd al-Rahman al-Tunisi, the JN leader in the Druze area of Jabal al-Summaq, and specifically his actions in the town of Qalb Lawzah. First, in middle and late 2014, Abu ʿAbd al-Rahman forced members of the Druze community to renounce their religion for Sunni Islam. Then, in early 2015, after perceiving this Druze commitment to be insincere—based on an alleged lack of devotion to "destroying shrines, teaching Islam with a particular focus on the youth, and adhering to sharia regulations on women's dress and gender-mixing"—he forced the community to restate its renunciation and rededicate itself to following these precepts.[49] And amid an altercation during a JN campaign in Qalb Lawzah to seize property from Druze previously loyal to the Assad regime, Abu 'Abd al-Rahman recruited henchman who subsequently massacred at least twenty individuals for alleged blasphemy.[50]

Tunisian Hazimis

In addition to the specific human rights violations that Tunisian foreign fighters were involved in, Tunisians have also been a part of and have taken a role in a specific intellectual and theological trend within IS. Although some in the Tunisian jihadosphere, especially those that are pro-AQ, claim that the spread of this trend among Tunisians is a consequence of the Tunisian government attempting to sully and divide the Tunisian jihadi movement, it is a bit more complicated than that.[51] As background, al-Hazimi did four different lecture series in Tunisia between December 2011 and May 2012 (see table 8.1) with the local jihadi milieu. Interestingly, the first series was announced on October 25, 2011, a mere two days after the Tunisian Constituent Assembly election, which al-Nahdah won as the leading political party.[52] Al-Hazimi's first three visits to Tunisia were in coordination with and sponsored by the Hay al-Khadra' Mosques Committee and the Islamic Good Society in Tunis. The committee was headed by Abu Muhanad al-Tunisi, who was a senior cleric in AST and also ran the al-Rahmah Mosque in Hay al-Khadra', a neighborhood in Tunis.[53] The al-Rahmah Mosque became an AST-run mosque following the 2011 revolution.[54] Abu Muhanad's first lecture promoted by AST at the al-Rahmah Mosque noted that it "is where the organization of the two previous sessions with Shaykh Ahmad Bin 'Umar al-Hazmi" took place since it happened in mid-February 2012.[55] As for the Islamic Good Society in Tunis, in May 2014 the head and some of its members were arrested for money laundering and terrorist financing.[56] This could suggest that this charity was involved with more than just spreading its interpretation of Islam but with assisting individuals involved in terrorism or helping finance travel abroad to Syria as well. Al-Hazimi's final lecture in Tunisia was at the Grand Mosque of Medenine, a city sixty-five miles northwest of the Tunisian-Libyan border.

Besides these courses, in early March 2012 al-Hazimi helped create and was the supervisor of the Ibn Abu Zayd al-Qayrawani Institute for Sharia Sciences.[57] It was based in Hay al-Khadra' and was named after the same historical Tunisian Maliki scholar mentioned in chapter 6 in the discussion of AST's religious lecture series. This institute was established in conjunction with the Hay al-Khadra' Mosques Committee, highlighting its connections to AST as well.

TABLE 8.1 Ahmad Bin 'Umar al-Hazimi's Visits to Tunisia

Dates	Location	Topics Covered
December 18–25, 2011	al-Rahmah Mosque, Hay al-Khadra', Tunis	*al-Usul al-Thalatha* (The Three Fundamental Principles); *Nawaqid al-Islam* (Nullifiers of Islam); and *Nazm 'Ubayd Rabah* (System of 'Ubayd Rabah), which is on grammar
January 23–28, 2012	al-Rahmah Mosque, Hay al-Khadra', Tunis	*Nawaqid al-Islam* (Nullifiers of Islam) and *Nazm al-Waraqat Li-l-Umrayti* (System of Papers for 'Umrayti), which is on legal theory
March 19–24, 2012	al-Rahmah Mosque, Hay al-Khadra', Tunis	*Sharah Kitab al-Tawhid* (Commentary of Muhammad Ibn 'Abd al-Wahhab's "The Book of Monotheism") by Shaykh 'Abd al-Rahman Bin Muhammad al-Qasim
May 14–16, 2012	Grand Mosque, Medenine	*Sharah Kitab A'lam al-Sunnah al-Manshurah fi A'tiqad al-Ta'ifah al-Mansurah* (Commentary of the Book "Highlights of the Sunni Knowledge on the Creed of the Victorious Sect") by Hafidh al-Hakami

Sources: al-Qabsi, "al-Dawrah al-'ilmiyah al-ula li-l-shaykh ahmad bin 'umar al-hazimi bi-tunis," *Ahl al-Hadith Forum*, October 25, 2011; Abu al-Zubayr al-Qabsi, "al-Dawrah al-'ilmiyah al-thaniyah li-l-shaykh ahmad bin 'umar al-hazimi bi-tunis," *Ahl al-Hadith Forum*, January 9, 2012; "al-Dawrah al-'ilmiyah al-thaniyah bi-tunis," *Mawqah al-Islam fi Tunis*, January 10, 2012; Abu 'Iyadh al-Tunisi, "al-Dawrah al-thalathah li-l-shaykh ahmad bin 'umar al-hazimi fi tunis," *Ahl al-Hadith Forum*, February 15, 2012; Muhammad al-Mu'amari, "al-Dawrah al-'ilmiyah al-thalathah bi-tunis li-l-shaykh ahmad bin 'umar al-hazimi," *Ahl al-Hadith Forum*, March 11, 2012; and "al-Dawrah al-'ilmiyah al-ula li-l-shaykh ahmad bin 'umar al-hazimi bi-madanin," *Mawqah al-Islam fi Tunis*, May 8, 2012.

After the institute opened registration on March 10, 2012, there was a specific institute in Tunisia that was teaching a curriculum that adhered to al-Hazimi's views on creedal matters (more on this below).[58] This is likely where many Tunisians became exposed to al-Hazimi's ideas beyond his in-person lecture series or his online presence.

Furthermore, AST promoted Hazimi's ideas on its official Facebook page via its sharia committee. In December 2012 AST published a list of content that "is obligatory to learn for members of AST" as part of their *dawa* efforts.[59] AST also republished this list on its official Facebook page as a reminder in mid-January 2013.[60] Besides al-Hazimi's content, the post suggested Abu

Muhammad al-Maqdisi's *Democracy: A Religion* and *The Religion of Abraham* as well as a Saudi Arabia Ministry of Islamic Affairs Dawa and Guidance book from 2004 called *Accessible Jurisprudence in Light of the Qur'an and Sunnah*.[61] The al-Hazimi content contained a six-part lecture series titled *al-Usul al-thalatha* (The three fundamental principles) exploring the ideas of "Who is your Lord?," "What is your religion?," and "Who is your Prophet?"; an eight-part lecture series titled *A'lam al-sunnah al-manshurah fi a'tiqad al-ta'ifah al-mansurah* (Highlights of the sunni knowledge on the creed of the victorious sect); and most importantly to the discussion related to extremism within the IS context, a four-part series titled *Nawaqid al-islam* (Nullifiers of Islam).

The latter lecture is based on a creedal work by the founder of Wahhabism, Muhammad Ibn 'Abd al-Wahhab, and relates to ten ways that nullify someone from being a true Muslim. In short, the third nullifier says, according to Cole Bunzel, that "one must pronounce *takfir* (excommunication) on those failing or hesitating to pronounce *takfir*" in relation to acts of polytheism.[62] *Takfir* in the jihadi context leads to the legitimization of killing those that fall outside the bounds of their interpretations of Islam. Within this third nullifier is where the shades of *takfir* between different jihadis, including within IS, is contested. Al-Hazimi believes in the idea of *takfir al-'adhir* (excommunication of the excuser), meaning those who follow *al-'udhr bi-l-jahl* (excusing someone from the duty of *takfir* on the basis of ignorance in what they are doing). This, according to those who opposed the followers of al-Hazimi within IS, would lead to a so-called endless chain of *takfir*. These ideas were thus promulgated in al-Hazimi's lectures in Tunisia and in the audio series AST posted online for its followers. This negates AQ-apologetic ideologues like Abu Lababah al-Tunisi or al-Maqalaat claiming that the growth in these ideas in Tunisia were a consequence of some conspiracy by the Tunisian government.[63] That being said, it is important to remember that AST's approach within Tunisia was not *takfiri* in any manner due to its *dawa*-first approach. It is clear, however, that these ideas by al-Hazimi did incubate within the minds of some and then were brought to fore more so in Syria once the Tunisian jihadists had joined ISIS/IS. Most notable among these figures was the aforementioned Abu Ja'afar al-Hatab who had been on AST's sharia committee.

Based on a reading of al-Hatab's publications with AST, al-Nahdah's crackdown upon AST following the government blocking AST from conducting its third annual conference in mid-May 2013 led al-Hatab down this ultra-extreme path. This is because al-Hatab was not writing anything along the lines of *takfir al-'adhir* for AST publications. Ahead of the third annual conference, there were signs that al-Nahdah was planning to shut it down, but based on its past behaviors as described in chapter 4, some within AST likely saw it as a bluff and were not necessarily taking it seriously. Despite these warnings, AST wanted to prepare its followers for the conference, so al-Hatab penned guidance and instruction on how to act. In particular, the third instruction illustrates that al-Hatab was not yet believing in such ultra-extreme ideas. He said, "We need to be humble whether alone or in groups. . . . Our brothers don't be arrogant especially with your brothers who have not joined AST. They are our brothers in faith. Be humble with them and invite them to attend our annual meeting. Even if they have disagreed with us, they still have the right to guardianship in Islam."[64]

Only six weeks after this al-Hatab wrote his treatise defending ISIS, saying the only legitimate *baya* was to Abu Bakr al-Baghdadi. This suggests that the al-Nahdah-led crackdown upon AST, which began in May 2013 and culminated in the group's eventual designation in August 2013, led al-Hatab to adopt more radical views over time. This was likely reinforced by JN's challenge to ISIS as well as reinforced once he made it to the war zone context in the summer of 2013. The failed AST experience of a *dawa*-first approach probably also pushed al-Hatab down a path of no compromise since the softer way did not work in Tunisia. This dynamic was seen with other Tunisians within ISIS too. For example, according to Rania Abouzaid, a Tunisian leader doing a Friday sermon in Syria equated JN's allegedly softening positions to his experience with al-Nahdah in Tunisia: "He had seen what he termed 'the reality of these people' in Tunisia, before his pilgrimage to Syria. 'They curse God and the Prophet and say it is freedom of expression. They walk around naked and say this is freedom! If you are a Muslim and express your opinion, you are a terrorist! If you call one of them an infidel, they say you are an extremist!.'"[65]

Within a year of joining ISIS, al-Hatab and other Tunisians who began to internalize al-Hazimi's ideas started to run afoul of the group, even though many Tunisians including al-Hatab came into important positions within the organization. For instance, when al-Hatab joined ISIS in the summer of 2013, he was a part of an early version of ISIS's sharia committee alongside Turki Binʿali, who became an arch nemesis of the Hazimi trend within ISIS, and Abu ʿAli al-Anbari.[66]

Based on my reading of WikiBaghdady, an alleged insider account and leaks on the inner workings of ISIS, which were published between December 2013 and June 2014, the ISIS infighting with JN helped cause the ascendancy of al-Hatab and other Tunisians within ISIS, which allowed for greater space for the Hazimi trend to grow.[67] While some within IS and AQ circles have skepticism about this source, a number of details from these leaks cohere with other information known about IS that has been independently written about since this time period.

In the early stages of the infighting between JN and ISIS, JN arrested two Tunisians, Abu Taj al-Sussi and Abu ʿUmar al-ʿAbadi, among others who were not Tunisian, due to their *takfiri* ways and loyalty to Abu Bakr al-Baghdadi.[68] In line with this, due to the loyalty of Tunisian foreign fighters during the fight with JN, a number of Tunisians were given more senior positions within ISIS, including al-Hatab. As a consequence of ISIS's violent infighting with JN, which became far more aggressive in January 2014, a number of foreign fighters soured on ISIS because they did not want to fight those they perceived as their brothers in JN, even if there were some political and strategic disagreements. In response, al-Baghdadi nominated al-Hatab to try to stem these losses by receiving new *bayat* from others who supported the group in Egypt, Libya, Tunisia, and Turkey.[69] Al-Hatab also took charge of attempting to persuade leaders of Syrian rebel factions to defect and join ISIS with a $1,500 incentive; however, this effort allegedly failed.[70] Furthermore, al-Baghdadi placed spies—trusty Iraqis and loyal Tunisians—"with each field commander to fortify ISIS from any defections and have an early notification to try to dissuade the dissidents or liquidate them."[71] Later on, al-Hatab became an official in IS's Diwan al-Ta'alim (Administration of Education).[72]

Shortly after providing more space to Tunisians due to their loyalty, their extreme positions on *takfir* came to light and increasingly became a problem for ISIS later in the year. In early March 2014 an audio leaked of a conversation between Abu Muhammad al-Tunisi, an ISIS sharia official in al-Hasakah, Syria; and Abu Mus'ab al-Tunisi, an ISIS sharia official in Deir al-Zour; and Abu Usamah al-Iraqi, the *wali* (governor) of al-Hasakah, during which they described the Taliban and Usamah Bin Ladin as infidels.[73] A couple of weeks later another audio leaked of Abu Mus'ab al-Tunisi, now doing *takfir* on AQIM and AST and claiming that only ISIS is part of *al-ta'ifah al-mansurah* (the victorious sect).[74] He also believes that "jihad will die" in Tunisia because of those two groups.[75] It should be noted that Tunisians were not the only ones associated with the Hazimi trend; in addition to al-Hatab, one of the early leaders in this trend was Abu 'Umar al-Kuwaiti.[76] In August 2017 an IS scholar named Abu 'Abd al-Malik al-Shami also highlighted that Egyptians, Saudis, Azerbaijanis, and Turks were among the early adopters of the Hazimi trend, along with Tunisians.[77] The increasing voice and strength of this trend, however, led to a backlash by some within the senior leadership of IS, who were worried about this excessive extremism in the use of *takfir*. This led to a series of arrests and then executions in August and September 2014, including of al-Hatab, Abu Mus'ab al-Tunisi, and Abu Suhayb al-Tunisi.[78] In the following years there were a number of other public incidents related to the Hazimi trend (see table 8.2) that Tunisians were involved in as well.

Likewise, behind the scenes, those who were against the Hazimi trend within IS wrote several letters and memos that have since been leaked online that included details on later manifestations of this trend, which also highlighted some more Tunisians among a broader grouping of people. Some of them had positions within IS, including Abu Hudhayfah al-Tunisi, a member of IS's Diwan al-I'alam (Administration of Media) and previously a judge of "real

TABLE 8.2 Extreme *Takfir*-Related Incidents with Tunisians in IS[1]

Dates	Names or Numbers of Those Involved	Details
September 2014	Abu Ja'afar al-Hatab (IS sharia committee and later IS official in its Diwan al-Ta'alim); Abu Mus'ab al-Tunisi (IS leader in Deir al-Zour); Abu Suhayb al-Tunisi	Executed for doing *takfir* on Abu Bakr al-Baghdadi and IS
February 2015	6 Tunisians	Executed to preserve IS's unity and were considered traitors
July 2016	Abu Ahmad al-Tunsi (IS head of *hisba* in al-Bab, Syria)	Executed for extreme position on *takfir*
January 2017	70 Tunisians	Were on a wanted list for extreme *takfiri* beliefs
March 2017	Tunisian field commander	Besieged in al-Mayadin, Syria, for having extreme *takfiri* thoughts
April 2018	Up to 50 Tunisians	Besieged in al-Ka'lah on the outskirts of Hajin, Syria, for doing *takfir* on Abu Bakr al-Baghdadi and IS. At least 6 were killed.
September 2018	Tunisian commander	Shot after IS accused him of being a *ghulat* (extremist)
September 2018	Several Tunisians	Attempted coup and execution attempt against Abu Bakr al-Baghdadi based on their extreme *takfiri* beliefs

Sources: Musalahah al-Tawhid, "Munasarah al-Ikhwah al-Ma'surin fi dawlah al-juhmiyah al-kafirin," August 16, 2014; "Islamic State Executes Prominent Members Who Planned Coup," *ARA News*, February 2, 2015; Jamie Dettmer, "ISIS Barbarians Face Their Own Internal Reign of Terror," *Daily Beast*, February 6, 2015; Islamic State, "Report on the Phenomenon of Extremism in the Islamic State"; Rodi Said, "Islamic State Turned on Dissenters as Raqqa Assault Neared," *Reuters*, June 28, 2017; "On the Eastern Banks of the Euphrates River, Fighting between 'Tunisian Khawirj' and ISIS Members," *SOHR*, April 15, 2018; "'Asharat al-muqatilin al-tunisiyin yuwasalun tumaridhum 'ala tanzim 'al-dawlah al-islamiyah' 'ind safaf al-furat al-sharqiyah ba'd 'takfir al-tanzim wa-qa'datuhu," *SOHR*, April 16, 2018; "September 6, 2018," *Daesh Daily*, September 6, 2018; and Martin Chulov, "'The Fighting Was Intense': Witness Tells of Two-Day Attempt to Kill Isis Leader," *Guardian*, February 10, 2019; Also see: https://justpaste.it/ISIS_takfiri; and https://twitter.com/memrijttm/status/757474726281371648/photo/1.

estate" in Wilayat al-Raqqah, and Abu Dhar al-Tunisi, the founder of IS's Military Academy, which had lectures on warfare and tactics.[79] Beyond these two individuals mentioned for their extremism in use of *takfir*, IS's Diwan al-Amn al-Am (Administration of General Security) notes some secret groups that came into being following the death of al-Hatab and his associates, including the Abu 'Abd Allah al-Tunisi group and the Abu Ayub al-Tunisi group.[80] The latter group had the support of the *wali* (governor) of Aleppo, making it difficult to go after them even if the *diwan* viewed them as dangerous. Therefore, even if the Hazimi trend is less open publicly within IS, there remains some remnants of it left as of the fall of 2019.

* * *

This chapter helps to explain why members of AST, which was an AQ group, decided to join ISIS and why, in turn, some among them became ultra-extremists. At the time it was not necessarily a taboo to go between AST and ISIS since there had yet to be an overt split between AQ and ISIS. Moreover, other figures who had been senior leaders within AST filled a leadership vacuum left by Abu 'Iyadh when he fled Tunisia for Libya. In particular, Abu Ja'afar al-Hatab, Kamal Zuruq, and Bilal al-Shawashi were promoting ISIS as the group to follow once one makes the trip to Syria. Furthermore, AST and Abu 'Iyadh had a relatively neutral stance on the infighting between AQ/JN and ISIS, even at one point suggesting al-Zawahiri should give *baya* to Abu Bakr al-Baghdadi. By the time he fully followed AQ's position on the issue, it was already too late.

Once in Syria, Tunisians earned a reputation for being extreme and brutal on two levels. One is related to human rights violations, which is not necessarily outside the norm among other foreign fighters, but since many Tunisians were in positions of power within ISIS, they got more attention. The second is related to specific theological and creedal positions and had to do with Ahmad Bin 'Umar al-Hazimi spreading extreme positions on *takfir* via four lecture series and the creation of a local sharia institute in Tunisia in 2011 and 2012. This exposed some, like al-Hatab, to these ideas, even though they were not necessarily internalized fully until after al-Nahdah's crackdown against AST in the spring and summer of 2013. This led to a growth in this belief system within ISIS in Syria as a consequence of Tunisians traveling there as a way to continue their jihadi activism.

Now that this context is understood, the next chapter explores the numbers behind how many Tunisians made it to Iraq and Syria as well as their motivations for going and what they actually were doing while they were in ISIS/IS.

CHAPTER 9

HONEST ONES AMONG THE *DAWA* PEOPLE MUST COME TO AL-SHAM

Two men in full black garb with their faces concealed drive a bulldozer in the middle of the desert on the Iraqi-Syrian border. The main person manning this vehicle is Taha Subhi Falahah, better known as Abu Muhammad al-Adnani, the Islamic State's (IS) official spokesperson and head of external operations. He maneuvers the machine to pick up the dirt and move it to the side. He is removing a twenty- to thirty-foot-high sand berm that demarcates the borders between Iraq and Syria. Symbolically, it shows that the Islamic State has broken the so-called Sykes–Picot border between the two states, illustrating the promise of a borderless Islamic state that does not rely upon the Western nation-state model. Rather, from its perspective, the Islamic State has succeeded in beginning a new world order. Several Islamic State members then kiss the ground and thank God for this victory. This symbolic border destruction continues with Islamic State military vehicles passing through this now borderless area. On top of the berm stands a grizzly looking man with long black hair and a long bushy black beard. He has a smile on his face and raises his right index finger, known as *isba' al-tawhid*, a gesture to signify the oneness of God, which is not exclusive to IS but many have come across it due to the ubiquity of its use in IS's propaganda videos. This man is Jamal al-Din Mallah (Jalal al-Din al-Tunisi and Abu Fatimah al-Tunisi), who is originally from Ras al-Jabal in the Bizerte governorate, about thirty-five miles north of Tunis. At this momentous occasion, Mallah explains:

> I tell the Muslim nation, we are now in Iraq. God destroyed the borders of Sykes and Picot and the Muslim is now able to enter Iraq without a passport. That is

because of God and because of jihad and mujahidin, God bless them. God have mercy on our Shaykh al-Zarqawi, God have mercy on our Shaykh Abu 'Umar al-Baghdadi, and God have mercy on our Shaykh Abu Hamzah al-Muhajir [all three are prior leaders of IS]. Those men were the reason behind the victory of God's religion. Those men were the reason behind the awakening of the Muslim nation. I tell everyone who talks against this state that he is a liar and a traitor, God liberated this land against the will of infidels.[1]

The fact that Mallah took part in this video and media event to showcase IS's successes illustrates his importance within IS alongside others like al-Adnani and 'Umar al-Shishani, IS's head military commander at the time who also spoke in the video. Mallah is also a key propagandist in another video that IS released four months later, which in some ways is an allusion to his Tunisian compatriots and what they had been doing the previous few years with AST. In this other message, he calls for "the honest ones among the *dawa* people must come to al-Sham, to the land of jihad and battles."[2] Although not specifically directed at Tunisians, it symbolically illustrates the continued through line between what Tunisians were up to with AST and how Tunisians took on roles in part of IS's structure once they made it to Syria beyond just fighting capacities.

* * *

This chapter explores the consequences of AST's recruitment campaign and how it fueled the growth in a new generation of foreign fighters—a third generation. There are several ways to understand this dynamic phenomenon, which is why this chapter clarifies the broader impact of this mobilization in terms of numbers related to how many actually went to Syria, motivations for why individuals joined, the roles taken on within IS, and connections to external operations plotting. This also helps to unfurl IS's use of Tunisians in its media campaign and gives a better understanding of people who went to join IS. I focus on Tunisians in IS over other groups due to ubiquity of them in IS in comparison with, say, Jabhat al-Nusra and its successor groups. This can best be summed up in a quote by Abu Khalid, an Islamic State intelligence officer: "Tunisia should really open its embassy in al-Raqqah, not Damascus. That's where its people are."[3]

However, before discussing Tunisians and IS in more depth, it is worth highlighting that Hay'at Tahrir al-Sham's current head official for foreign fighters is a Tunisian named Abu Hajr al-Tunisi, who has been in that position since at least 2015.[4] This is important to keep in mind for later discussions of whether Hay'at Tahrir al-Sham becomes a greater recruiter of foreign fighters or whether Abu Hajr changes groups. This is because Tunisians will continue to be connected with a key facilitation operator in the same way that was seen with individuals who took on key roles related to foreign fighters in Iraq, as discussed in chapter 3. While the focus of this chapter is on Tunisians and IS and on the fact that most Tunisians joined with IS, there are still other Tunisian jihadis with AQ-aligned or related groups, which could become more relevant in the years following this book's publication.

This chapter relies upon up to five thousand documents in multiple languages that I have collected since 2011 on foreign fighters. Thanks to the proliferation of jihadi primary sources on social media and intensive reporting on the war, unparalleled amounts of information have been released on these foreign fighters. I have also had access to the leaked IS border documents, which detail intake information from foreign fighters when they joined IS. These documents help provide official detail on Tunisians that joined IS between 2012 and 2014.

Data on Tunisian Foreign Fighters

In 2011, before jihadi groups officially announced their presence in Syria, foreign fighters began mobilizing to Syria with the Free Syrian Army. But after Jabhat al-Nusra (JN) formally released its first video in January 2012, reports of jihadi involvement by foreign fighters rose dramatically both in the press and within the jihadi movement. This would continue until the flow of foreign fighters began waning in 2015–16. As for the announcement of foreign fighter martyrs, this began in February 2012, with the posting of the first recorded martyrdom notice on the jihadi forum Shamukh al-Islam. This announcement was long delayed because the fighter in question, a Kuwaiti named Husam al-Mutayri, died August 29, 2011, while fighting with the Free Syrian Army in Damascus.[5] Besides the forums, a jihadi-run Facebook page and website called *al-Ghuraba'* (The strangers) began releasing information on foreign fighters killed in Syria. This is when the presence of Tunisians first became widely known. On April 19, 2012, the deaths of two Tunisians from Ben Gardane, Husayn Mars and Bulababah Buklash, were announced as having occurred in Idlib and Homs, respectively, marking the first known cases of Tunisians dying in the Syrian war.[6]

Overall Information

Over the next five to six years, nearly 30,000 Tunisians attempted to go to Iraq and Syria, with thousands arriving successfully, hundreds getting killed, and a thousand eventually returning to Tunisia (see table 9.1). The latter is explored in greater detail in the next chapter. This means that while 2,900 made it to their

TABLE 9.1 Tunisian Foreign Fighter Mobilization to Iraq and Syria

Date	Total prevented from mobilizing by this date	Total mobilized by this date	Total returned by this date	Total killed by this date
April 2012		Earliest reported fighters		
December 2012		100		37
March 2013		300		120
May 2013		800	150	
September 2013	6,000			269
April 2014	8,000	1,800		360
June 2014		2,400		389
July 2014	8,800			
October 2014	9,000	2,560		438
January 2015		2,800	570	
April 2015	12,000			
February 2016	15,000			508
March 2016			700	
April 2016	16,000			
December 2016		2,900	800	531
April 2017	27,000			
March 2018			970	552
February 2019			1,000	554

desired destinations, the Tunisian government prevented 27,000 individuals from going from the start of the mobilization until about April 2017.

While some observers have estimated that Tunisian foreign fighter activity in Iraq and Syria is as many as 6,000 individuals, my analysis of thousands of documents shows that this higher figure does not add up.[7] In fact, the original location where the 6,000 figure was written was never substantiated by any source, placing more doubt on its veracity, even though others then began citing it as gospel. The Tunisian government has never claimed such a number, and organizations such as the Soufan Group have lowered their estimates into the range suggested here.[8]

Most Tunisians who mobilized to join groups in Iraq and Syria did so between March 2013 and June 2014. This date range is perhaps surprising given that it predated the announcement of the IS caliphate. Several factors explain the surge in this period—and not later:

- The heightening showdown between AST and the Tunisian government in the spring of 2013, prompting many Tunisian jihadis to seek to fulfill their aspirations in Iraq and Syria rather than struggling with new challenges at home.
- The April 2013 announcement of ISIS operations in Syria, which was just as motivating for recruitment as the later caliphate declaration. After the 2013 news, most Tunisians formerly with JN switched to ISIS.
- A lack of friction due to the as-yet-unconsolidated efforts by the Tunisian government to prevent prospective jihadis from leaving the country. These efforts intensified only later.
- The rise of the Libyan theater, where, by the spring and summer of 2014, IS was already sending Tunisian operatives to build up its infrastructure ahead of its official November 2014 declaration extending its writ beyond Iraq and Syria to outlying "provinces." The jihad in Libya attracted many Tunisian fighters, given its proximity to Tunisia—providing yet another explanation for the peak of foreign fighters prior to the creation of the caliphate. Tunisians in IS in Libya and how this affected the Tunisian homeland is discussed in the next chapter.

Likewise, most publicly recorded Tunisian deaths in Iraq and Syria—based on both internal jihadi releases and press reporting in Arabic, English, and French—occurred by September 2014, the start of the U.S.-led Global Coalition to Defeat ISIS (as known in its current iteration). By the next month, October 2014, when Operation Inherent Resolve was formalized, an estimated 438 Tunisians had been killed (out of 554 killed over the entire period up to February 2019). The relatively low overall death count for Tunisians may be because of Tunisians' high representation in administrative roles, both before and after the announcement of the caliphate. Furthermore, eventual territorial setbacks for the jihadist group in late 2015 to early 2016 drove higher numbers of Tunisian recruits home. By February 2019, according to the Tunisian government, a thousand had returned. Additionally, the Rescue Association of Tunisians Trapped Abroad believes 400–500 Tunisians have returned undetected, mainly via the Libyan border.[9] Of those 2,900 Tunisians to make it to Iraq or Syria, the identities of 1,552 are known. It is likely that hundreds among the remaining 1,348 moved on to the Libyan battlefield between the spring of 2014 and December 2016, when IS was operating there, with many hundreds more remaining in Iraq or Syria with IS and, to a lesser extent, al-Qaeda and other jihadist groups operating in northwest Syria.

Tunisian-origin fighters from Europe figure much less prominently in open source documentation than do native-born ones, as borne out in table 9.2. This is in part because European nations do not necessarily classify such individuals by ethnicity or dual nationality. Nor does the local press automatically mention an individual's country of origin. Therefore, the numbers are likely higher. The grand total of these Tunisian-origin fighters is thirty-eight hailing from six countries, with France, Italy, and Germany most represented. Of these, the French mobilization was the largest. This likely can be traced to the legacy of Bubakr al-Hakim, the French Tunisian jihadi who belonged to al-Zarqawi's Iraq network in 2003, and to AST following the Tunisian Revolution. Al-Hakim had historical ties to French jihadi networks as well as a senior leadership role within IS after he returned to Syria in 2013. But the flow from France ended as a result of IS territorial setbacks and al-Hakim's death by a U.S. drone in late November 2016. By way of comparison, fewer Tunisian-origin Europeans went to Iraq and Syria than the number (thirty-nine) who went to Afghanistan during the period between the end of the Soviet occupation and 9/11 (1990–2001), but the figure exceeded those that mobilized to Iraq during the 2002–11 period (twenty).

In the early stages of the mobilization to Syria, a number of French jihadis, including French Tunisians traveled to Syria via Tunisia—some even joined AST before heading to Syria.[10] For example, the French Tunisian Abu Mus'ab and the French convert Wilson took part in the attack against the U.S. Embassy in Tunis in September 2012.[11] Over time, individuals like Wilson felt that AST's *dawa*-first methodology was too soft and decided to go to Syria: "When the prophet [Muhammad] is insulted, there is no *dawa*, we act and that's all!"[12] By mid-2013 most French jihadis began to travel from France straight to Turkey and then Syria instead of an intermediate stay in Tunisia and Libya.[13] Part of this could also be due to local Tunisians allegedly defrauding French jihadis with fake *tazkiyat* (assurances) for joining jihadi groups in Syria and losing €750 in the process.[14]

Leaked IS border documents shed greater detail on Tunisians living in other locales who went to Syria.[15] According to the documents, they came from these

TABLE 9.2 Mobilization of European-Based Tunisians to Iraq and Syria

Country	Numbers	Years of Mobilization
France	15	2012–16
Italy	8	2012–15
Germany	8	2013–17
Sweden	3	2012–14
Belgium	2	2013
Denmark	2	2013
Total	**38**	**2012–17**

Source: Western Jihadists 1993–Present: An Archive and Database Charting the Evolution of Jihadi-inspired Terrorist Networks and Recruitment in Western States. Principal Investigator: Jytte Klausen (Waltham, MA: Brandeis University).

locales in Europe: France (sixteen), Germany (four), Denmark (one), Belgium (one), Sweden (one), Austria (one), and Britain (one). Other Tunisian-origin fighters had lived in Libya (two), Saudi Arabia (two), Afghanistan (one), Pakistan (one), Bahrain (one), and Chechnya (one) prior to joining IS. Unsurprisingly, the two Tunisians based in Afghanistan and Pakistan had been fighting in those countries' insurgencies before going to Syria.

These IS border documents are extremely useful in garnering details on the individuals who joined the group (see figure 9.1).[16] For example, in a recent report, David Sterman and Nate Rosenblatt examine the socioeconomic backgrounds of individuals based on their city/town of origin, educational background, and prior jobs.[17] Still, not all news organizations and researchers appear to be working from the full data set provided by the border documents, based on a look at the distillation by Sterman and Rosenblatt, which is notably transparent about its information sources relative to other studies. For instance, when stripping out the duplicates and data on Tunisians living abroad, my numbers show 639 Tunisians in the IS border control documents, versus 589 in the Sterman and Rosenblatt report. Among the 639, 19 of them were under the age of eighteen.[18] And when broken down by governorate, some data in Sterman and Rosenblatt (Tunis, Sousse, Sidi Bouzid, al-Qayrawan, Gabes, Sfax, and Jendouba) is more robust, while other governorates in my data set contain more information (Bizerte, Ariana, Kasserine, Medenine, Gafsa, Manouba, Mahdia,

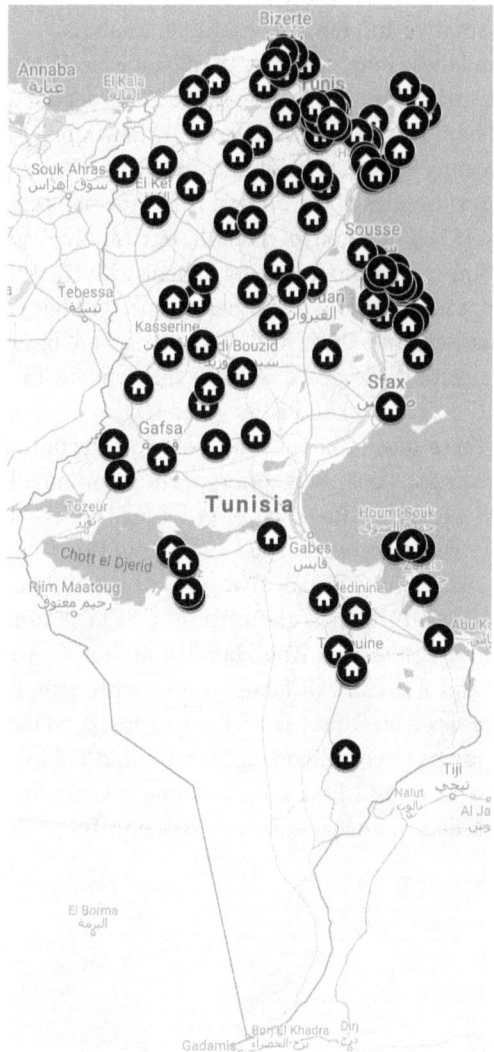

9.1 Location of Origin of Tunisian Foreign Fighters in Islamic State Border Documents

Kebili, Ben Arous, Monastir, Tataouine, Nabeul, Siliana, Zaghouan, El Kef, and Béja). This suggests an asymmetry in how different news organizations and researchers likely obtained different parts of the overall IS border document database. This is not to diminish the content, which has been verified by governments and several individuals in the database have been identified, but it does highlight the limitations in potential generalizability of the information since each individual who has access to the content might not be seeing the entire scope of the data. Due to the size of the data, however, it is still likely somewhat representative and remains useful for analysis.

Keeping in mind these imperfections, the data is especially useful as it relates to facilitation networks. The information in the IS border documents helps elucidate where and how Tunisians moved from Turkey into Syria (see figure 9.2). Particularly interesting is the revelation that the IS infrastructure spanned both the Turkish and Syrian sides of the border, with Tunisians checked in on both sides. Thus, while IS did not control or claim territory in Turkey, it did man a vital parastatal point of operations leading fighters to Syria. On the Turkish side were five main stops for Tunisians and other prospective fighters: Antakya, Reyhanli, Kilis, Gaziantep, and Urfa. Most Tunisians were based in Urfa before passing into Syria, with the largest check-ins occurring in Tal Abyad (204) followed by Reyhanli–Atme (149) and Kilis–Azaz (122).

In addition to these specific cities, some files note the individuals who facilitated border crossings, a task that differs from recommending the individual and giving IS assurance (*tazkiya*) of one's legitimacy. Along with other nationalities, nine Tunisians were listed as holding this facilitation role: Abu 'Umar al-Tunisi, Abu Muhammad al-Tunisi, Abu al-'Abbas al-Tunisi, Abu 'Ubaydah al-Tunisi, Abu Dujanah al-Tunisi, Abu Sa'id al-Tunisi, Abu Basir al-Tunisi, Abu Zayd al-Tunisi, and Abu Hamzah al-Tunisi. Although these are noms de guerre and therefore difficult to link with actual individuals, the available evidence ties Abu 'Umar with Tariq al-Harzi, as mentioned in prior chapters. After a long career in jihad, al-Harzi would finally die in an American airstrike in Syria in mid-June 2015, less than twenty-four hours after his brother 'Ali was killed in an American airstrike in Iraq.[19] It is also possible,

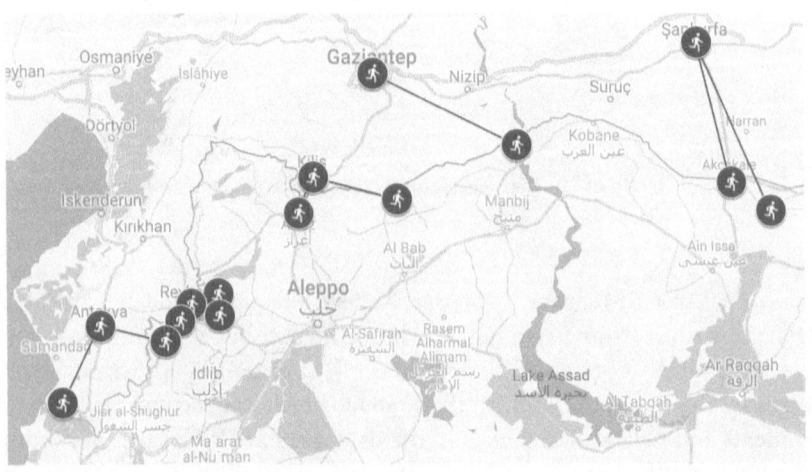

9.2 Where Tunisians Entered Syria from Turkey

though unconfirmed since it is a common *kunya*, that the Abu Muhammad al-Tunisi listed here helped with facilitation between Syria and Iraq during the last decade, when an individual so named provided access to foreign fighters from France.[20] In any case, this material illustrates that a number of Tunisians took part in border facilitation networks between Turkey and Syria when IS was at its peak.

Counting the Dead

Of the 554 recorded Tunisian deaths in Iraq and Syria since 2012, information on 447 came from internal jihadi announcements with the other 107 sourced from press reports. Breaking these numbers down further, within the jihadi announcements, 344 were of Tunisians who died in Syria and 103 in Iraq. Announcements on those killed in Iraq were released exclusively by the Islamic State and its predecessor groups, ISI and ISIS, and not any other organization. Because IS does not normally release information on these individuals unless they are granted a martyr biography in the weekly *al-Naba* newsletter—a distinction usually reserved for senior leaders—very little is known about who they are and where they came from beyond the possible location killed. Based on the system of "provinces" (*wilayat*) established by IS, Tunisians in Iraq died in ten of these provinces, with the location of five deaths remaining unknown. The most deaths occurred in al-Anbar (32), with others relatively evenly distributed among Ninawa (14), Diyala (13), Shamal Baghdad (13), and Salah al-Din (11) and smaller numbers in the provinces of Baghdad (5), al-Janub (3), Fallujah (2), al-Jazirah (2), and Dijlah (1).

IS did note that one Tunisian, Abu Yasin al-Tunisi, who was killed August 9, 2016, in Wilayat Ninawa, was a member of its media apparatus.[21] Beyond IS itself, some media organizations did report on a few of these individuals. Perhaps most notable is the case of Abu Ayub al-Nurwiji, a Tunisian who had previously lived in Oslo, Norway, and whose real name was Jamal Mahmud. After being killed on July 27, 2014, in Wilayat Shamal Baghdad, Abu Ayub was dubbed by the Norwegian press as "Norway's first suicide bomber."[22] Another case is that of Imad Bin 'Abd al-Razaq Bin Salah (aka Abu 'Abd Allah al-Tunisi, Abu 'Umar al-Tunisi, Abu 'Umar al-Faransi), who was killed in Mosul on March 14, 2017.[23] Born in 1971 and originally from Sfax, Bin Salah worked as a mechanical engineer at a car company in France before returning to Tunisia after the 2011 revolution. Little detail is available on how he got involved in the jihadi movement, but on March 21, 2013, he was arrested in Nasr City in Cairo for possessing fake passports and helping facilitate the travel of individuals to fight in Syria.[24] This was the same network mentioned in chapters 3 and 7, when a group of Libyans and Tunisians were arrested in January 2011 attempting to join ISI in Iraq. Bin Salah would be deported back to Tunisia a week later and be questioned by Tunisia's border police but would be released for alleged lack of evidence.[25] He would eventually make his way to IS territory in July 2014.[26]

Information on Tunisians who died in Syria is far more abundant, especially before the IS ascendance and the group's embargo on specific information about deaths. Of the 344 martyrdom notices in Syria, 244 (71 percent) noted the individual's location of death (see figure 9.3), 200 (58 percent) stated the group to which the individual belonged, and 134 (39 percent) provided the individual's city of origin. Therefore, the data has varied strength as to whether it can be generalized.

Unsurprisingly, most Tunisian fighters in Syria died in the Aleppo governorate, where some of the fiercest fighting against the Assad regime has occurred. In particular, many Tunisians died in the battle for Kobane, when IS endured its first defeat after the global coalition began assisting the Kurds in northern Syria. Furthermore, areas where IS has been strong (the Deir al-Zour, Raqqa, Homs, and al-Hasakah governorates) are all represented relatively well (see figure 9.3). But the numbers further illustrate that many Tunisians, by the

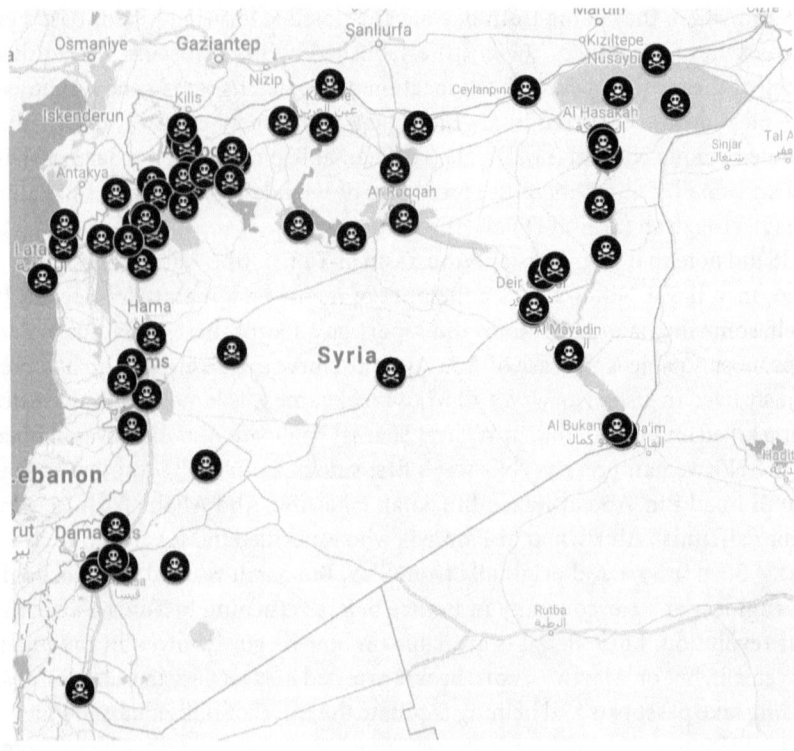

9.3 Location of Tunisian Foreign Fighter Deaths in Syria

time the battles in those provinces had accelerated, likely had moved on to Libya or returned home, since those casualties pale in comparison to Aleppo ones. Although Latakia has seen less fighting than most governorates during the war, a military campaign called "Cleansing the Coast"—aimed particularly at ethnically cleansing Alawite villages around Latakia—led to many Tunisian deaths among both IS and JN ranks. The deaths in the Idlib governorate highlight more of an association with JN, its successor groups, and its allies since they have controlled this territory since the spring of 2015.

Tunisians, however, have died fighting with IS (and associated groups) far more than with any other bloc, including JN (see table 9.3). As noted earlier, many Tunisian fighters defected to IS when it announced its presence in Syria in April 2013. This also helps explain the absence of substantial Tunisian deaths in JN's successor groups, Jabhat Fatah al-Sham and Hay'at Tahrir al-Sham. Many deaths with the AQ affiliate predated the ISIS announcement.

As displayed in figure 9.4, deceased fighters in Syria represent nineteen of Tunisia's twenty-four governorates. The five governorates for which deaths have not been recorded are Béja, Gafsa, Siliana, Tozeur, and Zaghouan, which are among the eight least populous in the country, none with a significant history of jihadi or foreign fighter participation. Still, of the Tunisians reportedly killed, only 39 percent mention their location of origin. And IS border control documents indicate that Tunisians joined IS from all five of those governorates, except Tozeur, which itself appears to have been touched by jihadi activism. For instance, on February 23–25, 2013, AST conducted an instructional session on *al-ruqyah al-sharia* (Islamic exorcism, or ridding oneself of jinni [spirits]) with Khalifah Qarawi, who had previously been a part of the so-called Sulayman Group in 2006–2007, at the al-Rahmah mosque in Nefta, an oasis town in southwest Tunisia.[27] Moreover, in mid-April 2016 the Tunisian government arrested a returned Tunisian foreign fighter from Tozeur who had fought in both Syria and Libya.[28] More recently still, in late May 2018 Tunisian security officials arrested a women in Tozeur for communicating via social media with terrorist elements abroad and possessing jihadi videos.[29] These examples illustrate the importance of triangulating with numerous sources, rather than focusing on just one, to try to achieve a complete picture of the phenomenon.

Deaths fit an expected pattern. For instance, Greater Tunis, which encompasses the Tunis, Ariana, Manouba, and Ben Arous governorates, was home to the largest grouping of individuals to die in Syria. These are followed by other areas of rich recruitment such as the Bizerte, Sidi Bouzid, Sousse, Medenine (Ben Gardane), and al-Qayrawan governorates. Similarly, less populous governorates like Kebili and Tataouine have a greater relative representation.

As the next section shows, a qualitative approach complements the statistical one, casting interesting light on the Tunisian foreign fighter phenomenon.

TABLE 9.3 Deaths of Tunisian Foreign Fighters by Group

The Islamic State	**140**
The Islamic State	82
Islamic State of Iraq and al-Sham	52
Katibat al-Battar al-Libi	6
Hay'at Tahrir al-Sham	**42**
Jabhat al-Nusra	34
Jabhat Fatah al-Sham	7
Hay'at Tahrir al-Sham	1
Other Groups	**19**
Jaysh Muhammad in Bilad al-Sham	3
Harakat Ahrar al-Sham al-Islamiyah	2
Jama'at Ansar al-Islam	2
Katibat al-Muhajirin	2
Katibat Suqur al-'Izz	2
al-Fatihun	1
Ansar al-Tawhid	1
Huras al-Din	1
Jaysh al-Muhajirin wal-Ansar	1
Katibat al-Hamzah bin 'Abd al-Mutalib	1
Katibat al-Khadra'	1
Liwa' al-Muhajirin wal-Ansar	1
Liwa' al-Mutah	1

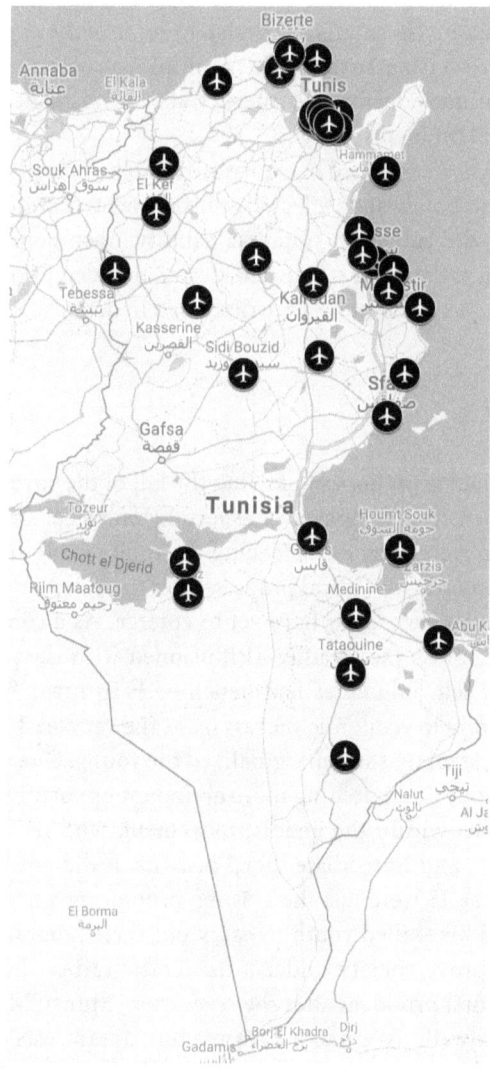

9.4 Origin of Killed Tunisian Foreign Fighters in Syria

Tunisian Motivations for Mobilizing to Syria

The explanations behind the Tunisian mobilization to Syria are complex and multicausal. Successful recruitment was not restricted to one geographical location or clustered in rural or urban locales. Mohamed Iqbal Ben Rejeb, president of the Rescue Association of Tunisians Trapped Abroad, has noted, "The problem of recruitment for the Syrian war transcends social class."[30] Certain reasons for the mobilization are specific to the Tunisian context while others are more universal. It also entails an overlap in some of the explanations as the Tunisian Faysal (Abu Islam) explains his multiple reasons for joining the jihad abroad: "The salafi movements, the Internet, the friends gone, the situation in Syria, the personal problems, etc."[31]

The main drivers are outlined here (organized alphabetically): altruism, anticolonial sentiment, bandwagon effect, disillusionment, economic opportunity, establishment of the caliphate, impressionability, open conditions, personal tragedy, prison radicalization, recidivism, desire for redemption, religious void, and sectarianism. A few of interest are discussed in detail.

Disillusionment

Many Tunisians had great hopes following the fall of the government of President Bin 'Ali in 2011. These hopes were especially prevalent among highly educated youth, who were then experiencing unemployment at extremely high rates. Yet, despite gradual political progress over the years since, the economic fruits that so many yearned for have yet to emerge. As a consequence, many young people have become steadily disillusioned with the political process, from which they felt only elites had benefited.[32] In turn, Tunisians sought alternative pathways to economic success or, at the very least, pursued significance outside a system that still marginalized the young. One way was through migration to Europe and pursuing more abundant opportunities there, while others sought relief within the jihadist movement, with its sense of mission, infusions of pride, and immediate social benefits. It did not hurt that groups like AST and, later, IS were just then rising, promoting a new form of governance that called for skilled youth to carry out their program, which sought ostensibly to improve society under a theocratic rather than a democratic rubric. Tunisia's first president after the revolution, Munsif Marzuqi, summed up this dilemma well: "We had a dream—our dream was called the Arab Spring. And our dream is now turning into a nightmare. But the young people need a dream, and the only dream available to them now is the caliphate."[33] Nabil Seliti, from Douar Hicher, an underdeveloped suburb of Tunis, explains: "I can't build anything in this country. But the Islamic State gives us the chance to create, to build bombs, to use technology."[34]

A young Tunisian filmmaker whose cousin was then fighting in Syria confirmed this sentiment when he was asked whether joining IS seemed normal to him: "If you lived in Tunisia and you're experiencing daily subjugation and injustice, and you have ideas, and you have principles, and you have objectives, and you have a vision for the future, and if you live in a state that doesn't embrace you, then it's the opposite. It's very normal."[35]

The Establishment of the Caliphate

When the Islamic State announced it had reestablished the caliphate, the news was greeted with support by many in the jihadist movement, regardless of whether the announcement carried much legitimacy in the broader Muslim community. Some saw a new opportunity for justice wherein Muslims were once again on top instead of being bullied through colonialism or disregarded by their local Arab secular, military, or monarchical authoritarian systems. This is why a Tunisian named Ahmad supported IS: "The Islamic State is a true caliphate, a system that is fair and just, where you don't have to follow somebody's orders because he is rich or powerful. . . . It is action, not theory, and it will topple the whole game."[36] Likewise, Ridha from Jendouba, who traveled to Syria in 2013, said he wanted to join IS because he was "attracted by their radical ideology [and was] convinced that he would be on the front lines of defending his faith and bringing sharia to the masses."[37] Ridha, however, would later escape after claiming members of the group had abused him sexually, returning to Tunisia in 2015.[38]

Such attitudes are not surprising given that the IS state-building message focused on enjoining followers to help create a utopian society. This prospect drew in more women, whereas previous recruitment calls for foreign travel to jihadist groups were based solely on the imperative to fight, an endeavor generally seen among jihadists as taboo for women. Therefore, being part of the administrative and services cadre of the caliphate project broadened opportunities and interest among women as well as some men who wanted to help by using skills other than fighting.

Desire for Redemption

Another reason Tunisians and others mobilized to fight in Syria is to atone for perceived past sins. To be sure, several individuals with criminal pasts have joined groups like IS to redeem themselves, echoing a pitch made by recruiters. According to Ahmad, the Tunisian IS adherent mentioned earlier, after his brother Rashid went to Syria, he saw online that this was a means of recruitment. He explained: "The jihadi recipe begins simmering in the minds of young men when they confess past sins to their clerics, sins that mainly revolve around dating a girl, drinking alcohol, or frequenting bars. The cleric then begins to exaggerate the seriousness of those sins, transforming them into unpardonable offenses that the young man must atone for through certain deeds, the culmination of which is to fight the jihad in Syria."[39]

These examples demonstrate many potential factors behind Tunisians' decision to travel to Syria. But, as already noted, these reasons can also be interlinked, illustrating the complexity of the process and the trickiness of fingering a single explanation. Indeed, any commentator who boils jihadist mobilization down to one particular cause should not be taken seriously.

With the potential motivations surveyed, the next section explores what Tunisians actually did with the Islamic State in Syria as well as in Iraq to illustrate Tunisians' importance within IS's the broader ecosystem.

What Did Tunisians Do with IS While in Iraq and Syria?

The notes column within the Islamic State border documents remark on specific skills of interest offered by Tunisians and others. For instance, Qaʻqaʻa al-Tunisi was trained in street fighting and kung fu, Abu Musa al-Tunisi had experience in transferring money and importing goods, Abu Saʻad al-Tunisi worked as a smuggler in Libya and Algeria, Abu Yusuf al-Tunisi knew the Montage video program and software piracy programs, and Abu Mujahid al-Tunisi was an expert in hacking encrypted sites. This shows how border documents were used not only to identify individuals entering IS territory but also to spot and channel talent for various elements of the state-building enterprise.

At a senior level, Fathi Bin Awn al-Murad al-Tunisi (Abu Sayaf al-Tunisi) was head of the IS's Diwan al-Rikaz (Administration of Precious Things from the Ground) in Wilayat al-Khayr (Deir al-Zour governorate) and Wilayat al-Barakah (al-Hasakah governorate) until he was killed in May 2016 during a U.S. Army Delta Force operation.[40] Abu Sayaf originally joined IS when Abu Musab al-Zarqawi established JTWJ in the aftermath of the 2003 U.S. invasion of Iraq.[41] This once again highlights the continuity between the older generation of foreign fighters and the more recent flow, similar to the case mentioned earlier of Abu ʻUmar al-Tunisi.

Elsewhere in the IS administrative machine, Abu Anas al-Tunisi was the deputy head of *hisba* (moral policing and consumer protection) in the village of Tayana, in Wilayat al-Khayr.[42] Abu Anas arrested individuals for smoking, wearing their clothing or hair inappropriately, having unacceptable songs or pictures on their phone, or leaving shops open during prayer time.[43] Another Tunisian named Luqman was in charge of receiving *jizya* payments (yearly tax on non-Muslim "people of the book") from Syrian Christians, a practice that had been eliminated from modern Muslim states between the mid-eighteenth and twentieth centuries but was reinstated by IS.[44]

In the IS military apparatus, a number of Tunisians served as trainers or commanders in Iraq and Syria. One of the group's military training camps for children was actually named after Shadad al-Tunisi, an IS commander who was killed in al-Bab, Syria, in January 2014 as fighting between IS and other Sunni insurgent factions began to take form.[45] Another component of IS's military division was its research and development shop. In it, one Tunisian was involved in developing the IS drone program,[46] which provided a key asymmetric weapon in the organization's arsenal, especially when fighting comparatively local adversaries that might lack a monopoly over airspace, particularly at lower altitudes. During a reporting trip in northern Syria, Jenan Moussa obtained internal IS documents, including one on the Islamic State's drone plans by one of its developers, Fadhl Mansi (Abu Yusri al-Tunisi).[47] Interestingly, until his assassination in December 2016 by Israel, another Tunisian, Muhammad al-Zawari, was a main engineer for Hamas's drone program.[48] As Moussa noted, though, there is no information on whether these two men knew each other. Beyond drones, a Tunisian named Muhammed S., who studied chemistry and physics at two universities in Tunisia, was helping IS "develop biological weapons and how to weaponize the bubonic plague from infected animals."[49]

Another job filled by Tunisians was as intermediaries between the mother ship in Iraq or Syria and its external provinces and affiliates. In the winter of 2013 a Tunisian named 'Ali acted as a courier on behalf of IS between Syria and Tunisia. According to 'Ali, he would relay important news back to IS elements in Tunisia, bring money to cells in Tunisia, and provide propaganda videos so that local Tunisian IS cells could recruit individuals.[50] Although 'Ali eventually quit the organization, others likely preceded and followed him in the role. More important, the case illustrates that as early as 2013, even before the announcement of the caliphate, IS was planning for its campaign to recruit Tunisians. Similarly, in August 2014 IS emir Abu Bakr al-Baghdadi allegedly dispatched Abu Hatim al-Tunisi to northern Mali to scout prospects for jihadi insurgent factions there joining his group. In particular, Abu Hatim hoped to meet Hamadu Uld Khayr, the leader of Jama'at al-Tawhid wal-Jihad fi Gharb Ifriqiya (the Movement for the Unicity of God and Jihad in West Africa), and Iyad Agh Ghali, the head of Ansar al-Din in Mali.[51] It is difficult to know whether this was successful since Ansar al-Din eventually merged with AQIM, although some Jama'at al-Tawhid wal-Jihad fi Gharb Ifriqiya factions that supported Adnan Abu Walid al-Sahrawi later swore *baya* to Abu Bakr al-Baghdadi in May 2015.[52] Whether Abu Hatim had any role in this remains unknown.

In terms of media work and logistics, when IS first set up in Wilayat Dimashq (Damascus Province), on May 18, 2015, the office of the province's *wali* (leader) asked al-Fida' al-Tunisi "to secure a dwelling for the brothers in the media office to be a base for media in Wilayat Dimashq. That is on account of the necessity of work while we have no place to work. If possible, we ask this request to be fulfilled as soon as possible."[53] Such media messaging is, as amply documented, central to IS communications to the outside world to illustrate its strength. The May 2015 date of this directive is additionally relevant because the previous month it had taken over its first territory in the region, the Yarmuk refugee camp, which was evidently not considered a safe location.[54] Therefore, this

Tunisian had been given an important task, which appears to have been fulfilled since the group began releasing even more video messages afterward.[55]

Even more important on the media front was IS's use of many Tunisians in its propaganda apparatus when releasing video messages from the territories it controlled in Iraq and Syria (see table 9.4). Between January 2013 and September 2017, Tunisians appeared in forty-eight IS videos, and fifty-three different individuals were featured within them, whether as ideologues, workers in IS's administrative apparatus, fighters, or suicide bombers ahead of their attacks. Abu Waqas al-Tunisi, who is mentioned in chapter 7, appeared in five IS videos, which was most among the whole cohort, followed by the aforementioned Jamal al-Din Mallah (three) and Bilal al-Shawashi (two).

Female Involvement

Beyond Tunisian men getting involved with ISIS/IS, Tunisian women also joined and played a role. Yet, within Islam in general and jihadism in particular, the role of women in fighting, militant groups, and doing *hijra* (emigration) to battlefields is debated. Much of this surrounds the question of whether a woman needs a *mahram* (male guardian) in order to travel.

Within this context, most relevant are two texts, one by AST's head sharia official, Abu Ja'afar al-Hatab, and the other by the Austrian senior IS ideologue Muhammad Mahmud (Abu Usamah al-Gharib). Regarding the former, al-Hatab wrote a ruling on determining the legitimacy of women making *hijra* and joining the jihad in Syria in late March 2013, a few weeks prior to ISI officially going into Syria and becoming ISIS. Therefore, this was in the context of JN being the preeminent jihadi group in the theater, and it is also prior to the al-Nahdah-led government's crackdown upon AST beginning in May 2013.

According to al-Hatab, it is forbidden for women to travel without a *mahram* unless it is *wajib* (obligatory) and one is going from *dar al-harb* (the abode of war) to *dar al-Islam* (the abode of Islam)—in this case, from Tunisia to Syria.[56] Since the leaders of JN have not called upon women to join them, it is not *wajib*.[57] As a result, it is advised that the woman should go with her husband if she wants to go to Syria, or her husband should provide a safe passage way if he is already in Syria and wants to meet him there.[58] In contrast, Mahmud says in a mid-September 2014 ruling, two months after the announcement of the caliphate, that "migration is a must for all!"[59] He explains that those who are against the migration of women without a *mahram* are simply fearful of them and illiterate of Islamic history.[60] Because of these two contrasting rulings, there were greater numbers of women who went and joined with ISIS/IS over JN. While limited in scope to a four-month period, an IS registry for women notes that twenty-two Tunisian women joined during the unspecified time period.[61]

TABLE 9.4 Tunisians in IS Propaganda Videos from Iraq and Syria

Date	Video Name	Media Office	Tunisians Named in Videos
January 11, 2013	"Clanging of the Swords," Part 3	al-Furqan Media	Abu Ziyad al-Bahar
July 25, 2013	"Press Coverage of One of the Da'wah Tents in the State of Aleppo #2"	al-Furqan Media	Abu Waqas al-Tunisi
September 7, 2013	"A Window Upon the Land of Epic Battles #7"	al-I'tisam Media	Abu Waqas al-Tunisi
September 20, 2013	"A Window Upon the Land of Epic Battles #11"	al-I'tisam Media	Abu Waqas al-Tunisi
September 20, 2013	"A Window Upon the Land of Epic Battles #12"	al-I'tisam Media	Abu Fatimah al-Tunisi (Jalal al-Din al-Tunisi, Jamal al-Din Mallah)
October 21, 2013	"A Window Upon the Land of Epic Battles #20"	al-I'tisam Media	Abu Waqas al-Tunisi
October 24, 2013	"A Window Upon the Land of Epic Battles #21"	al-I'tisam Media	Abu Jihad al-Tunisi
December 7, 2013	"A Window Upon the Land of Epic Battles #33"	al-I'tisam Media	Abu Waqas al-Tunisi
June 29, 2014	"Breaking of the Borders"	al-I'tisam Media	Abu Fatimah al-Tunisi (Jalal al-Din al-Tunisi, Jamal al-Din Mallah)

(continued)

TABLE 9.4 Tunisians in IS Propaganda Videos from Iraq and Syria (*continued*)

Date	Video Name	Media Office	Tunisians Named in Videos
October 18, 2014	"Flashes in the Shade of the Caliphate, #2: Interview with the Abu Fatimah al-Tunisi"	Wilayat al-Barakah Media Office	Abu Fatimah al-Tunisi (Jalal al-Din al-Tunisi, Jamal al-Din Mallah)
December 17, 2014	"Message to the People of Tunisia"	al-I'tisam Media	Abu Musʿab al-Tunisi, Abu Muhammad al-Tunisi, Abu Muqatil al-Tunisi (Bubakr al-Hakim)
March 10, 2015	"And Wretched Is That Which They Purchased"	al-Furqan Media	Sabri Isid and his nephew
March 11, 2015	"Joy of the Muslims in Wilayat al-Raqqah with the Bayaʿ of the Mujahidin in Nigeria"	Wilayat al-Raqqah Media Office	Unknown
March 25, 2015	"Aspects from the Battle in Rural ʿAyn al-Islam"	Wilayat Halab Media Office	Abu Mujahid al-Tunisi
March 31, 2015	"Incinerator of the Safavids"	Wilayat Salah al-Din Media Office	Abu Qasim al-Tunisi
April 8, 2015	"Incinerator of the Safavids #4"	Wilayat Salah al-Din Media Office	Abu ʿUmar al-Tunisi
May 24, 2015	"The Raid of al-Maʾamir/Zawbaʿ"	Wilayat al-Janub Media Office	Abu Fatimah al-Tunisi
June 10, 2015	"The Defiant Glorious Castle"	Wilayat Salah al-Din Media Office	Abu Ahmad al-Tunisi

Date	Title	Media Office	Attributed to
June 16, 2015	"The Control and Inspection Office"	Wilayat al-Khayr Media Office	Abu Ahmad al-Tunisi
June 25, 2015	"Repent Before We Apprehend You"	Wilayat Dimashq Media Office	N/A
July 12, 2015	"Holding Wounds of Their Nation #5"	Wilayat Salah al-Din Media Office	Abu Ahmad al-Tunisi
July 19, 2015	"The Atmosphere of 'Id al-Fiṭr in the City of al-Raqqah"	Wilayat al-Raqqah Media Office	Unknown
August 24, 2015	"The Raid of Abu Ḥasan al-Khathaʿmi: The Liberation of al-Qaraytayn"	Wilayat Dimashq Media Office	Abu Hafs al-Tunisi
October 2, 2015	"A Group of Committed Muslims and Their Imām"	Wilayat al-Furat Media Office	Abu Ibrahim al-Tunisi
October 9, 2015	"al-Ramadi: The Epic Battles of Jihad"	Wilayat al-Anbar Media Office	Abu Malik al-Tunisi
December 8, 2015	"Message to the Monotheists After the Bombing of the Apostates in Tunisia"	Wilayat al-Barakah Media Office	Abu ʿAbd Allah al-Tunisi (Bilal al-Shawashi), Abu Musʿab al-Tunisi, Abu Muhammad al-Tunisi
December 13, 2015	"Progress of the Battle with the Nusayri Army"	Wilayat Halab Media Office	Abu ʿAbd Allah al-Tunisi
December 30, 2015	"Determination of the Brave #2"	Wilayat al-Anbar Media Office	Abu Muthana al-Tunisi

(continued)

TABLE 9.4 Tunisians in IS Propaganda Videos from Iraq and Syria (*continued*)

Date	Video Name	Media Office	Tunisians Named in Videos
January 19, 2016	"Land of the Conquests"	Wilayat al-Raqqah Media Office	Abu Yusuf al-Tunisi
January 19, 2016	"They Bewitched the Eyes of the People and Struck Terror into Them"	Wilayat al-Khayr Media Office	Abu Layth al-Tunisi, Abu Ishaq al-Tunisi, Abu Ibrahim al-Tunisi
January 20, 2016	"Then There Is to Be No Aggression Except Against the Oppressors"	Wilayat Dimashq Media Office	Abu Sayf al-Tunisi
January 20, 2016	"To the Knights of the Islamic Maghrib"	Wilayat al-Furat Media Office	Abu al-Walid al-Tunisi
January 21, 2016	"The Countries of the Islamic Maghrib: The New Mardin"	Wilayat al-Barakah Media Office	Abu 'Abd al-Rahman al-Ifriqi
January 21, 2016	"Message to the Land of the Islamic Maghrib"	Wilayat al-Jazirah Media Office	Abu Yusuf al-Tunisi
January 21, 2016	"Message from the Vultures to the Brave in the Islamic Maghrib"	Wilayat al-Anbar Media Office	Abu Hudhayfah al-Tunisi, Abu Ayub al-Tunisi, Abu Isma'il al-Tunisi
April 3, 2016	"A Tour in the Administrations of the State"	Wilayat al-Raqqah Media Office	Abu Ammar al-Tunisi
May 5, 2016	"Sinai of Pride and Defiance"	Wilayat al-Jazirah Media Office	Abu Ahmad al-Tunisi

Date	Title	Media Office	Attributed to
June 16, 2016	"Foothold of the Conquerors"	Wilayat al-Raqqah Media Office	Abu Hammam al-Muhajir (Bilal al-Shawashi)
August 6, 2016	"The Demolished Structure"	Wilayat al-Khayr Media Office	Abu Asad al-Tunisi
August 9, 2016	"The Will to Fight"	Wilayat al-Anbar Media Office	Abu Muqatil al-Tunisi (not Bubakr al-Hakim)
August 26, 2016	"The Crumbling Nations"	Wilayat al-Raqqah Media Office	Abu al-Bara' al-Tunisi
October 19, 2016	"Seekers of Life"	Wilayat Halab Media Office	Abu Luqman al-Tunisi
January 3, 2017	"The Caravan of Light"	Wilayat Ninawa Media Office	Abu 'Abd Allah al-Tunisi
July 22, 2017	"Revered Glory #2"	Wilayat al-Khayr Media Office	Abu Isma'il al-Tunisi
July 30, 2017	"Death Rattle from the Tribes"	Wilayat al-Raqqah Media Office	Abu Ahmad al-Tunisi
August 16, 2017	"Dust of the Battle"	Wilayat al-Raqqah Media Office	Abu Muhammad al-Tunisi
August 31, 2017	"The Fertile Nation #5"	Wilayat al-Raqqah Media Office	Abu 'Abd Allah al-Tunisi
September 5, 2017	"Indeed, They Are [to Be] Drowned"	Wilayat al-Raqqah Media Office	Abu Mu'az al-Tunisi

Tunisian women helped shape the vision of Islamic State society, and most joined for religious and ideological reasons. Umm Fatimah al-Tunisi contested the idea that women joined IS for *jihad al-nikah* (a euphemism for providing sex to male militants; literally "jihad of marriage"), a notion propagated by the Tunisian government.[62] Undoubtedly, IS engaged in sexual abuse, but no credible evidence has emerged to suggest women joined IS specifically to "comfort" fighters, as indicated by Tunis.[63] For her part, the Tunisian Khadijah 'Umri said she went to Syria with her husband in the "hope of leading the kind of religious lifestyle they had long dreamt of."[64] It was "for jihad, for sharia and the Islamic State.... I really believed that there was a state where we could live like the Prophet."[65] Similarly, Umm Bara' al-Tunisi said she "came to Syria as a woman wanting to be empowered by Islamic principles."[66] It is also no surprise that the Tunisian Sabrine justifies their actions and reasons for going by stating: "Isn't Syria also our country?"[67]

The founder of the IS's infamous female-led al-Khansa' Brigade, which began operating on February 2, 2014, was a Tunisian women named Umm Rayan al-Tunisi.[68] She would also help establish the al-Khansa' Brigade in Libya after IS took control of Sirte, moving there from Syria in September 2015.[69] Among the initial thirty-five members of the group in Syria, seven were Tunisian. Umm Rayan's vision, instituted immediately, included stationing women at checkpoints to make sure those under the *niqab* were not men disguised for an ambush; securing marriages for foreigners who joined IS; standardizing displays for women's clothes and mannequins in stores; replacing all male OB-GYN doctors with women; and helping develop school curricula for girls.[70]

In turn, women within the brigade were led to recruit others already in Syria or abroad to help build al-Khansa's capacities. Among those to join were Umm Hajar al-Tunisi, who was responsible for sharia classes and helped recruit women for the group's Diwan al-Ta'alim (Administration of Education) and Diwan al-Siha (Administration of Health) for an estimated monthly salary of $100–$200.[71] There is also Asma' Bin Salim, from Tunis, who requested that the Islamic State employ her as a teacher for girls, according to the border documents submitted by her husband when they entered IS territory with their son on October 5, 2013. Lastly, there is Umm 'Abd al-Rahman al-Tunisi, who helped facilitate arranged marriages in al-Mayadin, Syria.[72]

External Operations

Tunisians served as senior leaders in the Islamic State's internal and external intelligence operations, most commonly referred to as al-Amn al-Khariji. At one point, Abu 'Abd al-Rahman al-Tunisi led this entity, helping to plan the infiltration and activation of sleeper cells within Syrian rebel groups to undermine them from within.[73] This in turn allowed IS to build up its capacities and take over locales more quickly in 2013–14. The group also enacted a public intimidation component to this takeover. For instance, Abu Usamah al-Tunisi was responsible for posting names of wanted Free Syrian Army members on the doors of mosques in al-Dana and Darat Izzah and ordering all Free Syrian Army members in his area of control to swear *baya* to al-Baghdadi and hand over their weapons, illustrating both a public and private approach to instilling fear in the local populace.[74]

Outside Syria, in the realms of intelligence and planning, Bubakr al-Hakim, the French Tunisian previously mentioned, was a senior leader in al-Amn al-Khariji and directly involved in the planning of key IS external operations in Europe and North Africa.[75] French officials believe he had a role in both the January 2015 Hypercacher grocery store attack and the November 2015 multipronged attack as well as influencing other plots that were broken up in France, Morocco, and Algeria.[76] Within Tunisia, al-Hakim assisted indirectly in the March 2015 Bardo National Museum and June 2015 Sousse beach attacks, having created the training camps in Sabratha, Libya, where the perpetrators trained beforehand.[77] The attack campaign within Tunisia is described in greater detail in the next chapter. These activities show al-Hakim's reach to be far regarding larger IS external operations. On top of al-Hakim's connections to plots and attacks outside IS's core territory, several other Tunisians were involved in plots and attacks coordinated or inspired by IS between 2014–18 (see table 9.5).

There are a few plots worth expanding upon that Bubakr al-Hakim was not involved in or are less well-known in comparison to the Brussels bombings, Bastille Day attack, and Berlin Christmas Market attack (the latter attack was also connected to IS in Libya and not Syria and therefore is discussed in greater detail in the next chapter). For example, the first plot that ISIS helped coordinate was the Cannes returnees plot, which included the French Tunisian 'Abd al-Qadir Talibah and the French Algerian Ibrahim Budina.[78] Both men had been involved previously with the Cannes-Torcy jihadi network that perpetrated a grenade attack against the Sarcelles kosher market outside Paris in September 2012. In the aftermath of the attack, the two men fled to Syria as French police began arresting those within the broader network.[79] These two men were part of a broader cluster of French and Belgian jihadis in Syria affiliated with an ISIS front group at the time called Katibat al-Muhajirin and were interested in conducting external operations back at home.[80] Talibah and Budina were arrested two weeks apart in January 2014 attempting to sneak into Europe via Greece and Italy. Their ultimate target was the Nice carnival attack.[81]

There were also a number of small-scale attacks that became signatures of IS-inspired attacks involving car rammings or stabbing types of attacks,

TABLE 9.5 Tunisians Involved in Plots and Attacks Coordinated or Inspired by IS

Date	Plot	Country	Tunisians Involved
January 16, 2014	Cannes returnees plot	France	ʿAbd al-Qadir Talibah
January 9, 2015	Hypercacher kosher supermarket siege	France	Bubakr al-Hakim
November 13, 2015	Paris attacks	France	Bubakr al-Hakim, Sufyan Ayari
January 1, 2016	Valence soldier attack	France	Raʿuf al-Ayab
January 7, 2016	Rue de la Goutte d'Or police attack	France	Tariq Bilqasim
March 22, 2016	Brussels bombings	Belgium	Sufyan Ayari
July 14, 2016	Bastille Day attack	France	Muhammad Lahuwij Buhlal, Shukri Shafrud, Ramzi Arifah
August 11, 2016	The Leaning Tower of Pisa plot	Italy	Bilal Shihawi
November 16, 2016	Strasbourg sleeper cell plot	France	Bubakr al-Hakim, Sami B. Z.
December 19, 2016	Berlin Christmas Market attack	Germany	Anis Amri, Bilal Bin Ammar, Mahir D.
June 19, 2017	Champs-Élysées attack	France	Adam Lutfi Jaziri
June 12, 2018	Cologne ricin plot	Germany	Sayf Allah Hammami

including the Valence soldier attack, in which Raʿuf al-Ayab attempted to run over with his car four soldiers guarding a mosque; the Rue de la Goutte d'Or police attack, wherein Tariq Bilqasim, on the one-year anniversary of the Charlie Hebdo attacks, approached a police station with a meat cleaver, fake explosives, and shouting *allahu akbar* (God is the greatest) before he was shot dead by police; and the Champs-Élysées attack, when Adam Lutfi Jaziri drove a car filled with gas canisters, automatic weapons, a taser, and handguns into the side of a police van.[82]

In addition to successful attacks, the most noteworthy thwarted plot was the one in which Sayf Allah Hammami attempted to conduct a ricin attack. Having failed twice in making it to Syria and joining IS when he was turned back in Turkey, Hammami decided to instead, based on online IS instructional manuals, conduct a ricin attack in Germany. Although he was arrested prior to his attack being actualized, according to the German investigative reporter Florian Flade, "[Hammami's plot] was the first time a jihadi in the West has successfully produced the toxic biological agent," highlighting the seriousness of the plot, had it been actualized.[83]

* * *

This chapter breaks down the number of Tunisians who went to Iraq and Syria and shows why the true number who went was just below three thousand. It also examines which groups they joined (primarily IS) and how many died. The data also concluded again that Tunisian jihadism is a national phenomenon and not sequestered to one or two areas within the country; rather, individuals from all governorates have been exposed to it at differing rates. To better get at the broader phenomenon, the chapter also explains why so many Tunisians were interested in joining the jihad in Syria, and IS in particular. There are a complex array of reasons why individuals decided to travel and fight, and many have more than one reason, illustrating that one cannot distill the reason to one particular cause, which shows why IS was so successful in recruiting foreign fighters. Once in Syria, Tunisians took part in the usual fighting functions of the jihadi group but also took major roles in its administrative infrastructure and assisted in the propaganda efforts of IS by appearing in almost fifty videos over a four-and-a-half year period. The chapter also highlights that, unlike in the past, women took on key roles within IS, and Tunisian women in particular had a leading role in entities such as the al-Khansa' Brigade. Lastly, as shown in chapters 2 and 3, Tunisians continued to be involved with the planning and execution of plots and attacks against Western nations, whether directed or inspired by IS.

On top of the external operations and inspired attacks that Tunisians were involved in within Europe, beginning in the spring and summer of 2014, IS began sending operatives from Syria—mostly Libyans and Tunisians—to Libya to help build up its capacities ahead of the November 2014 announcement that the caliphate was extending its writ there alongside other locales in the Arab world. This would have a major effect on the security inside of Tunisia due to the training camps on the other side of the border in Libya as well as the building up of a homegrown network in the central part of the country. The next chapter in this book explores these dynamics and what happened inside of the Tunisia following the designation of AST and how the growth in jihadism within Libya affected its trajectory. It also examines how the Tunisian government and civil society responded to the challenges wrought by a series of large-scale terrorist attacks in Tunisia in 2015–16.

CHAPTER 10

WE ARE HERE TO PROTECT YOU FROM THIS NONBELIEVER GOVERNMENT

Allahu akbar. . . . ashahadu an la ilaha illa Allah. . . . ashahadu anna Muhammadan rasulu Allah. . . . Hayya ala al-salah. . . . Hayya ala al-falah. . . . al-Salatu khayrun min al-nawm. . . . Allahu akbar. . . . La ilaha illa Allah.[1]

This is the Muslim call to prayer. It is also how the Islamic State (IS) cynically used regular Muslim practice that has nothing to do with extremism to begin the attack on Ben Gardane at 5:30 a.m. on March 7, 2016. When the *mu'azin* (one who does the call to prayer) at al-Jalal Mosque on the western outskirts of town did the call to prayer that morning, it was a signal to start the takeover of the entire town by the Islamic State.[2] This raid was planned in Sabratha, Libya, which Bubakr al-Hakim helped establish following the 2011 revolution. In the intervening time, these camps transformed from being pro-Ansar al-Sharia in Tunisia and Libya to Islamic State–run camps. According to the testimony of Tunisian foreign fighter Muhammad Bin Muhsin al-Gharbi (aka Abu Zayd), who was arrested by the Tripoli-based RADA Special Deterrence Forces, training took place in the city's al-Dabashi neighborhood.[3] He also noted that up to two hundred individuals were involved in the failed takeover. The purpose of the attack on this day was to try to take over territory that spanned the Tunisian-Libyan border, similar to the breaking of the borders scene described in Iraq and Syria at the beginning of the previous chapter. Not only is Ben Gardane the closest major city to the Libyan border, but it also has had a history of Tunisians from it that have been involved with foreign fighting in Iraq following the American invasion in 2003 and more recently with flows of individuals fighting in Iraq, Libya, and Syria since the Arab uprisings. Ben Gardane is significant to the Islamic State because its founder, Abu Mus'ab al-Zarqawi once remarked regarding the Tunisians who came to Iraq after 2003, "A city called Ben Gardane is found in southern Tunisia, but if it had been located on the borders of Iraq, then Iraq would have been liberated years earlier."[4]

According to Tunisian journalist, Naji al-Zairi, the planning for this takeover allegedly began in late December 2015.[5] There were signs that those who were not already in their place ahead of the attack began trying to infiltrate Tunisian territory. As early as February 20, two weeks prior to the attempted takeover, the Tunisian government arrested five individuals who had come from Sabratha and received training there to conduct an operation in Ben Gardane.[6] Moreover, another group of five individuals traversing the border were spotted on March 2, which led this time to clashes and four of the individuals being killed and fifth blowing himself up so as not to be captured.[7]

Although IS did not succeed in taking over Ben Gardane, it was a well-thought out plan, having cased the locations of the homes of members of the security forces.[8] Similarly, IS also recruited a street vendor whose sole purpose was to supervise security and military patrols in the city.[9] Following the attack, in one of the IS safehouses in Ben Gardane, Tunisian security found a list of names of citizens and civil society activists to be assassinated following the takeover.[10] The would-be "Wilayat Tunis," if the operation had gone to plan, was the work of Tunisian IS members Mu'az al-Fizani, Nur al-Din Shushan, Miftah Manita, Adl Ghandri, and Shukri 'Abd al-Qawi. The planning, in particular, is believed to have occurred largely at Ghandri's house in Sabratha.[11] Interestingly, the last stand for many also took place at Ghandri's house in Ben Gardane, where many IS operatives were killed.[12] If everything went according to plan, Manita was to be the proto-province's leader, 'Abd al-Qawi its sharia judge, and Ghandri its treasurer.[13]

Al-Fizani and Shushan, alongside Yahya Bin al-'Arabi Bin Muhammad al-Ghazali and Shams al-Din Bin 'Abd al-Rahman Bin Sharif Sandi, were also instrumental in planning two other major IS attacks in Tunisia.[14] The first strike was on the Bardo National Museum in Tunis on March 15, 2015, in which IS operatives Yasin Labidi (Abu Zakaria al-Tunisi) and Jabir Khashnawi (Abu Anas al-Tunisi) killed twenty tourists and two Tunisians while injuring fifty others; and the second strike was the Sousse mass shooting on June 26, 2015, when a lone gunman, Sayf al-Din Rizguwi Ya'qubi (Abu Yahya al-Qayrawani), killed thirty-eight and injured thirty-nine beachgoers at the Hotel Riu Imperial Marhaba.[15]

On the day of the Ben Gardane attack, IS activated sleeper cells while other cells crossed the border from Libya and began an assault on the gendarmerie and army barracks in Ben Gardane. A group also took to loudspeakers to explain the situation to local residents.[16] According to a witness, an IS fighter said, "Don't worry. We are the Islamic State. We are here to protect you from this non-believer government."[17] In addition, IS fighters created checkpoints where they questioned drivers and examined their identify cards, even killing an individual identified as a customs official at one such stop.[18] Most of the attackers that day were Tunisian.[19]

Had the takeover worked, it would likely have attracted other Tunisians (and possibly foreigners) to move from their hometowns to the newly liberated areas. For instance, an individual from Jelma, a village of 5,500 people twenty miles north of Sidi Bouzid, was arrested and "confessed that he was on his way to Ben Gardane to take up arms alongside [IS]."[20] No doubt, this would have become a larger trend. Another way IS attempted to motivate its followers was through online media operations to encourage them to join and assist their "brothers" in the fight against what they described as the *taghut* (tyrannical) Tunisian government and security forces. That is why, starting March 8, 2016, when the battle was seen to be losing steam, IS's official media channel on the encrypted application Telegram called Nashir released a call of "intense effort to interact with the campaign to encourage targeting of infidels and apostates in Tunisia."[21] The campaign was named *arhab tawaghit tunis* (terrorize the tyrants of Tunisia).[22] Subsequently, IS released a number of infographics with aspirational and inciting messages to inspire individuals to take up arms and help as well as to motivate those still fending off the Tunisian security forces.[23] Similarly, a number of articles were published or republished via various unofficial but auxiliary IS media accounts to evoke the same type of emotion and call for people to maintain their perseverance in the fight and to also join in the battle (see table 10.1). This online propaganda effort is a testimony to the systematic and organized nature of IS's plan preceding the attempted takeover and suggests it was a high priority from IS itself.

However, despite painstaking planning on the ground and in the online sphere, the attempted conquest failed owing to resistance from locals. This pushback likewise legitimized a sweep by the Tunisian military, during which it sought to kill or banish remaining IS elements from the city. Allegedly, residents even began throwing stones at IS fighters.[24] According to a twenty-year old resident named 'Umar, "This is our country and if we don't protect it, nobody else will."[25] Such developments shocked the IS leadership, given the infamy of Ben Gardane in previously furnishing the group and its predecessors with foreign fighters. In the following weeks and months a number of individuals related to the attack and who escaped were either arrested or killed in clashes with security forces in various locales, including Al Sammar, Baten, Beniri, Bouhajla,

TABLE 10.1 Auxiliary IS Media Releases During the Battle of Ben Gardane

Date	Title of the Release	Media Foundation
March 3, 2015	"Oh People of Monotheism; You Have to Leave Our Prisoners in the Land of al-Qayrawan"	al-Wafa' Media Foundation
January 6, 2016	"The Atlantic Breeze from the Tunisian Messages"	al-Wafa' Media Foundation
March 8, 2016	"They Were Left Between the Mujahidin and the Tawaghit"	Hafidat 'A'ishah Media Foundation
March 8, 2016	"Now, Now Comes the Fighting Oh Lions of al-Qayrawan"	Hafidat 'A'ishah Media Foundation
March 8, 2016	"They Have Displaced the Nakedness of the Cross"	Hafidat 'A'ishah Media Foundation
March 8, 2016	"God Loves the Patient"	Hafidat 'A'ishah Media Foundation
March 8, 2016	"Guidance to Make Jihad Possible"	al-Wafa' Media Foundation
March 8, 2016	"Ben Gardane and al-Zarqawi Cultivated His Ripened Fruits"	al-Wafa' Media Foundation
March 8, 2016	"Rise Oh Brothers of Tawhid in Tunisia"	al-Wafa' Media Foundation
March 8, 2016	"Oh Descendants of 'Uqbah, Ride the Steed"	al-Wafa' Media Foundation
March 8, 2016	"Ben Gardane, The Beginning of the Flood"	al-Wafa' Media Foundation
March 8, 2016	"Our Brothers the Monotheists in Tunisia"	al-Wafa' Media Foundation
March 8, 2016	"Oh People of Tunisia, Strike Above the Neck"	al-Wafa' Media Foundation
March 9, 2016	"Our Faith Will Prevail Over Their Disbelief in Tunisia"	al-Sumud Media Foundation

Date	Title of the Release	Media Foundation
March 9, 2016	"Five Messages to the Fearless Tunisia"	al-Sumud Media Foundation
March 9, 2016	"To Tunisia of al-Qayrawan"	al-Wafa' Media Foundation
March 10, 2016	"And in Tunisia . . . Descendants of Conquerors"	Hafidat 'A'ishah Media Foundation
March 10, 2016	"Tunisia from the Spark of the Revolution . . . to the Flames of Jihad"	al-Batar Media Foundation
March 10, 2016	"Terrorize the Tyrants of Tunisia"	al-Batar Media Foundation
March 10, 2016	"The Victorious in the Time of Displacement"	al-Batar Media Foundation
March 10, 2016	"Message to the Mujahidin of Tunisia"	al-Batar Media Foundation

Chareb Errajel, Djerba, Gabes, Gafsa, Hajeb Layoun, Kriba, Medenine, Mnihla, Oued Fessi, Remada, Sayah, Tabii, Tataouine, Tazarka, and Zarzis.[26]

The failed takeover of Ben Gardane was the height of IS's powers in relation to Tunisia. It was not only a turning point for IS's designs on Tunisia but also a major boost to the Tunisian government and military fight against IS due to the failures in the previous year, whether in the mountainous areas near the Algerian border or in the cities with large-scale attacks against civilians. What led to this crossroads, how did everything unfold in the aftermath of this, and where is the situation today? This chapter addresses these questions and examines the changing environment in relation to jihadism in Tunisia following Ansar al-Sharia in Tunisia.

✳ ✳ ✳

As the calendar turned over to 2014, the Tunisian government was beginning to consolidate the democratic transition by completing the Constitution, which was finally adopted on January 26, 2014, after two and a half years of negotiations.[27] This led to a transition from the al-Nahdah-led government to a technocratic one until the October 2014 parliamentary election and November and December 2014 presidential election. Furthermore, the domestic problem of Ansar al-Sharia in Tunisia (AST) was beginning to recede, as described in chapter 7, with the organization no longer conducting public events after December 2013. Yet, even if much of the Tunisian jihadi movement was operating outside its borders in Syria, some within the movement remained active within the country, just in a much different form than AST's open *dawa*-first style. According to Yusuf Mazuz, a former leader in AST's youth wing, past members continued to organize secretly in mosques to continue their educational work.[28] AST also maintained a presence online, although no longer via Facebook but primarily through the jihadi forums and Twitter until around August 2014. Much of it was motivational and ideological in nature and not as dynamic or specifically about what members of the group were doing on a day-to-day basis.[29] It was, in essence, a way to try to maintain supporters without on the ground effort. Due to the lack of actual activity, it is unsurprising that such online efforts exhausted themselves, especially considering that Tunisians had alternatives to act locally, whether with Katibat 'Uqbah Bin Nafi (KUBN) or IS, which began to build up its network within Tunisia in late spring 2014. IS's growth within Tunisia as well as next door in Libya began to undermine the momentum KUBN had been building in 2013 and into early 2014.

Therefore, this and the concluding chapter examine what happened within Tunisia to the local networks following the designation of AST and how that affected the trajectory of the Tunisian jihadi movement up to the present day. This chapter in many ways is a bookend to chapter 4, by highlighting what happened once the conditions for open mobilization changed. In many ways, the Tunisian government was attempting to put the "original sin" of the revolution, as described in chapter 4, back in Pandora's box. Beyond the story of the jihadi movement in Tunisia from January 2014 to October 2019, the chapter helps to shed light on how the Tunisian government slowly but eventually gained a better grasp of handling the local jihadi mobilization. It also explores briefly how Tunisia's civil society has dealt with this problem set as a new public actor in the postrevolution stage of democracy and how that could strengthen the country's ability to deal with potential future mobilizations in contrast to other Arab countries where much of the policy is wholly securitized and authoritarian.

Like other chapters, this one and the concluding one relies upon hundreds of primary sources from KUBN and IS in Libya and Tunisia. Similarly, I have access to internal governmental documents from the Libyan Attorney General's Office (on Tunisian foreign fighters in their country) and from Tunisia's Ministry of Interior (on Tunisian foreign fighter returnees from Iraq, Libya, and Syria). Furthermore, this chapter relies upon a database of information that I created since the designation of AST, based on publicly available information from the Tunisian government and local media that includes all known arrests related to jihadism, attacks (officially claimed and unclaimed), Tunisian military activity against insurgent forces within Tunisia, governmental policies, issues related to humanitarian questions surrounding the fight against jihadis, trial prosecutions, jihadis "wanted" by the state, detailed dossiers on the Bardo, Sousse, and Ben Gardane attacks (the latter described above), and Tunisian jihadis who have been financially sanctioned by the government. Due to the inherent nature of tracking information in the open source, it is plausible that not everything is in these databases. However, I am confident, based on the comprehensiveness of these databases, that they are more than sufficient to inform analysis and conclusions.

The Islamic State Infiltration of KUBN

When KUBN was formed in late 2012, it did not have a presence online, unlike many other jihadi groups, to release its propaganda or announce operations it conducted. Therefore, there was a gap in information on the organization in the first year and a half of its existence. This is likely because AQIM did not want to publicize this project. Recall from chapter 7 that the Tunisian government uncovered this front group. Therefore, the reports are plausible that KUBN, beyond conducting low-level insurgent attacks inside Tunisia, was also being used to attract more Tunisians to AQIM and was therefore providing initial training before sending these fighters to more advanced AQIM camps in Algeria or Libya.[30]

KUBN only began to establish a presence online on July 11, 2014, when it created a Facebook page and Twitter account called Fajr al-Qayrawan.[31] This was ahead of an attack on the Tunisian military five days later, which killed fourteen Tunisian soldiers and left twenty wounded.[32] The attack is considered the most deadly attack against the Tunisian military since the country's independence in 1956. Moreover, KUBN only disclosed that it was part of AQIM in January 2015, when a martyrdom notice that KUBN released included "AQIM" under "KUBN" at the bottom of the statement. Both the creation of the presence online as well as the announcement of overt affiliation as an AQIM front group was due to the Islamic State's advances in Iraq and Syria and, consequently, within Tunisia.

In the lead-up to and following the announcement of IS's caliphate in late June 2014, the proto-state promoted various pledges of allegiance and support to IS's leader, Abu Bakr al-Baghdadi, as well as to the broader project of resurrecting the historical form of Islamic government. For instance, in late March 2014 AQIM's central region came out in support of IS.[33] This grouping formed the basis of what eventually became a "province" of IS called Wilayat al-Jaza'ir (Algeria Province) following Abu Bakr al-Baghdadi's mid-November 2014 speech expanding IS's provincial system outside its core in Iraq and Syria.[34] This same dynamic occurred in mid-September 2014, when an alleged KUBN statement was released by Ifriqiya Media that stated, "The mujahidin brothers in KUBN from the land of al-Qayrawan show support, help, and aid for the Islamic Caliphate State.... Give victory to the Islamic State, raise its banner and unite the ranks of the mujahidin in every place."[35]

This statement, however, did not represent KUBN as an organization. In hindsight, it is known that a group of KUBN members who were pro-IS were attempting to agitate for the organization to defect and were buttressing IS's claims over the homegrown Tunisian jihadi movement. Another important aspect to point out is that the majority of insurgent attacks from IS in Tunisia, once they officially began conducting them in the spring of 2015, have been carried out in Jabal al-Maghilah and Jabal Sallum in the Kasserine governorate near the Algerian border.[36] This is where KUBN cells that defected to IS had previously been located. It also helps explain the pattern of operations in the Kasserine governorate, where IS maintains a base in those two locales, while those that remained loyal to KUBN continue to operate cells and conduct attacks in Jabal Chambi and Jabal Samamah.

The dynamics in Tunisia between KUBN and IS cells in the Kasserine governorate, where both groups mainly operate, is different and less hostile militarily than how the situation played out in Syria and elsewhere. Ifriqiya Media explains the nuanced nature of the local relationship between KUBN and IS: "We work in silence without any disagreements between us, we cooperate together, and the goals in different stages differ between every one of them."[37] Therefore, the groups had their own agendas and each focused on them, but sometimes they would cooperate since both were operating in the same non-conducive environment due to the Tunisian government's efforts against both groups.

That said, Ifriqiya Media, a Tunisian jihadi online media outlet that was founded in mid-June 2014 and was posting content that supported both IS and AQ-affiliated groups, had a clear agenda and information operation campaign. Ifriqiya Media was pro-IS and was only posting KUBN content since it was holding out hope that members of KUBN would pledge *baya* to Abu Bakr al-Baghdadi. Therefore, by posting both IS and KUBN content, Ifriqiya Media was hoping to expose their fellow pro-AQ jihadis to IS content and to convince them to commit to the correct side in the competition between IS and AQ.[38] Ifriqiya Media was hoping to undermine AQIM's project in Tunisia: "We were the first to support and spread the news about jihadi operations in Tunisia during a time when the official jihadi media platforms were being passive due to some orders given."[39] This is a slight against AQIM and a reference to what was discussed earlier, since KUBN did not have an overt presence online in the first year and a half of its existence. Fajr al-Qayrawan, KUBN's official outlet at the time, was established only a month after the creation of Ifriqiya Media. That said, Fajr al-Qayrawan went dormant in mid-October 2014 following the arrest of its administrator.[40]

This arrest, though, provided greater space to the pro-IS elements in KUBN because, for whatever reason—possibly a lack of qualified individuals with the necessary skill set to run a media outlet—KUBN did not create a new media apparatus or replace someone to run the Fajr al-Qayrawan online accounts. As a result, over time, more and more of the Ifriqiya Media content was pro-IS, and less and less highlighted pro-AQ/KUBN-related content. It is only after the death of KUBN's leader, Khalid Sha'ib, and KUBN's reaffirmation that it was still a part of AQIM, both in late March 2015, that Ifriqiya Media began fully posting 100 percent pro-IS and IS in Tunisia propaganda.[41] It is no wonder, then, that within two weeks of these developments, KUBN established its own Facebook page under the group's name for the first time in order to reclaim its autonomy and legitimacy.[42]

Ifriqiya Media's information operations are also likely why the Tunisian government originally claimed that KUBN was responsible for the Bardo Museum attack in March 2015 even though it was IS that conducted the attack.[43] The Tunisian government may not have fully comprehended by that point the split within KUBN itself. Therefore, IS's infiltration of KUBN hurt KUBN's capacity as well as its membership base due to the defections between late summer 2014 and early 2015, when IS began to overtly promote through its official propaganda organs that it was indeed IS that was involved in attacks, most notably the March 2015 and June 2015 Bardo Museum and Sousse Beach attacks. Tunisia's military, as part of its response to those two IS attacks, also picked up its operations against KUBN, due to the original confusion, to show that it was doing something against the militant threat. By July 2015, according to Tunisia's interior minister at the time, Najim Gharsalli, 90 percent of KUBN's membership had been killed.[44]

While IS was building up a base within Tunisia in the latter half of 2014, the Islamic State had its first overt message directed at the Tunisian state and its people in mid-December 2014.[45] In particular, Bubakr al-Hakim (who went by Abu al-Muqatil in the video) claimed responsibility for the assassination of Tunisia's secular leftist politicians in 2013: "Yes, tyrants, we are the ones who killed Chokri Belaid and Mohamed Brahmi."[46] This confirmed the al Nahdah-led government's accusation that al-Hakim was involved. Beyond calling for more violence and for Tunisians to remember its imprisoned brothers and sisters, al-Hakim also called upon the Tunisian people to pledge *baya* to Abu Bakr al-Baghdadi, noting that they should raise the banner of *tawhid* high and rip the flags of Charles de Gaulle and Napoleon down (alluding to colonialism and the historically close relations between Tunisia and France). This was the beginning of IS's campaign against Tunisia. It also coincided with the buildup of IS forces in Libya and the reinvigoration of the Tunisian cell that was based in Sabratha, Libya. Tunisians within IS in Libya also helped project the organization's power into Europe with the Berlin Christmas Market attack and into

Nigeria with Tunisian jihadis communicating online with Nigerian jihadis, which helped to facilitate Jama'at Ahl al-Sunnah li-Dawa wa-l-Jihad (better known as Boko Haram) join IS.

Tunisians with IS in Libya

Both of the large-scale attacks in Tunisia at Bardo in March 2015 and Sousse in June 2015 were directly connected to IS's infrastructure in Libya, particularly the town of Sabratha, which is about sixty miles east of the Tunisian border.[47] As described in chapter 7, Tunisian foreign fighters had been going to Libya since the beginning of the uprising against al-Qadhafi in 2011, but once IS established itself in Libya in a more concrete manner between the spring and fall of 2014, the infrastructure to export terrorism back into Tunisia became more sophisticated and formalized. That said, the first attack a Tunisian carried out with IS in Libya was by Abu Ibrahim al-Tunisi, alongside Abu Sulayman al-Sudani, against the Corinthia Hotel Tripoli in late January 2015, which led to the deaths of ten individuals and injury of five others.[48]

While there were certainly Tunisian leaders and foot soldiers with IS's operation in Darnah, Benghazi, and Sirte, much of the Tunisian contingent had their own network of activities based in Sabratha and, to a lesser extent, in Zuwarah, Libya, which are both close to the Tunisian border (see table 10.2). The individuals involved included Tunisians who had returned from Syria with IS's Libya front, Katibat al-Batar; Tunisians already in Libya who decided to switch allegiances from Ansar al-Sharia in Libya to IS; and Tunisian foreign fighters who were new to Libya.

Similar to Syria, IS in Libya also attempted to attract Tunisian fighters to join its ranks via its online media campaign (see table 10.3). IS made its first public call for Tunisians to join up in Libya on April 7, 2015. In a video released by its Wilayat Tarabulus Media Office, Abu Yahya al-Tunisi urged Tunisians to join the Islamic State in Libya, with the intention of gaining training and knowledge so that they would then return to Tunisia to conduct attacks as well as of establishing and extending the writ of the Islamic State crossing the two borders.[49]

Due to these online calls, the legacy of Tunisians already in Libya from the AST/ASL days, and the movement of Tunisian foreign fighters from Syria into Libya, up to 1,500 Tunisians went to Libya, including up to 300 women, at the height of IS in Libya, according to the Tunisian government.[50] In terms of the Tunisian women, the most known among them are the sisters Ghufran and Rahmah al-Shikhawi, who were both in their late teens when they joined. They were originally from the impoverished Tunis neighborhood of Ettadhamen and were recruited to the jihadi milieu through AST at its *dawa* tents and mosques

TABLE 10.2 Tunisians in Positions of Leadership Within IS in Libya

Name	Position	Department	Location
Abu Jabal al-Tunisi	Head of the Tunisian borders	Emigration and Borders Department	Sirte
Abu ʿUmar al-Qayrawani	Head of the Sharia courts	Judiciary and Grievances Department	Sirte
Marwan al-Amari Muhammadi (Anas al-Tunisi)	Head Sharia official	N/A	Sabratha
Yahya al-Arabi al-Ghazali (Saʿd al-Tunisi)	Head improvised explosive device official	N/A	Sabratha
Nazim al-Surati (Khalid al-Tunisi)	Head military official	N/A	Sabratha
ʿAtif ʿAbd al-Aziz al-Matiri (Abu Musʿab)	Western Tunisia official	N/A	Sabratha
Muhammad ʿAli Bin Taji (Ahmad al-Binqardani)	Head Tunisian border official	N/A	Sabratha
ʿUmar Bin Muhammad al-Akhdhar (Kamal al-Dhayb)	Head financial official	N/A	Sabratha
Sufyan al-Suhbi al-Saʿidi (Abu Usamah al-Tunisi)	Head emigration official	N/A	Sabratha

in Sousse. A few years later, in September 2014, the sisters decided to join IS in Libya.[51] Ghufran is currently raising a toddler in Libyan detention, while Rahmah married the earlier-noted senior Tunisian IS leader Nur al-Din Shushan, who was killed in a U.S. airstrike in Sabratha in February 2016.[52]

While the sisters may have been most known within Tunisia, the most important was Umm Rayan al-Tunisi, the founder of the al-Khansa' Brigade. Having helped to establish the brigade in al-Raqqah in February 2014, Umm Rayan set about, upon arriving in Libya, facilitating training for IS-affiliated women not only in *hisba* (moral policing) patrols but allegedly even as fighters.

TABLE 10.3 Tunisians Appearing in IS Libya Videos

Date	Name of Individual	Video Name
April 7, 2015	Abu Yahya al-Tunisi	"Message to Our Brothers in Tunisia"
July 30, 2015	Abu al-Bara' al-Tunisi	"Messages from Sirte"
September 29, 2015	Shaykaw al-Tunisi	"Support of the Captives"
January 16, 2016	Abu al-Yaqin al-Tunisi	"Benghazi: The Meaning of Stability #2"
May 18, 2016	Abu Musa al-Tunisi	"And That He Will Surely Establish for Them [Therein] Their Religion"
May 29, 2016	Khabab al-Tunisi	"From Humiliation to Glory"

According to Rahmah, potential women fighters received weapons training for three weeks, with many among them allegedly also trained to become suicide bombers.[53] According to an account from Umm 'Umar al-Tunisi (Zaynab), who is originally from Sfax, sometime after arriving in Libya through IS's facilitation network, she began training on a beach where she learned how to use an AK-47. She noted that the women involved could choose other weapons on which to be trained, including rocket-propelled grenades, PKT machine guns, and DShK machine guns. Moreover, Umm 'Umar explained that IS gave every woman their own explosive belt.[54]

Tunisians with IS in Libya Project Power Abroad

Based on IS's media campaign, which included other foreigners in addition to the Tunisians featured in the videos mentioned above, IS sought to use its recruitment successes to project power in other parts of Africa, especially in Nigeria and Somalia. In the former case, which is most relevant to this research, a Tunisian member of IS in Libya, Abu Malik Shaybah al-Hamad, who was associated with Ifriqiya Media, helped facilitate the *baya* of Boko Haram leader Abu Bakr al-Shikaw to Abu Bakr al-Baghdadi. Al-Hamad was the go-between a Boko Haram media official and IS's central media, which began in earnest in November 2014. Prior to his defection to IS, al-Hamad had been in AST and was "task[ed] [with] contacting the rest of the jihadi groups and Islamic emirates in the name of AST."[55] In particular, al-Hamad was in contact with the

Islamic State of Iraq, Jabhat al-Nusra, AQIM, AQAP, and the Islamic Emirate of the Caucasus as well as jihadi groups in Gaza, Sinai, Libya, Iran, and jihadi groups and sleeper cells in Europe and North America. Therefore, he was well placed to gain access to potential contacts in Boko Haram.[56] Furthermore, it is also conceivable that, while al-Hamad was in AST, he became acquainted with a Nigerian member of KUBN, Abu Muslim, who could have connected al-Hamad to a Boko Haram media official as well.[57]

Based on his experiences with Ifriqiya Media, al-Hamad assisted Boko Haram's media official with the creation of al-Urwah al-Wuthqa Media Foundation on January 18, 2015.[58] This development helped professionalize operations for Boko Haram. Previously, Boko Haram had been terrible at its media operations: producing grainy, low-quality video graphics; releasing them very sporadically; and sometimes just sending them straight to media organizations like the Agence France-Presse without posting them online. This changed quickly to a much better product after al-Hamad's assistance. Moreover, after Boko Haram became Wilayat Gharb Ifriqiya following al-Baghdadi's affirmation of al-Shikaw's *baya*, this transition allowed Boko Haram's media activities to be subsumed more easily by IS's central media system.[59]

Although this may not seem relevant to the broader story of the Tunisian jihadi movement, these connections could become more relevant in the future as there is more integration between North and West African jihadi groups and the movement of members between various fronts. For example, the Tunisian Wanas al-Faqih was captured by Nigerien security forces in November 2016 and extradited from Niger to Tunisia in January 2017 on twenty-nine charges related to terrorism.[60] Al-Faqih had previously been a part of AST's clerical network and was a religious leader based in Mahdia, a coastal city southeast of Sousse.[61] Following the designation of AST, he joined AQIM and helped it with its regional activities.[62] Additionally, Tunisia's minister of defense at the time, Farhat Hurshani, claimed that as IS was losing control over Sirte, Libya, in the fall of 2016, some jihadists fled to Nigeria to join IS there.[63] Therefore, it is important to understand these linkages even if at the time they seem random or irrelevant; they can become much more important in the future, depending on the course of events. This is an important lesson that should be drawn from the details in chapters 2 and 3 regarding jihadi connections prior to the revolution and how that played out later.

Based on available information, we know that Anis Amri, a Tunisian, was the perpetrator of the Berlin Christmas Market attack. With his connections to extremists in Germany, he conducted what could be described as a remote-controlled attack, meaning he was guided via encrypted messaging from IS members—in this case, from Libya.[64] According to the North Rhine–Westphalian State Office of Criminal Investigation, Amri had been in contact since February 2016 with two Tunisian IS members in Libya on Telegram.[65] In particular, Amri spoke with Mu'adh al-Tunisi over Telegram in the weeks leading up to the attack.[66] They were even in conversation as Amri was beginning the attack, with Amri talking to Mu'adh about securing the truck after killing the individual who had previously been using it and sending him pictures. The German government began trying to figure out who this individual was using clues from the Telegram channel, which Mu'adh connected to several Facebook accounts. One of these accounts stopped transmitting information on January 4, 2017, a day before Libyan Special Forces announced they had killed an individual named Abu Mu'adh al-Tunisi.[67]

In mid-September 2017 more information came to light when Tunisian officials in its National Guard told German officials and prosecutors that they believe they identified who was guiding Amri: an individual named Mahir D. According to Mahir's brother Shakr D., who acted as a financial middleman between Amri and Mahir, his brother was indeed in IS in Libya. However, Shakr did not disclose whether Mahir was dead or alive.[68] A month after the attack the U.S. military conducted an airstrike on an IS training camp and base twenty-eight miles southwest of Sirte, claiming the attack was in response to security threats emanating from the group against European allies.[69] U.S. officials and Libyan intelligence also suggest that the IS members in touch with Amri were based at this location, perhaps hinting at why U.S. forces chose the target.[70]

The Not So "Wilayat Tunis"

While these two ventures were important in expanding IS's influence and terror abroad, IS's Tunisian network within Libya was mainly focused on actualizing an attack campaign within Tunisia itself. As noted at the beginning of this chapter, the key organizers and planners for the two large-scale attacks against civilians were Mu'az al-Fizani, Nur al-Din Shushan, Yahya Bin al-'Arabi Bin Muhammad al-Ghazali, and Shams al-Din Bin 'Abd al-Rahman Bin Sharif Sandi. It did not take long for IS to strike in Tunisia following Bubakr al-Hakim's December 2014 video. Only a few months later, on March 18, 2015, was the Bardo National Museum attack, for which IS claimed responsibility: "For in a holy invasion God is pleased, because it was upon one of the nests of infidelity and corruption in Muslim Tunisia, launched by two knights sent from the knights of the state of the Caliphate, and they are: Abu Zakaria al-Tunisi and Abu Anas al-Tunisi."[71]

In the aftermath of the Bardo National Museum attack, knowing that the deaths of foreigners at a tourist site would hurt Tunisia's tourism industry, the Tunisian government and citizenry promoted a campaign online with the hashtag #IWillComeToTunisiaThisSummer to try to garner support for

Tunisia and to maintain its role as a popular tourist destination from Europe.[72] Any hit to the industry in general massively hurts Tunisia's economy and its population. Unsurprisingly, IS attempted to take advantage of this online campaign by flipping the popular meme #IWillComeToTunisiaThisSummer on its head by spelling out the hashtag using bullets and weapons and signing it in Arabic: the Islamic State in Tunisia. These threats against Tunisia intimated that the Bardo attack was just the beginning. And it is now known that IS did indeed conduct another large-scale attack against civilians in Tunisia when they attacked tourists at the beach in Sousse a few months later, in June 2015. Furthermore, in the third issue of IS's French-language magazine, *Dar al-Islam*, al-Hakim explained in an interview that the Bardo attack "healed our hearts" and encouraged further operations.[73]

Between the Bardo and Sousse attacks, IS's internal network within Tunisia began an insurgent campaign against Tunisia's security forces and claimed to have conducted six attacks. IS's first claim of responsibility for an insurgent attack occurred in Jabal al-Maghilah near the town of Sbeitla where they conducted an ambush, killing four and injuring twelve Tunisian soldiers on April 8.[74] In the lead-up to the Sousse attack, it appeared that IS was planning to upgrade its Tunisian network to an official IS branch, which would have been called Wilayat Tunis. On May 15, for example, IS's central media put out an audio message from a group of IS in Tunisia members giving *baya* to Abu Bakr al-Baghdadi:

> If disagreement weakens us, then imagine what division does to our strength. We can't unite if we are working for different parties and under different flags. Only one Caliph can unite all of us under one banner based on Qur'an and *sharia*. Unity is not only a religious obligation but a necessity based on the current dynamics we are living today. We can't fight evil if we are divided. That's why the western Crusades attacked our Muslim world in all of their strength to demolish the Caliphate. They demolished the Caliphate. But thank God the Caliphate is now back. That made monotheists happy and Jews afraid. Our dream come true. That's why we have to obey God and his Prophet and unite with one another. We are the mujahidin of Tunisia pledging *baya* to Abu Bakr al-Baghdadi. We ask all Muslims to do the same. God help Islam and Muslims and defeat infidels.[75]

The graphic used to promote this message as well as the language of the message itself followed a similar pattern to what was seen by prior local networks and groups that eventually became official IS branches. Therefore, when the Tunisian IS network claimed responsibility for their next attack, on the barracks at the Bouchoucha military base a mere ten days later on May 25, it was noteworthy that the claim came from a so-called Wilayat Tunis.[76] This portended to the possibility that IS was formalizing another official branch. However, for whatever reason, that never came to fruition and this was only a one-time occurrence.

As of October 2019, IS has yet to confer provincial status to its Tunisian network. Even in Abu Bakr al-Baghdadi's April 29, 2019 video message, which showed the group's various locales of operation, every one said "Wilayat X," including Turkey; yet, when the video showed Tunisia, it only said Tunisia without a *wilayah* being mentioned at all.[77] This is confounding, considering the number of attacks IS has conducted and claimed in Tunisia as well as the number of foreign fighters who have joined the group in Iraq, Libya, and Syria. However, it is likely that, had IS taken over Ben Gardane, IS would have begun to use the Wilayat Tunis moniker officially. That failure was a turning point for IS and for the Tunisian government and its people.

Since the height of IS's campaign against Tunisia, with eleven attacks in 2015, the Tunisian government has been able to degrade the network's ability to conduct mass-casualty attacks against civilians while also degrading the group's insurgent capacity in the mountainous area along the Algerian border. While the insurgents have not been defeated, there have been four attacks each year between 2016 and 2018. While IS has lost capacities, it remains a threat to security forces. Similarly, while never as strong as IS, KUBN has also retained a low-level insurgency, having conducted just three attacks per year between 2016 and 2018.

It did take some time for the Tunisian government to gain some level of credibility in its fight against jihadis. As discussed in earlier chapters, the al-Nahdah-led government had a light touch policy toward AST. However, the conservative-nationalist Nida Tunis-led government, which came to power following victories in the parliamentary and presidential elections at the end of 2014, while rhetorically more aggressive in fighting jihadis, still did not come off as serious, especially in the aftermath of IS's early attacks. For example, following the Sousse beach attack, when Tunisia's president, Muhammad al-Baji Qa'id al-Sibsi, announced the reimplementation of the government's state of emergency, he stated that "if similar attacks occur again, the state will collapse."[78] Not only was this comment the height of irresponsibility, it was also quite amateurish. Instead of reassuring the public, he was using fear as well as essentially egging on jihadis to conduct another attack to test his theory. Moreover, on the same day, the spokesman for the Ministry of Interior explained that the ministry did not want to blame the attack in Sousse on IS because advertising their involvement would radicalize the public.[79] Instead it blamed AST, which had more or less been defunct for a year by then. This follows from when the Tunisian government blamed the Bardo attack a few months earlier on KUBN, even though all evidence pointed to IS and the IS-run training camps in Sabratha, Libya.[80] Over time, the Tunisian government has improved in public messaging as well as its counterterrorism and counterinsurgency policies.

The Tunisian Government Responds to IS

While the effectiveness as well as the ability to discern changes in jihadi capacity did not begin to manifest itself until after IS failed to take over Ben Gardane, the Tunisian government since the designation of AST in August 2013 did begin to take steps to counter remnants of AST and the growing insurgent capacities of KUBN and IS from 2014 to 2016. In many ways, Tunisia's fight against its domestic jihadi movement, beginning with AST's designation until it began having a better grasp on it by 2016–17, was an attempt to put the "original sin" following the revolution back into its proverbial Pandora's box.

From AST's Designation to the Ben Gardane Victory

One of the earliest policies enacted by the Tunisian government following AST's designation was to create a "wanted" list so citizens could assist if they knew any information on individuals of interest. The first individuals added to this list were announced on October 30, 2013, about two months following the AST designation. Since then, as of early July 2019, there have been 137 individuals added to this wanted list.[81] Among this group, based on open source information, 15 are currently imprisoned, 32 have been killed, and 90 remain elusive in the mountainous areas of the border region with Algeria or abroad in Iraq, Libya, Mali, Syria, or elsewhere. Besides this early step, the Tunisian government began to enact various policies:

- March 3, 2014: The ministries of religious affairs, interior, and justice began coordinating the establishment of a list of extremist mosques to be recovered by the state.[82]
- April 3, 2014: The United States and Tunisia launched the first-ever U.S.–Tunisia Strategic Dialogue. The dialogue is focused on areas in which the United States and Tunisia can expand their relationship to address challenges facing Tunisia: economy and investment, security, governance, and partnerships.[83]
- April 16, 2014: Jabal Chambi, Jabal Samamah, Jabal Sallum, and Jabal al-Maghilah in the Kasserine governorate were declared "zones closed for military operations."[84]
- May 7, 2014: Tunisian president Munsif Marzuqi said his security council approved amnesty and reconciliation laws for militants who did not kill Tunisians.[85]

- July 24, 2014: The U.S. State Department approved the sale of twelve Sikorsky UH-60M Black Hawk helicopters to Tunisia, worth $700 million, including equipment, parts, training, and logistical support.[86]
- August 26, 2014: The United States stated it would give Tunisia $60 million worth of military aid to help it fight KUBN. Some of the money would be for equipment to detect improvised explosive devices, new boats, and training.[87]
- February 17, 2015: Tunisia's defense minister, Farhat Hurshani, announced that security along the border with Libya had been reinforced to prevent any incursion by jihadis. The army was being backed up by units from the Tunisian National Guard in an operation covering the entire border to stop incursions from Libya.[88]
- February 27, 2015: The United States announced that Tunisia would get eight Black Hawks for its fight against jihadis.[89]
- March 2015: The Ministry of Interior instructed all border police to require any Tunisian citizen under the age of thirty-five to receive their father's authorization for to travel to Turkey, Morocco, Algeria, or Libya.[90]
- March 16, 2015: The Tunisian army received Russian-made air-to-surface missiles from Algeria. The air-to-surface missiles would be used in attacking armed groups hiding in mountainous areas.[91]
- April 2, 2015: Tunisia said it planned to reopen a consulate in Syria and offered to invite the Syrian ambassador back to Tunisia in part to help track an estimated three thousand Tunisian militants fighting in Iraq and Syria. Tunisia would also reestablish diplomatic relations with neighboring Libya.[92]
- April 10, 2015: The United States announced plans to increase military aid to Tunisia threefold and to help train its troops.[93]
- May 13, 2015: Tunisia's minister of religious affairs, Batikh 'Uthman, created a specialized register to keep tabs on those who run and preach at the mosques in the country. The government also announced the launch of a religious reeducation program in the country's prisons.[94]
- May 21, 2015: Following U.S. president Barack Obama's meeting with Tunisian president al-Sibsi, it was announced that Tunisia would be named a "major non-NATO ally" of the United States. This designation provided Tunisia access to extra military assistance.[95]
- June 23, 2015: Algeria agreed to help train Tunisian special security forces to better patrol their shared border.[96]
- June 28, 2015: Tunisian security officials said they were deploying 1,400 extra police officers to tourist sites and beaches following the Sousse attack.[97]
- July 8, 2015: The Tunisian government announced plans to build a wall along its border with Libya to counter jihadis traversing the border. The wall would extend about a third of the 310-mile border and was expected to be completed by the end of the year.[98]

- July 25, 2015: The Tunisian parliament adopted a new "antiterror" law, with 172 members of parliament voting in favor and 10 abstentions. The new law imposes the death penalty as a possible sentence for a range of "terror" offenses and allows authorities to detain terror suspects for up to fifteen days without access to a lawyer. It also makes public expressions of support for terrorism a jailable offense. It makes it easier for investigators to use phone-tapping. The law grants security and intelligence services powers of surveillance, interception of communication, recording of phone conversations, and infiltration of suspected terrorist groups by policemen (provided they obtain advance judicial approval, and for a period not to exceed four months). During the last voting session, Parliament added a safeguard against abuse by making state agents liable to a one-year prison sentence if they conduct surveillance or infiltrate groups without judicial authorization.[99]
- September 15, 2015: Tunisian authorities and hotel companies began doing more security spot checks, and the government had the power to close any hotels that were not complying with new tougher security provisions.[100]
- October 3, 2015: Tunisia joined the U.S.-led military coalition fighting against the Islamic State in Syria and Iraq mainly to "exchange information." According to Tunisian prime minister Habib Essid, the coalition "includes countries with more information than us."[101]
- November 8, 2015: Tunisia's Ministry of Transport announced a new series of security measures in response to the crash of a Russian commercial aircraft in the Sinai and to strengthen the security policy in Tunisian aircrafts and airports. Within Tunisia, these measures include increased continuous control of aircraft entrances, luggage security, and equipment used for aircraft maintenance; increased control of travelers and hand luggage; additional control of the baggage of the travelers by the canine brigades; systematic checks of all employees before entering the airports; and greater use of x-ray equipment to search baggage on planes and dog brigades for checked baggage. Regarding measures taken for Tunisian aircraft coming from foreign airports, new measures include reinforcing control of returning planes, searching the entire planes after the departure of employees and before the boarding of new travelers, and surveilling the aircraft during the preparation of the next flight.[102]
- December 8, 2015: Tunisia's Ministry of Religious Affairs established a counternarrative campaign "We Are Islam." The movement aimed to reach young people over social media platforms like Twitter and Facebook. Najit Hammami of the ministry said, "We need to use technology in the same way" as the jihadis do.[103]
- February 1, 2016: Tunisia launched the program Ambassadors Against Terrorism, which was organized by the local youth and sports commissioner as part of the national program in Sidi Bouzid. The program aimed to mobilize youth to express rejection of terrorism in all forms and consolidated the

concept of civil defense, highlighted the culture of life as opposed to that of death, and raised youths awareness about the importance of solidarity and cohesion among civil society.[104]

- February 19, 2016: It was announced that German and U.S. contractors would install electronic surveillance equipment on strategic points along the completed border barrier with Libya to detect any breaches.[105]
- February 29, 2016: The United Kingdom sent a training team of some twenty troops from the 4th Infantry Brigade to Tunisia to help counter illegal cross-border movement from Libya in support of the Tunisian authorities.[106]

Based on these actions, it is unsurprising that by the time IS attempted to take over the town of Ben Gardane in March 2016, the Tunisian government was far more prepared and had greater warning systems. As was mentioned at the beginning of this chapter, Tunisian security services intercepted various cells attempting to traverse the border in late February and early March ahead of the planned assault.

On top of the more military-related approaches, Tunisia's law enforcement also began to take more assertive and proactive measures against those supporting KUBN, IS in Tunisia, or jihadis abroad. Between the beginning of 2014 and the end of September 2019, based on press releases by Tunisia's Ministry of Interior and cross-checked with local Tunisian media reports, Tunisia's law enforcement conducted 1,460 arrests related to jihadism within Tunisia.[107] While there are basic details on these arrests, a number of the arrests are of repeat offenders, so it is difficult to ascertain how many individuals in total have actually been arrested in this time span. Moreover, data tracking arrests of specific individuals and then later information on them being prosecuted is difficult to come by due to the opaque process that occurs between the Ministry of Interior and Ministry of Justice and what is shared publicly. However, there was a clear upward trend from 2014 to 2018 in the number of arrests related to jihadism: 32 in 2014, 163 in 2015, 262 in 2016, 404 in 2017, and 521 in 2018.[108]

Confoundingly, the pace of arrests began to drop precipitously since November 2018, with numbers for 2019 through the end of September only garnering 78 arrests, which would add up to 104 on an annual basis.[109] This figure would make it the least amount of arrests related to jihadism in Tunisia since 2014. While this might sound like good news and would seem that Tunisian law enforcement has become more discriminant and better led by intelligence rather than arresting anyone related to a particular incident or individual involved in terrorism, it is also possible that Tunisia's Ministry of Interior is not being as transparent in disclosing arrests publicly as it had previously. In the aftermath of an IS-inspired lone-actor attack by a woman in central Tunis in October 2018, information related to arrests suddenly began to dissipate.[110]

From the Ben Gardane Victory Through Mid-2019

Beyond the aggressive arrest campaign that began in earnest following the Bardo, Sousse, and Ben Gardane attacks, Tunisia continued to tweak and enhance its broader policies against the jihadi movement internally:

- June 2016: U.S. Air Force Reaper drones began flying out of a Tunisian airbase (likely at the Sidi Ahmed Air Base in Bizerte north of Tunis) and played a role in the U.S. air campaign against IS in Libya. The drones were unarmed and used to collect intelligence on IS in Sirte. The Pentagon deployed about seventy military personnel to oversee drone operations. Under the memorandum of understanding, the U.S. committed to helping build up Tunisia's intelligence collection capabilities.[111]
- July 9, 2016: NATO began providing advice to the Tunisian authorities on the development of the Tunisian Intelligence Fusion Center and helping to train Tunisian Special Operations Forces.[112]
- November 7, 2016: Tunisia's national security council adopted a strategy to fight terrorism and extremism. The president, in a statement, said the "national strategy to fight against extremism and terrorism" is built around four points: prevention, protection, judicial proceedings, and retaliation.[113]
- December 20, 2016: Tunisia established a national intelligence center whose mission will be to collect and analyze information and coordinate actions between the various intelligence services. The national intelligence center will define under what circumstances international intelligence cooperation can take place and will create a national intelligence plan.[114]
- February 2, 2017: Tunisia's armed forces received six U.S.-made military Bell OH-58D Kiowa Warrior helicopters. The helicopters will reinforce the army's reconnaissance and attack capabilities, and the aircraft are equipped for both day and night operations against terrorists.[115]
- October 30, 2017: India and Tunisia agreed to jointly combat terrorism and extremism while ramping up cooperation in the field of security.[116]
- February 2018: Justice Minister Ghazi Jeribi announced that the state would launch a massive prison construction project to reduce overcrowding in existing prisons. Jeribi said, "We want to give more space to each prisoner, to meet international standards, which stipulate four square metres per person." The plan is to create space for 7,265 individuals by 2020.[117]
- February 23, 2018: The U.S. Pentagon, with the assistance of Germany, plans to add nearly $20 million in high-tech sensors to Tunisia's border security.[118]
- April 12, 2018: Col. Lasad Bashuwil, a member of the Tunisian National Commission for the Fight Against Terrorism, affirmed that the commission is in the process of establishing a national list of persons involved in terrorism

cases. This list is in collaboration with the Commission of Financial Analysis and the ministries of finance, justice, and interior. The bank accounts of individuals appearing on this list will be frozen. However, the affected individuals will be able to appeal the government's decision.[119]

- May 17, 2018: Justice Minister Jeribi proposed the creation of a judiciary dedicated to crimes of terrorism among children and adolescents, noting that this sector does not exist in the judicial component of the fight against terrorism.[120]
- July 17, 2018: Government officials from Algeria and Tunisia met in Tunis and agreed to create a new joint military and security operations room for their shared border, with direct communications between commanders along the frontier.[121]
- November 23, 2018: Tunisia's Ministry of Higher Education and Scientific Research announced formal steps to tackle terrorism in higher education institutions. According to the ministry, it will help build a database of university expertise in the prevention of violent extremism and terrorism; awareness campaigns for students in the fields of citizenship, protection against polarization, and prevention of extremism; training programs for stakeholders on early responses to violent extremism and radicalization; and research on terrorism.[122]
- December 26, 2018: Japan agreed to help Tunisia improve the country's counterterrorism capabilities.[123]
- July 4, 2019: Funding contracts worth $10 million USD were signed for associations (Tunisia Tomorrow, We Love Sousse, and al-Jahiz Forum) in Tunisia's civil society to implement local projects to prevent violent extremism. They are designed to target vulnerable groups such as women, youth, and children. There will also be a process of monitoring and evaluation for these projects to assess their utility.[124]

Based on many of these measures, Tunisia's interior minister in mid-April 2019 argued that it has "enabled [Tunisia's] security and military institutions to move from the phase of the fight against terrorism to anticipation."[125] In other words, the minister is suggesting that Tunisia feels confident and comfortable with the threat level in early 2019 and with having a more proactive than reactive posture in its fight against IS and KUBN. This could also be an explanation for why the number of arrests related to jihadism has fallen. Moreover, this Tunisian governmental analysis is also why the country's prime minister, Yusuf Shahid, boasted when the government proactively stopped a potential "catastrophic" attack during Ramadan (May) 2019.[126]

Human Rights Concerns

There is no doubt that Tunisia's government and population should be lauded for its successes and accomplishments in improving its security and returning its tourism industry to levels above those prior to the terrorist attacks at Bardo and Sousse and even topping the prerevolution highs. These successes, however, have come at a cost according to several individuals within the human rights community. It is important to note that Tunisia now is nowhere near as regressive rights-wise as it had been prior to 2011, but with any security challenge, balancing the rule of law and security is not always easy, as can be seen in countries with far more history of democratic governance. Therefore, reports of renewed torture within the prison system is worrisome.[127] There are also concerns regarding the restrictive traveling policies allowed for men under the age of thirty-five and their ability to travel to countries like Turkey, Morocco, Algeria, or Libya—even when they might not have anything to do with jihadism or foreign fighting.[128] Furthermore, Tunisia's inclusion of an option for a death penalty provision in the 2015 counterterrorism law, even though Tunisia has not executed anyone since 1991, was seen as very controversial within the human rights community.[129] More worrisome from the perspective of attempting to build a free press postrevolution, some journalists have been arrested or detained for their coverage of terrorism-related events, which the state has argued is against the counterterrorism law even though they are only attempting to educate and contextualize events for the public.[130]

Relatedly, in terms of prosecuting those arrested for terrorism-related charges, according to the United Nations, the process was extremely slow and the judicial apparatus was overwhelmed as of early 2017.[131] However, based on my collection of data from local media, there have been a lot more publicly disclosed prosecutions of various terrorism-related offenses since early 2019. As context, there were two prosecutions in 2014, two in 2015, four in 2016, one in 2017, three in 2018, and eighteen in the first nine months of 2019.[132] It should be noted that many of these prosecutions had more than one individual involved. The uptick in 2019 suggests a more streamlined process, which will hopefully alleviate pressure on the judiciary and become more of an efficient trend going forward.

* * *

This chapter has identified what happened within Tunisia and among Tunisia's jihadi movement domestically following the designation of AST in late August 2013. Although KUBN was gaining momentum with insurgent attacks against Tunisia's security forces in 2013–14 as AST became less relevant, pro-IS members of KUBN hurt the organization from within and eventually defected to create a separate IS network and organization within Tunisia. Similarly, in Libya, IS also gained defections from ASL as well as incubated its organization in Libya with returned Libyan and Tunisian foreign fighters from Syria. The Tunisians built their own cell in Sabratha, Libya, that helped provide training to Tunisians who carried out the Bardo and Sousse attacks in 2015, and the cell was the staging ground for the planned takeover of the Tunisian city of Ben Gardane in March 2016. The failure to execute this plan not only was a turning point for IS in Tunisia but also provided a victory to the Tunisian government and helped push it forward in its fight against IS (and KUBN).

The final chapter highlights that although IS lost territory in Iraq, Libya, and Syria beginning in 2015, KUBN has not been able to take advantage of IS's losses due to the incoherence between its rhetoric and actions. This has helped to narrow the focus for the Tunisian government on continuing to deter and suppress militant activity by both IS and KUBN in the mountainous areas along the Algerian border, and to focus on other issues such as jihadi prisoners, returnees who have yet to come back home, and those still fighting abroad.

CHAPTER 11

THE FUTURE OF THE TUNISIAN JIHADI MOVEMENT

There are several aspects of the Tunisian jihadi movement to consider when looking at the future. Of course, it is impossible to predict what is going to happen, but there are a number of trends or current processes worth exploring: the status of KUBN with the fall of IS's territorial control in Iraq, Libya, and Syria; the question of foreign fighter returnees from Iraq, Libya, and Syria; the movement within Tunisia's prison system; and other less-discussed foreign fighter destinations Tunisians could join in the near future. While this latter aspect of the history of the Tunisian jihadi movement is incomplete, in many ways, the movement itself is at its weakest since the 2011 revolution. While that might sound reassuring, the relative weakness now is still stronger than it had been pre-2011, which hints to the challenges ahead.

KUBN's Inability to Take Advantage of IS's Losses

As IS began to lose territory in Iraq and Syria in the spring of 2015, many who studied jihadism argued that al-Qaeda would take advantage of IS's misfortunes.[1] In a general or overall sense that might be true to a certain extent, but within the Tunisian context, AQ's official branch in Tunisia has not been able to do so. Why is that?

As discussed earlier in the previous chapter, by mid-2015 KUBN had been severely degraded by Tunisian security forces. In response the organization put out a statement in late August 2015, with a new official logo to try to rebrand

and boost its efforts. In many ways it was also a reintroduction of the group to the Tunisian public due to its past policy of little online engagement over social media or even releasing its propaganda. It had a message for a few audiences in the statement:

> The Tunisian government (which it called taghut [tyrants]) and its soldiers: "their repressive measures against the Katibah and against all Muslims will only strengthen their resolve to continue their jihad."
> Their "mujahidin" brothers and especially those in the prisons of the tyrants: "offering them support and encouragement."
> The people of Tunisia: "the freedom promised by their revolution is being stolen. The Katibah will not shed innocent Muslim blood, and they are only targeting the tyrants."[2]

This last line is the most consequential aspect of the message. It would come back to hurt the organization since it has been unable to fully live up to its claim that it does not shed "innocent Muslim blood." A crucial point to understand when exploring KUBN as an organization today and its ability to position itself vis-à-vis IS's network in Tunisia is that the group is not connected to the pulse of the Tunisian jihadi movement, is not innovative in the way it operates, and alienates the local population it is attempting to curry favor with. Some might argue that this is the case for IS in Tunisia as well, but IS, unlike AQ, has never claimed that it is attempting to cultivate hearts and minds. Therefore, this is due to KUBN's network disconnection, the changed experiences of Tunisian jihadis since the Arab uprisings, and KUBN's inability to align propaganda with action, therefore losing hearts and minds of the local populace.

Network Disconnection

KUBN has had the disadvantage of positioning itself in areas that did not have much historic connection to jihadi activism. It is true that AQIM's predecessor groups, the Groupe salafiste pour la prédication et le combat and the Groupe islamique armé, conducted attacks along the Algerian-Tunisia border three times between 1995 and 2001.[3] But most historical Tunisian jihadi networks as discussed throughout this book were closer to the coastal region (Ariana, Bizerte, and Tunis) and Libyan border (Ben Gardane). This is in contrast to KUBN's network, which hugs the Algerian border in Kasserine and to a lesser extent in El Kef and Jendouba. Moreover, following the Tunisian Revolution, when AST was active and building local branches of its organization in various governorates, cities, and villages, the governorates where KUBN has operated were some of the least active within AST's network. On a per capita basis as it relates to events that AST organized by governorate (of twenty-four governorates in Tunisia), El Kef (nineteenth), Jendouba (twenty-second), and Kasserine (twenty-fourth) were at the bottom.[4] The main takeaway from this is that those locales were not deeply penetrated by jihadi networks and influence. Therefore, those three governorates, with Kasserine being the most relevant, were not fertile ground to easily recruit and penetrate the local milieus. Instead, KUBN has mostly been holed up in different mountainous areas in these regions, with Jabal Chambi and Jabal Samamah as the most relevant—both of which are in the Kasserine governorate.

Beyond the limited nature of AST's activism within those three governorates, as described in chapter 8, the areas that were more richly organized and mobilized were later co-opted for recruitment to fight in Libya and Syria with the AST successor Shabab al-Tawhid network to IS. Moreover, many of the key figures in the leadership of KUBN had previously come from AQIM's network in Algeria and Mali. The latter were mainly Tunisians who had been foreign fighters in Mali. The former, including the group's leaders (Khalid Sha'ib, Murad Sha'ib, and Bilal Kobi), were Algerian. Therefore, they were not necessarily as plugged into the new scene that emerged in Tunisia with AST after the revolution and were more used to the methodology of AQIM's network in Algeria. Therefore, if one compares the modus operandi of KUBN with AQIM's activities in Algeria over the past decade, they appear to be very similar: small groups of cells that primarily lay ambushes and are deeply clandestine in rural and mountainous areas. While this might bode well for survival, it does not necessarily help with winning hearts and minds of the local population. Nor does this approach bode well for KUBN's propaganda products garnering an audience, especially if the frame alignment is off due to differences between what is said and what its actions show.

From Terrorism and Insurgency to Social Movement and Service Provision

In addition to network disconnection, AST's experience, which seamlessly led into the mobilization for IS, highlights a key structural change that happened to the jihadi movement, which this book touches upon regarding the post-Arab uprising environment: namely, a growth in *dawa* activities as well as the provision of social services and in some cases governance. This was a paradigm shift and moved the jihadi movement forward due to the greater opportunities to appeal directly to the local populace in a face-to-face manner versus only through online videos. These new conditions brought in a larger pool of individuals who may have not joined if it had been a purely violent and underground movement. Therefore, the expectations within the broader movement altered to presume a certain type of organizational operation. This also shows that jihadi groups could not only talk about implementing some type of theocratic vision sometime in the future but could actually carry it out in the real world to varying degrees.

Consequently, Tunisian jihadis became accustomed to a certain type of jihadism, one that included population outreach and service, beyond just violence. This historical process, especially with the experience of the Tunisian jihadi movement since the revolution, is key to also understanding why KUBN has not been able to succeed as much with the local population as one might think. It does not help, either, that their ideological messaging to the population does not completely align with what has happened on the ground.

Losing Hearts and Minds

With this in mind, a few points are worth considering: first, the type of messages that KUBN and AQIM have been pushing to the Tunisian population seems distant and from an era prior to the Arab uprisings; second, KUBN has been unable to ingratiate itself with the local population; and finally, any possible goodwill has been hurt due to KUBN's penchant for stealing provisions from locals homes, raiding local businesses for supplies, and setting up mines that are likely supposed to target Tunisian security forces but have in many cases killed local civilians in the areas they operate. In the end, KUBN and AQIM are proffering a message against the current Tunisian government and those who believe in the process of democratization but are not offering anything in return beyond terrorizing and alienating the local community, a community that they are not even close to because they are hiding in the mountains.

For example, ahead of Tunisia's municipal election in May 2018, KUBN/AQIM released a statement that notes, "In every election to date all political parties market the next elections as a turning point as if it's a 'magic cane,' which will change the circumstances of the country, and allow the country to escape its economic and political crises."[5] It is true that many Tunisians are still waiting for economic benefits from the revolution, but this particular election was part of a process to get those gains in the longer term. By decentralizing power to the local level, instead of a centralized apparatus that is distant to the population, this election provides more local agency over budgets and other types of services and advantages that only someone from that particular area might be able to render since they do care about the area they came from. This is in contrast to some outsider from the capital who has no connection to the rural and interior parts of Tunisia. Therefore, KUBN/AQIM are criticizing a measure that in the medium to long term will be beneficial to the local populations. This is especially the case in areas where KUBN operates like Kasserine, since local residents will have more control over and say in their own lives and future, with the hope of alleviating more of the economic burden. As a result, the same playbook that AQ-aligned groups might use to delegitimize faux elections in authoritarian systems in the Arab world prior to the uprisings falls short and impedes the wishes of the locals whom the group is attempting to sway.

More importantly, KUBN/AQIM do not provide much alternative to what it is criticizing beyond rhetorical flourishes about the need for Islamic law and for individuals to fight jihad. These positions are attached to another key element of its messaging related to the fact that it claims it does not attack civilians. In at least four statements, KUBN/AQIM tries to convince Tunisians that it does not spill the blood of innocent individuals (which is part of a broader campaign that AQ has promoted since Ayman al-Zawahiri's September 2013 "General Guidelines for the Work of a Jihadi," covered in chapter 5):

> We tell our people in Tunisia that we do not target the Tunisian people.... We only target those who attack us.... We are not responsible for attacks on our Muslim Tunisian Families.... We ask our mujahidin to do their best and be up to the task and warn them about infallible blood.[6]

> [KUBN] will not shed innocent Muslim blood, and they are only targeting the tyrants.[7]

> It reiterates to the people of Tunisia that KUBN's fight is with the tyrants and their soldiers, not with ordinary Muslims. And it warns the local population to be cautious about moving around KUBN areas with weapons in case the group mistakes them for enemy soldiers. It also informs local inhabitants that they can expect to be searched and to undergo identity checks so that KUBN can determine that they are not members of the army or on their list of supporters of the tyrants. KUBN also assert their right to defend themselves if they are attacked, even if the attacker is Muslim.[8]

> We promise our people in Tunisia that we do not target any innocent Muslim who is not fighting us. And we confirm that our war is against those who oppressed and assaulted us like the army and other security bodies.[9]

Also, AQIM's 'Abd al-Rahman al-Jaza'iri in December 2016 released an advice booklet to leaders and fighters in KUBN on how to operate in the mountainous areas where they are based. It notes the following key directions:

> Getting to know many people as much as you can and gain their affection, if you gain their affection they will aid you in many things.... They will not snitch on you and will hide you, and mislead your enemies. You will gain influence in the

area and will be able to mobilize as you wish. Gain information about the enemy anytime. And best you will gain and benefit from is the issue of recruiting. You will guarantee logistical support in all kinds (such as: provisions, clothes, and everything you need from military supplies).... And reminding everyone of the bombs, because it might be a danger to them, this is part of maintaining the safety of Muslims.[10]

This counsel about being close to the local population, along with KUBN/AQIM's own propaganda about not targeting innocent civilians has not been heeded. Instead, KUBN is not close to the local residents but rather is hiding in the mountains. More importantly, KUBN has killed a number of residents either on purpose or by accident and has also ransacked individuals' homes and businesses to survive, which runs counter to the second point in al-Jaza'iri's guidance manual.

As a consequence of KUBN's direct murder of local residents, including Salih al-Firjani, Haddah Rihimi, and Lamjad Griri, it has released statements as part of a public relations gambit, attempting to justify the group's actions and whitewashing the deaths that were seen locally as inexcusable.[11] Based on a database that I created, between May 2016 and July 2019, there have been twenty cases where landmines laid by KUBN have been set off by civilians, leading to at least four deaths, two amputations, and other various injuries.[12] Less lethal but no less worrisome to local residents, KUBN has been involved in twenty cases of breaking into people's homes and local businesses to steal provisions, supplies, and eat home-cooked meals, and they have attacked or assaulted locals for information on the Tunisian military between October 2015 and July 2019.[13]

It is no surprise, then, that many local residents do not look too fondly upon KUBN and its fight against the Tunisian government and security forces. Not only is KUBN not close to the local residents and is not attempting to gain favor with them via service provision, it has instead killed, injured or harassed many civilians. Therefore, KUBN has undermined its own potential base. This helps provide a greater explanation for why KUBN is unlikely to overtake IS as the most popular jihadi group in Tunisia. Plus, the broader Tunisian jihadi network is pro-IS, whether breaking it down by those that are based abroad (Syria, Libya, Europe) or those who are internal (prison system). The reality is, IS's message still has greater appeal because it can rely on a nostalgic narrative of what it did in Iraq, Libya, and Syria, unlike KUBN, which just discusses what could be. All IS has to do is point to the exploits it was able to accomplish in Libya, Iraq, and Syria in terms of administration, governance, and services to show what could be a possibility in Tunisia if given the proper conditions, in contrast to a negative lived experience with KUBN.

For these reasons, it is worthwhile to now explore those who have returned home to Tunisia from the battlefields of Iraq, Libya, and Syria; those currently imprisoned; and those still on battlefields abroad.

Returnees

According to the Tunisian government, there are one thousand individuals who have returned home, and five hundred of them are under house arrest.[14] Based on documents that I was able to access from Tunisia's Ministry of Interior, the ministry has a dossier on six hundred of these individuals, which suggests the government has a grasp on what these individual were up to when they were foreign fighters abroad.[15]

Muhammad Iqbal Bin Rajab, president and founder of the Rescue Association of Tunisians Trapped Abroad, explains that Tunisians decide to return home for three primary reasons: the experience of "becoming disenchanted by the war, ... being cajoled by their distraught families, or in the hope to recruit their fellow countrymen."[16] The last of these comes with sparse specifics, due to the clandestine nature of recruitment by returnees. Yet public cases exist, such as one in April 2014 when two Tunisian returnees from Syria were arrested for attempting to build a bomb in Ain Charfi, seven miles northwest of Sfax.[17] Other reasons also come up, like in the alleged case of Abu Fatimah al-Tunisi, a local leader in eastern Deir al-Zour, Syria, who stole $25,000 in *zakat* (religiously obligated tax) funds, fled IS territory, and later mocked his former comrades on Twitter: "What state? What Caliphate? You idiots."[18]

Most Tunisians attempting to return do so in one of three logistical ways: (1) a direct flight from Turkey; (2) a flight via Turkey then Morocco, where they burn their passports, get new ones at the embassy in Rabat, and then fly home, aiming to cover their past indiscretions; or (3) by sneaking over the Libyan border in hopes of remaining undetected, unharassed, and free from a possible trial and jail time upon their return.[19] While many do make it back to Tunisia, others are either killed outright by IS when fleeing,[20] are taken into custody by the Kurdish-led Syrian Democratic Forces (SDF) in northeast Syria,[21] or are arrested by Turkish authorities when attempting to traverse the Syrian-Turkish border to catch a flight home from Ankara or Istanbul.[22]

Once you are in Syria, you are at the mercy of jihadi groups, as the Tunisian Faysal explains: "Now that you're far from home, they know you cannot go back."[23] According to Umm Bara' al-Tunisi, who was introduced in the previous chapter and is a former female IS member held in the SDF Ain Issa camp where many captured IS members are placed, "The punishment for foreign families who tried to escape was severe. Many times the Islamic State killed its own fighters suspected of disloyalty."[24] For example, one Tunisian was allegedly thrown into a well and left to rot after expressing an interest in leaving IS.[25] As noted by Khadijah 'Umri, also in the Ain Issa camp, "You couldn't speak freely or criticize IS, you didn't know who was listening."[26] She also noted that seventy Tunisians were on an Islamic State hit list.[27]

Iman Tariqi, a lawyer representing returned Tunisian foreign fighters, affirmed that "60 percent of those who come back profess disappointment."[28] A number of such returnees have spoken out on their disillusionment and desire for detachment from events in Syria. There are two primary reasons: infighting between Jabhat al-Nusra and IS and the latter group's failure to live up to its own professed standards on governance. For example, Sharf al-Din Hasni, an IS supporter who remained in Tunisia but had multiple friends who traveled to Syria, noted from his interactions with them that "they thought it would be like joining the side of the Prophet Muhammad, but they found it was divided into these small groups with a lot of transgressions they did not expect, like forcing people to fight [between IS and JN]."[29] Furthermore, an aspiring combatant named Ghayth, who returned to Tunisia, said, "It was totally different from what they said jihad would be like. . . . It's not a revolution or jihad, it's a slaughter."[30] Moreover, Faysal explains that "between the image they give themselves in their videos on the internet—that of the companions of the prophet—and what they really are, cold and calculating, there is a gap."[31] Lastly, the returned Tunisian 'Ali expressed that "I feel like I was a terrorist, I was shocked by what I did. . . . It's not Islam. Don't give your life up for nothing."[32]

Many women such as 'Umri also were disappointed regarding their yearning to live in a pristine Islamic state. "My husband and I made a huge mistake by coming there," she explained. "And I advise you not to believe those who say that IS is an Islamic state."[33] In addition, 'Umri complained that after her first husband was killed, she was placed in a dormitory where a supervisor named Umm Adab mistreated her and her children, as well as others, by denying them diapers and medicine.[34] 'Umri concluded that such abuse could be a tactic to lead widows, seeking to protect themselves and their children, into remarriage with other IS fighters.[35] Umm Bara' felt similarly, remarking, "I quickly became horrified by the executions and killings committed by IS, but by then it was too late to leave."[36]

Some expressions of disenchantment might not be wholly genuine, instead reflecting an acknowledgment of the Islamic State's loss of territory. For example, after IS began ceding ground, some, like Anwar Bayudh, evidently began to see IS members as "monsters," but for whatever reason he and others did not express such sentiments when the group's situation appeared promising.[37] Similarly, Muhammad Amruni, after IS began losing al-Raqqah, reached out to his family about returning home. His brother Ajmi said Muhammad "begged for my forgiveness."[38] This is part of the dilemma with returning foreign fighters writ large: determining whether their remorse is genuine. Expressing disillusionment with the IS experience paired with hesitating to disavow the broader ideology and a focus on poor implementation presents a special quandary. This is likely why someone like Umm Bara' still says that, "given my choice I would stay here in Syria . . . rather than go home and go to prison there."[39] Those who do end up returning home and have a similar mindset can create security and human rights dilemmas for local actors.

Once home, returnees also face the stigma of having joined a jihadi group, now wearing a proverbial scarlet letter. A former combatant named Rajab concurs that "even the ones that express regret are outcast and marginalized by society."[40] Because these returnees have no alternative social network in Tunisia, they risk relapsing out of the desire for solidarity and purpose that fomented their mobilization in the first place. In some sense, this is why Ajmi Amruni's expression in reference to his brother Muhammad, who is seeking to return home via extradition from an SDF camp—"Insh'Allah. He is not a threat"—encapsulates the approach taken by Tunisia and other countries to the broader dilemma of returning foreign fighters.[41] Tunis is essentially hoping that everything just works out because as of October 2019, it has yet to offer a comprehensive governmental-level rehabilitation or reintegration initiative for individuals who fought in Syria—with some returnees out in society and others detained in prison. According to Tunisian media reports, those who have returned from battlefields and are currently out of prison and in society are mainly based in Tunis (Douar Hicher, Oued Ellil, Hay al-Intilaka, El Kabaria, and La Marsa), Sidi Bouzid, Kasserine, Sousse, Monastir, Ben Gardane, and Tataouine.[42]

Before discussing the current status of jihadis in prison, which the Tunisian government has agency in dealing with, Tunisian foreign fighters stuck abroad in detention or refugee camps, particularly in Syria, present a far more tricky issue, considering the complexity of who might be there and what it could mean if they are returned home. As of May 2019 numbers on Tunisian male fighters with IS who have been detained is not available, but Tunisia's Ministry of Women and Children has identified about two hundred children and one hundred women held abroad in Iraq, Libya, and Syria.[43] Although IS lost its claim over territory by the end of March 2019, within the al-Hawl Camp, the main SDF camp housing the women and children of IS, women are continuing to act as if they are in positions of power and creating a gang-like atmosphere. It should come as no surprise, considering Tunisian women's prior role as leaders in the al-Khansa' Brigade, that Tunisian women, alongside Russians, are continuing to enforce morality laws within al-Hawl. According to the Swedish detainee Lisa Andersson, "If you go outside the tent without your burqa, or say something to the management, they beat you or your children up. They threaten to burn your tent."[44] Similarly, a Belgian detainee at al-Hawl noted the Tunisian womens extreme beliefs, explaining that "talking to the guards, or requesting to go to the market, can make us infidels."[45] This could suggest that some of the Tunisian women at al-Hawl follow the Hazimi trend, which is discussed in chapter 8. As a result of this, Tunisian authorities view these women as incubators of extremist jihadi thought to their children.[46] Besides the women, there are also the male members of IS; four hundred of them are housed in the SDF-run maximum-security Derik Central Prison, and some are Tunisians.[47] There are also a number of Tunisian male fighters in Iraqi prisons; however, there is very little detail as of October 2019 related to them.

Part of the dilemma is the fact that there is not a lot of appetite, by the government or even among many in the citizenry, to bring back Tunisia's foreign fighters. As early as January 2017 there were protests against the return of foreign fighters to Tunisia, with slogans such as "no return, no freedom for savage (IS) bands" and "no repenting, no pardon for terrorists."[48] This is why Tunisian authorities have been hesitant to bring back detained fighters (male, female, and their children) who had joined IS in Libya.[49] Even among al-Nahdah politicians like Usamah Sagha'ir, there is not much sympathy, and the government is creating barriers for the return of young children: "How do we know these kids are Tunisian? They were born outside the law in a country where there is no registration of birth. If they can prove they are Tunisian, we're going to do what we can to bring them back."[50] The government has proposed the potential for DNA tests but has also told detained individuals to get in touch with the Tunisian Embassy and consulates in Turkey.[51] But this is nearly impossible since they are detained. At the time this book went to press, a policy related to those still abroad has yet to be formulated beyond the ad hoc nature of governmental statements.

The Status of the Prisons

In many ways the future of Tunisian jihadism is now brewing within the country's prison system. While some Tunisian jihadis are still active fighting in the mountainous region near the Algerian border or abroad (more on this shortly), the vast majority are now within Tunisia's prison system. One can only hope that the Tunisian government does not demonstrate the disinterest in this population that the Bin 'Ali government showed in its latter years. During that era, as described in chapter 5, Tunisia's imprisoned jihadis developed a plan that led to the formation of what became AST and all that followed.

Similar to that time period, Tunisia's prison system now also retains not only domestic Tunisians but also Tunisians of dual nationality who have been expelled from their country of residence or have been extradited from places where they have been arrested for involvement in terrorism. This is the same dynamic discussed in chapter 3 in the decade prior to the Tunisian Revolution, which allowed many Tunisians from different generations and various places to connect and plan what would happen if they were ever let out of prison. For instance, a Tunisian arrested and sentenced to death by Mali's judiciary for involvement in terrorism-related crimes in Mali and Niger was extradited back to Tunisia in June 2014.[52] More notably, Mu'az al-Fizani, one of the architects of the Bardo and Sousse attacks, fled Libya for Sudan following the failure of the Ben Gardane takeover in March 2016. However, due to Italian interest in him from his past jihadi activities as part of the Milan network in the 1990s and 2000s and through Italian intelligence, al-Fizani was arrested in Khartoum in mid-November 2016.[53] He was later extradited to Tunisia in late December 2016.[54]

More recently, Fahmi Lasuwidah, a half-Tunisian and half-Libyan national, who had been a commander with IS in Syria, was arrested in Manila, Philippines, in mid-February 2018 after having been in the Philippines since July 2016.[55] Based on this timeline it is possible Lasuwidah provided assistance to the upstart IS branch in the Philippines ahead of their takeover of the town of Marawi in May 2017. There have also been reports of other Tunisians with IS in the Philippines, but in Mindanao.[56] Once through the judicial process, the Filipino government said they would deport Lasuwidah.[57] Similarly, a twenty-two-year old Tunisian who had previously been a member of AST and was now sympathetic to IS was arrested and later deported from Malaysia in early March 2019.[58]

Besides these cases related to places that are currently in war or dealing with insurgency, there has been a growth in Europe in preventative expulsions where governments expel individuals with dual nationalities based on their extremist views and their potential for violence in the future or once they have served jail sentences related to jihadism. While Germany and France have done this on a small scale, Italy has been very aggressive in its jihadi-related expulsion policy since 2015. Based on a database I created from Italian Ministry of Interior press releases and Italian media reports on expulsions, as of July 2019, Italy has expelled seventy-five Tunisians back to Tunisia for jihadi-related reasons since 2015.[59] Those who have been expelled from Europe are believed to now be imprisoned within Tunisia; however, once expelled, little public detail has been gleaned within Tunisia on what happened to these individuals. Therefore, it is plausible that some might not be imprisoned, such as the case of the Tunisian Sami Aydudi from Germany, who was previously Usamah Bin Ladin's bodyguard in Afghanistan.[60]

In addition to those imprisoned in Tunisia after being expelled, extradited, or deported, there are many top individuals within the movement in Tunisia's prison system who were arrested by Tunisian authorities. One in particular is Adl Ghandri, who took part in the planning for the Ben Gardane takeover. During his trial for involvement in the assault and other activities with IS, Ghandri attacked the judge with the judge's own gavel.[61] Therefore, even though Ghandri was sentenced to life imprisonment,[62] it is individuals like him who maintain an extreme ideology that could help maintain the purity among prisoners with shorter sentences or could help incubate new thinking in prisoners that were arrested for petty criminality and unrelated to jihadism. Even more extreme within the prison system are figures like Abu Muhanad al-Tunisi, who had previously been part of AST's cleric establishment. Following the crackdown on AST he followed the ideological path of the Hazimi movement and his fellow Tunisian Abu Ja'far al-Hatab. As recently as late April 2019, Abu Muhanad denounced IS for its crackdown on those who followed the Hazimi trend.[63] Tunisia has to contend with not only those affiliated with or sympathetic to AQ or IS but also individuals who view both AQ and IS as not extreme enough in their beliefs. These dynamics, whichever trend gains an upper hand among the others within the prison system, does not portend well considering the conditions of the prison system as of October 2019. The prisons in Tunisian are overflowing with individuals, and they lack resources to maintain facilities or provide adequate services to the inmates.[64]

There were already reports as early as March 2016 that jihadis "held complete control [of the prison], and they beat up anyone who challenged them."[65] A Tunisian politician in early 2017 even described some prison blocks as having turned into mini-emirates.[66] More recently, in April 2018 a former prisoner named Hisham who was imprisoned for theft explained that while he was in prison, "The [jihadi] recruiters are everywhere; in the corridors, the walkways, the cells. They approached me dozens of times. They said if I wanted an easy time of it, it would be best for me to follow the path they were going to show me."[67]

Even though Tunisia's police and military have gained excellent experience in law enforcement and counterterrorism and have done a remarkable job in keeping Tunisia safe since 2015 following the Islamic State campaign against the country, a purely kinetic response does not resolve broader underlying issues. That is why the government recently introduced the "rehabilitation of minds" program at Rabta Prison, a program that "deconstructs the jihadi mode of thinking to allow suspects to be progressively re-introduced into society."[68] This pilot program in one prison could be a first step in building capacity and a more comprehensive plan to better integrate individuals back into their communities. Unlike in other Arab states, which are undemocratic, Tunisia has the possibility to harness its robust civil society to help with these issues on the front and back ends. A number of organizations have formed in recent years specifically to focus on topics related to countering violent extremism, such as prevention, off-ramping, rehabilitation, and reintegration.[69] Besides the Rescue Association of Tunisians Trapped Abroad, which is one group dealing with foreign fighters abroad and helping returnees safely come home, there are other less prominent ventures that are also attempting to help.[70] As with any such program, it is difficult to estimate their impact, but at least they are attempting to better the situation. Organizations and initiatives should be given a chance to help at a local level rather than a purely governmental-run, top-down process at a national level that does not concern itself with the various reasons why youths join in the first place and the local dynamics that play differently between the various governorates. As these organizations learn and grow, they could help get peoples lives back after they serve their prison sentences and could prevent individuals from joining in the first place.

Tunisians have also been involved abroad in other fronts besides Iraq, Libya, and Syria. This should not be lost in the debates about the domestic aspects of dealing with the Tunisian jihadi movement going forward since those who are abroad are outside the reach of the state and can continue to help incite and recruit new Tunisians to join the fight abroad or conduct an attack at home.

Remaining Fighters Abroad and Internally

Among the locales that are less focused on but have Tunisian foreign fighters, Afghanistan continues to be a place that attracts individuals. According to a senior Taliban official, Tunisians are among a cadre of 2,000–3,000 foreign fighters in their midst including others from Chechnya, China, Iraq, Saudi Arabia, Tajikistan, Uzbekistan, and Yemen.[71] There are also reports that Tunisians are currently fighting in the Sinai, although there are few details.[72] On the other hand, there are far more details on Tunisians continuing to fight and die alongside AQIM and its front group in Mali (as well as in Chad and Niger) called Jama'at Nusrat al-Islam wa-l-Muslimin (JNIM). For example, in late March 2015, Abu Abbas al-Tunisi died in Mali.[73] Moreover, two Tunisians were arrested in Taboye, Mali, about forty miles north of Gao, in mid-October 2017 with a large amount of money and weapons.[74] Only two months later another Tunisian in JNIM was arrested in Tilmesi, Mali, close to the Mauritanian border.[75]

More substantially, on February 21, 2019, Abu 'Iyadh al-Tunisi, the founder of AST, was reported to have died unceremoniously in a French operation that also killed JNIM's deputy leader, Yahya Abu al-Hamam, and a Tunisian poet, al-Sha'ir al-Qayrawani, near the border of Mauritania in El Aklé, about 185 miles northwest of Timbuktu, Mali.[76] This was the first time hearing meaningful reports about what Abu 'Iyadh had been up to since the leaked video of him praying over the dead body of ASL founder Muhammad al-Zahawi in late 2014. While the United States claims to have killed Abu 'Iyadh in an airstrike outside Ajdabiya, Libya, in mid-June 2015,[77] there was never any proof and jihadis never confirmed his death. This time key AQ-aligned online activists such as al-Muhajir al-Khurasani and Shibl al-Qaeda confirmed these reports.[78] Moreover, the pro-AQ essayist Abu Hudhayfah al-Sudani wrote about the deaths, which was distributed widely within the AQ online ecosystem on the encrypted application Telegram.[79] As Heni Nsaibia notes, Abu 'Iyadh's death also confirms the Tunisian media outlet Akhir Khabar's reports that Abu 'Iyadh fled Darnah, Libya, in the spring of 2016 to Mali, which would suggest that Abu 'Iyadh had been fighting in Mali with AQIM/JNIM for two and a half years.[80]

Likewise, north of Mali in Libya, a couple of Tunisian commanders with AQIM have been killed in the past few years. Most recently was the case of Ramzi Mansur (Ramzi al-Tunisi) who was killed in a late July 2018 airstrike in the southern Libyan town of Ubari, which had previously been a base of Mukhtar Bilmukhtar ahead of the In Amenas attacks in Algeria.[81] More substantial was the death of Mukhtar 'Akuri (Abu 'Umar al-Tunisi), who was also killed in an airstrike in mid-November 2016 in Gardhah al-Shati north of the central Libyan town of Sebha.[82] While he was a leader with AQIM in Libya, 'Akuri founded the AQIM Arabic-language magazine *al-Huda*; however, due to his death the magazine only lasted one issue.[83] More significantly, he was part of the so-called Sulayman Group that fought Tunisian security in December 2006–January 2007; following the revolution and the prisoner amnesty, he joined KUBN before assisting AQIM in Libya, illustrating again the long residual effect of older networks and what that could mean for more recent ones in the future.[84]

More worrisome is the fact that Libya's Khalifah Haftar, who is fighting a military campaign against Islamists and jihadis, has admitted that after capturing Tunisian IS members, he has released them without handing them back to the Tunisian government, which means they could be anywhere in Libya or elsewhere now.[85] Similarly, there have been reports that the current head of IS in Libya is the Tunisian Jamal al-Din Mallah, who was involved with "breaking the border" between Iraq and Syria in June 2014, as described in the beginning of chapter 9.[86]

Other Tunisians remain active in battlefields, which keeps the movement alive outside the prison system. One of the most important of these individuals is the previously discussed Bilal al-Shawashi (Abu Dhar al-Tunisi and Abu 'Abd Allah al-Tunisi), who played an important role in the recruitment of Tunisians to fight in Syria. Following his departure from Tunisia, he joined Jabhat al-Nusra, then defected to IS when it announced the caliphate, then defected again back to Jabhat al-Nusra in late 2016, which was calling itself Jabhat Fatah al-Sham by then and would again change its name a few months later to Hay'at Tahrir al-Sham.[87] As of late 2017, al-Shawashi was Hay'at Tahrir al-Sham's head sharia official for the Syrian town of Kafr Nabl.[88] This could implicate al-Shawashi in the assassination of Syrian activist Raed Fares since al-Shawashi allegedly harassed and tried to exile Fares in the year preceding his murder.[89] Besides al-Shawashi, there are even rumors that IS's current official spokesperson, Abu Hasan al-Muhajir, is a Tunisian, although some believe he is from Saudi Arabia.[90] If he is Tunisian, that would place him at a very powerful position within IS, which could become beneficial to other Tunisians within the organization and to the broader IS movement worldwide in the future.

Within Tunisia itself, as of mid-January 2019, based on information the Tunisian government shared with the United Nations, eighty insurgents remain in the mountainous areas along the Algerian border.[91] KUBN "employs only about 50 fighters, with activities limited to the mountainous areas of Kasserine and Jendouba."[92] And IS in Tunisia is "a relatively inactive group of approximately 30 fighters in the mountainous region."[93] Therefore, even if the security situation related to jihadism within Tunisia and outside Tunisia is not as urgent as it was between 2013 and 2016, as of October 2019, there still remains loyal members of the jihadi movement to fight in the cause of AQ or IS and to attempt to create an Islamic state abroad or at home.

Potential for greater destabilization in Algeria due to uprisings and continued civil war in Libya could be wild cards as well in the short to medium term. It is nearly impossible to completely eradicate the allure of jihadism, but answers on the future trajectory of the Tunisian jihadi movement will depend whether Tunisia is able to create a sustainable solution.

* * *

A lot has changed in the nine years since I stumbled across a jihadi forum post announcing Ansar al-Sharia as a new jihadi group in Tunisia. No longer do individuals necessarily find it surprising that Tunisian jihadis are involved in foreign fighting abroad and terrorist plotting in Tunisia or Europe. While many now know about Tunisian involvement in jihadism, many still have deeper questions about the reasons behind the sudden emergence and magnitude of involvement. This book aims to explore the history of Tunisian jihadism through the lens of AST and what came afterward with the rise of IS. Far from simply providing an empirically grounded and historically enriched book, my aim has been to go beyond the history of Tunisian jihadism to shed light on issues applicable to postcolonial religious reforms, diaspora networks, democratization, jihadi strategy, jihadi organizational structure, social movement theory's applicability in explaining jihadi groups, jihadi governance, jihadi messaging, militant learning across theaters, and how jihadis survive and adapt when their operating environments change.

This research elucidates what was described as "jihadi operational art," which helped al-Qaeda overcome command-and-control issues following 9/11 and the Iraq War for its branches and front groups. This could be relevant when looking at the future of the Islamic State now that it does not control physical territory but has a network of "provinces" and supporters worldwide. Furthermore, this research refines and strengthens ideas on leadership structure within jihadi organizations—going beyond the leader-led versus leaderless debate, which is applicable more to jihadism as it relates to terrorism in the West—and how this better understanding allows militants to operate locally when given space. This is relevant when looking at similar types of jihadi organizations currently operating in regional safe havens.

The dispersion of learning among militant groups happens, especially due the highly transnational nature of the jihadi movement. AST's propaganda distributed through social media, local outreach, and social service/governance methodology that it conducted between 2011 and 2013 was emulated both by its sister organization, Ansar al-Sharia in Libya, but also the Islamic State via advisors and alumni of AST. This study shows how jihadi networks evolve over time depending on the changing dynamics and circumstances in the environments they operate. This illustrates the utility of parts of social movement theory in helping explain the movement and changes within it. Without understanding local conditions that allow or negate the ability to mobilize, it would be more difficult to pinpoint why movements arise or decline. The designation of AST as a terrorist organization by the Tunisian government in August 2013, which ended its ability to operate openly in society, did not eliminate Tunisian jihadism. The case of Tunisian jihadism historically has morphed between a fluid diaspora network that mainly was involved in criminal support networks, facilitation, and external operation plotting and attacking as well as post-prison planning to a local organization following the revolution to currently a traveling band of foreign fighters in a number of locales along with a return to a diaspora network and an imprisoned movement.

In this book I have sought to answer the question of why jihadism grew and became so relevant in Tunisia following the Tunisian Revolution. It is my hope that this research will allow others in the field to better understand the reasons behind Tunisian jihadi involvement in Iraq and Syria and the underlying processes that led to it. It also provides a sturdy base on which other researchers can build, refine, or expand upon these book's broader ideas in the future.

AUTHOR'S NOTE ON TERMINOLOGY

This section explores the terms Islamism, salafism, jihad, jihadi-salafism, *dawa*, and *hisba*, with the particular goal of elucidating how they should be read in this book.[1]

Islamism

According to Peter Mandaville, Islamism is an ideology and political project that has as its goal "the establishment of the Islamic political order in the sense of a state whose governmental principles, institutions, and legal system derive directly from the sharia."[2] During the colonial period and following independence, a vacuum was created in many Muslim Arab nations when the state co-opted the *'ulama* (clerical establishment), which led to a loss of the *'ulama*'s legitimacy. In its place, Islamist groups like the Muslim Brotherhood (MB), beginning in the late 1920s, would take advantage of this gap. Nelly Lahoud argues, however, that Islamists lacked the necessary training and background in classical Islamic doctrine, leading to its misuse for their own political aims.[3] Islamists decontextualized the original meaning and purpose and applied them to the current circumstance.[4] Over time this new "lay-led" grassroots social movement, which first began in Egypt, became relevant within political systems across the Arab world—including Tunisia—and challenged the status quo.

The man who would transform Islamism into a more extreme ideology was an Egyptian named Sayyid Qutb. In response to the harsh torture that he endured in Egyptian prisons, Qutb shifted away from MB founder Hasan al-Banna's program, which focused primarily on building the MB's organizational and social structures.[5] Instead, Qutb created an intellectual argument that gave credence to the idea that Egyptian leaders, along with other Arab or Muslim leaders who strayed from "true" sharia and broke God's *hakimiya* (sovereignty), were in fact not true Muslims but rather those who lived in a state of *jahiliya* (pre-Islamic ignorance).[6]

Qutb's ideas inspired a new generation of proto-jihadis from the late 1960s to the early 1980s. This generation included his own cell, organized in prison, as well as a number of other organizations, including Salih Siriyyah's al-Gama'at al-Shabab Muhammad, which ultimately led to a failed coup against the Egyptian state on April 18, 1974 (almost a decade after Qutb's death); Shukri Mustafa's al-Gama'at al-Muslimin, which was destroyed after a botched kidnapping of the former minister of *awqaf* (religious endowments), Muhammad al-Dhahabi, on July 3, 1977; and Shaykh 'Umar 'Abd al-Rahman's al-Gama'ah al-Islamiyyah and Muhammad 'Abd al-Salam Farag's Tanzim al-Jihad, which were responsible for the assassination of Egypt's president, Anwar al-Sadat, on October 6, 1981.[7]

Although Farag drew inspiration from the thoughts articulated by Qutb, he was critical of Qutb's methodology. In particular, in Farag's seminal work *al-Jihad al-farida al-gha'iba* (Jihad: The neglected duty), he took issue with Qutb's call for spiritual training ahead of any physical or military action. Instead, Farag promoted the singularity of jihad in Islam. As he saw it, jihad was a "neglected duty," so it was necessary to rebel against the "near enemy"(the Egyptian regime of President al-Sadat, in this case). Once this goal was accomplished, it was one's obligation to create an Islamic state.[8]

Although the notion of jihad first may be taken for granted today, it helped propel individuals into the contemporary phenomenon of global jihadism. Before discussing global jihadism in greater depth, it is necessary to review the concept of salafism. The theology of salafism, combined with the sociorevolutionary ways of the MB, provide the essential elements of what later became the ideology of al-Qaeda, the Islamic State, and their various branches, provinces, affiliates, and inspired individuals.

Salafism

Within salafism there are many contours, interpretations, and evolutions as a theo-ideological construct and project. The term itself is derived from the Arabic word *al-salaf al-salih*, which refers to the pious predecessors, primarily, the first three generations of Muslims. Individuals that believe in salafism "try to emulate *al-salaf al-salih* as closely and in as many spheres of life as possible and construct their beliefs, their behavior and their reading of the sources of Islam to further that goal."⁹ Therefore, in contrast to the MB, salafism's "emphasis is on doctrinal purity and not politics."¹⁰

Further, Bernard Haykel explains the key components of salafi thought:

> Salafism can be understood by looking at three constitutive elements of the movement: theology, which is encapsulated by the concept of *tawhid* [the unicity of God]; law, which is centered on the question of *ijtihad* [independent reason] and whether one should adhere to the teachings of a particular school of law; and politics, which is determined by the particular *manhaj* [methodology] or way salafis choose to engage in the world. On matters of theology the movement's members appear to be in unanimous agreement on the creedal tenets that define salafism. On questions of legal theory and practice, the consensus frays somewhat, though most salafis are of the view that *ijtihad* is a requirement, and that *taqlid* [following past precedent] should be avoided, even by the unschooled Muslim. The divisions within the movement are most prominent as is to be expected perhaps, on how to make salafi teachings pertinent to political life and questions of power.¹¹

These differences have led scholars such as Quintan Wiktorowicz to categorize salafism into three key trends: quietists, politicos, and jihadis. According to Wiktorowicz, quietists focus on nonviolent forms of *dawa* (propagation of Islam) and spiritual purification; politicos attempt to implement the salafi *aqidah* (creed) to political life; and jihadis call for violent warfare to upend society and institute its brand of Islam.¹²

The most relevant religious leader to this discussion is Shaykh Abu Muhammad al-Maqdisi, who used the ideas of salafism to turn salafi ideas against the Saudi state—a Salafi theocracy—in the 1980s. Al-Maqdisi believes Saudi Arabia does not live up to or uphold true Islam as interpreted by past salafi scholars. Therefore, like Qutb but within a salafi construct, al-Maqdisi believes it is necessary to conduct jihad against the *murtad* (apostate) Saudi regime (and any others not living up to salafi creed). Accordingly, Joas Wagemakers explains that al-Maqdisi "mostly treats jihad as a tool to oppose *kufr* [disbelief] and *shirk* [polytheism] in order to advance the cause of Islam embodied in *tawhid*, and therefore does not limit jihad to just fighting, but rather sees *dawa* as a form of struggle ('jihad of the tongue') through which this goal can be achieved."¹³

Jihad

In its raw form, the Arabic root for the term "jihad", *j-h-d*, means to strive or to struggle. Therefore, etymologically, jihad does not mean holy war. Rather, if one were to translate the term "holy war" into Arabic, it would be *al-harb al-muqaddas*.[14] That being said, Michael Bonner notes:

> When followed by the modifying phrase *fi sabil Allah*, "in the path of God," or when-as often-this phrase is absent but assumed to be in force, jihad has a specific sense of fighting for the sake of God. In addition, several other Arabic words are closely related to jihad in meaning and usage. These include *ribat*, which denotes pious activity, often related to warfare, and in many contexts seems to constitute a defensive counterpart to a more activist, offensive jihad.... *Ghazw, ghazwa,* and *ghaza'* have to do with raiding. *Qital*, or "fighting," at times conveys something similar to jihad/ribat, at times not. *Harb* means "war" or "fighting," usually in a more neutral sense, carrying less ideological weight than the other terms.[15]

Further, Bonner explains that jihad refers to a legal doctrine within Islam contained in sharia manuals by Islamic scholars. These manuals include a "book of jihad."[16] Some scholars such as Muhammad Abdel Haleem have argued that jihad was mainly a defensive measure within a Qur'anic framework. Historically, however, Haleem explains that "there is no denying that the classical legal literature as a whole recognized offensive as well as defensive warfare. There is no denying that Islamic states, such as the caliphate of the Umayyads and 'Abbasids and the Ottoman empire, regularly sent raiding expeditions into non-Muslim territory, in addition to large-scale expeditions of conquest that they undertook from time to time."[17] This explanation is important because both Qutb and Farag believed in the idea of offensive jihad. Later, jihadis such as 'Abd Allah 'Azzam, a Palestinian graduate of al-Azhar University considered to be the first leader of the global jihadi movement, believed that orthodox Islam more strongly aligned with defensive jihad.

In 'Azzam's book *al-Dafa'a 'an ard al-muslimin* (Defense of Muslim lands), he explains the differences and obligations between offensive and defensive jihad. According to 'Azzam, an offensive jihad is fought only in the context of an Islamic state and when one is fighting in the disbelievers' territory. Therefore, in that context, jihad is *fard al-kifayah* (a collective obligation), meaning that not all Muslims need to fight. More important for 'Azzam was defensive jihad, which seeks to "expel the infidels from our [Muslim] land." It is considered *fard al-'ayn* (individual obligation).[18] 'Azzam's main departure from the orthodox understanding of *fard al-'ayn* is his argument that it is the duty of all Muslims anywhere to come and help their fellow Muslims in need. In the past, it was an individual obligation for those within the territory that had been attacked or occupied to fight jihad against the enemy. 'Azzam's new interpretation created what became the contemporary phenomenon of jihadi foreign fighting.[19]

Jihadi-Salafism

The anti-Soviet Afghan jihad of the 1980s brought Muslims from all over the world to fight alongside local Afghan insurgents against the invading and occupying Soviet Union. This conflict helped fuse the Qutb-inspired sociorevolutionary Islamist movements with the more doctrinal and legalistic theology of salafism.

Lahoud and Daniel Lav contrast MB-style Islamism and purist-salafism with jihadi-salafism. Lahoud explains that the key difference in the former is that more mainstream Islamists emphasize the community, while jihadism focuses more on the individual.[20] Lav emphasizes that there are two creedal issues separating the more mainstream "purist" salafi school with the newer "jihadi" school:

> The extent to which they do or do not adhere exclusively to neo-Hanbali [one of the four Sunni Muslim schools from which much of salafi doctrine derives] doctrine of faith, and the extent to which they view it as applicable to the issue of governance.... Thus the period of the emergence of the salafi jihadi school was marked both by a struggle against the quietists to prove that the issue of *hakimiyyah* was a legitimate salafi one, and also by an internal struggle within the radical camp to arrive at a correct reformulation of the issue.[21]

These two points, in addition to the convergence of Qutb's revolutionary ideas and the theology of salafism, led to what many describe today as jihadism, jihadi-salafism, or global jihadism. As Lav further highlights, these points show "it to be a total ideology that subsumes all these variations under a global, even cosmic, battle between faith and unbelief."[22]

While the ideology has been consolidated over the past few decades, key disputes and differences related to doctrinal purity and military strategy continue within the global jihadi community. A fissure in this book's discussion of Ansar al-Sharia in Tunisia relates to al-Maqdisi's critiques of Abu Mus'ab al-Zarqawi, the founder of what is now called the Islamic State's predecessor. One of the main critiques that al-Maqdisi presents, and from which he hopes to create a course correction within the jihadi movement, is his differentiation between *qital al-nikayya* (fighting to hurt or damage the enemy) and *qital al-tamkin* (fighting to consolidate one's power). Al-Maqdisi expounds upon these concepts in his book *Waqafat ma'a thamrat al-jihad* (Stances on the fruits of jihad), published in 2004.[23] He argues that the former provides only short-term tactical victories that often amount to little long-term success, while the latter provides a framework for consolidating an Islamic state. In doing so, al-Maqdisi highlights the importance of planning, organization, education, and *dawa* (calling individuals to Islam) activities.

Dawa and *Hisba*

Dawa can refer to a number of concepts, from calling individuals to Islam to outreach and proselytization. According to the *Encyclopedia of the Qur'an*, *dawa* is "the exhortation to heed the qur'anic message. The Qur'an issues its basic invitation to all people: worship and serve the sovereign and unique God alone and practice true religion. Invitations come through messengers and prophets to their peoples."[24] Sohirin M. Solihin further argues that humans then become the vicegerents of God to spread the message, which is based on the example of the Prophet Muhammad.[25]

While *dawa* sometimes displays a softer or more pragmatic side of jihadis, other concepts emphasize the harsher aspects—namely, the use of *hisba* (forbidding wrong as conceived by one of the preeminent Sunni scholars in history, Muhammad al-Ghazzali), which members of AST took part in. According to Michael Cook, *hisba* is derived from a number of Qur'anic verses: "'Let there be one community of you, calling to good, and commanding right and forbidding wrong [*al-amr bi-l-ma'ruf wa 'n-nahi 'an al-munkar*]; those are the prosperous' [Q3:104, 3:119, 3:114, 7:157, 9:71, 9:112, 22:41, 31:17]; the two phrases scarcely appear in isolation from each other."[26] Furthermore, Roel Meijer notes an important hadith that states, "'Whoever sees a wrong, and is able to put it right with his hand (*bi-l-yad*), let him do so; if he cannot then with his tongue (*bi-l-lisan*); if he cannot then with his heart (*bi-l-qalb*). That is the bare minimum of faith.' . . . According to the classical doctrine of Muslim scholars, putting things right (*taghyir*) with the hand is the prerogative of the political authorities, with the tongue of scholars and in (or with) the heart for the common people."[27]

The idea behind *hisba* has evolved since the classical period into a more activist instrumentalization over the past few decades. Cook has argued that "the core of the old conception was a personal duty to right wrongs committed by fellow-believers as and when one encountered them; the core of the new conception is a systematic and organized propagation of Islamic values both within and outside the community."[28] Moreover, Meijer states that "by linking *hisba* with the concept of *tawhid al-rububiyyah*, the necessity to completely submit to God's sovereignty, it was developed into an activist 'programme of changing evil by force' (*manhaj taghyir al-munkar bi-l-quwwah*)."[29]

Governments such as those in Saudi Arabia, the Islamic Emirate of Afghanistan, the Islamic State, Iran, and Hamas-led Gaza have used religious police to administer *hisba* policy and punishments. In nonstate cases like AST, *hisba* has been used as a vigilante tactic to spread fear among particular groups' opponents. Some examples include the smashing of alcohol, forcible closure of restaurants that serve on Ramadan, compulsory wearing of the *niqab* (full body cover), and attacks on brothels and theater artists, among other things.

NOTES

Introduction

1. Abu 'Iyadh al-Tunisi, "Opening Statement at the Ansar al-Sharia Forum," May 21, 2011.
2. Abu Muhammad al-Maqdisi, *Waqafat ma' thamrat al-jihad*, Minbar al-Tawhid wa-l-Jihad, 2004; and 'Umar 'Abd alHakim (Abu Mus'ab alSuri), *Mulahazat hawla al-tajriba al-jihadiyya fi Suriyya*. Peshawar, May 1991.
3. Aaron Y. Zelin, "Maqdisi's Disciples in Libya and Tunisia," *Foreign Policy's Middle East Channel*, November 14, 2012.
4. Lorenzo Vidino, "Sharia4: From Confrontational Activism to Militancy," *Perspectives on Terrorism* 9, no. 2 (2015).
5. al-Qa'ida in the Islamic Maghrib, "Journalistic Encounter with the Director of al-Andalus Media Foundation," al-Andalus Media Foundation, April 18, 2013.
6. Marion Boulby, "The Islamic Challenge: Tunisia Since Independence," *Third World Quarterly* 10, no. 2, *Islam & Politics* (April 1988): 590–614; Nikki R. Keddie, "The Islamist Movement in Tunisia," *Maghreb Review* 1, no. 1 (1986): 26–39; Bruce Maddy-Weitzman, "The Islamic Challenge in North Africa," *Terrorism and Political Violence* 8, no. 2 (June 1996): 171–88; Susan Waltz, "Islamist Appeal in Tunisia," *Middle East Journal* 40, no. 4 (Autumn 1986): 651–70; and Susan E. Waltz, "The Islamists Challenge in Tunisia," *Journal of Arab Affairs* 3 (1984): 99–105.
7. Anne Wolf, *Political Islam in Tunisia: The History* (London: Hurst, 2017); and Rory McCarthy, *Inside Tunisia's al-Nahda: Between Politics and Preaching* (Cambridge: Cambridge University Press, 2018).
8. Alaya Allani, "The Islamists in Tunisia Between Confrontation and Participation: 1980–2008," *Journal of North African Studies* 14, no. 2 (June 2009): 257.
9. Francesco Cavatorta and Fabio Merone, "Moderation Through Exclusion? The Journey of the Tunisian Ennahda from Fundamentalist to Conservative Party," *Democratization* 20, no. 5 (August 2013): 857.

10. Anne Wolf, "An Islamist 'Renaissance?' Religion and Politics in Post-Revolutionary Tunisia," *Journal of North African Studies* 18, no. 4 (September 2013): 560.
11. Khaled Elgindy, "The Rhetoric of Rashid Ghannushi," *Arab Studies Journal* 3, no. 1 (Spring 1995): 101–19; and Abdullah Saeed, "Rethinking Citizenship Rights of Non-Muslims in an Islamic State: Rashid al-Ghannūshi's Contribution to the Evolving Debate," *Islam and Christian–Muslim Relations* 10, no. 3 (October 1999): 307–23.
12. Rikke Hostrup Haugbølle, "New Expressions of Islam in Tunisia: An Ethnographic Approach," *Journal of North African Studies* 20, no. 3 (2015): 319–35.
13. Stefano M. Torelli, "The Multi-Faceted Dimensions of Tunisian Salafism," in *Salafism After the Arab Awakening: Contending with People's Power*, ed. by Francesco Cavatorta and Fabio Merone (Oxford: Oxford University Press, 2016), 159.
14. Fabio Merone and Francesco Cavatorta, "Salafist mouvance and sheikh-ism in the Tunisian Democratic Transition," *Centre for International Studies*, Dublin City University, Working Paper no. 7 (2012).
15. Stefano M. Torelli, Fabio Merone, and Francesco Cavatorta, "Salafism in Tunisia: Challenges and Opportunities for Democratization," *Middle East Policy* 19, no. 4 (Winter 2012): 140–54.
16. Francesco Cavatorta, "Salafism, Liberalism, and Democratic Learning in Tunisia," *Journal of North African Studies* 20, no. 5 (2015): 770–83.
17. Monica Marks, "Youth Politics and Tunisian Salafism: Understanding the Jihadi Current," *Mediterranean Politics* 18, no. 1 (March 2013): 104–11.
18. John Horgan, *The Psychology of Terrorism*, 2nd ed. (Abingdon, U.K.: Routledge, 2014).
19. Alison Pargeter, "North African Immigrants in Europe and Political Violence," *Studies in Conflict & Terrorism* 29, no. 8 (December 2006): 731–47.
20. Alison Pargeter, "Radicalisation in Tunisia," in *Islamist Radicalisation in North Africa: Politics and Process*, ed. by George Joffe, 71–94 (Abingdon, U.K.: Routledge, 2011).
21. Marc Lynch, "The New Salafi Politics," in *Arab Uprisings: The New Salafi Politics*, POMEPS Studies, no. 2 (October 16, 2012).
22. Daveed Gartenstein-Ross and Tara Vassefi, "Perceptions of the 'Arab Spring' Within the Salafi-Jihadi Movement," *Studies in Conflict & Terrorism* 35, no. 12 (2012): 831–48; and Donald Holbrook, "Al-Qaeda's Response to the Arab Spring," *Perspectives on Terrorism* 6, no. 6 (2012).
23. William F. McCants, "Al Qaeda's Challenge: The Jihadists' War with Islamist Democrats," *Foreign Affairs* 90, no. 5 (September/October 2011).
24. Daveed Gartenstein-Ross, "Al-Qaeda Is Winning," *Atlantic*, September 8, 2011.
25. Alex S. Wilner, "Opportunity Costs or Costly Opportunities? The Arab Spring, Osama Bin Laden, and Al-Qaeda's African Affiliates," *Perspectives on Terrorism* 5, no. 3–4 (2011): 50–62.
26. Shiraz Maher and Peter R. Neumann, *Al-Qaeda at the Crossroads: How the Terror Group Is Responding to the Loss of Its Leaders & the Arab Spring* (International Centre for the Study of Radicalisation and Political Violence, August 2012), 7 and 15.
27. Clinton Watts, "What If There Is No Al-Qaeda? Preparing for Future Terrorism," *Foreign Policy Research Institute*, E-Notes, July 2012.
28. Leah Farrall, "Some Quick Thoughts on Reports Abu Yahya al-Libi Has Been Killed," *All Things Counterterrorism* (blog), June 6, 2012, https://allthingscounterterrorism.com/2012/06/06/some-quick-thoughts-on-reports-abu-yahya-al-libi-has-been-killed/.
29. Daveed Gartenstein-Ross and Amichai Magen, "The Jihadist Governance Dilemma," *Washington Post*, July 18, 2014.

30. Brian Fishman, *Fourth Generation Governance: Sheikh Tamimi Defends the Islamic State of Iraq* (West Point, N.Y.: Combating Terrorism Center, Harmony Program, March 23, 2007).
31. Brian Fishman, *Dysfunction and Decline: Lessons Learned from Inside Al-Qa'ida in Iraq* (West Point, N.Y.: Combating Terrorism Center, Harmony Project, March 16, 2009).
32. Brian Fishman, *Redefining the Islamic State: The Fall and Rise of Al-Qaeda in Iraq* (Washington, D.C.: New America Foundation, National Security Studies Program Policy Paper, August 2011).
33. Daveed Gartenstein-Ross, "The Deadly Cycle of Terror That Has Iraq and Syria in Its Grip," *Spectator*, June 21, 2014.
34. Aaron Y. Zelin, "The ISIS Guide to Building An Islamic State," *Atlantic*, June 13, 2014; and Aaron Y. Zelin, "The Islamic State's Territorial Methodology," Washington Institute for Near East Policy, *Research Notes*, no. 29 (January 2016).
35. Twitter discussion between ShamiWitness and Marwan-el-Tounisi (archived by author): https://twitter.com/ShamiWitness/status/360382067562921985.
36. Rukmini Callimachi, "Yemen Terror Boss Left Blueprint for Waging Jihad," Associated Press, August 9, 2013.
37. Callimachi, "Yemen Terror Boss."
38. Abu Zubayr 'Adil Bin 'Abd Allah al-Abab, "Gains and Benefits of Control Over Parts of Abyan and Shabwah," *Minbar al-Tawhid wa-l-Jihad*, July 7, 2012.
39. Christopher Anzalone, "Insurgency, Governance, and Legitimacy in Somalia: A Reassessment of Harakat al-Shabab al-Mujahideen, its Rhetoric & Divisions," *al-Wasat*, December 6, 2010.
40. Robin Simcox, "Ansar al-Sharia and Governance in Southern Yemen," *Current Trends in Islamic Ideology* 14 (January 2013), https://www.hudson.org/research/9779-ansar-al-sharia-and-governance-in-southern-yemen.
41. Aaron Y. Zelin, "Jihadi Soft Power in Tunisia: Ansar al-Shari'ah's Convoy Provides Aid to the Town of Haydrah in West Central Tunisia," *al-Wasat*, February 21, 2012.
42. Marc Sageman, *Leaderless Jihad: Terror Networks in the Twenty-First Century* (Philadelphia: University of Pennsylvania Press, 2008), 132.
43. Sageman, *Leaderless Jihad*, 133.
44. Bruce Hoffman, "The Myth of Grass-Roots Terrorism: Why Osama bin Laden Still Matters," *Foreign Affairs* 87, no. 3 (May/June 2008).
45. Hoffman, "The Myth of Grass-Roots Terrorism."
46. Bruce Hoffman, "The Leaderless Jihad's Leader: Why Osama Bin Laden Mattered," *Foreign Affairs*, May 13, 2011.
47. Eliane Tschaen Barbieri and Jytte Klausen, "Al Qaeda's London Branch: Patterns of Domestic and Transnational Network Integration," *Studies in Conflict and Terrorism* 35, no. 6 (June 2012): 427.
48. Barbieri and Klausen, "Al Qaeda's London Branch."
49. Peter Neumann, Ryan Evans, and Raffaello Pantucci, "Locating Al Qaeda's Center of Gravity. The Role of Middle Managers," *Studies in Conflict and Terrorism* 34, no. 11 (November 2011): 829.
50. Neumann, Evans, and Pantucci, "Locating Al Qaeda's Center of Gravity," 828.
51. Neumann, Evans, and Pantucci, "Locating Al Qaeda's Center of Gravity," 829.
52. John Gerring, "Mere Description," *British Journal of Political Science* 42, no. 4 (October 2012): 721–46.

53. Max Besbris and Shamus Khan, "Less Theory. More Description," *Sociological Theory* 35, no. 2 (2017), https://doi.org/10.1177%2F0735275117709776.
54. Sidney Tarrow, *Power in Movement: Social Movements and Contentious Politics*, 3rd ed. (Cambridge: Cambridge University Press, 2011), 9.
55. Carrie Rosefsky Wickham, *Mobilizing Islam: Religion, Activism, and Political Change in Egypt* (New York: Columbia University Press, 2002), 4.
56. Quintan Wiktorowicz, ed., *Islamic Activism: A Social Movement Theory Approach*, Bloomington: Indiana University Press, 2004.
57. Quinn Mecham, *Institutional Origins of Islamist Political Mobilization* (Cambridge: Cambridge University Press, 2017), 15.
58. Charles Tilly, *Democracy* (Cambridge: Cambridge University Press, 2007).
59. Erica Chenoweth, "Terrorism and Democracy," *Annual Review of Political Science* 16 (2013): 355–78.
60. Donna della Porta and Mario Diani, *Social Movements: An Introduction*, 2nd ed. (Oxford: Blackwell, 2006); Charles Tilly, *Contentious Politics* (Oxford: Oxford University Press, 2006); Sidney Tarrow, *The New Transnational Activism* (Cambridge, Cambridge University Press, 2005); Doug McAdam, John D. McCarthy, and Mayer N. Zald, eds., *Comparative Perspectives on Social Movements: Political Opportunities, Mobilizing Structures, and Cultural Framings* (Cambridge: Cambridge University Press, 1996); and Tarrow, *Power in Movement*; and Jeff Goodwin and James M. Jasper, eds., *The Social Movements Reader: Cases and Concepts*, 2nd ed. (Hoboken, N.J.: Wiley-Blackwell, 2009).
61. della Porta and Diani, *Social Movements*, 31.
62. Tarrow, *Power in Movement*, 195–214.
63. To look at the Freedom House Reports more in full, see https://freedomhouse.org/report/freedom-world/2011/tunisia, https://freedomhouse.org/report/freedom-world/2012/tunisia, https://freedomhouse.org/report/freedom-world/2013/tunisia, https://freedomhouse.org/report/freedom-world/2014/tunisia, and https://freedomhouse.org/report/freedom-world/2015/tunisia.
64. McAdam, McCarthy, and Zald, *Comparative Perspectives on Social Movements*, 3.
65. Wickham, *Mobilizing Islam*, 8.
66. Heather S. Gregg, "Religious Resources and Terrorism," *Numen* 65, no. 2–3 (2018), https://doi.org/10.1163/15685276-12341494.
67. Robert D. Benford and David A. Snow, "Framing Processes and Social Movements: An Overview and Assessment," *Annual Review of Sociology* 26 (2000): 615.
68. "Letter to Mullah Mohammed 'Omar from Usama bin Ladin," June 5, 2002. Located in the United States Military Academy's Combatting Terrorism Center's online Harmony Database, Document #: AFGP-2002-600321.
69. Jeffry R. Halverson, H. L. Goodall Jr., and Steven R. Corman, *Master Narratives of Islamist Extremism* (New York: Palgrave McMillan, 2011), 13.
70. Michael Page, Lara Challita, and Harris, Alistair, "Al Qaeda in the Arabian Peninsula: Framing Narratives and Prescriptions," *Terrorism and Political Violence* 23, no. 2 (February 2011): 150–72.
71. Thomas Hegghammer, "Why Terrorists Weep," Paul Wilkinson Memorial Lecture, University of St. Andrews, April 16, 2015, https://web.archive.org/web/20180820134435/http://hegghammer.com:80/_files/Hegghammer_-_Wilkinson_Memorial_Lecture.pdf.
72. Adam Dolnik, "Conducting Field Research on Terrorism: A Brief Primer," *Perspectives on Terrorism* 5, no. 2 (2011): 31–32.

1. The Generation of Zaytunah

1. "Al-Habib burqibah yakhla' al-hijab min 'ala ru'us al-tunisiyyat," *YouTube*, https://www.youtube.com/watch?v=JTBgjxlKbt4.
2. Kenneth J. Perkins, "'The Masses Look Ardently to Istanbul': Tunisia, Islam, and the Ottoman Empire, 1837–1931," in *Islamism and Secularism in North Africa*, ed. John Reudy, 23–36 (London: Palgrave Macmillan, 1996), 30.
3. Michael J. Willis, *Politics and Power in the Maghreb: Algeria, Tunisia, and Morocco from Independence to the Arab Spring* (London: Hurst, 2012), 28.
4. Anne Wolf, *Political Islam in Tunisia: The History* (London: Hurst, 2017), 7.
5. 'Abd Elbaki Hermassi, "La Société tunisienne au miroir islamiste," *Maghreb-Machrek*, January/February/March, 1984, 1.
6. Sarah J. Feuer, *Regulating Islam: Religion and the State in Contemporary Morocco and Tunisia* (Cambridge: Cambridge University Press, 2018), 18.
7. "Nobody's Man, But the Man of Islam," *Arabia* 4, no. 44 (April 1985): 18.
8. Rory McCarthy, *Inside Tunisia's al-Nahda: Between Politics and Preaching* (Cambridge: Cambridge University Press, 2018), 14.
9. Marion Boulby, "The Islamic Challenge: Tunisia since Independence," *Third World Quarterly* 10, no. 2, Islam and Politics (April 1988: 592.
10. Wolf, *Political Islam in Tunisia*, 23.
11. Anne Wolf, "An Islamist 'Renaissance?' Religion and Politics in Post-Revolutionary Tunisia," *Journal of North African Studies* 18, no. 4 (October 2013): 562.
12. Arnold H. Green, "Political Attitudes and Activities of the Ulama in the Liberal Age: Tunisia as an Exceptional Case," *International Journal of Middle East Studies* 7, no. 2 (April 1976): 209–41; and Leon Carl Brown, "The Islamic Reformist Movement in North Africa," *Journal of Modern African Studies* 2, no. 1 (March 1964): 55–63.
13. Robert D. Lee, "Tunisian Intellectuals: Responses to Islamism," *Journal of North African Studies* 13, no. 2 (June 2008): 160.
14. Lee, "Tunisian Intellectuals."
15. Interview with Rashid Ghannushi, *Arabia*, April 1985.
16. Sana Ben Achour, "Le CSP, 50 ans après: Les dimensions de l'ambivalence," *L'annèe du Maghreb, Dossier: Femmes, Familles et Droit* 2 (2005–2006): 55–70.
17. Mohammed Elihachimi Hamdi, *The Politicisation of Islam: A Case Study of Tunisia* (Boulder, Colo.: Westview, 1998), 13.
18. Wolf, *Political Islam in Tunisia*, 30.
19. Wolf, *Political Islam in Tunisia*, 30.
20. David Bonderman, "Modernization and Changing Perceptions of Islamic Law," *Harvard Law Review* 81, no. 6 (April 1968): 1184.
21. Lee, "Tunisian Intellectuals," 160.
22. Willis, *Politics and Power in the Maghreb*, 158.
23. Noura Boursali, *Bourguiba wa-l-masa'la al- dimaqratiyah* (Tunis: Arabesques, 2016).
24. Edward Webb, "The 'Church' of Bourguiba: Nationalizing Islam in Tunisia," *Sociology of Islam* 1 (2013): 17.
25. Barbara DeGorge, "The Modernization of Education: A Case Study of Tunisia and Morocco," *European Legacy* 7, no. 5 (2002): 587.
26. Willis, *Politics and Power in the Maghreb*, 21.
27. Webb, "The 'Church' of Bourguiba," 19.
28. Webb, "The 'Church' of Bourguiba," 39.

29. Rikke Hostrup Haugbølle, "New Expressions of Islam in Tunisia: An Ethnographic Approach," *Journal of North African Studies* 20, no. 3 (2015): 319–35.
30. Emad Eldin Shahin, "The Rise and Repression of an Islamic Movement: Harakat al-Nahda in Tunisia," in *Political Ascent: Contemporary Islamic Movements in North Africa* (Boulder, Colo.: Westview, 1997), 67.
31. Shahin, "The Rise and Repression of an Islamic Movement," 63.
32. Willis, *Politics and Power in the Maghreb*, 159.
33. Boulby, "The Islamic Challenge," 599.
34. Hamdi, *The Politicisation of Islam*, 18–19; and Shahin, "The Rise and Repression of an Islamic Movement," 70.
35. McCarthy, *Inside Tunisia's al-Nahda*, 22.
36. Alaya Allani, "The Islamists in Tunisia Between Confrontation and Participation: 1980–2008," *Journal of North African Studies* 14, no. 2 (June 2009): 258.
37. Shahin, "The Rise and Repression of an Islamic Movement," 70.
38. Hamdi, *The Politicisation of Islam*, 20–21.
39. François Burgat, *L'islamisme au Maghreb: La voix du Sud (Tunisie, Algérie, Libye, Maroc)* (Paris: Karatha, 1988), 206–7.
40. Shahin, "The Rise and Repression of an Islamic Movement," 78.
41. McCarthy, *Inside Tunisia's al-Nahda*, 34–35.
42. Rashid al-Ghannushi, *Harakat al-Ittijah al-Islami fi Tunis* (Kuwait: Dar al-Qalam, 1989), 109–10.
43. Shahin, "The Rise and Repression of an Islamic Movement," 79.
44. Wolf, *Political Islam in Tunisia*, 46.
45. Hamdi, *The Politicisation of Islam*, 26.
46. Burgat, *L'islamisme au Maghreb*, 209.
47. Wolf, *Political Islam in Tunisia*, 44.
48. Hermassi, "La Société tunisienne au miroir islamiste," 50.
49. Shahin, "The Rise and Repression of an Islamic Movement," 75.
50. Hamdi, *The Politicisation of Islam*, 33.
51. Hamdi, *The Politicisation of Islam*, 34.
52. Boulby, "The Islamic Challenge," 603.
53. Shahin, "The Rise and Repression of an Islamic Movement," 83.
54. Shahin, "The Rise and Repression of an Islamic Movement," 85.
55. Susan Waltz, "Islamist Appeal in Tunisia," *Middle East Journal* 40, no. 4 (Autumn 1986): 653.
56. Hamdi, *The Politicisation of Islam*, 35.
57. Wolf, *Political Islam in Tunisia*, 37.
58. Hamdi, *The Politicisation of Islam*, 37.
59. Hamdi, *The Politicisation of Islam*, 39.
60. Muhammad al-Hashimi al-Hamadi, *Ashwaq al-Huriyyah* (Kuwait: Dar al-Qalam, 1989), 78.
61. Wolf, *Political Islam in Tunisia*, 57.
62. Hamdi, *The Politicisation of Islam*, 43.
63. Ghannushi, *Harakat al-Ittijah al-Islami fi Tunis*, 151–52.
64. Allani, "The Islamists in Tunisia Between Confrontation and Participation," 262.
65. Alison Pargeter, "Radicalisation in Tunisia," in *Islamist Radicalisation in North Africa: Politics and Process*, edited by George Joffe (Abingdon, U.K.: Routledge, 2011), 77.
66. McCarthy, *Inside Tunisia's al-Nahda*, 56.
67. Hamdi, *The Politicisation of Islam*, 47.
68. Shahin, "The Rise and Repression of an Islamic Movement," 88.

69. Boulby, "The Islamic Challenge," 606.
70. Shahin, "The Rise and Repression of an Islamic Movement," 96.
71. Hamdi, *The Politicisation of Islam*, 50–51.
72. 'Abd Elbaki Hermassi, "The Islamist Movement and November 7," in *Tunisia: The Political Economy of Reform*, ed. by I. William Zartman (Boulder: Lynne Rienner, 1991), 196.
73. Shahin, "The Rise and Repression of an Islamic Movement" 90.
74. Hamdi, *The Politicisation of Islam*, 49.
75. Hamdi, *The Politicisation of Islam*, 52.
76. Shahin, "The Rise and Repression of an Islamic Movement," 97.
77. Wolf, *Political Islam in Tunisia*, 64.
78. Sharan Grewal, "Tunisia's Foiled Coup: The November 8th Group," Working Paper, August 19, 2018, 5.
79. Grewal, "Tunisia's Foiled Coup," 13.
80. Wolf, *Political Islam in Tunisia*, 65.
81. Hamdi, *The Politicisation of Islam*, 62.
82. *November 7: al-Thawra al-Hudi'a* (Tunis: A. Ben Abdallah for Publishing and Distribution, 1992), 402–21.
83. Feuer, *Regulating Islam*, 109.
84. François Burgat and William Dowell, *The Islamic Movement in North Africa* (Austin: Center for Middle Eastern Studies, University of Texas, 1993), 234.
85. Shahin, "The Rise and Repression of an Islamic Movement," 101.
86. Wolf, *Political Islam in Tunisia*, 72.
87. Hamdi, *The Politicisation of Islam*, 70.
88. Qusayy Salih Darwish, *Yahduthu fi Tunis* (Paris: al-Tabah al-Faransiyah, 1987), 184.
89. Wolf, "An Islamist 'Renaissance?'," 564.
90. Wolf, *Political Islam in Tunisia*, 75.
91. Abdullah Anas, *To the Mountains My Life in Jihad, from Algeria to Afghanistan*, with Tam Hussein (London: Hurst, 2019), 223–24.
92. Rashid Ghannushi interview, *al-Da'wa*, Islamabad, December 16, 1993.
93. Allani, "The Islamists in Tunisia Between Confrontation and Participation," 265.
94. Esen Kirdiş, "Wolves in Sheep Clothing or Victims of Times? Discussing the Immoderation of Incumbent Islamic Parties in Turkey, Egypt, Morocco, and Tunisia," *Democratization* 25, no. 5 (2018): 901–18.
95. Wolf, *Political Islam in Tunisia*, 100–101.
96. Wolf, *Political Islam in Tunisia*, 100–101.
97. Rikke Hostrup Haugbølle and Francesco Cavatorta, "Will the Real Tunisian Opposition Please Stand Up? Opposition Coordination Failures Under Authoritarian Constraints," *British Journal of Middle Eastern Studies* 38, no. 3 (2011): 337.
98. Wolf, *Political Islam in Tunisia*, 119.
99. "Case Information: Hamadi Jebali," Committee on Human Rights, n.d., https://web.archive.org/web/20150906003802/http://www7.nationalacademies.org/humanrights/Cases/CHR_051858.htm.
100. Interview with Mahmoud Kammoun, son-in-law of former prime minister Hamadi al-Jabali and an Ennahda activist, Sousse, Tunisia, February 18, 2013.
101. Wolf, *Political Islam in Tunisia*, 5.
102. McCarthy, *Inside Tunisia's al-Nahda*, 107.
103. McCarthy, *Inside Tunisia's al-Nahda*, 126.
104. All information is gathered from Shaykh al-Khatib al-Idrisi's official Facebook page's biography.

105. Haugbølle, "New Expressions of Islam in Tunisia."
106. McCarthy, *Inside Tunisia's al-Nahda*, 111.
107. Fabio Merone, "Between Social Contention and Takfirism: The Evolution of the Salafi-Jihadi Movement in Tunisia," *Mediterranean Politics* 22, no. 1 (2017): 71–90.
108. Hédi Yahmed, *Taht rayyat al-uqub: Salafiyyun jihadiyyun tunisiyyun* (Tunis: Diwan li-l-nashir, 2015).
109. Faraj Isma'il, "Khartah al-tayyarat al-islamiyyah fi Tunis min al-Ghannushi ila al-Dhurayr," *Al Arabiya*, January 19, 2011, https://www.alarabiya.net/articles/2011/01/19/134222.html; 'Ali 'Abd al 'Al, "al-Salafiyyin fi Tunis ... wa-l-mutaghayrat al-jadidah," *'Ali 'Abd al 'Al's Blog*, January 18, 2011, available at http://ali-abdelal.maktoobblog.com.
110. McCarthy, *Inside Tunisia's al-Nahda*, 118.
111. McCarthy, *Inside Tunisia's al-Nahda*, 118.

2. A Scattered Group with a Less-Than-Perfect Image

1. David Collier, "Understanding Process Tracing," *PS: Political Science & Politics* 44, no. 4 (October 2011): 823.
2. Collier, "Understanding Process Tracing," 824.
3. Fahd al-Qahtani, *Ziljal Juhayman fi al-Makkah* (London: Munazzamat al-Thawra al-Islamiyya fi al-Jazira al-Arabiyya, 1987), 23.
4. James Bruce, "Arab Veterans of the Afghan War," *Jane's Intelligence Review* 7, no. 4 (April 1995); and Imtiaz Hussein, "Osama Prepares List of Arab Martyrs of Afghan Jihad," *Frontier Post*, May 24, 2000.
5. 'Umar 'Abd al-Hakim (Abu Mus'ab al-Suri), *Da'wat al-Muqawamah al-Islamiyyah al-'Alamiyyah* (2004), 756–59. Al-Suri further explained that Tunisians again failed to establish an organization in Sudan and on its return to Afghanistan in 1996. Moreover, in 1995, one of the GIA's founding members, Qa'iri Sa'id, attempted to expand its writ by bringing a number of the North African jihadi movements together, including calling for the Tunisians to establish the Tunisian Islamic Fighting Group à la the Libyan Islamic Fighting Group. Similar to the prior attempts in Afghanistan to band Tunisians together into an organization, this too failed. Alison Pargeter, "Radicalisation in Tunisia," ed. George Joffé, *Islamist Radicalisation in North Africa: Politics and Process* (New York: Routledge, 2012), 77.
6. Pargeter, "Radicalisation in Tunisia," 76–77.
7. Most from Tunisia and North Africa in general did not start to come until after 1987–88: Anthony Davis, "Foreign Combatants in Afghanistan," *Jane's Intelligence Review* 5, no. 7 (July 1993).
8. Hamad al-Qatari, "From Stories of the Arab Martyrs #40: 'Abd al-Hadi al-Tunisi," http://saaid.net/Doat/hamad/32.htm.
9. Qatari, "From Stories of the Arab Martyrs #40."
10. Abu Ja'afar al-Masri al-Qandahari, *Memoirs of the Arab-Afghans* (Cairo: Dar al-Sharuq, 2002), 232.
11. Qandahari, *Memoirs of the Arab-Afghans*, 261–62.
12. Qandahari, *Memoirs of the Arab-Afghans*, 115, 269.
13. Mohamed Mokeddem, *Les Afghans Algériens: De la Djamaâ À la Qa'ida* (Alger: ANEP, 2002). Ahmad would later be imprisoned in Algeria in 1993. While there are no specific details about it, due to his prior experiences it is quite possible he got caught up with the insurgency in the Algerian civil war.

14. *al-Bunyan al-Marsus*, no. 15–16 (Spring 1987), 32.
15. Pargeter, "Radicalisation in Tunisia," 77.
16. "Saudi-Owned Al-Arabiya Deletes Story on 'Erdoğan's Ties with Warlords' amid Gulf Crisis," *Turkish Minute*, June 10, 2017; originally released at, but then deleted (the author retains an original copy), "Erdogan, Ghannouchi Ties with Hekmatyar Show Islamists' Links with Warlords," *Al-Arabiya*, June 9, 2017.
17. Anne Wolf, *Political Islam in Tunisia: The History* (London: Hurst, 2017), 93–94.
18. Ahmad Muaffaq Zaidan, *The "Afghan Arabs" Media at Jihad* (Islamabad: ABC Printers, 1999), 61–64; and Barnett R. Rubin, "Arab Islamists in Afghanistan," in *Political Islam: Revolution, Radicalism, or Reform?*, ed. by John L. Esposito, 179–206 (Boulder: Lynne Rienner, 1997), 182–83.
19. *al-Bunyan al-Marsus*, no. 18 (February 1988): 43–48; and *al-Bunyan al-Marsus*, no. 19 (March 1988): 44.
20. *al-Bunyan al-Marsus*, no. 15–16 (Spring 1987): 35.
21. 'Abd Allah 'Azzam, *'Ashaq al-Hur*, 7–9.
22. "Tunis tajud bi-awal shahid a'iyaha 'ala ardh Afghanistan al-mujahidah: al-shahid Abu 'Uqbah," *Majallat al-Jihad*, no. 20 (1986): 20–21.
23. Mustafa Hamid and Leah Farrall, *The Arabs at War in Afghanistan* (London: Hurst, 2015), 90.
24. Basil Muhammad, *Safahat min Sajil al-Ansar al-Arab fi Afghanistan* (Riyadh: Lajnat al-birr al-Islamiyya, 1992), 199.
25. Muhammad, *Safahat min Sajil al-Ansar al-Arab fi Afghanistan*, 176–77.
26. Muhammad, *Safahat min Sajil al-Ansar al-Arab fi Afghanistan*, 90.
27. Muhammad, *Safahat min Sajil al-Ansar al-Arab fi Afghanistan*, 92.
28. Muhammad, *Safahat min Sajil al-Ansar al-Arab fi Afghanistan*, 194.
29. Hamid and Farrall, *The Arabs at War in Afghanistan*, 166–69.
30. Davis, "Foreign Combatants in Afghanistan."
31. Hamid and Farrall, *The Arabs at War in Afghanistan*, 155, 161–62.
32. Hamid and Farrall, *The Arabs at War in Afghanistan*, 164–65.
33. Hamid and Farrall, *The Arabs at War in Afghanistan*, 170.
34. Hamid and Farrall, *The Arabs at War in Afghanistan*, 140.
35. Mustafa Hamid, *al-Hamaqah al-Kubra aw harb al-mu'iz*, August 11, 1997, 4.
36. Fadl Harun, *The War Against Islam: Fadil Harun's Story*, Markaz Dirasat Qidhaya al-'Alam al-Islami, vol. 1 (February 26, 2009), 200.
37. Wisam Fu'ad, "al-Afghan al-'arab bayna wahdat al-manhaj al-tarbuwi wa taditid al-manarhij al-harakiyyah," *Mirkaz al-Mustaqbil Li-l-Dirasat wa-l-Abhath*, June 2000, http://www.moragaat.com/moragaat/jun2000/g04.htm.
38. Hamid and Farrall, *The Arabs at War in Afghanistan*, 242.
39. Harun, *The War Against Islam*, 467.
40. "In the Hearts of Green Birds: Stories of Foreign Mujahidin Killed in Bosnia" (Azzam Publications, 1996), https://web.archive.org/web/20010217045039/http:/azzam.com/html/storiessalmanalfarsi.htm.
41. Harun, *The War Against Islam*, 302 and 601.
42. Hamid and Farrall, *The Arabs at War in Afghanistan*, 204.
43. Harun, *The War Against Islam*, 200.
44. Hamid, *al-Hamaqah al-Kubra aw harb al-mu'iz*.
45. Alison Pargeter, *The New Frontiers of Jihad: Radical Islam in Europe* (Philadelphia: Pennsylvania University Press, 2008), 113; and Pargeter, "Radicalisation in Tunisia," 77.
46. Pargeter, "Radicalisation in Tunisia," 77.

47. Mehdi Mabrouk, "Tunisia: The Radicalization of Religious Policy," ed. George Joffé, *Islamist Radicalisation in North Africa: Politics and Process* (New York: Routledge, 2012), 56.
48. Pargeter, "Radicalisation in Tunisia," 77.
49. Mohamed Ali Harrath's official Facebook page.
50. Catherine Mayer, "Tunisian Elections: From Yesterday's Most Wanted to Tomorrow's Leaders," *Time*, October 21, 2011.
51. Mayer, "Tunisian Elections."
52. U.S. Department of State, Office of the Coordinator for Counterterrorism, "Patterns of Global Terrorism 1995," April 1996.
53. Ahmad Nazif, "Tunis: al-Salafiyya wa Ikhwatuha al-Halaqa al-Ula: al-Salafiyya al-Ilmiyya wa-l-Harakiyya," *Taqadoumiya*, January 23, 2012.
54. U.S. Department of State, Office of the Coordinator for Counterterrorism, "Patterns of Global Terrorism 1995."
55. Christopher Harmon, Andrew Pratt, and Sebastian Gorka, *Toward a Grand Strategy Against Terrorism* (New York: McGraw Hill Professional, 2010), 352.
56. Sean K. Anderson and Stephen Sloan, *Historical Dictionary of Terrorism* (Lanham, Md.: Scarecrow Press, 2009), 325.
57. Wolf, *Political Islam in Tunisia*, 123.
58. Western Jihadists 1993–Present: An Archive and Database Charting the Evolution of Jihadi-inspired Terrorist Networks and Recruitment in Western States. Principal Investigator: Jytte Klausen. Waltham, Mass.: Brandeis University.
59. Thomas Hegghammer, *Jihad in Saudi Arabia: Violence and Pan-Islamism Since 1979* (Cambridge: Cambridge University Press, 2010), 48–49.
60. Lorenzo Vidino, *al-Qaeda in Europe: The New Battleground of International Jihad* (New York: Prometheus, 2006), 216, 219.
61. Pargeter, *The New Frontiers of Jihad*, 34–39. The other group was led by al-Zubayr al-Hayli, who was also a Saudi and Afghan veteran.
62. Evan Kohlmann, *al-Qaida's Jihad in Europe: The Afghan-Bosnian Network* (Oxford: Berg, 2004), 17–18.
63. Pargeter, *The New Frontiers of Jihad*, 60.
64. Pargeter, *The New Frontiers of Jihad*, 19.
65. These documents were obtained from Bosnian government records by J. M. Berger for research on the documentary *Sarajevo Ricochet* (Febris Film, 2010). Berger emailed me a picture of a pie chart breakdown on June 3, 2013.
66. Kohlmann, *al-Qaida's Jihad in Europe*; and Thomas Hegghammer, "The Rise of Muslim Foreign Fighters: Islam and the Globalization of Jihad," *International Security* 35, no. 3 (Winter 2010/11): 53–94.
67. "Daily Says 741 Afro-Asians Who Pose Security Risk Have Bosnian Citizenship," *BBC News*, February 4, 2015.
68. Hamad al-Qatari, "From Stories of the Arab Martyrs #72: Abu al-Shahid al-Tunis," http://saaid.net/Doat/hamad/62.htm.
69. Pargeter, *The New Frontiers of Jihad*, 35.
70. Kohlmann, *al-Qaida's Jihad in Europe*, 198.
71. Evan Kohlmann, "Abu el-Ma'ali," *Global Terror Alert*, August 29, 2005.
72. Kohlmann, *al-Qaida's Jihad in Europe*, 198.
73. "Suspects in Murder Attempt Against Pope Still Have Bosnian Citizenship—Daily," *BBC News*, February 4, 2015.
74. Aimen Dean, Paul Cruikshank, and Tim Lister, *Nine Lives: My Time as MI6's Top Spy Inside al-Qaeda* (London: Oneworld, 2018), 149.

75. Dean, Cruikshank, and Lister, *Nine Lives*, 149.
76. Kohlmann, *al-Qaida's Jihad in Europe*, 64 and 89.
77. Kohlmann, *al-Qaida's Jihad in Europe*, 125, 131, 135, and 137. Operation Black Lion was the first of the three battles, but there are no public records that Tunisians were involved, although it is quite possible that they were considering their involvement in the other two.
78. Hegghammer, *Jihad in Saudi Arabia*, 48–49; and Kohlmann, *al-Qaida's Jihad in Europe*, 23.
79. Kohlmann, *al-Qaida's Jihad in Europe*, 23.
80. John Schindler, *Unholy Terror: Bosnia, al-Qa'ida, and the Rise of Global Jihad* (St. Paul, Minn.: Zenith, 2007), 267–68.
81. Schindler, *Unholy Terror*, 267–68.
82. Guido W. Steinberg, *German Jihad: On the Internationalization of Islamist Terrorism* (New York: Columbia University Press, 2013), 64.
83. Western Jihadists 1993–Present.
84. Dean, Cruikshank, and Lister, *Nine Lives*, 78.
85. For more background on Islamism in Algeria and the evolution of the war from the FIS to the GIA, see these two books: Michael Willis, *The Islamist Challenge in Algeri* (New York: New York University Press, 1999); and Camille Tawil, *al-Harakah al-Islamiyah al-musallahah fi al-Jaza'ir: Min al-Inqadh ila al-Jama'ah* (Beirut: Dar al-Nahar, 1998).
86. Hamid and Farrall, *The Arabs at War in Afghanistan*, 166–67.
87. "The Knight Abu Fatah Dismounts After a Long Jihad: Condolences on His Death and His Brothers upon the Land of Tunisia," *Ifriqiyyah al-Muslimah*, July 11, 2015.
88. Pargeter, *The New Frontiers of Jihad*, 83 and 85.
89. Omar Nasiri, *Inside the Jihad: My Life With al-Qaeda* (New York: Basic Books, 2006), 92.
90. Anneli Botha, "Terrorism in Maghreb: The Transnationalisation of Domestic Terrorism," *Institute for Security Studies*, ISS Monograph Series, no. 144 (June 2008), 149.
91. Nasiri, *Inside the Jihad*, 92.
92. Frida Dahmani, "Tunisie: Abou Iyadh, l'ennemi public numéro un," *Jeune Afrique*, October 1, 2002.
93. Asim Qureishi, "Interview with the Wife of Sayfullah Ben Hassine—Tunisian Political Prisoner Sentenced to 60 Years by Ousted President Ben Ali," *Cage Prisoners*, January 19, 2011, https://web.archive.org/web/20150103075013/http://www.cageprisoners.com/our-work/interviews/item/162-interview-with-the-family-of-sayfallah-ben-hassine.
94. Brynjar Lia, *Architect of Global Jihad: The Life of al-Qaida Strategist Abu Mus'ab al-Suri* (New York: Columbia University Press, 2008), 182.
95. Lia, *Architect of Global Jihad*, 185.
96. Nasiri, *Inside the Jihad*, 265.
97. Sean O'Neill and Daniel McGory, *The Suicide Factory: Abu Hamza and the Finsbury Park Mosque* (London: Harper Perennial, 2006), 134.
98. Abu Qatadah al-Filistini, "Important and Urgent Message to Ansar al-Shari'ah in Tunisia," al-Bayyariq Foundation for Media, January 20, 2014.
99. Nasiri, *Inside the Jihad*, 272–73.
100. Camille Tawil, *Brothers in Arms: The Story of al-Qa'ida and the Arab Jihadists* (London: Saqi Books, 2010), 134–35.
101. al-Jama'ah al-Salafiyyah Li-l-Da'wah wa-l-Qital, "al-Wahdah: al-Jama'ah Rahmah," September 16, 1998, https://web.archive.org/web/20071026121902/http://www.qmagreb.org:80/pages/wihda.html.

102. U.S. Department of State, Office of the Coordinator for Counterterrorism, "Patterns of Global Terrorism 1998," April 1999.
103. Western Jihadists 1993–Present.
104. Western Jihadists 1993–Present.
105. Western Jihadists 1993–Present.
106. Western Jihadists 1993–Present.
107. Botha, "Terrorism in Maghreb," 42.
108. Botha, "Terrorism in Maghreb," 66; and Vidino, al-Qaeda in Europe, 143.
109. Jean-Charles Brisard, Zarqawi: The New Face of Al-Qaeda (New York: Other Press, 2005), 69.
110. Botha, "Terrorism in Maghreb," 135.
111. Vidino, al-Qaeda in Europe, 370.
112. Vidino, al-Qaeda in Europe, 219.
113. Vidino, al-Qaeda in Europe, 147; and "Apprehension of a Suspect of a Crime," Indictment of Tarek Maaroufi, Essid Sami Ben Khemais, et al. Public Prosecutor's Office, Dr. Stefano Dambruoso, Penal Proceeding No. 13016/99 RGNR (A4/DIGOS/sez, 3/C), Milan, Italy, April 2, 2001.
114. Hamid and Farrall, The Arabs at War in Afghanistan, 229 and 231.
115. Harun, The War Against Islam, 870.
116. Hamid and Farrall, The Arabs at War in Afghanistan, 166–67.
117. Hamid and Farrall, The Arabs at War in Afghanistan, 166–67.
118. Raffaello Pantucci, "We Love Death as You Love Life": Britain's Suburban Terrorists (London: Hurst, 2015), 134.
119. Hamid and Farrall, The Arabs at War in Afghanistan, 257–61.
120. Kohlmann, al-Qaida's Jihad in Europe, 204–5.
121. Kohlmann, al-Qaida's Jihad in Europe, 206.
122. Lia, Architect of Global Jihad, 249.
123. Hamid and Farrall, The Arabs at War in Afghanistan, 259–60.
124. Brisard, Zarqawi, 69.
125. Brisard, Zarqawi, 70.
126. Brisard, Zarqawi, 71.
127. Carlotta Gall and Eric Schmitt, "Jihadist from Tunisia Died in Strike in Libya, U.S. Official Says," New York Times, July 2, 2015.
128. Isaac J. Martin, "El poeta tunecino y ex reclutador de Al Qaeda en Molenbeek," El Mundo, May 17, 2016.
129. "Mohamed Ben Riadh Nasri," The Guantánamo Docket, New York Times, https://www.nytimes.com/interactive/projects/guantanamo/detainees/510-mohamed-ben-riadh-nasri.
130. Ashraf al-Tabib, "Qiyadi Salafi Jihadi Sayf Allah bin Hasin (Abu 'Iyadh) yatahadath l-al-usubu'i: sir khatir wara' ahadath Sijnan . . . al-Astul al-Sadis al-Amriki yurid iqama qa'idah tansat fiha," al-Sabah, March 26, 2012.
131. Scott Sayare, "The Ultimate Terrorist Factory Are French Prisons Incubating Extremism?," Harpers, January 2016.
132. Hadi Yahmad, "Hiwar ma' Sayf Allah bin Hasin (Abu 'Iyadh)," Jaridat al-Haqa'iq al-Tunisiyyah, December 11, 2011.
133. Hamid and Farrall, The Arabs at War in Afghanistan, 272.
134. Martin, "El poeta tunecino y ex reclutador de Al Qaeda en Molenbeek."
135. Malikah al-Arud, Les soldats de lumière (2003), 10 and 71, https://ia800200.us.archive.org/27/items/lumiere_580/LESSOLDATSDELUMIERE.pdf.

136. Abdullah Anas, *To the Mountains My Life in Jihad, from Algeria to Afghanistan*, with Tam Hussein (London: Hurst, 2019), 246.
137. Nasiri, *Inside the Jihad*, 93; and Botha, "Terrorism in Maghreb," 163.
138. The Guantánamo Docket, *New York Times*, last update June 13, 2015, http://projects.nytimes.com/guantanamo.
139. "Lotfi Bin Ali," The Guantánamo Docket, *New York Times*, https://www.nytimes.com/interactive/projects/guantanamo/detainees/894-lotfi-bin-ali.
140. "Adel Bin Ahmed Bin Ibrahim Hkiml," The Guantánamo Docket, *New York Times*, https://www.nytimes.com/interactive/projects/guantanamo/detainees/168-adel-bin-ahmed-bin-ibrahim-hkiml; and "Mohamed Ben Riadh Nasri," The Guantánamo Docket.
141. "Abdul Bin Mohammed Bin Abess Ourgy," The Guantánamo Docket, *New York Times*, https://www.nytimes.com/interactive/projects/guantanamo/detainees/502-abdul-bin-mohammed-bin-abess-ourgy/documents/4.
142. Western Jihadists 1993–Present; Vidino, *al-Qaeda in Europe*, 162; Frazer Egerton, *Jihad in the West: The Rise of Militant Salafism* (Cambridge: Cambridge University Press, 2011), 102–10; and Peter Bergen, *The Osama bin Ladin I Know: An Oral History of al-Qaeda's Leader* (New York: Free Press, 2006), 269.
143. Harun, *The War Against Islam*, 1,331.
144. Harun, *The War Against Islam*, 278.
145. Harun, *The War Against Islam*, 657; and "Ridah Bin Saleh al Yazidi," The Guantánamo Docket, *New York Times*, https://www.nytimes.com/interactive/projects/guantanamo/detainees/38-ridah-bin-saleh-al-yazidi.
146. al-Qaeda, "Resurgence Magazine #2," al-Sahab Media, June 25, 2015.
147. "Mohamed Ben Riadh Nasri," The Guantánamo Docket.
148. Vidino, *al-Qaeda in Europe*, 226.
149. "Spain Indicts Eight 9/11 Suspects," *CBS News*, January 17, 2005.
150. Thomas H. Kean, Lee Hamilton, and the National Commission on Terrorist Attacks upon the United States, *The 9/11 Commission Report: Final Report of the National Commission on Terrorist Attacks upon the United States* (Washington, D.C.: National Commission on Terrorist Attacks upon the United States, 2004), 235 and 527.
151. Nasser al-Bahri, *Guarding Bin Laden: My Life in al-Qaeda: My Life in al-Qaeda* (London: Thin Man Press, 2013), 185.
152. Kean et al., *The 9/11 Commission Report*, 527.
153. "Seeking Information: Abderraouf Jdey," FBI's Most Wanted List, https://www.fbi.gov/wanted/terrorinfo/abderraouf-jdey/@@download.pdf.
154. Harun, *The War Against Islam*, 1,303.
155. Bahri, *Guarding Bin Laden*, 88–89.
156. Bahri, *Guarding Bin Laden*, 94–95.
157. Harun, *The War Against Islam*, 1,303.
158. Harun, *The War Against Islam*, 1,302.
159. Harun, *The War Against Islam*, 254.
160. Harun, *The War Against Islam*, 305.
161. Harakat al-Shabab al-Mujahidin, "Interview with Shaykh Mukhtar Abu al-Zubayr," *Radio al-Andalus*, January 1, 2012, https://archive.org/details/ghjttt.
162. Ali Soufan, *The Black Banners: The Inside Story of 9/11 and the War Against Al-Qaeda* (New York: Norton, 2011), 345.
163. Soufan, *The Black Banners*, 545; Clint Watts, Jacob Shapiro, and Vahid Brown, *al-Qa'ida's (Mis)adventure's in the Horn of Africa* (West Point, N.Y.: Combating Terrorism Center, July 2, 2007), 137–42.

164. Harun, *The War Against Islam*, 556.
165. Ali Soufan, *Anatomy of Terror: From the Death of bin Laden to the Rise of the Islamic State* (New York: Norton, 2017), 151.
166. Abu 'Ubaydah al-Maqdisi, "Shuhada' fi zaman al-ghuraba," al-Fajr Media, 2008.
167. Maqdisi, "Shuhada' fi zaman al-ghuraba."
168. Maqdisi, "Shuhada' fi zaman al-ghuraba."
169. Kohlmann, *al-Qaida's Jihad in Europe*, 44. For more background on al-Muwafaq Foundation, see "State Department Cables on Muwafaq Foundation," September 16, 2010, IntelWire, http://news.intelwire.com/2010/09/state-department-cables-on-muwafaq.html.
170. Material on al-Ayadi is available on the Office of Foreign Assets Control website, https://sdnsearch.ofac.treas.gov/Details.aspx?id=635; "Security Council Al-Qaida Sanctions Committee Deletes Entry of Shafiq ben Mohamed ben Mohamed Al-Ayadi from Its List," United Nations, October 17, 2011, https://www.un.org/press/en/2011/sc10413.doc.htm; and "Kadi Wins His Second ECJ Case Removing Him from the UN and EU Counter-Terrorist Sanctions Lists," *Brick Court Chambers*, July 22, 2013.
171. "QDe.090: Tunisian Combatant Group," United Nation's ISIL (Da'esh) & Al-Qaida Sanctions Committee Resolution 1267 List.
172. Jeff Israely, "The Second Time Around," *Time*, February 25, 2002.
173. Western Jihadists 1993–Present.
174. Martín, "El poeta tunecino y ex reclutador de Al Qaeda en Molenbeek."
175. Western Jihadists 1993–Present.
176. "Blast at Tunisian Synagogue Kills Five," *BBC*, April 11, 2002.
177. French and Spanish court documents on the Djerba attack obtained by the author show that Khalid Sheikh Mohammed was the mastermind behind the attack.
178. Marc Sageman, *Understanding Terror Networks* (Philadelphia: University of Pennsylvania Press, 2004), 189.
179. Chris Hedges, "Tunisian Killed in Synagogue Blast Was Unlikely Convert to Militancy," *New York Times*, June 9, 2002.
180. Hedges, "Tunisian Killed in Synagogue Blast."
181. Harun, *The War Against Islam*, 1,092, 1,335; and David Malet, *Foreign Fighters: Transnational Identity in Civil Conflicts* (Oxford: Oxford University Press, 2013), 191.
182. "Hassan Mohammed Ali Bin Attash," The Guantánamo Docket, *New York Times*, https://www.nytimes.com/interactive/projects/guantanamo/detainees/1456-hassan-mohammed-ali-bin-attash.
183. Harun, *The War Against Islam*.
184. French Prosecution of the Djerba Bombings, November 8, 2006, Cour d'Appel de Paris, Tribunal de Grande Instance de Paris, Parquet du Procureur de la République, No. Parquet: P.02.107.3901/2, No. Instruction: 029/02/1432, p. 76.
185. Bruce Crumley, "French Terror Conviction: Lesson for U.S.?" *Time*, February 6, 2009.
186. Crumley, "French Terror Conviction: Lesson for U.S.?"
187. Piotr Smolar, "De la Haute-Silésie à Médine, l'itinéraire d'un 'haut responsable d'Al-Qaida' arrêté en France En savoir plus sur," *Le Monde*, July 12, 2005.
188. Steinberg, *German Jihad*, 44–48; and French Prosecution of the Djerba Bombings, 81–83. Shadi 'Abd Allah himself met Ganczarski in Afghanistan in early 2000. Jama'at Tawhid wa-l-Jihad was the name of the group that Abu Mus'ab al-Zarqawi led before it became a part of AQ in October 2004 (and, subsequently, the Islamic State). Steinberg, *German Jihad*, 44–48; and French Prosecution of the Djerba Bombings, 81–83.

189. French Prosecution of the Djerba Bombings, 77, 91; and "German Terror Link: Djerba Bombing Trial Begins in Paris," *Der Spiegel*, January 5, 2009.
190. al-Bahri, *Guarding bin Laden*, 88–89.
191. "German Terror Link: Djerba Bombing Trial Begins in Paris."
192. French Prosecution of the Djerba Bombings, 64.
193. Audiencia Nacional, Juzgado Central de Instrucción no. 2, Senencia 20/2006, 11–12.
194. French Prosecution of the Djerba Bombings, 64.
195. French Prosecution of the Djerba Bombings, 68.
196. French Prosecution of the Djerba Bombings, 68.
197. "Deadly Attack Keeps World on Alert," *Guardian*, September 3, 2002.
198. David S. Cloud and Ian Johnson, "Hunt for al Qaeda Misses the Likes of Nizar Nawar," *Wall Street Journal*, August 20, 2002; and Botha, "Terrorism in Maghreb," 118.
199. "Le kamikaze tunisien de Djerba avait bénéficié de l'aide de sa famille en France en savoir plus sur," *Le Monde*, February 11, 2003.
200. "Le kamikaze tunisien de Djerba."
201. French Prosecution of the Djerba Bombings, p. 115.
202. Audiencia Nacional, Juzgado Central de Instrucción no. 2, Senencia 20/2006, 5.
203. Audiencia Nacional, Juzgado Central de Instrucción no. 2, Senencia 20/2006, 12.
204. Audiencia Nacional, Juzgado Central de Instrucción no. 2, Senencia 20/2006, 11.
205. Audiencia Nacional, Juzgado Central de Instrucción no. 2, Senencia 20/2006, 11.
206. Audiencia Nacional, Juzgado Central de Instrucción no. 2, Senencia 20/2006, 13–14.
207. Audiencia Nacional, Juzgado Central de Instrucción no. 2, Senencia 20/2006, 15.
208. Audiencia Nacional, Juzgado Central de Instrucción no. 2, Senencia 20/2006, 15.
209. Audiencia Nacional, Juzgado Central de Instrucción no. 2, Senencia 20/2006, 15.
210. Hedges, "Tunisian Killed in Synagogue Blast."
211. French Prosecution of the Djerba Bombings, 115.
212. French Prosecution of the Djerba Bombings, 115; and Cloud and Johnson, "Hunt for al Qaeda Misses the Likes of Nizar Nawar."
213. Ahmad Muwafiq al-Zaydan, "Tanzim qarib min 'al-Qa'idah' yutabna 'amaliyyat kanis jerbah," *Al-Hayat*, April 16, 2002.
214. Zaydan, "Tanzim qarib min 'al-Qa'idah' yutabna 'amaliyyat kanis jerbah."
215. "Tanzim al-qa'ida yuwa'id al-amrikiyyin," *BBC Arabic*, June 23, 2012.
216. Hamid and Farrall, *The Arabs at War in Afghanistan*, 320.
217. Joby Warick, *Black Flags: The Rise of ISIS* (New York: Doubleday, 2015), 65.
218. Audiencia Nacional, Juzgado Central de Instrucción no. 6, "Sumario 20/2004," November 7, 2006, 14.
219. Lia, *Architect of Global Jihad*, 205–6.
220. French Prosecution of the Casablanca Bombings, April 2, 2007, Cour d'Appel de Paris Tribunal de Grande Instance de Paris Parquet du Procureur de la Republique, No. Parquet: P 01.253.3902/2, No. Instruction: 1417, p. 33.
221. Fernando Reinares, *¡Matadlos!: Quién estuvo detrás del 11-M y por qué se atentó en España* (Barcelona: Galaxia Gutenberg/Círculo de Lectores, 2014), 69–84.
222. Botha, "Terrorism in Maghreb," 143; Pargeter, *The New Frontiers of Jihad*, 126; and Vidino, *al-Qaeda in Europe*, 309.
223. Botha, "Terrorism in Maghreb," 143.
224. Pargeter, *The New Frontiers of Jihad*, 127.
225. Vidino, *al-Qaeda in Europe*, 309.
226. Fernando Reinares, "The 2004 Madrid Train Bombings," in *The Evolution of the Global Terrorist Threat: From 9/11 to Osama bin Laden's Death*, ed. by Bruce Hoffman and

Fernando Reinares, 29–60 (New York: Columbia University Press, 2014), 46; and Lia, *Architect of Global Jihad*, 201.
227. Lia, *Architect of Global Jihad*, 138.
228. Lia, *Architect of Global Jihad*, 137.
229. Lia, *Architect of Global Jihad*, 144.
230. Reinares, "The 2004 Madrid Train Bombings," 34.
231. Lia, *Architect of Global Jihad*, 142; and Reinares, "The 2004 Madrid Train Bombings," 34.
232. Lia, *Architect of Global Jihad*, 203–4.
233. Lia, *Architect of Global Jihad*, 207; Reinares, "The 2004 Madrid Train Bombings," 46; and Schindler, *Unholy Terror*, 297.
234. Reinares, "The 2004 Madrid Train Bombings," 46.
235. Reinares, "The 2004 Madrid Train Bombings," 33, 37.
236. Reinares, "The 2004 Madrid Train Bombings," 41.
237. Egerton, *Jihad in the West*, 102–3.
238. Pargeter, *The New Frontiers of Jihad*, 127.
239. Pargeter, *The New Frontiers of Jihad*, 139.

3. Come Do Jihad

1. Louisa Loveluck, "Planting the Seeds of Tunisia's Ansar al Sharia," *Foreign Policy*, September 27, 2012.
2. Mary Anne Weaver, "The Short, Violent Life of Abu Musab al-Zarqawi," *Atlantic*, July/August 2006.
3. Weaver, "The Short, Violent Life of Abu Musab al-Zarqawi."
4. Jean-Charles Brisard, *Zarqawi: The New Face of Al-Qaeda* (New York: Other Press, 2005), 93–96.
5. Fazel Hawramy, "Iran's jihadi gambit," *al-Monitor*, January 10, 2018; and Weaver, "The Short, Violent Life of Abu Musab al-Zarqawi."
6. Brisard, *Zarqawi*, 108, 189. Zarqawi also traveled during this time to the Palestinian Ayn al-Hilweh refugee camp in Lebanon and non-Kurdish Iraq.
7. Brisard, *Zarqawi*, 118–19.
8. "al-Kashaf 'an huwaya 'al-ab al-ruhi' li-l-qa'ida fi al-'iraq al-tanzim walad qabal 2003 wa musayr majhul," *Baghdad al-Yawm*, September 11, 2018, available at https://baghdadtoday.news.
9. Brisard, *Zarqawi*, 108, 114–15, 156.
10. Lorenzo Vidino, *al-Qaeda in Europe: The New Battleground of International Jihad* (New York: Prometheus, 2006), 244.
11. Aaron Y. Zelin and Oula Alrifai, "The Islamic State in Southern Syria," *CTC Sentinel* 8, no. 11, November/December 2015, https://ctc.usma.edu/app/uploads/2015/12/CTCSentinel-Vol8Iss114.pdf.
12. Anneli Botha, "Terrorism in Maghreb: The Transnationalisation of Domestic Terrorism," *Institute for Security Studies*, ISS Monograph Series, no. 144 (June 2008): 163.
13. Vidino, *al-Qaeda in Europe*, 263–64.
14. Vidino, *al-Qaeda in Europe*, 265–66.
15. Botha, "Terrorism in Maghreb," 168.
16. Botha, "Terrorism in Maghreb," 163.
17. Botha, "Terrorism in Maghreb," 163.

18. Jean-Pierre Filiu, "Ansar al-Fatah and 'Iraqi' Networks in France," in *The Evolution of the Global Terrorist Threat: From 9/11 to Osama bin Ladin's Death*, ed. by Bruce Hoffman and Fernando Reinares (New York: Columbia University Press, 2014), 360.
19. "Statement by Pentagon Press Secretary Peter Cook on Coalition Strike Against Boubaker al-Hakim," U.S. Department of Defense, News Release, No. NR-435-16, December 10, 2016.
20. Islamic State, "Message to the People of Tunisia," al-I'tisam Media, December 17, 2014.
21. Karim Baouz, *Plognee au coeur de la fabrique djihadiste enquete sur les filieres du terrorisme francais* (Paris: First Document, 2016), 97–98; Timothy Holman, "Belgian and French Foreign Fighters in Iraq 2003–2005: A Comparative Case Study," *Studies in Conflict and Terrorism* 38, no. 8 (2015): 3; and Filiu, "Ansar al-Fatah and 'Iraqi' Networks in France," 361.
22. Kevin M. Woods and James Lacey, *Iraqi Perspectives Project: Saddam and Terrorism: Emerging Insights from Captured Iraqi Documents* (Alexandria, Va.: Institute for Defense Analysis, 2008), 16.
23. Jim Yardley, "Jihadism Born in a Paris Park and Fueled in the Prison Yard," *New York Times*, January 11, 2015.
24. Filiu, "Ansar al-Fatah and 'Iraqi' Networks in France," 362.
25. Filiu, "Ansar al-Fatah and 'Iraqi' Networks in France," 363.
26. "Djihâd en Tunisie: Interview du frère Abou Mouqâtil At-Tounsî," *Dar al-Islam Magazine*, no. 3, June 2015.
27. After the uprisings of course the entity would once again rename itself to the Islamic State of Iraq and al-Sham (ISIS) in April 2013 and then the Islamic State in June 2014.
28. Patrick B. Johnston, Jacob N. Shapiro, Howard J. Shatz, Benjamin Bahney, Danielle F. Jung, Patrick K. Ryan, and Jonathan Wallace, *Foundations of the Islamic State Management, Money, and Terror in Iraq, 2005–2010* (Santa Monica, Calif.: RAND, 2016), https://www.rand.org/pubs/research_reports/RR1192.html.
29. Brian Fishman and Joseph Felter, *al-Qa'ida's Foreign Fighters in Iraq: A First Look at the Sinjar Records* (West Point, N.Y.: Combating Terrorism Center, January 2, 2007), 8.
30. Fishman and Felter, *al-Qa'ida's Foreign Fighters in Iraq*, 9.
31. Fishman and Felter, *al-Qa'ida's Foreign Fighters in Iraq*, 20.
32. Evan Kohlmann, "Foreign Fighters Reported Killed in Iraq: June 2003–June 2005," *Global Terror Alert*, June 2005; and Reuven Paz, "Arab Volunteers Killed in Iraq: An Analysis," The Project for the Research of Islamist Movements at Global Research in International Affairs (GLORIA) Center, PRISM Series of Global Jihad, no. 1/3 (March 2005).
33. Lisa Meyers, "Who Are the Foreign Fighters?" *MSNBC*, June 20, 2005.
34. Alan B. Krueger, "The National Origins of Foreign Fighters in Iraq," presentation at the annual meeting of the American Economic Association, Chicago, Illinois, January 5, 2007, 3–4; and Joseph Felter and Brian Fishman, "Becoming a Foreign Fighter: A Second Look at the Sinjar Records," in ed. Brian Fishman, *Bombers, Bank Accounts and Bleedout: al-Qa'ida's Road In and Out of Iraq*, Combating Terrorism Center, July 22, 2008, 35–36.
35. "More Than 1,000 People in Tunisia Arrested," *Majallat Minbar Suriya al-Islami*, no. 3, October 2005. The magazine used to be hosted at these websites, which are now defunct: www.nnuu.org and www.islam-syria.com.
36. Craig S. Smith, "North Africa Feared as Staging Ground for Terror," *New York Times*, February 20, 2007.

37. Thomas Hegghammer, "The Rise of Muslim Foreign Fighters: Islam and the Globalization of Jihad," *International Security* 35, no. 3 (Winter 2010/11): 61.
38. Some of the foot soldiers included Abu al-Walid al-Tunisi, Abu Samir al-Tunisi, Abu Musʻab al-Tunisi, Abu Radwan al-Tunisi, Abu Tariq al-Tunisi (Ziyad al-Mahrazi), and a former foreign fighter in Afghanistan, Abu ʻAbd al-Rahman al-Tunisi. Evan Kohlmann, "The Foreign Mujahideen "Martyrs" of Iraq: 2003–2004," *Global Terror Alert*, January 2005; Mohamed Hafez, *Suicide Bombers in Iraq: The Strategy and Ideology of Martyrdom* (Washington, D.C.: United States Institute of Peace, 2007), 251–54; Mushrad al-Filistini, "Isma' al-Shuhada' al-ʻArab fi al-ʻIraq (Manqul)," *Shabkah Filisin Li-l-Hiwar*, February 12, 2005; Abu Ismaʻil al-Muhajir, "Min Sir Aʻ'Alam al-Shuhada' #26: Abu Radwan al-Tunisi," al-Furqan Media, October 10, 2006; and Abu Ismaʻil al-Muhajir, "Min Sir Aʻ'Alam al-Shuhada' #29: Abu Tariq al-Tunisi," al-Furqan Media, March 10, 2007.
39. Karim, "Qisah Kumandir Abu Ibrahim al-Tunisi," al-Hisbah Forum, April 28, 2006.
40. Karim, "Qisah Kumandir Abu Ibrahim al-Tunisi."
41. Karim, "Qisah Kumandir Abu Ibrahim al-Tunisi."
42. ʻAbd Allah al-Aʻala al-Madhri, "Min Sir Aʻ'Alam al-Shuhada' #42: Abu Basir al-Tunisi," *al-Furqan Media*, March 22, 2010.
43. "Biography of an al-Qaeda Operative 'Martyred' in Iraq: Abu Usama al-Tunisi," July 2006, https://web.archive.org/web/20061021081705/http://www.globalterroralert.com/pdf/0706/iraqmartyr0706-2.pdf.
44. ʻAbd Allah al-Aʻala al-Madhri, "Min Sir Aʻ'Alam al-Shuhada' #38: Abu Usamah al-Tunisi," al-Furqan Media, November 29, 2009.
45. Bill Roggio, "Senior al Qaeda in Iraq Leader Killed in Airstrike," *Long War Journal*, September 29, 2007.
46. Information originally posted to the al-Firdaws Forum and subsequently reported by Daniele Raineri on Twitter, January 17, 2017: https://twitter.com/DanieleRaineri/status/821315966663585793.
47. Charles Lister, *The Syrian Jihad: Al-Qaeda, the Islamic State and the Evolution of an Insurgency* (London: Hurst, 2015), 57.
48. Muʻawiyya al-Qahtani, "Martyrs of the Land of al-Qayrawan #1: Abu Qudamah al-Tunisi (Yusri al-Tariqi)," al-Qayrawan Media Foundation, January 4, 2012.
49. Qahtani, "Martyrs of the Land of al-Qayrawan #1."
50. Joel D. Rayburn and Frank K. Sobchak, eds. *The U.S. Army in the Iraq War*, vol. 1: *Invasion, Insurgency, Civil War, 2003–2006* (Carlisle Barracks, Penn.: U.S. Army War Press, 2019).
51. Botha, "Terrorism in Maghreb," 168.
52. Qahtani, "Martyrs of the Land of al-Qayrawan #1."
53. Hafez, *Suicide Bombers in Iraq*, 206.
54. Brisard, *Zarqawi*, 171; and "Desarticulada en Italia una supuesta red de terroristas," *Diario Córdoba*, November 29, 2003.
55. Clint Watts, "Discussion of Countries? Appendix B," *PJ Sage* (blog), 2008.
56. Joel D. Rayburn and Frank K. Sobchak, eds. *The U.S. Army in the Iraq War*, vol. 2: *Surge and Withdrawal, 2007–2011* (Carlisle Barracks, Penn.: U.S. Army War Press, 2019).
57. U.S. Department of the Treasury, "Treasury Designates Twelve Foreign Terrorist Fighter Facilitators," press release, September 24, 2014, https://www.treasury.gov/press-center/press-releases/Pages/jl2651.aspx.
58. Filiu, "Ansar al-Fatah and 'Iraqi' Networks in France," 359; and Murad Batal al-Shishani, "Al-Zarqawi's Legacy Seen in Trial of Jordanian al-Qaeda Cell," *Terrorism Focus* 6, no. 4 (February 6, 2009).

59. Bill Roggio, "Turkey," *Long War Journal*, December 5, 2006.
60. "Case of Charahili v. Turkey," European Court of Human Rights, Application Number 46605/07, Strasbourg, April 13, 2010, http://hudoc.echr.coe.int/eng?i=001-98256.
61. Holman, "Belgian and French Foreign Fighters in Iraq 2003–2005," 6.
62. "Case of Charahili v. Turkey."
63. Holman, "Belgian and French Foreign Fighters in Iraq 2003–2005," 7.
64. Holman, "Belgian and French Foreign Fighters in Iraq 2003–2005," 7.
65. Katharina Von Knop, "The Female Jihad: Al Qaeda's Women," *Studies in Conflict & Terrorism* 30, no. 5, 2007; and Anne Speckhard, "Female Suicide Bombers in Iraq," *Democracy and Security* 5, no. 1, 2009.
66. "La veuve de l'assassin du commandant Massoud et pionnière de la djihadosphère est déchue de sa nationalité belge," *La Libre*, December 1, 2017.
67. Western Jihadists 1993–Present: An Archive and Database Charting the Evolution of Jihadi-inspired Terrorist Networks and Recruitment in Western States. Principal Investigator: Jytte Klausen (Waltham, Mass.: Brandeis University).
68. Western Jihadists 1993–Present.
69. Gilles Kepel, *Terror in France: The Rise of Jihad in the West* (Princeton, N.J.: Princeton University Press, 2017), 75.
70. Abu 'Umar al-Baghdadi, "Fa-ama al-zabad fa-yadhhabu jufa,'" al-Furqan Media, December 4, 2007, copy held in the author's archives.
71. Jim Michaels, "Foreign Fighters Leaving Iraq, Military Says," *USA Today*, March 21, 2008.
72. Michaels, "Foreign Fighters Leaving Iraq"; Karen DeYoung, "Fewer Foreigners Crossing into Iraq from Syria to Fight," *Washington Post*, September 16, 2007; and "More Foreign Fighters Enter Iraq via Syria: US," *al-Arabiya*, May 12, 2009.
73. Bernard Rougier, *The Sunni Tragedy in the Middle East: Northern Lebanon from al-Qaeda to ISIS* (Princeton, N.J.: Princeton University Press, 2015), 124–70.
74. Rougier, *The Sunni Tragedy in the Middle East*, 94.
75. Botha, "Terrorism in Maghreb," 129; Tine Gade, *Fatah al-Islam in Lebanon: Between Global and Local Jihad*, Norwegian Defence Research Establishment (FFI), May 12, 2007, 24.
76. "More Foreign Fighters Enter Iraq via Syria"; and Lara Jakes and Qassim Abdul-Zahra, "More Foreign Fighters Seen Slipping Back into Iraq," Associated Press, December 5, 2010.
77. Jakes and Abdul-Zahra, "More Foreign Fighters Seen Slipping Back into Iraq."
78. Brian Fishman, *Redefining the Islamic State: The Fall and Rise of Al-Qaeda in Iraq* (Washington, D.C.: New America Foundation, August 2011), 12; "String of Bombings in Iraq Underscores Fragile Situation," *PBS News Hour*, April 24, 2009; and Mike Mount, "With Exit Deadline Looming, U.S. Battles Insurgents in Mosul," *CNN*, May 8, 2009.
79. *United States of America v. Faruq Khalil Muhammad 'Isa: Indictment*, United States District Court, Eastern District of New York, December 9, 2011; *United States of America v. Faruq Khalil Muhammad 'Isa: Criminal Complaint*, United States District Court, Eastern District of New York, January 14, 2011; and Bill Roggio, "US, Iraqi Forces Target Syrian-Based Network," *Long War Journal*, May 16, 2009.
80. Mount, "With Exit Deadline Looming"; and Bill Roggio, "Iraq," *Long War Journal*, May 26, 2009.
81. Jakes and Abdul-Zahra, "More Foreign Fighters Seen Slipping Back into Iraq"; and "Iraq: Al Qaeda Planning Holiday Attacks in West," *CBS News*, December 15, 2010.

82. Johannes Saal, "The Rise and Fall of Majd—Part II: Adolescence in Switzerland," *The German Jihad* (blog), July 12, 2018, https://germanjihad.wordpress.com/2018/07/12/the-rise-and-fall-of-majd-part-2-adolescence-in-switzerland/.
83. Lorenzo Vidino, "Jihadist Radicalization in Switzerland," *ETH Zürich*, November 2013; see also Sylvain Besson, "Les enfants perdus d'Al-Qaida en Suisse," *Le Temps*, September 5, 2011.
84. Vidino, "Jihadist Radicalization in Switzerland"; and Besson, "Les enfants perdus d'Al-Qaida en Suisse."
85. Vidino, "Jihadist Radicalization in Switzerland"; and Besson, "Les enfants perdus d'Al-Qaida en Suisse."
86. Abu Hamzah al-Muhajir, "al-Nabi al-Qa'id," *al-Fajr Media*, November 7, 2008, https://ia802702.us.archive.org/28/items/al-naibeyalqied1/al-nbey-alqaied.pdf, 67.
87. "Hiwar ma' walidah al-shahid Abu Sa'd al-Tunisi," al-Ma'sadat Media Foundation, August 25, 2010.
88. Western Jihadists 1993–Present.
89. French Court of Appeals, Court Trial Division of Paris, Department of the Public Prosecutor of the Republic, Department no. P96 253 390L2, Investigation no. 59 and 30.
90. Western Jihadists 1993–Present.
91. Western Jihadists 1993–Present.
92. Botha, "Terrorism in Maghreb," 153–54.
93. Marcel Rosenbach and Holger Stark, "The Istanbul Connection: Teenager Smuggled Bomb Plot Detonators to Germany," *Der Spiegel*, October 8, 2007.
94. Alexander G. Higgins, "Germans Concerned About Muslim Converts," Associated Press, September 7, 2007.
95. Guido W. Steinberg, *German Jihad: On the Internationalization of Islamist Terrorism* (New York: Columbia University Press, 2013), 71.
96. Steinberg, *German Jihad*, 73.
97. Steinberg, *German Jihad*, 103–5.
98. Rosenbach and Stark, "The Istanbul Connection."
99. Western Jihadists 1993–Present.
100. "Tahawwur Rana Sentenced to 14 Years in Prison for Supporting Pakistani Terror Group and Terror Plot in Denmark," FBI Chicago, 2013.
101. "Tahawwur Rana Sentenced to 14 Years."
102. Morten Storm, Paul Cruickshank, and Tim Lister, *Agent Storm: My Life Inside al Qaeda and the CIA* (New York: Grove, 2014), 232.
103. Western Jihadists 1993–Present.
104. "Islamist Website Owners Found Guilty," *SwissInfo*, June 21, 2007.
105. Steven Erlanger, "Terror Arrests Ahead of E.U. Summit," *New York Times*, December 11, 2008.
106. Paul Cruickshank, "Love in the Time of Terror," *Marie Claire*, May 15, 2009.
107. Cruickshank, "Love in the Time of Terror."
108. Erlanger, "Terror Arrests Ahead of E.U. Summit."
109. Erlanger, "Terror Arrests Ahead of E.U. Summit."
110. Angel Rabasa and Cheryl Benard, *Eurojihad: Patterns of Islamist Radicalization and Terrorism in Europe* (Cambridge: University of Cambridge Press, 2015), 122.
111. "On the Departure of the Commander and Scholar from the Flag of Jihad Mu'az al-Gharsalawi al-Qayrawani," *Ghorfah Minbar al-Ansar*, October 17, 2012.
112. Bill Roggio and Lisa Lundquist, "Jund al Khilafah Emir Killed in 'Treacherous Raid,'" *Long War Journal*, October 17, 2012.

113. Jund al-Khilafah, "On the French Operations," Minbar Media, March 22, 2012; and Abu Qa'qa' al-Andalusi, "Yusuf al-Faransi As I Knew Him," *Jund al-Khilafah*, March 31, 2012.
114. Marcel Rosenbach and Yassin Musharbash, "Inhaftierte Reisegruppe: Pakistan lässt mutmaßliche deutsche Islamisten ausreisen," *Der Spiegel*, October 21, 2009.
115. Islamic Movement of Uzbekistan, "Glad Tidings from Pakistan Part 1," *Jund Allah Studies*, January 17, 2011.
116. "Un islamiste présumé expulsé d'Ethiopie en garde à vue à la DST," *RTL*, August 30, 2007.
117. Fadl Harun, *The War Against Islam: Fadil Harun's Story*, vol. 2, Markaz Dirasat Qidhaya al-'Alam al-Islami, February 26, 2009, 583.
118. Harun, *The War Against Islam*, 2:583.
119. Harun, *The War Against Islam*, 2:591; and Sihem Bensedrine, "Tunisie: Quatre Tunisiens prisonniers de l'armée éthiopienne," *AllAfrica*, July 25, 2007.
120. Botha, "Terrorism in Maghreb," 118–19.
121. "Que faisait l'internaute de Zarzis tué en Somalie?," *Jeune Afrique*, August 6, 2007.
122. Botha, "Terrorism in Maghreb," 64.
123. Storm, Cruickshank, and Lister, *Agent Storm*, 37 and 43.
124. Filiu, "Ansar al-Fatah and 'Iraqi' Networks in France," 365–66.
125. Abu Mus'ab 'Abd al-Wadud, "Isha'ar bi-taghayyir al-tasmiyyah," qmagreb.org, January 24, 2007, https://web.archive.org/web/20070620152835/http://www.qmagreb.org/pages/tasmiya.html; and Ayman al-Zawahiri, "Realities of the Conflict Between Islam and Unbelief," *As-Sahab Media*, December 29, 2006.
126. "An Interview with Abdelmalek Droukdal," *New York Times*, July 1, 2008.
127. Alison Pargeter, "Radicalisation in Tunisia," in *Islamist Radicalisation in North Africa: Politics and Process*, ed. George Joffe, 71–94 (Abingdon, U.K.: Routledge, 2011), 77.
128. Botha, "Terrorism in Maghreb," 120.
129. Botha, "Terrorism in Maghreb," 120.
130. Botha, "Terrorism in Maghreb," 120.
131. Botha, "Terrorism in Maghreb," 60.
132. "L'ANP décapite le GSPC," *algerie-dz*, June 21, 2004, http://www.algerie-dz.com/article811.html; and Abu Mus'ab 'Abd al-Wadud, "To Usamah Bin Ladin About the Leadership of the Organization," U.S. Director of National Intelligence, Abbatabad files, retrieved from Bin Ladin's computer, https://www.dni.gov/files/documents/ubl2016/arabic/Arabic%20The%20Leadership%20of%20the%20Organization.pdf.
133. "L'armée encercle "l'émir du Sahara" Djouadi à El Oued," *Ennahar*, January 29, 2010. They would both, along with another deputy, be arrested by Algerian forces on January 28, 2010.
134. Botha, "Terrorism in Maghreb," 50.
135. Alison Pargeter, "The Suleiman Affair—Radicalism and Jihad in Tunisia," *Jane's Intelligence Review* 23, no. 1 (2011).
136. Interview with Montassar Anas Jemmali, youth activist, Tunis, Tunisia, August 30, 2013.
137. Interview with former senior governmental minister, Le Kram, Tunisia, February 16, 2013.
138. A year after Sassi left Italy, Tunisian courts sentenced him to twenty years in prison in absentia. Similarly, three years after that, Sassi was charged by an Italian court in the Milan Tunisian Group II plot with providing military clothing and money to the GSPC as well as financing and planning suicide attacks in Italy.
139. Pargeter, "The Suleiman Affair."

140. Pargeter, "The Suleiman Affair."
141. Craig S. Smith, "Tunisia Says Suspects in Gun Battle Had Blueprints of Embassies," *New York Times*, January 14, 2007.
142. Jean-Luc Marret, "Al-Qaeda in the Islamic Maghreb: A 'Glocal' Organization," *Studies in. Conflict and Terrorism* 31, no. 6 (June 2008): 543.
143. "Tadhakir al-qaʻimah li-mamuʼah sulayman mutmatiʼun bi-l-ʼafu al-tashriʼi al-ʼam yutazʼmun majmuʼat irhabiyah takhtit li-istihadaf masalih haywiyah," *Akhir Khabar*, May 15, 2016, available at http://www.akherkhabaronline.com.
144. "Tadhakir al-qaʻimah."
145. Where AST's leadership/religious figures spoke database, created by Aaron Y. Zelin, available at http://tunisianjihadism.com. Last updated August 10, 2016.
146. AST Facebook page, March 3, 2013. Author retains archive of post.
147. Aaron Y. Zelin, "Wanas al-Faqih Designated as a Terrorist by U.S. Department of State," *Tunisian Jihadism*, January 5, 2018.
148. Botha, "Terrorism in Maghreb," 120.
149. Botha, "Terrorism in Maghreb," 119.
150. Botha, "Terrorism in Maghreb," 120.
151. Botha, "Terrorism in Maghreb," 121.
152. Botha, "Terrorism in Maghreb," 121.
153. Botha, "Terrorism in Maghreb," 121.
154. Botha, "Terrorism in Maghreb," 121.
155. Botha, "Terrorism in Maghreb," 194.
156. Botha, "Terrorism in Maghreb," 75.
157. "Iʼtiqal shakhsayn fi shamal bilad li-l-ishtibah fi ʻilaqathuma bi-tanzim al-qaʼidah," *Wa-Kallah Nuwakashut Li-l-Anba*,' January 9, 2010, https://web.archive.org/web/20100112121811/http://www.ani.mr/?menuLink=9bf31c7ff062936a96d3c8bd1f8f2ff3&idNews=7908.
158. Botha, "Terrorism in Maghreb," 164.
159. Botha, "Terrorism in Maghreb," 122.
160. Botha, "Terrorism in Maghreb," 121.
161. Botha, "Terrorism in Maghreb," 49.
162. Botha, "Terrorism in Maghreb," 119.
163. Botha, "Terrorism in Maghreb," 121.
164. Alex Thurston, "AQIM Kidnappings and Murders in the Sahel, 2007–Present," *Sahel Blog*, January 18, 2011.
165. Western Jihadists 1993–Present.
166. "Explosions Rock Algerian Capital," *BBC News*, April 12, 2007.
167. Western Jihadists 1993–Present.
168. Javier Jordán, "The Foiled Attacks in Italy in 2006," in *The Evolution of the Global Terrorist Threat: From 9/11 to Osama bin Laden's Death*, ed. by Bruce Hoffman and Fernando Reinares, 273–88 (New York: Columbia University Press, 2014), 274.
169. Jordán, "The Foiled Attacks in Italy in 2006," 275.
170. Jordán, "The Foiled Attacks in Italy in 2006," 278.
171. Jordán, "The Foiled Attacks in Italy in 2006," 273.
172. Jordán, "The Foiled Attacks in Italy in 2006," 278.
173. Botha, "Terrorism in Maghreb," 101.
174. Botha, "Terrorism in Maghreb," 100.
175. "L'auteur de l'attentat au Mali est un Tunisien ayant 'la haine de la France,'" *TF1*, January 6, 2011.

176. Matthieu Suc, "Les confessions du "stagiaire" d'Al-Qaïda," *Media Part*, May 14, 2017.
177. Suc, "Les confessions du "stagiaire" d'Al-Qaïda."
178. Suc, "Les confessions du "stagiaire" d'Al-Qaïda."
179. Suc, "Les confessions du "stagiaire" d'Al-Qaïda."
180. Suc, "Les confessions du "stagiaire" d'Al-Qaïda."
181. Suc, "Les confessions du "stagiaire" d'Al-Qaïda."
182. Farah Samti, "Young Tunisian Sentenced to Death in Mali," *Tunisia Live*, December 4, 2011.
183. Houda Mzioudet, "Arrest Warrant Against Extradited Tunisian From Mali," *Tunisia Live*, January 2, 2012.
184. Hédi Yahmed, *Taht rayyat al-uqub: Salafiyyun jihadiyyun tunisiyyun* (Tunis: Diwan li-l-nashir, 2015).
185. "Abdullah Bin Omar," The Guantánamo Docket, *New York Times*, https://www.nytimes.com/interactive/projects/guantanamo/detainees/721-abdullah-bin-omar; and "Lufti Bin Swei Lagha," The Guantánamo Docket, *New York Times*, https://www.nytimes.com/interactive/projects/guantanamo/detainees/660-lufti-bin-swei-lagha.
186. Western Jihadists 1993–Present.
187. Hadi Yahmad, "Hiwar ma' Sayf Allah bin Hasin (Abu 'Iyadh)," *Jaridat al-Haqa'iq al-Tunisiyyah*, December 11, 2011.
188. Decree Law No. 1 for the Year 2011 on the Date of February 19, 2011, Relating to the General Amnesty, *Journal Officiel de la République Tunisienne*, Year 154, no. 12, February 22, 2011, http://www.iort.gov.tn/WD120AWP/WD120Awp.exe/CTX_5436-26-LxtITUmekq/AfficheJORT/SYNC_1580747203, p. 183; and *Report of the Special Rapporteur on the Promotion and Protection of Human Rights and Fundamental Freedoms While Countering Terrorism*, Martin Scheinin, UN General Assembly, Human Rights Council, Twentieth Session, Agenda Item 3, March 14, 2012, p. 7.

4. Sons of Tunisia

1. Alexis Arieff, "Political Transition in Tunisia," *Congressional Research Service*, April 15, 2011.
2. Lufti Hajji, "The 18 October Coalition for Rights and Freedoms in Tunisia," *Arab Reform Initiative*, Arab Reform Bulletin, October 13, 2006, 3–4.
3. "Tunisie: Tous les prisonniers politiques auraient été libérés," *Le Monde*, March 2, 2011.
4. *Tunisia: Violence and the Salafi Challenge*, International Crisis Group, Middle East/North Africa Report No.137, February 13, 2013, https://d2071andvipowj.cloudfront.net/tunisia-violence-and-the-salafi-challenge.pdf, p. 14.
5. Fabio Merone and Francesco Cavatorta, "The Emergence of Salafism in Tunisia," *Jadaliyya*, August 17, 2012.
6. Erik Churchill, "A Note on "Jihadi Soft Power in Tunisia," *Kefteji*, February 22, 2012.
7. Alexis Arieff, "Political Transition in Tunisia," *Congressional Research Service*, September 20, 2011; and Aaron Y. Zelin, "The Rise of Salafists in Tunisia After the Fall of Ben Ali," *CTC Sentinel*, August 2011.
8. Arieff, "Political Transition in Tunisia," April 15, 2011.
9. Sabina Henneberg, "Governing Uncertainty: Challenges for the First Tunisian Provisional Administration of 2011 and Its Impacts in 2012–2014," *British Journal of Middle Eastern Studies*, July 2018, http://dx.doi.org/10.1080/13530194.2018.1493375.
10. Arieff, "Political Transition in Tunisia," September 20, 2011.

11. Monica Marks, "Ennahda's Rules of Engagement," *Sada*, October 18, 2012.
12. Jaridat al-Haqa'iaq al-Tunisiyyah interview with Abu 'Iyadh al-Tunisi, December 22, 2011.
13. "Tunisian Islamist Leader Says Salafis Must Not Be Demonized," Reuters, October 18, 2012.
14. Monica Marks, "Tunisia's Ennahda: Rethinking Islamism in the Context of ISIS and the Egyptian Coup," Project on US Relations with the Islamic World at Brookings, Rethinking Islamism Series, Working Paper, August 2015, p. 5.
15. Denise Yamin, "al-Jabal li-al-safir: lam ya't al-salafiyyun min al-marrikh … wa lan nadha'hum fi al-sijn," *al-Safir*, May 11, 2012, http://assafir.com/Article/275055/Archive.
16. "Tunisia: Violence and the Salafi Challenge," 30.
17. Merone and Cavatorta, "The Emergence of Salafism in Tunisia."
18. Ansar al-Sharia in Tunisia, "About the Tunisian Elections," October 22, 2011. Maintained in my archives.
19. Aaron Y. Zelin, "The Salafi Challenge to Tunisia's Nascent Democracy," *Washington Institute for Near East Policy*, Policy Watch #1879, December 8, 2011.
20. "Tunisia: Violence and the Salafi Challenge," 31.
21. Syrine Guediche, "Tunisie: Le double discours de Rached Ghannouchi à propos des Salafistes," *Tunisie Numerique*, September 24, 2012.
22. "Rached Ghannouchi: Le salafisme tel qu'on le voit en Tunisie est un projet de guerre civile," *Business News Tunisia*, March 28, 2012.
23. "Il n'appartient pas à l'Etat d'imposer un mode particulier de se vêtir, de se nourrir, de consommer des boissons ou de suivre des coutumes," *La Presse de Tunisie*, July 31, 2012.
24. Marks, "Ennahda's Rules of Engagement."
25. Marks, "Tunisia's Ennahda," 6.
26. Interview with founding member of AST, August 29, 2013, Le Lac, Tunisia.
27. The video was originally on YouTube at this link: https://www.youtube.com/watch?v=151rBh6ok5s. It has since been taken down but has been reported upon extensively in the Tunisian press.
28. Tarek Amara, "Tunisia Islamist Causes Outcry with 'Caliphate' Talk," Reuters, November 15, 2011.
29. "Tunisia: Violence and the Salafi Challenge," 7.
30. Erik Churchill, "Shaping Ennahda's Re-Election Strategy," *Foreign Policy's Middle East Channel*, March 27, 2012.
31. Rory McCarthy, "Protecting the Sacred: Tunisia's Islamist Movement Ennahdha and the Challenge of Free Speech," *British Journal of Middle Eastern Studies* 42, no. 4 (February 2015), 457.
32. "Tunisia: Violence and the Salafi Challenge," 2.
33. "Tunisia: Violence and the Salafi Challenge," 7.
34. "Tunisia: Violence and the Salafi Challenge," 35.
35. Marks, "Ennahda's Rules of Engagement."
36. Erik Churchill, "After Extremists Riot, Political Brinkmanship Creates Major Risks for Tunisian Revolution," *Kefteji*, June 13, 2012.
37. Paul Schemm, "Tunisian Islamists Spark Fear of Culture War," Associated Press, March 9, 2012.
38. Schemm, "Tunisian Islamists Spark Fear of Culture War."
39. Erik Churchill, "Standing up for a Salafist—Defending Offensive Speech in Tunisia," *Kefteji*, May 10, 2012.
40. Erik Churchill, "Tunisian Transition Leader Speaks Out—A Must Read Interview," *Kefteji*, April 13, 2012.

41. Erik Churchill, "Thug Violence vs. Salafist Violence—Do Definitions Really Matter?," *Kefteji*, June 19, 2012.
42. Churchill, "Thug Violence vs. Salafist Violence."
43. "Tunisia: Violence and the Salafi Challenge," 36.
44. "Tunisia: Violence and the Salafi Challenge," 37.
45. "Tunisia: Violence and the Salafi Challenge," 38.
46. Sarah Leah Whitson, "Letter to Tunisian Minister of Interior and Minister of Justice," Human Rights Watch, October 14, 2012, https://www.hrw.org/news/2012/10/14/letter-tunisian-minister-interior-and-minister-justice.
47. "Islamist Leader Attacked at 'Tolerance in Islam' Conference," *Tunisia Live*, August 6, 2012.
48. Marks, "Tunisia's Ennahda," 6.
49. Hédi Yahmed, *Taht rayyat al-uqub: salafiyyun jihadiyyun tunisiyyun* (Tunis: Diwan li-l-nashir, 2015).
50. Jamal al-Farshishi, "Tunis: Shuru wa abu 'iyadh wajaha lujahu," *al-Sabah*, October 1, 2012.
51. Marks, "Ennahda's Rules of Engagement."
52. Habib Sayah, "The Next Insurgency in Tunisia," *Fikra Forum*, February 12, 2013.
53. Monica Marks, "Tunisia in Turmoil," *Foreign Policy's Middle East Channel*, July 26, 2013.
54. "Tunisia PM Links Ansar al-Sharia Islamists to 'Terror,'" Agence France-Presse, May 20, 2013.
55. Andrew Lebovich, "Confronting Tunisia's Jihadists," *Foreign Policy's Middle East Channel*, May 16, 2013.
56. Aaron Y. Zelin, "Tunis Designates Ansar al-Sharia in Tunisia," *al-Wasat*, August 28, 2013.
57. "Bushra sara li-l-muwahidin // qariban iftaah mu'wassaat al-qayrawan al-i'alami—in sha allah," al-Qayrawan Media Foundation (blog), April 27, 2011, http://www.al-qayrawan.blogspot.com/2011/04/blog-post.html.
58. "#Khabar muhim# bushra sara || inaq'ad miltaqa ansar al-shari'ah || bi-tunis al 'asimah 18 jumada al-thaniyyah 1432—in sha allah," al-Qayrawan Media Foundation (blog), May 15, 2011, http://www.al-qayrawan.blogspot.com/2011/05/18-1432.html.
59. Yahmed, *Taht rayyat al-uqub*.
60. "Abderraouf Ayadi: 'Je suis honoré d'avoir soutenu les salafistes,'" *Shems FM*.
61. Facebook post of Miltiqa Ansar al-Shari'ah (originally located at https://www.facebook.com/Molta9a.Ansar.Alchari3a), October 9, 2011. Maintained in my archives.
62. Facebook post #2 of Miltiqa Ansar al-Shari'ah, October 9, 2011. Maintained in my archives.
63. Facebook post of Miltiqa Ansar al-Shari'ah, October 11, 2011. Maintained in my archives.
64. Iris Kolman, "Gender Activism in Salafism: A Case Study of Salafi Women in Tunisia," in *Salafism After the Arab Awakening: Contending with People's Power*, ed. by Francesco Cavatorta and Fabio Merone (Oxford: Oxford University Press, 2016), 193.
65. Facebook post of Miltiqa Ansar al-Shari'ah, October 18, 2011. Maintained in my archives.
66. Wiem Melki, "Owner of Nessma TV Fined 2,400 Dinars in Persepolis Trial, *Tunisia Live*, May 3, 2012.
67. Roxane Farmanfarmaian, "Media and the politics of the sacral: freedom of expression in Tunisia after the Arab Uprisings," *Media, Culture & Society* 39, no. 7, 2017, https://doi.org/10.1177%2F0163443717690817.

68. Monica Marks, "Tunisia's Student Salafis," *Foreign Policy's Middle East Channel*, January 6, 2012.
69. Interview with Habib Kazdaghli, Dean of the School of Letters, Arts, and Humanities at Manouba College, February 16, 2013.
70. "Tunisian Detainee Dies After Hunger Strike," *al-Jazeera*, November 17, 2012.
71. Interview with Habib Kazdaghli.
72. "Tunisia Secular, Islamist Students Clash on Campus," Reuters, November 29, 2011.
73. Hassassi Hend, "Classes Cancelled but Clashes Continue at Tunisian University," *Tunisia Live*, November 30, 2011.
74. *al-Shuruq al-Tunisiyyah* interview with Abu 'Iyadh, March 17, 2012.
75. Facebook post of Miltiqa Ansar al-Shari'ah, March 8, 2012. Maintained in my archives.
76. Facebook post of Miltiqa Ansar al-Shari'ah, March 8, 2012.
77. Asma Ghribi, "Tunisians Erupt in Anger over Desecration of Flag," *Tunisia Live*, March 9, 2012.
78. Interview with Nabil Cherni, English teacher at the School of Letters, Arts, and Humanities at Manouba College, February 16, 2013.
79. Ali Houissa, "Tunisian Student Stands up to Salafists Over Flag," Cornell University Middle East & Islamic Studies Collection (blog), March 29, 2012.
80. Churchill, "Thug Violence vs. Salafist Violence."
81. Marks, "Tunisia's Student Salafis."
82. Marks, "Tunisia's Student Salafis."
83. "Tunisia: Fundamentalists Disrupting College Campuses," Human Rights Watch, December 9, 2011, https://www.hrw.org/news/2011/12/09/tunisia-fundamentalists-disrupting-college-campuses.
84. Sana Ajmi, "Man Accused of Desecrating Tunisian Flag Turns Himself In," *Tunisia Live*, April 5, 2012.
85. Houda Mzioudet, "Mosque Tagged with Red Star of David and Quran Desecration Highlights Islamist-Secularist Divide in Tunisia," *Tunisia Live*, March 18, 2012.
86. Tarek Amara, "Tunisian Islamists Step up Demand for Islamic State," Reuters, March 25, 2012.
87. Ansar al-Shari'ah in Tunisia, "Nusrah al-shari'ah fi tunis al-islam," al-Bayyariq Media, March 25, 2012.
88. Ahmad Ellali, "Several Thousand Salafists Demonstrate for Islamic Law, Attack Dramatists in Tunisia," *Tunisia Live*, March 25, 2012.
89. Ellali, "Several Thousand Salafists Demonstrate."
90. Habib Toumi, "Al Nahda's Decision on Legislation Source Sparks Controversy in Tunisia," *Gulf News*, March 27, 2012.
91. *al-Shuruq al-Tunisiyyah* interview with Abu 'Iyadh.
92. Jaridat al-Haqa'iaq al-Tunisiyyah interview with Abu 'Iyadh al-Tunisi.
93. For more on other incidents, see Daveed Gartenstein-Ross, "Stringtime for Salafists," *Foreign Policy*, March 26, 2013.

5. Tunisia Is a Land of *Dawa*

1. Muhammad 'Ali Khalifah, "Abu 'Iyadh fi hadith khasa wa-muthir li-l-Shuruq," *Jaridat al-Shuruq al-Tunisiyyah*, March 17, 2012.
2. Hadi Yahmad, "Hiwar ma' Sayf Allah bin Hasin (Abu 'Iyadh)," *Jaridat al-Haqa'iq al-Tunisiyyah*, December 11, 2011.

3. Brynjar Lia and Thomas Hegghammer, "Jihadi Strategic Studies: The Alleged Al Qaida Policy Study Preceding the Madrid Bombings," *Studies in Conflict and Terrorism* 27, no. 5, 2004.
4. Steven Brooke, "Jihadist Strategic Debates before 9/11," *Studies in Conflict and Terrorism* 31, no. 3 (2008): 201–26.
5. Joas Wagemakers, "Reclaiming Scholarly Authority: Abu Muhammad al-Maqdisi's Critique of Jihadi Practices," *Studies in Conflict and Terrorism* 34, no. 7 (2011): 523–39; and Joas Wagemakers, "Protecting Jihad: The Sharia Council of the Minbar al-Tawhid wa-l-Jihad," *Middle East Policy* 18, no. 2 (Summer 2011).
6. Michael W. S. Ryan, *Decoding al-Qaeda's Strategy: The Deep Battle Against America* (New York: Columbia University Press, 2013); Kenneth Payne, "Building the Base: Al Qaeda's Focoist Strategy," *Studies in Conflict and Terrorism* 34, no. 2 (2011): 124–43; Mark Stout, "In Search of Salafi Jihadist Strategic Thought: Mining the Words of the Terrorists," *Studies in Conflict and Terrorism* 32, no. 10 (2009): 876–92; and Daveed Gartenstein-Ross, Jason Fritz, Bridget Moreng, and Nathaniel Barr, "Islamic State vs. al-Qaeda: Strategic Dimensions of a Patricidal Conflict," *New America Foundation*, December 2015.
7. Dima Adamsky, "Jihadi Operational Art: The Coming Wave of Jihadi Strategic Studies," *Studies in Conflict and Terrorism* 33, no. 1 (2009): 1–19.
8. Ayman al-Zawahiri, "General Guidelines for the Work of a Jihadi," al-Sahab Media, September 14, 2013.
9. Abu 'Ubayd al-Qurashi, "al-Hurub al-Thawriyyah," *Majallat Al-Ansar*, January 15, 2002, 10–15.
10. Ryan, *Decoding al-Qaeda's Strategy*, 143–46.
11. Yahmad, "Hiwar ma' Sayf Allah bin Hasin (Abu 'Iyadh)."
12. George Packer, "Exporting Jihad: The Arab Spring Has Given Tunisians the Freedom to Act on Their Unhappiness," *New Yorker*, March 28, 2016.
13. Packer, "Exporting Jihad."
14. Brian H. Fishman, *The Master Plan: ISIS, al-Qaeda, and the Jihadi Strategy for Final Victory* (New Haven, Conn.: Yale University Press, 2016), 38.
15. Abu Bakr Naji, "Idarat al-tawahush: Akhtar marhalah satamuru biha al-ummah," 2005, 15, https://archive.org/details/dorarr.blogspot.com-books/page/n1.
16. Naji, "Idarat al-tawahush," 11.
17. Ryan, *Decoding al-Qaeda's Strategy*, 244–45.
18. Christopher Anzalone, "Missionaries of Jihad," *Foreign Policy*, June 3, 2011.
19. Naji, "Idarat al-tawahush," 2005, 7.
20. Abu Mus'ab al-Suri, *The Global Islamic Resistance Call*, published online at https://archive.org/details/The-call-for-a-global-Islamic-resistance/page/n13 (2005).
21. al-Suri, *The Global Islamic Resistance Call*.
22. Daveed Gartenstein-Ross and Tara Vassefi, "Perceptions of the 'Arab Spring' Within the Salafi-Jihadi Movement," *Studies in Conflict and Terrorism* 35, no. 12 (December 2012): 831–48.
23. William McCants, "Militant Ideology Atlas," Combating Terrorism Center, November 1, 2006, https://ctc.usma.edu/app/uploads/2012/04/Atlas-ResearchCompendium1.pdf.
24. Wagemakers, "Reclaiming Scholarly Authority," 524.
25. Abu Muhammad al-Maqdisi, *Waqafat ma' thamrat al-jihad* (Minbar al-Tawhid wa-l-Jihad), 2004.
26. Aaron Y. Zelin, "Maqdisi's Disciples in Libya and Tunisia," *Foreign Policy's Middle East Channel*, November 14, 2012.

27. Assaf Moghadam and Brian Fishman, eds., *Fault Lines in Global Jihad: Organizational, Strategic, and Ideological Fissures* (London: Routledge, 2013); Camille Tawil, *Brothers In Arms: The Story of al-Qa'ida and the Arab Jihadists* (London: Saqi Books, 2011); Mustafa Hamid and Leah Farrall, *The Arabs at War in Afghanistan* (London: Hurst, 2015); and Barak Mendelsohn, *The al-Qaeda Franchise: The Expansion of al-Qaeda and Its Consequences* (Oxford: Oxford University Press, 2016).
28. Suri, *The Global Islamic Resistance Call*.
29. Thomas Hegghammer, "The Ideological Hybridization of Jihadi Groups," *Current Trends in Islamist Ideology*, no. 9 (November 2009).
30. Zawahiri's Letter to Zarqawi, July 9, 2005, private letter intercepted by the U.S. military, available at Combating Terrorism Center, https://ctc.usma.edu/harmony-program/zawahiris-letter-to-zarqawi-original-language-2/.
31. Zawahiri's Letter to Zarqawi.
32. Zawahiri's Letter to Zarqawi.
33. 'Atiyat Allah's Letter to Zarqawi, December 12, 2005.
34. 'Atiyat Allah's Letter to Zarqawi.
35. Gadahn's Letter suggesting letting go of ISI, late January 2011, obtained by the U.S. military from Bin Ladin's computer at Abbotobad, available at http://www.jihadica.com/wp-content/uploads/2012/05/SOCOM-2012-0000004-Orig.pdf.
36. Christopher Anzalone, "Revisiting Shaykh Atiyyatullah's Works on Takfir and Mass Violence," *CTC Sentinel* 5, no. 4 (April 2012).
37. Khalifah, "Abu 'Iyadh fi hadith khasa wa-muthir li-l-Shuruq."
38. For his full archive, see "Category: Khālid bin 'Abd al-Raḥman al-Husaynān [Abū Zayd al-Kūwaytī]," at *Jihadology*, http://jihadology.net/category/individuals/ideologues/khalid-bin-abd-al-ra%E1%B8%A5man-al-husaynan-abu-zayd-al-kuwayti.
39. For his full archive, see "Category: Hārith bin Ghāzī al-Naẓāri [Muḥammad al-Mirshadī]," at *Jihadology*, http://jihadology.net/category/individuals/ideologues/harith-bin-ghazi-al-na%E1%BA%93ari-mu%E1%B8%A5ammad-al-mirshadi.
40. For their full archives, see "Category: Shaykh al-Ḥasan Rashīd al-Bulaydī," at *Jihadology*, http://jihadology.net/category/individuals/ideologues/shaykh-al-%E1%B8%A5asan-rashid-al-bulaydi; and "Category: Dr. Sāmī al 'Arīdī," at *Jihadology*, http://jihadology.net/category/individuals/ideologues/dr-sami-al-aridi.
41. Mona Ben Gamra, "Exclusif: Le leader des salafistes djihadistes, Seif Allah Ben Hassine alias Abou Yadh au 'Temps,'" *Le Temps*, March 30, 2012.
42. Yahmad, "Hiwar ma' Sayf Allah bin Hasin (Abu 'Iyadh)."
43. Yahmad, "Hiwar ma' Sayf Allah bin Hasin (Abu 'Iyadh)."
44. Yahmad, "Hiwar ma' Sayf Allah bin Hasin (Abu 'Iyadh)."
45. Yahmad, "Hiwar ma' Sayf Allah bin Hasin (Abu 'Iyadh)."
46. Louisa Loveluck, "Planting the Seeds of Tunisia's Ansar al Sharia," *Foreign Policy's Middle East Channel*, September 27, 2012.
47. Interview with founding member of AST, August 29, 2013, Le Lac, Tunisia.
48. Francesco Cavatorta, "Salafism, Liberalism, and Democratic Learning in Tunisia," *Journal of North African Studies* 20, no. 5 (2015): 770–83.
49. Ashraf al-Tabib, "Qiyadi Salafi Jihadi Sayf Allah bin Hasin (Abu 'Iyadh) yatahadath l-al-usubu'i: Sir khatir wara' ahadath Sijnan . . . al-Astul al-Sadis al-Amriki yurid iqama qa'idah tansat fiha," *al-Sabah*, March 26, 2012.
50. Interview with founding member of AST, August 29, 2013.
51. Yahmad, "Hiwar ma' Sayf Allah bin Hasin (Abu 'Iyadh)."
52. Abu 'Iyadh al-Tunisi, "Bi-munasimah al-mu'tamar al-sanuwi al-thalith li-ansar al-shari'ah bi-tunis," al-Bayyariq Media, May 23, 2013.

53. Robert D. Benford and David A. Snow, "Ideology, Frame Resonance, and Participant Mobilization," *International Social Movement Research* 1 (1988): 200–201.
54. Shaykh Abu al-Mundhir al-Shinqiti, "Question About How Things Happened in Tunisia," *Minbar al-Tawhid wa-l-Jihad*, January 19, 2011.
55. Shaykh Abu Basir al-Tartusi, "Fall of the Idol Zayn, the Devil Named Zayn al 'Abidin," January 19, 2011, https://jihadology.net/2011/01/19/new-statement-from-shaykh-abu-basir-al-%e1%b9%adar%e1%b9%adusi-fall-of-the-idol-zayn-the-devil-named-zayn-al-abidin.
56. Abu Muslim al-Jaza'iri, "To Our Brothers and Families in Tunisia," *Minbar al-Tawhid wa-l-Jihad*, February 8, 2011, https://jihadology.net/2011/02/08/new-article-from-abu-muslim-al-jazairi-of-minbar-at-taw%e1%b8%a5id-wal-jihad-to-our-brothers-and-families-in-tunisia.
57. al-Qaeda in the Islamic Maghrib, "To Our People in Tunisia: The Tyrant Has Fled but the Infidel and Tyrannical System Remains," al-Andalus Media, January 28, 2011.
58. Shaykh Ibrahim bin Sulayman al-Rubaysh, "Ben 'Ali and Ibn Sa'ud," al-Malahim Media, February 26, 2011.
59. Hamzah bin Muhammad al-Bassam, "First Installment: The Sociable Benefits and the Uprisings Across Egypt and Tunisia," *Nukhbat al-I'alam al-Jihadi*, February 26, 2011.
60. Bassam, "First Installment."
61. Jaza'iri, "To Our Brothers and Families in Tunisia."
62. Cavatorta, "Salafism, Liberalism, and Democratic Learning in Tunisia."
63. Originally available on YouTube in December 2011 at this link: https://www.youtube.com/watch?v=ycEWYknD9kI.
64. Originally available on You Tube in December 2011 at this link: https://www.youtube.com/watch?v=ycEWYknD9kI.
65. Letter from Usamah Bin Ladin to 'Atiyat Allah al-Libi, April 26, 2011, obtained by the U.S. military from Bin Ladin's computer at Abbotobad, available athttps://ctc.usma.edu/app/uploads/2013/10/Letter-from-UBL-to-Atiyatullah-Al-Libi-2-Original.pdf.
66. Shinqiti, "Question About How Things Happened in Tunisia."
67. Shinqiti, "Question About How Things Happened in Tunisia."
68. al-Qaeda in the Islamic Maghrib, "To Our People in Tunisia."
69. 'Atiyyat Allah Abu 'Abd ar-Rahman al-Libi, "The Popular Revolution and the Fall of the Corrupt Arab System," al-Fajr Media, February 24, 2011.
70. SOCOM-2012-0000010.
71. Interview with members of AST, Sousse, Tunisia, February 19, 2013.
72. Yahmad, "Hiwar ma' Sayf Allah bin Hasin (Abu 'Iyadh)."
73. Jaza'iri, "To Our Brothers and Families in Tunisia."
74. Abu Muslim al-Jaza'iri, "Urgent Questions Concerning the Situation of Tunisia," *Minbar al-Tawhid wa-l-Jihad*, February 25, 2011.
75. Shaykh Abu al-Mundhir al-Shinqiti, "What Is the Ruling for Formal Affiliation with al-Nahdah?," *Minbar al-Tawhid wa-l-Jihad*, March 7, 2011.
76. Shaykh Abu al-Mundhir al-Shinqiti, "Ruling on Joining al-Nahdah the Tunisian Party for Structural Reform," *Minbar al-Tawhid wa-l-Jihad*, May 10, 2011.
77. Shaykh Abu al-Mundhir al-Shinqiti, "Is It Permissible to Vote for al-Nahdah?," *Minbar al-Tawhid wa-l-Jihad*, September 24, 2011; and Shaykh Abu al-Mundhir al-Shinqiti, "Some Questions About the Elections in Tunisia," *Minbar al-Tawhid wa-l-Jihad*, October 10, 2011.
78. Ayman al-Zawahiri, "Oh People of Tunisia Support Your Shari'ah," al-Sahab Media, June 11, 2012.
79. Interview with founding member of AST, August 29, 2013.

80. Abu Mus'ab 'Abd al-Wadud ('Abd al-Malik Drukdil), "In Support of the Intifadah of our People in Tunisia," al-Andalus Media, January 13, 2011.
81. Jaza'iri, "To Our Brothers and Families in Tunisia."
82. Loveluck, "Planting the Seeds of Tunisia's Ansar al Sharia."
83. Yahmad, "Hiwar ma' Sayf Allah bin Hasin (Abu 'Iyadh)."
84. Khalifah, "Abu 'Iyadh fi hadith khasa wa-muthir li-l-Shuruq."
85. Tabib, "Qiyadi Salafi Jihadi Sayf Allah bin Hasin (Abu 'Iyadh)."
86. Gamra, "Exclusif."
87. "Osama bin Laden Wanted to Change al-Qaeda's Name for Marketing Reasons," *Telegraph*, June 24, 2011.
88. "Liqa' maftuh ma' Shaykh Abu Zubayr 'Adil bin 'Abd Allah al-Abab," Ghorfah Minbar al-Ansar, April 19, 2011.
89. Shaykh Abu al-Mundhir al-Shinqiti, "We Are Ansar al-Shari'ah," *Minbar al-Tawhid wa-l-Jihad*, June 18, 2012.
90. Abu 'Iyadh al-Tunisi, "Answer to the Essay of Abu Maysarah al-Shami: Letters to Dr. Ayman al-Zawahiri," Hidayyah Media, January 6, 2016.

6. Hear from Us, Not About Us

1. Diana Kendall, *Sociology in Our Times* (Independence, Ky.: Thomson Wadsworth, 2016), 601.
2. Peter Neumann, Ryan Evans, and Raffaello Pantucci, "Locating Al Qaeda's Center of Gravity: The Role of Middle Managers," *Studies in Conflict and Terrorism* 34, no. 11 (November 2011): 825–42.
3. Ansar al-Shari'ah in Tunisia, "First Da'wah Forum in Hammam-Lif," al-Bayyariq Media, March 31, 2013.
4. Francesco Cavatorta, "Salafism, Liberalism, and Democratic Learning in Tunisia," *Journal of North African Studies* 20, no. 5 (2015): 770–83.
5. Interview with founding member of AST, Le Lac, Tunisia, August 29, 2013.
6. Rory McCarthy, *Inside Tunisia's al-Nahda: Between Politics and Preaching* (Cambridge: Cambridge University Press, 2018), 149.
7. "Tunisie: Cinq morts suite à une vague de froid "exceptionnelle,"" *L'Obs*, February 12, 2012.
8. Farah Samti, "Tunisian North West Regions Endure Cold Waves and Economic Hardships," *Tunisia Live*, December 21, 2011.
9. Ansar al-Shari'ah in Tunisia, "Untitled Video of Abu 'Iyadh Speech," al-Bayyariq Media, February 20, 2012.
10. Ansar al-Shari'ah in Tunisia, "'The Believers Are but Brothers': Aid Convoy to Haydrah," al-Bayyariq Media, February 20, 2012. For more on that particular campaign, see Aaron Y. Zelin, "Jihadi Soft Power in Tunisia: Ansar al-Shari'ah's Convoy Provides Aid to the Town of Haydrah in West Central Tunisia," *al-Wasat* (blog), February 12, 2012, https://thewasat.wordpress.com/2012/02/21/jihadi-soft-power-in-tunisia-ansar-al-shariahs-convoy-provides-aid-to-the-town-of-haydrah-in-west-central-tunisia-with-pictures.
11. AST's branches that organized convoys outside their home locations: Al-Qayrawan, Bekalta, Ben Arous, Béni Khiar, Bizerte, Cité El Khadra, El Krib, El Ouardia, Hammam Al Agzaz, Hammamet, Jemmal, Mahdia, Mateur, Menzel Bourguiba, Manzil Bu Zalafah, Monastir, Northern Suburbs, Sfax, Sidi Bouzid, Sousse, Southern Suburbs, Western Suburbs, Tunis, and Zaghouan.

12. Anne Wolf, *Political Islam in Tunisia: The History* (London: Hurst, 2017), 139–40.
13. Interview with founding member of AST.
14. Nineteen of the activities were in unknown locations.
15. Michael Marcusa, "My Two Weeks with the Jihadists," *Atlantic*, August 15, 2013.
16. International Crisis Group, "Tunisia's Borders: Jihadism and Contraband," International Crisis Group, Report No. 148, November 28, 2013.
17. Andrew Lebovich, "Confronting Tunisia's Jihadists," *Middle East Channel*, May 16, 2013.
18. Michael Marcusa, "Radicalism on the Periphery: History, Collective Memory, and the Cultural Resonance of Jihadist Ideology in Tunisia," *Comparative Politics* 51, no. 2 (January 2019).
19. Christopher Barrie and Neil Ketchley, "Is Protest a Safety Valve Against ISIS in Tunisia?," *Washington Post*, December 10, 2018, https://www.washingtonpost.com/news/monkey-cage/wp/2018/12/10/is-protest-a-safety-valve-against-isis-in-tunisia/?utm_term=.5d7556e13903.
20. Ansar al-Sharia in Tunisia, "Receiving and Carrying Yusri al-Tariqi's Body," al-Bayyariq Media, November 23, 2011.
21. Ansar al-Sharia in Tunisia, "Helping Refugees at Tunisian-Libyan Border," al-Bayyariq Media, March 2–4, 2011.
22. Their website is not live, but an archived version is available here: https://web.archive.org/web/20140328003024/http://azzahrawi.org.tn.
23. Ansar al-Sharia in Tunisia, "Medical Services in Ksour Essef," al-Bayyariq Media, April 22, 2012.
24. Ansar al-Sharia in Tunisia, "Medical Services in Sidi Bouzid," al-Bayyariq Media, November 11, 2012.
25. Eric Reidy, "Tunisia Cracks Down on Radicalization," *al-Monitor*, May 19, 2015.
26. McCarthy, *Inside Tunisia's al-Nahda*, 145.
27. Anne Wolf, "The Radicalization of Tunisia's Mosques," *CTC Sentinel* 7, no. 6 (June 2014).
28. Reidy, "Tunisia Cracks Down on Radicalization."
29. Reidy, "Tunisia Cracks Down on Radicalization."
30. "State Wrests Back Control of Last Mosque Beyond Control (Minister)," *Tunisian African Press*, July 2, 2016.
31. 1/1000 of a Tunisian dinar.
32. Ansar al-Sharia in Tunisia, "Yawm al-thalatha' in sha' allah satanataliq hawiyah tuhamil al-wasa'il al-daw'iyah ila tunis," al-Qayrawan Media, December 19, 2011.
33. Ansar al-Sharia in Tunisia, "Showing al-Qaeda Video 'The West and the Tunnel' at La Cagna Mosque," *al-Bayyariq Media*, January 5, 2013; and Ansar al-Sharia in Tunisia, "Showing al-Qaeda Video 'The West and the Tunnel' at al-Taqwa Mosque in El Ouardia," *al-Bayyariq Media*, January 14, 2013.
34. Based on AST's public pronouncements, it organized at least thirteen *dawa* tents and distributed AST literature at schools in the following locations: Le Kram, Jemmal (twice), La Marsa, Bou Mhel el-Bassatine, Téboulba, Sabalat Ouled Asker, Sfax, Béni Khiar, Sijoumi, al-Qayrawan, Ariana, and Borj Louzir.
35. Ansar al-Shari'ah in Tunisia, "Cubs of Ansar al-Sharia in Sfax," al-Bayyariq Media, June 2, 2013.
36. Ansar al-Sharia in Tunisia, "Soccer Lesson for the Cubs of Islam in Mateur," al-Bayyariq Media, October 28, 2012.
37. *The Islamic Imagery Project: Visual Motifs in Jihadi Internet Propaganda* (West Point, N.Y.: Combating Terrorism Center, March 2006), 29–32.

38. Ansar al-Sharia in Tunisia, "Sports Tournament for the Cubs of the Supporters in El Krib," al-Bayyariq Media, March 28, 2013; Ansar al-Sharia in Tunisia, "Leisure Trip of the Children Towards Natural Attractions of the Region from Douar Hicher," al-Bayyariq Media, April 29, 2013; and Ansar al-Sharia in Tunisia, "Cubs of Tawhid Camp in Alataya," al-Bayyariq Media, June 23, 2013.
39. Ansar al-Shari'ah in Tunisia, "Surat al-Mariyyam Contest in Tunis," al-Bayyariq Media, January 1, 2013; Ansar al-Shari'ah in Tunisia "Awards to Children at al-Salam Neighborhood School in Bou Mhel el-Bassatine," al-Bayyariq Media, March 15, 2013; and Ansar al-Shari'ah in Tunisia, "Children Refresher Day in the Northern Suburbs," al-Bayyariq Media, May 1, 2013.
40. Ansar al-Shari'ah in Tunisia, "Cubs of Tawhid at a Party in Menzel Bourguiba," al-Bayyariq Media, June 4, 2011; Ansar al-Shari'ah in Tunisia "Children's Party for the End of Ramadan in El Krib," al-Bayyariq Media, August 4, 2013; and Ansar al-Shari'ah in Tunisia, "Party at Conclusion of Children's Session 'In the Shadow of the Qur'an' in Kalaa Kebira," al-Bayyariq Media, August 4, 2013.
41. Ansar al-Shari'ah in Tunisia, "Main Road Maintenance Campaign in Ariana," al-Bayyariq Media, March 10, 2013; Ansar al-Shari'ah in Tunisia, "Cleaning Campaign in Ez Zahra," al-Bayyariq Media, March 27, 2013; and Ansar al-Shari'ah in Tunisia, "Da'wah Tour in the Neighborhoods of al-Mitlawi," al-Bayyariq Media, June 1, 2013.
42. Jonathan A. C. Brown, *Misquoting Muhammad: The Challenge and Choices of Interpreting the Prophet's Legacy* (London: Oneworld, 2014), 279–80.
43. For more on The Islamic State's use of Wahhabi heritage, see Cole Bunzel, *The Kingdom and the Caliphate: Duel of the Islamic States* (Washington, D.C.: Carnegie Endowment for International Peace, February 2016), https://carnegieendowment.org/files/CP_265_Bunzel_Islamic_States_Final.pdf; and Jacob Olidort, *Inside the Caliphate's Classroom: Textbooks, Guidance Literature, and Indoctrination Methods of the Islamic State*, Washington Institute for Near East Policy, Policy Focus, no. 147 (August 2016), https://www.washingtoninstitute.org/uploads/Documents/pubs/PolicyFocus147-Olidort-5.pdf.
44. Robert D. Benford and David A. Snow, "Ideology, Frame Resonance, and Participant Mobilization," *International Social Movement Research* 1 (1988): 200–201.
45. Arie W. Kruglanski, Michele J. Gelfand, Jocelyn J. Bélanger, Anna Sheveland, Malkanthi Hetiarachchi, and Rohan Gunaratna, "The Psychology of Radicalization and Deradicalization: How Significance Quest Impacts Violent Extremism," *Advances in Political Psychology* 35, S1 (2014): 73.
46. Graham Usher, "That Other Tunisia," *Nation*, August 24, 2011.
47. Hadi Yahmad, "Hiwar ma' Sayf Allah bin Hasin (Abu 'Iyadh)," *Jaridat al-Haqa'iq al-Tunisiyyah*, December 11, 2011.
48. Jeff Goodwin and James M. Jasper, "Emotions and Social Movements," in *Handbook of the Sociology of Emotions*, ed. by Jan E. Stets and Jonathan H. Turner (New York: Springer, 2006), 625.
49. Fabio Merone, "Salafism in Tunisia: An Interview with a Member of Ansar al-Sharia," *Jadaliyya*, April 11, 2013.
50. Leila Fadel, "Tunisia's Salafis: 'A Danger' or Preachers of God's Law?," *NPR*, January 29, 2013.
51. Ansar al-Shari'ah in Tunisia, "Graphic Announcing the Second Annual Conference," al-Bayyariq Media, April 25, 2012.
52. Ansar al-Shari'ah in Tunisia, "Helping Needy Families in Ariana," al-Bayyariq Media, June 2, 2013.

53. Ansar al-Shari'ah in Tunisia, "Da'wah Forum in Le Kram," al-Bayyariq Media, May 11, 2013.
54. The Qur'anic verses used by AST when promoting its activities were 2:281, 3:31, 3:104, 3:139, 3:140, 5:32, 6:153, 8:39, 9:32, 9:40, 14:5, 47:7, 48:29, 49:10, 51:50, 61:8, and 61:14.
55. Lorne L. Dawson, "Challenging the Curious Erasure of Religion from the Study of Religious Terrorism," *Numen* 65, nos. 2–3 (2018), https://doi.org/10.1163/15685276-12341492.
56. Jeffry R. Halverson, R. Bennett Furlow, and Steven R. Corman, *How Islamic Extremists Quote the Qur'an*, Center for Strategic Communication at Arizona State University, Report no. 1202, July 9, 2012, 2.
57. Halverson, Furlow, and Corman, *How Islamic Extremists Quote the Qur'an*.

7. Tunisians Can Be Found Everywhere in the Land of Jihad

1. Ansar al-Sharia in Tunisia Facebook post, September 13, 2012. Author retains copy in his archives.
2. David Thompson, *Les français jihadistes* (Paris: Les Arènes, 2014), 150.
3. Interview with U.S. Embassy in Tunis official, February 21, 2013.
4. Interview with U.S. Embassy in Tunis official, February 21, 2013.
5. Abu Turab al-Tunisi's pictures, posted on September 16, 2012. Author retains copy in his archives.
6. Abu Turab al-Tunisi's pictures.
7. Thompson, *Les français jihadistes*, 153.
8. Thompson, *Les français jihadistes*, 157.
9. Interview with U.S. Embassy in Tunis official, February 21, 2013.
10. Interview with U.S. Embassy in Tunis official, February 21, 2013.
11. Donatella della Porta, "Radicalization: A Relational Perspective," *Annual Review of Political Science* 21 (2018): 461–74.
12. Abu 'Iyadh al-Tunisi, "The Dangers of the Rawafidh," al-Bayyariq Media, May 9, 2012.
13. al-Qayrawan Media Facebook post, February 24, 2012.
14. The poem in full can be found here: https://web.archive.org/web/20181210014413/http://shamela.ws:80/browse.php/book-7533/page-10.
15. "Tunisia: Female Sufi Saint Targeted by Salafis," *ANSAmed*, March 6, 2012; "Tunisia: Attackers Set Fire to Muslim Saint Shrine," Associated Press, October 16, 2012; "Tunisia Arrests Salafist Suspects Over Sufi Shrine Attack," Agence France-Presse, December 5, 2012; and "Tunisian Court Jails Salafists for Burning Sufi Shrine," Reuters, June 18, 2013.
16. "Incendie du mausolée de Sidi Bou Saïd: 'Des Coran précieux sont partis en fumée,'" *France 24*, January 14, 2013.
17. "Man Jailed for Desecrating Tunisia Leader's Tomb," Agence France-Presse, September 26, 2012; "Le mausolée Sidi Abdekader à Menzel Bouzalfa fermé par les salafistes," *ShemsFM*, September 20, 2012; and "Sufi Shrines Targeted in Tunisian Salafist Upsurge," Agence France-Presse, October 15, 2012.
18. Abu al-Mundhir al-Shinqiti, "What Is the Ruling on Burning Shrines of Righteous People in Tunisia?," *Minbar al-Tawhid wa-l-Jihad*, February 21, 2013.
19. "Tunisia Salafists Halt Iranian Concert at Sufi Festival," Agence France-Presse, August 17, 2012.
20. Afifa Ltifi, "Three Performances Cancelled After Salafist Interruptions," *Tunisia Live*, August 17, 2012; and Sana Ajmi, "Arrest of Four Salafists Involved in Art Show Attack," *Tunisia Live*, August 17, 2012.

21. Manel Derbeli, "Abou Yadh s'insurge contre la conquête chiite et appelle le gouvernement à la contrer," *Tunisie numerique*, August 21, 2012.
22. Ansar al-Shari'ah in Tunisia, "Burning the Flag of the Majus Iran in Gabes," al-Bayyariq Media, August 18, 2012; and Manel Derbeli, "Tunisie: La ligue tunisienne pour la défense des Droits de l'Homme dénonce les violences entre un groupe chiite et les habitants de la région," *Tunisie numerique*, August 21, 2012.
23. Houda Mzioudet, "Tunisia: Head of Leftist Independent List Assaulted During Political Meeting in Southwestern Region," *Tunisia Live*, April 22, 2012.
24. Farah Samti, "Tunisian Leftist Coalition Member Assaulted by 'Salafists,'" *Tunisia Live*, July 13, 2012.
25. Racha Haffar, "Political Violence Targets Opposition Alliance," *Tunisia Live*, February 4, 2012.
26. Ati Metwaly, "Tunisian Universities Face Pressure from Salafists," *Ahram Online*, January 4, 2012.
27. "Tunisia: Fundamentalists Disrupting College Campuses," Human Rights Watch, December 9, 2011.
28. "Tunisia: Fundamentalists Disrupting College Campuses."
29. "Tunisia: Fundamentalists Disrupting College Campuses."
30. "Tunisia: Fundamentalists Disrupting College Campuses."
31. Khawla Ammar, "Molotov Cocktail Thrown at Higher Institute of Fine Arts in Sousse," *Tunisia Live*, June 12, 2012.
32. Houda Trabelsi, "Tunisia: Salafists Clash with Students in Tunisia," *Magharebia*, November 14, 2012.
33. "Islamists Attack Tunisia School Over ban," Reuters, April 11, 2013.
34. Lilia Weslaty, "Des salafistes détruisent des œuvres artistiques au Palais Abdellia," *Nawaat*, June 11, 2012.
35. "Salafists Block Tunisia Comedy Show That 'Offends Islam,'" Agence France-Presse, August 15, 2012; and "Tunisia: Salafists Attempt to Block Humorist Lotfi Abdelli's Show at Sfax Municipal Theatre," *Tunis Afrique Presse*, August 18, 2012.
36. "Salafists Fail to Stop 'Harlem Shake' in Tunisia," Agence France-Presse, February 27, 2013; "Fresh Harlem Shake Scuffles in Tunisia," Agence France-Presse, February 28, 2013; and Haifa Zaaiter, "al-Raqs yuthir janun salafi tunis: 'muslim shayk' huwa al-hal," *al-Safir*, March 4, 2013.
37. Afifa Ltifi, "Salafists Burn Down Bars, Liquor Stores While Police Are Passive in Sidi Bouzid," *Tunisia Live*, May 20, 2012; and Sana Ajmi, "Salafists Burn Bars and Police Station in Tunisia's Northwest," *Tunisia Live*, May 26, 2012.
38. "Tunisie: Des "jihadistes" derrière l'attaque d'un hôtel, l'enquête piétine," Agence France-Presse QBC, September 5, 2012; "Tunisian Salafis Attack Alcohol Sellers in Capital," Reuters, October 28, 2012; and "Tunisie: Des salafistes ont attaqué le bar d'un hôtel à Sbeitla," *Slate Afrique*, December 14, 2012.
39. Habib Toumi, "Tunisian Salafists Cut Off Man's Fingers for Selling Alcohol," *Gulf News*, October 30, 2012.
40. Sami-Joe Abboud, "Tunisie—Les policiers réquisitionnés pour fermer les restaurants à Carrefour," *Business News*, July 25, 2012.
41. Interview with Habib Sayah, a Tunisian specialist on jihadism, over email, July 7, 2016.
42. Ansar al-Shari'ah in Tunisia, "Ardh li-riyadhah al-zamaqtal," al-Bayyariq Media, May 24, 2012.
43. Ansar al-Shari'ah in Tunisia, "An Invitation to All Brothers," al-Bayyariq Media, October 6, 2012.

44. Ansar al-Shari'ah in Tunisia's Facebook page, February 7, 2013.
45. Amira Masrour, "Salafist Security Patrols Divide Tunisians," *Tunisia Live*, February 13, 2013.
46. Alice Fordham, "Tunisian Islamist Revolutionaries Patrol Streets, Undermining Police," *National*, February 13, 2013.
47. Fordham, "Tunisian Islamist revolutionaries patrol streets."
48. Hadi Yahmad, "Hiwar ma' Sayf Allah bin Hasin (Abu 'Iyadh)," *Jaridat al-Haqa'iq al-Tunisiyyah*, December 11, 2011.
49. Yahmad, "Hiwar ma' Sayf Allah bin Hasin (Abu 'Iyadh)."
50. Yahmad, "Hiwar ma' Sayf Allah bin Hasin (Abu 'Iyadh)."
51. "L'Appel de Tunisie de Béji Caïd Essebsi," *Business News*, April 20, 2012.
52. "Tunisian Salafis Attack Alcohol Sellers in Capital."
53. Ansar al-Shari'ah in Tunisia, "Da'wah Forum in Douar Hicher," al-Bayyariq Media, April 6, 2013; Ansar al-Shari'ah in Tunisia, "Lecture by Kamal Zuruq," al-Bayyariq Media, April 24, 2013; Ansar al-Shari'ah in Tunisia, "Lecture by 'Atif al-Matiri," al-Bayyariq Media, June 18, 2013; and Ansar al-Shari'ah in Tunisia, "Da'wah Tabling in Douar Hicher," al-Bayyariq Media, July 25, 2013.
54. Hend Hassassi, "National Guard Official Injured in Brawl with 'Salafists' in Douar Hicher," *Tunisia Live*, October 30, 2012.
55. Hana Zbeiss, "Tunis: al-salafiyyun wajahan li-wajahu ma' shartah wa-l-nahdah 'ala hayad," *al-Hayat*, November 10, 2012.
56. Kevin Ivey, "Another Night of Violence in Manouba Leaves One Dead, Three Wounded," *Tunisia Live*, October 31, 2012.
57. "Tunisian Imam Dies of Wounds After Attack on Police," Agence France-Presse, October 31, 2012.
58. I retain a copy of the interview, which had been available on YouTube.
59. Abu 'Iyadh al-Tunisi, "About the Recent Events (Douar Hicher)," al-Bayyariq Media, November 2, 2012.
60. al-Tunisi, "About the Recent Events (Douar Hicher)."
61. "Intervista: Hassan Ben Brik, Stato islamico non con la forza . . . per ora," *Globalist*, September 24, 2012.
62. "Jihadists Hunted in Tunisia 'Former Mali Fighters,'" Agence France-Presse, May 8, 2013.
63. al-Qa'ida in the Islamic Maghrib, "To the Wise Men of the Islamist Movement in Tunisia," al-Andalus Media, October 22, 2012.
64. al-Qa'ida in the Islamic Maghrib, "Call to the Youth of Islam: To Those Who Aspire to Hijrah in the Way of God in the Islamic Maghrib in General and Tunisia in Particular," al-Andalus Media, March 17, 2013.
65. Abu Yahya al-Shinqiti, "Oh People of Tunisia of al-Qayrawan Be Supporters of Shari'a al-Rahman," al-Andalus Media, May 18, 2013.
66. al-Qa'ida in the Islamic Maghrib, "To the Wise Men."
67. Abu Yahya al-Shinqiti, "Oh People of Tunisia."
68. Abu 'Iyadh al-Tunisi, "Congratulations on the Occasion of the Month of Ramadan," al-Bayyariq Media, July 9, 2013.
69. "Two Suspected Qaeda Affiliates Arrested in Tunisia," Agence France-Presse, May 15, 2011; "Six Killed in Tunisian Clashes Near Algeria: Diplomat," Agence France-Presse, September 23, 2011; Kouichi Shirayanagi, "Tunisian Authorities Break Up Alleged Al Qaeda Terror Cell," *Tunisia Live*, February 13, 2012; and Pesha Magid, "Tunisian Ministry of Defense Confirms Destruction of Armed Camp," *Tunisia Live*, June 23, 2012.

70. Abu 'Iyadh al-Tunisi, "Commenting on the Event of the American Embassy," al-Bayyariq Media, September 18, 2012.
71. Tarek Amara, "Tunisian Salafist Leader Escapes Arrest for Film Protest," Reuters, September 17, 2012.
72. Masrour, "Salafist Security Patrols Divide Tunisians."
73. "Tunisia: Violence and the Salafi Challenge," *International Crisis Group*, Middle East/North Africa Report No. 137, February 13, 2013, https://d2071andvipowj.cloudfront.net/tunisia-violence-and-the-salafi-challenge.pdf, p. 39.
74. "The In Amenas Attack," *Statoil*, September 12, 2013, 39; and "Les salafistes annoncent l'implication d'un Tunisien dans un attentat terroriste au Niger," *Niamey*, September 11, 2013.
75. Amira Masrour, "Circumstances of Death Arise After Algerian Border Attack," *Tunisia Live*, December 11, 2012; Amira Masrour, "National Guard in Pursuit of Suspects in Algerian Border Attack," *Tunisia Live*, December 12, 2012; and "Tunisia Arrests 11 After Deadly Border Attack," Agence France-Presse, December 12, 2012.
76. "16 Qaeda Suspects Arrested in Tunisia: Minister," Agence France-Presse, December 21, 2012.
77. Abu 'Umar al-Maghribi, "Sons of 'Uqbah Pull Your Courage Swords Out," *Masama' al-Khayr l-l-Inshad*, May 28, 2013.
78. "Tunisie: Les djihadistes préparaient une vingtaine d'homicides," Agence France-Presse, August 28, 2013.
79. "Minister: Tunisia Salafis Get Orders from al-Qaida," Associated Press, August 29, 2013.
80. "'Ansar al-Sharia' Was Planning More Assassinations, Bombings (Interior Ministry official)," Agence Tunis Afrique Presse, August 29, 2013.
81. "'Ansar al-Sharia' Was Planning More Assassinations."
82. Alexandra Hartmann, "Tunisian Government Links Ansar al-Sharia to Assassinations and al-Qaeda," *Tunisia Live*, August 28, 2013.
83. Hartmann, "Tunisian Government Links Ansar al-Sharia."
84. Abu Maysarah al-Shami, "The Jews of Jihad: Qa'idat al-Zawahiri," January 4, 2016, https://jihadology.net/2016/01/04/new-release-from-abu-maysarah-al-shami-the-jews-of-jihad-al-qaidat-al-%e1%ba%93awahiri.
85. Islamic State, "Message to the People of Tunisia," al-I'tisam Media, December 17, 2014.
86. "Interview with Abu Muqatil," *Dabiq Magazine*, no. 8, al-Hayat Media Center (March 30, 2015), 59–62.
87. Monia Ghanmi, "Tunisia rejects al-Qaeda, Salafist Violence," *Magharebia*, June 7, 2012; and Abou Chadha, "Al Qaïda projette de mener des opérations en Tunisie," *Tunisie Numerique*, June 5, 2012.
88. Suzanne Kelly, Pam Benson, and Elise Labott, "US Intel Believes Some Benghazi Attackers Tied to al Qaeda in Iraq," *CNN*, October 24, 2012.
89. "Interview with Abu Muqatil."
90. Aaron Y. Zelin, "The Tunisian-Libyan Jihadi Connection," *ICSR Insight*, July 6, 2015; Eli Lake, "Benghazi Suspect Held in Tunisia," *Daily Beast*, October 23, 2012
91. Walid al-Mejri, "'Ali al-harzi, mutahim fi muqatil al-safir al-amriki wa ahad al-mutahimin fi qidhayyah bil'aid wa-l-brahimi, birratah wizarat al-bahiri wa lahaqtahu wizarah bin jiddu," *Nawaat*, August 7, 2013; "Treasury Designates Twelve Foreign Terrorist Fighter Facilitators," *U.S. Department of the Treasury*, September 24, 2014.
92. Della Porta, "Radicalization: A Relational Perspective."

93. Matthieu Suc, "The Threat from Islamic State's 'Fifth Column' in Europe," *MediaPart*, November 12, 2017.
94. "The Cost of Leaving Islamic State: Death or Jail," *Associated Press*, February 3, 2015.
95. al-Qa'ida in the Islamic Maghrib, "Revenge For the Free Tunisia: Targeting the Interior Minister 'Lutfi Bin Jiddu,'" *al-Andalus Media*, June 13, 2014.
96. "Tunisie: neuf militaires tués dans un accrochage près de la frontière avec l'Algérie," *TSA*, July 30, 2013; "Le groupe terroriste Abou Fida, derrière l'attentat du Chaâmbi, selon les autorités sécuritaires algériennes," *Turess*, July 29, 2013; and Asma Smadhi, "Suspect in Chaambi Killings Arrested," *Tunisia Live*, August 12, 2013.
97. Aaron Y. Zelin, "Tunis Designates Ansar al-Sharia in Tunisia," *al-Wasat*, August 28, 2013.
98. Isabelle Mandraud, "Ali Larayedh: 'Je veux redonner confiance aux Tunisiens,'" *Le Monde*, March 26, 2013.
99. Abu 'Iyadh al-Tunisi, "Urgent Message to the Wise Men of al-Nahdah," *al-Bayyariq Media Foundation*, March 27, 2013.
100. AST's Facebook page, May 10–13; "Tunisia police clash with Salafists in Tunis," Agence France-Presse, May 12, 2013; "Tunisie: la police disperse par la force des prédicateurs salafistes près de Tunis," *RFI*, May 12, 2013; Borzou Daragahi, "Tunisia cracks down on Ansar al-sharia militants after clashes," *Financial Times*, May 12, 2013; and "Almurazaqah (Nabeul)/a'awan al-aman yamn'un intisab tawilah da'wiyyah li-ansar al-shari'ah," *ShemsFM*, May 12, 2013.
101. Abu 'Iyadh al-Tunisi, "Statement from Ansar al-Shari'ah," *al-Bayyariq Media Foundation*, May 13, 2013.
102. "Tunisie: Un rassemblement à l'appel d'un groupe salafiste interdit," *Le Monde*, May 15, 2013.
103. "Tunisie: Un rassemblement à l'appel d'un groupe salafiste interdit."
104. "Tunisie: Un rassemblement à l'appel d'un groupe salafiste interdit."
105. Lilia Weslaty, "Meeting with Supporters of Ansar Sharia in Kairouan: Between 'Islamic Revolution' and Social Injustice," Nawaat, May 30, 2013
106. Robert Tuttle, "Tunisia's Ansar al-Sharia Must Obey Law, Prime Minister Says," Bloomberg, May 19, 2013.
107. Abu al-Mundhir al-Shinqiti, "What Is Your Advice with Regard to the Annual Conference to be Held by the Brothers in Ansar al-Shari'ah in Tunisia?," *Minbar al-Tawhid wa-l-Jihad*, May 17, 2013.
108. Abu 'Iyadh al-Tunisi, "On the Occasion of the Third Annual Conference," al-Bayyariq Media Foundation, May 23, 2013.
109. Jamel Arfaoui, "Ansar al-Sharia Leader Sparks Ramadan Row in Tunisia," *Magharebia*, July 19, 2013.
110. Daveed Gartenstein-Ross and Oren Adaki, "Ansar al-Sharia in Tunisia's Social Media Activity in 2014," *Jihadology*, June 6, 2014.
111. Natasha Turak, "Medical Student Fatma Zouaghi, Alleged Ansar Al Sharia Member, Arrested, *Tunisia Live*, October 15, 2014; and "Tunisia: Young Girl Led Propaganda Cell of Ansar Al-Sharia and Okba Ibn Nafaa Brigade," *Tunis Afrique Presse*, October 14, 2014.
112. Lara Jakes and Qassim Abdul-Zahra, "More Foreign Fighters Seen Slipping Back into Iraq," Associated Press, December 5, 2010
113. Jakes and Abdul-Zahra, "More Foreign Fighters Seen Slipping Back into Iraq."
114. Bill Roggio, "Egypt," *Long War Journal*, January 25, 2011.

115. Wiem Melki, "Tunisian-Born Al Qaeda Leader Killed in Iraq," *Tunisia Live*, December 16, 2011.
116. Bouazza Ben Bouazza, "Tunisian Radicals Travel to Syria," Associated Press, June 21, 2012; and Tunisian Martyrs in Syria Database, curated by Aaron Y. Zelin, available at http://tunisianjihadism.com, last updated January 25, 2017.
117. Bill Roggio, "Tunisia," *Long War Journal*, September 23, 2011; "Accusé de terrorisme, un tunisien est arrêté par les autorités algériennes," *Tuniscope*, July 30, 2012; Nouara Bachouche, "Terrorist's Confessions: Belaouer's Group Planned to Smuggle Foreign Hostages to Libya," *Echorouk*, January 24, 2013; "Un dangereux terroriste a pu traverser la frontière algéro-tunisienne: l'Algérie boucle sa frontière dans la wilaya d'El Oued," *El Watan*, July 27, 2013; Hatem Bourial, "Arrestation d'un dangereux djihadiste à la frontière tuniso-algérienne," *Webdo*, July 28, 2013; "Yemen Air Strikes Kill Four al Qaeda Suspects: Witnesses," *Reuters*, July 3, 2012; "Yemen to Unleash Four Egyptian al-Qaeda Suspects," *Yemen Post*, August 7, 2012; "Qaeda Bomb-Maker and Six Arab Operatives Killed in Yemen," *Saba Net*, August 7, 2012; Bill Roggio, "Jihadist Identifies Tunisian Fighter Killed in Recent US Drone Strike in Yemen," *Long War Journal*, August 17, 2012; "Yemeni Court Sentences 7 al-Qaeda Members to 2–5 Years," *Saba Net*, April 7, 2013; Florian Flade, "German Jihadi Militant Killed in Drone Strike," *Jih@d*, April 29, 2012; and Islamic Movement of Uzbekistan, "The King Of Setterich," *Jund Allah Studio*, April 10, 2013.
118. Abu Mus'ab 'Abd al-Wadud, "In Support of the Intifâḍah of our People in Tunisia," al-Andalus Media, January 13, 2011.
119. Yahmad, "Hiwar ma' Sayf Allah bin Hasin (Abu 'Iyadh)."
120. Yahmad, "Hiwar ma' Sayf Allah bin Hasin (Abu 'Iyadh)."
121. Yahmad, "Hiwar ma' Sayf Allah bin Hasin (Abu 'Iyadh)."
122. Ansar al-Shari'ah in Tunisia, "Dialogue of Shaykh Abu 'Iyadh al-Tunisi with the Journalist Nasr al-Din Bin Hadid," al-Bayyariq Media Foundation, January 30, 2013.
123. Interview with a founding member of AST, Le Lac, Tunisia, August 29, 2013.
124. Fabio Merone, "Between Social Contention and Takfirism: The Evolution of the Salafi-Jihadi Movement in Tunisia," *Mediterranean Politics* 22, no. 1.
125. Ansar al-Shari'ah in Tunisia, "Ihda' ila jabhat al-nusrah ji'inakum bi-l-fatah al-jawlani," al-Bayyariq Media Foundation, January 24, 2013.
126. Ansar al-Shari'ah in Tunisia, "Tahiyyah min ashbal ansar al-shari'ah ila jabhat al-nusra bi-bilad al-sham," Ansar al-Shari'ah in Tunisia's Facebook page, April 28, 2013.
127. Some examples include "Istishahid mu'az hizm," Ansar al-Sharia in Tunisia's Facebook page, November 29, 2012; and "Irtiqa' al-akh isma'il min madinat al-sayjumi ardh al-rijal," Ansar al-Sharia'h in Tunisia's Facebook page, June 20, 2013.
128. Hazim al-Amin, "'Al-Mujahidun' al-tunisiyun fi suriya: khafaf al-hijrah fi dhil al-ta'shirah al-turkiyah wa taht a'yin 'al-nahdhdah,'" *al-Hayat*, October 28, 2014.
129. Ben Bouazza, "Tunisian Radicals Travel to Syria."
130. "Tunisia PM Says Country Cannot Legally Prevent Citizens from Going to Syria," *Al Arabiya*, March 24, 2013.
131. Salma Bouzid, "Syrian Opposition Asked to Address Plight of Tunisian Fighters," *Tunisia Live*, March 27, 2013.
132. Farah Samti, "Tunisians in Syria Report Neglect by Home Government," *Tunisia Live*, April 25, 2013.
133. "Tunisia PM says Country Cannot Legally Prevent Citizens from Going to Syria."
134. "Khatir jidan," Ansar al-Shai'iah in Tunisia's Facebook page, May 31, 2012.

135. "Radical Mosques Invite Young Tunisians to Jihad in Syria," Agence France-Presse, May 18, 2012.
136. Maria Abi-Habib, "Young Tunisians Embrace Jihad, Raise Tension at Home," *Wall Street Journal*, December 17, 2013.
137. Tunisian Foreign Fighters in Libya Database, curated by Aaron Y. Zelin, available at http://tunisianjihadism.com, last updated December 12, 2016.
138. Jamel Arfaoui, "Tunisians join Mourabitounes terrorist group," *Magharebia*, September 30, 2013.
139. Malik Aït-Aoudia, "Tunisie: Qui protège les camps jihadistes?," *Marianne*, October 23, 2012.
140. Mischa Benoit-Lavelle, "Tunisian Salafis on the Rise," *al-Monitor*, January 31, 2013.
141. Benoit-Lavelle, "Tunisian Salafis on the Rise."
142. Nick Meo, "Aggressive Salafist Islamists Threaten Tunisia's Dream of Freedom," *The Telegraph*, September 22, 2012.
143. Ansar al-Shari'ah in Tunisia, "Helping Refugees at Tunisian-Libyan Border," March 2–4, 2011, copy retained in the author's archives.
144. Ansar al-Shari'ah in Tunisia, "Active Contribution to the Brothers in the Refugee Tents at the Tunisian-Libyan Border—The Caravan of Victory," March 2–4, 2011, copy retained in the author's archives.
145. International Crisis Group, "Tunisia's Borders: Jihadism and Contraband," *Middle East/North Africa Report* No. 148, November 28, 2013, 17.
146. International Crisis Group, "Tunisia's Borders: Jihadism and Contraband."
147. Olfa Lamloum, "Marginalisation, Insecurity and Uncertainty on the Tunisian–Libyan Border Ben Guerdane and Dhehiba from the Perspective of Their Inhabitants," *International Alert*, December 2016.
148. Aaron Y. Zelin, "The Role of Tunisians," in *Beyond Syria and Iraq: Examining Islamic State Province*, edited by Katherine Bauer, *Policy Focus* no. 149 (Washington, DC: Washington Institute for Near East Policy, November 2016).
149. Mourad S., "Opération terroriste de Ben Guerdane: Un chef, ancien de Guantanamo, parmi les victimes des assaillants," *Tunisie Numerique*, March 7, 2016; and Patrick Markey and Tarek Amara, "As Fighters Return from Libya, Tunisia Faces Growing Challenge," Reuters, March 24, 2016.
150. International Crisis Group, "Tunisia's Borders: Jihadism and Contraband," 22.
151. International Crisis Group, "Tunisia's Borders: Jihadism and Contraband," 23.
152. "Interview with Abu Muqatil," 62.
153. Tunisian Jihadi Activities Database, curated by Aaron Y. Zelin, available at http://tunisianjihadism.com, last updated September 30, 2016.
154. Pictures from the Ansar al-Mujahidin Arabic Forum, March 28, 2011; author retains copy in his archives. Ansar al-Shari'ah in Darnah created its first Facebook page on December 7, 2011, and Katibat Ansar al-Shari'ah in Benghazi claimed on its Facebook page that it launched on February 17, 2012.
155. For more on this, see Aaron Y. Zelin, "Maqdisi's Disciples in Libya and Tunisia," *Foreign Policy's Middle East Channel*, November 14, 2012.
156. Ansar al-Shari'ah in Tunisia, "The Moment of Our Brother 'Ali al-Harzi's Release from Prison," al-Bayyariq Media, January 8, 2013.
157. Mischa Benoit-Lavelle, "Tunisian Islamist Violence Spills Across Libyan Border," *Tunisia Live*, June 18, 2012; and Houda Mzioudet, "Failed Attack on Tunisian Consulate in Tripoli," *Tunisia Live*, June 26, 2012.

158. The video can be found here: https://www.facebook.com/ObservatoryLY/videos/1846319362269997.
159. "Abou Yadh a fui le territoire tunisien avec l?aide d?un caporal de la garde nationale," *ShemsFM*, October 27, 2013.
160. Interview with one of the twenty original members/founders of AST in prison, Le Lac, August 29, 2013.
161. "Letter from 'Atiyah to Abu Basir," March 27, 2011, Bin Laden's Bookshelf, Declassified Material—January 19, 2017, Director of National Intelligence, https://www.dni.gov/index.php/features/bin-laden-s-bookshelf.
162. For more on the detainees, see Aaron Y. Zelin, "New Evidence on Ansar al-Sharia in Libya Training Camps," *al-Wasat*, August 8, 2013.
163. Houda Mzioudet, "Tunisians 'Not Involved' in Benghazi Clashes Claims Salafist," *Libya Herald*, November 25, 2013.
164. Bearer of the Sword, "Is a Transnational Rival Network of Al Qaaidah Emerging?," *Islamic Awakening Forum*, May 30, 2012, copy retained in the author's archives.
165. Maria Abi-Habib, "Young Tunisians Embrace Jihad, Raise Tension at Home," *Wall Street Journal*, December 17, 2013; and Carlotta Gall, "Worry in Tunisia Over Youths Who Turn to Jihad," *New York Times*, December 18, 2013.
166. International Crisis Group, "Tunisia's Borders: Jihadism and Contraband," 28.
167. "Tunisia Sending Terrorists to Syria via Turkey," Fars News Agency, December 19, 2012; and Ahmed Maher, "Syria Conflict: Why Did My Tunisian Son Join the Rebels?," *BBC News*, May 15, 2013. According to leaked Islamic State files, there were 374 Tunisians who, by the end of 2013, had registered with the leader who ran IS's border control. There are limitations with the data since it is only a snapshot and does not include the full universe of IS recruits. There were likely multiple IS leaders that registered individuals at the border. Therefore, the number of Tunisians with IS by the end of 2013 was much higher.
168. "Tunisian Girls Return Home Pregnant After 'Sexual Jihad' in Syria," *Al Arabiya*, September 20, 2013.
169. Timothy Holman, "'Gonna Get Myself Connected': The Role of Facilitation in Foreign Fighter Mobilizations," *Perspectives on Terrorism* 10, no. 2 (2016).
170. Interview with member of Ansar al-Sharia in Tunisia, al-Zahra', Tunisia, September 3, 2013.
171. Jamel Arfaoui, "Tunisia Arrests Hundreds in Syria Recruit Probe," *Magharebia*, April 29, 2013.
172. Abi-Habib, "Young Tunisians Embrace Jihad, Raise Tension at Home."
173. Maher, "Syria Conflict."
174. Maher, "Syria Conflict."
175. Thomas Hegghammer and Aaron Y. Zelin, "How Syria's Civil War Became a Holy Crusade," *Foreign Affairs*, July 7, 2013.
176. "Tahiyyid al-masjid fi tunis," al-Tasia'a Massa'a, *YouTube*, November 7, 2012, https://www.youtube.com/watch?v=Eohr7yrw5Zo; and "al-Qahwah: Ma' juhur bin mubarak wa bilal al-shuwashi," Shabakat Tunis al-Ikhbariyyah, *YouTube*, December 11, 2012, https://www.youtube.com/watch?v=ZuEj3Gku4q8.
177. "Tunisie: L'imam salafiste Bilel Chaouachi écroué pour 'incitation à la violence,'" *Kapitalis*, November 6, 2012; and Islamic State, "Foothold of the Conquerors," Wilayat al-Raqqah Media Office, June 16, 2016.
178. Ben Bouazza, "Tunisian Radicals Travel to Syria."
179. Bilal Chaouachi Facebook Page, June 30, 2014.

180. Abu Sufyan al-Sulami, "al-Rihlah al-dawa'iyyah ila tunis," *YouTube*, September 21, 2012, copy retained in the author's archives; and Ansar al-Shari'ah in Tunisia, "Khutbah by Abu Sufyan al-Sulami [Turki Bin'ali]," al-Bayyariq Media, June 21, 2013.
181. Ansar al-Shari'ah in Tunisia, "Khutbah by Abu Sufyan al-Sulami [Turki Bin'ali]."
182. Shaykh Kamal Zuruq, "Appeal to Support the Islamic State of Iraq and al-Sham," Shabab al-Tawhid Media, June 4, 2014.
183. Tunisian Martyrs in Syria Database, created by Aaron Y. Zelin, available at http://tunisianjihadism.com, last updated January 25, 2017.
184. Tunisian Martyrs in Syria Database.
185. Islamic State of Iraq and al-Sham, "Press Coverage of One of the Da'wah Tents in the State of Aleppo #2," al-Furqan Media, July 25, 2013; Islamic State of Iraq and al-Sham, "A Window upon the Land of Epic Battles #7," al-I'tisam Media, September 7, 2013; Islamic State of Iraq and al-Sham, "A Window upon the Land of Epic Battles #11," al-I'tisam Media, September 20, 2013; Islamic State of Iraq and al-Sham, "A Window upon the Land of Epic Battles #20," al-I'tisam Media, October 21, 2013; Islamic State of Iraq and al-Sham, "A Window upon the Land of Epic Battles #33," al-I'tisam Media, December 7, 2013; and Islamic State of Iraq and al-Sham, "Series of the Life From the Words of the 'Ulama' on the Project of the Islamic State #1: Shaykh Anwar al-'Awlaqi," al-I'tisam Media, December 10, 2013.
186. Interview with members of AST's dawa program, Sousse, Tunisia, February 19, 2013.
187. Islamic State of Iraq and al-Sham, "The Voice of al-Shām Magazine #2," al-Shām Foundation, September 6, 2013, 7.
188. Jaysh al-Muhajirin wa-l-Ansar, "Inciting Words from the Brother Abu 'Abd Allah al-Tunisi," *YouTube*, copy retained in the author's archives. A number of members of Jaysh al-Muhajirin wa-l-Ansar would eventually join up with ISIS.
189. Islamic State of Iraq and al-Sham, "A Window Upon the Land of Epic Battles #21," al-I'tisam Media, October 24, 2013.
190. Olfa Lamloum, *Politics on the Margins in Tunisia: Vulnerable Young People in Douar Hicher and Ettadhamen*, International Alert, March 2016, https://www.international-alert.org/sites/default/files/Tunisia_PoliticsOnTheMargins_EN_2016.pdf.

8. It Was Mostly the Tunisians Who Were Involved in *Takfir*

1. "Birnamij hamuna 4—al-halaqah al-sadisah—tujarib shabab mugharar bi-him," *Saudi Channel 1*, *YouTube*, March 5, 2014, https://www.youtube.com/watch?v=1Q8SS1HmT2o.
2. Aaron Y. Zelin, "Tunisian Foreign Fighters in Iraq and Syria," Washington Institute for Near East Policy, *Policy Notes*, no. 55 (November 2018).
3. al-Qaeda's General Command, "On the Relationship of Qa'idat al-Jihad and the Islamic State of Iraq and al-Sham," al-Fajr Media Center, February 2, 2014.
4. Jean-Charles Brisard, *Zarqawi: The New Face of Al-Qaeda* (New York: Other Press, 2005), 71.
5. Shaykh Abu Ja'far al-Hatab, "Bay'at al-amsar li-l-imam al-mukhtar: ahkam al-bay'ah fi al-islam wa-tatarayliha 'ala bay'ah ahl al-sham," al-Bayyariq Media, June 26, 2013.
6. Abu Hamam Bakr Bin 'Abd al-'Aziz al-Athari, "Extend Our Hands in Bay'ah to al-Baghdadi," *Minbar al-Tawhid wa-l-Jihad*, August 5, 2013.
7. S. J., "The Salafist Struggle," *Economist*, January 1, 2014.
8. "An Important Message and Advice to the New Nafirin (Those Who Heeded the Call to Jihad)," Shabab al-Tawhid Media, March 11, 2014.

9. "Its Knights Are Conquering Foreign Lands While It Is a Hostage," Shabab al-Tawhid Media, October 24, 2014.
10. Aaron Y. Zelin, "Shabab al-Tawhid: The Rebranding of Ansar al-Sharia in Tunisia?," Washington Institute for Near East Policy, *Policy Watch*, no. 2250 (May 9, 2014); and Aaron Y. Zelin, "The Clairvoyant: Update on Shabab al-Tawhid and Creation of al-Midrar Media," *Jihadology*, May 12, 2014, https://jihadology.net/2014/05/12/the-clairvoyant-update-on-shabab-al-tawhid-and-creation-of-al-midrar-media/.
11. Central Division of al-Qaeda in the Islamic Maghrib, "Munasirah min maghrib al-islam li-dawlah al-islamiyah fi 'iraq wa-l-sham," Shabab al-Tawhid Media, March 22, 2014.
12. Abu Suhayb al-Muhajir, "Hukum nakath al-bay'ah wa-minhum ahl al-hal wa-l-'aqd," Shabab al-Tawhid Media, March 16, 2014; and Abu Suhayb al-Muhajir, "Masa'lah bayn bay'at al-tanzim wa-bay'at al-dawlah al-islamiyah," Shabab al-Tawhid Media, March 21, 2014.
13. Shaykh Kamal Zuruq, "Appeal to Support the Islamic State of Iraq and al-Sham," Shabab al-Tawhid Media, June 4, 2014.
14. Shabab al-Tawhid location database, created by Aaron Y. Zelin, available at http://tunisianjihadism.com, last updated May 12, 2014.
15. Ansar al-Sharia in Tunisia, "Regarding the Disagreement in al-Sham," al-Bayyariq Media, July 15, 2013.
16. Abu 'Iyadh al-Tunisi, "Qar'ah mawdhu'iyah waqi'yah li-hal al-tayar al-jihadi wa-l-tahadiyat al-lati tawajahahu," May 1, 2014, copy retained in the author's archives.
17. Abu 'Iyadh al-Tunisi, "Inspired by the Conquests of Iraq," al-Bayyariq Media, June 13, 2014.
18. Bilal al-Shawashi, "Haqa'iq maduwiyah: li-l-daw'iyah al-tunisi bilal al-shawashi al-ladhi iltihaq bi-jabhat al-nusrah," April 23, 2014, copy retained in the author's archives.
19. Abu 'Iyadh al-Tunisi, "Answer to the Essay of Abu Maysarah al-Shami: Letter to Dr. Ayman al-Zawahiri," Hidayyah Media Foundation, January 6, 2016.
20. Tunisi, "Answer to the Essay."
21. Tunisi, "Answer to the Essay."
22. Tunisi, "Answer to the Essay."
23. Tunisi, "Answer to the Essay."
24. Tunisi, "Answer to the Essay."
25. Abu Qatadah al-Filistini, "Important and Urgent Message to Ansar al-Sharia in Tunisia," al-Bayyariq Media, January 20, 2014.
26. Abu Maysarah al-Shami, "The Jews of Jihad: Qa'idat al-Zawahiri," January 4, 2016, https://jihadology.net/2016/01/04/new-release-from-abu-maysarah-al-shami-the-jews-of-jihad-al-qaidat-al-%e1%ba%93awahiri.
27. Haïfa Mzalouat and Malek Khadhraoui, "Fayçal, du jihad en Syrie à la désillusion," *Inkyfada*, August 31, 2018; Lina Sinjab, "al-Qaeda's Brutal Tactics in Syria Force Out Moderates," *BBC News*, November 27, 2013; Mansour Omari, "Two Years an ISIS Slave," *Daily Beast*, December 22, 2015; Yaroslav Trofimov, "In Islamic State Stronghold of Raqqa, Foreign Fighters Dominate," *Wall Street Journal*, February 4, 2015; and Charlie Savage, "As ISIS Fighters Fill Prisons in Syria, Their Home Nations Look Away," *New York Times*, July 18, 2018.
28. Guy Taylor, "Arab Spring Star Tunisia Emerges as Islamic State's No. 1 Source for Foreign Fighters," *Washington Times*, September 14, 2016. You can find a picture of Maghrawi with his arm around al-Kasasbah's neck here: https://twitter.com/GuyVanVlierden/status/1082185656649089024.

29. George Packer, "Exporting Jihad: The Arab Spring Has Given Tunisians the Freedom to Act on Their Unhappiness," *New Yorker*, March 28, 2016.
30. Ahmad Ibrahim, "The Story of Hajer & ISIS' All-Female Battalion," *Raqqa Is Being Slaughtered Silently*, August 29, 2017.
31. Wladimir Van Wilgenburg, "Secrets of the Black Stadium: In Raqqa, Inside ISIS' House of Horror," *Daily Beast*, October 24, 2017.
32. Taylor, "Arab Spring Star Tunisia Emerges."
33. Kassem Hamadé, "ISIS Commander on the Run Tells of the Terror Inside the Terrorist Sect," *Expressen*, October 11, 2017.
34. Pieter Van Ostaeyen, "Katibat al-Battar and the Belgian Fighters in Syria," January 21, 2015, https://pietervanostaeyen.com/2015/01/21/katibat-al-battar-and-the-belgian-fighters-in-syria/; and Oliver Holmes and Suleiman al-Khalidi, "Islamic State Executed 700 People from Syrian Tribe: Monitoring Group," Reuters, August 16, 2014.
35. Liz Sly, "Syria Tribal Revolt Against Islamic State Ignored, Fueling Resentment," *Washington Post*, October 20, 2014; and Islamic State, "Report from Wilayat al-Khayr," Wilayat al-Khayr Media Office, August 27, 2014.
36. Mona al-Mohammad, "Flogged by the Islamic State," *Syria Stories*, January 19, 2016.
37. Marwan Hisham and Molly Crabapple, *Brothers of the Gun: A Memoir of the Syrian War* (New York: Penguin Random House, 2018), 268.
38. "'They Came to Destroy': ISIS Crimes Against the Yazidis," UN Human Rights Council, A/HRC/32/CRP.2, June 15, 2016.
39. "'They Came to Destroy'."
40. Interview with Ahmet Yayla over Skype, February 2, 2018.
41. "Shadhudh jinsi wa ughtasab fi safuf al-tandhim yu'akas haqiqah 'anasirahu," *Sawt wa Surah*, September 1, 2015, http://sound-and-picture.com/?p=1070.
42. "Tandhim da'ish yu'adam ithnayn min 'anasiruhu bi-tahmah al-zina," *Sawt wa Surah*, July 27, 2017, http://sound-and-picture.com/?p=2217.
43. "Li-l-marat al-ula . . . mujhulun yuqatilun amir al-hisbah fi al-mayadin khanqan," *Qasioun*, April 8, 2016, available at http://www.qasioun.net.
44. Josie Ensor and Magdy Samaan, "The Town Nicknamed 'Little London' at the Heart of Islamic State's War," *Telegraph*, January 11, 2016.
45. Benoit Faucon and Margaret Coker, "The Rise and Deadly Fall of Islamic State's Oil Tycoon," *Wall Street Journal*, April 24, 2016.
46. Ben Taub, "The Real Value of the ISIS Antiquities Trade," *New Yorker*, December 4, 2015.
47. Taub, "The Real Value of the ISIS Antiquities Trade."
48. "Adhaba fi Madinat Salqin ba'd Atada Anasir Tunisiyin min Jabhat al-Nusra 'ala Imarah," *al-Durar al-Shamiyah*, June 26, 2016, https://eldorar.com/node/99850.
49. Aymenn Jawad al-Tamimi, "Additional Notes on the Druze of Jabal al-Summaq," October 6, 2015; and Daveed Gartenstein-Ross and Aymenn Jawad al-Tamimi, "Druze Clues," *Foreign Affairs*, October 5, 2015.
50. "Al-Qaeda's Syria Affiliate Kills 20 Druze," Agence France-Presse, June 11, 2015.
51. Abu Lababah al-Tunisi, "Series About the Causes of the Spread of Extremism in the Tunisian Youth: Why Are Tunisia's Youth the Most Extreme in the Ranks of the State Organization?, Parts 2, 3, 4," September 3, 2015, https://jihadology.net/2015/09/03/new-article-from-abu-lababah-al-tunisi-series-about-the-causes-of-the-spread-of-extremism-in-the-tunisian-youth-why-are-tunisias-youth-the-most-extreme-in-the-ranks-of-the-state-or; and al-Maqalaat, "Tunisia: A Reason For the Current Extremism in the Jihadi Movement," November 19, 2015, copy retained in the author's archives.

52. Abu al-Zubayr al-Qabsi, "al-Dawrah al-'ilmiyah al-ula li-l-shaykh ahmad bin 'umar al-hazimi bi-tunis," *Ahl al-Hadith Forum*, October 25, 2011; and "Dawrah 'ilmiyah: Shaykh ahmad bin 'umar al-hazimi," *Mawqah al-Islam fi Tunis*, October 29, 2011, https://islamentunisie.com/?p=453.
53. See https://masejed.weebly.com/index.html.
54. Ansar al-Sharia in Tunisia's Clerical Establishment Database, created by Aaron Y. Zelin, available at http://tunisianjihadism.com, last updated August 10, 2016.
55. Ansar al-Sharia in Tunisia, "Khutbah of Abu Muhanad al-Tunisi," al-Bayyariq Media, February 17, 2012.
56. Salwa al-Tarhuni, "Bitaqah ida'a bi-sijin fi haqq ra'yis jami'ah al-khayr al-islamiyah bi-tuhamah tamwil al-irhab," *Tunisien*, May 14, 2014, available at http://www.tunisien.tn.
57. "Bayan bi-khasus iftitah ma'had ibn abu zayd al-qayrawani li-l-'ulum al-shari'ah," March 1, 2012, http://majles.alukah.net/t97703.
58. "Tariqah al-tasjil fi ma'had ibn zayd al-qayrawani li-l-'ulum al-shari'ah," March 1, 2012, http://majles.alukah.net/t97703.
59. Ansar al-Sharia in Tunisia Facebook page, December 22, 2012.
60. Ansar al-Sharia in Tunisia Facebook page, January 15, 2013.
61. As linked to by AST on its official Facebook page: *Fiqh al-Muyasar fi Dhu' al-Kitab wa-l-Sunnah*, Saudi Arabia: Ministry of Islamic Affairs, Dawah and Guidance, 2004, https://ia800204.us.archive.org/10/items/fikh_moyasar1/fikh_moyasar1.pdf.
62. Cole Bunzel, "Ideological Infighting in the Islamic State," *Perspectives on Terrorism* 13, no. 1 (February 2019): 13–22.
63. Tunisi, "Series About the Causes of the Spread of Extremism; and al-Maqalaat, "Tunisia: A Reason For the Current Extremism in the Jihadi Movement."
64. Abu Ja'afar al-Hatab, "Stance Ahead of the Third Annual Conference," al-Bayyariq Media, May 13, 2013.
65. Rania Abouzeid, *No Turning Back: Life, Loss, and Hope in Wartime Syria* (New York: Norton, 2018), 515–17.
66. Bunzel, "Ideological Infighting in the Islamic State."
67. WikiBaghdady, December 14, 2013–June 13, 2014, originally posted here: https://twitter.com/wikibaghdady, and archived here: https://docs.google.com/document/d/1wEQ0FKosa1LcUB3tofeub1UxaT5A-suROyDExgV9nUY.
68. WikiBaghdady.
69. WikiBaghdady.
70. WikiBaghdady.
71. WikiBaghdady.
72. Islamic State, "Report on the Phenomenon of Extremism in the Islamic State," November 14, 2015, http://www.jihadica.com/wp-content/uploads/2018/11/zahirat-al-ghuluww.pdf.
73. "Shari'iyun da'ish yukafirun harakat taliban wa usamah bin ladin khatir jidan," *YouTube*, June 28, 2015, https://www.youtube.com/watch?v=t_LANfh2BOU.
74. "al-Dawlah al-islamiyah 'da'ish' wa 'aqidat al-takfir—da'ish tadu'i anaha al-ta'ifah al-mansurah wa ansar al-shari'ah 'ala khata,'" March 13, 2014, originally available here: https://www.youtube.com/watch?v=pvHnfeaBQ9E, author maintains a copy in his archives.
75. "al-Dawlah al-islamiyah 'da'ish' wa 'aqidat al-takfir."
76. Tore Hamming, "The Extremist Wing of the Islamic State," *Jihadica*, June 9, 2016.
77. Abu 'Abd al-Malik al-Shami, "Sighs from the Islamic State Buried Alive," August 2017, copy retained in the author's archives.

78. Islamic State, "Report on the Phenomenon of Extremism in the Islamic State."
79. "Message of the 'Council of 'Ilm' on the State of the Extremists in the Media Diwan," al-Turath al-'Ilmi Foundation, 2018; and Abu 'Abd al-Malik al-Shami, "Sighs from the Islamic State Buried Alive."
80. The Islamic State, "Report on the Phenomenon of Extremism in the Islamic State." Other members of the Abu Ayub group included Abu al-Darda' al-Tunisi, Abu al-Yaman al-Tunisi, Abu Qatadah al-Tunisi, Abu 'Abd al-Rahman al-Libi, Abu Khalid al-Tunisi, Abu al-Mu'tasim al-Tunisi, and Jahabdhah al-Tunisi.

9. Honest Ones Among the *Dawa* People Must Come to al-Sham

1. Islamic State of Iraq and al-Sham, "Breaking of the Borders," al-I'tisam Media, June 29, 2014.
2. The Islamic State, "Flashes in the Shade of the Caliphate #2: Interview with the Abu Fatimah al-Tunisi," Wilayat al-Barakah Media Office, October 28, 2014.
3. Michael Weiss, "How ISIS Picks Its Suicide Bombers," *Daily Beast*, November 16, 2015.
4. Tunisian Foreign Fighter Signatories to AQ-Linked Statements During Times of Discord Database, created by Aaron Y. Zelin, available at http://tunisianjihadism.com, last updated February 6, 2019.
5. "Awal Shuhada Jazira al-Arab fi Suriyya (Hussam al-Mutayri)," Shamukh al-Islam Forum, February 17, 2012. Author retains archive of post.
6. This information was originally posted on Facebook at https://www.facebook.com/photo.php?fbid=359430794174612&set=a.126014154182945.22702.122217594562601&type=1; and https://www.facebook.com/Strangers.sy4/posts/224215384416156. Author retains archive of posts. The posts are no longer available.
7. Yaroslav Trofimov, "How Tunisia Became a Top Source of ISIS Recruits," *Wall Street Journal*, February 25, 2016.
8. Richard Barrett, *Beyond the Caliphate: Foreign Fighters and the Threat of Returnees*, The Soufan Center, October 2017, https://www.jstor.org/stable/resrep10782.
9. Sarah Souli, "Tunisia: Why Foreign Fighters Abandon ISIL," *Al Jazeera*, March 3, 2016.
10. Angelique Chrisafis, "Radicalised French Woman Who Followed Son to Syria Jailed for 10 Years," *Guardian*, October 6, 2017; and Gilles Kepel, *Terror in France: The Rise of Jihad in the West* (Princeton, N.J.: Princeton University Press, 2017), 84.
11. David Thompson, *Les français jihadistes* (Paris: Les Arènes, 2014), 155–56.
12. Thompson, *Les français jihadistes*, 168.
13. Thompson, *Les français jihadistes*, 171; and David Thompson, *Les revenants: Ils étaient partis faire le jihad, ils sont de retour en France* (Paris: Éditions du Seuil, 2016), 11.
14. Thompson, *Les français jihadistes*, 170.
15. Ammar Cheikh Omar, Richard Engel, and Ben Plesser, "Leaked ISIS Personnel Files Paint Picture of Group's Recruits," *NBC News*, March 10, 2016.
16. For more details and an appendix of a variety of information from the border documents, see Aaron Y. Zelin, "Tunisian Foreign Fighters in Iraq and Syria," Washington Institute for Near East Policy, *Policy Notes*, no. 55 (November 2018).
17. David Sterman and Nate Rosenblatt, *All Jihad Is Local*, vol. 2, *ISIS in North Africa and the Arabian Peninsula* (New America Foundation, April 2018).
18. Dakota Foster and Daniel Milton, "Children at War: Foreign Child Recruits of the Islamic State," *CTC Sentinel* 11, no. 6 (June/July 2018), https://ctc.usma.edu/app/uploads/2018/06/CTC-SENTINEL-062018_1.pdf.

19. Islamic State, "Among the Believers Are Men: Abu 'Umar al-Tunisi," *Dabiq Magazine*, no. 10 (July 13, 2015), 41.
20. Jean-Pierre Filiu, "Ansar al-Fatah and 'Iraqi' Networks in France," in *The Evolution of the Global Terrorist Threat: From 9/11 to Osama bin Laden's Death*, ed. by Bruce Hoffman and Fernando Reinares (New York: Columbia University Press, 2014), 359.
21. Islamic State, "The Brother Abu Yasin al-Tunisi (May God Accept Him)," Wilayat Ninawa Media Office, August 9, 2016.
22. Eirik Linaker Berglund and Camilla Huuse, "Denne Selvmordsbomberen Skal ha Bodd Flere år i Oslo," *VG*, July 27, 2014.
23. "Daech: Le Terroriste Tunisien Imed Ben Salah tué en Irak," *Kapitalis*, March 15, 2017.
24. Emine M'tiraoui, "Al-Shaykh Imad bin Salih al-Malqab bi-Abu Abd Allah al-Tunisi Yasul ila Tunis ba'd Taraduhu min Misr," *Nawaat*, April 4, 2013, http://nawaat.org/portail/2013/04/04/الشيخ-عماد-بن-صالح-الملقب-بأبو-عبد-الله/.
25. "Tunisia Frees Salafist Sheikh Expelled by Egypt," Agence France-Presse, April 5, 2013.
26. "Daech."
27. Ansar al-Sharia in Tunisia, "Learning Session in the Preparation of al-Ruqyah al-Sharia," al-Bayyariq Media Foundation, February 23–25, 2013.
28. "Tozeur: Arrestation d'un Terroriste Classé Dangereux," *Shems FM*, April 15, 2016.
29. "Une jeune fille arrêtée pour appartenance à un mouvement terroriste," *Mosaique FM*, May 30, 2018.
30. Imen Blioua, "Syrian Conflict Drawing in Tunisia's Youth," *Tunisia Live*, July 10, 2014.
31. Haifa Mzalouat and Malek Khadhraoui, "Fayçal, du jihad en Syrie à la désillusion," *Inkyfada*, August 31, 2018.
32. "Disillusioned with Revolution, Tunisian Youths Head to Syria to Fight," Agence France-Presse, October 1, 2014.
33. Trofimov, "How Tunisia Became a Top Source of ISIS Recruits."
34. George Packer, "Exporting Jihad: The Arab Spring Has Given Tunisians the Freedom to Act on Their Unhappiness," *New Yorker*, March 28, 2016.
35. Shadi Hamid, "Why Jihadists Fight," *Foreign Policy*, June 13, 2016.
36. David D. Kirkpatrick, "New Freedoms in Tunisia Drive Support for ISIS," *New York Times*, October 21, 2014.
37. "Ridha le Tunisien, Esclave Sexuel des Jihadistes en Syrie," *Kapitalis*, November 3, 2016.
38. "Ridha le Tunisien, Esclave Sexuel des Jihadistes en Syrie."
39. "Who Is the 'Typical' Tunisian Jihadist?" *al-Hayat*, November 3, 2014.
40. Benoit Faucon and Margaret Coker, "The Rise and Deadly Fall of Islamic State's Oil Tycoon," *Wall Street Journal*, April 24, 2016; and Ben Taub, "The Real Value of the ISIS Antiquities Trade," *New Yorker*, December 4, 2015.
41. Faucon and Coker, "The Rise and Deadly Fall of Islamic State's Oil Tycoon"; and Taub, "The Real Value of the ISIS Antiquities Trade."
42. "Deir al-Zour 24 Tatamakin min Kashafa Huwiyah qa Makan Iqamah Amir al-Hisba fi Madinat Deir al-Zour," *DeirEzzour24*, August 12, 2015.
43. "Deir al-Zour 24 Tatamakin."
44. Tam Hussein, "Paradise Lost: The Rise and Fall of Abu Bakr al-Baghdadi," *Syria Comment*, April 14, 2017.
45. "Picture Tour Inside Shadad al-Tunisi Military Training Camp for Training and Graduation of Cubs of the Islamic State," Wilayat Halab Media Office, February 21, 2015. The announcement of Shadad al-Tunisi's death can be found here: https://www.facebook.com/Labyek.Bashar.Al.Asad/posts/641652845895593.

46. Don Rassler, *The Islamic State and Drones: Supply, Scale, and Future Threats* (West Point, N.Y.: Combating Terrorism Center, July 11, 2018).
47. Jenan Moussa, "Al-Hawiyah wal-Ism al-Kamil li-Matur Ta'irat Da'ish al-Masirah Takashafaha Akhbar al-An," *Akhbar al-An*, March 29, 2017, available at https://www.akhbaralaan.net.
48. "Hamas Accuses Israel of Killing Its Tunisian Drone Expert," *BBC News*, December 17, 2016.
49. Harald Doornbos and Jenan Moussa, "Found: The Islamic State's Terror Laptop of Doom," *Foreign Policy*, August 28, 2014.
50. "The Cost of Leaving Islamic State: Death or Jail," Associated Press, February 3, 2015.
51. "Al-Baghdadi Yukalaf Amiran Tunisiyan bi-Tawhid al-Jamaat li-Tanfidh Amaliyat Irhabiyah," *Arabesque*, August 12, 2014, available at http://www.arabesque.tn.
52. Adnan Abu Walid al-Sahrawi, "Announcing a New Amir and Giving Bay'ah to al-Baghdadi," May 13, 2015, https://jihadology.net/2015/05/13/new-audio-message-from-al-murabi%e1%b9%aduns-adnan-abu-walid-al-%e1%b9%a3a%e1%b8%a5rawi-announcing-a-new-amir-and-giving-bayah-to-al-baghdadi.
53. Aymenn Jawad al-Tamimi, "Specimen 19T: Request from the Office of the *Wali* of Wilayat Dimashq," Archive of Islamic State Administrative Documents, #2.
54. Aaron Y. Zelin and Oula A. Alrifai, "The Islamic State in Southern Syria," *CTC Sentinel* 8, no. 11 (November/December 2015), https://ctc.usma.edu/app/uploads/2015/12/CTCSentinel-Vol8Iss114.pdf.
55. An archive of IS's Wilayat Dimashq content can be found here: https://jihadology.net/category/the-islamic-state/wilayat-dimashq.
56. Abu Ja'afar al-Hatab, "Provisions of Emigration and Jihad for Women," al-Bayyariq Media, March 23, 2013.
57. Hatab, "Provisions of Emigration and Jihad for Women."
58. Hatab, "Provisions of Emigration and Jihad for Women."
59. Abu Usamah al-Gharib, "Arbitrating on Women Doing Hijrah Without a Mahram," al-Ghuraba' Media, September 18, 2014.
60. Gharib, "Arbitrating on Women Doing Hijrah Without a Mahram."
61. Daniel Milton and Brian Dodwell, "Jihadi Brides? Examining a Female Guesthouse Registry from the Islamic State's Caliphate," *CTC Sentinel* 11, no. 5 (May 2018), https://ctc.usma.edu/app/uploads/2018/05/CTC-Sentinel_Vol11Iss5.pdf.
62. Steven Erlanger, "In West, ISIS Finds Women Eager to Enlist," *New York Times*, October 23, 2014.
63. "Tunisia's 'Sexual Jihad'—Extremist Fatwa or Propaganda?" *BBC News*, October 27, 2013.
64. Rodi Said, "Islamic State Turned on Dissenters as Raqqa Assault Neared," *Reuters*, June 28, 2017; see also Borzou Daragahi, "We Spoke to Women Who Married into ISIS in Syria. These Are Their Regrets," *BuzzFeed*, July 20, 2017.
65. Sara Manisera, "'I Came for the Jihad:' Women Tell of Life in the Islamic State," *Syria Deeply*, September 29, 2017.
66. Anthony Loyd, "Hundreds of ISIS Widows Trapped in Syria as Caliphate Falls," *Times*, December 16, 2017.
67. Iris Kolman, "Gender Activism in Salafism: A Case Study of Salafi Women in Tunisia," in *Salafism After the Arab Awakening: Contending with People's Power*, ed. by Francesco Cavatorta and Fabio Merone (Oxford: Oxford University Press, 2016).
68. Ahmad Ibrahim, "The Story of Hajer & ISIS' All-Female Battalion," *Raqqa Is Being Slaughtered Silently*, August 29, 2017.

69. "Min al-Khansa ila al-Hailah wa 'Saja' wa Umm 'Rayan:' Antha al-Dawa'ish' fi Muhimat al-Istiqatab wal-Uqab," *Attounissia*, December 12, 2015, http://www.turess.com/attounissia/162646.
70. Ibrahim, "The Story of Hajer & ISIS' All-Female Battalion."
71. "Tandhim al-Dawlah Yuftah Bab al-Tajnid al-Nisa wa Yabhath an al-Muta'lamat," *Sawt wa Surah*, August 17, 2015, http://sound-and-picture.com/?p=1009.
72. Ghoulay Zaza, "Mudhafat al-Nisa fi Deir al-Zour . . . al-Mujtama al-Muthali li-Da'ish," *Raseef22*, August 26, 2017.
73. Weiss, "How ISIS Picks Its Suicide Bombers"; and Kim Sengupta, "Confessions of an ISIS Killer: British Jihadis Shunned Frontline in Favour of Torture Squads," *Independent*, December 29, 2016.
74. "Abu Usama al-Tunisi Yuqim Imaratuhu fi Suriya ala Jamajim al-Munfadhin Dhid al-Asad," *Azzaman*, July 8, 2013, https://www.azzaman.com/?p=38689.
75. Mattieu Suc, "Boubakeur el-Hakim, Vie et Mort d'un Émir Français," *Mediapart*, December 14, 2016.
76. Suc, "Boubakeur el-Hakim."
77. Islamic State, "Interview with Abu Muqatil," *Dabiq Magazine*, no. 8 (March 30, 2015): 59–62.
78. Western Jihadists 1993–Present: An Archive and Database Charting the Evolution of Jihadi-inspired Terrorist Networks and Recruitment in Western States. Principal Investigator: Jytte Klausen. Waltham, MA: Brandeis University.
79. Western Jihadists 1993–Present.
80. Jean-Charles Brisard and Kévin Jackson, "The Islamic State's External Operations and the French-Belgian Nexus," *CTC Sentinel* 9, no. 11 (November/December 2016): 8–15.
81. Brisard and Jackson, "The Islamic State's External Operations."
82. Western Jihadists 1993–Present.
83. Florian Flade, "The June 2018 Cologne Ricin Plot: A New Threshold in Jihadi Bio Terror," *CTC Sentinel* 11, no. 7 (August 2018), https://ctc.usma.edu/app/uploads/2019/01/CTC-SENTINEL-082018-final.pdf.

10. We Are Here to Protect You from This Nonbeliever Government

1. Translation: God is the greatest. . . . I acknowledge that there is no deity but God. . . . I acknowledge that Muhammad is the Messenger of God. . . . Hasten to the prayer. . . . Hasten to the salvation. . . . Prayer is better than sleep. . . . God is greatest. . . . There is no deity but God.
2. Tarek Amara and Patrick Markey, "Border Attack Feeds Tunisia Fears of Libya Jihadist Spillover," Reuters, March 13, 2016; "Commandant à l'armée: des tirs venaient de la mosquée lors de l'attaque de Ben Guerdene," *Shems FM*, March 14, 2016; and "Un lieutenant-colonel de l'armée confirme l'utilisation du minaret de la mosquée Jalel à Ben Guerdane par les terroristes," *Shems FM*, March 14, 2016.
3. "I'tirafat li-Muhammad bin Muhsin al-Gharbi al-Makanni bi-Abu Zayd Tunisi al-Jinsiyyah," Quwat al-Rada al-Khasah, February 23, 2016, https://www.facebook.com/QwtAlradaAlhaast/videos/1159313520755270.
4. Abu 'A'isha, "Ben Gardane and al-Zarqawi Cultivated His Ripened Fruits," al-Wafa' Media, March 8, 2016.

5. "Naji al-Zairi Yufajrha: Liday Wathiqah Tukashaf al-Takhtit li-Amaliyyat bin Qardan Mindhu Disimbur al-Madhi . . . wa-al-Sultat Kanat ala Ilm," *al-Sabah*, March 7, 2016, available at http://www.assabahnews.tn.
6. "Ben Guerden: Arrestation d'une cellule terroriste ayant planifié l'intrusion sur le territoire tunisien," *Shems FM*, February 20, 2016.
7. "Affrontements à Ben Guerdane: 4 terroristes tués le 5ème s'est fait exploser," *Mosaïque FM*, March 2, 2016.
8. "Un témoin oculaire: 'Les terroristes connaissaient les maisons des sécuritaires,'" *Shems FM*, March 7, 2016.
9. "Ben Guerdane: Il se faisait passer pour un marchand ambulant pour surveiller les unités sécuritaires," *Mosaïque FM*, March 11, 2016.
10. "Ben Guerdane: Des militants de la société civile et des citoyens visés par un plan d'assassinat," *Mosaïque FM*, March 10, 2016.
11. Emily Estelle, "Desknote: ISIS's Tunisian Attack Cell in Libya," *Critical Threats Project*, March 8, 2016.
12. "Bin Qardan: al-Irhabiyun yutahasilun bi-manzil al-irhabi 'adl al-ghandri," *Mosaique FM*, March 7, 2016, available at https://www.mosaiquefm.net.
13. See the MENASTREAM Twitter post, March 13, 2016, https://twitter.com/MENASTREAM/status/709188293636837376.
14. Greg Botelho and Barbara Starr, "49 Killed in U.S. Airstrike Targeting Terrorists in Libya," *CNN*, February 20, 2016; and Heni Nsaibia, "MENASTREAM ID #1: Moez Ben Abdelkader Ben Ahmed Fezzani," MENASTREAM, February 9, 2016.
15. "Tunisia Beach Killer Trained with Museum Gunmen," Associated Press, June 30, 2015.
16. Raouf Ben Hédi and Mohamed Garoui, "Les terroristes passent aux aveux: Leur plan pour instaurer l'Émirat de Ben Guerdène," *Business News*, March 8, 2016.
17. Sudarsan Raghavan, "Islamic State, Growing Stronger in Libya, Sets Its Sights on Fragile Neighbor Tunisia," *Washington Post*, May 13, 2016.
18. Raghavan, "Islamic State, Growing Stronger in Libya."
19. "Attaque terroriste de Ben Guerdane: Identification de 38 cadavres de terroristes," *Shems FM*, March 15, 2016.
20. "Gabes: Arrestation d'un individu qui voulait rallier les terroristes à Ben Guerdane," *Shems FM*, March 12, 2016.
21. Islamic State, "#Akhbar_al-khilafah #arhab_tawghit_tunis al-himmah fi al-tafa'il ma' al-hamlah tahridhiya 'ala istihadaf al-kufar wa-l-murtadin fi #tunis," *Nashir*, March 9, 2019.
22. Islamic State, "#Akhbar_al-khilafah."
23. The Islamic State—Tunisia Database, created by Aaron Y. Zelin, available at http://tunisianjihadism.com, last updated April 19, 2019.
24. Hédi and Garoui, "Les terroristes passent aux aveux."
25. Asma Ghribi, "Trouble in the Wild East," *Foreign Policy*, August 7, 2016.
26. Details on the Ben Gardane Takeover Attempt Database, created by Aaron Y. Zelin, available at http://tunisianjihadism.com, last updated April 23, 2019.
27. Tristan Dreisbach, "New Tunisian Constitution Adopted," *Tunisia Live*, January 26, 2014.
28. S. J., "The Salafist Struggle," *The Economist*, January 1, 2014.
29. Daveed Gartenstein-Ross and Oren Adaki, "Ansar al-Sharia in Tunisia's Social Media Activity in 2014," *Jihadology*, June 6, 2014.

30. Benjamin Roger, "Tunisie: Sur la trace des djihadistes de mont Chaambi," *Jeune Afrique*, May 7, 2013.
31. Fajr al-Qayrawan Facebook page, accessed July 11, 2014.
32. Jacob Jaffe, "14 Tunisian Soldiers Killed, 20 wounded in Chaambi Attack," *Tunisia Live*, July 17, 2014.
33. Central Division of al-Qaeda in the Islamic Maghrib, "Munasirah min maghrib al-islam li-dawlah al-islamiyah fi 'iraq wa-l-sham," Shabab al-Tawhid Media, March 22, 2014.
34. Abu Bakr al-Hussayni al-Qurayshi al-Baghdadi, "Although the Disbelievers Dislike It," *al-Furqan Media*, November 13, 2014.
35. Katibat 'Uqbah Bin Nafi, "al-Qayrawan Support for the Islamic State," *Ifriqiya Media*, September 16, 2014.
36. Aaron Y. Zelin, "Islamic State Attacks in Tunisia," *Tunisian Jihadism*, June 6, 2018.
37. Ifriqiya Media, "A Brief Explanation of What Is Going on in the Tunisian Field," March 31, 2015.
38. Ifriqiya Media, "Information, Reminders, Coded Messages, Advice, and Warning," December 17, 2014.
39. Ifriqiya Media, "Information, Reminders, Coded Messages."
40. Natasha Turak, "Medical Student Fatma Zouaghi, Alleged Ansar Al Sharia Member, Arrested," *Tunisia Live*, October 15, 2014; and "Tunisia: Young Girl Led Propaganda Cell of Ansar Al-Sharia and Okba Ibn Nafaa Brigade," *Tunis Afrique Presse*, October 14, 2014.
41. Ifriqiya Media, "Good Night in This Life and Immortality in Paradise," March 29, 2015; and Ifriqiya Media, "A Brief Explanation of What Is Going On."
42. Katibat 'Uqba Bin Nafi Facebook page, accessed April 16, 2015.
43. Patrick Markey, "Tunisia Signals Local al Qaeda Links to Bardo Museum Attack," Reuters, March 26, 2015.
44. Tarek Amara, "Tunisia Says Almost Wipes Out al Qaeda Group After Attacks," Reuters, July 13, 2015.
45. Islamic State, "Message to the People of Tunisia," al-I'tisam Media, December 17, 2014.
46. Islamic State, "Message to the People of Tunisia."
47. "Tunisia Beach Killer Trained with Museum Gunmen."
48. Abu Ibrahim al-Tunisi's martyrdon notice was originally posted here: https://twitter.com/spg9_c5k_rpg7/status/560131525891870721/photo/1, accessed January 27, 2015.
49. Islamic State, "Message to Our Brothers in Tunisia," Wilayat Tarabulus Media Office, April 7, 2015.
50. Office of the UN High Commissioner for Human Rights, "Preliminary Findings by the United Nations Working Group on the Use of Mercenaries on Its Official Visit to Tunisia—1 to 8 July 2015," https://www.ohchr.org/EN/NewsEvents/Pages/DisplayNews.aspx?NewsID=16219; and Bel Trew, "Hundreds of Jihadi Brides Sent for Combat Training," *Times*, April 19, 2016.
51. "Les Terroristes Gofrane et Rahma," *Shems FM*, September 18, 2015.
52. Trew, "Hundreds of Jihadi Brides."
53. Trew, "Hundreds of Jihadi Brides."
54. "#Amaliyat_Albunyan_al-Marsus: Qisah Umm Umar al-Tunisi Kama Ruwaytuha... Juz al-Thalath," *Markaz al-I'alami li-Amaliyat al-Bunyan al-Marsus*, November 29, 2016, https://www.facebook.com/BMCLY/photos/a.1000960909987714.1073741828.1000646256685846/1160462377370899.

55. Abu Malik Shaybah al-Hamad, "Scattered Words and Authentication for the Important Period Prior to Shaykh al-Shikaw's Allegiance Which Made the Islamic Nation Happy," Ifriqiya Media, March 27, 2015.
56. al-Hamad, "Scattered Words and Authentication."
57. Abu Muslim is on Tunisia's wanted list. See https://www.facebook.com/ministere.interieur.tunisie/photos/a.940857442608299/940868662607177.
58. Aaron Y. Zelin, "Boko Haram's Media and the Islamic State Connection?" *Jihadology*, January 27, 2015; and Jacob Zenn, "Wilayat West Africa Reboots for the Caliphate," *CTC Sentinel* 8, no. 8 (August 2015).
59. Abu Bakr Shikaw, "Bay'ah Jama'at Ahl al-Sunnah li-l-Da'wah wa-l-Jihad to the Caliph of the Muslims Abu Bakr al-Baghdadi," al-Urwah al-Wuthqa Foundation, March 7, 2015.
60. "Le terroriste Ouanes Fekih livré par le Niger à la Tunisie," *Kapitalis*, January 1, 2017; and "Extradition vers la Tunisie du terroriste et ancien Émir d'Ansaar Charia à Mahdia, Wannes Fekih Ahmed," *Shems FM*, January 1, 2017.
61. Ansar al-Sharia in Tunisia's Clerical Establishment Database, created by Aaron Y. Zelin, available at http://tunisianjihadism.com, last updated August 10, 2016.
62. U.S. Department of State, Office of the Spokesperson, "State Department Terrorist Designations of Muhammad al-Ghazali, Abukar Ali Adan, and Wanas al-Faqih," January 4, 2018, https://www.state.gov/state-department-terrorist-designations-of-muhammad-al-ghazali-abukar-ali-adan-and-wanas-al-faqih/.
63. "Tunisia Fears Jihadists Returning Home from Libya, Seeks Joint Action," Reuters, September 6, 2016.
64. Georg Heil, "The Berlin Attack and the 'Abu Walaa' Islamic State Recruitment Network," *CTC Sentinel* 10, no. 2 (February 2017), https://ctc.usma.edu/app/uploads/2017/02/CTC-Sentinel_Vol10Iss228.pdf.
65. Florian Flade, "Was das LKA bei Amris Terror-Chat Mitlas," *Welt*, March 27, 2017.
66. Florian Flade, "Der Einflüsterer von Anis Amri," *Welt*, June 14, 2018.
67. Flade, "Der Einflüsterer von Anis Amri."
68. Flade, "Der Einflüsterer von Anis Amri."
69. Terri Moon Cronk, "U.S. Airstrikes Kill 80 ISIL Fighters in Libya, Carter Says," U.S Department of Defense, January 19, 2017.
70. Paul Cruickshank and Nic Robertson, "U.S. Bombing in Libya Was Linked to Berlin Truck Attack," *CNN*, January 24, 2017.
71. Islamic State, "Adopting the Bardo Museum Operation in Islamic Tunisia," March 19, 2015, https://jihadology.net/2015/03/19/new-statement-from-the-islamic-state-adopting-the-bardo-museum-operation-in-islamic-tunisia.
72. About 12 percent of Tunisia's population relies upon wages from the tourism sector, and tourism accounts for about 7 percent of the country's gross domestic product. Hazel Heyer, "Tunisia Tourism Moves Forward by Sticking to the Old," *E-Turbo News*, March 12, 2008.
73. "Djihâd en Tunisie: Interview du frère Abou Mouqâtil At-Tounsî," *Dar al-Islam Magazine*, no. 3 (April 2015).
74. Islamic State, "Akhbar al Yawm: al Jumu'ah, 21 Jumadi al-Akhirah 1436 H," *Idha'at al-Bayan*, April 9, 2015.
75. Mujahidin of Tunisia of al-Qayrawan, "Baya to the Caliph of the Muslims Abu Bakr al-Baghdadi and Joining the Islamic State," May 18, 2015, https://jihadology.net/2015/05/18/new-audio-message-from-mujahidin-of-tunisia-of-al-qayrawan-bayah-to-the-caliph-of-the-muslims-abu-bakr-al-baghdadi-and-joining-the-islamic-state.

76. "Tunisia: Monitoring the Presence of Security and Armored Vehicles in the Capital," Wilayat Tunis Media Office, June 2, 2015.
77. Abu Bakr al-Hussayni al-Qurayshi al-Baghdadi, "In the Hospitality of the Leader of the Faithful," al-Furqan Media, April 29, 2019.
78. Conor McCormick-Cavanagh, "Tunisia's President Warns of State Collapse if Another Attack Takes Place," *Middle East Eye*, July 4, 2015.
79. "Masu'ul hukumi: Ansar al-sharia wara' hujum sussah al-irhabi," *Jawhara FM*, July 4, 2015, available at https://www.jawharafm.net.
80. Markey, "Tunisia Signals Local al Qaeda Links."
81. For more details on the wanted list, see Aaron Y. Zelin, "Tunisia's Most Wanted Terrorists," *Tunisian Jihadism*, April 3, 2019.
82. Mounir Souissi, "Tunisia Seeks to Wrest Back Control of Radicalized Mosques," Agence France-Presse, March 14, 2014.
83. U.S. Embassy in Tunis, "U.S.-Tunisia Strategic Dialogue," April 3, 2014, https://tn.usembassy.gov/us-tunisia-strategic-dialogue/.
84. "Tunisia Declares Mountainous Area 'Military Zone,'" Agence France-Presse, April 16, 2014.
85. Safa Ben Said, "Marzouki Promises Conditional Pardon to Gunmen on Mount Chaambi," *Tunisia Live*, May 7, 2014.
86. Defense Security Cooperation Agency, "Tunisia—UH-60M Black Hawk Helicopters," July 24, 2014, https://www.dsca.mil/major-arms-sales/tunisia-uh-60m-black-hawk-helicopters.
87. "Washington to Give Tunisia Military Aid to Battle Islamists," Reuters, August 26, 2014.
88. Houda Mzioudet, "Tunisia and Algeria Send Military Reinforcements to Borders with Libya," *Libya Herald*, February 17, 2015.
89. "Tunisia to Get 8 Black Hawks for Fight Against Militants," Agence France-Presse, February 27, 2015.
90. "Tunisia: Arbitrary Travel Restrictions," Human Rights Watch, July 10, 2015.
91. "Algeria Sends Air-to-Surface Missiles to Tunisia," *Middle East Monitor*, March 16, 2015.
92. Tarek Amara, "Tunisia Says Plans to Renew Ties with Syria to Help Track Fighters," Reuters, April 2, 2015.
93. Tarek Amara, "U.S. to Triple Military Aid to Tunisia," Reuters, April 10, 2015.
94. Conor Sheils, "Game over for Tunisia's Extremist Preachers?," *Tunisia Live*, May 13, 2015.
95. Nahal Toosi, "U.S. to Upgrade Tunisia's Ally Status," *Politico*, May 21, 2015.
96. "Tunisia: Algeria to Train Tunisian Special Forces," *AnsaMed*, June 23, 2015.
97. Tamer El-Ghobashy and Radhouane Addala, "How a Gunman Brought Terror to a Tunisian Resort," *Wall Street Journal*, June 28, 2015.
98. Aditya Tejas, "Tunisia to Build Libya Border Wall After ISIS Attacks," *International Business Times*, July 8, 2015.
99. "Tunisia Passes Anti-Terror Laws After Deadly Attacks," *al-Jazeera*, July 25, 2015.
100. "Tunisia Eyes Enhanced Security to Win Back Tourists," Reuters, September 15, 2015.
101. "Tunisia Joining US-Led Coalition Against IS: PM," Agence France-Presse, October 3, 2015.
102. "Min. du Transport: Nouvelles mesures sécuritaires dans les aéroports," *Shems FM*, November 8, 2015.
103. Christine Petré, "How Tunisia's Moderate Imams Are Seeking to Reclaim Islam from Extremists," *al-Monitor*, December 8, 2015.

104. "Tunisia Launches 'Ambassadors Against Terrorism' Program," *al-Bawaba*, February 1, 2016.
105. Oscar Nkala, "Tunisia to Install Surveillance Gear on New Libyan Border Wall," *Defense News*, February 19, 2016.
106. "Britain Sends Troops to Help Guard Libya-Tunisia Border," *DW*, February 29, 2016.
107. Tunisian Arrests Related to Jihadism Since 2014 Database, created by Aaron Y. Zelin, available at http://tunisianjihadism.com, last updated May 8, 2019.
108. Tunisian Arrests Related to Jihadism Since 2014 Database.
109. Tunisian Arrests Related to Jihadism Since 2014 Database.
110. Aaron Y. Zelin, "Tunisia's Female Jihadists," Washington Institute for Near East Policy, *Policy Watch*, no. 3032 (October 31, 2018).
111. Adam Entous and Missy Ryan, "U.S. Has Secretly Expanded Its Global Network of Drone Bases to North Africa," *Washington Post*, October 26, 2016.
112. "NATO Steps Up Efforts to Project Stability and Strengthen Partners," NATO, July 9, 2016, https://www.nato.int/cps/en/natohq/news_133804.htm.
113. "Tunisia Adopts Strategy to Fight 'Terrorism,'" Agence France-Presse, November 7, 2016.
114. "Youssef Chahed Decides to Set Up National Intelligence Centre," *TAP*, December 20, 2016.
115. "Tunisia Gets 6 US Combat Helicopters to Fight 'Terror,'" Agence France-Presse, February 6, 2017.
116. "India, Tunisia Vow to Combat Terror, Extremism," *India Times*, July 12, 2018.
117. Jeremy Felkowsky, "Radicalisation in Prison Cells in France and Tunisia," *al-Araby*, April 16, 2018.
118. Jack Detsch, "Pentagon Partners with Germany on Tunisia Border Security," *al-Monitor*, February 23, 2018.
119. "La Tunisie gèlera les comptes bancaires des terroristes," *Mosaique FM*, April 12, 2018.
120. "Crime de terrorisme: Création d'une magistrature pour les enfants," *Shems FM*, May 17, 2018.
121. "Algeria and Tunisia Agree to Fight Cross-Border Terrorism," *Middle East Monitor*, July 17, 2018.
122. Wagdy Sawahel, "In Wake of Bombing, Plan to Fight Extremism on Campuses," *University World News*, November 23, 2018.
123. "Japan, Tunisia Agree on Anti-Terror Measures," *NHK*, December 26, 2018.
124. "Tawqiy'a 'aqud tamwil li-fa'idah (05) khams jama'iyat min al-mujtama'a al-madani al-tunisi," *Tunisia's National Counterterrorism Commission*, July 5, 2019.
125. "Terrorisme en Tunisie: Après la lutte place à l'anticipation," *Mosaique FM*, April 13, 2019.
126. "Chahed: On a évité des attentats terroristes pendant le ramadan," *Mosaique FM*, May 9, 2019.
127. "Tunisia Efforts to Eradicate Torture 'Disappointing:' UN," Agence France-Presse, June 7, 2014; and "Tunisia: New Evidence of Torture Five Years on from 'Jasmine Revolution,'" *Amnesty International UK*, January 14, 2016.
128. "Tunisia: Arbitrary Travel Restrictions."
129. "Tunisia: Counterterror Law Endangers Rights," Human Rights Watch, July 31, 2015.
130. Zeinab Marzouk, "Government Uses Anti Terror Law to Prosecute Journalists," *Tunisia Live*, November 19, 2015.
131. "UN Expert: Tunisia Must Speed Up Reviews of Terror Cases," Associated Press, February 9, 2017.

132. Tunisian Terrorism Prosecutions Since 2014 Database, created by Aaron Y. Zelin, available at http://tunisianjihadism.com, last updated May 10, 2019.

11. The Future of the Tunisian Jihadi Movement

1. Bruce Hoffman, "Al-Qaeda's Resurrection," *Council on Foreign Relations*, March 6, 2018; Daveed Gartenstein-Ross and Nathaniel Barr, "How Al-Qaeda Works: The Jihadist Group's Evolving Organizational Design," *Current Trends in Islamist Ideology* 23 (June 2018); Julia McQuaid, Jonathan Schroden, Pamela G. Faber, P. Kathleen Hammerberg, Alexander Powell, Zack Gold, David Knoll, and William Rosenau, *Independent Assessment of U.S. Government Efforts against Al Qaeda* (Arlington, Va.: Center for Naval Analysis, October 2017); and Aaron Y. Zelin, "How al-Qaeda Survived Drones, Uprisings, and the Islamic State," Washington Institute for Near East Policy, *Policy Focus*, no. 153 (June 2017).
2. Katibat 'Uqbah Bin Nafi, "So Wait; Indeed We, Along with You, Are Waiting," August 21, 2015, https://jihadology.net/2015/08/21/new-statement-from-katibat-uqbah-ibn-nafi-so-wait-indeed-we-along-with-you-are-waiting.
3. Aaron Y. Zelin, "Jihadi Attacks in Tunisia Prior to 2011," *Tunisian Jihadism*, October 22, 2018.
4. Ansar al-Sharia in Tunisia's Activities Database, created by Aaron Y. Zelin, available at http://tunisianjihadism.com, last updated February 18, 2019.
5. al-Qaeda in the Islamic Maghrib, "The Mirage of Elections in Tunisia," al-Andalus Media, May 4, 2018.
6. al-Qaeda in the Islamic Maghrib, "Revenge For the Free Tunisia: Targeting the Interior Minister 'Lutfi Bin Jiddu,'" al-Andalus Media, June 13, 2014.
7. Katibat 'Uqbah Bin Nafi, "So Wait."
8. Katibat 'Uqbah Ibn Nafi, "Clarification and Warning About the Killing of the Missionary Salih al-Firjani," September 3, 2015, https://jihadology.net/2015/09/03/new-statement-from-katibat-uqbah-ibn-nafi-clarification-and-warning-about-the-killing-of-the-missionary-%e1%b9%a3ali%e1%b8%a5-al-firjani.
9. Katibat 'Uqbah Ibn Nafi, "Denial: Innocence of the Mujahidin From the Murder of 'Haddah Rihimi,'" April 4, 2016, https://jihadology.net/2016/04/04/new-statement-from-katibat-uqbah-ibn-nafi-denial-innocence-of-the-mujahidin-from-the-murder-of-%e1%b8%a5addah-ri%e1%b8%a5imi.
10. 'Abd al-Rahman al-Jaza'iri, "Message to the Lions of al-Qayrawan," *Ifriqiya al-Muslimah*, December 4, 2016.
11. Katibat 'Uqbah Ibn Nafi, "Clarification and Warning"; Katibat 'Uqbah Ibn Nafi,' "Denial"; and Katibat 'Uqbah Ibn Nafi, "Explanation of the Circumstances for the Loss of the Shepherd 'Lamjad al-Qariri,'" June 26, 2018, https://jihadology.net/2018/06/26/new-statement-from-katibat-uqbah-ibn-nafi-explanation-of-the-circumstances-for-the-loss-of-the-shepherd-lamjad-al-qariri-lamjed-griri.
12. Jihadi Attacks in Tunisia Since 2014 Database, created by Aaron Y. Zelin, available at http://tunisianjihadism.com, last updated May 10, 2019.
13. Jihadi Attacks in Tunisia Since 2014 Database.
14. "Tunisia Wrestles with the Return of Its Isis Orphans," *Times*, April 3, 2019.
15. Tunisia Ministry of Interior Returnee Dossiers, accessed April 14, 2019; copy maintained in my archives.
16. Sarah Souli, "Tunisia: Why Foreign Fighters Abandon ISIL," *Al Jazeera*, March 3, 2016.

17. "Tunisie-Société: Explosion d'une bombe artisanale près de Sfax," *Kapitalis*, April. 6, 2014.
18. Erika Solomon, "ISIS Proves Vulnerable to Its Own 'Ghost Armies,'" *Financial Times*, December 20, 2015.
19. Souli, "Tunisia: Why Foreign Fighters."
20. Rahma Guettari, "Tunisian Man Speaks of Being Serially Sexual Abused Within ISIS Ranks," *Tunisia Live*, November 4, 2016.
21. Rodi Said, "Islamic State Turned on Dissenters as Raqqa Assault Neared," Reuters, June 28, 2017.
22. "Quand Daech embrigade le fils et tue le père," *Mosaique FM*, June 29, 2016; "Gaziantep'te IŞİDçi Polise Gidince Yakalandı," *Vatan*, April 8, 2015; and "Son Dakika Haberleri: Atatürk Havalimanı'nda DAEŞ'li Yolcu Paniği," *Milliyet*, October 21, 2016.
23. Haïfa Mzalouat and Malek Khadhraoui, "Fayçal, du jihad en Syrie à la désillusion," *Inkyfada*, August 31, 2018.
24. Anthony Loyd, "Hundreds of ISIS Widows Trapped in Syria as Caliphate Falls," *Times*, December 16, 2017.
25. A. Agron, "Cracks in the Caliphate: Western ISIS Members Complain About Life in the Islamic State," *Middle East Media Research Institute*, November 12, 2015.
26. Said, "Islamic State Turned on Dissenters."
27. Said, "Islamic State Turned on Dissenters."
28. David D. Kirkpatrick, "New Freedoms in Tunisia Drive Support for ISIS," *New York Times*, October 21, 2014.
29. Kirkpatrick, "New Freedoms in Tunisia Drive Support for ISIS."
30. "The Cost of Leaving Islamic State," Associated Press, February 3, 2015.
31. Mzalouat and Khadhraoui, "Fayçal, du jihad en Syrie à la désillusion."
32. "The Cost of Leaving Islamic State."
33. Taha Abed al-Wahed, "ISIS Wives Live in Oppression, Slavery," *Asharq al-Awsat*, July 16, 2017.
34. Borzou Daragahi, "We Spoke to Women Who Married into ISIS in Syria: These Are Their Regrets," *BuzzFeed*, July 20, 2017.
35. Sara Manisera, "'I Came for the Jihad:' Women Tell of Life in the Islamic State," *Syria Deeply*, September 29, 2017.
36. Loyd, "Hundreds of ISIS Widows Trapped."
37. "Tunisia to Put on Trial Son of Istanbul Attack Victim for Joining Islamic State," Agence France-Presse, July 2, 2016.
38. Lindsey Snell, "The ISIS Volunteer Who Won't Be Coming Home," *Daily Beast*, March 20, 2018.
39. Loyd, "Hundreds of ISIS Widows Trapped."
40. Guettari, "Tunisian Man Speaks."
41. Snell, "The ISIS Volunteer."
42. "al-Asimah fi al-sadarah, al-'a'idun min bu'ur al-tawatr wa tuwazi'ahum al-jaghrafi hasab al-wilayat fi tunis," *Akhir Khabar*, December 30, 2016, available at http://www.akherkhabaronline.com.
43. Sudarsan Raghavan, "No Nationality Heeded the Call to Come Fight for ISIS Like Tunisians Did: Now They're Stuck," *Washington Post*, May 11, 2019.
44. Martin Chulov and Bethan McKernan, "Hoda Muthana 'Deeply Regrets' Joining Isis and Wants to Return Home," *Guardian*, February 17, 2019.
45. Tony Gamal-Gabriel, "In Syria's Al-Hol Camp, Ultra-Extremists Fuel Fear," Agence France-Presse, March 31, 2019.

46. Raghavan, "No Nationality Heeded the Call."
47. Amberin Zaman, "Inside the Prison Holding IS Detainees in Northeast Syria," *al-Monitor*, March 15, 2019.
48. "1,000 Tunisians Fearing Return of Jihadis March to Say 'No,'" Associated Press, January 8, 2017.
49. "Libya Ready to Extradite ISIS Affiliates, Tunisia Refuses to Receive them," *Libya Herald*, May 15, 2016.
50. Raghavan, "No Nationality Heeded the Call."
51. Raghavan, "No Nationality Heeded the Call."
52. "Un terroriste condamné à mort au Mali vient de rentrer en Tunisie," *Business News*, June 20, 2014.
53. "Sudan: Arrestato Fezzani, il reclutatore dell'Isis in Italia," *TGCom 24*, November 14, 2016.
54. "Sudan Extradites Senior Tunisian Islamic State Suspect: State Media," Reuters, December 23, 2016.
55. Emily Rauhala, "Philippine Police Arrest Man Suspected of Recruiting for the Islamic State," *Washington Post*, February 19, 2018; and "Philippine Police Say Arab Militant Suspect Won't Be Freed," Associated Press, March 9, 2018.
56. Zam Yusa, "Philippines: 100 Foreign Fighters Joined ISIS in Mindanao Since the Marawi Battle," *Defense Post*, November 5, 2018.
57. "Philippine Police Say Arab Militant Suspect Won't Be Freed."
58. Melissa Goh, "Malaysia on Alert After Arrests of 9 Terror Suspects, Including Foreigners," *Channel News Asia*, March 10, 2019.
59. Tunisians Deported from Italy Database, created by Aaron Y. Zelin, available at http://tunisianjihadism.com, last updated March 19, 2019.
60. "Tunisia Releases Suspected bin Laden Bodyguard, Citing Lack of Evidence," Reuters, July 27, 2018.
61. "Un terroriste agresse un juge militaire," *Mosaique FM*, February 26, 2019.
62. "Le terroriste Adel Ghandri condamné à la perpétuité incompressible," *Shems FM*, February 27, 2019.
63. See Romain Caillet Twitter post, April 23, 2019, https://twitter.com/RomainCaillet/status/1120824548952297473.
64. "Tunisian Prisons Are Overpopulated, Justice Minister," *North Africa Post*, January 3, 2017; and Nadia Bentamansourt, "Tunisie: 45% des prisons tunisiennes ne sont pas médicalisées," *African Manager*, March 16, 2016.
65. George Packer, "Exporting Jihad: The Arab Spring Has Given Tunisians the Freedom to Act on Their Unhappiness," *New Yorker*, March 28, 2016.
66. "H. Hammami: Un bloc de la prison de Mornag, transformé en émirat," *Mosaique FM*, January 3, 2017.
67. Felkowsky, "Radicalisation in Prison Cells in France and Tunisia."
68. Felkowsky, "Radicalisation in Prison Cells in France and Tunisia."
69. Lydia Letsch, "Countering Violent Extremism in Tunisia—Between Dependency and Self-Reliance," *Journal for Deradicalization*, no. 17 (Winter 2018): 163–95.
70. Other groups include Tunisia's Action Against Exclusion and Marginalization Association, which aims to rehabilitate and integrate youth prisoners into society and professional life and protect them from extremism; the National Youth Initiative Against Terrorism, which provides poor youths with activities at recreation centers and offers counselling sessions against jihad; and Salam: Preventing Violent Extremism in Tunisia, which has five key missions: strengthening the observatory on the prevention of

violent extremism in Tunisia as a platform of dialogue and proposals for civil society in public policies against violent extremism, contributing to the development of knowledge on the deep causes of violent fundamentalism, promoting the participation of women and the young in the creation of targeted public policies, helping the young against imams preaching violence, and working to implement a strategy against violent extremism in prisons.

71. F. Brinley Bruton and Mushtaq Yusufzai, "9/11 Hangs Over Taliban Talks and Assurances Militant Group Has Changed," *NBC News*, December 17, 2018.
72. "1000 terroristes de retour en Tunisie," *Realities*, February 19, 2019.
73. See Gilles N. Twitter post, March 28, 2015, https://twitter.com/VegetaMoustache/status/581956889170280448/photo/1.
74. "GAO: Deux présumés djihadistes ont été arrêtés hier à Taboye," *Studio Tamani*, October 15, 2017.
75. "Gao: Un cadre du JNIM échappe à un raid de Barkhane à Tilemsi," *Kibaru*, December 14, 2017.
76. Heni Nsaibia, "Exclusive: End of the Run for Tunisian Ansar al-Sharia Founder Abu Iyadh al-Tunisi," *MENASTREAM*, February 23, 2019; "Exclusive for Kibaru: Abu Al-Hammam Was Shot Down by French Forces, According to His Relatives," *Kibaru*, February 22, 2019; and "Al-Qaeda Supporters Downplay Impact of Leaders' Deaths in Mali," *BBC Monitoring*, February 27, 2019.
77. Carlotta Gall and Eric Schmitt, "Jihadist from Tunisia Died in Strike in Libya, U.S. Official Says," *New York Times*, July 2, 2015.
78. al-Muhajir al-Khurasani and Shibl al-Qaeda Telegram channels.
79. Shaykh Abu Hudhayfah al-Sudani, "The Sun Rises in Mali," February 27, 2019, https://jihadology.net/2019/02/27/new-release-from-shaykh-abu-%e1%b8%a5udhayfah-al-sudani-the-sun-rises-in-mali.
80. Nsaibia, "Exclusive: End of the Run"; and "Abu 'iyadh yumkin mn al-kharuj min libiya wa huwa muqim fi hadha al-makan," *Akhir Khabar*, May 28, 2016, available at http://www.akherkhabaronline.com.
81. Heni Nsaibia, "Libya: Tunisian AQIM Commander Killed in Ubari Airstrike," *MENASTREAM*, August 3, 2018, http://menastream.com/tunisian-aqim-commander-ubari.
82. Heni Nsaibia, "Libya: Air Raid by Unknown Aircraft in Gardhah al-Shati," *MENASTREAM*, November 15, 2016.
83. Heni Nsaibia, "MENASTREAM ID #3: Tunisian AQIM Veteran Mokhtar Akkouri Announced Dead," *MENASTREAM*, April 10, 2017.
84. Nsaibia, "MENASTREAM ID #3."
85. "Interview with Libya's Military Strongman Khalifa Haftar," *France 24*, July 27, 2017.
86. This is based on research from the Italian journalist Daniele Raineri and Spanish researcher Marco Arnaboldi.
87. "Wasalu ila idlib: inshiqaq al-irhab al-tunisi bilal al-shawashi wa 4 amra' 'an 'da'ish,'" *al-Chourouk*, December 7, 2016, available at http://archive.alchourouk.com.
88. Interview with Syrian activist from Kafr Nabl, November 7, 2017.
89. Interview with Syrian activist from Kafr Nabl, November 7, 2017.
90. See @SakeOfTawhid__, post March 19, 2019, https://twitter.com/sakeoftawhid__/status/1108009925899444229?s=12. Author maintains a copy in his archives.
91. "Twenty-Third Report of the Analytical Support and Sanctions Monitoring Team Submitted Pursuant to Resolution 2368 (2017) Concerning ISIL (Da'esh), Al-Qaida and Associated Individuals and Entities," United Nations Security Council, S/2019/50,

January 15, 2019, https://www.un.org/sc/ctc/wp-content/uploads/2019/02/N1846950_EN.pdf.
92. "Twenty-Third Report of the Analytical Support and Sanctions Monitoring Team."
93. "Twenty-Third Report of the Analytical Support and Sanctions Monitoring Team."

Author's Note on Terminology

1. For a more in depth analysis on these terms and the intellectual history behind them, see Aaron Y. Zelin, "From the Archduke to the Caliph: The Islamist Evolution That Led to 'The Islamic State,'" in *The First World War and Its Aftermath: The Shaping of the Middle East*, ed. by T. G. Fraser (London: Gingko Library, 2015).
2. Peter Mandaville, *Global Political Islam* (New York: Routledge, 2007), 57.
3. Nelly Lahoud, *The Jihadis' Path to Self-Destruction* (New York: Columbia University Press, 2010), 105–6.
4. Lahoud, *The Jihadis' Path to Self-Destruction*.
5. Brynjar Lia, *The Society of the Muslim Brothers in Egypt: The Rise of an Islamic Mass Movement 1928–1942* (Reading, U.K.: Ithaca Press, 2006).
6. Sayed Khatab, *The Political Thought of Sayyid Qutb: The Theory of Jahiliyyah*, London: Routledge, 2006; and Sayed Khatab, *The Power of Sovereignty: The Political and Ideological Philosophy of Sayyid Qutb* (London: Routledge, 2006).
7. For more on Qutb's legacy, see Aaron Y. Zelin, "al-Farīḍa al-Ghā'iba and al-Sadat's Assassination, a 30 Year Retrospective," *International Journal for Arab Studies* 3, no. 2 (July 2012).
8. Muhammad 'Abd al-Salam Farag, *al-Jihad al-Farida al-Gha'iba* (n.p., n.d.).
9. Joas Wagemakers, *A Quietist Jihadi: The Ideology and Influence of Abu Muhammad al-Maqdisi* (New York: Cambridge University Press, 2012), 3.
10. Roel Meijer, "Introduction," in *Global Salafism: Islam's New Religious Movement*, ed. by Roel Meijer, 1–32 (New York: Columbia University Press, 2009), 13.
11. Bernard Haykel, "On the Nature of Salafi Thought and Action," in *Global Salafism: Islam's New Religious Movement*, ed. by Roel Meijer, 33–51 (New York: Columbia University Press, 2009), 50–51.
12. Quintan Wiktorowicz, "Anatomy of the Salafi Movement," *Studies in Conflict & Terrorism* 29, no. 3 (August 2006): 208.
13. Wagemakers, *A Quietist Jihadi: The Ideology and Influence of Abu Muhammad al-Maqdisi*, 58.
14. Mu'assasat Āl al-Bayt lil-Fikr al-Islāmī, *Jihad and the Islamic Law of War* (Amman, Jordan: Royal Aal Al-Bayt Institute for Islamic Thought, 2007), 1.
15. Michael Bonner, *Jihad in Islamic History: Doctrines and Practice* (Princeton, N.J.: Princeton University Press, 2006), 2–3.
16. Bonner, *Jihad in Islamic History*. More specifically, the book of jihad usually discusses "law governing the conduct war, which covers treatment of non-belligerents, division of spoils among the victors, and such matters. Declaration and cessation of hostilities are discussed, raising the question of what constitutes proper authority. A Book of Jihad will also include discussion of how the jihad derives from the Quran and the Sunna, or in other words, how the jihad has been commanded by God" (2–3).
17. Muhammad Abdel Haleem, *Understanding the Qur'an: Themes and Style* (London: I. B. Tauris, 1999), 60–62; and Bonner, *Jihad in Islamic History*, 160.
18. 'Abd Allah 'Azzam, *Defense of Muslim Lands* (Kingdom of Saudi Arabia: Maktaba Dar-us-Salam, 1993), 14–15.

19. For more on this phenomenon, see Thomas Hegghammer, "The Rise of Muslim Foreign Fighters: Islam and the Globalization of Jihad," *International Security* 35, no. 3 (Winter 2010/11): 53–94.
20. Lahoud, *The Jihadis' Path to Self-Destruction*, 118 and 121.
21. Daniel Lav, *Radical Islam and the Revival of Medieval Theology* (New York: Cambridge University Press, 2012), 122 and 128.
22. Lav, *Radical Islam and the Revival of Medieval Theology*, 201.
23. Wagemakers, *A Quietist Jihadi*, 84.
24. A. H. Mathias Zahniser, "Invitation," in *Encyclopedia of the Qur'an*, vol. 2, ed. by Jane Dammen McAuliffe (Leiden: Brill, 2001), 557.
25. Sohirin M. Solihin, *Islamic Da'wah: Theory and Practice* (Kuala Lumpur: IIUM Press, 2008).
26. Michael Cook, *Commanding Right and Forbidding Wrong in Islamic Thought* (Cambridge: Cambridge University Press, 2000), 13.
27. Roel Meijer, "Commanding Right and Forbidding Wrong as a Principle of Social Action: The Case of the Egyptian al-Jama'a al-Islamiyya," in *Global Salafism: Islam's New Religious Movement*, ed. by Roel Meijer, 189–220 (New York: Columbia University Press, 2009), 191, 205.
28. Cook, *Commanding Right and Forbidding Wrong*, 515
29. Meijer, "Commanding Right and Forbidding Wrong," 194.

BIBLIOGRAPHY

Primary Sources

Primary Sources Authored by Tunisian Jihadis

"#Amaliyat_Albunyan_al-Marsus: Qisah Umm Umar al-Tunisi Kama Ruwaytuha . . . Juz al-Thalath." *Markaz al-I'alami li-Amaliyat al-Bunyan al-Marsus*, November 29, 2016, https://www.facebook.com/BMCLY/photos/a.1000960909987714.1073741828.1000646256685846/1160462377370899.

"al-Dawlah al-islamiyah 'da'ish' wa 'aqidat al-takfir—da'ish tadu'i anaha al-ta'ifah al-mansurah wa ansar al-shari'ah 'ala khata.'" March 13, 2014. Originally available on YouTube: https://www.youtube.com/watch?v=pvHnfeaBQ9E. Author maintains a copy in his archives.

"al-Dawrah al-'ilmiyah al-thaniyah bi-tunis." *Mawqah al-Islam fi Tunis*, January 10, 2012, https://islamentunisie.com/?p=1372.

"al-Dawrah al-'ilmiyah al-ula li-l-shaykh ahmad bin 'umar al-hazimi bi-madanin." *Mawqah al-Islam fi Tunis*, May 8, 2012, https://islamentunisie.com/?p=2675.

al-Qaeda in the Islamic Maghrib. "The Mirage of Elections in Tunisia." al-Andalus Media, May 4, 2018.

"al-Qahwah: ma' juhur bin mubarak wa bilal al-shuwashi." Shabakat Tunis al-Ikhbariyyah, *YouTube*, December 11, 2012. https://www.youtube.com/watch?v=ZuEj3Gku4q8.

al-Shuruq Interview with Abu 'Iyadh, March 17, 2012.

"An Important Message and Advice to the New *Nafirin* (Those Who Heeded the Call to Jihad)." Shabab al-Tawhid Media, March 11, 2014.

Ansar al-Sharia in Tunisia. "About the Tunisian Elections," October 22, 2011. Author maintains a copy in his archives.

———. "Active Contribution to the Brothers in the Refugee Tents at the Tunisian-Libyan Border—The Caravan of Victory," March 2–4, 2011. Author maintains a copy in his archives.

———. "An Invitation to All Brothers." al-Bayyariq Media, October 6, 2012.
———. "Ardh li-riyadhah al-zamaqtal." al-Bayyariq Media, May 24, 2012.
———. "Awards to Children at al-Salam Neighborhood School in Bou Mhel el-Bassatine." al-Bayyariq Media, March 15, 2013.
———. "'The Believers Are But Brothers:' Aid Convoy to Haydrah." al-Bayyariq Media, February 20, 2012.
———. "Burning the Flag of the Majus Iran in Gabes." al-Bayyariq Media, August 18, 2012.
———. "Children Refresher Day in the Northern Suburbs." al-Bayyariq Media, May 1, 2013.
———. "Children's Party for the End of Ramadan in El Krib." al-Bayyariq Media, August 4, 2013.
———. "Cleaning Campaign in Ez Zahra." al-Bayyariq Media, March 27, 2013.
———. "Cubs of Ansar al-Sharia in Sfax." al-Bayyariq Media, June 2, 2013.
———. "Cubs of Tawhid Camp in Alataya." al-Bayyariq Media, June 23, 2013.
———. "Cubs of Tawhid at a Party in Menzel Bourguiba." al-Bayyariq Media, June 4, 2011.
———. "Da'wah Forum in Douar Hicher." al-Bayyariq Media, April 6, 2013.
———. "Da'wah Forum in Le Kram." al-Bayyariq Media, May 11, 2013.
———. "Da'wah Tabling in Douar Hicher." al-Bayyariq Media, July 25, 2013.
———. "Da'wah Tour in the Neighborhoods of al-Mitlawi." al-Bayyariq Media, June 1, 2013.
———. "Dialogue of Shaykh Abu 'Iyadh al-Tunisi with the Journalist Nasr al-Din Bin Hadid." al-Bayyariq Media, January 30, 2013.
———. "First Da'wah Forum in Hammam-Lif." al-Bayyariq Media, March 31, 2013.
———. "Graphic Announcing the Second Annual Conference." al-Bayyariq Media, April 25, 2012.
———. "Helping Needy Families in Ariana." al-Bayyariq Media, June 2, 2013.
———. "Helping Refugees at Tunisian-Libyan Border." al-Bayyariq Media, March 2–4, 2011.
———. "Ihda' ila jabhat al-nusrah ji'inakum bi-l-fatah al-jawlani." al-Bayyariq Media, January 24, 2013.
———. "Khutbah of Abu Muhanad al-Tunisi." al-Bayyariq Media, February 17, 2012.
———. "Khutbah by Abu Sufyan al-Sulami [Turki Bin'ali]." al-Bayyariq Media, June 21, 2013.
———. "Learning Session in the Preparation of al-Ruqyah al-Sharia." al-Bayyariq Media, February 23–25, 2013.
———. "Lecture by 'Atif al-Matiri." al-Bayyariq Media, June 18, 2013.
———. "Lecture by Kamal Zuruq." al-Bayyariq Media, April 24, 2013.
———. "Leisure Trip of the Children Towards Natural Attractions of the Region from Douar Hicher." al-Bayyariq Media, April 29, 2013.
———. "Main Road Maintenance Campaign in Ariana." al-Bayyariq Media, March 10, 2013.
———. "Medical Services in Ksour Essef." al-Bayyariq Media, April 22, 2012.
———. "Medical Services in Sidi Bouzid." al-Bayyariq Media, November 11, 2012.
———. "The Moment of Our Brother 'Ali al-Harzi's Release from Prison." al-Bayyariq Media, January 8, 2013.
———. "Nusrah al-shari'ah fi tunis al-islam." al-Bayyariq Media, March 25, 2012.
———. "Party at Conclusion of Children's Session 'In the Shadow of the Qur'an' in Kalaa Kebira." al-Bayyariq Media, August 4, 2013.
———. "Receiving and Carrying Yusri al-Tariqi's Body." al-Bayyariq Media, November 23, 2011.
———. "Regarding the Disagreement in al-Sham." al-Bayyariq Media, July 15, 2013.
———. "Showing al-Qaeda Video 'The West and the Tunnel' at La Cagna Mosque." al-Bayyariq Media, January 5, 2013.
———. "Showing al-Qaeda Video 'The West and the Tunnel' at al-Taqwa Mosque in El Ouardia." al-Bayyariq Media, January 14, 2013.

———. "Soccer Lesson for the Cubs of Islam in Mateur." al-Bayyariq Media, October 28, 2012.
———. "Sports Tournament for the Cubs of the Supporters in El Krib." al-Bayyariq Media, March 28, 2013.
———. "Surat al-Mariyyam Contest in Tunis." al-Bayyariq Media, January 1, 2013.
———. "Tahiyyah min ashbal ansar al-shari'ah ila jabhat al-nusra bi-bilad al-sham." Ansar al-Shari'ah in Tunisia's Facebook Page, April 28, 2013.
———. "Untitled Video of Abu 'Iyadh Speech." al-Bayyariq Media, February 20, 2012.
———. "Yawm al-thalatha' in sha' allah satanataliq hawiyah tuhamil al-wasa'il al-daw'iyah ila tunis." al-Qayrawan Media, December 19, 2011.
"Bayan bi-khasus iftitah ma'had ibn abu zayd al-qayrawani li-l-'ulum al-shari'ah." March 1, 2012. http://majles.alukah.net/t97703.
"Bushra sara li-l-muwahidin // qariban iftaah mu'wassaat al-qayrawan al-i'alami—in sha allah." al-Qayrawan Media (blog), April 27, 2011. http://www.al-qayrawan.blogspot.com/2011/04/blog-post.html.
"Dawrah 'ilmiyah: shaykh ahmad bin 'umar al-hazimi." *Mawqah al-Islam fi Tunis*, October 29, 2011. https://islamentunisie.com/?p=453.
"Djihâd en Tunisie: Interview du frère Abou Mouqâtil At-Tounsî." *Dar al-Islam Magazine*, no. 3 (April 2015).
Hamad, Abu Malik Shaybah al-. "Scattered Words and Authentication for the Important Period Prior to Shaykh al-Shikaw's Allegiance Which Made the Islamic Nation Happy." Ifriqiya Media, March 27, 2015.
Hatab, Abu Ja'far al-. "Bay'at al-amsar li-l-imam al-mukhtar: Ahkam al-bay'ah fi al-islam wa-tatarayliha 'ala bay'ah ahl al-sham." al-Bayyariq Media, June 26, 2013.
———. "Provisions of Emigration and Jihad for Women." al-Bayyariq Media, March 23, 2013.
———. "Stance Ahead of the Third Annual Conference." al-Bayyariq Media, May 13, 2013.
"I'tirafat li-Muhammad bin Muhsin al-Gharbi al-Makanni bi-Abu Zayd Tunisi al-Jinsiyyah." Quwat al-Rada al-Khasah, February 23, 2016. https://www.facebook.com/QwtAlrada Alhaast/videos/1159313520755270.
Ifriqiya Media. "A Brief Explanation of What Is Going on in the Tunisian Field." March 31, 2015.
———. "Good Night in This Life and Immortality in Paradise." March 29, 2015.
———. "Information, Reminders, Coded Messages, Advice, and Warning." December 17, 2014.
"Intervista: Hassan Ben Brik, Stato islamico non con la forza . . . per ora." *Globalist*, September 24, 2012.
"Irtiqa' al-akh isma'il min madinat al-sayjumi ardh al-rijal." Ansar al-Sharia'h in Tunisia's Facebook Page, June 20, 2013.
Islamic State. "Adopting the Bardo Museum Operation in Islamic Tunisia." March 19, 2015. https://jihadology.net/2015/03/19/new-statement-from-the-islamic-state-adopting-the-bardo-museum-operation-in-islamic-tunisia/.
———. "#Akhbar_al_khilafah #arhab_tawghit_tunis al-himmah fi al-tafa'il ma' al-hamlah tahridhiya 'ala istihadaf al-kufar wa-l-murtadin fi #tunis." *Nashir*, March 9, 2019.
———. "Akhbar al-Yawm: al-Jumu'ah, 21 Jumadi al-Akhirah 1436 H." *Idha'at al-Bayan*, April 9, 2015.
———. "Among the Believers Are Men: Abu 'Umar al-Tunisi." *Dabiq Magazine*, no. 10 (July 13, 2015).
———. "The Brother Abu Yasin al-Tunisi (May God Accept Him)." Wilayat Ninawa Media Office, August 9, 2016.
———. "Foothold of the Conquerors." Wilayat al-Raqqah Media Office, June 16, 2016.

——. "Flashes in the Shade of the Caliphate #2: Interview with the Abu Fatimah al-Tunisi," Wilayat al-Barakah Media Office, October 28, 2014.
——. "Interview with Abu Muqatil." *Dabiq Magazine*, no. 8, March 30, 2015.
——. "Message to Our Brothers in Tunisia," Wilayat Tarabulus Media Office, April 7, 2015
——. "Message to the People of Tunisia." al-I'tisam Media, December 17, 2014.
——. "Report from Wilayat al-Khayr." Wilayat al-Khayr Media Office, August 27, 2014.
"Istishahid mu'az hizm." Ansar al-Sharia in Tunisia's Facebook Page, November 29, 2012.
"Its Knights Are Conquering Foreign Lands While It Is a Hostage." Shabab al-Tawhid Media, October 24, 2014.
Katibat 'Uqbah Bin Nafi. "al-Qayrawan Support for the Islamic State," Ifriqiya Media, September 16, 2014.
——. "Clarification and Warning About the Killing of the Missionary Salih al-Firjani." September 3, 2015. https://jihadology.net/2015/09/03/new-statement-from-katibat-uqbah-ibn-nafi-clarification-and-warning-about-the-killing-of-the-missionary-%e1%b9%a3ali%e1%b8%a5-al-firjani/.
——. "Denial: Innocence of the Mujahidin from the Murder of 'Haddah Rihimi.'" April 4, 2016. https://jihadology.net/2016/04/04/new-statement-from-katibat-uqbah-ibn-nafi-denial-innocence-of-the-mujahidin-from-the-murder-of-%e1%b8%a5addah-ri%e1%b8%a5imi/.
——. "Explanation of the Circumstances for the Loss of the Shepherd 'Lamjad al-Qariri.'" June 26, 2018. https://jihadology.net/2018/06/26/new-statement-from-katibat-uqbah-ibn-nafi-explanation-of-the-circumstances-for-the-loss-of-the-shepherd-lamjad-al-qariri-lamjed-griri/.
——. "So Wait; Indeed We, Along with You, Are Waiting." August 21, 2015. https://jihadology.net/2015/08/21/new-statement-from-katibat-uqbah-ibn-nafi-so-wait-indeed-we-along-with-you-are-waiting/.
"#Khabar muhim# bushra sara || inaq'ad miltaqa ansar al-shari'ah || bi-tunis al 'asimah 18 jumada al-thaniyyah 1432—in sha allah." al-Qayrawan Media (blog), May 15, 2011. http://www.al-qayrawan.blogspot.com/2011/05/18-1432.html.
Khalifah, Muhammad 'Ali. "Abu 'Iyadh fi hadith khasa wa-muthir li-l-Shuruq." *Jaridat al-Shuruq al-Tunisiyyah*, March 17, 2012. https://shamikh1.biz/vb/showthread.php?p=1058981998.
"Khatir jidan." Ansar al-Shai'iah in Tunisia's Facebook Page, May 31, 2012.
Mu'amari, Muhammad al-. "al-Dawrah al-'ilmiyah al-thalathah bi-tunis li-l-shaykh ahmad bin 'umar al-hazimi." *Ahl al-Hadith Forum*, March 11, 2012. https://www.ahlalhdeeth.com/vb/showthread.php?t=278069.
Mujahidin of Tunisia of al-Qayrawan. "Baya to the Caliph of the Muslims Abu Bakr al-Baghdadi and Joining the Islamic State," May 18, 2015. https://jihadology.net/2015/05/18/new-audio-message-from-mujahidin-of-tunisia-of-al-qayrawan-bayah-to-the-caliph-of-the-muslims-abu-bakr-al-baghdadi-and-joining-the-islamic-state/.
"Picture Tour Inside Shadad al-Tunisi Military Training Camp for Training and Graduation of Cubs of the Islamic State," Wilayat Halab Media Office, February 21, 2015.
Qabsi, Abu al-Zubayr al-. "al-Dawrah al-'ilmiyah al-ula li-l-shaykh ahmad bin 'umar al-hazimi bi-tunis." *Ahl al-Hadith Forum*, October 25, 2011. https://www.ahlalhdeeth.com/vb/showthread.php?t=264332.
——."al-Dawrah al-'ilmiyah al-taniyah li-l-shaykh ahmad bin 'umar al-hazimi bi-tunis." *Ahl al-Hadith Forum*, January 9, 2012. https://www.ahlalhdeeth.com/vb/showthread.php?t=272070.
Qahtani, Mu'awiyya al-. "Martyrs of the Land of al-Qayrawan #1: Abu Qudamah al-Tunisi (Yusri al-Tariqi)." al-Qayrawan Media, January 4, 2012.

"Qiyadi Salafi Jihadi Sayf Allah bin Hasin (Abu 'Iyadh) yatahadath l-al-usubu'i: sir khatir wara' ahadath Sijnan . . . al-Astul al-Sadis al-Amriki yurid iqama qa'idah tansat fiha." *al-Sabah*, March 26, 2012. https://web.archive.org/web/20130625084412/http://www.assabah.com.tn/article-66317.html.

"Shari'iyun da'ish yukafirun harakat taliban wa usamah bin ladin khatir jidan." *YouTube*, June 28, 2015. https://www.youtube.com/watch?v=t_LANfh2BOU.

Shawashi, Bilal al-. "Haqa'iq maduwiyah: li-l-daw'iyah al-tunisi bilal al-shawashi al-ladhi iltihaq bi-jabhat al-nusrah." April 23, 2014. https://justpaste.it/f7ar.

"Tahiyyid al-masjid fi tunis." al-Tasia'a Massa'a, *YouTube*, November 7, 2012. https://www.youtube.com/watch?v=Eohr7yrw5Zo.

"Tariqah al-tasjil fi ma'had ibn zayd al-qayrawani li-l-'ulum al-shari'ah." March 1, 2012, http://majles.alukah.net/t97703.

Tunisi, Abu 'Iyadh al-. "About the Recent Events (Douar Hicher)." al-Bayyariq Media, November 2, 2012.

———. "al-Dawrah al-thalathah li-l-shaykh ahmad bin 'umar al-hazimi fi tunis." *Ahl al-Hadith Forum*, February 15, 2012, https://www.ahlalhdeeth.com/vb/showthread.php?t=275911.

———. "Answer to the Essay of Abu Maysarah al-Shami: Letters to Dr. al-Zawahiri, Ayman." Hidayyah Media, January 6, 2016.

———. "Bi-munasimah al-mu'tamar al-sanuwi al-thalith li-ansar al-shari'ah bi-tunis." al-Bayyariq Media, May 23, 2013.

———. "Commenting on the Event of the American Embassy." al-Bayyariq Media, September 18, 2012.

———. "Congratulations on the Occasion of the Month of Ramadan." al-Bayyariq Media, July 9, 2013.

———. "The Dangers of the Rawafidh." al-Bayyariq Media, May 9, 2012.

———. "Inspired by the Conquests of Iraq." al-Bayyariq Media, June 13, 2014.

———. "On the Occasion of the Third Annual Conference." al-Bayyariq Media, May 23, 2013.

———. "Qar'ah mawdhu'iyah waqi'yah li-hal al-tayar al-jihadi wa-l-tahadiyat al-lati tawajahahu." May 1, 2014. Author maintains a copy in his archives.

———. "Statement from Ansar al-Shari'ah." al-Bayyariq Media, May 13, 2013.

———. "Urgent Message to the Wise Men of al-Nahdah." al-Bayyariq Media, March 27, 2013.

Tunisi, Abu Lababah al-, "Series About the Causes of the Spread of Extremism in the Tunisian Youth: Why Are Tunisia's Youth the Most Extreme in the Ranks of the State Organization?, Parts 2, 3, 4," September 3, 2015. https://jihadology.net/2015/09/03/new-article-from-abu-lababah-al-tunisi-series-about-the-causes-of-the-spread-of-extremism-in-the-tunisian-youth-why-are-tunisias-youth-the-most-extreme-in-the-ranks-of-the-state-or/.

"Tunisia: Monitoring the Presence of Security and Armored Vehicles in the Capital," Wilayat Tunis Media Office, June 2, 2015.

Yahmad, Hadi. "Hiwar ma' Sayf Allah bin Hasin (Abu 'Iyadh)." *Jaridat al-Haqa'iq al-Tunisiyyah*, December 11, 2011.

Zuruq, Kamal. "Appeal to Support the Islamic State of Iraq and al-Sham." Shabab al-Tawhid Media, June 4, 2014.

Primary Sources Authored by Non-Tunisians

Abab, Abu Zubayr 'Adil bin 'Abd Allah al-. "Gains and Benefits of Control Over Parts of Abyan and Shabwah." *Minbar al-Tawhid wa-l-Jihad*, July 7, 2012.

Abu 'A'isha. "Ben Gardane and al-Zarqawi Cultivated His Ripened Fruits." *al-Wafa' Media*, March 8, 2016.
Andalusi, Abu Qa'qa' al-. "Yusuf al-Faransi As I Knew Him." *Jund al-Khilafah*, March 31, 2012.
Arud, Malikah al-. *Les Soldats de Lumière*, 2003. https://ia800200.us.archive.org/27/items/lumiere_580/LESSOLDATSDELUMIERE.pdf.
Athari, Abu Hamam Bakr Bin 'Abd al-'Aziz al- (Turki Bin'ali). "Extend Our Hands in Bay'ah to al-Baghdadi." *Minbar al-Tawhid wa-l-Jihad*, August 5, 2013.
al-Jama'ah al-Salafiyyah Li-l-Da'wah wa-l-Qital. "al-Wahdah: al-Jama'ah Rahmah." September 16, 1998. https://web.archive.org/web/20071026121902/http://www.qmagreb.org:80/pages/wihda.html.
al-Maqalaat. "Tunisia: A Reason for the Current Extremism in the Jihadi Movement," November 19, 2015. Author maintains a copy in his archives.
al-Qaeda. "Resurgence Magazine #2." al-Sahab Media, June 25, 2015.
al-Qaeda's General Command. "On the Relationship of Qa'idat al-Jihad and the Islamic State of Iraq and al-Sham." al-Fajr Media Center, February 2, 2014.
al-Qaeda in the Islamic Maghrib. "Call to the Youth of Islam: To Those Who Aspire to Hijrah in the Way of God in the Islamic Maghrib in General and Tunisia in Particular." al-Andalus Media, March 17, 2013.
———. "Journalistic Encounter with the Director of al-Andalus Media Foundation." al-Andalus Media Foundation, April 18, 2013.
———. "Revenge for the Free Tunisia: Targeting the Interior Minister 'Lutfi Bin Jiddu.'" al-Andalus Media, June 13, 2014.
———. "To Our People in Tunisia: The Tyrant Has Fled but the Infidel and Tyrannical System Remains." al-Andalus Media, January 28, 2011.
———. "To the Wise Men of the Islamist Movement in Tunisia." al-Andalus Media, October 22, 2012.
'Azzam, 'Abd Allah. *Defense of Muslim Lands*. Kingdom of Saudi Arabia: Maktaba Dar-us-Salam, 1993.
Baghdadi, Abu Bakr al-Hussayni al-Qurayshi al-. "Although the Disbelievers Dislike It." al-Furqan Media, November 13, 2014.
———. "In the Hospitality of the Leader of the Faithful." al-Furqan Media, April 29, 2019.
Baghdadi, Abu 'Umar al-. "Fa-ama al-zabad fa-yadhhabu jufa.'" al-Furqan Media, December 4, 2007, http://up1430.com/central-guide/pencil/elit/the_sum/the_sum_3/pages/emir/6/index.php. Author maintains a copy in his archives.
Bassam, Hamzah bin Muhammad al-. "First Installment: The Sociable Benefits and the Uprisings Across Egypt and Tunisia." *Nukhbat al-I'alam al-Jihadi*, February 26, 2011.
Bearer of the Sword. "Is a Transnational Rival Network of Al Qaaidah Emerging?" Islamic Awakening Forum, May 30, 2012. http://forums.islamicawakening.com/f18/is-transnational-rival-network-al-qaaidahemerging-59127. Author maintains a copy in his archives.
"Biography of an al-Qaeda Operative 'Martyred' in Iraq: Abu Usama al-Tunisi." July 2006. https://web.archive.org/web/20061021081705/http://www.globalterroralert.com/pdf/0706/iraqmartyr0706-2.pdf.
"Birnamij hamuna 4—al-halaqah al-sadisah—tujarib shabab mugharar bi-him." *Saudi Channel 1, YouTube*, March 5, 2014, https://www.youtube.com/watch?v=lQ8SS1HmT2o.
Central Division of al-Qaeda in the Islamic Maghrib. "Munasirah min maghrib al-islam li-dawlah al-islamiyah fi 'iraq wa-l-sham." Shabab al-Tawhid Media, March 22, 2014.
Dabiq Magazine, no. 8, al-Hayat Media Center, March 30, 2015.

Filistini, Abu Qatadah al-. "Important and Urgent Message to Ansar al-Shari'ah in Tunisia." al-Bayyariq Media, January 20, 2014.
Filistini, Mushrad al-. "Isma' al-Shuhada' al-'Arab fi al-'Iraq (Manqul)." *Shabkah Filisin Li-l-Hiwar*, February 12, 2005. https://www.paldf.net/forum/showthread.php?t=25970.
Fiqh al-Muyasar fi Dhu' al-Kitab wa-l-Sunnah, Saudi Arabia: Ministry of Islamic Affairs, Dawah and Guidance, 2004, https://ia800204.us.archive.org/10/items/fikh_moyasar1/fikh_moyasar1.pdf.
Ghannushi, Rashid al-. *Harakat al-Ittijah al-Islami fi Tunis*. Kuwait: Dar al-Qalam, 1989.
Gharib, Abu Usamah al-. "Arbitrating on Women Doing Hijrah Without a Mahram." al-Ghuraba' Media, September 18, 2014.
Farag, Muhammad 'Abd al-Salam. *al-Jihad al-Farida al-Gha'iba*. N.p., n.d.
Hakim, 'Umar 'Abd al (Abu Mus'ab alSuri). *Da'wat al-Muqawamah al-Islamiyyah al-'Alamiyyah*, 2004. Author maintains a copy in his archives.
———. *Mulahazat hawla al-tajriba al-jihadiyya fi Suriyya*. Peshawar, May 1991.
Hamid, Mustafa. *al-Hamaqah al-Kubra aw harb al-mu'iz*, August 11, 1997, 4. Author maintains a copy in his archives.
Harun, Fadl. *The War Against Islam: Fadil Harun's Story*, Vol. 1, Markaz Dirasat Qidhaya al-'Alam al-Islami, February 26, 2009.
———. *The War Against Islam: Fadil Harun's Story*, Vol. 2, Markaz Dirasat Qidhaya al-'Alam al-Islami, February 26, 2009.
Harakat al-Shabab al-Mujahidin. "Interview with Shaykh Mukhtar Abu al-Zubayr." *Radio al-Andalus*, January 1, 2012. https://archive.org/details/ghjjttt.
Harmon, Christopher, Andrew Pratt, and Sebastian Gorka. *Toward a Grand Strategy Against Terrorism*. New York: McGraw Hill Professional, 2010.
"Hiwar ma' walidah al-shahid Abu Sa'd al-Tunisi," al-Ma'sadat Media, August 25, 2010.
"In the Hearts of Green Birds: Stories of Foreign Mujahidin Killed in Bosnia," *Azzam Publications*, 1996, https://web.archive.org/web/20010217045039/http://azzam.com/html/storiessalmanalfarsi.htm.
Islamic Movement of Uzbekistan. "Glad Tidings from Pakistan Part 1," *Jund Allah Studies*, January 17, 2011.
———. "The King of Setterich." *Jund Allah Studio*, April 10, 2013.
Islamic State. "Report on the Phenomenon of Extremism in the Islamic State." November 14, 2015. http://www.jihadica.com/wp-content/uploads/2018/11/zahirat-al-ghuluww.pdf.
Islamic State of Iraq and al-Sham. "Breaking of the Borders." al-I'tisam Media, June 29, 2014.
———. "Press Coverage of One of the Da'wah Tents in the State of Aleppo #2." al-Furqan Media, July 25, 2013.
———. "Series of the Life From the Words of the 'Ulama' on the Project of the Islamic State #1: Shaykh Anwar al-'Awlaqi," al-I'tisam Media, December 10, 2013.
———. "The Voice of al-Shām Magazine #2," al-Sham Foundation, September 6, 2013.
———. "A Window upon the Land of Epic Battles #7." *al-I'tisam Media*, September 7, 2013.
———. "A Window upon the Land of Epic Battles #11." al-I'tisam Media, September 20, 2013.
———. "A Window upon the Land of Epic Battles #20." al-I'tisam Media, October 21, 2013.
———. "A Window upon the Land of Epic Battles #21." al-I'tisam Media, October 24, 2013.
———. "A Window upon the Land of Epic Battles #33." al-I'tisam Media, December 7, 2013.
Jawziyya, Ibn Qayyim al-. *Nuniyah al-Qahtani*, n.d. https://web.archive.org/web/20181210014413/http://shamela.ws:80/browse.php/book-7533/page-10.
Jaysh al-Muhajirin wa-l-Ansar. "Inciting Words from the Brother Abu 'Abd Allah al-Tunisi." *YouTube*, July 18, 2013. https://www.youtube.com/watch?v=IEDSXDRje4Y.

Jaza'iri, 'Abd al-Rahman al-. "Message to the Lions of al-Qayrawan." *Ifriqiya al-Muslimah*, December 4, 2016.

Jaza'iri, Abu Muslim al-. "To Our Brothers and Families in Tunisia." *Minbar al-Tawhid wa-l-Jihad*, February 8, 2011.

———. "Urgent Questions Concerning the Situation of Tunisia." *Minbar al-Tawhid wa-l-Jihad*, February 25, 2011.

Jund al-Khilafah. "On the French Operations." Minbar Media, March 22, 2012.

Karim. "Qisah Kumandir Abu Ibrahim al-Tunisi." al-Hisbah Forum, April 28, 2006.

"The Knight Abu Fatah Dismounts After a Long Jihad: Condolences on His Death and His Brothers Upon the Land of Tunisia." *Ifriqiyyah al-Muslimah*, July 11, 2015.

Letter from 'Atiyah to Abu Basir." March 27, 2011, Bin Laden's Bookshelf, Declassified Material—January 19, 2017. Director of National Intelligence. https://www.dni.gov/index.php/features/bin-laden-s-bookshelf.

Madhri, 'Abd Allah al-A'ala al-. "Min Sir A'Alam al-Shuhada' #38: Abu Usamah al-Tunisi." al-Furqan Media, November 29, 2009.

———. "Min Sir A'Alam al-Shuhada' #42: Abu Basir al-Tunisi." al-Furqan Media, March 22, 2010.

Maghribi, Abu 'Umar al-. "Sons of 'Uqbah Pull Your Courage Swords Out." *Masama' al-Khayr l-l-Inshad*, May 28, 2013.

Muhajir, Abu Isma'il al-. "Min Sir A'Alam al-Shuhada' #26: Abu Radwan al-Tunisi." al-Furqan Media, October 10, 2006.

———. "Min Sir A'Alam al-Shuhada' #29: Abu Tariq al-Tunisi." al-Furqan Media, March 10, 2007.

Muhajir, Abu Hamzah al-. "al-Nabi al-Qa'id." *al-Fajr Media*, November 7, 2008. https://ia802702.us.archive.org/28/items/al-naibeyalqied1/al-nbey-alqaied.pdf.

Muhajir, Abu Suhayb al-. "Hukum nakath al-bay'ah wa-minhum ahl al-hal wa-l-'aqd." Shabab al-Tawhid Media, March 16, 2014.

———. "Masa'lah bayn bay'at al-tanzim wa-bay'at al-dawlah al-islamiyah." Shabab al-Tawhid Media, March 21, 2014.

Maqdisi, Abu Muhammad al-. *Waqafat ma' thamrat al-jihad*. Minbar al-Tawhid wa-l-Jihad, 2004.

Maqdisi, Abu 'Ubaydah al-. "Shuhada' fi zaman al-ghuraba." al-Fajr Media, 2008.

"Message of the 'Council of 'Ilm' on the State of the Extremists in the Media Diwan." al-Turath al-'Ilmi Foundation, 2018.

Muhammad, Basil. *Safahat min Sajil al-Ansar al-Arab fi Afghanistan*. Riyadh: Lajnat al-birr al-Islamiyya, 1992.

Naji, Abu Bakr. "Idarat al-tawahush: akhtar marhalah satamuru biha al-ummah," 2005. https://archive.org/details/dorarr.blogspot.com-books/page/n11.

"On the Departure of the Commander and Scholar from the Flag of Jihad Mu'az al-Gharsalawi al-Qayrawani." *Ghorfah Minbar al-Ansar*, October 17, 2012.

Qahtani, Fahd al-. *Ziljal Juhayman fi al-Makkah*. London: Munazzamat al-Thawra al-Islamiyya fi al-Jazira al-Arabiyya, 1987.

Qandahari, Abu Ja'afar al-Masri al-. *Memoirs of the Arab-Afghans*. Cairo: Dar al-Sharuq, 2002.

Qatari, Hamad al-. "From Stories of the Arab Martyrs #40: 'Abd al-Hadi al-Tunisi." http://saaid.net/Doat/hamad/32.htm.

———. "From Stories of the Arab Martyrs #72: Abu al-Shahid al-Tunisi." http://saaid.net/Doat/hamad/62.htm.

Qurashi, Abu 'Ubayd al-. "al-Hurub al-Thawriyyah." *Majallat Al-Ansar*, January 15, 2002.

Qureishi, Asim, "Interview with the Wife of Sayfullah Ben Hassine—Tunisian Political Prisoner Sentenced to 60 Years by Ousted President Ben Ali." *Cage Prisoners*, January 19, 2011. https://web.archive.org/web/20150103075013/http://www.cageprisoners.com/our-work/interviews/item/162-interview-with-the-family-of-sayfallah-ben-hassine.

Rahman, 'Atiyat Allah Abu 'Abd al-. "The Popular Revolution and the Fall of the Corrupt Arab System." al-Fajr Media Center, February 16, 2011.

Rubaysh, Ibrahim bin Sulayman al-. "Ben 'Ali and Ibn Sa'ud." al-Malahim Media, February 26, 2011.

Sahrawi, Adnan Abu Walid al-. "Announcing a New Amir and Giving Bay'ah to al-Baghdadi," May 13, 2015. https://jihadology.net/2015/05/13/new-audio-message-from-al-murabi%e1%b9%aduns-adnan-abu-walid-al-%e1%b9%a3a%e1%b8%a5rawi-announcing-a-new-amir-and-giving-bayah-to-al-baghdadi/.

Shami, Abu 'Abd al-Malik al-. "Sighs from the Islamic State Buried Alive." August 2017. Author maintains a copy in his archives.

Shami, Abu Maysarah al-. "The Jews of Jihad: Qa'idat al-Zawahiri." January 4, 2016. https://jihadology.net/2016/01/04/new-release-from-abu-maysarah-al-shami-the-jews-of-jihad-al-qaidat-al-%e1%ba%93awahiri/.

Shami, Abu Muhammad al-'Adnani al-. "This Is Not Our Manhaj, Nor Will It Ever Be." al-Furqan Media, April 17, 2014.

Shikaw, Abu Bakr. "Bay'ah Jama'at Ahl al-Sunnah li-l-Da'wah wa-l-Jihad to the Caliph of the Muslims Abu Bakr al-Baghdadi." al-Urwah al-Wuthqa Foundation, March 7, 2015.

Shinqiti, Abu al-Mundhir al-. "Is It Permissible to Vote for al-Nahdah?," *Minbar al-Tawhid wa-l-Jihad*, September 24, 2011.

———. "Question About How Things Happened in Tunisia." *Minbar al-Tawhid wa-l-Jihad*, January 19, 2011.

———. "Ruling on Joining al-Nahdah the Tunisian Party for Structural Reform." *Minbar al-Tawhid wa-l-Jihad*, May 10, 2011.

———. "Some Questions About the Elections in Tunisia." *Minbar al-Tawhid wa-l-Jihad*, October 10, 2011.

———. "We Are Ansar al-Shari'ah." *Minbar al-Tawhid wa-l-Jihad*, June 18, 2012.

———. "What Is the Ruling on Burning Shrines of Righteous People in Tunisia?," *Minbar al-Tawhid wa-l-Jihad*, February 21, 2013.

———. "What Is the Ruling for Formal Affiliation with al-Nahdah?," *Minbar al-Tawhid wa-l-Jihad*, March 7, 2011.

———. "What Is Your Advice with Regard to the Annual Conference to Be Held by the Brothers in Ansar al-Shari'ah in Tunisia?," *Minbar al-Tawhid wa-l-Jihad*, May 17, 2013.

Shinqiti, Abu Yahya al-. "Oh People of Tunisia of al-Qayrawan Be Supporters of Shari'a al-Rahman." al-Andalus Media, May 18, 2013.

Sudani, Abu Hudhayfah al-. "The Sun Rises in Mali," February 27, 2019. https://jihadology.net/2019/02/27/new-release-from-shaykh-abu-%e1%b8%a5udhayfah-al-sudani-the-sun-rises-in-mali/.

Sulami, Abu Sufyan al- (Turki Bin'ali). "al-Rihlah al-dawa'iyyah ila tunis." *YouTube*, September 21, 2012, https://www.youtube.com/watch?v=FI8Gyo1ecMk. Author maintains a copy in his archives.

Suri, Abu Mus'ab al-. *The Global Islamic Resistance Call*. Published online at https://archive.org/details/The-call-for-a-global-Islamic-resistance/page/n13 (2005).

Tartusi, Abu Basir al-. "Fall of the Idol Zayn, the Devil Named Zayn al 'Abidin," January 19, 2011. https://jihadology.net/2011/01/19/new-statement-from-shaykh-abu-basir-al-%e1%b9%adar%e1%b9%adusi-fall-of-the-idol-zayn-the-devil-named-zayn-al-abidin/.

Tawhid, Musalahah al-. "Munasarah al-Ikhwah al-Ma'surin fi dawlah al-juhmiyah al-kafirin," August 16, 2014. Author maintains a copy in his archives.

Wadud, Abu Mus'ab 'Abd al- ('Abd al-Malik Drukdil). "In Support of the Intifadah of Our People in Tunisia." al-Andalus Media, January 13, 2011.

——. "Isha'ar bi-taghayyir al-tasmiyyah," January 24, 2007. https://web.archive.org/web/20070620152835/http://www.qmagreb.org/pages/tasmiya.html.

——. "To Usamah Bin Ladin About the Leadership of the Organization." Director of National Intelligence, files retrieved from Bin Ladin's computer. https://www.dni.gov/files/documents/ubl2016/arabic/Arabic%20The%20Leadership%20of%20the%20Organization.pdf.

Zawahiri, Ayman al-. "And Be Neither Weakened nor Saddened." as-Sahab Media Foundation, August 15, 2011.

——. "General Guidelines for the Work of a Jihadi." al-Sahab Media, September 14, 2013.

——. "Oh People of Tunisia Support Your Shari'ah." al-Sahab Media, June 11, 2012.

——. "Realities of the Conflict Between Islam and Unbelief." al-Sahab Media, December 29, 2006.

Interviews

Ahmet Yayla, chief of counterterrorism in Sanliurfa, Turkey, between 2010 and 2013. Skype, February 2, 2018.

AST activists, Sousse, Tunisia, February 19, 2013.

Executive board of Nida Tunis, Le Lac, Tunisia, August 28, 2013.

Former senior Tunisian governmental minister during the Ben 'Ali era, Le Kram, Tunisia, February 16, 2013.

Founding member of AST, August 29, 2013, Le Lac, Tunisia.

Habib Kazdaghli, Dean of the School of Letters, Arts, and Humanities at Manouba College, Manouba, Tunisia, February 16, 2013.

Habib Sayah, a Tunisian specialist on jihadism, email, July 7, 2016.

Mahmoud Kammoun, son-in-law of former prime minister Hamadi Jebali and al-Nahdah student president, Sousse, Tunisia, February 18, 2013; September 1, 2013.

Marwa Roumani, Nida Tunis youth activist, Sousse, Tunisia, February 18, 2013.

Member of AST, Ez Zahra, Tunisia, September 3, 2013.

Member of Ansar al-Sharia in Tunisia, al-Zahra', Tunisia, September 3, 2013.

Members of AST's dawa program, Sousse, Tunisia, February 19, 2013.

Montassar Anas Jemmali, youth activist, Tunis, Tunisia, August 30, 2013.

Nabil Cherni, English teacher at the School of Letters, Arts, and Humanities at Manouba College, Manouba, Tunisia, February 16, 2013.

Radwan Masmoudi, president of the Center for the Study of Islam and Democracy, Tunis, Tunisia, February 22, 2013.

Returned Tunisian foreign fighter who fought in Syria, Manzil Bu Zalafah, August 31, 2013.

Salafi taxi driver, Sousse, Tunisia, September 3, 2013.

Sonia Karma, Nida Tunis—general secretary, Tunis, Tunisia, February 15, 2013.

Syrian activist from Kafr Nabl, Skype, November 7, 2017.

U.S. Embassy in Tunis, official, Tunis, Tunisia, February 21, 2013.

U.S. Embassy in Tunis, officials, Le Lac, Tunisia, August 29, 2013.

Bibliography 349

Court Documents

"Apprehension of a Suspect of a Crime." Indictment of Tarek Maaroufi, Essid Sami Ben Khemais, et al. Public Prosecutor's Office; Dr. Stefano Dambruoso, Penal Proceeding No. 13016/99 RGNR (A4/DIGOS/sez, 3/C), Milan, Italy, April 2, 2001.
Audiencia Nacional. Juzgado Central de Instrucción no. 2, Senencia 20/2006.
Audiencia Nacional. Juzgado Central de Instrucción no. 6, "Sumario 20/2004," November 7, 2006.
"Case Information: Hamadi Jebali." National Academies of Science, Engineering, Medicine, Committee on Human Rights. https://web.archive.org/web/20150906003802/http://www7.nationalacademies.org/humanrights/Cases/CHR_051858.htm.
"Case of Charahili v. Turkey." European Court of Human Rights, Application No. 46605/07, Strasbourg, April 13, 2010. http://hudoc.echr.coe.int/eng?i=001-98256.
Dr. Stefano Dambruoso, Penal Proceeding No. 13016/99 RGNR (A4/DIGOS/sez, 3/C), Milan, Italy, April 2, 2001.
French Prosecution of the Casablanca Bombings, April 2, 2007. Cour d'Appel de Paris Tribunal de Grande Instance de Paris Parquet du Procureur de la Republique, No. Parquet: P.01.253.3902/2, No. Instruction: 1417.
French Prosecution of the Djerba Bombings, November 8, 2006. Cour d'Appel de Paris, Tribunal de Grande Instance de Paris, Parquet du Procureur de la République, No. Parquet: P.02.107.3901/2, No. Instruction: 029/02/1432.

Government Documents

"Criminal Intelligence Summary." Department of the Army: United States Army Criminal Investigation Command, May 3, 2002.
Cronk, Terri Moon, "U.S. Airstrikes Kill 80 ISIL Fighters in Libya, Carter Says," U.S Department of Defense, January 19, 2017.
Decree Law No. 1 for the Year 2011 on the Date of February 19, 2011 Relating to the General Amnesty, *Journal Officiel de la République Tunisienne*, Year 154, no. 12, February 22, 2011, http://www.iort.gov.tn/WD120AWP/WD120Awp.exe/CTX_5436-26-LxtITUmekq/AfficheJORT/SYNC_1580747203.
Defense Security Cooperation Agency. "Tunisia—UH-60M Black Hawk Helicopters," July 24, 2014. https://www.dsca.mil/major-arms-sales/tunisia-uh-60m-black-hawk-helicopters.
Kean, Thomas H., Lee Hamilton, and the National Commission on Terrorist Attacks upon the United States. *The 9/11 Commission Report: Final Report of the National Commission on Terrorist Attacks upon the United States*. Washington, D.C.: National Commission on Terrorist Attacks upon the United States, 2004.
"NATO Steps Up Efforts to Project Stability and Strengthen Partners." NATO, July 9, 2016. https://www.nato.int/cps/en/natohq/news_133804.htm.
Office of the UN High Commissioner for Human Rights. "Preliminary Findings by the United Nations Working Group on the Use of Mercenaries on Its Official Visit to Tunisia—1 to 8 July 2015." https://www.ohchr.org/EN/NewsEvents/Pages/DisplayNews.aspx?NewsID=16219.
Report of the Special Rapporteur on the Promotion and Protection of Human Rights and Fundamental Freedoms While Countering Terrorism, Martin Scheinin. United Nations General Assembly, Human Rights Council, Twentieth Session, Agenda Item 3, March 14, 2012.

"Security Council Al-Qaida Sanctions Committee Deletes Entry of Shafiq ben Mohamed ben Mohamed Al-Ayadi from Its List," United Nations, October 17, 2011. https://www.un.org/press/en/2011/sc10413.doc.htm.

"Seeking Information: Abderraouf Jdey." FBI's Most Wanted List. https://www.fbi.gov/wanted/terrorinfo/abderraouf-jdey/@@download.pdf.

"'They Came to Destroy:' ISIS Crimes Against the Yazidis," *UN Human Rights Council*, A/HRC/32/CRP.2, June 15, 2016.

United Nations Security Council. "Twenty-Third Report of the Analytical Support and Sanctions Monitoring Team Submitted Pursuant to Resolution 2368 (2017) Concerning ISIL (Da'esh), Al-Qaida and Associated Individuals and Entities." S/2019/50, January 15, 2019. https://www.un.org/sc/ctc/wp-content/uploads/2019/02/N1846950_EN.pdf.

U.S. Department of State, Office of the Coordinator for Counterterrorism. "Patterns of Global Terrorism 1995," April 1996.

——. "Patterns of Global Terrorism 1998," April 1999.

U.S. Department of State, Office of the Spokesperson. "State Department Terrorist Designations of Muhammad al-Ghazali, Abukar Ali Adan, and Wanas al-Faqih," January 4, 2018. https://www.state.gov/state-department-terrorist-designations-of-muhammad-al-ghazali-abukar-ali-adan-and-wanas-al-faqih/.

U.S. Department of the Treasury. "Treasury Designates Twelve Foreign Terrorist Fighter Facilitators." Press release, September 24, 2014. https://www.treasury.gov/press-center/press-releases/Pages/jl2651.aspx.

U.S. Embassy in Tunis. "U.S.–Tunisia Strategic Dialogue." April 3, 2014. https://tn.usembassy.gov/us-tunisia-strategic-dialogue/.

Secondary Sources

Abdel Haleem, Muhammad. *Understanding the Qur'an: Themes and Style*. London: I. B. Tauris, 1999.

Abouzeid, Rania. *No Turning Back: Life, Loss, and Hope in Wartime Syria*. New York: W. W. Norton, 2018.

Achour, Sana Ben. "Le Code tunisien du statut personnel, 50 ans après: Les dimensions de l'ambivalence." *L'anne´e du Maghreb, Dossier: Femmes, Familles et Droit* 2 (2005–2006): 55–70.

Adamsky, Dima. "Jihadi Operational Art: The Coming Wave of Jihadi Strategic Studies." *Studies in Conflict and Terrorism* 33, no. 1 (2009): 1–19.

Allani, Alaya. "The Islamists in Tunisia Between Confrontation and Participation: 1980–2008." *Journal of North African Studies* 14, no. 2 (June 2009): 257–72.

Anas, Abdullah. *To the Mountains My Life in Jihad, from Algeria to Afghanistan*, with Tam Hussein. London: Hurst, 2019.

Anderson, Sean Kendall, and Stephen Sloan. *Historical Dictionary of Terrorism*. Lanham, Md.: Scarecrow, 2009.

Anzalone, Christopher. "Insurgency, Governance, and Legitimacy in Somalia: A Reassessment of Harakat al-Shabab al-Mujahideen, Its Rhetoric & Divisions." *al-Wasat*, December 6, 2010.

——. "Missionaries of Jihad." *Foreign Policy*, June 3, 2011.

——. "Revisiting Shaykh Atiyyatullah's Works on Takfir and Mass Violence." *CTC Sentinel* 5, no. 4 (April 2012).

Arieff, Alexis. "Political Transition in Tunisia." *Congressional Research Service*, April 15, 2011.

———. "Political Transition in Tunisia." *Congressional Research Service*, September 20, 2011.
Bahri, Nasser al-. *Guarding Bin Laden: My Life in al-Qaeda*. London: Thin Man Press, 2013.
Baouz, Karim. *Plongée au coeur de la fabrique djihadiste enquete sur les filieres du terrorisme francais*. Paris: First Document, 2016.
Barbieri, Eliane Tschaen, and Jytte Klausen. "Al Qaeda's London Branch: Patterns of Domestic and Transnational Network Integration." *Studies in Conflict and Terrorism* 35, no. 6 (June 2012): 411–31.
Barrett, Richard. *Beyond the Caliphate: Foreign Fighters and the Threat of Returnees*. The Soufan Center, October 2017. https://www.jstor.org/stable/resrep10782.
Benford, Robert D., and David A. Snow, "Framing Processes and Social Movements: An Overview and Assessment." *Annual Review of Sociology* 26 (August 2000): 611–39.
———. "Ideology, Frame Resonance, and Participant Mobilization." *International Social Movement Research* 1 (1988): 197–217.
Bergen, Peter. *The Osama bin Ladin I Know: An Oral History of al-Qaeda's Leader*. New York: Free Press, 2006.
Berry, Randal K., ed. "Arabic: ALA-LC Romanization Tables: Transliteration Schemes for Non-Roman Scripts." Washington, D.C.: Library of Congress, 1997.
Besbris, Max, and Shamus Khan. "Less Theory. More Description." *Sociological Theory* 35, no. 2 (2017). https://doi.org/10.1177%2F0735275117709776.
Bonderman, David. "Modernization and Changing Perceptions of Islamic Law." *Harvard Law Review* 81, no. 6 (April 1968): 1161–93.
Bonner, Michael. *Jihad in Islamic History: Doctrines and Practice*. Princeton, N.J.: Princeton University Press, 2006.
Botha, Anneli. "Terrorism in Maghreb: The Transnationalisation of Domestic Terrorism." *Institute for Security Studies*, ISS Monograph Series, no. 144, June 2008.
Boulby, Marion. "The Islamic Challenge: Tunisia Since Independence." *Third World Quarterly* 10, no. 2, *Islam & Politics* (April 1988): 590–614.
Boursali, Noura. *Bourguiba wa-l-masa'la al- dimaqratiyah*. Tunis: Arabesques, 2016.
Brisard, Jean-Charles. *Zarqawi: The New Face of Al-Qaeda*. New York: Other Press, 2005.
Brisard, Jean-Charles, and Kévin Jackson. "The Islamic State's External Operations and the French-Belgian Nexus." *CTC Sentinel* 9, no. 11 (November/December 2016): 8–15.
Brooke, Steven. "Jihadist Strategic Debates Before 9/11." *Studies in Conflict and Terrorism* 31, no. 3 (2008): 201–26.
Brown, Jonathan A. C. *Misquoting Muhammad: The Challenge and Choices of Interpreting the Prophet's Legacy*. London: Oneworld, 2014.
Brown, Leon Carl. "The Islamic Reformist Movement in North Africa." *Journal of Modern African Studies* 2, no. 1 (March 1964): 55–63.
Bruce, James. "Arab Veterans of the Afghan War." *Jane's Intelligence Review* 7, no. 4 (April 1995): 175–79.
Bunzel, Cole. "Ideological Infighting in the Islamic State." *Perspectives on Terrorism* 13, no. 1 (February 2019): 13–22.
———. *The Kingdom and the Caliphate: Duel of the Islamic States*. Washington, D.C.: Carnegie Endowment for International Peace, February 2016. https://carnegieendowment.org/files/CP_265_Bunzel_Islamic_States_Final.pdf.
Burgat, François. *L'islamisme au Maghreb: La voix du Sud (Tunisie, Algérie, Libye, Maroc)*. Paris: Karatha, 1988.
Burgat, François, and William Dowell. *The Islamic Movement in North Africa*. Austin: Center for Middle Eastern Studies, University of Texas, 1993.

Cavatorta, Francesco. "Salafism, Liberalism, and Democratic Learning in Tunisia." *Journal of North African Studies* 20, no. 5 (2015): 770–83.
Cavatorta, Francesco, and Fabio Merone. "Moderation Through Exclusion? The Journey of the Tunisian Ennahda from Fundamentalist to Conservative Party." *Democratization* 20, no. 5 (August 2013): 857–75.
Chenoweth, Erica. "Terrorism and Democracy." *Annual Review of Political Science* 16 (2013): 355–78.
Churchill, Erik. "Shaping Ennahda's Re-Election Strategy." *Foreign Policy's Middle East Channel*, March 27, 2012.
Collier, David. "Understanding Process Tracing." *PS: Political Science & Politics* 44, no. 4 (October 2011): 823–30.
Cook, Michael. *Commanding Right and Forbidding Wrong in Islamic Thought*. Cambridge: Cambridge University Press, 2000.
Crumley, Bruce. "French Terror Conviction: Lesson for U.S.?" *Time*, February 6, 2009.
Darwish, Qusayy Salih. *Yahduthu fi Tunis*. Paris: al-Tabah al-Faransiyah, 1987.
Davis, Anthony. "Foreign Combatants in Afghanistan." *Jane's Intelligence Review* 5, no. 7 (July 1993): 327–31.
Dawson, Lorne L. "Challenging the Curious Erasure of Religion from the Study of Religious Terrorism." *Numen* 65, nos. 2–3 (2018). https://doi.org/10.1163/15685276-12341492.
Dean, Aimen, Paul Cruikshank, and Tim Lister. *Nine Lives: My Time as MI6's Top Spy Inside al-Qaeda*. London: Oneworld, 2018.
DeGorge, Barbara. "The Modernization of Education: A Case Study of Tunisia and Morocco." *European Legacy* 7, no. 5 (2002): 579–96.
della Porta, Donatella. "Radicalization: A Relational Perspective." *Annual Review of Political Science* 21 (2018): 461–74.
della Porta, Donatella, and Mario Diani. *Social Movements: An Introduction*, 2nd ed. Oxford: Blackwell, 2006.
Denoeux, Guilian. "The Forgotten Swamp: Navigating Political Islam." *Middle East Policy* 9, no. 2 (2002). https://doi.org/10.1111/1475-4967.00057.
Dolnik, Adam. "Conducting Field Research on Terrorism: A Brief Primer." *Perspectives on Terrorism* 5, no. 2 (2011): 3–35.
Egerton, Frazer. *Jihad in the West: The Rise of Militant Salafism*. Cambridge: Cambridge University Press, 2011.
Elgindy, Khaled. "The Rhetoric of Rashid Ghannushi." *Arab Studies Journal* 3, no. 1 (Spring 1995): 101–20.
Esposito, John L. *Political Islam: Revolution, Radicalism, or Reform?* Boulder, Colo.: Lynne Rienner, 1997.
Farmanfarmaian, Roxane. "Media and the Politics of the Sacral: Freedom of Expression in Tunisia After the Arab Uprisings." *Media, Culture & Society* 39, no. 7 (2017). https://doi.org/10.1177%2F0163443717690817.
Farrall, Leah. "Some Quick Thoughts on Reports Abu Yahya al-Libi Has Been Killed." *All Things Counterterrorism* (blog), June 6, 2012. https://allthingscounterterrorism.com/2012/06/06/some-quick-thoughts-on-reports-abu-yahya-al-libi-has-been-killed/.
Feldman, Noah. *The Fall and the Rise of the Islamic State*. Princeton, N.J.: Princeton University Press, 2008.
Felter, Joseph, and Brian Fishman. "Becoming a Foreign Fighter: A Second Look at the Sinjar Records," in *Bombers, Bank Accounts and Bleedout: al-Qa'ida's Road In and Out of Iraq*, ed. by Brian Fishman (West Point, N.Y.: Combating Terrorism Center, July 22, 2008), 35–36.

Feuer, Sarah J. *Regulating Islam: Religion and the State in Contemporary Morocco and Tunisia*. Cambridge: Cambridge University Press, 2018.
Filiu, Jean-Pierre. "Ansar al-Fatah and 'Iraqi' Networks in France." In *The Evolution of the Global Terrorist Threat: From 9/11 to Osama bin Laden's Death*, ed. by Bruce Hoffman and Fernando Reinares. New York: Columbia University Press, 2014.
Fishman, Brian, ed. *Bombers, Bank Accounts and Bleedout: al-Qa'ida's Road in and out of Iraq*. West Point, N.Y.: Combating Terrorism Center, July 22, 2008.
———. *Dysfunction and Decline: Lessons Learned from Inside Al-Qa'ida in Iraq*. West Point, N.Y.: Combating Terrorism Center, Harmony Project, March 16, 2009.
———. *Fourth Generation Governance: Sheikh Tamimi Defends the Islamic State of Iraq*. West Point, N.Y.: Combating Terrorism Center, Harmony Program, March 23, 2007.
———. *The Master Plan: ISIS, al-Qaeda, and the Jihadi Strategy for Final Victory*. New Haven, Conn.: Yale University Press, 2016.
———. *Redefining the Islamic State: The Fall and Rise of Al-Qaeda in Iraq*. Washington, D.C.: New America Foundation, National Security Studies Program Policy Paper, August 2011.
Fishman, Brian, and Joseph Felter. *al-Qa'ida's Foreign Fighters in Iraq: A First Look at the Sinjar Records*. West Point, N.Y.: Combating Terrorism Center, January 2, 2007.
Flade, Florian. "The June 2018 Cologne Ricin Plot: A New Threshold in Jihadi Bio Terror." *CTC Sentinel* 11, no. 7 (August 2018). https://ctc.usma.edu/app/uploads/2019/01/CTC-SENTINEL-082018-final.pdf.
Foster, Dakota, and Daniel Milton. "Children at War: Foreign Child Recruits of the Islamic State." *CTC Sentinel* 11, no. 6 (June/July 2018). https://ctc.usma.edu/app/uploads/2018/06/CTC-SENTINEL-062018_1.pdf.
Gade, Tine. *Fatah al-Islam in Lebanon: Between Global and Local Jihad*. Norwegian Defence Research Establishment (FFI), May 12, 2007.
Gartenstein-Ross, Daveed. "Al-Qaeda Is Winning." *Atlantic*, September 8, 2011.
———. "The Deadly Cycle of Terror That Has Iraq and Syria in Its Grip." *Spectator*, June 21, 2014.
———. "Springtime for Salafists." *Foreign Policy*, March 26, 2013.
Gartenstein-Ross, Daveed, and Oren Adaki. "Ansar al-Sharia in Tunisia's Social Media Activity in 2014." *Jihadology*, June 6, 2014.
Gartenstein-Ross, Daveed, and Nathaniel Barr. "How Al-Qaeda Works: The Jihadist Group's Evolving Organizational Design." *Current Trends in Islamist Ideology* 23 (June 2018).
Gartenstein-Ross, Daveed, Jason Fritz, Bridget Moreng, and Nathaniel Barr. "Islamic State vs. al-Qaeda: Strategic Dimensions of a Patricidal Conflict." *New America Foundation*, December 2015.
Gartenstein-Ross, Daveed, and Aymenn Jawad al-Tamimi. "Druze Clues." *Foreign Affairs*, October 5, 2015.
Gartenstein-Ross, Daveed, and Tara Vassefi. "Perceptions of the 'Arab Spring' Within the Salafi-Jihadi Movement." *Studies in Conflict and Terrorism* 35, no. 12 (December 2012): 831–48.
Gerges, Fawaz. *The Far Enemy: Why Jihad Went Global*. Cambridge: Cambridge University Press, 2009.
Gerring, John. "Mere Description." *British Journal of Political Science* 42, no. 4 (October 2012): 721–46.
Goodwin, Jeff, and James M. Jasper. "Emotions and Social Movements." In *Handbook of the Sociology of Emotions*, ed. by Jan E. Stets and Jonathan H. Turner. New York: Springer, 2006.

———, eds. *The Social Movements Reader: Cases and Concepts*, 2nd ed. Hoboken, N.J.: Wiley-Blackwell, 2009.

Green, Arnold H. "Political Attitudes and Activities of the Ulama in the Liberal Age: Tunisia as an Exceptional Case." *International Journal of Middle East Studies* 7, no. 2 (April 1976): 209–41.

Gregg, Heather S. "Religious Resources and Terrorism." *Numen* 65, no. 2-3 (2018). https://doi.org/10.1163/15685276-12341494.

Grewal, Sharan. "Tunisia's Foiled Coup: The November 8th Group." Working Paper, August 19, 2018.

Hafez, Mohamed. *Suicide Bombers in Iraq: The Strategy and Ideology of Martyrdom*, Washington, D.C.: United States Institute of Peace, 2007.

Hajji, Lufti. "The 18 October Coalition for Rights and Freedoms in Tunisia." *Arab Reform Initiative*, Arab Reform Bulletin, October 13, 2006.

Halverson, Jeffry R., R. Bennett Furlow, and Steven R. Corman. *How Islamic Extremists Quote the Qur'an*. Center for Strategic Communication at Arizona State University, Report No. 1202, July 9, 2012.

Halverson, Jeffry R., H. L. Goodall Jr., and Steven R. Corman. *Master Narratives of Islamist Extremism*. New York: Palgrave McMillan, 2011.

Hamadi, Muhammad al-Hashimi al-. *Ashwaq al-Huriyyah*. Kuwait: Dar al-Qalam, 1989.

Hamdi, Mohammed Elihachimi. *The Politicisation of Islam: A Case Study of Tunisia*. Boulder, Colo.: Westview, 1998.

Hamid, Mustafa, and Leah Farrall. *The Arabs at War in Afghanistan*. London: Hurst, 2015.

Hamming, Tore. "The Extremist Wing of the Islamic State." *Jihadica*, June 9, 2016.

Haugbølle, Rikke Hostrup. "New Expressions of Islam in Tunisia: An Ethnographic Approach." *Journal of North African Studies* 20, no. 3 (2015): 319–35.

Haugbølle, Rikke Hostrup, and Francesco Cavatorta. "Will the Real Tunisian Opposition Please Stand Up? Opposition Coordination Failures Under Authoritarian Constraints." *British Journal of Middle Eastern Studies* 38, no. 3 (2011): 323–41.

Hegghammer, Thomas. "The Ideological Hybridization of Jihadi Groups." *Current Trends in Islamist Ideology*, no. 9 (November 2009).

———. *Jihad in Saudi Arabia: Violence and Pan-Islamism Since 1979*. Cambridge: Cambridge University Press, 2010.

———. "The Rise of Muslim Foreign Fighters: Islam and the Globalization of Jihad." *International Security* 35, no. 3 (Winter 2010/11): 53–94.

———. "Why Terrorists Weep: The Socio-Cultural Practices of Jihadi Militants." Paul Wilkinson Memorial Lecture, University of St. Andrews, April 16, 2015.

Hegghammer, Thomas, and Aaron Y. Zelin. "How Syria's Civil War Became a Holy Crusade." *Foreign Affairs*, July 7, 2013.

Heil, Georg. "The Berlin Attack and the 'Abu Walaa' Islamic State Recruitment Network." *CTC Sentinel* 10, no. 2 (February 2017). https://ctc.usma.edu/app/uploads/2017/02/CTC-Sentinel_Vol10Iss228.pdf.

Henneberg, Sabina. "Governing Uncertainty: Challenges for the First Tunisian Provisional Administration of 2011 and Its Impacts in 2012–2014." *British Journal of Middle Eastern Studies*, July 2018. http://dx.doi.org/10.1080/13530194.2018.1493375.

Hermassi, 'Abd al-Latif al-. *al-Harakah al-Islamiyyah fi Tunis: al-Yasar al-Ishtiraki, al-Islam, wa al-Harakah al-Islamiyyah*. Tunis: Bayram li al-Nashr, 1985.

Hermassi, 'Abd Elbaki. "The Islamist Movement and November 7." In *Tunisia: The Political Economy of Reform*, ed. by I. William Zartman, 193–204. Boulder: Lynne Rienner, 1991.

——. "La Société tunisienne au miroir islamiste." *Maghreb-Machrek*, January/February/March 1984.
Hisham, Marwan, and Molly Crabapple. *Brothers of the Gun: A Memoir of the Syrian War*. New York: Penguin Random House, 2018.
Hoffman, Bruce. "Al-Qaeda's Resurrection." *Council on Foreign Relations*, March 6, 2018.
——. "The Leaderless Jihad's Leader: Why Osama Bin Laden Mattered." *Foreign Affairs*, May 13, 2011.
——. "The Myth of Grass-Roots Terrorism: Why Osama bin Laden Still Matters." *Foreign Affairs* 87, no. 3 (May/June 2008).
Hoffman, Bruce, and Fernando Reinares, ed. *The Evolution of the Global Terrorist Threat: From 9/11 to Osama bin Ladin's Death*. New York: Columbia University Press, 2014.
Holbrook, Donald. "Al-Qaeda's Response to the Arab Spring." *Perspectives on Terrorism* 6, no. 6 (2012).
Holman, Timothy. "Belgian and French Foreign Fighters in Iraq 2003–2005: A Comparative Case Study." *Studies in Conflict and Terrorism* 38, no. 8 (2015): 603–21.
——. "'Gonna Get Myself Connected:' The Role of Facilitation in Foreign Fighter Mobilizations." *Perspectives on Terrorism* 10, no. 2 (2016).
Horgan, John. *The Psychology of Terrorism*, 2nd ed. Abingdon, U.K.: Routledge, 2014.
International Crisis Group. "Tunisia's Borders: Jihadism and Contraband." *Middle East/North Africa Report*, Report No. 148, November 28, 2013.
The Islamic Imagery Project: Visual Motifs in Jihadi Internet Propaganda. West Point, N.Y.: Combating Terrorism Center, March 2006. https://ctc.usma.edu/app/uploads/2010/06/Islamic-Imagery-Project.pdf.
Israely, Jeff. "The Second Time Around." *Time*, February 25, 2002.
Johnston, Patrick B., Jacob N. Shapiro, Howard J. Shatz, Benjamin Bahney, Danielle F. Jung, Patrick K. Ryan, and Jonathan Wallace. *Foundations of the Islamic State Management, Money, and Terror in Iraq, 2005–2010*. Santa Monica, Calif.: RAND, 2016. https://www.rand.org/pubs/research_reports/RR1192.html.
Joffé, George, ed. *Islamist Radicalisation in North Africa: Politics and Process*. Abingdon, U.K.: Routledge, 2011.
Jordán, Javier. "The Foiled Attacks in Italy in 2006." In *The Evolution of the Global Terrorist Threat: From 9/11 to Osama bin Laden's Death*, ed. by Bruce Hoffman and Fernando Reinares, 273–88. New York: Columbia University Press, 2014).
Keddie, Nikki R. "The Islamist Movement in Tunisia." *Maghreb Review* 11, no. 1 (1986): 26–39.
Kendall, Diana. *Sociology in Our Times*. Independence, Ky.: Thomson Wadsworth, 2016.
Kennedy, Jonathan, and Gabriel Weimann. "The Strength of Weak Terrorist Ties." *Terrorism and Political Violence* 23, no. 2 (2011): 201–12.
Kepel, Gilles. *Terror in France: The Rise of Jihad in the West*. Princeton, N.J.: Princeton University Press, 2017.
Khatab, Sayed. *The Political Thought of Sayyid Qutb: The Theory of Jahiliyyah*. London: Routledge, 2006.
——. *The Power of Sovereignty: The Political and Ideological Philosophy of Sayyid Qutb*. London: Routledge, 2006.
——. *Understanding Islamic Fundamentalism*. New York: American University in Cairo Press, 2011.
Kirdiş, Esen. "Wolves in Sheep Clothing or Victims of Times? Discussing the Immoderation of Incumbent Islamic Parties in Turkey, Egypt, Morocco, and Tunisia." *Democratization* 25, no. 5 (2018): 901–18.

Kohlmann, Evan. "Abu el-Ma'ali." *Global Terror Alert*, August 29, 2005.
———. *al-Qaida's Jihad in Europe: The Afghan-Bosnian Network*. Oxford: Berg, 2004.
———. "Foreign Fighters Reported Killed in Iraq: June 2003–June 2005." *Global Terror Alert*, June 2005.
———. "The Foreign Mujahideen "Martyrs" of Iraq: 2003–2004." *Global Terror Alert*, January 2005.
Kolman, Iris. "Gender Activism in Salafism: A Case Study of Salafi Women in Tunisia." In *Salafism After the Arab Awakening: Contending with People's Power*, ed by Francesco Cavatorta and Fabio Merone, 187–204. Oxford: Oxford University Press, 2016.
Kramer, Martin. "Coming to Terms: Fundamentalists or Islamists?" *Middle East Quarterly*, Spring 2003.
Kruglanski, Arie W., Michele J. Gelfand, Jocelyn J. Bélanger, Anna Sheveland, Malkanthi Hetiarachchi, and Rohan Gunaratna. "The Psychology of Radicalization and Deradicalization: How Significance Quest Impacts Violent Extremism." *Advances in Political Psychology* 35, S1 (2014): 69–93.
Krueger, Alan B. "The National Origins of Foreign Fighters in Iraq." Presentation at the annual meeting of the American Economic Association, Chicago, Illinois, January 5, 2007.
Lahoud, Nelly. *The Jihadis' Path to Self-Destruction*. New York: Columbia University Press, 2010.
Lahoud, Nelly, Stuart Caudill, Liam Collins, Gabriel Koehler-Derrick, Don Rassler, and Muhammad al-`Ubaydi. "Letters from Abbottabad: Bin Ladin Sidelined?" West Point, N.Y.: Combating Terrorism Center, Harmony Program, May 3, 2012.
Lamloum, Olfa. *Marginalisation, Insecurity and Uncertainty on the Tunisian–Libyan Border Ben Guerdane and Dhehiba from the Perspective of Their Inhabitants*. International Alert, December 2016. https://www.international-alert.org/sites/default/files/Tunisia Libya_MarginalisationInsecurityUncertaintyBorder_EN_2016.pdf.
———. *Politics on the Margins in Tunisia: Vulnerable Young People in Douar Hicher and Ettadhamen*. International Alert, March 2016. https://www.international-alert.org/sites/default/files/Tunisia_PoliticsOnTheMargins_EN_2016.pdf.
Lav, Daniel. *Radical Islam and the Revival of Medieval Theology*. New York: Cambridge University Press, 2012.
Lebovich, Andrew. "Confronting Tunisia's Jihadists." *Foreign Policy's Middle East Channel*, May 16, 2013.
Lee, Robert D. "Tunisian Intellectuals: Responses to Islamism." *Journal of North African Studies* 13, no. 2 (June 2008).
Letsch, Lydia. "Countering Violent Extremism in Tunisia—Between Dependency and Self-Reliance." *Journal for Deradicalization*, no. 17 (Winter 2018/19): 163–95.
Lia, Brynjar. *Architect of Global Jihad: The Life of al-Qa`ida Strategist Abu Mus`ab al-Suri*. Oxford: Oxford University Press, 2009.
———. *The Society of the Muslim Brothers in Egypt: The Rise of an Islamic Mass Movement 1928–1942*. Reading, U.K.: Ithaca Press, 2006.
Lia, Brynjar, and Thomas Hegghammer. "Jihadi Strategic Studies: The Alleged Al Qaida Policy Study Preceding the Madrid Bombings." *Studies in Conflict and Terrorism* 27, no. 5 (2004): 355–75.
Lister, Charles. *The Syrian Jihad: Al-Qaeda, the Islamic State and the Evolution of an Insurgency*. London: Hurst, 2015.
Lumbard, Joseph E. B., ed. *Islam, Fundamentalism, and the Betrayal of Tradition: Essays by Western Muslim Scholars*. Bloomington, Ind.: World Wisdom, 2004.

Lynch, Marc. "The New Salafi Politics." In *Arab Uprisings: The New Salafi Politics. POMEPS Studies*, no. 2, October 16, 2012.
Mabrouk, Mehdi. "Tunisia: The Radicalization of Religious Policy," ed. by George Joffé, *Islamist Radicalisation in North Africa: Politics and Process*. New York: Routledge, 2012.
Maddy-Weitzman, Bruce. "The Islamic Challenge in North Africa." *Terrorism and Political Violence* 8, no. 2 (June 1996): 171–88.
Maher, Shiraz, and Peter R. Neumann. *Al-Qaeda at the Crossroads: How the Terror Group Is Rsponding to the Loss of Its Leaders & the Arab Spring*. International Centre for the Study of Radicalisation and Political Violence, August 2012.
Malet, David. *Foreign Fighters: Transnational Identity in Civil Conflicts*. Oxford: Oxford University Press, 2013.
Mandaville, Peter. *Global Political Islam*. New York: Routledge, 2007.
Marcusa, Michael. "My Two Weeks with the Jihadists." *Atlantic*, August 15, 2013.
———. "Radicalism on the Periphery: History, Collective Memory, and the Cultural Resonance of Jihadist Ideology in Tunisia." *Comparative Politics* 51, no. 2 (January 2019).
Marks, Monica. "Ennahda's Rules of Engagement." *Sada*, October 18, 2012.
———. "Tunisia in Turmoil." *Foreign Policy's Middle East Channel*, July 26, 2013.
———. "Tunisia's Ennahda: Rethinking Islamism in the Context of ISIS and the Egyptian Coup." Project on US Relations with the Islamic World at Brookings, Rethinking Islamism Series, Working Paper, August 2015.
———. "Tunisia's Student Salafis." *Foreign Policy's Middle East Channel*, January 6, 2012.
———. "Youth Politics and Tunisian Salafism: Understanding the Jihadi Current." *Mediterranean Politics* 18, no. 1 (March 2013): 104–11.
Marret, Jean-Luc. "Al-Qaeda in the Islamic Maghreb: A 'Glocal' Organization." *Studies in Conflict and Terrorism* 31, no. 6 (June 2008): 541–52.
Mayer, Catherine, "Tunisian Elections: From Yesterday's Most Wanted to Tomorrow's Leaders," *Time*, October 21, 2011.
McAdam, Doug, John D. McCarthy, and Mayer N. Zald, eds. *Comparative Perspectives on Social Movements: Political Opportunities, Mobilizing Structures, and Cultural Framings*. Cambridge: Cambridge University Press, 1996.
McAuliffe, Jane Dammen, ed. *Encyclopedia of the Qur'an*, Vol. 2. Leiden: Brill, 2001.
———. *Encyclopedia of the Qur'an*, Vol. 3. Leiden: Brill, 2001.
McCants, William. "Al Qaeda's Challenge: The Jihadists' War with Islamist Democrats." *Foreign Affairs* 90, no. 5 (September/October 2011).
———. "Militant Ideology Atlas." West Point, N.Y.: Combating Terrorism Center, November 1, 2006. https://ctc.usma.edu/app/uploads/2012/04/Atlas-ResearchCompendium1.pdf.
McCants, William, and Jarret Brachman. "The Militant Ideology Atlas." West Point, N.Y.: Combating Terrorism Center, November 2006.
McCarthy, Rory. *Inside Tunisia's al-Nahda: Between Politics and Preaching*. Cambridge: Cambridge University Press, 2018.
———. "Protecting the Sacred: Tunisia's Islamist Movement Ennahdha and the Challenge of Free Speech." *British Journal of Middle Eastern Studies* 42, no. 4 (February 2015): 447–64.
McQuaid, Julia, Jonathan Schroden, Pamela G. Faber, P. Kathleen Hammerberg, Alexander Powell, Zack Gold, David Knoll, and William Rosenau. *Independent Assessment of U.S. Government Efforts against Al Qaeda*. Arlington, Va.: Center for Naval Analysis, October 2017.
Mecham, Quinn. *Institutional Origins of Islamist Political Mobilization*. Cambridge: Cambridge University Press, 2017.

Meijer, Roel. "Commanding Right and Forbidding Wrong as a Principle of Social Action: The Case of the Egyptian al-Jama'a al-Islamiyya." In *Global Salafism: Islam's New Religious Movement*, ed. by Roel Meijer, 189–220. New York: Columbia University Press, 2009.

———, ed. *Global Salafism: Islam's New Religious Movement*. New York: Columbia University Press, 2009.

Mendelsohn, Barak. *The al-Qaeda Franchise: The Expansion of al-Qaeda and Its Consequences*. Oxford: Oxford University Press, 2016.

Merone, Fabio. "Between Social Contention and Takfirism: The Evolution of the Salafi-Jihadi Movement in Tunisia." *Mediterranean Politics* 22, no. 1 (2017): 71–90.

———. "Salafism in Tunisia: An Interview with a Member of Ansar al-Sharia." *Jadaliyya*, April 11, 2013.

Merone, Fabio, and Francesco Cavatorta. "The Emergence of Salafism in Tunisia." *Jadaliyya*, August 17, 2012.

———. "Salafist mouvance and sheikh-ism in the Tunisian Democratic Transition." Centre for International Studies, Dublin City University, Working Paper No. 7, 2012.

Milton, Daniel, and Brian Dodwell. "Jihadi Brides? Examining a Female Guesthouse Registry from the Islamic State's Caliphate." *CTC Sentinel* 11, no. 5 (May 2018). https://ctc.usma.edu/app/uploads/2018/05/CTC-Sentinel_Vol11Iss5.pdf.

Mitchell, Richard P. *The Society of the Muslim Brothers*. Oxford: Oxford University Press, 1993.

Moghadam, Assaf, and Brian Fishman, ed. *Fault Lines in Global Jihad: Organizational, Strategic, and Ideological Fissures*. London: Routledge, 2013.

Mokeddem, Mohamed. *Les Afghans algériens: De la Djamaâ À la Qa'ida*. Alger: ANEP, 2002.

Mu'assasat Āl al-Bayt lil-Fikr al-Islāmī. *Jihad and the Islamic Law of War*. Amman, Jordan: Royal Aal Al-Bayt Institute for Islamic Thought, 2007.

Nasiri, Omar. *Inside the Jihad: My Life With al-Qaeda*. New York: Basic Books, 2006.

Neumann, Peter, Ryan Evans, and Raffaello Pantucci. "Locating Al Qaeda's Center of Gravity: The Role of Middle Managers." *Studies in Conflict and Terrorism* 34, no. 11 (November 2011): 825–42.

"Nobody's Man-But the Man of Islam." *Arabia* 4, no. 44 (April 1985).

November 7: al-Thawra al-Hadi'a. Tunis: A. Ben Abdallah for Publishing and Distribution, 1992.

Olidort, Jacob. *Inside the Caliphate's Classroom: Textbooks, Guidance Literature, and Indoctrination Methods of the Islamic State*. Washington Institute for Near East Policy, Policy Focus, no. 147 (August 2016). https://www.washingtoninstitute.org/uploads/Documents/pubs/PolicyFocus147-Olidort-5.pdf.

O'Neill, Sean, and Daniel McGory. *The Suicide Factory: Abu Hamza and the Finsbury Park Mosque*. London: Harper Perennial, 2006.

Packer, George. "Exporting Jihad: The Arab Spring Has Given Tunisians the Freedom to Act on Their Unhappiness." *New Yorker*, March 28, 2016.

Page, Michael, Lara Challita, and Alistair Harris. "Al Qaeda in the Arabian Peninsula: Framing Narratives and Prescriptions." *Terrorism and Political Violence* 23, no. 2 (February 2011): 150–72.

Pantucci, Raffaello. *"We Love Death as You Love Life": Britain's Suburban Terrorists*. London: Hurst, 2015.

Pargeter, Alison. *The New Frontiers of Jihad: Radical Islam in Europe*. Philadelphia: Pennsylvania University Press, 2008.

———. "North African Immigrants in Europe and Political Violence." *Studies in Conflict & Terrorism* 29, no. 8 (December 2006): 731–47.
———. "Radicalisation in Tunisia." In *Islamist Radicalisation in North Africa: Politics and Process*, ed. George Joffe, 71–94. Abingdon, U.K.: Routledge, 2011.
———. "The Suleiman Affair—Radicalism and Jihad in Tunisia." *Jane's Intelligence Review* 23, no. 1 (2011).
Payne, Kenneth. "Building the Base: Al Qaeda's Focoist Strategy." *Studies in Conflict and Terrorism* 34, no. 2 (2011): 124–43.
Paz, Reuven. "Arab Volunteers Killed in Iraq: An Analysis." The Project for the Research of Islamist Movements at Global Research in International Affairs (GLORIA) Center, PRISM Series of Global Jihad, no. 1/3, March 2005.
Perkins, Kenneth J. "'The Masses Look Ardently to Istanbul': Tunisia, Islam, and the Ottoman Empire, 1837–1931." In *Islamism and Secularism in North Africa*, ed. John Reudy, 23–36. London: Palgrave Macmillan, 1996.
Rabasa, Angel, and Cheryl Benard. *Eurojihad: Patterns of Islamist Radicalization and Terrorism in Europe*. Cambridge: University of Cambridge Press, 2015.
Rassler, Don. *The Islamic State and Drones: Supply, Scale, and Future Threats*. West Point, N.Y.: Combating Terrorism Center, July 11, 2018.
Rayburn, Joel D., and Frank K. Sobchak, eds. *The U.S. Army in the Iraq War*. Vol. 1: *Invasion, Insurgency, Civil War, 2003–2006*. Carlisle Barracks, Penn.: U.S. Army War Press, 2019.
———, eds. *The U.S. Army in the Iraq War*. Vol. 2: *Surge and Withdrawal, 2007–2011*. Carlisle Barracks, Penn.: U.S. Army War Press, 2019.
Reinares, Fernando. *¡Matadlos!: Quién estuvo detrás del 11-M y por qué se atentó en España*. Barcelona: Galaxia Gutenberg/Círculo de Lectores, 2014.
———. "The 2004 Madrid Train Bombings." In *The Evolution of the Global Terrorist Threat: From 9/11 to Osama bin Laden's Death*, ed. by Bruce Hoffman and Fernando Reinares, 29–60. New York: Columbia University Press, 2014.
Reudy, John. *Islamism and Secularism in North Africa*. London: Palgrave Macmillan, 1996.
Rougier, Bernard. *The Sunni Tragedy in the Middle East: Northern Lebanon from al-Qaeda to ISIS*. Princeton, N.J.: Princeton University Press, 2015.
Rubin, Barnett R. "Arab Islamists in Afghanistan." In *Political Islam: Revolution, Radicalism, or Reform?*, ed. by John L. Esposito, 179–206. Boulder: Lynne Rienner, 1997.
Ryan, Michael W. S. *Decoding al-Qaeda's Strategy: The Deep Battle Against America*. New York: Columbia University Press, 2013.
Saal, Johannes. "The Rise and Fall of Majd—Part II: Adolescence in Switzerland." *The German Jihad* (blog), July 12, 2018. https://germanjihad.wordpress.com/2018/07/12/the-rise-and-fall-of-majd-part-2-adolescence-in-switzerland/.
Saeed, Abdullah. "Rethinking Citizenship Rights of Non-Muslims in an Islamic State: Rashid al-Ghannūshi's Contribution to the Evolving Debate." *Islam and Christian-Muslim Relations* 10, no. 3 (October 1999): 307–23.
Sageman, Marc. *Leaderless Jihad: Terror Networks in the Twenty-First Century*. Philadelphia: University of Pennsylvania Press, 2008.
———. *Understanding Terror Networks*. Philadelphia: University of Pennsylvania Press, 2004.
Sayah, Habib. "The Next Insurgency in Tunisia." *Fikra Forum*, February 12, 2013.
Schindler, John. *Unholy Terror: Bosnia, al-Qa'ida, and the Rise of Global Jihad*. St. Paul, Minn.: Zenith, 2007.

Shahin, Emad Eldin. "The Rise and Repression of an Islamic Movement: Harakat al-Nahda in Tunisia." In *Political Ascent: Contemporary Islamic Movements in North Africa*. Boulder, Colo.: Westview, 1997.

Shishani, Murad Batal al-. "Al-Zarqawi's Legacy Seen in Trial of Jordanian al-Qaeda Cell." *Terrorism Focus* 6, no. 4 (February 6, 2009).

Silber, Mitchell. *The Al Qaeda Factor: Plots Against the West*. Philadelphia: University of Pennsylvania Press, 2012.

Simcox, Robin. "Ansar al-Sharia and Governance in Southern Yemen." *Current Trends in Islamic Ideology* 14 (January 2013). https://www.hudson.org/research/9779-ansar-al-sharia-and-governance-in-southern-yemen.

Solihin, Sohirin M. *Islamic Da'wah: Theory and Practice*. Kuala Lumpur: IIUM Press, 2008.

Soufan, Ali. *Anatomy of Terror: From the Death of bin Laden to the Rise of the Islamic State*. New York: Norton, 2017.

——. *The Black Banners: The Inside Story of 9/11 and the War Against Al-Qaeda*. New York: Norton, 2011.

Spataro, Armando. "Facets of Islamic Terrorism in Italy." *Circunstancia* 7, no. 18 (January 2009).

Speckhard, Anne. "Female Suicide Bombers in Iraq." *Democracy and Security* 5, no. 1 (2009).

Steinberg, Guido W. *German Jihad: On the Internationalization of Islamist Terrorism*. New York: Columbia University Press, 2013.

Sterman, David, and Nate Rosenblatt. *All Jihad Is Local*. Volume 2, *ISIS in North Africa and the Arabian Peninsula*. New America Foundation, April 2018.

Stets, Jan E., and Jonathan H. Turner, ed. *Handbook of the Sociology of Emotions*. New York: Springer, 2006.

Storm, Morten, Paul Cruickshank, and Tim Lister. *Agent Storm: My Life Inside al Qaeda and the CIA*. New York: Grove, 2014.

Stout, Mark. "In Search of Salafi Jihadist Strategic Thought: Mining the Words of the Terrorists." *Studies in Conflict and Terrorism* 32, no. 10 (2009): 876–92.

Suc, Matthieu. "The Threat from Islamic State's 'Fifth Column' in Europe." *MediaPart*, November 12, 2017.

Tarrow, Sidney. *The New Transnational Activism*. Cambridge, Cambridge University Press, 2005.

——. *Power in Movement: Social Movements and Contentious Politics*, 3rd ed. Cambridge: Cambridge University Press, 2011.

Tawil, Camille. *al-Harakah al-Islamiyah al-musallahah fi al-Jaza'ir: Min al-Inqadh ila al-Jama'ah*. Beirut: Dar al-Nahar, 1998.

——. *Brothers in Arms: The Story of al-Qa'ida and the Arab Jihadists*. London: Saqi Books, 2010.

Thompson, David. *Les français jihadistes*. Paris: Les Arènes, 2014.

——. *Les revenants: Ils étaient partis faire le jihad, ils sont de retour en France*. Paris: Éditions du Seuil, 2016.

Tilly, Charles. *Contentious Politics*. Oxford: Oxford University Press, 2006.

——. *Democracy*. Cambridge: Cambridge University Press, 2007.

Thurston, Alex. "AQIM Kidnappings and Murders in the Sahel, 2007–Present," *Sahel Blog*, January 18, 2011.

Torelli, Stefano M. "The Multi-Faceted Dimensions of Tunisian Salafism." In *Salafism After the Arab Awakening: Contending with People's Power*, ed. by Francesco Cavatorta and Fabio Merone. Oxford: Oxford University Press, 2016.

Torelli, Stefano M., Fabio Merone, and Francesco Cavatorta. "Salafism in Tunisia: Challenges and Opportunities for Democratization." *Middle East Policy* 19, no. 4 (Winter 2012): 140–54.

Tunisia: Violence and the Salafi Challenge, International Crisis Group, Middle East/North Africa Report No. 137, February 13, 2013. https://d2071andvipowj.cloudfront.net/tunisia-violence-and-the-salafi-challenge.pdf.

Usher, Graham. "That Other Tunisia." *Nation*, August 24, 2011.

Vidino, Lorenzo. *al-Qaeda in Europe: The New Battleground of International Jihad*. New York: Prometheus, 2006.

———. "Jihadist Radicalization in Switzerland." *ETH Zürich*, November 2013.

———. "Sharia4: From Confrontational Activism to Militancy." *Perspectives on Terrorism* 9, no. 2 (2015).

Von Knop, Katharina. "The Female Jihad: Al Qaeda's Women." *Studies in Conflict & Terrorism* 30, no. 5 (2007): 397–414.

Wagemakers, Joas. "Protecting Jihad: The Sharia Council of the Minbar al-Tawhid wa-l-Jihad." *Middle East Policy* 18, no. 2 (Summer 2011).

———. *A Quietist Jihadi: The Ideology and Influence of Abu Muhammad al-Maqdisi*. New York: Cambridge University Press, 2012.

———. "Reclaiming Scholarly Authority: Abu Muhammad al-Maqdisi's Critique of Jihadi Practices." *Studies in Conflict and Terrorism* 34, no. 7 (2011): 523–39.

Waltz, Susan. "Islamist Appeal in Tunisia." *Middle East Journal* 40, no. 4 (Autumn 1986).

———. "The Islamists Challenge in Tunisia." *Journal of Arab Affairs* 3 (1984): 99–105.

Warick, Joby. *Black Flags: The Rise of ISIS*. New York: Doubleday, 2015.

Watts, Clint. "Discussion of Countries? Appendix B." *PJ Sage*, 2008.

Watts, Clinton. "What If There Is No Al-Qaeda? Preparing for Future Terrorism." *Foreign Policy Research Institute*, E-Notes, July 2012.

Watts, Clint, Jacob Shapiro, and Vahid Brown. *al-Qa'ida's (Mis)adventure's in the Horn of Africa*. West Point, N.Y.: Combating Terrorism Center, July 2, 2007.

Webb, Edward. "The 'Church' of Bourguiba: Nationalizing Islam in Tunisia." *Sociology of Islam* 1, no. 1–2 (2013). https://doi.org/10.1163/22131418-00101002.

Weslaty, Lilia. "Meeting with Supporters of Ansar Sharia in Kairouan: Between 'Islamic Revolution' and Social Injustice." *Nawaat*, May 30, 2013.

Whitson, Sarah Leah. "Letter to Tunisian Minister of Interior and Minister of Justice." Human Rights Watch, October 14, 2012. https://www.hrw.org/news/2012/10/14/letter-tunisian-minister-interior-and-minister-justice.

Wickham, Carrie Rosefsky. *Mobilizing Islam: Religion, Activism, and Political Change in Egypt*. New York: Columbia University Press, 2002.

Wiktorowicz, Quintan. "Anatomy of the Salafi Movement." *Studies in Conflict & Terrorism* 29, no. 3 (August 2006): 207–39.

———, ed. *Islamic Activism: A Social Movement Theory Approach*. Bloomington: Indiana University Press, 2004.

Willis, Michael J. *The Islamist Challenge in Algeria*. New York: New York University Press, 1999.

———. *Politics and Power in the Maghreb: Algeria, Tunisia, and Morocco from Independence to the Arab Spring*. London: Hurst, 2012.

Wilner, Alex S. "Opportunity Costs or Costly Opportunities? The Arab Spring, Osama Bin Laden, and Al-Qaeda's African Affiliates." *Perspectives on Terrorism* 5, no. 3–4 (2011): 50–62.

Wolf, Anne. "An Islamist 'Renaissance?' Religion and Politics in Post-Revolutionary Tunisia." *Journal of North African Studies* 18, no. 4 (September 2013): 560–73.
———. *Political Islam in Tunisia: The History*. London: Hurst, 2017.
———. "The Radicalization of Tunisia's Mosques." *CTC Sentinel* 7, no. 6 (June 2014).
Woods, Kevin M., and James Lacey. *Iraqi Perspectives Project: Saddam and Terrorism: Emerging Insights from Captured Iraqi Documents*. Alexandria, Va.: Institute for Defense Analysis, 2008.
Yahmed, Hédi. *Taht rayyat al-uqub: Salafiyyun jihadiyyun tunisiyyun*. Tunis: Diwan li-l-nashir, 2015.
Zaidan, Ahmad Muaffaq. *The "Afghan Arabs" Media at Jihad*. Islamabad: ABC Printers, 1999.
Zartman, I. William, ed. *Tunisia: The Political Economy of Reform*. Boulder, Colo.: Lynne Rienner, 1991.
Zenn, Jacob. "Wilayat West Africa Reboots for the Caliphate." *CTC Sentinel* 8, no. 8 (August 2015).
Zelin, Aaron Y. "al-Farīḍa al-Ghā'iba and al-Sadat's Assassination, a 30 Year Retrospective," *International Journal for Arab Studies* 3, no. 2 (July 2012).
———. "Boko Haram's Media and the Islamic State Connection?" *Jihadology*, January 27, 2015.
———. "From the Archduke to the Caliph: The Islamist Evolution That Led to 'The Islamic State.'" In *The First World War and Its Aftermath: The Shaping of the Modern Middle East*, ed by. T. G. Fraser, 159–73. London: Gingko Library, 2015.
———. "How al-Qaeda Survived Drones, Uprisings, and the Islamic State." Washington Institute for Near East Policy, *Policy Focus*, no. 153 (June 2017).
———. "The ISIS Guide to Building an Islamic State." *Atlantic*, June 13, 2014.
———. "Islamic State Attacks in Tunisia." *Tunisian Jihadism*, June 6, 2018.
———. "The Islamic State's Territorial Methodology." Washington Institute for Near East Policy, *Research Notes*, no. 29 (January 2016).
———. "Jihadi Attacks in Tunisia Prior to 2011." *Tunisian Jihadism*, October 22, 2018.
———. "Jihadi Soft Power in Tunisia: Ansar al-Shari'ah's Convoy Provides Aid to the Town of Haydrah in West Central Tunisia." *al-Wasat* (blog), February 21, 2012. https://thewasat.wordpress.com/2012/02/21/jihadi-soft-power-in-tunisia-ansar-al-shariahs-convoy-provides-aid-to-the-town-of-haydrah-in-west-central-tunisia-with-pictures.
———. "Know Your Ansar al-Sharia." *Foreign Policy*, September 21, 2012.
———. "Maqdisi's Disciples in Libya and Tunisia." *Foreign Policy's Middle East Channel*, November 14, 2012.
———. "New Evidence on Ansar al-Sharia in Libya Training Camps." *al-Wasat*, August 8, 2013.
———. "The Others: Foreign Fighters in Libya." Washington Institute for Near East Policy, *Policy Note*, no. 45, January 2018.
———. "The Rise of Salafists in Tunisia After the Fall of Ben Ali." *CTC Sentinel*, August 2011.
———. "The Role of Tunisians." In *Beyond Syria and Iraq: Examining Islamic State Province*, ed by Katherine Bauer. *Policy Focus*, no. 149. Washington, D.C.: Washington Institute for Near East Policy, November 2016.
———. "The Salafi Challenge to Tunisia's Nascent Democracy." Washington Institute for Near East Policy, *Policy Watch* #1879, December 8, 2011.
———. "Shabab al-Tawhid: The Rebranding of Ansar al-Sharia in Tunisia?" Washington Institute for Near East Policy, *Policy Watch*, no. 2250 (May 9, 2014).
———. "Tunis Designates Ansar al-Sharia in Tunisia." *al-Wasat*, August 28, 2013.
———. "Tunisian Foreign Fighters in Iraq and Syria," Washington Institute for Near East Policy, *Policy Notes*, no. 55 (November 2018).

———. "The Tunisian-Libyan Jihadi Connection." *ICSR Insight*, July 6, 2015.
———. "Tunisia's Female Jihadists." Washington Institute for Near East Policy, *Policy Watch*, no. 3032, October 31, 2018.
———. "Tunisia's Most Wanted Terrorists." *Tunisian Jihadism*, April 3, 2019.
———. "The Clairvoyant: Update on Shabab al-Tawhid and Creation of al-Midrar Media." *Jihadology*, May 12, 2014, https://jihadology.net/2014/05/12/the-clairvoyant-update-on-shabab-al-tawhid-and-creation-of-al-midrar-media/.
———. "Wanas al-Faqih Designated as a Terrorist by U.S. Department of State." *Tunisian Jihadism*, January 5, 2018.
———. "The War Between ISIS and al-Qaeda for Supremacy of the Global Jihadist Movement." Washington Institute for Near East Policy, *Research Notes*, no. 20, June 2014.
Zelin, Aaron Y., and Oula A. Alrifai. "The Islamic State in Southern Syria." *CTC Sentinel* 8, no. 11 (November/December 2015). https://ctc.usma.edu/app/uploads/2015/12/CTCSentinel-Vol8Iss114.pdf.

INDEX

'Abd Allah 'Azzam, 43, 46, 276
'Abd al-'Aziz al-Muqrin, 116
'Abd Elbaki Hermassi, 24
Abdelli, Lotfi, 165–66
'Abd al-Fatah, Shukri, 182
'Abd al-Hadi al-Tunisi, 43
'Abd al-Latif al-Hermassi, 30
'Abd al-Malik Drukdal, 11, 125–26, 131
'Abd al-Nasir, Gamal, 28–29
'Abd al-Rahman al-Jaza'iri, 261–62
'Abd al-Ra'uf al-'Ayadi, 106
Abouzaid, Rania, 200
Abu 'Abd Allah al-Tunisi, 186, 203
Abu 'Abd al-Rahman al-Tunisi, 228–29
Abu Ahmad al-Tunisi, 87–88
Abu 'Ali al-Anbari, 200
Abu Anas al-Tunisi, 220
Abu Ayub al-Nurwiji, 213
Abu Ayub al-Tunisi, 127–28, 203
Abu Basir al-Tunisi, 77, 126
Abu Fatimah al-Tunisi, 263
Abu Hafs al-Tunisi, 86
Abu Hajr al-Tunisi, 205
Abu Hamzah al-Masri, 53
Abu Hamzah al-Muhajir, 77
Abu Hasan al-Muhajir, 270–71
Abu Hatim al-Tunisi, 221

Abu Hudhayfah al-Sudani, 269–70
Abu Ibrahim al-Tunisi, 76, 242
Abu Ishaq al-Shinqiti, 92–93
Abu 'Iyadh al-Tunisi, 1, 52–56, 58, 68–69, 93, 99–100; Abu Mus'ab 'Abd al-Wadud and, 174; AQ and, 57, 115, 133–34, 192–94; on AST managing the stages, 127, 132, 168, 170, 187; Bin'ali and, 185; on *dawa*, 114, 117, 131–32, 168, 171; on Iraq jihad, 179; on ISIS, 192–94; on jihad, 139; in Mali, 270; Mar'akat al-azan fi-l-sujun and, 124; al-Nahdah and, 154, 169, 172–73, 176–77; on *niqab* ban, 109; on *Persepolis*, 107; in prison, 124–25, 129; on *rawafidh*, 162; on sharia demonstration, 112; on *takfir*, 123; on Tunisian foreign fighters, 179–80; on Tunisian jihadis in IS, 194; al-Zahawi and, 183; al-Zarqawi and, 189; al-Zawahiri and, 133, 174, 193–94
Abu Mu'adh al-Tunisi, 245–46
Abu Muhammad al-Adnani, 204
Abu Muhanad al-Tunisi, 197, 268
Abu al-Mundhir al-Shinqiti, 100, 126, 128, 130, 133, 163–64, 177
Abu Mus'ab 'Abd al-Wadud, 174
Abu Mus'ab al-Tunisi, 201
Abu Qatadah al-Filistini, 53–56, 58, 69, 194

Abu Shahid al-Tunisi, 49–50, 52–53
Abu Taj al-Sussi, 200
Abu Tariq al-Tunisi, 61
Abu Turab al-Tunisi, 160
Abu 'Umar al-Baghdadi, 81
Abu 'Umar al-Tunisi, 78, 212
Abu Usamah al-Tunisi, 229
Abu Usamah Walid Uld al-Habat al-Tunisi, 77
Abu al-Waqas al-Tunisi, 11, 185–86
Abu Yasin al-Tunisi, 213
Abu Zayd al-Tunisi, 46–47, 61, 196
Abu Zubaydah, 55–56, 69
Abu Zubayr 'Adil Bin 'Abd Allah al-Abab, 11
Adamsky, Dima, 115
al-Adl, Sayf, 46, 61, 117
Afghanistan, 54–62, 66–67, 72, 76, 121–22
Afghan jihad, 33, 40–45, 47, 85–86, 277
Ain Issa camp, 263–64
al-Akari, Muhammad, 174
'Akuri, Mukhtar, 270
al-Alawi, Nasr al-Din, 169
alcohol, 166–68
Algeria, 90–91, 101, 122, 173
Algerian civil war, 52
Algerian jihad, 51–55
Allani, Alaya, 4, 146
al-Nazari, Harith bin Ghazi, 123
Amduni, Ayman, 169
al-Amduni, Mahriz Bin Sassi, 51
Amri, Anis, 245–46
Amruni, Ajmi, 264–65
Amruni, Muhammad, 264–65
Andersson, Lisa, 265
al-Ansar, 53, 116
Ansar al-Islam, 73, 83
Ansar al-Mujahidin Arabic Forum, 1–3
Ansar al-Sharia in Libya (ASL), 159, 175, 183
Ansar al-Sharia in Tunisia (AST), 1–2, 271–72; activities, by governorate, 141, *142–43*, 143; activities organized by, 143, *144–45*, 145–53; alternative voices within, 189–90; AQ and, 115, 123–26, 128, 132–34, 149–50; AQIM and, 8–9, 141, 170–71, 173–74, 182–83; after Arab uprisings, 11; association network of, 146–47; Avenue Bourguiba clock tower protest of, 110–12; Bin Ladin to, 128–29; black flag of, 103, 108–9, 111, 159–60;

charitable activities of, 145–46; collective action frame of, 17; on Constituent Assembly elections, 2011, 100, 106–7; convoy campaign, 139; downfall of, 160–61, 171–78, 186, 237–38; Facebook page, 135–36, 140, 149, 159, 162, 167, 180–81, 198–99; failure to manage the stages, 168–71, 187; founding of, 106–7; framing narratives of, 16–17, 153; on Ghannushi, R., 100–101; al-Hatab and, 199–200; on al-Hazimi, 198–99; *hisba* and, 161–66, *163*, 168–70; IS and, 10–11, 21–22; ISIS and, 185–86, 188–93, 203; on Islam, 154–55; on Islamic state, 156; on jihad, 164, 168–69; jihadism of, 6; JN and, 180, 184–86, 192–93; KUBN and, 173, 258–59; leaders, previous jihadi activity of, 41, 43; leadership structure, 136, *137*, 138; literature distributed by, 149; in Manouba College *niqab* protest, 108–10; Marufi in, 62; medical convoys of, 145–46; members, interviewed, 19; messaging by, 119, 153–57; middle managers in, 14; military wing, structure of, 174; mosque network, 147, *148*; narratives of, 16–17, 153–57; neighborhood committees, 167–69; network plans of, 131; organization of, 136, *137*, 138–41, 143, 157–58; outreach to children and teenagers, 150–51, 154–55; on *Persepolis* airing on Nessma TV, 107–8; publicly released materials by, 18; Qur'an and, 149, 157; at al-Rahmah Mosque, 197; Ramadan aid by, 147–48; recruitment by, 3; recruitment campaign, 205; religion and, 17; religious lectures program of, *151*, 151–53; resource mobilization by, 16–17, 136, 147; security committees, 166–69; sharia committee, 189–90; slogans, 154–57; SMT and, 14–15; social services of, 12, 121, 145; ST and, 190–91; terrorist organization designation by Tunisian government, 9, 11, 16, 96–97, 105, 160–61, 176–78, 187, 249–52; on Tunisian foreign fighters, 179–81; Tunisian government on, 9, 20, 94–95, 98–99, 132, 168, 176, 237–38; Tunisian jihadis and, 94–95, 98; after Tunisian revolution, 20, 41; Tunisian

transitional government and, 98–99; U.S. Embassy attack, 3, 171. *See also* Abu ʻIyadh al-Tunisi
Ansar al-Sharia in Tunisia (AST), *dawa* and, 17; Abu Ayub al-Tunisi on, 127–28; Abu ʻIyadh on, 117, 131–32, 171; AQ advice on, 125–26; IS and, 10–11; jihad and, 164; literature by, 123–24, 138, 149; al-Nahdah and, 100, 105, 176–77; program for, 11–12, 139–41, 143, 149, 154, 171; refugee aid, 182; social services through, 12, 15; strategy, as *dawa*-first, 21, 121, 128, 132, 134–35, 153, 187; Tunisian locals in campaign of, 14
Ansar al-Sharia in Tunisia (AST), al-Nahdah and, 96–97, 111–13, 117, 129–30; Abu ʻIyadh and, 172–73, 176–77; *dawa* and, 100, 105, 176–77; al-Hatab and, 199; *hisba* and, 161–62; jihadi policy, 99–105; sharia and, 140; Tunisian foreign fighters, 180
anti-Gulf War protests, 36
Anzalone, Christopher, 11, 118–19
AQ. *See* al-Qaeda
AQAP. *See* al-Qaeda in the Arabian Peninsula
AQI. *See* al-Qaeda in Iraq
AQIM. *See* al-Qaeda in the Islamic Maghrib
Arab uprisings, 2–3, 6–9, 11, 118–20
al-Arud, Malikah, 58, 85–86
ASL. *See* Ansar al-Sharia in Libya
al-Assad, Bashar, 74, 78–79, 81, 180–81, 184
AST. *See* Ansar al-Sharia in Tunisia
Avenue Bourguiba clock tower protest, 110–12
al Awaʼir, Burawi, 57–58
al-Ayadi, Shafiq Bin Muhammad, 62
Azmaraʼi, Usamah, 45

al-Baghdadi, Abu Bakr, 185, 201, 221, 239, 248; *baya* to, 189–91, 193, 200, 229, 240–41, 244–45, 247
al-Bahri, Nasir, 61
Bakhti, Muhammad, 89, 108–9, 160
al-Banna, Hasan, 30, 273–74
Bardo National Museum attack, 175, 229, 234, 241–42, 246–47
Barrie, Christopher, 143

al-Bassam, Hamzah Bin Muhammad, 127
baya, 189–91, 193, 200, 229, 240–41, 244–45, 247
Bayudh, Anwar, 264
Beghal, Jamal, 57
Benford, Robert D., 17, 153
Ben Gardane attack, 233–35, 236–37, 238, 248–49, 252–53
Benghazi, Libya, 175, 181–83
Benotman, Noman, 43
Benyettou, Farid, 74
Berlin Christmas Market attack, 229, 241–42, 245–46
Bilaʼid, Shukri, 105, 156, 164, 167
Bilmukhtar, Mukhtar, 9, 173
Binʼali, Turki, 185, 190, 200
Bin ʻAli, 34–39, 47–48, 92, 96–100, 125–26
Bin Hasan, Bashir, 184
Bin Hasin, Sayf Allah. *See* Abu ʻIyadh al-Tunisi
Bin Jiddu, Lutfi Bin, 176
Bin Khamis, Sami Isid, 47, 54, 60, 62, 73, 176
Bin Ladin, Usamah, 17, 43, 45–46, 55; Abu Tariq and, 61; to AST, 128–29; on *dawa*, 129; death of, 13; to TCG, 57
Bin Muhammad Tlili, Lahzar, 91
Bin Rajab, Muhammad Iqbal, 217, 263
Bin Salah, Imad Bin ʻAbd al-Razaq, 213–14
Bin Salim, Asmaʼ, 228
Bin Salim, Munsif, 37, 110
Bin Sassi, ʻAli, 78, 299n138
Black Hawk Down, 61
Black Thursday, 31
Boko Haram, 244–45
Bologna, Italy, 51, 58, 83
Bonner, Michael, 276, 336n16
border documents, of IS, 18, 210–12, 211, 220, 318n167
Bosnian jihad, 49–51
Boulby, Marion, 25, 28
Bourguiba, Habib, 23, 28, 31–34; educational reforms of, 26–27; Islamic reforms by, 24–27, 40; al-Nahdah after, 35–36
Brahmi, Muhammad, 164, 173–74, 176
Bread Riots, 33
al-Briguwi, Yasin, 109–10
al-Brik, Hasan, 71–72, 124–25, 131, 160, 169–70
Brooke, Steven, 115

Bu'amra, Ahmad, 44
Budhiba, Hidi Bin Yusuf, 60
Budina, Ibrahim, 229
al-Bunyan al-Marsus, 44
Buyahiya, Mahir, 78

Callimachi, Rukmini, 11
Call to Global Islamic Resistance (al-Suri), 118, 121
Casablanca bombings, 68–69
Cavatorta, Francesco, 4–5
Chebbi, Ahmed Najib, 164
Chenoweth, Erica, 15
Churchill, Erik, 102, 110
Clausewitz, Carl von, 13–14
Code du statut personnel, 25–26
Collier, David, 42
Congrés pour la république (CPR), 37
convoy campaign, of AST, 139
Cook, Michael, 278
Corman, Steven R., 17, 157
counterterrorism policies, of Tunisian government, 248–55
CPR. *See* Congrés pour la république
Cremona Cathedral plot, 83

Dabiq (magazine), 174–76
Dahmani, 'Abd al-Satar, 57–58
dawa, 3, 9; Abu 'Iyadh on, 114, 117, 131–32, 168, 171; AQIM on, 170–71; AQ on, 123, 125, 129; of ASL, 183; Bin Ladin on, 129; defining, 278; of IS, 10–11; of ISIS, 185–86; in jihadi movement, 259; JT on, 28; al-Qurashi on, 117; in Tunisia, 114, 131–32, 170; Tunisian jihadis and, 115, 126, 128–29. *See also* Ansar al-Sharia in Tunisia (AST), *dawa* and
Dawson, Lorne L., 157
Dean, Aimen, 50
Degauque, Muriel, 79
Deir al-Zour, 195–96
Della Porta, Donatella, 16, 175
Denmark, 84–85
Djerba synagogue bombing, 64–68
Dolnik, Adam, 19
Douar Hicher, Tunis, 169

educational reforms, of Bourguiba, 26–27
Egypt, 7–8, 28–29, 32, 49

Ethiopia, 86
Europe: Tunisian foreign fighters based in, mobilizing, 209–10, 210; Tunisian jihadis in, 48–49, 68; Tunisian jihadis in plots in, 2005-2010, 83–85. *See also specific countries*
Evans, Ryan, 13–14, 136

Faenza Mosque, in Bologna, 83
Fajr al-Qayrawan, 239–40
Fakhit, Sarhan Bin 'Abd al-Majid, 69–70
al-Faqih, Wanas, 89, 245
Farag, Muhammad 'Abd al-Salam, 274, 276
Farmanfarmaian, Roxane, 108
Farrall, Leah, 8
Fatah al-Islam, 81
female Tunisian jihadis, in IS, 222, 228, 242–44
Feuer, Sarah J., 24
Firjani, Sa'id, 103, 110
FIS. *See* al-Jabhah al-Islamiyah Li-l-Inqadh
Fishman, Brian, 10
FIT. *See* Tunisian Islamic Front
al-Fizani, Mu'az, 50, 267
Flade, Florian, 231
framing narratives, of AST, 16–17, 153
France, 48, 52, 54; colonial period, in Tunisia, 25; Mali and, 170, 173, 182; Tunisian foreign fighters from, 209
Free Syrian Army, 206, 229
Furlow, R. Bennett, 157

Gadahn, Adam, 60, 123
al-Gama'ah al-Islamiyyah, 49
Ganczarski, Christian, 65–66
Gartenstein-Ross, Daveed, 7, 10, 120
Gelowicz, Fritz, 83
Germany, 83–84
Gerring, John, 14
Ghandri, Adl, 267–68
Ghannushi, Muhammad, 97
Ghannushi, Rashid: Abu 'Iyadh and, 176–77; AST on, 100–101; al-Nahdah and, 24–25, 27–29, 31–34, 36, 39, 44, 100–101
al-Gharsalawi, Mu'az al-Din, 85–86
Gharsalli, Najim, 241
GIA. *See* Groupe islamique armé
global jihadi movement, 8–10, 12–14, 43, 179

Goodall, H. L., Jr., 17
grassroots organizing, 13–14
Gregg, Heather S., 17
Groupe islamique armé (GIA), 48–49, 51–55, 87, 122
Groupe salafiste pour la prédication et le combat (GSPC), 48–49, 51, 53–55, 87–94
GSPC. *See* Groupe salafiste pour la prédication et le combat
Guantánamo files, WikiLeaks, 58
Gulf War, 36

habus, 26
Haftar, Khalifah, 270
al-Hakim, Bubakr, 241; on Bardo attack, 229, 247; Brahmi assassination by, 174, 176; *Dabiq* interview with, 174–76; in French jihadi mobilization, 209; in Iraq, 74; IS, Tunisian jihadis and, 185; on Libya, 182; in 19th arrondissement network, 74, 79; in prison, 74–75
Hakimi, 'Adl Bin Ahmad Bin Ibrahim, 58
halaqat, 28–29
Haleem, Muhammad Abdel, 276
Halverson, Jeffry R., 17, 157
al-Hamad, Abu Malik Shaybah, 244–45
Hamdi, Mohammed Elihachimi, 29, 31
Hamid, Mustafa, 45, 55, 57, 189
Hammami, Sayf Allah, 231
Hanashi, Ra'uf, 56
Harakat al-Shabab al-Mujahidin, 9–11, 61, 86, 132–33
Harakat al-Ittijah al-Islami (MTI), 32–35
Harakat al-Nahdah. *See* al-Nahdah
Harrath, Muhammad 'Ali, 47–48
Harris, Alistair, 17
Harun, Fadhl, 60–62, 65, 86
al-Harzi, 'Ali Bin al-Tahar Bin al-Falih, 175, 183
al-Harzi, Tariq, 41, 71, 78, 94, 212
Hasni, Sharf al-Din, 264
Hatab, Hasan, 53, 87
al-Hatab, Abu Ja'afar, 189–91, 199–201, 222, 268
Haugbølle, Rikke Hostrup, 4, 237
al-Hawl Camp, 265–66
Hay al-Khadra' Mosques Committee, 197
Hay'at Tahrir al-Sham, 205
Haykel, Bernard, 275

al-Hazimi, Ahmad Bin 'Umar, 194–95, 197–200, *198*
Hazimis, 197–201, 203, 266
Headley, David Coleman, 84
Hegghammer, Thomas, 19, 115, 121
Henneberg, Sabina, 99
hijra, 222
hisba, 15, 21, 171, 278; AST and, 161–66, *163*, 168–70; al-Nahdah and, 161–62; salafis and, 162–66
Hoffman, Bruce, 12–13
Holman, Timothy, 184
Homs, Syria, 81–82, 178, 206
Human Rights Council, UN, 195–96
human rights violations: in Iraq, 195–97; by IS, 195–96; in Syria, 195–97, 203; by Tunisian government, concerns about, 254–55
Human Rights Watch, 104, 110
Hurshani, Farhat, 245
al-Husaynan, Khalid bin 'Abd al-Rahman, 123
Husni, Jamal, 78
Hussein, Saddam, 74

Ibn Abu Zayd al-Qayrawani Institute for Sharia Sciences, 197–98
Ibn Shaykh al-Libi, 56
ICI. *See* Islamic Cultural Institute
al-Idrisi, Shaykh al-Khatib, 38–39, 127, 131
Ifriqiya Media, 239–41
ijtihad, 26
Independent Students initiative, 37
International Crisis Group, 102, 182
Iran, 164
Iranian Revolution of 1979, 31–32
Iraq, 39, 122, 178, 193; al-Hakim in, 74; Syria border, 204, 270; Tunisian foreign fighters in, 206, *207*, 208–9, *210*, 213; Tunisian jihadis committing human rights violations in, 195–97; Tunisian jihadis in, 220–22, 223–27, 228–31; Tunisian jihadis in IS propaganda videos from, 222, 223–27. *See also* Islamic State of Iraq; Islamic State of Iraq and al-Sham; al-Qaeda in Iraq
Iraq jihad: Abu 'Iyadh on, 179; AQIM, ISI in, 175–76; *takfir* in, 114; Tunisian jihadis in, 71–79, *80*, 90–91

Iraq War, 10, 72–78, 81
IS. *See* Islamic State
ISI. *See* Islamic State of Iraq
Isid, Sabri, 79, 81
ISIS. *See* Islamic State of Iraq and al-Sham
Islam, 9; AST on, 154–55; sharia and, 25; in Tunisia, 20, 23
Islamic Courts Union, 86
Islamic Cultural Institute (ICI), 49, 54, 73, 91–92
Islamic Good Society, 197
Islamic Jihad Union, 83, 86
Islamic law, 25
Islamic Movement of Uzbekistan, 86
Islamic reforms, by Bourguiba, 24–27, 40
Islamic social movements, 15, 37
Islamic State (IS), 6–8, 10, 114, 174; AQ and, 57, 122, 175–76, 189, 200, 268, 271; AQIM and, 191; AST and, 10–11, 21–22; attacks in Tunisia, 229; Bardo National Museum attack by, 241–42, 246–47; Ben Gardane attack by, 233–35, *236–37*, 238, 248–49, 252–53; border documents, 18, 210–12, *211*, 220, 318n167; caliphate, 185, 219, 239; captured members, in Ain Issa camp, 263–64; *dawa* program of, 10–11; on deaths of Tunisian foreign fighters, 213–14; external operations, 228–31; female Tunisian jihadis in, 222, 228, 242–44; human rights violations by, 195–96; on Iraq-Syria border, 204, 270; ISIS and, 175, 189, 194, 199, 203, 222; JN and, 264; KUBN and, 177, 238–42, 248, 255–63; in Libya, 50; Mallah in, 204–5; returnees to Tunisia from, 263–66; Sousse Beach attack by, 241–42, 247; *takfir* and, 201, *202*, 203; territory losses, KUBN and, 257–63; Tunisia attacks by, 246–49; Tunisian government and, 249–55; at Turkish-Syrian border, 212; Wilayat Tunis and, 247–48. *See also* Tunisian jihadis, in IS
Islamic State of Iraq (ISI), 10, 75–79, 81–82; AQ and, 123, 175–76; AQIM and, 123, 175–76; foreign fighters in, 178; ISIS and, 123, 175, 189; KUBN and, 175; in Syria, 179; in Tunisia, expanding operations, 174–75; al-Zarqawi and, 123

Islamic State of Iraq and al-Sham (ISIS): Abu 'Iyadh on, 192–94; AQ and, 191–94; AST and, 185–86, 188–93, 203; *dawa* program of, 185–86; IS and, 175, 189, 194, 199, 203, 222; ISI and, 123, 175, 189; JN and, 185–86, 190–93, 200–201; Tunisian jihadis in, 188–91, 200–201, 203
Islamism, 20, 273–74. *See also* Tunisian Islamism
Islamist activism, 15, 38
Islamist groups, 15, 25
Italy, 78; Bologna, 51, 58, 83; Milan, 48–49, 54, 62, 91; Tunisian jihadis in, 49–51, 54, 58, 62, 74, 83
#IWillComeToTunisiaThisSummer campaign, 246–47

al-Jabali, Hamadi, 33, 37, 100–101, 105, 124–25
JABF. *See* Jund Asad Bin al-Furat
al-Jabhah al-Islamiyah Li-l-Inqadh (FIS), 48, 52
Jabhat al-Nusra (JN), 9, 179; AST and, 180, 184–86, 192–93; IS and, 264; ISIS and, 185–86, 190–93, 200–201; Tunisian foreign fighters in, 206, 215; Tunisian jihadis in, 188–89, 196–97
Jalalabad school, 45–46, 50, 56–57, 68–69, 189–94
al-Jama'ah al-Islamiyyah (JI), 29–32
Jama'at Nusrat al-Islam wa-l-Muslimin (JNIM), 269
Jama'at al-Tabligh (JT), 28–29
Jama'at al-Tawhid wa-l-Jihad (JTWJ), 74–76, 78–79
Jama'iah Abu al-Qasim al-Zahrawi, 145–46
Jarraya, Khalil, 83
al-Jawlani, Abu Muhammad, 189–90
al-Jaza'iri, Abu Muslim, 127, 129–31
JI. *See* al-Jama'ah al-Islamiyyah
Jiday, 'Abd al-Ra'uf, 60–61
jihad: Abu 'Iyadh on, 139; Afghan, 33, 40–45, 47, 85–86, 277; Algerian, 51–55; of AQ, as corrective, 121–24; AST on, 164, 168–69; Bosnian, 49–51; leader-led *versus* leaderless, 12–14; al-Maqdisi protecting, 120–21; meaning of, 275–76; in Syria, 184–85. *See also* Iraq jihad
jihad al-nikah, 228

jihadi policy: of al-Nahdah, 99–105; of Tunisian transitional government, 97–99

jihadis: Arab uprising and, 2–3; AST leaders' previous activity as, 41, 43; *dawa* in movement of, 259; global movement, 8–10, 12–14, 43, 179; metastization, post-Arab uprisings, 7–9; operational art of, 115–16; social services and governance, 9–12; terrorist attacks by, 171, *172*; theory of resistance, 118; Tunisian Revolution and, 1, 16. *See also* Tunisian jihadis

jihadi-salafis, 100, 102–5, 110, 114, 120

jihadi-salafism, 277

jihadism: of AST, 6; in West, 5, 13. *See also* jihad; Tunisian jihadis

JN. *See* Jabhat al-Nusra

JNIM. *See* Jama'at Nusrat al-Islam wa-l-Muslimin

JT. *See* Jama'at al-Tabligh

JTWJ. *See* Jama'at al-Tawhid wa-l-Jihad

Jund Asad Bin al-Furat (JABF), 39, 88–89

Jund al-Islam, 72–73

Jund al-Sham, 72

al-Jurshi, Salah al-Din, 27–28, 30

Jyllands-Posten attack, 84

Kar, Mevlüt, 84

Karkar, Salah, 32–35, 44

Karoui, Nabil, 107–8

Karray Kamal Bin 'Ali, 50

al-Kasasbah, Mu'adh, 195

Kashmiri, Ilyas, 84

Katibat 'Uqbah Bin Nafi (KUBN), 18–19, 21–22, 88, 105, 271; AQIM and, 161, 170, 239–41, 259–62; AST and, 173, 258–59; Fajr al-Qayrawan and, 239–40; hearts and minds, lost by, 260–63; Ifriqiya Media and, 239–41; IS and, 177, 238–42, 248, 255–63; ISI and, 175; after IS' losses of territory, 257–63; al-Nahdah and, 173; network disconnection, 258–59; on Tunisian government, 258; Tunisian jihadis and, 260

Kazdaghli, Habib, 108–9

Kendall, Diana, 136

Kenya, 86

Ketchley, Neil, 143

Khalden network, 55–56, 68

Khalid Shaykh Muhammad (KSM), 44, 60–61, 64–67

Kirdiş, Esen, 37

Klausen, Jytte, 5, 18

Krekar, Mullah, 72–73

Kruglanski, Arie W., 153

KSM. *See* Khalid Shaykh Muhammad

KUBN. *See* Katibat 'Uqbah Bin Nafi

Kurdistan, 72–73

Lahoud, Nelly, 273, 277

Larayedh, 'Ali, 105, 172, 176–77, 180

Lasuwidah, Fahmi, 267

Lav, Daniel, 277

leader-led *versus* leaderless jihad, 12–14

Lebanon, 81

Lee, Robert D., 25–26

leftists, Tunisian, 28–31, 103, 164

leftist strategists, 115

Lia, Brynjar, 115

al-Libi, 'Atiyat Allah 'Abd al-Rahman, 122–23, 128–29, 183

Libya, 8–9, 19; AQIM in, 270; ASL in, 159, 175, 183; Benghazi, 175, 181–83; Civil War, 181–82; al-Hakim on, 182; IS in, 50; refugees from, 145; Tunisia border with, 233–34; Tunisian foreign fighters in, 181–84, 208–9; Tunisian jihadis with IS in, 242–46, *243*, *244*

Libyan Islamic Fighting Group, 53

al-Luz, Habib, 102

Lynch, Marc, 7

Madrid train bombings, 68–70, 92

Magen, Amichai, 10

Maghrawi, Hamzah, 195

Mahmud, Muhammad, 222

mahram, 222

Majlis Shura al-Mujahidin (MSM), 75–79

Maktab al-Khidamat al-Mujahidin (MAK), 43

Mali, 11, 92–93, 266–67; Abu 'Iyadh in, 270; France and, 170, 173, 182

Mallah, Jamal al-Din, 204–5, 270

Management of Savagery, The (Naji), 117

Mandaville, Peter, 273

Manitah, Miftah, 182

Manouba College *niqab* protest, 108–10

Mao Tse-Tung, 116–17
al-Maqdisi, Abu Muhammad, 114–16, 120–21, 126–27, 149, 198–99, 275, 277
Mar'akat al-azan fi-l-sujun, 124
Marcusa, Michael, 141, 143
al-Ma'rifa magazine, 29–30, *30*
Marks, Monica, 5, 100, 103–5
Marufi, Tariq, 47, 52, 54, 57, 62, 85
Marzuqi, Munsif, 93, 110, 218
Masahil, Muhammad Bin al-Hadi, 92
Mas'ud, Ahmad Shah, 57–58, 60, 73
Mazuz, Yusuf, 190, 238
MB. *See* Muslim Brotherhood
McAdam, Doug, 16
McCants, William, 7, 120
McCarthy, John D., 16–17
McCarthy, Rory, 4, 38, 138
Mecham, Quinn, 15
media halo, 119
medical convoys, of AST, 145–46
Meijer, Roel, 278
Merah, Muhammad, 79, 81, 86
Merone, Fabio, 4–5
Mibaza'a, Fu'ad, 98
middle managers, 13–14, 136
Milan, Italy, 48–49, 54, 62, 91
Minbar al-tawhid wal-jihad (website), 120–21
Morocco, 92
Moussa, Jenan, 221
MSM. *See* Majlis Shura al-Mujahidin
MTI. *See* Harakat al-Ittijah al-Islami
Muhammad (prophet), 84, 104, 159, 278
al-Mujahidun, 44
Murshidi, Kamal, 73
Muru, 'Abd al-Fatah, 32–33, 36, 104
Muslim Brotherhood (MB): al-Nayfar on, 30; al-Banna in, 30, 273–74; Egyptian, 29, 32; ideology, 29; organizations like, 1–2, 6, 15, 37, 126, 138; Syrian, 28–29, 180
Muslim practices, 25–26

al-Nahdah, 1–2, 4, 7, 16, 20; Abu 'Iyadh and, 154, 169, 172–73, 176; on Afghan jihad, 44; AQIM on, 170–71; Bin 'Ali and, 35–36, 99–100; CPR and, 37; expansion phase, 1973–1979, 29–31; fatwa against, 100; five phases of, 28–38; formative phase, 1960s-1973, 28–29; Ghannushi, R., and, 24–25, 27–29, 31–34, 36, 39, 44, 100–101; al-Jabali and, 33, 37; JABF and, 39; JI and, 29–32; jihadi policy of, 99–105; JT and, 28–29; Karkar in, 44; KUBN and, 173; MTI and, 32–35; al-Nayfar and, 27–31; after 9/11, 37; organizational infrastructure of, 36–37; political normalization phase, 2001–2010, 36–38; politicization phase, 1979–1987, 31–35; post-Bourguiba phase, 1987–2000, 35–36; on salafi movement, 39, 99–100; Shahin on phases of, 27–28; al-Shinqiti on, 130; on Tunisian government, 36; Tunisian jihadis and, 129–30; Tunisian Revolution and, 28; U.S. and, 168, 171. *See also* Ansar al-Sharia in Tunisia (AST), al-Nahdah and
Naji, Abu Bakr, 115, 117–19
Naqash, Anis, 167–68
narratives, 16–17, 153–57
Nasiri, Omar, 55
Nasri, Muhammad Bin Riyadh, 57–58, 60
National Association for the Preservation of the Qur'an, 28–29
National Guard, of Tunisia, 169
Nawar, Nizar Bin Muhammad Nasar, 64–67
Nawar, Walid, 66–67
al-Nayfar, Hamidah, 27–31
Nessma TV, 99, 107–8
Neumann, Peter, 13–14, 136
Nida Tunis, 168
9/11, 37–39; aftermath, 61–62; AQ in, 121–22; successful attacks after, 64–70; Tunisian jihadis and, 60–62, *63–64*
19th arrondissement network, 74, 79
niqab, 108–10, 228, 278
Nsaibia, Heni, 270
Al-Nur Mosque, 169

October 18 Collectif, 37
Ouerghi, Munsif, 166

Page, Michael, 17
Palestinian Liberation Organization (PLO), 43–44
Pantucci, Raffaello, 13–14, 136
Pargeter, Alison, 5, 43
Perkins, Kenneth J., 23

Persepolis (2007), 99, 107–8, 165
Peshawar, 43
PLO. *See* Palestinian Liberation Organization
police, Tunisian, 103–4
prison, Tunisian jihadis in, 70, 72, 93–94, 124–25, 129, 266–69
prisoner amnesty, 20, 96–98, 106, 114
propaganda videos, Tunisian jihadis in, 222, 223–27, 244

al-Qadhafi, Mu'ammar, 181–83
qadis, 26
al-Qaeda (AQ), 2–3, 37; Abu 'Iyadh and, 57, 115, 133–34, 192–94; Abu Zayd in, 46–47; in Afghanistan, 55, 57, 121; Arab uprisings and, 7–8; AST and, 115, 123–26, 128, 132–34, 149–50; corrective jihad, 121–24; on *dawa*, 123, 125–26, 129; defeat of, 7–8; in Djerba synagogue bombing, 64–68; Ganczarski in, 65; global jihad and, 12; IS and, 57, 122, 175–76, 189, 194, 200, 268, 271; ISI and, 123, 175–76; ISIS and, 191–94; leader-led, leaderless jihad and, 12–13; media strategy, 119; middle managers in, 13–14; narratives of, 17; Nawar, N., in, 64–67; in 9/11, 121–22; al-Qurashi and, 116; al-Suri and, 118–19; TCG and, 60; theory of resistance, 118; training camps, 46; Tunisian jihadis in, 57–58, 60–61, 188–89, 194, 206; Waddani in, 73; Zakariyya in, 61
al-Qaeda in Iraq (AQI), 75–76, 78–79
al-Qaeda in the Arabian Peninsula (AQAP), 11, 133
al-Qaeda in the Islamic Maghrib (AQIM), 3, 87–94, 126–27, 129; AST and, 8–9, 141, 170–71, 173–74, 182–83; on *dawa*, 170–71; IS and, 191; ISI and, 123, 175–76; KUBN and, 161, 170, 239–41, 259–62; in Libya, 270; on al-Nahdah, 170–71; Tunisian foreign fighters and, 178–79; weapons smuggling, 171, 182–83
al-Qaradawi, Yusuf, 184
Qarawi, Khalid, 169
Qarawi, Khalifah, 89
al-Qatari, Muhammad, 43
al-Qayrawan Media, 127

qital al-nikayya versus *qital al-tamkin*, 120
Qur'an, AST and, 149, 157
al-Qurashi, Abu 'Ubayd, 116–17
Qutb, Sayyid, 34, 273–74, 276–77

al-Rahmah Mosque, 197
Ramadan, 26, 147–48, 166
Ramda, Rashid, 52
Rashidi, Khawla, 109–10
rawafidh, 162
Razouane, Karim, 168
religion, in social movements, 17
religious lectures program, of AST, 151, 151–53
resistance, theory of, 118
resource mobilization, 16–17, 136, 147
Rida Bin Salih al-Yazidi, 60
Rihani, Lufti, 73
Rissam, Ahmad, 56
Riyabi, Zayd, 91
Riyabi, Zuhayr, 91
Rosenblatt, Nate, 210–11
al-Rubaysh, Ibrahim Bin Sulayman, 127
Ryan, Michael W. S., 116

Sa'adi, Fadhl, 58, 73
al-Sadat, Anwar, 29, 49
Sadiq al-Tunisi, 43–44
Sageman, Marc, 12–13
al-Sahab Media, 119
Sahrawi, Nabil, 87
sahwa movement, 10
Sakka, Luay, 68, 72, 78, 84
salafis: *hisba* violence by, 162–66; jihadi-salafis, 100, 102–5, 110, 114, 120; at Sayeda Aicha Manoubia Sufi shrine, 162–63; against Shias, 163–64
salafism, 40; defining, 274–75; jihadi-salafism, 277; al-Nahdah on, 39, 99–100; in Tunisia, 4–5, 7–8, 38–39, 128
Salih, Shaykh Adnan Muhammad, 69
Sana Ben Achour, 26
Sassi, Shaykh Lassad, 88
Satrapi, Marjane, 107
Sauerland plot, 83
Sawaysh, Bilal, 184
Sayah, Habib, 105
Sayeda Aicha Manoubia Sufi shrine, 162–63
SDF. *See* Syrian Democratic Forces

secularism, 23–25
security committees, of AST, 166–69
sefsari, 23, 25–26
Seliti, Nabil, 218
Sfaxi, Ayub, 86
Shabab al-Tawhid (ST), 190–91, *192*
Shaban, Shaykh Anwar, 49–51, 54, 62
Shafiq al-Tunisi, 45
Shahid, Yusuf, 254
Shahin, Emad Eldin, 27–28
Sha'ib, Khalid, 241
al-Shaitat tribe, 195
Shammam, Muhammad, 34
Sharahili, Malik, 78–79
sharia, 25, 140, 273–74
sharia committee, of AST, 189–90
sharia show of strength, Avenue Bourguiba clock tower protest, 110–12
al-Shawashi, Bilal, 117, 160, 184–85, 270
Shia and Sunni Muslims, 77–78, 162–64
al-Shikaw, Abu Bakr, 244–45
al-Shikhawi, Ghufran, 242–43
al-Shikhawi, Rahmah, 242–44
Shilindi, 'Umar Faruq, 86
Shuru, al-Sadiq, 104, 106
al-Sibsi, Muhammad al-Baji Qa'id, 97, 168, 248
Siege of Mecca, 1979, 42
Simcox, Robin, 11
Sinun, Bashir, 92–93
Six-Day War, 1967, 28–29
slogans, of AST, 154–57
SMT. *See* social movement theory
Snow, David A., 17, 153
socialism, 28, 31
social movements, 14–17
social movement theory (SMT), 14–16
social services, 9–12, 15, 121, 145
Solihin, Sohirin M., 278
Somalia, 11, 86
Sousse Beach attack, 241–42, 247
Spain, 68–70, 92
ST. *See* Shabab al-Tawhid
Stade de France, 54
Sterman, David, 210–11
Stevens, J. Christopher, 159
Sughir, Bilal, 79
Sulayman Group, 5, 108–9, 182

Sultan, 'Adl Bin, 60
al-Suri, Abu Mus'ab, 43, 56, 115, 117–19, 121, 286n5
al-Susi, Amin, 180
Sweden, 86
Switzerland, 85–86
Syria, 6–10; al-Assad regime, 74, 78–79, 81, 180–81, 184; *baya* and, 189–90; Free Syrian Army, 206, 229; Homs, 81–82, 178, 206; Iraq border, 204, 270; ISI in, 179; jihad in, 184–85; MB in, 28–29, 180; ST and, 190–91; Tunisian jihadis committing human rights violations in, 195–97, 203; Tunisian jihadis in, 76, 78–79, 220–22, 223–27, 228–31; Tunisian jihadis in IS propaganda videos from, 222, *223–27*; Turkey border, *212*, 212–13. *See also* Tunisian foreign fighters, in Syria
Syrian Civil War, 79
Syrian Democratic Forces (SDF), 263–66

TADA. *See* Tunisian Association for Drama Arts
Ta'ib, 'Ala al-Din, 84
takfir, 52–53; Abu 'Iyadh on, 123; extreme incidents related to, *202*; in Iraq jihad, 114; IS and, 201, *202*, 203; Tunisian jihadis and, 45–47, 199–201, *202*
Taliban, 54–56, 76
Tanzania, 67
Tariqi, Iman, 264
al-Tariqi, Yusri Bin Fakhr, 77–78
Tarrow, Sidney, 14–16
TCG. *See* Tunisian Combatant Group
thawrat al-talibah, 109, 164–65
Thompson, David, 160
Tilly, Charles, 15
Tora Bora, 56–59, 68
Torelli, Stefano M., 5
al-Trabilsi, Nizar, 85
Tunis, 26, 34, 36, 110–12; Bardo National Museum attack in, 175, 229, 234, 241–42, 246–47; Douar Hicher suburb of, 169; Islamic Good Society in, 197; U.S. embassy in, 3, 140, 159–60, 168, 171–72, 185
al-Tunisi, Munir, 87

Tunisia: Bourguiba's Islamic reforms in, 24–27; *dawa* in, 114, 131–32, 170; French colonial period in, 25; governorates, 141, *142–43*, 143, *172*; Harakat al-Nahdah in, 1–2; al-Hazimi lectures in, 197–99, *198*; al-Idrisi in, 38–39; independence of, 25; IS attacks in, 229, 246–49; ISI in, 174–75; Islam in, 20, 23; leftists in, 28–31, 103, 164; Libya border with, 233–34; National Guard of, 169; PLO in, 43–44; political prisoners of, 97–98; politicization of, 39; prison system, 70, 72, 97–98, 266–69; religion in, 23; returnees to, 263–66; salafism in, 4–5, 7–8, 38–39, 128; secularism in, 23–25; *sefsari* in, 23, 25–26; socialism in, 28, 31; ST network in, *192*. *See also* Ansar al-Sharia in Tunisia; al-Nahdah; *specific topics*

Tunisian Association for Drama Arts (TADA), 111

Tunisian Combatant Group (TCG), 42–43, 52, 54; in Afghanistan, 57–58, 60–61; AQ and, 60; Bin Ladin to, 57; Marufi in, 85; organizational chart, 59

Tunisian foreign fighters, 269–71; Abu 'Iyadh on, 179–80; AQIM and, 178–79; AST, al-Nahdah and, 180; AST and, 179–81; data on, 206, *207*, 208–15, *216*; deaths of, 208–9, 213–15, *216*, *217*; desire for redemption, 219–20; disillusionment of, 218; European-based, mobilization of, 209–10, *210*; from France, 209; in Iraq, 206, *207*, 208–9, *210*, 213; on IS caliphate, 219; in JN, 206, 215; in Libya, 181–84, 208–9; location of origin of, 210, *211*; returnees to Tunisia, 263–66; ST and, 190–91; Tunisian jihadis as, 78–79, 81–82, 178–90; Tunisian Revolution and, 178. *See also* Tunisian jihadis

Tunisian foreign fighters, in Syria, 184–87, 194; AST on, 179–81; AST sharia committee on, 189–90; deaths of, 208–9, 213–15, *214*, *216*, *217*; European-based, mobilization of, 209–10, *210*; in Homs, 178; mobilization of, 206, *207*, 208–10, 217–20; returnees to Tunisia from, 263–65; ST and, 190–91; Turkish border, 212, *212*

Tunisian General Union of Students, 34, 36

Tunisian government: on AST, 9, 20, 94–95, 98–99, 132, 168, 176, 237–38; on AST as terrorist organization, 9, 11, 16, 96–97, 105, 160–61, 176–78, 187, 249–52; Ben Gardane victory of, 252–53; Constituent Assembly election for, 97–98, 100, 102, 106–7, 166–67; counterterrorism policies of, 248–55; human rights concerns about, 254–55; IS and, 249–55; #IWillComeToTunisiaThisSummer campaign of, 246–47; KUBN on, 258; Ministry of Interior, 248, 250, 252; prisoner amnesty, 20, 96–98, 106, 114; transitional, jihadi policy of, 97–99; U.S. and, 249–52. *See also* Ansar al-Sharia in Tunisia (AST), al-Nahdah and; al-Nahdah

Tunisian Islamic Front (FIT), 47–49

Tunisian Islamism, 20; in campus clashes, 30–31; jihadism and, 4–6, 24; new forms of, 38–39; '*ulama* in, 27. *See also* al-Nahdah

Tunisian jihadis, 1–2, 20; in Afghanistan, 56–62; Afghan jihad and, 33, 40–45, 47, 85–86; in Algerian jihad, 51–55; in AQ, 57–58, 60–61, 188–89; in AQI, 75–76, 78–79; AQIM and, 126–27, 129; AST and, 94–95, 98; in Bosnian jihad, 49–51; in broken-up Iraq jihad networks, 79, 80; communal relations of, 131; complacency warning to, 126–27; *dawa* and, 115, 126, 128–29 (*See also* Ansar al-Sharia in Tunisia (AST), *dawa* and); in Djerba synagogue bombing, 64–68; in Europe, 48–49, 68; in European plots, 2005–2010, 83–85; extradition of, 93; FIT, 47–49; as foreign fighters, 78–79, 81–82, 178–90; in GSPC and AQIM, 87–94; as Hazimis, 197–201, 203; human rights violations by, 195–97, 203; in Iraq, 39; in Iraq jihad, 71–79, *80*, 90–91; in ISI, 75–79, 81–82; in ISIS, 188–91, 200–201, 203; in Italy, 49–51, 54, 58, 62, 74, 83; in JABF, 88–89; in Jalalabad school, 45–46, 50, 56–57, 68–69, 189–94; in JN, 188–89, 196–97; in JTWJ, 74–76, 78–79; in Khalden network, 55–56, 68; in Krekar network, 72–73; KUBN and, 260; in Lebanon, 81;

Tunisian jihadis (*continued*)
in Madrid train bombings, 69–70; in Mas'ud assassination, 57–58, 60, 73; in MSM, 75–79; al-Nahdah and, 129–30; 9/11 attack and, 60–62, 63–64; North and West African jihadi groups and, 245; operations in Tunisia, 238; organization plan of, 127–28; in prison, 70, 72, 93–94, 124–25, 129, 266–69; in Somalia, 86; strategic advice for, 125–31; in Syria, 76, 78–79; *takfir* and, 45–47, 199–201, 202; after terrorist organization designation, 177–78; Tunisian Islamism and, 4–6, 24; Tunisian Revolution and, 41–42, 98; at Turkish base, 68–69; ultra extremism among, 194–201, 202, 203; in Yemen, 87; youth, 100; in al-Zarqawi network, 72–73

Tunisian jihadis, in IS, 18–19, 21–22; Abu 'Iyadh and, 194; AQ and, 194, 206; attacks and plots, 229–31, *230*; deaths of, 213–15, *216*; external operations, 228–31; extreme *takfir*-related incidents with, 202; female, 222, 228, 242–44; al-Hakim and, 185; in Iraq and Syria, 220–22, 223–27, 228–31; in Libya, 242–46, *243*, *244*; Mallah, 204–5; positions of leadership, 242, *243*; in propaganda videos, 222, 223–27, *244*

Tunisian Revolution, 40, 154, 266–67; AST after, 20, 41; jihadis in, 1, 16; al-Nahdah and, 28; Tunisian foreign fighters and, 178; Tunisian jihadis and, 41–42, 98

Tunisians: locals, in AST *dawa* campaign, 14; police, 103–4; youth, 154. *See also* Tunisian jihadis

al-Turabi, Hassan, 36

Turkey, 84, *212*, 212–13

Turkish base, 68–69

2000 millennium plot, 55–56

UGTT. *See* L'Union générale tunisienne du travail

'*ulama*, 25–27, 273

ultra extremism, among Tunisian jihadis, 194–201, 202, 203

umma, 8–9

Umm 'Abd al-Rahman al-Tunisi, 228

Umm Bara' al-Tunisi, 228, 263–65

Umm Hajar al-Tunisi, 228

Umm Rayan al-Tunisi, 195, 228, 243

Umm 'Umar al-Tunisi, 244

'Umri, Khadijah, 228, 264

UN. *See* United Nations

L'Union générale tunisienne du travail (UGTT), 31

United Nations (UN), 195–96, 255, 271

United States (U.S.): in Afghanistan, 121–22; in Bin Ladin death, 13; Embassy, in Tanzania, 67; Embassy, in Tunis, 3, 140, 159–60, 168, 171–72, 185; in Iraq War, 10, 81; in Middle East, 37–38; al-Nahdah and, 168, 171; Tunisian government and, 249–52

University of Manouba, 32, 164–65

University of Tunis, 34

U.S. *See* United States

Vassefi, Tara, 120

Waddani, Habib, 73

al-Wadhan, Habib, 61–62

Wagemakers, Joas, 115, 120, 275

al-Wahhab, Muhammad Ibn 'Abd, 152–53

Wahhabism, 120

Waqafat ma' thamrat al-jihad (al-Maqdisi), 120

Watts, Clinton, 8

weapons smuggling, 171, 182–83

Webb, Edward, 26–27

Weslaty, Lilia, 176

Westergaard, Kurt, 84

Western Jihadism Project, 5, 18

Western social movements, 15

Wickham, Carrie Rosefsky, 15, 17

al-Wihayshi, Nasir, 11

WikiLeaks, 58

Wiktorowicz, Quintan, 5, 275

Wilayat Tunis, 247–48

Willis, Michael, 23

Wilner, Alex S., 7

Wolf, Anne, 4, 23–25, 35, 38, 48, 140

Yahmed, Hédi, 104

Yarkas, Imad al-Din Barakat, 69–70

Yayla, Ahmet, 196

Yazidis, 195–96

Yemen, 11, 87

al-Zahawi, Muhammad, 183
Zakariyya al-Tunisi, 61–62
Zaluti, Sahbi, 84
al-Zarqawi, Abu Mus'ab, 56, 77; Abu 'Iyadh and, 189; on Ben Gardane, 234; ISI and, 123; JTWJ of, 75; al-Libi and, 122–23; al-Maqdisi and, 120; network of, 70, 72–74; al-Zawahiri and, 122

al-Zawahiri, Ayman, 57, 92, 115; Abu 'Iyadh and, 133, 174, 193–94; al-Zarqawi and, 122
zawiyyas, 25
Zaytunah University, 26
Zimmuri, Yusuf, 74
Zoghlami, Yamina, 173
Zuruq, Kamal, 151–52, 185, 190–91, 193, 203

COLUMBIA STUDIES IN TERRORISM AND IRREGULAR WARFARE
Bruce Hoffman, Series Editor

This series seeks to fill a conspicuous gap in the burgeoning literature on terrorism, guerrilla warfare, and insurgency. The series adheres to the highest standards of scholarship and discourse and publishes books that elucidate the strategy, operations, means, motivations, and effects posed by terrorist, guerrilla, and insurgent organizations and movements. It thereby provides a solid and increasingly expanding foundation of knowledge on these subjects for students, established scholars, and informed reading audiences alike.

Ami Pedahzur, *The Israeli Secret Services and the Struggle Against Terrorism*
Ami Pedahzur and Arie Perliger, *Jewish Terrorism in Israel*
Lorenzo Vidino, *The New Muslim Brotherhood in the West*
Erica Chenoweth and Maria J. Stephan, *Why Civil Resistance Works: The Strategic Logic of Nonviolent Conflict*
William C. Banks, editor, *New Battlefields/Old Laws: Critical Debates on Asymmetric Warfare*
Blake W. Mobley, *Terrorism and Counterintelligence: How Terrorist Groups Elude Detection*
Jennifer Morrison Taw, *Mission Revolution: The U.S. Military and Stability Operations*
Guido W. Steinberg, *German Jihad: On the Internationalization of Islamist Terrorism*
Michael W. S. Ryan, *Decoding Al-Qaeda's Strategy: The Deep Battle Against America*
David H. Ucko and Robert Egnell, *Counterinsurgency in Crisis: Britain and the Challenges of Modern Warfare*
Bruce Hoffman and Fernando Reinares, editors, *The Evolution of the Global Terrorist Threat: From 9/11 to Osama bin Laden's Death*
Boaz Ganor, *Global Alert: The Rationality of Modern Islamist Terrorism and the Challenge to the Liberal Democratic World*
M. L. R. Smith and David Martin Jones, *The Political Impossibility of Modern Counterinsurgency: Strategic Problems, Puzzles, and Paradoxes*
Elizabeth Grimm Arsenault, *How the Gloves Came Off: Lawyers, Policy Makers, and Norms in the Debate on Torture*
Assaf Moghadam, *Nexus of Global Jihad: Understanding Cooperation Among Terrorist Actor*
Bruce Hoffman, *Inside Terrorism*, 3rd edition
Stephen Tankel, *With Us and Against Us: How America's Partners Help and Hinder the War on Terror*
Wendy Pearlman and Boaz Atzili, *Triadic Coercion: Israel's Targeting of States That Host Nonstate Actors*
Bryan C. Price, *Targeting Top Terrorists: Understanding Leadership Removal in Counterterrorism Strategy*
Mariya Y. Omelicheva and Lawrence P. Markowitz, *Webs of Corruption: Trafficking and Terrorism in Central Asia*

GPSR Authorized Representative: Easy Access System Europe, Mustamäe tee 50, 10621 Tallinn, Estonia, gpsr.requests@easproject.com